ETHNOMUSICOLOGY

Published with the support of the
Prins Bernhard Fonds and the Royal Tropical Institute, Amsterdam, under
the auspices of the International Folk Music Council

ETHNOMUSICOLOGY

A study of its nature, its problems, methods and representative
personalities to which is added a bibliography

by

JAAP KUNST

Honorary member of the staff of the Department of Cultural and Physical
Anthropology of the Royal Tropical Institute, Amsterdam,
reader in Ethnomusicology at the University of Amsterdam
and member of the
Royal Netherlands Academy of Sciences

Third much enlarged edition of 'Musicologica'

THE HAGUE
MARTINUS NIJHOFF
1959

TO KATY
WHO KNOWS WHY

PRINTED IN THE NETHERLANDS

PREFACE TO THE FIRST EDITION

This booklet hardly needs a preface; the contents, I think, speak for themselves. It contains a short and carefully brought up to date résumé of all that I, as a private University Lecturer in Amsterdam, have tried to teach my pupils.

It is intended as a general introduction to ethnomusicology, before going on to the study of the forms of separate music-cultures.

I sincerely hope that those, who wish to teach themselves and to qualify in this branch of knowledge, will find a satisfactory basis for selftuition in the matter here brought together.

Regarding the possibility of a new edition, any critical remarks or information as to possible desiderata would be very gratefully received.

J. K.

PREFACE TO THE SECOND EDITION

My request for critical remarks and desiderata has not been ignored. My sincere thanks to all who took the trouble to let me know what they missed in my booklet. Through their collaboration the contents have undergone a considerable improvement and enlargement as compared to the original edition issued in 1950 by the Royal Tropical Institute, Amsterdam, under the title 'Musicologica'.

I have taken care to add many particulars from non-European sources, with the result that now the book is no longer so Europe-centric as it was.

Furthermore, I have done my best to mention in a special bibliography all the more important ethnomusicological publications, with the exception of those issued in the Russian, Arabic, Chinese, Indonesian, Javanese, Sundanese and Japanese languages and in the languages of the Indian subcontinent. Besides, inserted are only books and articles specialized in the field of ethnomusicology, and not the (numerous) reports and studies on ethnology in general, in which are included some (often important) data concerning the music of the peoples treated. Nor are inserted articles containing too many faulty data and those that are quite antiquated or too superficial. Admittedly, often I had to make a rather subjective choice; it has already become an impossibility to give a really complete bibliography. For many more titles I may refer the reader to the lists found in the works marked by an asterisk, especially – for the musics of Asia – to the excellent and comprehensive bibliography by RICHARD WATERMAN c.s. (4307) [1]; for Indonesia to 2399, 2417 and 2418; for India to 43; for Negro Africa to 4196 and 2853; for China to 4531a, and for American Indian music (but only till 1909) to 4088.

Finally, I feel impelled to thank Messrs MARTINUS NIJHOFF for the great care they have given to my booklet and the patience they have shown in regard to my wishes.

Amsterdam, 1st January, 1955. J. K.

[1] Figures printed in bold type refer to the publications contained in the bibliography on p. 79 et seq.

PREFACE TO THE THIRD EDITION

The second edition was soon exhausted, so now I have the opportunity to add many new (and many abusively omitted old) titles, and to correct some mistakes.

The capitals A – M behind many titles in the bibliography, representing resp. eight Dutch libraries, one Belgian, two English, one Danish and one German, indicate where the publications thus marked can be found. As far as the library of the British Museum (represented, by the capital I) is concerned, only books and pamphlets have been indicated in this way; publications in periodicals may easily be found by consulting the *British Union Catalogue of periodicals* by JAMES D. STEWART, MURIEL E. HAMMOND and ERWIN SAENGEN (London, 1955 onward). For publications in periodicals to be found in the libraries of the U.S.A. and Canada, the reader should consult WINIFRED GREGORY, *Union list of serials in libraries of the U.S.A. and Canada* (New York, 2/1943).

As for my own publications, I have omitted – as I have done in the second edition – those which have served as preliminary studies only and which therefore are no longer required, being incorporated, often in a better form, in the publications referred to in this bibliography. This bibliographic list, now containing about 5200 entries, goes up to September 1st, 1958. For publications of a later date I may refer to the bibliographies, issued three times a year in the periodical 'Ethnomusicology' of the 'Society for Ethnomusicology' (1134) (of which everybody interested in this field of study should be a member, as well as of the 'International Folk Music Council').

In preparing this new edition I, again, owe many thanks to many people, in the first place to Miss MAUD KARPELES, hon. secr. of the Intern. Folk Music Council, who purified the text from idiomatic blunders and 'hollandisms' and gave many a good hint; to Miss MARIJKE CHARBON, who made, on her own initiative, that very useful Index of periodicals; to Miss EVA-BRITT HELLIESEN, assistant at the Royal Library, Copenhagen; to Miss ELISABETH SMIT, ass.-librarian at the Library of the University, Groningen; to Dr. OLGA BOONE, curator at the Congo Museum, Tervueren, Belgium; to Dr. G. D. VAN WENGEN of the Rijksmuseum voor Volkenkunde, Leyden; to professor MARIUS SCHNEIDER, head of the Institute of Musical Sciences, Cologne, and his assistant ROBERT GÜNTHER; to Dr. D. A. GROSHEIDE, librarian of Utrecht University; to Miss MARIANNE REYERS, assistant at the Library of the Department of Cultural and Physical Anthropology of the Royal Tropical Institute, Amsterdam, and to my assistant FELIX VAN LAMSWEERDE. Many others also, who, I hope, will not resent their being not mentioned here *nominatim*, can be sure of my lasting gratitude.

Amsterdam, 1st September, 1958.   J. K.

N.B. The author wishes to appeal to the clemency of his readers should they occasionally stumble on an inaccuracy: it was found impossible to check each separate item of the generously submitted contributions.

CONTENTS

Wer sich selbst und andre kennt,
Wird auch hier erkennen:
Orient und Occident
Sind nicht mehr zu trennen.

Sinnig zwischen beiden Welten
Sich zu wiegen, lass' ich gelten;
Also zwischen Ost und Westen
Sich bewegen sei's zum besten!

(GOETHE, 'Epigrammatisch')

'Wer die dominierende Stellung der Musik in primitiveren Kultur-
zuständen, die Vielheit ihrer Formen, die überraschenden Ähn-
lichkeiten und Unterschiede, wer den Zusammenhang der darauf
bezüglichen Untersuchungen mit den allgemeinsten Fragen nach
den Ursprüngen und Formen menschlicher Zivilisation, nach der
Entwicklung und Ausbreitung der Menschenrassen bedenkt, für
den bedarf die Wichtigkeit der Erforschung aussereuropäischer
Musik für die allgemeine Ethnologie und Geschichte des Menschen-
geschlechts keines Beweises. Auch jeder Psychologe, jeder Ästhe-
tiker, der aus dem Bannkreis der Gelehrtenstube und der Selbst-
beobachtung hinausstrebt, um seinen Horizont durch objektive
Untersuchung menschlichen Denkens und Fühlens in andern
Zeiten und Räumen zu erweitern, sieht hier fruchtbare Aufgaben
vor sich. Je unaufhaltsamer europäische Kultur in fremde Erdteile
eindringt und abweichende Formen, wenn nicht sogar ihre Träger,
zum Absterben zwingt, um so mehr ist es an der Zeit, jene Formen
zu sammeln und zu studieren.'

CARL STUMPF

The study-object of ethnomusicology, or, as it originally was called:
comparative musicology, is the _traditional_ music and musical instruments
of all cultural strata of mankind, from the so-called primitive peoples to
the civilized nations. Our science, therefore, investigates all tribal and folk
music and every kind of non-Western art music. Besides, it studies as well
the sociological aspects of music, as the phenomena of musical acculturation,
i.e. the hybridizing influence of alien musical elements. Western art- and
popular (entertainment-) music do not belong to its field.

The original term 'comparative musicology' (vergleichende Musikwissenschaft) fell into disuse, because it promised more – for instance, the
study of mutual influences in Western art-music – than it intended to comprise, and, moreover, our science does not 'compare' any more than any
other science.

The importance of this, still young, science of ethnomusicology for our
own musical culture is as yet insufficiently realized in wide circles which
really ought to be better informed. There is among Westerners an inclination
to regard all exotic music, even in its highest forms, as nothing more than
either expressions of inferior, more primitive civilizations, or as a kind of
musical perversion. It is not sufficiently realized that Western music, after
all, is based on older forms which are identical with – or, at any rate, comparable to – those found today outside Europe and 'European' America. Neither
is it generally understood that, as far as the higher musical forms of expression of the Asiatic civilized nations are concerned, their extremely refined

I

specialization renders them difficult to grasp for us Westerners, who are equally specialized, but in a different direction. The differences are frequently felt as deficiencies, and strike the hearer more forcibly than the elements which both types of music have in common.

The position, after all, is that each race, each population group has its own manner of musical expression, and this special manner strikes a different race or people, on first acquaintance, as strange. This manner of expression, characteristic of a race or people, is not only bound to its specific psychic structure, but is also physiologically conditioned. The problems which this situation raises constitute a field of investigation *par excellence* of ethnomusicology. WILHELM HEINITZ (1649–1684) in his article *Musikwissenschaft und Völkerkunde* (1680), formulated this principle – with real German thoroughness – as follows: 'In Wirklichkeit kann es eine grundlegende Musikwissenschaft nur geben, wenn man die musikalische Gestaltung ansieht als korrelativ bedingte Transgredation seelisch-körperlicher Bewegungsprozesse, die kategorisch ihr subjectives Gleichgewicht finden in dem funktionellen Bezugsystem biologischer Dynamik'. (i.e.: Actually, there cannot exist any well-founded musicology unless one regards musical formation as a correlatively conditioned transposition of psychophysiological motorial processes, which categorically find their equilibrium in the organic-functional relative system of biological dynamics). We in the Netherlands have a simpler interpretation of the condition laid down in this pronouncement, namely that 'elk vogeltje zingt zoals het gebekt is', i.e. each bird is known by its song.

Ethnomusicology, as it has developed as an independent science during the last seventy years, counts only a relatively small number of investigators as its principal exponents. It is usual to regard the British mathematician and philologist A. J. ELLIS as its founder (fig. 1).

ALEXANDER JOHN ELLIS – whose original name was SHARPE – was born in 1814. His real subject was phonetics, his main work being *Early English Pronunciation with special reference to Shakespeare and Chaucer* (1868–1889, in 5 vols.). But it is through his musicological investigations that he still lives im the memory of later generations (1070–1082). A remarkable fact, when one takes into account that ELLIS was known to be totally tone-deaf.[1]

The two works which have remained the best known of his writings are *The History of Musical Pitch* (1880/'81), very much worth while, but difficult to obtain, and then the work to which he owes the designation 'Father of ethno-musicology': *Tonometrical Observations on some existing*

---

[1] On the personality of ELLIS see 2411.

2

non-harmonic Scales, (1884), revised and enlarged a year later, and published, under the title of *On the Musical Scales of Various Nations*, in the 'Journal of the Society of Arts'. In 1922, ERICH VON HORNBOSTEL gave an excellent German translation of it in the first volume of the 'Sammelbände für vergleichende Musikwissenschaft' (1924).

ELLIS, in his treatise – originally an address with demonstrations – gives an account and the results of his tone-measurements, made on a large number of exotic instruments with fixed scales and on string- and wind-instruments tuned by experts, and preceded by a survey of some theoretically known Arabian and Indian scales. He was assisted in his measurings by the musically gifted ALFRED JAMES HIPKINS (1826–1903) (1841–1844).

ELLIS concludes with a summary of what their investigation taught them, in which he says: 'The final conclusion is that the Musical Scale is not one, not 'natural', nor even founded necessarily on the laws of the constitution of musical sound so beautifully worked out by HELMHOLTZ, but very diverse, very artificial, and very capricious' (1082, p. 526).

In more than one respect ELLIS and HIPKINS did pioneering work with their investigation. Not only because they at last opened the eyes of European musicologists to the fact there could exist, apart from Western scale constructions, other ones built on totally different principles, which, by ears accustomed to them, were experienced as normal and logical, but they were also the first to apply a method of representing intervals which, since then, has found general acceptance, because it offers the Westerner advantages far exceeding all other methods of presentation.

I should like to go into this point in some detail. *The pitch of a tone* is determined by the number of vibrations, i.e. the number of movements made by some part of the material which is made to sound (string, key, aircolumn, tongue, membrane etc.), during one second: the so-called c.p.s. (= cycles per second) or double vibrations (in French: *vibrations doubles* (v.d.), in German: *hertz* (H.)), counting the swing to both sides as a single movement. An *interval* is expressed by a fraction, of which the vibration figures of the two tones bordering the interval are the numerator and denominator.

In certain cases this fraction will, of course, be a simple one; thus, the octave may be represented by the fraction $2 : 1$, the perfect fifth by $3 : 2$, the perfect fourth by $4 : 3$ – which is to say that the higher tone of each of these pairs forming the intervals has, respectively, 2, $1^1/_2$ and $1^1/_3$ times as many vibrations as the lower.

When, however, the vibration figures of two tones have no largest common divisor, the numerator and denominator remain unsurveyable large numbers. The so-called Pythagorean comma, i.e. the excess of twelve successive leaps of a perfect fifth over seven octaves, for instance,

3

has to be expressed by the fraction $(^3/_2)^{12} : 2^7 = 531441 : 524288$, or, which may be easier to grasp, by the decimal fraction 1,0136. Often, it is also impossible, without the aid of intricate computations, to determine which of two intervals is the larger; for instance, the fact that the intervals 799 : 634 and 592 : 470 are equally large, can hardly be realized at first sight.

It has been attempted in different ways to simplify this presentation of intervals; in the first place by the use of logarithms. By this method the ratios are reduced to a single figure. This method also removes the complication of the increase of the number of vibrations in respect to the same interval towards the treble (each next-higher octave having twice the number of vibrations of the preceding one).

Although this does, indeed, facilitate the getting of a mental picture of a given ratio, the result is not yet quite satisfying. For, it still remains impossible to see at a glance what the relation is between a given interval and the tone-distances in common use in European music – which, after all, to Westerners, constitutes the basis of all musical determination of intervals.

For this reason another method was adopted; namely, that of dividing the octave, theoretically, into a large number of very small equal parts, as units in which to express the size of intervals. Thus, for instance, the French physicist SAVART (1791–1841), who, because log. 2 is 0.301(03), proposed a division of the octave in 301 intervals of equal size (called, after him, *savart*). In the 19th century this interval-representation in *savarts* has also been accepted by other investigators, but later on it was generally superseded by other systems, among which I may mention one that, for obvious reasons, uses the *milli-octave* (M.O.) ($^{1000}\sqrt{2}$) as a unit. By applying this M.O.-system it is possible, without further mathematical computations, to form a mental image of, at any rate, some of the most important intervals; as, for example, the tempered tritone of 500 M.O., the tempered major third of 333, and the tempered sléndro-interval of 200 M.O. Other intervals, on the other hand, do not convey much to the mind when expressed in M.O.; which means that we cannot directly compare their size with that of the intervals already known to us; – the fifth, for instance, which is such an important interval, being rendered by the completely meaningless figure 583.

Now it is ELLIS' great merit to have proposed and put into practice, in this *cents* system, a manner of representation that creates the possibility of immediate comparison with all our western scale-steps. For he took – it was the egg of Columbus! – the tempered European semitone as unit of measurement, and divided this into 100 equal parts called *cents* ($^{100}\sqrt{^{12}\sqrt{2}} = ^{1200}\sqrt{2}$).

4

The expression of intervals in *cents* is sufficiently accurate, both theoretically and in practice (cf. below p. 11).

The only remaining difficulty is that the conversion of intervals into *cents* is rather a time-devouring task which, moreover, is not everybody's job, as it requires the knowledge and manipulation of logarithmic tables.

A logarithm table for the conversion of ratios (and therefore of intervals) into *cents* and *vice versa* is given by ELLIS himself in his treatise, referred to above: *On the Musical Scales of Various Nations* (p. 487). A description of the same process is also to be found in Appendix XX of the *second* edition (from 1885) of ELLIS' translation of HELMHOLTZ' *Lehre von den Tonempfindungen (Sensations of tone)* (1074) ; in VON HORNBOSTEL's German translation of ELLIS' treatise [1], and, in a slightly different and perhaps clearer form, originating from T. B. W. SPENCER, in A. H. FOX STRANGWAYS, *The Music of Hindostan* (1283), pp. 115 and 116. In the treatise *Vorschläge für die Transkription exotischer Melodien* (1895), written in collaboration between OTTO ABRAHAM (1882–1885, 1889, 1895, 1931) and ERICH VON HORNBOSTEL, one will find this same kind of table, but in a slightly simplified form.

In the first four publications mentioned, also a second – arithmetical – procedure is given which, besides, is reproduced in GROVE's *Dictionary of Music and Musicians*, 3rd. ed., vol. II, p. 718a, and in CURT SACHS, *The Rise of Music in the Ancient World, East and West* (3567, p. 28). This second process, however, is not so accurate as the other one, apart from its taking more time.

Here follows ELLIS' exposition of the two processes:

'If of the two numbers expressing the interval ratio, 3 times the larger is *not* greater than 4 times the smaller, multiply 3,477 by their difference, and divide by their sum to the nearest whole number, adding 1 to the result if over 450. Thus, if the ratio is 4 : 5 (where 3 times 5 the larger number = 15, is less than 4 times the smaller number = 16), the difference is 1, and sum 9, and dividing 3,477 by 9, the result is 386, the *cents* required.

If the ratio is greater than 3 : 4 and less than 2 : 3, multiply the larger number by 3, and the smaller by 4, proceed as before, and finally add 498 to the result. Thus for 32 : 45, multiply 45 by 3, and 32 by 4, giving 128 : 135, difference 7, sum 263. Then 7 × 3,477 : 263 gives 92, and 92 + 498 gives 590, the *cents* required.

Lastly, if the ratio exceeds 2 : 3, multiply the larger number by 2 and the smaller by 3, and proceed as in the first case, adding 702 to the result. Thus for 5 : 8, take 3 × 5 : 2 × 8 or 15 : 16; difference 1, sum 31; then

---

[1] 1924, p. 8, note 1.

5

3,477 : 31 = 112, and this added to 702, gives 814, the required number of *cents*.

This process is sometimes very convenient, but tedious when a large number of results have to be obtained. In this case, those who can use logarithms, will find the following table very simple, and it will give the result to one-tenth of a *cent*.

TO CONVERT LOGARITMHS INTO CENTS AND CONVERSILY

cents	log.	cents	log.	cents	log.	cents	log.
100	.02509	10	.00251	1	.00025	.1	.00003
200	.05017	20	.00502	2	.00050	.2	.00005
300	.07526	30	.00753	3	.00075	.3	.00008
400	.10034	40	.01003	4	.00100	.4	.00010
500	.12543	50	.01254	5	.00125	.5	.00012
600	.15051	60	.01505	6	.00151	.6	.00015
700	.17560	70	.01756	7	.00176	.7	.00018
800	.20069	80	.02007	8	.00201	.8	.00020
900	.22577	90	.02258	9	.00226	.9	.00023
1000	.25086						
1100	.27594						
1200	.30103						

Subtract the logarithms of the pitch numbers or of the numbers of their ratio. Thus for 32 : 45, log. 45 = 1.65321, log. 32 = 1.50515, difference .14806, the next least log. in the table, .12543, gives 500 C. Subtract this from former log., result. 02263, next least .02258, giving 90 C., total 590 C. to the nearest *cent* as before. We can now, if we wish, go a step farther, and subtracting the two last logs, we get .00005, which in the last column corresponds to .2 C. Final result 590.2 C. It is, as a general rule, unnecessary to go beyond the nearest whole number of *cents'*.

This second process also, though easier to manipulate than the other, remains for non-mathematicians a rather thorny path. Fortunately, ERICH VON HORNBOSTEL has obliged the musicological world by once and for all making the necessary computations and combining these in a handy table. Since then there is not one musicologist left who knows how to handle a logarithm table ....

On VON HORNBOSTEL's table, the size of all intervals formed by tones between 340 and 809 v.d. may be found at a glance.

I believe that I work in the spirit of VON HORNBOSTEL by here reproducing (on p. 232) his table – which has been of such great help to our

6

science, but which has hitherto been concealed in a somewhat inaccessible periodical (1923) – together with its author's commentary:

'The reduction of logarithms, even when done with the aid of the familiar tables, suggested by ELLIS, is always a boring and time-devouring affair. The methods described by ELLIS and T. B. W. SPENCER, i.e. the direct conversion of ratio figures into *cents* without the use of logarithms, are both complicated and inaccurate. It is possible, however, to make the whole business much easier by means of a very simple expedient. This is the computation, once and for all, of the ratios between all integers from n to $2n$, and n into *cents*. We shall then find that the *cents* figure for the ratio between any two numbers $p : q$ (between n and $2n$) is equal to the difference between the *cents* figure for $p : n$ and $q : n$, since $q/n : p/n = q/p$. The criterion for the choice of n must be the degree of accuracy needed in the computations, and further the absolute magnitude of the numbers most generally involved. The table attached hereto is intended to serve the need of the acoustic specialist who wishes to determine vibration figures chiefly in the middle register, say, between 400 and 800 v.d., neglecting, as a rule, interval differences of 5 C. in the lower, and 2 C. in the higher part of this register. Numbers outside the range covered by the computation should first be either multiplied or divided (octave transposition) by $2n$; for this reason it was thought desirable to extend the range of the table over more than one octave; it covers – without thereby becoming unwieldy – a minor tenth (*1500* C.).[1] The tens of the vibration figures are placed right and left, the units above and below in the margin. Finding the *cents* figures is simplified by means of group-lines and different letter-types.

Here follow a few examples to illustrate the manner of using the table.

I. CONVERSION OF NUMERICAL RATIOS INTO CENTS

(1) Having measured the vibration figures 435 (a') and 652 v.d., we wish to find the *cents* figure (z) for the ratio. For 652 we find in the table *1126* C.; for 435, *426* C.; so $z = 1126 - 426 = 700$ C. (tempered fifth).

(2) Given 290,3 : 435, wanted z. The smaller number has to be brought within the range of the table by octave transposition: $2 \times 290,3 = 580,6$; we then get, instead of the interval wanted, its extension into the octave: $1200 - z = 926 - 426 = 500$; $z = 700$ C. (The value for 580,6 is found by interpolation). Or, direct: $z = (1200 + 426) - 926 = 700$ C.

(3) What is the *cents*-number that corresponds to the perfect fifth 2 : 3? Answer: $2 : 3 = 400 : 600$; $z = 983 - 281 = 702$ C.

---

[1] The cents-figures are further on printed in *italics*.

II. CONVERSION OF CENTS INTO RATIOS

(4) What is the numerical ratio that approximately corresponds to the tempered fifth *700* C.? Answer: *1500 − 700 = 800; 700* C. ∼ 540 : 809.

(5) Which tone (*n*) is the tempered major third (*400* C.) of *c′* = 256 v.d.? Answer: 256 × 2 = 512; *708 + 400 = 1108; n =* 645 : 2 = 322,5 v.d.

(6) By how many vibrations does the perfect major third (*386* C.) differ from the tempered one at the beginning of the one-lined octave? Answer: *400 − 386 = 14* C.; *708* (table value for *c″* = 512 v.d.) *+ 14 = 722;* (516 − 512) : 2 = 2 v.d.

III. TRANSPOSITION

(7) Find the interval 443 : 541 based on 613 v.d. (N.B. All numbers in these problems are prime-numbers). Answer: *804 − 458 = 346* C. (one of the 'neutrals' that occur so often in exotic music, i.e. an interval between a major and a minor third); *1020 + 346 = 1366;* 443 : 541 = 613 : 749.

(8) Calculate a cycle of fifths of *678* C. (too small by a Pythagorean comma = *22* C.), downwards from the Chinese diapason (pitch-tone) 732 v.d., gathering all the tones within the range of a single octave. To this end we alternately go down *678* C., and upward by *1200 − 678 = 522* C.; *1327 − 678 = 649; 649 + 522 = 1171,* etc.; we then get: 732, 494^1/$_2$, 669 v.d., etc.

(9) Calculate the Siamese scale of seven equal steps as from 378 v.d.: *1200* : 7 = *171,43* C.; *183 + 171,43 = 354,43; 354,43 + 171,43 = 525,86;* .... *697,3; 868,7; 1040; 1311,6* C. Result: 378; 417^1/$_2$; 461; 509; 562; 620; 685 v.d.

(10) Enlarge a curve by the ratio 509 : 571. What parameter *p²* does the point *p¹* = 601 get in the new scale? Answer: *897 − 698 = 199; 986 + 199 = 1185; p² = 674^1/$_2$.'*

In 1939, Prof. R. W. YOUNG has given, in his pamphlet *A table relating Frequency to Cents* (4456), a method of calculation, starting from the equally tempered scale on *a′* = 440 c.p.s. This table insures great accuracy, but appears to me to be rather difficult for a non-mathematically trained musicologist to manipulate.

Another, very practical method of converting intervals into *cents* and *cents* into intervals, a method that eliminates all cyphering, has, some years ago, been offered and described by Professor M. REINER of Technical College, Haifa, in his article *The Music Rule* (3369) and by Dr. E. GERSON-KIWI of the Conservatory of Music, Jerusalem (fig. 26), in her treatise *Towards an exact transcription of Tone-relations* (1401).

In the last named treatise Mrs. GERSON says:

'A decisive step in this direction (i.e. the direction of avoidance of lengthy and troublesome logarithmic or arithmetic calculations) has recently been done by the construction of a technical device, worked out by M. REINER (of Technical College, Haifa), and called the 'Music Rule'. Generally, logarithmic calculation can be facilitated by using the slide rule. In a similar way, the Music Rule consists of two separate double-scales the first of which (A–B) confronts the vibration numbers (scale A) in *hertz* with the respective *cent*-numbers (or *ellis*) (scale B) in a way, that any required pitch can be read off directly, without calculation. The second double-scale (C–D) confronts the *ellis*-number (scale C) with the main musical intervals (scale D) (p 234, fig. 64).

The scale A represents the tones $c' — c''$ with frequencies of 264 to 528 *hertz*. Each division on scale A is equivalent to 2 *hertz*, and each division on scale B to 10 *ellis*. (As for other octave ranges one has to multiply or divide the figures of scale A by 2 (or adding or subtracting 1200 on scale B).) Now shift the C-scale against the A-scale, until the base-line of the C-scale is opposite the vibration number of the lower tone of the interval to be measured. Then read directly from the C-scale, opposite the vibration number of the higher tone of the interval to be measured, the size of that interval expressed in *ellis'*.

Another recent contribution in this field, made by the Hamburg musicologist HEINRICH HUSMANN, excels in that it meets all possible demands of exactness and is especially useful for those unaccustomed to intricate calculations. His publication has been issued under the title *Fünf- und siebenstellige Centstafeln zur Berechnung musikalischer Intervalle* (2003).

Then there is FRITZ BOSE's system (430). It closely resembles that of Prof. REINER, mentioned above.

And recently, CURT SACHS has shown us in his book *Our musical heritage* (3578), p. 12 ff., a simple and easy way of interval calculation.

*   *   *

How is the pitch of a tone measured? For this, some or other measuring instrument is indispensable. However sharp one's musical ear may be, however firmly one may be convinced of the infallibility of one's 'absolute pitch', without a measuring instrument it is impossible to objectivate one's auditory experience more accurately than by recording, say, $a' +$; 'between e and f', or, as regards intervals, 'a fourth on the small side', 'fifth-like intervals'; 'about $3/4$ of a tone', and so on.

Our organ of hearing, moreover, has an unconscious inclination to 'correct' tones and intervals that do not fit in with our own familiar tonal

9

system, in such a way that they will appear to fit in with it. Hence the mistaken idea on the part of musically gifted, retired officials from Indonesia that the Javanese sléndro scale can be truly played on the five black keys of the piano. In other words: without recourse to a measuring instrument it is absolutely impossible to fathom the nature, the structure of an exotic scale and to communicate it to others.

In the course of time, the sciences of phonetics and musicology have developed and obtained the use of a large number of such measuring instruments. Of these, it may broadly be asserted that their precision is in inverse proportion to their usefulness in 'field work', which after all, demands that the instrument shall be easily transportable, of a simply manipulated construction, and able to stand a certain amount of knocking about. It should further, for preference, not be too expensive to buy and maintain: musicologists do not, as a rule, excel as possessors of earthly riches, and only a very few are privileged to receive adequate financial assistance from scientific institutions or interested private persons.

In a modernly equipped laboratory it is possible to perform tone-measurements with amazing accuracy. The so-called 'electric eye' allows of determinations of pitches down to particles of vibrations. Other instruments are, for instance, tuning forks with adjustable weights that change the pitch as they are shifted, and with a scale-division on the prongs; APPUNN's tonometer (sequences of reed-pipes); tuning- or pitch-pipes; slide- or piston-pipes (i.e. with an air-column of adjustable length) with scale-division (e.g., the Tonvariator of W. STERN, that made by Messrs. PHILIPS, and other types); the 'Schwebungstongenerator' (heterodyne tone generator) of W. LEHMANN [1]; VON HORNBOSTEL's 'Reisetonometer' (a small wind instrument with freely vibrating reed, adjustable air-column length and graduation scale indicating pitches). We further know the method followed by E. W. SCRIPTURE (enlargement and analysis of gramophone curves) [2], the oscilloscope method of GRÜTZMACHER and LOTTERMOSER [3], the so-called 'soot method' of MARBE [4], METFESSEL's method of phonophotography (2866), the chromatic stroboscope as described by R. W. YOUNG and A. LOOMIS [5] and the ingenious photographic method used by OLAV GURVIN (1560). ELLIS, in his classic investigations, used a – very extensive – series of tuning forks [6].

My own experience has taught me that, as regards field work, the most

[1] WERNER LEHMANN, Helv. Phys. Acta 6, p. 18 ff. (1933).
[2] E. W. SCRIPTURE, Researches in Experimental Phonetics (1906). Cf. also STUMPF, Die Anfänge der Musik (3995), p. 80/81.
[3] 'Akustische Zeitschrift' 1937, p. 247 ff.; ibid. 1938, p. 183 ff.
[4] 'Zeitschrift für Psychologie', Vol. 49, p. 206 ff.
[5] In 'Journal Acoust. Soc. Amer'. X, p. 112 ff. (1938). See about this apparatus also FRITZ A. KUTTNER (2445) and MILTON E. METFESSEL (2867).
[6] ELLIS, 1082, p. 486.

satisfactory instrument is the old, well-tried monochord, fitted with a proper graduation scale. This instruments embodies a generally acceptable compromise: (1) fairly great precision; (2) easy transportability; (3) it is practically unbreakable; (4) has good resistance to climatologic influences; (5) is quickly and easily operated, (6) the cost of purchase is small and cost of maintenance nil (fig. 59).

The results obtained with the monochord may in most cases be deemed sufficiently accurate for musicological purposes. Instrumental tone-sequences – such as played, for instance, on the melody-instruments of Javanese, Balinese or Siamese orchestras – show slight internal differences in pitch which are not intended, and, therefore, do not require the use of a more precise measuring-instrument.

Among the sources of errors in measurements such as these, we must mention in the first place the investigator's organ of hearing, since there are limits to its precision. He bases himself on the sharpness of his musical ear:

(a) when, in tuning the string of the monochord to a calibrated tuning fork, identity of tuning is attempted between a vibrating metal rod and a string; (in this, the difference in tone-quality (timbre) is a disturbing factor);

(b) in equalizing the pitch of the monochord string with that of the tone to be measured (here, too, there is usually difference in both material and timbre).

There are further the following unfavourable factors:

(c) *always* the relative inaccuracy of the graduation scale attached to the monochord, and

(d) *sometimes* the extra source of error arising as soon as a tone has to be measured which lies outside the register covered by the monochord. For in this case one has to have recourse to the next higher or lower octave; and the equalization of the tone to be measured with its octave on the monochord – as has been proved empirically – cannot be effected with the same precision that can be obtained in equalizing two tones in the same octave-register.

In causing to correspond, first, the tones of the tuning fork and the monochord string, and, later, that of the latter with the sound-source to be measured, attention should be given to the 'beats' which are heard as soon as the two tones approach each other. When the beats have disappeared, equality has been attained. If beats are still audible, their number per second should be estimated as nearly as possible. This number is equal to the difference between the respective numbers of vibration per second of the two tones.

It is further advisable to repeat, if possible, the measurements after some time. It will then be seen that the results slightly differ here and there. One may be better disposed at one time than at another; I have also noticed that the state of the weather (extreme moisture or drought, excessive heat or cold) may influence either the investigator's hearing, the instrument to be measured or the monochord in some way or other; the sources of error mentioned above may make themselves felt, now in this, now in that direction. It is, therefore, advisable, to measure twice, with an interval of some days in between, to add the results of both measurements and divide the sum by 2, or, better still, a third measurement is made with the hope that this will confirm the relative accuracy of one of the two preceding ones.

* * *

Ethnomusicology could never have grown into an independent science if the gramophone had not been invented. Only then was it possible to record the musical expressions of foreign races and peoples objectively; it was no longer necessary to make do with notations made by ear on the spot, which notations, however well-intended, usually fell short in every respect – i.e. both rhythmically and as regards pitch. And in addition it now became possible to incorporate the style of performance – that extremely important element – into the subject-matter of the investigation.

Truly, it is not only the intervals and the rhythm which, next to the special musical forms, are characteristic of the manifestations of a race. The manner, the style, of performance is at least as important. One must have heard them to realize this to the full extent: the mobile, amazingly fast *melos* of the pygmies, sung with a high head-voice; the passionately 'pinched' vocal sound of the Japanese and Chinese actors; the nasalized melodics of the Indonesian women; the pathos in the vocal rendering of the American Indians; the vital jollity as well as the sonorous seriousness of the Negro singing – one must have heard them to realize to the full the degree to which a race is characterized by its style of interpretation. More and more this is being acknowledged and understood. An important treatise in this special field is WERNER DANCKERT's *Musikwissenschaft und Kulturkreislehre* (793). I would further mention, in the same connexion, GEORG HERZOG's article *The Yuman Musical Style* (1702); VON HORNBOSTEL's review in 'Baessler Archiv' (1947); VON HORNBOSTEL and LACHMANN, *Asiatische Parallelen zur Berbermusik* (1956); EICHENAUER, *Musik und Rasse* (1058); WILHELM HEINITZ' articles *Die vergleichende Musikwissenschaft im Dienste der Völkerkunde* (1665), *Die vergleichende Musikwissenschaft als Instrument der Stil- und Rassenkunde* (1676), *Was kann die vergleichende Musikwissenschaft zur Indogermanenfrage beitragen?* (1678), *Die Erforschung rassischer Merkmale aus der Volksmusik* (1681) and *Rassische*

Merkmale an afrikanischem Musikgut (1683) ; G. WALDMANN, *Musik und Rasse* (4269) ; BÉLA BARTÓK's *Rassenreinheit in der Musik* (278) ; HERBERT HÜBNER's study *Die Musik im Bismarck-archipel* (1987) ; ROBERT LACH, *Das Rassenproblem in der vergleichenden Musikwissenschaft* (2472) ; MARIUS SCHNEIDER's *Geschichte der Mehrstimmigkeit* (*passim*) (3734) ; by the same author : *Die musikalischen Beziehungen zwischen Urkulturen, Altpflanzern und Hirtenvölkern* (3745), and par. V of his contribution *Die Musik der Naturvölker* (3773), FRITZ BOSE's *Klangstile als Rassenmerkmale* (424) and *Messbare Rassenunterschiede in der Musik* (438b) ; and, finally, E. KLUSEN's article *Der Stammescharakter in den Weisen neuerer deutscher Volkslieder* (2248).

Ethnomusicology derives still further advantages from the invention of the gramophone. The phonographic method makes it possible to collect vastly more material in the available – usually awkwardly restricted – time, than formerly, when everything heard had to be noted down then and there – a very troublesome and wearying task. At the same time, too, the strain on the patience of the players and singers is reduced to a minimum. Formerly, whenever the melody to be recorded was very complicated, these people would be asked to repeat it many times over, if possible in bits at a time ; a proceeding which, in actual practice, mostly amounted to starting right from the beginning over and over again (since the repetition of a passage in the middle of a piece, as one may imagine, causes considerable difficulty). Now, on the contrary, the players can usually content themselves – and the recorder – with 'doing their stuff' once only.

As in the case of tone-measurement, so with the sound-recording there exist a number of different apparatuses, and here, too, the same applied until recently, i.e. that the technically best method proved less useful in practice, owing to the size, weight, fragility and costliness of the apparatus demanded by it.

Until World War II, therefore, – at any rate when dealing with a territory where conditions had remained more or less primitive (lacking for instance motor roads and electric current), and especially in difficult mountainous or wooded parts where carriers were the only possible means of transport – the general opinion was that the old-fashioned springdriven phonograph with wax-cylinders, recorder and reproducer, such as the 'Edison-Amberola' and the 'Excelsior', was the proper instrument for this purpose.

Since then, this situation has undergone a remarkable change, as everybody knows. Various electromagnetic systems, by which the pieces are recorded on metal wire or on a metallized paper or plastic strip or band (called 'coated tape'), have summarily caused all other recording methods to become antiquated. For a survey of various systems in existence I refer the reader to S. J. BEGUN, *Magnetic Recording* [1]. The new apparatuses not

---

[1] New York/Toronto, 1951.

only enable us to obtain an infinitely better rendering – hardly, if at all, inferior to the original performance; they also allow of uninterrupted recording lasting, if desired, several hours; their manipulation is simple; they are readily transportable and not very vulnerable or fragile, and, last not least, their purchase price, although higher than that of the phonograph or gramophone, is not an unsurmountable obstacle, whereas their cost of maintenance is even less. The only thing most of them require is the presence of a power source. If there is no local electric network to which the recording apparatus (which also reproduces the sound) can be connected, one has to have a transportable power source at one's disposal.

However, recently several new types of tape recorders have appeared, especially suited for research in areas without electric power. This type of recorder, made both in the United States and in Germany and Switzerland, is powered by dry cell batteries (for the microphone) and has a mechanical drive. The weight and the bulk have been reduced seizably. According to reports this new type is greatly facilitating field recording.

For the spoken word, the wire- and tape-recordings are equally satisfactory; for the recording of music it appears that a tape-apparatus is preferable, the more so as it seems that wire-recording has a 'constitutional' drawback in so far that the wire is subject to the danger of getting tangled. [1]

Now whatever apparatus the field worker may have at his disposal, one thing is certain: on arriving in the locality of his researches, he will often find himself faced with a certain diffidence and even suspicion on the part of the population. He will not always find someone who is immediately eager or even prepared to play or sing to the visiting stranger with his mysterious-looking instruments. The general – quite understandable – tendency is 'to wait for the cat to jump'.

All the same, my experience is that it is not so difficult to get the people to sing, or dance, unless abnormal circumstances – such as, in North-Nias, the fear of the Christian mission's hostility to the ancient folk-song and -dance – have gained the upper hand over the people's natural curiosity and willingness to perform. The well-tried recipe: first to perform a tune oneself, say, a European folk-song or a piece on the violin, or to execute a Western folk-dance, has often worked wonders among the Indonesian peoples in whose midst I have made my investigations. They didn't like to be left behind; they, too, wanted to let you hear or show you something of their own – and this the sooner, once they found that every performance was followed by some little reward.

---

[1] See on the question, which recording equipment one should buy, also the article by ALAN P. MERRIAM (2854) and the Manual, edited for the I.F.M.C. and the R. Anthrop. Inst. by MAUD KARPELES (2144a). – For historic data concerning the recording of sound I may refer to ROLAND GILATT, *The story of the gramophone from tinfoil to high fidelity* (London, 1956).

As regard these rewards: a systematic record of the preference on the part of a given population group for particular objects would be most useful. The old Dutchmen – crafty traders as they were – realized the desirability of this policy right from the start, and acted accordingly. The *Corte Verclaeringhe per* CORNELIS DE HOUTMAN *van de Landen ghenaemt Oost Indien ofte Conquisten van Portugal* – the report of a study trip to Portugal in preparation of 'D'Eerste Schipvaert' of 1595–'97 – already contains a lengthy list of articles which, from Portuguese experience, were readily accepted by the peoples of the Archipelago in exchange for their products [1].

For those who contemplate making a study trip to Nias or to Flores, the following suggestions may prove useful.

I found that, in Nias, the people were most impressed by necklaces of 'gold' beads (which were made of coloured glass); the red coral necklaces, which, in my eyes, were much prettier, found but scant favour there; and neither did flashlights, unless they were longer than two batteries. In Flores, on the contrary, they sniffed at the 'golden' beads, whereas the red corals were all the rage. They also fell violently in love with a rather complicated type of pocket-knife, while the smaller flashlights were also much in favor. Tobacco, in the form of lumps of chewing tobacco, and cigarettes, as well as chocolate drops and sweet biscuits, proved a universally appreciated reward; I could not bring a sufficient store of these to satisfy all demands. In South-Nias, the 'Bensdorp' flat round chocolate drops were at first taken to be some sort of money, as they were wrapped in silver paper.

A most important factor for the success of a musicological expedition is *some* knowledge of the language current in the territory of your investigation. You should at least know a sufficient number of words and expressions to enable you to ask a person to sing at the right moment and in the right way, or that will be helpful in establishing a friendly contact with the person you are talking to. In Nias, for example, a set of fourteen terms have helped me through many difficulties and smoothed my way towards obtaining the goodwill of the population. I was able to say 'yes' (*la'u*) and 'no' (*lö'ö*); express thanks (*sauhagölö*); welcome somebody (*ya'ugö;* literally: ('is that) you?') and say good-day (*yahö*); express my admiration for a fine song- or dance-performance (*söchi-söchi* = 'fine, fine!'), and my affection by a friendly tap on the shoulder while pronouncing the word *sifahuhu* (= 'friend'). Singing into the horn of the phonograph was directed by the words *löna* ('not yet'), *taborogo* ('start'), *honögö* ('stop, silence'), *alio* ('quick'), *balo'i* (North Nias) or *besé'o* (Central Nias) (= 'wait

[1] See: J. C. M. WARNSINCK, *De wetenschappelijke voorbereiding van onze eerste schipvaart naar Oost-Indië* (inaugural address), 1936, p. 9.

a moment'), *é bua ö liu* ('louder!'); while I was able to express sympathy with the experimental persons at the end of the singing or dancing, by asking in kind, thoughtful tones: *érégé dödö?* or *marasé?*, meaning 'are you tired now?'.

For the rest there is needed a little tactful handling, a lot of patience, a smile at the right moment, and the sympathy which will enable you to detect whether your informants' initial shyness is giving way to some sort of confidence, whether he is getting tired and in consequence a little irritable or easily distracted, and whether the psychological moment has arrived to show a little generosity – in short, intuition and tact, one either has them or has them not, but they are indispensable if satisfactory results are to be obtained.

* * *

The first phonograms of exotic music to benefit our science were made by Dr. WALTER FEWKES in 1889, from the singing of the Passamaquoddy and Zuñi Indians. These records were passed on for analysis and elaboration to Dr. B. I. GILMAN of Harvard University, and this led to the publication of his study *Zuñi Melodies* (1438), which paper has served as example to many later treatises based on phonographic material.

Once the importance and necessity of phonographic recording was generally realized, many larger and smaller phonogram-archives came into being; the oldest established being in the U.S.A. Some American universities now have extensive collections. The American stock of phonograms was estimated in 1933 at about 17.000 different records, including Honolulu. The majority of these are recordings of American Indian vocal music, and are mostly, as far as I know, on cylinders. [1]

Since then the important and rapidly growing collection of records of the Library of Congress, Washington D.C., the majority of which were recorded by means of the most modern apparatuses, have been added to these as well as the splendid collection, brought together by GEORGE HERZOG, formerly at Columbia University, New York, and afterwards transferred by him to the Anthropology Department of the University of Indiana, Bloomington (Ind.), where he is now teaching.

This material has been gathered, studied and still is studied by a number of meritorious ethnomusicologists. I already mentioned the names of FEWKES, GILMAN and GEORG HERZOG (1702–1750). Next to them worked FRANCES DENSMORE (fig. 11) (855–949), HELEN H. ROBERTS (fig. 28) (3430–3451), EDWARD SAPIR (3648, 3649), FREDERICK R. BURTON (554),

---

[1] See: 'Zeitschrift für vergleichende Musikwissenschaft', Vol. I (1933), p. 58.

CHARLES K. WEAD (4315–4317), ROSE BRANDEL (468–470a), GERTRUDE P. KURATH (1225, 1226, 2419–2438), WILLARD RHODES (3399–3405a), ALAN P. MERRIAM (fig. 43) (2845–2860), DAVID MCALLESTER (2797–2802), E. R. CLARK (686), RICHARD A. WATERMAN (1701, 4307–4312) and many others. After 1933 American ethno-musicology received a fresh impetus when, owing to the rise of Nationalsocialism in Germany, SACHS (fig. 3) (1913, 3526–3579g), VON HORNBOSTEL (figs. 12 and 18) (1882–1963) and BUKOFZER (fig. 31) (533–538) came to the United States and were called to university chairs. In 1952 MANTLE L. HOOD (fig. 44) from the University of California, Los Angeles, came to Europe and specialized in Indonesian music (1877–1879).

French Canada, also, boasts a large and excellent collection of phonograms of French-Canadian, English-Canadian and (more than 2600) Canadian-Indian folksongs, brought together by M. MARIUS BARBEAU (fig. 19) (233–242, 1360) and housed in the National Museum of Canada at Ottawa.

As far as Europe is concerned, the best known and most important collections were found in Vienna and Berlin. Of these two, the Viennese one – the property of the Academy of Sciences – is the older. Its establishment dates from about 1900; apart from a few thousand speech- and language-phonograms, it contained, in 1933, about 1500 music records.[1] The Academy issued many ethnomusicological studies, based on its phonogram collection. Of those I may mention the publications by EXNER and PÖCH (1139), TREBITSCH (4139–4141), FELBER (1217–1222), VAN OOST (3066–3069), MURKO (4934, 4935), BIRO (361), IDELSOHN (2018, 2020), LACH (fig. 17) (2460–2462, 2480–2485, 2493), NADEL (2956, 2960), GRAF (1488), JANSKY (2067) and TRUBETSKOY (4152). Recently Dr. WALTER GRAF has been appointed as its director.

The Berlin archives – which were destroyed or, at least, dispersed without the slightest chance of getting them together again [2], during the second world war – were much larger. They were established in 1902, at the instigation of the great physiologist and psychologist CARL STUMPF (fig. 2), and were at first – until 1932 – housed in the Psychological Institute of the University of Berlin, and later in the Staatliche Hochschule für Musik; after 1933 they have been incorporated with the collections of the Museum für Völkerkunde [3].

STUMPF, as far as his musicological work is concerned, lives on in the grateful remembrance of ethnomusicologists not only on account of having founded this richest and best organized of all European phonogram archives,

---

[1] Ibid., p. 15.
[2] Dr. EMSHEIMER told me that four crates with about 1300 cylinders have been recovered; the rest, packed in 20 crates, the Russians took with them and, therefore, it is lost for Western science. – See also KURT REINHARD (3376).
[3] Since 1948 some young musicologists, in the first place KURT REINHARD (3370–3388b) and HANS HEINZ DRÄGER (1007–1009a), try to revive this Berlin centre by lecturing at the recently founded 'Freie Universität' and rebuilding the phonogram-archives.

but also as the man who, in collaboration with Dr. OTTO ABRAHAM (1882–1885, 1889, 1895, 1931), made the first musicological phonographic records in Germany (from the music of the Siamese court-orchestra which was performing in Berlin at the time), and also as the author of that masterly treatise *Tonsystem und Musik der Siamesen* (3993), of a larger work, *Anfänge der Musik* (3997), and a number of other publications (3984–3999).

However, the extraordinary growth of the Berlin phonographic archives is not so much due to STUMPF's work, but rather to that of his pupil and younger friend ERICH M. VON HORNBOSTEL – *facile princeps* among all those who have made ethnomusicology the chosen subject of their study. Under his direction the phonographic collection grew rapidly, until, in 1933, when VON HORNBOSTEL left Berlin, it comprised no less than 10.000 records.

VON HORNBOSTEL – at first with the co-operation of Dr. OTTO ABRAHAM, later alone – published a series of brilliant studies, based on the analysis and transcription of the phonograms acquired by the Berlin Archives, and dealing with the musical expressions of peoples from all parts of the world (1882–1963, 2509, 2510, see also 2373 and 3579b). Unfortunately these studies are scattered over countless periodicals and accounts of travels, often difficult to obtain. The author never got as far as publishing that part of his life's work in a single volume of 'Collected Musicological Essays'; only his articles dating from before 1908 may be found together in the first volume of the 'Sämmelbände für vergleichende Musikwissenschaft'. [1]

The marvellous clarity of mind and wellnigh infallible intuition with which VON HORNBOSTEL penetrated into the – at the time practically virgin – field of exotic musical cultures will rarely be equalled. He was for all of us a shining example and unattainable ideal.

The remarkable thing is that his greatest service to the science of ethnomusicology was probably the fact that he put forward a theory which might be considered untenable – that is, if later investigators, MANFRED F. BUKOFZER (534, 535, 537) and KATHLEEN SCHLESINGER (3719), who have attempted to disapprove it, (though with, in my opinion, unsufficient arguments) are right – but which has, at any rate, succeeded in bringing clarity into certain very thorny problems in connexion with the structure of, and possible relationship between, instrumental scales of different peoples living remote from each other, and of both former and present times. I am of course referring to VON HORNBOSTEL's famous hypothesis of the cycle of blown fifths, which the reader no doubt knows by name. For the content of this hypothesis, and the criticism levelled at it, I may refer those interested to my brochure *Around Von Hornbostel's theory of the cycle of blown fifths*

---

[1] A complete bibliography of VON HORNBOSTEL has been published in Newsletter No. 2 (Aug. 1954) of the Society of Ethnomusicology (1134).

(2394) and to the articles by Handschin (fig. 12) (1593) and Lloyd (2639).

Von Hornbostel trained a number of talented pupils, several of whom worked for some years as his assistants. I would mention Georg Herzog (fig. 4ca) (1702–1750), now a prominent authority on North American Indian Music and attached to the University of Indiana, (as an anthropologist), and Robert Lachmann (fig. 20) (2496–2515) who specialized in the Japanese Noh- and the Arab and Berber music, and to whom we owe one of the cleverest and best written ethno-musicological publications, i.e. *Musik des Orients* (2502). There is further Walter Wiora (fig. 29), author of several elaborate and dependable essays on Central European folk-music, its nature and methods of investigation (4394–4420a) ; the prolific Hans Hickmann (fig. 30), an authority in the field of Egyptian and North African music (1753–1840c).; Heinrich Husmann (2000–2008a), and the many-sided Marius Schneider (fig. 24) (2785, 3734–3774b) who, in the first place, has occupied himself with typology of melodies and their transformation in the course of history, in the different cultures, races or by migration (3744, 3747, 3749, 3768, 3773) ; further with the formation of tonesystems (3767a), music philosophy (3769), symbolism in music (3750, 3752, 3753, 3756, 3764, 3770), sound-languages (3748, 3755), talking drums (3761), multipart music (3734) and the spreading of musical forms (3739, 3745, 3746, 3757). Also Mieczyslaw Kolinski (fig. 22) (2282–2292) may be reckoned among Von Hornbostel's pupils, as well as Fritz Bose (415–438a and 4492).

But his sphere of influence did not and does not confine itself to his direct pupils. Among those who have been inspired by his personality and publications I may mention, for instance, Heinrich Simbriger (3839, 3840), Manfred F. Bukofzer (533–538), Siegfried Nadel (2954–2961), and myself (2358–2418).

Von Hornbostel confined himself chiefly to 'home-work'. Most of his 'field-work' was done in the beginning of his career, among the Pawnee Indians. It is probable that his physique would not have stood the strain of much field-work. In other ways, however, he possessed all the necessary qualities for it, especially tact and intuition, and it is indeed to be regretted that circumstances finally forced him to work mainly at home. This was a pity – in the first place for himself. For it is precisely the variation between the two so diametrically opposed operations, in the field and in the study, which can make the life of an ethnomusicologist so rich and so eminently worth living. The man to whose lot it falls to be permitted the study of our science from both angles, may, indeed, consider himself lucky. He lives a 'double life' in the right sense of the word; on the one hand a life of adventure: enjoying contact with strange peoples, experiencing the enchantment of penetrating into less known regions; on the other hand his scientific and esthetic inclinations find satisfaction in thorough, far-reaching analysis of the material collected, which, moreover, is so much more alive for him, having gathered it himself, than for others who receive the records, musical instruments and comments by mail or investigate them in a museum.

However, experience teaches us that the position is often different in that the two aspects of ethnomusicological investigation must necessarily be kept apart. A. H. Fox Strangways (fig. 7) (1282–1290, 2515) the author of *Music of Hindostan* (1283) – that work beyond praise – in an opening article entitled *East and West* in the first volume of the 'Zeitschrift für vergleichende Musikwissenschaft', gave the following qualification of the two categories of ethnomusicologists: 'The workers are in two classes. There are those who have the health, energy and personality, provided they have the time and the means, to go and collect material. It is hard to say which of these is the most important, but the right personality is the rarest. Without the willing co-operation of the singers and dancers they will do little, and that willingness is only to be bought with unfeigned sympathy, inexhaustible curiosity, lively gratitude, untiring patience and a scrupulous conscience. It is easy to fake a tune till it fits a theory. It is easy to be content with a dozen specimens, and not to plough on and get the thirteenth which would have been worth them all. It is easy to think that it is we who confer the honour by collecting and recording, until a singer says, as she said to me, that she is not going to deliver her soul to a piece of wax which may get broken in the train.

And there are those who sit at home and shift and sort. Material comes in from diverse places and very various minds. How much credence are we to attach to each? How are we to fill the lacunae? How reconcile contradictions? What advice is to be given to young collectors? The bare facts are not of much use without the ideas on which to string them, and the natural enthusiasm of the collector benefits by being set in the proper proportions'.

In addition to the American and German phonogram-archives we should also briefly mention the French ones. Extensive collections of ethnomusicological records are in the possession of various organizations, particularly the 'Société d'Anthropologie', the 'Musée de l'Homme', the 'Bibliothèque musicale du Musée de la Parole et du Musée Guimet' [1] and the 'Phonothèque Nationale'.[2] They are chiefly on discs, i.e. made according to the gramophone process invented by Berliner, in which the recorder

---

[1] See 3951.

[2] In 1952 Unesco published a catalogue of the collection of the last named institute (123). It contains no less than 4564 numbers. In the same year appeared, under the auspices of the Ciap, Simone Roche's Catalogue of the collection of the Musée de l'Homme (3458).

does not, as in the case of the EDISON phonograph, move vertically, cutting deeper and less deep cuts into the sensitive wax cylinder, but is moved in a horizontal plane on a circular wax plate. (The Viennese archives, until recently, employed an intermediate form between phonograph and gramophone: with the former it had the variable depths of groove in common, with the latter the wax plates).

In Budapest there is the large collection of phonograms chiefly consisting of Hungarian and Rumanian folk music; it comprises over 30.000 records, collected for the greater part by the late BÉLA BARTÓK (fig. 9) (256–283) in collaboration with ZOLTÁN KODÁLY (fig. 10) (261, 265, 266, 283, 2267–2272).

The Musicological Institute at Stockholm (director: Dr. ERNST EMS-HEIMER) (fig. 26) (1091–1101), also possesses a collection of discs containing, among others, a series of valuable Mongolian and Caucasian records, whilst the Archives of Dialect and Folklore, Uppsala, contain a large collection of records of all Swedish provinces, including Lappland.

Further the phonogram archives of Leningrad must be mentioned, containing, it appears, mainly records of the music of the peoples living inside the borders of the Soviet Union. The scientific output of the Russian ethnomusicologists since the war is considerable. Because of their publications being written only in the Russian language and apparently not available for investigators on this side of the iron curtain, with a few exceptions they have not been included in the bibliography on p. 79 ff. Many of them, however, one can find in the bibliography of Asiatic musics by WATERMAN c.s. in 'Notes' (4307).

Many other national institutes also – for the greater part after World War II only – try to preserve on tape or wire the inheritance of traditional folk songs and folkdance melodies of their countries. So, for instance, in France (Paris) the 'Musée National des Arts et Traditions populaires' (CLAUDIE MARCEL-DUBOIS (fig. 31) and MAGUY ANDRAL); in England (London) the 'Music Department of the B.B.C.' (MARY SLOCOMB, PETER KENNEDY) and the 'British Institute of Recorded Sound' (HYATT KING, PATRICK SAUL); in the Netherlands (Amsterdam) the 'Netherlands Section of the International Folk Music Council' and the 'Codification Committee' of the 'Raad voor de Nederlandse Volkszang' (Father ELIS. BRUNING, JAAP KUNST, P. J. MEERTENS, JOP POLLMANN, WILL D. SCHEEPERS, MARIE VELDHUYZEN); in Scotland (Edinburgh) the 'School of Scottish Studies of Edinburgh University' (STEWART F. SANDERSON); in West-Germany (Regensburg) the 'Schallarchiv des Institutes für Musikforschung' (FELIX HOERBURGER) (1858) and in Freiburg i/Br. the 'Deutsches Volkslied-Archiv' (ERICH SEEMANN, WALTER WIORA (fig. 29)); in Italy (Rome) the 'Centro Nazionale Studi di Musica popolare' (GIORGIO NATALETTI); in

Yugoslavia the 'Serbian Academy of Sciences' in Beograd (MIODRAG VASILJEVIC) (fig. 41) and the Folkloristic Institutes at Zagreb (VINKO ŽGANEČ (fig. 35), ZORAN PALČOK), Sarajevo (CVJETKO RIHTMAN (fig. 36)), Skopje (GIVKO FIRFOV, EMANUIL CUČKOV), and Ljubljana (FRANCE MAROLT (†), VALENS VODUČEK (fig. 35)), e.t.q.

As for the study of folk music behind the Iron Curtain, I might quote the composer and musicologist ANDREY OLKHOVSKY, who, in his recent book *Music under the Soviets* [1], says: 'The organisation of Soviet folklore studies is concentrated chiefly in the Institutes of Folklore, attached to the All-Union and Republic Academies of Sciences and in the folklore departments of a number of conservatories (e.g. those of Moscow, Kiev, Kharkov, and Minsk). The most important work in the study of the theoretical problems of folk music has been done by a group of collaborators of the folklore department of the All-Union Academy of Sciences in Leningrad, particularly YE GIPPIUS and Z. EWALD; by K. KVITKA, a member of the folklore department of the Moscow Conservatory who specialized in the study of Ukrainian folklore; by the Kiev Institute of Folklore (especially Prof. HRINCHENKO); by the Kiev Conservatory (BEREGOVSKI), and by the Kharkov Conservatory (STEBLYANKO).'

At the time of writing it seems that the central position taken up by the Berlin phonogram archives until the second world war, will in future, at least partly, be occupied by the 'Archives internationales de musique populaire', established at Geneva under the auspices of the UNESCO and the CIA(T)P (= Commission Internationale des Arts et Traditions populaires). This institution is under the direction of Professor CONSTANTIN BRAILOIU (figs. 12 and 37) (458–467), formerly co-worker of BÉLA BARTÓK and, next to ZOLTÁN KODÁLY, *the* authority in the field of Rumanian and other East European musical folklore.

On reading an enumeration of the contents of the phonogram archives, [2] many will have wondered whether the large gramophone companies have not made very considerable contributions towards the work of recording what is still alive and being played in the way of exotic music. The answer to this question, it must be said, is rather disappointing; these companies, being run as they are on a purely commercial basis, have not rendered so much service to ethnomusicology as could be expected. The reason for this is threefold:

(*a*) the records of exotic music, which they have made, have usually been on sale only in the country in which the music was collected;

---

[1] New York, Praeger, 1955.
[2] A general survey also in: *Musique et chansons populaires* (ed. by the Intern. Inst. f. Intellectual Co-operation), Paris, 1934, in *Folklore musicale* (ed. by id.), Paris, 1939, and in the recent catalogue, edited for the Intern. Folk Music Council by NORMAN FRASER (1298).

(*b*) these companies were prepared to supply copies of the records in question elsewhere on condition that at least 25 copies were taken simultaneously, a condition which hardly suited the convencience of most musicologists or even museums;

(*c*) they usually only produced records when they had reason to expect them to be sold in quantities; in other words, they usually pandered completely to the – often regrettable – taste of the larger public and fought shy of the rarer musical expression-forms which are important by virtue of their being ancient, but (possibly for that very reason) no longer generally current, let alone popular. They also avoided, if possible, making records exceeding the limit of one side of a disc. There are but sporadic exceptions: Columbia has recorded Javanese vocal plays (*langendrya*) at Surakarta in the Mangku Nagaran in their entirety; the Karl Lindström Concern published an album of records, selected and with a commentary by Von Hornbostel, containing examples of Japanese, Chinese, Balinese, Siamese, Javanese, Sundanese, Indian, Persian, Egyptian and Tunesian music. And if the war had not intervened to spoil my own plans, I should have been given opportunity to produce, in collaboration with the Netherlands Indian Radio Omroepmaatschappij (Nirom), 60 large, double-sided records with examples of all the musical scales used in Java and Bali; of the sound produced by, and the manner of playing all instruments used by the native musicians in these islands, and of all types of orchestras and all forms of compositions.

If the gramophone companies had only heeded the examples mentioned above, they might have rendered inestimable services to the science of ethnomusicology. Now, they will have to hurry: for as fast as the recording processes are being perfected, the musical expressions eligibe for reproduction are, under the influence of western civilization and the intensificaton of world trafic, declining in purity and musical value. In the course of the years much that was once beautiful and remarkable has gone to perdition, without a trace or record remaining. Moreover, instead of giving (or selling) to a scientific institution the matrices of recordings which, after some years, have been deleted from their catalogues (often containing music that can no longer be found, even by field-workers), these companies usually have destroyed them, and so, also in this way, much irreplaceable material is lost for ever. [1]

---

[1] 'The gramophone companies had noteworthy classical renderings but of these even the master records had been subsequently destroyed. For the policy of the gramophone companies subsequently developed a new commercial outlook which had a bad effect on our art. On the one hand, they began to employ for renderings a bizarre background of a variety of instruments, and on the other, flooded the market with cheap cinema tunes and song hits' ... (V. Raghavan, 3302, p. 79).

'The preparation of a catalogue of recorded music in India is, in a way, a distressing task, for the best of the music recorded has been destroyed without any regard for its artistic value.

Further, the gramophone companies should always assure themselves of the cooperation of a specialist who is familiar with the music to be recorded – as Odeon, very luckily, did at the time, in Bali, where the gifted painter-musician WALTER SPIES acted as their advisor. This measure would not only ensure a correct and varied choice of recordings, but would also lead to a greater likelihood of the records turning out truer to reality. To give an example of this latter point: existing records of Javanese gamelan music which include the vocal element often allow the voice to be far too prominent, as if it were a solo with accompaniment, while in reality the solo- and choral voices are nothing more than equivalent elements in an otherwise instrumental tonal texture; in other words, the singers ought not to have been placed right in front of the microphone.

By utilizing the knowledge and advice of a musical specialist it will also be possible to prevent the titles on the records from containing such an annoyingly large number of spelling mistakes.

Fortunately, in this regard also, the last years have shown a noticeable improvement. We have already mentioned the widely known album 'Musik des Orients', issued by the Karl Lindström Concern, Berlin. ERICH VON HORNBOSTEL chose for it from among the records, published in previous years (more for commercial, rather than musicological purposes) by Odeon and Parlophon. [1]

After Worldwar II, however, there resulted, in the nick of time, from the fertile collaboration of ethnomusicologists with gramophone- or broadcastingcompanies a number of splendid collections. Of those I will cite the following:

a) issued by the **American Columbia** (799, 7th Avenue, New York) under the general editorship of ALAN LOMAX:

SL. 204. Ireland (rec. and ed. by SEAMUS ENNIS);
SL. 205. French Africa (regions: Hoggar, Fezzan, Upper Volta, Somaliland, Niger Territory, French Sudan, French Guinea, Madagascar, Togo, Gabon, Congo) (tribes: Ambilube, Babinga Babenzélé Pygmies, Babinga Bangombe Pygmies, Babinga Pygmies, Badouma, Bawanji, Bongli, Dankali, Dogon, Gwin, Jarma, Kabre, Koukouya, Kourroussa, N(o)gundi, Okande, Sakalava, Somali, Sonray, Tuareg, Vezo, Wara) (ed. by ANDRÉ SCHAEFF- NER (fig. 14) and GILBERT ROUGET (fig. 34));
SL. 206. England (ed. by PETER KENNEDY);
SL. 207. France (and Corsica) (instr.: barrel organ, accordeon, hurdy-gurdy, bag-pipe (*biniou*), *musette*, tamburine, *galoubet*, oboe, clarinet, *bombarde*) (ed. by CLAUDIE MARCEL-DUBOIS (fig. 30) and MAGUY ANDRAL));

Some of the most important recording companies were and still are mainly foreign concerns and have no responsible artistic adviser.

If the sales of a record fail to reach a certain figure during a three-monthly period, the record is automatically destroyed. .... Almost all the records of musicians of the past generation have been destroyed.' (ALAIN DANIÉLOU, 815, Foreword).

[1] Recently Decca has re-issued this collection on two L.P. records (No. DX 107).

SL. 208. Australia and New Guinea (regions and tribes: Arnhemland, Melville and Bathurst Island, Djuan, Unpelli, Karkar, Tami, Wabaga, Orokaiva, Yule Island, Gerebi, Kunimaipa, Fuyuge, Lake Murray region etc.) (instr.: *didjeridu*); (ed. by A. P. ELKIN, with contrib. by Father ANDRÉ DUPEYRAT and the Australian Broadcasting Coy.);

SL. 209. Scotland (regions: Hebrides, Barra, Lewis, Uist, Skye, Mull, Islay, Coll; Shetlands; Highlands, Lowlands) (ed. with the assistance of the MAC-LEANS of Raasay, HAMISH HENDERSON and WILLIAM MONTGOMERIE);

SL. 210. Indonesia (islands: East- and West-Guinea, Aru Islands, Babar, Manuwoko, Kai Islands, Banda, Ambon, Bali, Borneo (Dayak) and Java) (instr.: New Guinea: flute, jew's harp; Moluccos: gongs, drums, *gambus;* Borneo: *jerupai*) shawm with free tongue), drums, gongs, *sapoh* (lute); Bali: gamelans Angklung, Gong, Gambuh and Jogèd; gendèr wayang, flute, jew's harp; Java: the different instruments of the gamelan (ed. by J. KUNST);

SL. 211. Canada (tribes: French Canadians, English Canadians, Iroquois, Kwakiutl, Huron, Seneca, Cayuga, Scots-Gaelic, Caribou Eskimo) (ed. by MARIUS BARBEAU) (fig. 18);

SL. 212. Venezuela (tribes: a.o. Puinabe, Maquiritare, Guaharibo, Kalina, Yayuro, Piaroa) (instr.: bark horns, pan-pipes, bamboo horns, bull-roarers, nose-flutes, grass- oboe's', *birimbao, bandola, cuatro, maracas,* harp, stamping tubes, musical bow, guitar, drums (a.o. *mina*)) (ed. by JUAN LISCANO);

SL. 213. British East Africa (tribes: Bukusu, Chewa, Chopi, Ganda, Girimaya, Haya, Hehe, Karanga, Luba, Luo, Ndau/Garwe, Nyamwezi, Nyoro, Shona/Karanga, Shona/Ndau/Garwe, Sotho, Swahili, Zaramo, Zezuru) (instr.: drums, *sanza* (*mbira*), musical bow, flutes, zithers, lyres) (ed. by HUGH T. TRACEY) (fig. 23);

SL. 214. Japan, Ryu-kyu's, Formosa, Korea) (peoples and tribes: Japanese, Vunun, Saisett, Pyuma, Ami) (instr.: *shamisen, koto, shahuhuchi, fue, taiko, shirabe* or *shime-daiho, tuusumi, kane* or *surigane, samshin,* mouth-harp, *janggo,* Korean vertical flute, Korean transversal flute, harp) (rec. and ed. by GENJIRO MASU);

SL. 215. India (tribes and peoples: a.o. Gond) (instr.: *shahnai, dholak, jhori, nagara, dukkar, kasavar, do-tara, chang, ekatara, karatala, tippera, vina, sarangi, svaramandala, tampura, tabla*) (rec. and ed. by ALAIN DANIÉLOU);

SL. 216. Spain (provinces: Galicia, Asturias, Santander, Leon, Castilla, Andalucia) (instr.: a.o. bagpipe, castanets, drums, tamburine, guitar, *payecha* (scraped skillet), *ximbomba, rabel, pandero, banduria, oud*) (ed. ALAN LOMAX);

SL. 217. Yugoslavia (regions: Croatia, Slovenia, Macedonia, Bosnia, Hercegovina, Montenegro, Serbia) (instr.: *tamburiza* orchestra, different types of bagpipe (*dude, gajde, diple*), *sopele, gusle, dvojnice, tapan, tambura, frula, kaval, daire, kemane, darbuka, oud, mandola, def*) (rec. by PETER KENNEDY; notes by ALBERT LORD);

and by the same firm: 'Dancers of Bali' (instr.: gamelan Gong, gamelan Angklung, gendèr wayang) (notes by COLIN MCPHEE) (ML 4618);

b) issued by the **American Indian Soundchief**: a series of 78 and 33 rpm records 'Songs of the Redman' (tribes: Arapaho, Caddo, Canada Chippewa, Cherokee, Cheyenne, Chippewa, Choctaw-Chickasaw, Comanche, Creek-Seminoles, Crow, Geronimo Apaches, Kiowa, Montana Plain Cree, Navajo, Otoe, Pawnee, Ponca, Sioux, South Dacota Oglala Sioux, Taos Pueblo, Wichita, Zuñi Pueblo) (for more particulars see 1134 No. 9);

c) issued by the **Argo Record Company Ltd**. (George Street, London W 1): two L.P. records 'Music from Bali', played by the gamelan from Pliatan, South Bali, under the direction of ANAK ANAK GDÉ MANDÉRA (instr.: *gamelan Gong, gamelan Angklung*) (ARS 1006 and 1007) = B.A.M., Paris, Nos. L.D. 017 and 018;

d) recorded and edited by **Arthur S. Alberts**: Tribal, Folk and Café Music of West Africa (3 albums) with text and commentary by MELVILLE J. HERSKOVITS, DUNCAN EMRICH, RICHARD A. WATERMAN and MARSHALL W. STEARNS (Field Recordings, New York, 1950);

e) issued by the **Barclay Disques**, Paris: 'Musique pygmée' (rec. by the Ubangi-Congo Expedition) (No. 86.019);

f) issued by the '**Boîte à Musique**', (133 Boulevard Raspail, Paris): a series of Central African music, recorded by the Ogowé-Congo Mission (Messrs. A. DIDIER and GILBERT ROUGET) (regions: Middle-Congo, Gabon, Ogowé, Upper-Volta, as well Negro- as Pygmee-music) (instr.: a.o. *sanza*, musical bow, harp-zither, drums, trumpets, *marimba*); and further:

L.D. 014. 'Musique traditionelle de l'Inde';

L.D. 015. 'Musique religieuse de l'Inde' (both collected by DEBEN BHATTACHARYA);

L.D. 310. 'Chants folkloriques du Bengale' (sung by LOKENATH BHATTACHARYA);

L.D. 314. 'Musique de la haute forêt amazonienne' (rec. by FRANCIS MAZIÈRE) (tribes: Boni and Oayana);

L.D. 326. 'Tribus Proto-Indochinoises Moïs' (rec. by FRANTZ LAFOREST; notes by id. and L. BERTHE) (tribes: Bahnar, Dié, Maä, Sedang, Yarai) (instr.: bamboo xylophone (*latung*), bar-zither (*bro* or *tingning*), hydraulic bamboo carillon (*tang koa*), bamboo zither (*roding*), gong (*gok*); drum (*gorr*), small gongs (*tong-tieng*), small cymbals (*rong ruyh*), mouth-organ (*kom boät*), jew's harp (*toong*), handclapping-bamboos (*pah pung*));

L.D. 331. (M.) Musique du Nord-Cameroun (tribes: Foulbe, Kirdi, Lamido, Massa, Matakam, Moundang) (instr.: *agaita* (wooden trumpet), *kakaki* (long metal trumpet), *goundi* (harp), drums, flute, horns) (rec. and notes: JACQUES and CLAUDE BILTGEN and JEAN BRUGIAL);

g) issued by the Capitol firm: Music of Belgian Congo (Kasongo) (T 10005);

h) issued by '**Chant du Monde**' (32, rue Beaujon, Paris 8e): 'Mongolie/Sin-kiang' (tribes: Mongolians, Uigurs, Kazaks) (instr.: *ma ya li, tam po-euhr*) (LDY 4039) (rec. by CLAUDE ROY);

Grèce No. 2. Egina (rec. by DESPINA MAZARAKI, MELPO MERLIER, LOUIS BERTHE and PIERRE GOUGUIDIS; notes by LOUIS BERTHE) (instr.; violin, *lauto, santuri* (beaten zither, derived from the Persian *santur* and played like the Basque *tun-tun*));

Chansons populaires du Vietnam (notes: NGUYEN-NGHE) (LDY 4.046);

i) issued by the '**Club Français du Disque**': Rythmes et Mélodies de Turquie (instr.: different kinds of *saz, tulum* (bagpipe), *darbuka, mey* (shawm), *zurna, kemence*) (rec. and notes: BLAISE CALAME);

j) issued by the **Colosseum** firm:

No. 174. Caucasus (Azerbajjan);

No. 175. Caucasus (Georgia, Armenia);

No. 198. Central Asia (Turkmenia, Uzbekistan);

k) issued by the **Commodore** firm: Music of Belgian Congo (Comm. 30005);

l) issued by '**Contrepoint**' (52, rue Hauteville, Paris 10e):

MC 20.045. Music of the Malinké and the Baoulé tribes, Upper Guinea, French West Africa (instr.: a.o. *balafon*, harp, flute) (rec. by GILBERT ROUGET with the aid of JEAN KOROMA);

MC 20.093. Music of Dahomey (rec. by GILBERT ROUGET, in collaboration with PIERRE VERGER);

MC 20.103. 'Chants et danses folkloriques d'Arménie et du Caucase';

MC 20.110. 'Musique populaire de l'Inde du Nord' (rec. by DEBEN BATTACHARYA);

MC 20.112. 'Borneo' (tribe: Pnihing) (instr.: *suling, sapeh*, gongs, drums) (rec. by PIERRE IVANOFF);

26

MC 20.113. 'Bali' (rec. by PIERRE IVANOFF);
MC 20.119. Tibetans of Sikkim (rec. in 1953 by the expedition-BOURGUIGNON and ed. by GILBERT ROUGET);
MC 20.137. Brésil (tribes: Gorotire, Kubenkranken, Kwikuru, Yaulapiti, Kamayura, Kayapo, Kaingang) (rec. and notes by SIMONE DREYFUS-ROCHE);
MC 20.138. Brésil (music of the Negroes of Bahia) (instr.: musical bow (birimbau), flat drum (pandeiro), bamboo scraper (reco-reco), rattling instrument (caxixi)) (rec. and notes by SIMONE DREYFUS-ROCHE);
MC 20.146. Dahomey (musique du roi) et Guinée (tribe: Malinké) (instr. seron (harp-lute), kora (other type of harp-lute), drums, balafon, a.o.) (rec. and notes: GILBERT ROUGET);
EXTP 1033 and 1034). Musique Persane (instr.: tar, tabla (drum) (rec. and notes: NOËL BALLIF);

m) issued by the Cook Laboratories Inc. (101, 2nd Street, Stamford (Conn.) U.S.A.) 'The Japanese Koto' (LP 1132);

n) issued by the Discothèque Contemporaine (Place St. Jean 5, Brussels): a set of eight 78-records of Copt music (rec. during the Congress of Arab music, Cairo 1932) (Nos. HD 14–21);

o) issued by the Disques Africavox: a series of 78-records from all parts of the French African Empire: Niger-Sudan (tribes: Haussa, Songhai-Zerma, Sarakolé, Bambara, Senoufo); French Guinea (tribes: Bambara, Malinké, Toma); Upper-Volta (tribes: Senoufo, Dioula, Gwin); Ivory Coast (tribes: Baoulé, Ebrié, Kono); Senegal (tribes: Wolof, Lébou, Peul); Mauritania (Moors); Dahomey (tribes: Yoruba, Goun, Fon); Togo; Cameroons; French Equatorial Africa (Middle-Congo: tribes: Kuyu, Balali, Batéké, Mbochi, Ngundi; Ubangi-Chari-region (tribes: Baya, Bugongo); Gabon (tribes: Baduma, Bawanji, Boungomo, Okandi));

p) issued by Ducretet-Thomson (41, rue Washington, Paris 8e) an 'Anthologie de la musique classique de l'Inde' (performers: MOHIN UDDIN DAGAR, AMIN UDDIN DAGAR, RAVI SHANKAR, MISHRA SHYÂM LÂL, NÂRÂYAN DÂS MISHRA, D. R. PARVATIKAR, RADHA SHIRI RÂM, S. VIDYA, BÂLÂ SARASVATI, T. VISVANATHAN, MUTTU KUMARAM, CHATURLAL, ALI AKBAR KHAN, MUDI KONDAN C. VENKATARAMA IYER, D. K. PATTAMAL, DEVAKOTAI NÂRÂYANA IYENGAR, KALYÂNA KRISHNA BHAGAVATAR, RAGHUNÂTH PRASANNA, NANDAN PRASÂD, P. R. BÂLASUBRAHMANYAM, K. PICHIAPPA, KAMALÂ KRISHNAMURII, K. GANESHAN, BUDALUR KRISHNAMURTI SHASTRI) (instr.: shahnai, sitar, flute, sârangî, vinâ, mrḍangga, tablâ, sarode, nâgasvaram, gottuvâdyam); (rec. and notes by ALAIN DANIÉLOU); further: 'A travers la Grèce' (No. 260 V 062);

q) issued by Electra, Stratford: 'Voices of Haiti' (L.P. Ekl 5) (rec. by MAYA DEREN);

r) issued by Elektra Records (361, Bleecker Str., New York 14): Steelband music from Trinidad (EKL 139);

s) issued by the English Columbia: a series of 78-recordings, mostly from South-India, among which:
GA 731. (performer: RAJARATNAM PILLAI) (instr.: nagasvara, ottu, tavil);
GE 980. (perf.: VEENAI DHANAM) (instr.: vina);
GE 6173. (singer: PATTAMAL);
GE 6240. (singer: id.);
GE 6347. (singer: MADURA MANI IYER);
GE 17505. (perf.: ABDUL KARIM KHAN)) (instr.: vina) (North India!);
A 106. (singer: RAMANUJA IYENGAR) (instr.: violin, mrḍangga);
LBE 30. (singer: SUBRAHMANYA IYER) (instr. violin, mrḍangga);

t) issued by the English Decca: a series of L.P.-records, collected by HUGH T. TRACEY (fig. 23):
LF 1084. Songs and instrumental music of Tanganyika (tribes: Nyamwezi, Hehe, Haya; instruments a.o. sanza, ligombo (zither), nanga (trough zither), enkoito drums);

27

LF 1120. The drums of East Africa (tribes: Nyamwezi, Nyoro/Haya, Ganda, (Wa)tu(t)si; instruments a.o. *enkoito* drums, *entenga* drums);

LF 1121. Kenya (tribes: Nandi, Kipsigi, Luo, Nyika/Kambe, Nyika/Chonye, Nyika/Girimaya; instruments a.o. *kibukandet* (lyre), *chepkong* (lyre), *oruto* (lute), *thum* (lyre), *gara* (leg bells), *kayamba* (castanets), rattles);

LF 1169. Talking and Royal Tutsi (Watusi) drums; (tribes: Tutsi, Lokele);

LF 1170. The guitars of Africa (tribes: Swahili, Zulu/Ndebele, Nubi, Luo, Luba/Sanga, Ngala);

LF 1171. The African Music Society's choice (tribes: Luba/Sanga, Ganda, Mbunda, Medje, Zande/Bandiya, Nande, Tutsi, Luo; instruments a.o. guitar, *ennanga* (harp), *kathandi* (sanza), *neikembe* (id.), *kundi* (harp), *nyamulera* (flute));

LF 1172. Congo songs and dances (tribes: Genya, Tutsi, Zande, Luba, Bobwa, Buudu, Yogo, Mbuti Pygmies, Batwa, Zande/Bandiya; instruments a.o. *chizanshi* (xylophone), *lisanzo* (id.), drums, rattles, flutes, *kponingbo* (xylophone));

LF 1173. Music of the Uganda Protectorate (tribes: Ganda, Nyoro/Toro, Nyoro, Ganda/Soga, Bamba; instr.: drums, *mbira*, xylophone, flute, calabash-horn, harp, lyre);

LF 1224. Music of the Malinké, Baoulé, Yoruba, Swahili, Sudan, Ganda, Lonzo, Mulari, Ekondo, Tabwa;

LF 1225. Music of the Girimaya, Luo, Gogo, Thonga, Bembe, Ndebele-Zulu, Chopi, Sotho (Basutoland);

u) issued by the **Esoteric** firm:

Eso 513. Tribal music and dances of Africa;

Eso 537. Music from Dahomey;

Eso 547. Arabian music;

Eso 2004. Indians of the Upper Amazon;

v) issued by **Ethnic Folkways** (Folkways Records and Service Corp.) (117 W. 46th Street, New York 36, (N.Y.)):

FE 4401 (P 401). Music of the Sioux and the Navajo (rec. and notes by WILLARD RHODES);

FE 4402 (P 402). Music of Equatorial Africa (tribes: Baduma, Baya, Bongili, Kukuya, Mboko, Ngoundi, Okandi, Yaswa) (rec.: ANDRÉ DIDIER; notes: GILBERT ROUGET);

FE 4403 (P 403). Drums of Haiti (rec. and notes: HAROLD COURLANDER);

FE 4404 (P 404). Folk and traditional music of Turkey (instr.: *cura*, *baglama*, *bozuk*, *meydan sazi*, *asik saź* (5 different kinds of *saź*), *qanun*, *kemence* (bowed lute with 3 strings), *kasik* (castanets), *zil* (fingerbells), *zurna*, *kaval*, *darbuka*, *davul* (large drum)) (notes: TARIK BULUT);

FE 4405 (P 405). Folk music of Ethiopia (and Erithrea) (instr.: *begenna* (harp), *tcherawata* (fiddle), *m'bilta* (flute), *masonquo* (lyre), drum) (rec. and notes: HAROLD COURLANDER);

FE 4406 (P 406). Music of Indonesia (Java, Minangkabau, Batak, Bali, Malaya) (notes: R. SUWANTO);

FE 4407 (P 407). Folk music of Haiti (rec. and notes: HAROLD COURLANDER);

FE 4408 (P 408). Folk music of Palestine (Bokhara, Palestine, Yemen, Persia) (instr.: *doyra*, *tar*, *durbukki*, *qanun*) (rec. Dept. of Folk music Anthrop. Inst. of Israel; introd. by RAPHAEL PATAI; notes and transcriptions by MIECZYSLAW KOLINSKI);

FE 4409 (P 409). Folk music of India (Punjab, Bengal, Rajastan, South India) (instr.: *esraj*, *sitar*, flute, *gopijantra*, *dholak*, *surangi*, *pakavaj*, *kartal*, *vani*, *mrḍangga*, *shahnai*, *tabla*, *baya*, *tappu*) (notes: HAROLD COURLANDER);

FE 4410 (P 410). Cult music of Cuba (Lucumi, Abakwa, Kimbisa, Djuka, Arara) (rec. and notes: HAROLD COURLANDER);

FE 4411 (P 411). Music of Spain (Navarre, Galicia, Asturias, Catalonia, Majorca) (notes: EMILIO DE TORRE);

FE 4413 (P 413). Indian music of Mexico (tribes: Yaqui, Seri, Huichol, Cora, Tzotzil) (instr.: *huehuetl*, harp, flute, drum, violin, rasping sticks, water drum, music bow (*mitote*)); (rec. HENRIETTA YURCHENCO; notes: GORDON F. ECKHOLM and HENRIETTA YURCHENCO);

FE 4414 (P 414). Folk music of France (Berry, Normandy, Provence, Orleans, Bretagne, Vendée (Poitou), Anjou, Corsica, Angoulème) (instr.: *hurdy-gurdy, tamburine, fluviol (txistu, galoubet), tamboril (tun-tun), bagpipe*) (notes: PAUL ARMA);

FE 4415 (P 415). Music of Peru (Aymara, Quechua, Mestizos) (notes: HARRY TSCHOPIK);

FE 4416 (P 416). Music of the Russian Middle East (Azerbaijan, Armenia, Uzbekistan) (notes: HENRY COWELL);

FE 4417 (P 417). Negro Folk music of Alabama. I. secular (rec. and notes: HAROLD COURLANDER);

FE 4418 (P 418). Negro Folk music of Alabama. II. religious (rec. and notes: HAROLD COURLANDER);

FE 4419 (P 419). Folk music of Rumania (rec. BÉLA BARTÓK; notes: HENRY COWELL);

FE 4420 (P 420). Music of the American Indians of the Southwest (Navajo, Zuñi, Hopi, San Ildefonso, Taos, Western Apache, Yuma, Papago, Walapai, Havasupai) (rec. and notes: WILLARD RHODES);

FE 4421 (P 421). Music of South Arabia (Bedouin, Yemenite Jews) (rec. and notes: WOLF LESLAU);

FE 4422 (P 422). Traditional and classical music of India (instr.: *dholak, tabla, sitar, sarinda, algoza, tambura, gharghar, nugara*) (performers: TURAYUR M. RAJAGOPALA SARMA, KUMARI SHYAMALA, D. K. PATTAMAL, DATTO-PANT, KUMARI JUTHIKA RAY, and T. N. RAGARATHNAM PILLAI) (notes: HAROLD COURLANDER);

FE 4423 (P 423). Music of Southeast Asia (Thailand, Viet Nam, Laos, Cambodia, Burma, Malaya) (notes: HENRY COWELL);

FE 4424 (P 424). Folk and classical music of Korea (notes: KYUNG HO PARK);

FE 4425 (P 425). Folk music of Pakistan (rec. Government of Pakistan);

FE 4426 (P 426). Spanish and Mexican Music of New Mexico (rec. and notes: J. D. ROBB);

FE 4427 (P 427). Folk Music of the Western Congo (tribes: Bambala, Bunda, Kwesi, Pende, Pindi) (instr.: talking drums, *sanza*, horns, rattles, marimba's) (rec. and notes: LEO A. VERWILGHEN);

FE 4428 (P 428). Songs of the Watutsi (rec. and notes: LEO A. VERWILGHEN);

FE 4429 (P 429). Folk music of Japan (instr.: a.o. *samisen, koto, surigane*) (rec. and notes: EDWARD NORBECK);

FE 4430 (P 430). Songs and Pipes of the Hebrides (rec. and notes: POLLY HITCHCOCK);

FE 4431 (P 431). Religious music of India (a.o. Vedic chant) (instr. a.o. *ghungarus, karatali*) (performers: T. M. KRISHNASWAMI IYER, P. R. BALASUBRAH-MANYAM, pandit AMARNATHA MISRA, SRI TARAPADA KUNDU, Swami D. R. PARVATIKAR, pandit RAMJI SHASTRI DRAVIDA, SHYAM LAL, and KANHAIYA LAL) (rec. and notes: ALAIN DANIÉLOU);

FE 4432 (P 432). Songs and dances of Haiti (rec. and notes: HAROLD COURLANDER);

FE 4433 (P 433). Maori songs of New Zealand (rec. by the New Zealand Broadcasting Service; notes: HARRY TSCHOPIK and ULRIC WILLIAMS);

FE 4434 (P 434). Folk music of Yugoslavia (rec. LAURA BOLTON; notes by id. and M. S. FILIPOVIĆ);

FE 4435 (P 435). The Black Caribs of Honduras (rec. by PETER KITE SMITH; notes: DORIS STONE);

FE 4436 (P 436). Burmese folk and traditional music (instr. a.o. *patt waing, maung saing, saung, pattala, kim si daw, shwe-bo, do butt, o zi*) (notes: MAUNG THAN MYINT);

FE 4437 (P 437). Spain: flamenco music of Andalusia (introd. and notes: GILBERT CHASE);

FE 4439 (P 439). Tribal music of Australia (Arnhemland) (instr.: *didjeridu*) (rec. and notes: A. P. ELKIN);

FE 4440 (P 440). Religious songs and drums in the Bahamas (rec. and notes: MARSHALL W. STEARNS);

FE 4441 (P 441). Drums of the Yoruba of Nigeria (instr. a.o. *dundun, gungan, igbin, kanango, kerikeri, gudugudu, bata, shekere*) (rec. and notes: WILLIAM BASCOM);

FE 4442 (P 442). Music of the Falashas (instr.: gongs, drums) (rec. by WOLF LESLAU);

FE 4443 (P 443). Music of the Ukraine (instr. a.o. *duda* (bagpipe), *balalaika*) (notes: HENRY COWELL);

FE 4444 (P 444). The Eskimos of Hudson Bay and Alaska (tribes: Aevilikmiut, Okomiut), (rec. by LAURA BOULTON; notes by id. and HENRY COWELL);

FE 4445 (P 445). Songs and dances of the Flathead Indians (rec. by ALAN P. and BARBARA W. MERRIAM: notes: ALAN P. MERRIAM);

FE 4446 (P 446). Music from Mato Grosso (tribes: Camayura, Chavante, Iwalapeti, Kayabi) (rec. by EDWARD WEYER; notes: HARRY TSCHOPIK);

FE 4447 (P 447). Folk music of South Asia (Nepal, Pakistan, Kashmir, India);

FE 4448 (P 448). Folk music of the Amami islands (instr.: a.o. *jyabisen* (primitive *shamisen*) (rec. and notes: DOUGLAS G. HARING);

FE 4449 (P 449). Japanese Buddhist rituals (rec. and notes: DOUGLAS G. HARING);

FE 4450 (P 450). Music of Cape Breton Island (Nova Scotia) (Gaelic songs);

FE 4451 (P 451). Music of the Bulu of Cameroon (rec. and notes: EDWARD COUZENS);

FE 4453 (P 453). Folk music of Jamaica (rec.: EDWARD SEAGA);

FE 4454 (P 454). Folk music of Greece (Epirus, Rhodos, Cyprus, Naxos, Peloponnesos, Macedonia, Pontus) (instr.: Pontic lyre (*kemence*), Cretan lyre, lute, bagpipe (*gainda, askaulos, tzambuna, askomandura*), *pipiza, santuri, kanonion*, clarinet (*suravli, tzamara, phiamboli, pithkiavli*), drums, horns) (rec.: JAMES A. NOTOPOULOS; notes: G. A. MEGAS);

FE 4458 (P 458). Indian music of the Upper Amazone (tribes: Campa, Cocoma, Conibo, Shipibo) (rec.: HARRY TSCHOPIK; notes by id. and WLLARD RHODES);

FE 4460 (P 460). Temiar dream songs of Malaya (rec. and notes: D. NOONE);

FE 4461 (P 461). Jamaica cult rhythm (rec. and notes: GEORGE EATON SIMPSON);

FE 4462 (P 462). Wolof music of Senegal and Gambia (rec.: DAVID AMES);

FE 4464 (P 464). Indian music of the Canadian plains (tribes: Assiniboin, Blackfoot, Blood, Cree) (rec.: KEN PEACOCK);

FE 4465 (P 465). Music of Liberia (tribes: Bassa, Gio, Kpelle, Kru, Loma, Mandingo) (instr.: drums, slitdrums, musical bow, *balafon*) (rec.: PACKARD L. OKIE);

FE 4466 (P 466). Music of the Philippines (tribe: Hanunoo) (instr.: *gitgit* (3-stringed bowed lute), *kudyapi* (6-str. plucked lute), *lantuy* (flute), *agung* (gong), *tangkup, pitu* (whistles), *kudlung* (bamboo idiochord), *batiwtiw* (id.), *kalutang* (musical sticks) (notes: HAROLD CONKLIN and JOSÉ MACEDA);

FE 4467 (P 467). Folk dances of Greece (Epirus, Cyprus, Crete, Naxos, Peloponnesos, Macedonia, Pontus) (instr.: bagpipe, Cretan lyre, a.o.) (rec.: JAMES A. NOTOPOULOS; notes: SPYROS PERISTERES);

FE 4469 (P 469). Kurdish folk songs and dances (Iraq) (instr.: *juzale* (double clarinet) and *tapil* (drums)) (rec.: RALPH S. SOLECKI, LAWK, BESTA, and HAIRAN);

FE 4471-4474 (P 471-474). Negro folk music of Alabama III-VI (rec. and notes: HAROLD COURLANDER);

FE 4476 (P 476). The Baoule of the Ivory Coast (instr.: horns, whistles, flutes, harp, gourd, *balafon*, rattles, drums) (rec. and notes: DONALD THUROW);

FE 4480. Arabic and Druse music (Palestine) (instr.: *shabbabi, yaroul, durbakki*) (rec.: SAM ESKIN);

FE 4482. Folk music of French Canada (rec.: LAURA BOULTON, SAM GESSER and from the Archives of the National Museum of Canada; notes: MARIUS BARBEAU, BIDOU, prince EUGÈNE a.o.);

FE 4483. Music of the Ituri forest (tribes: Bandaka, Banguana, Bira, Mandaka, Mbudo, Mbuti) (instr.: drums, slitdrum, clappers, boardzither, guitar, musical bow, flute) (rec. and notes: COLIN T. TURNBULL and FRANCIS S. CHAPMAN);

FE 4500 (P 500). Negro folk music of Africa and America (tribes and countries: Anglo-Egyptian Sudan, Baduma, Erithrea, Ethiopia, Ibo, Yoruba, Zanzibar, Zulu; Brazil, Colombia, Cuba, Haiti, Puerto Rico, Trinidad, U.S.A.) (rec. by MELVILLE J. and FRANCES HERSKOVITS, ANDRÉ DIDIER, HAROLD COURLANDER, WOLF LESLAU, EMMA COURLANDER, RICARDO E. ALEGRIA, Odeon, Singer and FUENTES) (notes: HAROLD COURLANDER);

FE 4501A/D (P 501A/D). Folk music of the Mediterranean (Algeria, Sardinia, Albania, Syria, France, Egypt, Morocco, Italy, Tunis, Greece, Turkey, Spain, Serbia, Libya and Palestine) (instr.: beating sticks, double clarinet, oboe, drum, guitar, *oud, qanun, rebab tamburiza* orchestra, violin, accordeon, tamburine, fife (*galoubet, fishialetto*)) (selection and notes: HENRY COWELL);

FE 4502A/D (P 502A/D). African and Afro-American drums (Watusi, Baya, Yoruba, Madagascar, Bambala, Mahafaly, Haiti, Virgin islands, Puerto Rico, Jamaica, Cuba, Bahamas, Surinam, Brazil, Trinidad, U.S.A.) (notes: HAROLD COURLANDER and MIECZYSLAV KOLINSKI);

FE 4503 (P 503). Africa South of the Sahara (tribes: Amakwavi, Babinga, Bambara, Bashi, Bechuana, Boungomo, Bulu, Bushmen, Hororo, Ibani, Kwiri, Mahafaly, Makwa, Mbuti, Mboko, Pende, Pindi, Sudan, Twa, Wolof, Yoruba, Zulu) (ed.: HAROLD COURLANDER);

FE 4504 (P 504). Music of the world's peoples (Madagascar, Caucasus, Greece, Japan, Nigeria, India, Russia, U.S.A., Ireland, France, Bali, Arabia, Tahiti, Tibet, Iceland and Spain) (instr. a.o. *harp, koto, sho, sanai, esraj, jalatarang*) (selection and notes: HENRY COWELL);

FE 4505 (P 505). Music of the world's peoples, vol. II (Serbia, Iran, Albania, China, Congo, Finland, French Canada, Ukraine, Chile, Italy, Kashmir, Australia, Cuba, Azerbaijan, Palestine Jews, Sioux) (selection and notes: HENRY COWELL);

FE 4506 (P 506). Music of the world's peoples, vol. III (American Northwest Indians, Argentina, Brazil, Bulgaria, Dahomey, Egypt, England, Hungarian Gypsies, Mexico, Peru, Philippines, Puerto Rico, Serbia, Thailand Trinidad, Turkey, Vietnam, Zulu,) (selection and notes: HENRY COWELL);

FE 4520 (P 520). Folkmusic from Italy (Albanian villages in Southern Italy, Calabria, Campobasso, Capri, Frosinone, San Paolo Matese, Sardinia, Sicily) (instr.: *brocca, cornamusa*, flute, guitar, jew's harp, *organetto, zampogna, zufolo*) (rec.: WALTHER HENNING);

FE 4525 (P 525). Man's early musical instruments (instr.: foot stamping, hand clapping, tapping sticks, cymbals, pounding bamboos, beaten pots, rattles, scrapers, slit drum, finger drum, water drum, frame drum, hollow log drum, drum chimes (*patt vaing*), gong chimes (*chaing vaing*), bells, xylophone, sanza, jew's harp, trumpets, horns, oboe, clarinet,

31

double clarinet, bagpipe, accordeon, vertical flute, transverse flute, whistle flute, one hand flute, panpipe, nose flute, ground harp, musical bow, arched harp, stick zither, tubular zither, bowl zither, *langleik*, lyre, long lute, *samisen*, banjo, guitar, *gusla, surinda, hu ch'in*, spike fiddle, lira, Hardanger violin, hurdy-gurdy, gendèr wayang, Burmese orchestra, Siamese orchestra, Rumanian orchestra, *cobla*) (compiled and edited by CURT SACHS);

FM 4000 (P 1000). Hungarian folk songs (instr. a.o. *bagpipe*) (rec. BÉLA BARTÓK; notes: HENRY COWELL);

FM 4003 (P 1003). Songs and dances of Great Lake Indians (tribes: Algonquians (Meskwaki), Chippewa (Ojibwa), Ottawa, Iroquois (Onondaga, Cayuga, Tutelo)) (rec. and notes: GERTRUDE P. KURATH);

FM 4007 (P 1007). Lappish joik songs from Northern Norway (rec.: WOLFGANG LAADE and DIETER CHRISTENSEN);

FM 4008 (P 1008). Songs and dances of Norway (instr. a.o. *Hardanger fiddle, langleik*) (rec. by Norwegian Performing Rights Soc.; notes: O. M. SANDVIK);

FM 4009 (P 1009). Lithuanian folk songs (rec. and notes: JONAS BALYS);

FM 4011 (P 1011). The big drum dance of Carriacou (rec. and notes: ANDREW C. PEARSE);

FW 6808 (FP 8). Calypso, meringues, native music (Caribbean);

FW 6812 (FP 12). Chinese classical instrumental music (instr.: *ehr-hu, p'i-p'a, hsiao, t'i, yangchung, yuan, sin se*) (rec.: RAYMOND WONG; notes: HENRY COWELL);

FW 6815 (FP 15). Songs of Mexico;

FW 6817 (FP 17). Scottish bagpipe tunes, played by Pipe Major JOHN MACLELLAN;

FQ 8366 (FP 66). Classical music of India (perf.: NAZIR ALI JAIRAZBHON; introd.: RICHARD WATERMAN);

- FW 8801 (FP 80/1). Songs and dances of Turkey (instr.: clarinet, violin, drum, *cura, darbuka*, bagpipe (*tulum*), *baglama, saz, zurna, duval*, flute, *kaval, kemence*) (rec.: LAURA BOULTON);

FC 3576 (FP 76/1). Folk songs and dance tunes of the Netherlands (coll., harmonized, annotated, sung and played by JAAP KUNST, acc. by ERNST WOLFF);

FE 4438 (FP 438). Cajun songs from Louisiana;

FW 6802 (FP 802). Folk songs and dances of China;

FW 6805 (FP 805). Songs and dances of Yugoslavia (Bosnia, Hercegovina, Serbia, Macedonia, Croatia, Montenegro, Slovenia) (instr.: *gusle, tapan, zurla, frula, kaval, gajde, dude*) (rec. and notes: LAURA BOULTON);

FW 6806 (FP 806). Songs and dances of Armenia (instr.: *duduk, tar, kemenche, qanun*);

FW 6811 (FP 811). Haitian folk songs;

FW 6814 (FP 814). Songs and dances of Greece;

FW 6820 (FP 820). Russian folk songs;

FW 6830 (FP 830). Songs and dances of the Basques (instr.: *txistu, tun-tun* a.o.);

FW 6834 (FP 834). Folk music of Honduras (instr.: *marimba*)(notes by DORIS STONE);

FW 8850. Indian music of the Southwest (tribes: Apache, Hopi, Mohave, Navajo, Papago, Pima, San Ildefonso Indians, Santa Ana Indians, Taos, Zuñi) (rec. and notes: LAURA BOULTON);

FW 8851. Music of Indians of Mexico (tribes: Zapotecs, Otomi, Yaqui, Maya) (rec.: LAURA BOULTON);

FW 8852. African music (French Sudan, Southern Nigeria, Cameroon) (tribes: Bambara, Bini, Kwiri, Kru, Malinké, Tuareg) (instr.: drums, lute, musical bow, rattles, *balafon*) (rec.: LAURA BOULTON);

FW 8821. Yemenite Passover, the Hagadah (rec.: SAM ESKIN; notes: THEODOR GASTER);

FW 6840 (FP 840). Caribbean dances (Virgin Islands, Martinique, Guadeloupe, Trinidad, Antigua, Curaçao) (instr.: steelband, a.o.) (rec.: LISA and WALTER LEKIS);

FW 6865 (FW 865). Steelband. Trinidad Panharmonic Orchestra;

FW 6916 (FP 916). Folk music of the S.S.R. Middle East (Georgia, Tadjik, Daghstan, Kazak, Azerbaijan, Kabardinian, Tatar Tadjik) (instr.: *doira, dombara, dutar, duduk, kaval, kobuz, nagara, nai, tambur, zurna*) (notes: HENRI COWELL);

FW 6957 (FP 957). Yaqui dances (instr.: harp, violin, rattle) (rec.: SAMUEL B. CHARTERS; notes: JEAN ZEIGER);

FW 8811. Carribbean rhythms (San Andres) (instr.: mandolin, guitar, *maraca*, horse's jaw, 'tub'-stringbass) (rec.: THOMAS J. PRICE);

FG 3502. 'My life in recording Canadian Indian folklore' (by MARIUS BARBEAU);

FR 8975. Mushroom ceremony of the Meztec Indians of Mexico (rec. and notes: V. P. and R. G. WASSON);

w) issued by **His Master's Voice**:, some fine 78-records, mostly from North India, among which:

N 5961.   (instr.: *tabla, tampura, sarangi, kattyavana vina*) (performer: MANAHAR BARVÉ);

N 5994.   (instr.: flute) (perf.: D. AMEL);

N 6687.   (singer: KAMALA (JHARIA));

N 6982.   (instr.: *vichitra vina, tabla*) (perf.: ABDUL AZIZ KHAN);

N 14564. (instr.: *shahnai, duggi*) (perf.: BISMILLAH);

N 15906. (instr.: two-headed drum, *sarangi*) (perf.: KHAN SAHIB AHMADJANA THIRAKHAVA);

N 16764. (instr.: *sarode, tabla*) (perf.: ALI AKBAR KHAN);

N 16781. (instr.: *sarode, tabla*) (perf.: id.);

N 18219. (instr.: violin, *mṛdangga*) (singer: SM. N. C. VASANTHAKOKILAM) (South India!);

N 20027. (instr.: *sarangi, tabla*) (singer: RAVINDIA SHANKAR);

HQ 2.   (instr.: *sarangi, tabla*) (singer: BAI KESARBAI KERKAR);

HQ 83.   (instr.: *sarangi, tabla*) (perf.: BUNDU KHAN);

N 16622. Thibetan instrumental and vocal music; further some L.P.-recordings, of which I mention:

ALPC 2,   a really superb rendering of North Indian music, performed by ustad ALI AKBAR KHAN (*sarode*), pandit CHATUR LAL (*tabla*) and SHIRISH GOR (*tampura*), and preceded by an introduction by JEHUDI MENUHIN;

ALPC 7,. a no less excellent recording of the *sitar* playing of RAVI SHANKAR, acc. by CHATUR LAL (*tabla*) and PRODYOT SEN (*tanpura*);

OALP 7504 and 7505. Music of the Australian aboriginal (tribes of Arnhemland) (instr.: beating sticks, *didjeridu*) (rec. and notes: A. P. ELKIN);

x) issued by the **Malaya Broadcasting Corporation**: a collection of music from the Plé-Témiar, a small tribe of forest nomads in Pérak (rec. by the protector of aborigines, the late H. D. NOONE) (presumably = Ethnic Folkways No FE 4460 (P 460));

y) issued by **'Musica Viva'**, Cairo, more than 200 78-record of Egyptian and Sudanese (Shilluk) folk music and of an Ethiopian Mass;

z) issued by **'Musique Monde'** (29, rue Vernet, Paris): Chants Kalina (of the Coast-Caribs) and chants Oayana (from the Upper Marowijne (= Maroni), Dutch or French Guyana) (red.: G. CHARPENTIER);

aa) issued by **'Pacific'** (Paris): Chant religieux du Râab de Tlemcen (chanté en Yiddish) (Morocco) (No. CO 9009);

bb) issued by the **Period** firm (304 East, 74th Street, New York 21):

No. 1611. Armenian and Caucasian music;

No. 1612. Music from Borneo;

No. 1613. Music from Bali;

cc) issued by the **Philips Concern** (Baarn, Holland): 'Begdja, the Gamelan boy (a story of the Isle of Java, written and told by JAAP KUNST, with musical illustrations by the Study Group for Gamelan Music 'Babar layar') (N 00165 L); 'Féerie sud-Marocaine' (rec. and notes: JEAN MAZEL) (N 76.048 R);

dd) issued by the **Reeves Sound Studios Inc.**, New York: 6 records of African music, made by the DENIS/ROOSEVELT African Expedition (tribes: Man(g)betu, Babira, Bapere, Mbuti, Batwa, Watu(t)si, Bahutu) (instr.: the Royal Watusi drums, trumpets, xylophones, beating sticks a.o.);[1]

ee) issued by the **Riverside Records** (125, La Salle Str., New York 27 (N.Y.)):

RLP 4001. African Coast rhythms (tribes: Ashanti, Fanti, Ga (all Gold Coast), Ba'ule (Ivory Coast), Buzi or Loma, Mano (both Liberia), Bambara, Mossi (both Upper Volta), Kissi, Malinké (both French Guinea)), (instr.: drums, *balafon, gong-gong*, rebec, *kora* (harp), Kru-harp) (rec.: ARTHUR and LOIS ALBERTS; notes: MELVILLE J. HERSKOVITS and RICHARD A. WATERMAN) (this record is partly a dubbing from the album mentioned under d));

RLP 4002. 'Voice of the Congo' (instr.: trough zithers, *umunahi* (musical bow), Royal Tutsi drums, *ndingiti* (one-stringed violin), *ndongo* (7-str. harp), *boyeke* (scraper), *lukombe, menda* (blown jug)) (tribes: Bashi, Batwa, Ekondo, Hema, Hutu, Koga, Mbuti, Ngala, Rundi, Tutsi) (rec.: ALAN and BARBARA W. MERRIAM; notes: ALAN MERRIAM);

RLP 4006. Music of the Belgian Congo (tribe: Ekondo);

ff) issued by the **Stinson Records**:

SLP 50. Folk and devotional music of India (singer: SANGITHA VIDWAN BALA-KRISHNA) (notes: HANS STEFAN SANTESSON);

gg) issued by the **Tempo firm**:

TT 2252. Drums over Afghanistan (tribes: Pashtun, Parsi) (instr.: drums (resp. *daira, dholak, dumbek, tabla*), kettle drums (*dum tek*), plucked lute (*rebob*), *sarangi, sitar, dilruba, zurna*, triangle) (rec.: LEO SARKISIAN);

hh) issued by **'Vitadisc'**, Port of Spain, Trinidad: many steelband- and Calypso-recordings, among which some outstanding, as, for instance, TC 134 and TC 148;

ii) issued by **'Vogue'** (54, rue Hauteville, Paris 10e):

LDM 30.051. Espagne I (Baleares: Majorca, Ibiza) (rec.: ALAN LOMAX);

LDM 30.052. Espagne II (Jota Aragonaise and folk dances from Majorca) (rec.: ALAN LOMAX);

MC 20.147. Afghanistan and Iran (tribes: Afghans (Pashtun), Kurds, Tadjik, Turkmenes, Uzbek) (rec.: J. C. and S. LUBTCHANSKY);

LDM 30.057. Gavotte de Bretagne;

jj) issued by **Westminster** (375, 7th Avenue, New York 1):

WL 5332/4. Bedouin tribal songs from Oran;

XWN 2210. Music of India (perf.: GAURANG YODH (*sitar*) and DINESH PATEL (*tabla*));

XWN 18096. EDRIC CONNOR sings calypso;

WP 6037. JEAN RITCHIE sings songs from Kentucky (instr.: dulcimer);

XWN 2209. Music of Bali (gam. *Gong*, gam. *Angklung*) (leader: ANAK AGUNG GDÉ MANDÉRA);

WP 6055. Music of Kazakhstan, Kirghizia and Georgia;

kk) issued by the **World Collection of Recorded Folk Music** (p/a Unesco, Avenue Kléber, Paris 16e) (editor: CONSTANTIN BRAILOIU in collaboration with Unesco): albums with music resp. from:

I. the Haussa, German Switzerland, Scotland, Rumania, Italy;

II. Caribou Eskimo, (incl. Aevilikmiut, Padleirmiut), France, Serbia, the Spanish Jews, Greece;

---

[1] Re-issued by the Commodore firm as a L.P. record (DL 30.005).

34

III. Tuareg, Ireland, Turkey (Anatolia), Sardinia, Hindostan (Benares) (instr.:
bagpipe, *kaval, saz, launneddas*, a.o.);

IV. Fulah (Peul), Rumania, Flanders, Esthonia, Bosnia (instr.: *zazakual*
(flute), musical bow, carillon, jew's harp, bagpipe, bowed bow, *gusle,
dvojnice, tamburiza*);

V. Formosa (tribes: Bunun, Tsarisen, Sazek), England (Somerset, Oxford-
shire, Northhumberland, Norfolk, Wales), Bulgaria, Ukraine, Russia
(distr. Pskoff) (instr.: beakflute (flûte à bec), bagpipe, *gadulka*);

VI. Japan, France (Brittanny), Belgium (Wallonia), Austria (Tirol), Ethiopia
(Amhara, Kerker);

VII. Middle Congo (tribes: Ngundi, Babinga), Ivory Coast (tr.: Ba'ule), France
(Basques), Norway, Formosa, China (Canton), Algeria (Kabyls);

VIII. Georgia (West-), Corsica, Macedo-Rumanians (Greece), Portugal (Beira-
Baixa), Germany (Suebia, Bavaria, Saxony, Wolga-Germans, Czecho-
slovakian Germans) (instr.: drum, flute, violin, bagpipe);

ll) issued by IRAMA, the Indonesian Music Company Ltd.:

LPI 17501. Javanese gamelan music (region: Jogjakarta) (notes: Mr. KAWAT);

LPI 17506. Music of (South-)Bali (gamelan Gong, cond. by Tjokorda Mas)
(notes: Mr. KAWAT);

LPI 17503. Sundanese music (regions: Chiandjur, Sumedang) (performers: IBU
HADJI RESNA and ADJENG) (instr.: *kachapi, suling, tarawangsa*) (rec.
and notes: BERNARD IJZERDRAAT).

Also a number of scientific institutions have, during the past few years,
issued some collections of exotic records.

So, for instance, the Musée de l'Homme, to which the musicological world owes the
publication, first of a large series, on 78-records, of Malgassian music (recorded by the
CLERISSE mission); then, at the end of 1949 another, still larger one, containing music, instrumental and vocal, of Negro- and Pygmee-tribes from French Central Africa, recorded
by Mr. A. DIDIER during the Ogowé-Congo Mission (1946); in 1950 an album of Rumanian folk music, recorded by CONSTANTIN BRAILOIU; in 1952 an album of African music,
this time especially from the Hoggar, Fezzan, Adrar des Iforas, Tamasna and In
Salah (peoples: Tuareg and Arabian) (instr.: *amzad* (bowed lute)) (rec. by HENRI
LHOTE and ALAIN JOSET; notes by ANDRÉ SCHAEFFNER and GILBERT ROUGET);
in 1953 an album with music of the Upper Orinoco (tribes: Guarahibo, Maquiritare,
Piaroa and Puinave), recorded by PIERRE GAISSEAU; notes by SIMONE DREYFUS-
ROCHE (E 1–5); and another from the Niger (tribes: Haussa and Songhai/Zerma)
(rec. by J. ROUCH and R. ROSFELDER; notes by GILBERT ROUGET); further a record
from Dahomey (tribes: Fon, Goun) (rec. by GILBERT ROUGET); another from the
Sudan, rec. by Mrs. DIETERLEN; notes by SIMONE DREYFUS-ROCHE (Nos 1 and 2);
yet another, from the same region, rec. by Mrs. PÂQUES; notes by SIMONE DREYFUS-
ROCHE in 1954 and following years an album with music of the Upper Amazone
(tribes: Iawa, Bora) (rec. by BERTRAND FLORNOY; notes by SIMONE DREYFUS-ROCHE)
(L.D. 3); another album with music of French Guinea (tribe: Toma) (rec. by PIERRE
GAISSEAU, JEAN FICHTER and TONY SAULNIER; notes by SIMONE DREYFUS-ROCHE)
(L.D. 4); yet another from the Yayuro-tribe (Southern Venezuela) (rec. by
H. LE BESNERAIS; notes by SIMONE DREYFUS-ROCHE (L.D. 1); Musique Bantou
d'Afrique Equatoriale Française (tribes: Baduma, Bongili, Bongongo, Boungomo,
Kukuya, Mbeti, Mboko, Ngundi, Pomo, Yassua) (rec. by A. DIDIER; ed. by GILBERT
ROUGET) (L.D. 13); Musique pygmée de la Haute Sangha (tribes: Babinga, Babinga
Babenzélé, Bangombé) (rec. by A. DIDIER; ed. by GILBERT ROUGET) (L.D. 14);
Musique des Indiens du Rio Xingu et des Kaingang de Santa Catarina (rec. and notes
by SIMONE DREYFUS-ROCHE) (L.D. 15); Popular North Indian music (rec. by DEBAN
BHATTACHARYA; ed. by GILBERT ROUGET) (L.D. 8); Malaya, songs of the Semang and
Sakai and songs from New Caledonia, rec. resp. by JEANNE CUISINIER and MAURICE
LEENHARDT (Z. 1); Pondo kakou, musique de société secrète (tribes: Ba'ule and

others from French Guinea and Dahomey) (MC 20.141); Bushman music (rec. by the MARSHALL expedition 1953) and Pygmy music (rec. by the Ogowé-Congo expedition 1946) (tribes: !Kung Bushmen, Babinga pygmies) (notes by GILBERT ROUGET and YVETTE GRIMAUD; transc. by YVETTE GRIMAUD) (L.D. 9).

Of the Phonothèque Nationale, Paris (123) I may mention an interesting 78-recording from New Caledonia (Nos. 3970 and 3972).

The Intern. Library of African Music issued, among others, in 1957 African dances of the Witwatersrand Goldmines (Nos. LF 1254 and 1255) (tribes: Bacca, Mpondo, Mpondomisi, Ndau, Sotho, Xhosa, Zingili, Zulu) (for commentary see 4126).

Also the Library of Congress, Washington, caused many collections of exotic music to be made, of which I will mention the records, made of Zuñi and Sioux Songs and Dances (recorded by CHARLES HOFFMANN); of Iroquois songs (vol. VI, recorded by WILLIAM N. FENTON); of Indian and Negro Folk Music of Venezuela (vol. XV, recorded by JUAN LISCANO and CHARLES SEEGER); of Seneca Music (vol. XVII, recorded by WILLIAM N. FENTON); of Brazil (Afro-Bahian Religious Songs) (vol. XVIII, recorded by M. J. HERSKOVITS); of Mexico (vol. XIX, recorded by HENRIETTA YURCHENCO).

This Library has issued a series of L.P. records which were copied from the original recordings on wax-cylinders, made many years ago by FRANCES DENSMORE (855–949). These contain some hundreds of songs from different American Indian tribes: vol. XXII (Chippewa), XXIII (Sioux), XXIV (Yuma, Cocopa, Yaqui), XXV (Pawnee and Northern Ute), XXXI (Papago), XXXII (Nootka and Quileute), XXXIII (Menomenee, Mandan, and Hidatsa). To each of those volumes is added an excellent commentary written by FRANCES DENSMORE herself. This series has been followed in 1954 by yet another, recorded and with notes by WILLARD RHODES, containing American Indian music from the Northwest (Puget Sound) (tribes: Lummi, Makah, Quinault, Skokomish and Swinomish) (L 34); Kiowa (L 35), Indian songs of today (L 36), Delaware, Choctaw, Creek and Cherokee (L 37), Great Basin, Paiute, Washo, Ute, Bannock and Shoshone (L 38), Plain-Indians: Comanche, Cheyenne, Kiowa, Caddo, Wichita and Pawnee (L 39), Sioux (L 40), Navaho (L 41), Apache (L 42), Pueblo: Taos, San Ildefonso, Zuñi, Hopi (L 43).

The Kokusai Bunka Shinkokai (= Society for International Cultural Relations), Tokyo, issued in 1949 an album of Japanese music, containing music of all kinds (gagaku, Buddhist chant, noh-music, biwa-, koto-, samisen-music and many folk songs), with notes by KASHO MACHIDA (2686);

the Peabody Museum of Harvard University in 1952 an album 'Navajo Creation Chants' (notes by DAVID MCALLESTER) (2799);

the 'Institut Français d'Afrique Noire' (Dakar, Sénégal, A.O.F.) two albums, i.e. Musique Sosso et Malinké (Guinée Française) (instr.: balafon, kora, drums, flute) (rec.: MAURICE HOUIS and P. POTENTIER), and Musique Maure et Peule (resp. from Mauritania and French Guinea) (instr.: kerona (lute), gourd-rattles, one-stringed bowed lute, tobol (drum), tidinit (string-instrument) (rec. P. POTENTIER).

With regard to recordings of Asiatic music I may also refer to the Survey of recordings of Asiatic music in the United States (4308) and the Catalogue of recorded classical and traditional Indian music (815); for South African recordings to the large collection brought together under the auspices of the African Music Research, since 1946, by the Hon. Secretary of the African Music Society, the indefatigable HUGH T. TRACEY (23, 4115–4136); for Negro music in general to GAY's recent discography (1378), for the Belgian Congo to PIERRE DENYS' discography (950) and for Australia and New Guinea to the article in 'Oceania' by A. P. ELKIN (1063a).

In recent times the number of ethnic records has increased in such a way, that it has become almost impossible to mention them all in a booklet like this one. Fortunately, they are for the greater part incorporated in the catalogue made for the International Folk Music Council and Unesco by NORMAN FRASER (1298)[1]. For the Americas see also DUNCAN EMRICH (1090).

Starting with No. 8 of September 1956, the Society for Ethnomusicology regularly gives in its periodical lists of recently issued ethnic recordings (1134).

* * *

The transcription of exotic phonograms is one of the most difficult and intricate tasks which ethnomusicological research has ever put before its devotees. BÉLA BARTÓK says about this task: 'Although perfection cannot be attained in transcribing . . . folk music, we must always endeavour to approach an ideal of perfection . . . We should never tire of improving and changing our methods of work in order to accomplish this task as well as is humanly possible' (282, p. 20). Often, in the beginning, one finds oneself faced with apparently unsurmountable difficulties, inextricable rhythmic constructions, indeterminable tones.

Each individual investigator will invent his own method, manners and expedients. I only recount my own experiences in this field of work, where each is free to surmount the difficulties according to his own personal insight.

It is best, when proceeding to transcribe a phonogram, to start early in the morning; the fresher one feels, the sharper one's hearing, the greater one's patience, and the more subtle one's acoustic imagination. I would remind those who are blessed (or cursed) with 'absolute pitch' that fatigue causes the inner norm of hearing to rise; in other words, that, when one is tired, as at the end of a long day's work, one is inclined to hear everything slightly sharper (up to half a tone) than it sounds in reality.

When transcribing from flat gramophone records, one should, if at all possible, obtain the use of an electric gramophone with a pick-up; this obviates repeated interruption and rewinding of the mechanism, and in addition ensures constancy of speed, and, with that, of pitch.

One need not stress that the room in which transcription takes place can never be too quiet; the slightest outside sound distracts the ear and the mind; more or less 'musical' sounds even make transcription totally impossible. This is another reason why transcription should preferably be done in the very early morning, when most mortals are still asleep.

The gramophone, phonograph or recorder should be placed at one's left hand. Before setting anything on paper – apart from the title of the piece to be transcribed and the number of the phonogram – play the whole record

---

[1] to which supplements will from time to time be issued.

once through, so as to get a general impression of the piece, and to know whether to put a treble- or a bass-clef at the beginning of the stave. (Ultimately, one generally transcribes in the treble-clef as far as possible, if necessary with a note to the effect that everything sounds one octave lower or higher). Another advantage of this preliminary hearing is that it gives one an opportunity to learn something of the tonality, the rhythm and the general structure.

We then start on the actual work of transcription. We first play a few tones – say, a melodic fragment, somewhat rounded-off for preference, of a few seconds length – and endeavour to write this down at the right pitch and in the correct rhythm. We repeat this first attempt a few times, until we are perfectly sure that the transcription approximates melodically and rhythmically as closely as possible to the real thing, after which we take a step forward, also of a few tones, each time again playing the record right from the beginning and taking great pains to check up whether what has already been written down tallies with what one hears. The result will frequently be only an approximation – be it a rather close one – to reality. For, most exotic peoples use tonal sequences and intervals differing from those of us Westerners; and rhythmically ,too, they often do things that strike us as incomprehensibly complicated and inimitable. The difficulty in this, moreover, is to know *what* is essential in what we have heard, and *what* is due to imperfection of the singer's voice or the player's instrumental technique, or his rhythmic feeling. In the case of primitive peoples we may say: the way they perform a piece is the way it is intended; there is usually no standard model, no norm hallowed by tradition; what is played or sung is the emotion, rendered audible, of that particular person at that particular moment; a subsequent performance by the same player or singer of the same piece would turn out differently in many respects, because the performer's emotion at that moment would be different, for instance, it would be experienced either more or less intensely.

However, even apart from this difficulty, there is another, more or less akin to it: how far should the precision of the transcription be allowed to go? It is possible, by applying a mechanical-visual method of sound-registration (e.g., by recording the sound-curves on a rotating cylinder) to carry the exactitude of a transcription to a point where one cannot see the wood for trees, so that the structure of the piece transcribed has got completely out of hand. In my own view, the transcription by ear, in European notation, as nearly exact as possible, combined with the measurement of the actually used intervals is nearly always sufficient for ethnomusicological purposes. In that case, however, it is to be recommended, when publishing the results, to give some sort of account, by way of introduction to, and justification of, the transcription. For this purpose, I myself use the following method. On a set of horizontal lines, each representing the sound-continuum, I place (a) on one of them the tone-points of the European tempered scale (either all, or only those used in the transcription of the piece in question), and (b) on the other(s) the tone-points of the scales actually used by the performers of the piece transcribed. One of the tonal points of each of the respective scales is made equal to the other(s), and, therefore, placed on the same point on both (or, as the case may be, all) lines; and these corresponding tone-points are then connected by a vertical dotted line. From the other tone-points on the lines of the measured scales also vertical dotted lines, intersecting the European scale-line, are either raised or dropped, to show the extent to which the tones – and with those, the intervals – of the piece transcribed deviate from the European tones approximating them in the transcription. In addition, the sizes of the intervals are given in *cents*, and vibration figures of the scale-tones are also added.

The example on p. 233, fig. 62, in which a comparison is drawn between the Javanese pélog- and sléndro- and the European tempered chromatic scale, may clarify this.

Accidental, involuntary deviations in pitch may be indicated in the transcription itself by some mark or other above the notes to which they belong.

Apart from the exact rendering of pitch and rhythm, it may reasonably be expected that a good transcription gives as many indications as possible with regard to the style of interpretation. Experience has shown that the marks used for this purpose in our European notation are inadequate to this end.

This led OTTO ABRAHAM and ERICH VON HORNBOSTEL to the publication of their treatise *Vorschläge für die Transkription exotischer Melodien* (1895).

In spite of this, unification of the transcription is still far from being attained; and so, the CIAP finally convened, in July 1949, a conference of specialists at Geneva, with instructions to effect, if possible, this unification. Naturally the recommendations formulated at this conference possess no legal sanction and cannot be enforced; it remains to be seen whether ethnomusicologists in general will be prepared to avail themselves in future of the transcription-rules recommended by the conference. [1]

The musicologist's skill in transcribing must, of course, have attained a certain level of faithful interpretation if his rendering is to satisfy us. As we said before, practice plays a considerable part. I further believe that having 'absolute pitch' can be a factor of great utility in this work. Its possession, however, is no *conditio sine qua non;* those who do not enjoy this faculty – and they constitute the majority, also among the musically

---

[1] One will find a summary of the results, attained by this conference, in the CIAP-Information No. 15/16 of Nov./Dec. 1949 and in a brochure, issued by the same institution in 1952 (3044).

talented – have generally developed their relative hearing to a far finer pitch than their 'absolute' colleagues, and are able, it seems, to arrive at most acceptable results also by this means.

But for either of them the all-important thing is to have a perfectly open mind as regards the piece to be heard and transcribed. One must be on one's guard against the temptation to presuppose or imagine the presence, in exotic phonograms, of the particular rhythmics and the equality of bar-length typical of most Western music, or of involuntarily hearing the strange melody 'harmonically', i.e. as if it were based on unplayed harmonies.

For the sake of legibility, however, it is advisable to put a bar-line in those places where the rhythm seems to call for one (roughly, always before a prominent accent or 'down-beat'), as well as vertical dotted lines whenever the 'bars' created thereby contain complicated rhythmic formations – in order to indicate the more elementary rhythmic units. Greater melodic periods might be closed by a double bar-line.

No doubt one will frequently feel, when tackling the same phonogram some days later, an inclination to distribute the bar-lines differently. The reason for this is the fact that accentuation in the music of many exotic peoples is much weaker than that in Western music; in some cases this accentuation is put into it by the investigator, because we Westerners seem to feel the need of making what is heard more comprehensible by 'phrasing' it in some way or other.

When dealing with vocal records one should also try to get hold of the text which, especially in the case of the primitives, is anything but easy unless one masters the native language (as many missionaries do), so as to understand the words sung in spite of their being recorded only indistinctly by the phonogram. To ask for the text just sung, *after* the performance, will generally prove futile; for the texts are very often improvised during the performance itself. This difficulty is not present to the same extent in the case of peoples on a higher cultural level, for in their case one frequently has to deal with existing, standardized texts. But even there it is necessary to collate the text with the vocal tune on the spot (that is, if one has been able to put the melody approximately on paper during recording), since the manner in which the words are distributed over the notes usually deviates considerably from the way in which we Westerners would proceed. A correct knowledge of the text will often have influence on the manner in which one thinks the melody should be phrased.

The complexity and arbitrariness of the rhythm of some exotic melodies may be evident from the example on p. 234, fig. 63, which I transcribed some years ago from a phonogram taken in Central Flores. When in addition, the voice moves in intervals deviating from our own Western ones (which was *not* the case in the district in question), it is easy to imagine the trouble that must be taken before the melody has been faultlessly caught 'in the little cage of our musical staves' – as the late Father HEERKENS (1639), an authority on Florinese music, expressed it.

Recently many difficulties in the realm of rhythm have been eliminated by the ingenious contraption, constructed and used by Father A. M. JONES (2093, p. 59 ff.), whilst in regard to melody (and rhythm also), OLAV GURVIN's photographic method (1560) and SEEGER's Melograph (3797, 3800) deserve to be broadly known, as well as, in regard to the difficulties in general to be met with when transcribing phonograms of non-Western music, the clever article by ZYGMUNT ESTREICHER (fig. 12), *Une technique de transcription de la musique exotique* (1133).

I have further found – especially in the case of vocal, but also in string-instrumental performances – that the 'corresponding' tones are not quite stable. Moreover, the entire pitch is, on occasion, gradually raised or lowered in the course of the performance. In such cases it may be advisable to indicate this alteration of pitch in the transcription by inserting the vibration figures above different notes whose pitch could readily be determined (i.e. often those with a fairly long time-value).

This peculiarity is, for that matter, by no means a monopoly of exotic musical expressions. Western vocal music, including that sung by really good singers, knows similar deviations from the theoretical scale, as is clearly evident from the tone- and interval-measurements made by OTTO ABRAHAM from the performance of a song by a well-trained European singer. [1]

It may be apposite at this point to say a word or two about the fairytale of the 'simple ratios', which, according to the opinion of many, characterize the European tonal system as the perfect and chosen one. STUMPF [2], indeed, was able to prove that intervals which are heard and felt to be perfectly true by musically trained European ears, are precisely the ones that escape all attempts at representing them by one of the simple ratios in question; their constituent tones have only approximately such ratio; in reality, consonant intervals felt to be perfectly true proved to be slightly greater than those which could be represented by the simple proportions (while the subjective tendency to enlarge them increased in accordance with the size of the consonant intervals).

There are yet other deviations from this numerical simplicity to be noted in musical practice, apart from those just mentioned.

Thus, European music has for some centuries known the so-called 'equal' (better: 'proportional') temperament, i.e. the 12 steps into which the

---

[1] Dr. O. ABRAHAM, in 'Psychologische Forschungen', vol. 4, p. 1 ff. (1923).
[2] *Maassbestimmungen über die Reinheit consonanter Intervallen* (in collaboration) with M. MAYER) (3991).

space within one octave has been divided, have been made perfectly equal. The result of this was that nothing whatever was left of that simplicity of the vibration ratios, with the sole exception of that of the octave itself. Again, one tone, i.e. the tone preceding the tonic in the scale, is always taken sharp when, in melodics, the tonic immediately follows it; this tone (the 'leading note') is sung or played on a string-instrument in such a way that it forms, with the tonic that follows it, an interval considerably smaller than a semitone. The same applies to the tones that have a leading note function in respect to the tonic immediately below it, and in respect to the dominant.

Generally speaking, moreover, the seconds and sevenths in our tone-system are in themselves fairly unstable as it is. Professor BALTH. VAN DER POL, a Dutch acoustic specialist, in his published lecture *Muziek en elementaire getallentheorie* [1], quotes in this connexion the composer and theoretician PAUL HINDEMITH, who declares as follows: 'Die Sekunden und Septimen sind stärkeren Schwankungen unterworfen als alle anderen Intervalle; sie kommen in Melodik und Harmonik in den mannigfaltigsten Grössenabstufungen vor'. (i.e. 'The seconds and sevenths are subject to greater fluctuations than all other intervals; they occur in melodies and harmonies in the most multifarious dimensions'). [2]

In the summary of his above-mentioned address, Professor VAN DER POL declares: 'The correct relative pitch of any given note depends entirely upon the organic melodic and harmonic relation between that note and those surrounding it. Thus, two modulations, e.g., from *C* to *G*, may quite well lead to two different pitches of the respective *G*'s, according to the respective constructions of the two modulations. Ideally speaking, this fact alone creates certain *a priori* necessary variations in pitch, which are conditioned by the organic interconnexion'. [3]

Further, a good piano tuner invariably tunes the high register of a piano a trifle sharp, since it would give a flat impression if it were theoretically tuned correctly.

It should be perfectly clear from the above that Western musical practice is also far from adhering to the simple quantitative proportionalities of the so-called 'natural' intervals (which, as we know, are identical with those of the harmonic overtones). [4]

But even assuming that European music should actually have adhered strictly to this structure, which it postulates as the natural, as its credo, so to speak – i.e. the scale structure based on the principle of consonance –

[1] 'Archives du Musée Teyler', vol. 9, p. 597 ff. (p. 528), 1942.
[2] PAUL HINDEMITH, *Unterweisung im Tonsatz* (Mainz, 1937), vol. I, p. 95.
[3] *Op. cit.*, p. 532.
[4] *Vide* also, on this question, YVES CHARDON, *Essais à propos de la justesse attractive* ('La Revue Musicale', vol. XIII, p. 166 ff.), 1932.

even then the fact remains that other peoples have taken quite different principles as their starting point in constructing their tonal system; or, rather – since these words, in effect, represent the course of affairs in reverse order of sequence (i.e., -as if the scales came first and the music afterwards), and, moreover, attribute to the whole process a far too conscious and purposive character – that their musical expressions often appear to rest upon entirely deviating foundations: foundations which, in the last analysis, would sometimes seem to derive essentially from a *non-musical* source.

In many primitive musical expressions we may distinguish a number of 'Gerüsttöne' ('skeletal tones'), which are more or less consonant with respect to one another, and form the larger intervals (octaves, fifths, fourths); these are then subdivided by intermediary, not quite constant tones. In this subdivision, what is important is not so much the size of the intervals, but rather the *direction* (rising or falling) of the melodic line. To use a felicitous comparison of the musicologist ROBERT LACHMANN, it is something like the sketching of dance-steps: their direction and order of sequence, not the precise length of the steps, is what matters (2502, p. 10). Nevertheless, as VON HORNBOSTEL ascertained, it appears that the smaller intervals thus formed do divide the 'skeletal' intervals according to ratios found in intervals which are formed according to the consonance principle (2366, p. 14/15, note 24).

As one of the, in effect, non-musical elements referred to above, we may mention the visual-esthetic feeling which demands, for example, that the stops on a flute shall be placed at equal distances from each other, or – as on some bamboo flutes – always in the middle of each internode; or, again, that strings shall be subdivided in a certain manner according to some hieratic standard.

This latter point leads us to another non-musical element, namely the sanctity of a given standard of measurement or a given number. The fact that so many scales contain either 5 or 7 steps to the octave is sometimes attributed to the sanctity of the numbers 5 and 7. This belief in the holiness of certain numbers is found in large parts of the world; in the majority of cases it is the number 7. COMBARIEU, in his *Histoire de la Musique* (731, vol. I, p. 39), asserts this in respect of the Chinese, the Hindus, the Chaldeans (Babylonians), the Phoenicians, the Greeks, the Persians, the Arabs and the Turks. In the Indian archipelago, too, this special position of the number 7 is upheld. Dr. A. C. KRUYT, in his treatise *Measa, een bijdrage tot het dynamisme der Baré'e-sprekende Toradja's en enkele omwonende volken* [1], gives several examples of this. And as regards the sanctity of a linear measure I refer the reader to VON HORNBOSTEL's important article *Die Maassnorm als kulturgeschichtliches Forschungsmittel* (1941).

[1] Second part ('Bijdragen Taal-, Land- en Volkenkunde', Vol. 75 (1919), p. 36 ff. (114 ff.)).

Conceptions such as these hold that there is – or rather, that there ought to be – a relation between a tonal system and the structure of the universe; the harmony of the spheres must be reflected in the harmony of music. Also the contradistinction between the two basic principles of Life – i.e. the male and female principles, *Yang* and *Yin* – finds expression in certain scale systems, as, for instance, in the Chinese tonal system.

Tone systems resting on foundations other than the consonance principle often generate melodies which are essentially unsusceptible to harmonization, unless the deviation from the scales based on the consonance principle is so slight as to be negligible in practice, as in the case of the European tempered chromatic scale.

In contrast to this, West-European melodies are always susceptible to being harmonized; even the seemingly monodic West-European folk-music, in so far as it is not modal, is usually based on unsung and unplayed simple harmonies, and in this forms a sharp contrast with other, non-European, as well as many East-European, tunes, which in many cases are purely and simply melodic.

This, however, does not say that there exists no non-European multi-part music. On the contrary, Javanese and Balinese orchestral music – to mention only some very conspicuous examples – are there to prove the opposite. But this multi-part music is not a harmonic one; it knows of no teaching of the construction of chords; its harmony has, one might say, a more or less incidental character. Often we have to do with so-called 'heterophony', a term which, in this meaning, was first used by STUMPF [1] This heterophony is the result of the playing around, and making variations on, a nuclear theme by different instruments simultaneously. Besides this heterophony we often find multi-part music, based on 'overlapping' and so leading to primitive forms of polyphony, even real canons (2401).

Exotic music which gives the impression of being built entirely on the consonance principle, and in which, therefore, real fifths, fourths and thirds (including the notorious 'interlocking' and 'pendular' thirds) are heard, may be found, for instance, in places where a negroid element plays a rôle in the miscegenation, as, of course, in Negro Africa, but also in large parts of New Guinea (2402), in the districts Nagé and Ngada in midwest Flores (2383), and in Melanesia (cf., for instance, 1911).

* * *

About the beginning of the 20th century the gradually gathered fact-material had become already so extensive and variegated, that examination

---

[1] It may be noted that the term heterophony is used, in later years, again in the sense which it, apparently, originally had in PLATO's famous *locus* of the dialogue 'Laws' (812 D). Cf. J. HANDSCHIN, *Musikgeschichte* (Bâle, 1948), p. 61.

could be made regarding its serviceableness for investigation as to racial and cultural relationship.

Of the elements brought into question may be mentioned, in addition to the already discussed characteristics of musical expression (p. 12/13):

a) identity of scale systems, both as regards structure (identity of intervals), and as regards absolute pitch (identity of diapason) (cf. 1903, 1941 and 2394);

b) identity of melodies or of melodic fragments (cf. 1258, 2339, 2412 and 4405);

c) concurrence in structural melodic characteristics [1];

d) preference for certain rhythms, intervals and tone-successions [2];

e) the occurrence in different regions of the same, exceptionally formed, musical instruments [3];

f) the occurrence of musical instruments concurring not only in their essentiality, but also in typical details, which are absolutely unnecessary for the sound-production. [4]

A difficulty in connexion with these data is that it is often impossible to ascertain whether the stated concurrences find their origin in original race-relationship, or in later cultural influences. MARIUS SCHNEIDER's dictum 'Die Vortragsart ist ein Rassekriterium, der Vortragsstil ein Kulturkriterium' (3745) (i.e. the kind of expression is a racial, the style a cultural criterium) will not always help us sufficiently in drawing the borderline between those two elements.

The pioneers in this field were WILHELM TAPPERT, the author of *Wandernde Melodien* (4052), OSKAR FLEISCHER in his respectively from 1900 and 1902 dating treatises *Ein Kapitel vergleichender Musikwissenschaft* (1257) and *Zur vergleichender Musikforschung* (1258) and ERICH VON HORNBOSTEL who published an article in 1911, titled *Ueber ein akustisches Kriterium für Kulturzusammenhänge* (1903). The time, had however, apparently not yet come for such speculations; neither TAPPERT's and FLEISCHER's, nor VON HORNBOSTEL's treatises found any response. But when later, about 1921, the last mentioned divulged his hypothesis over the structure of the oldest pan-pipe- and xylophone-tuning, the later much

---

[1] Cf., for instance, the 'tiled' melodies of the Mamberamo Papuas and of some N.W. Australian tribes (2366, 2402).

[2] For instance the preference for the tritone, combined with ternary rhythms, of the East-Florinese, the South Nias-tribes and the Angami-Naga's and probably yet other peoples with a megalithic culture (2383, p. 35 ff.).

[3] F.i. those strangely formed metal instruments, which, in Java, are called *kemanak* (fig. 53) and do also occur in Central Africa (fig. 54) and N.E. Siberia (cf. J. KUNST, *De Toonkunst van Java* (2370), p. 131/132 = id., *Music in Java* (2399), p. 181/182).

[4] Cf., for instance, the 'pointed' flute (German: Spitzflöte) of Central Timor, called *féku* (fig. 55), which is identical with the *dunda* of the province of Sokoto (N. Nigeria) (fig. 56), also in its accessoria. (Cf. 2398, p. 9 and figs. 42 and 43).

contested 'Blasquintentheorie' (i.e. theory of blown fifths), the activity, also of other investigators, was roused.

In this connection I may mention the Frenchman GEORGES DE GIRONCOURT, who in his book *La Géographie musicale* (1445), an enthusiastically written synopsis of the differences in musical expression among the peoples of the world, time and again points out the common elements that suggest a (? racial, ?cultural) relation, a subject which he, in other publications [1], worked out at a later date. [2], [3].

* * *

How did music come into being? Theories galore have been propounded to explain this phenomenon; one might almost say, as many theories as there have been investigators of the problem.

Articles summarizing the various hypotheses may be found in, among other works, STUMPF's *Die Anfänge der Musik* (3995), and G. RÉVÉSZ'

---

[1] *Recherches de Géographie musicale en Indochine* (1448); *Recherches de Géographie musicale au Cambodge et à Java* (1449), and others.

[2] It is regrettable that the writer usually does not take into account possible differences in scale-structure; with a few exceptions he writes everything in European staff-notation without further diacritical signs or tone-measurements. After all that has already been mentioned, it will not be necessary to point out how this method of work, which reminds one of that used in the pre-phonographic period, *can* suggest concurrence, that in reality is not there, and miss relations, that exist. Though we must conclude – from the fact that Mr. DE GIRONCOURT speaks (in a laudatory manner) of other investigators in the same field (at least in his later writings) – that he was acquainted with their work, still he calls himself 'le créateur d'une nouvelle science, 'la géographie musicale" (i.e. the creator of a new science, 'musical geography'). This creation of his is then said to have taken place in 1927 in the November number of the periodical 'La Géographie' and during a lecture, held on May 25th 1928 for the 'Société de Géographie', Paris. Although Mr. DE GIRONCOURT in the eyes of other ethno-musicologists occasionally seems to be a little bit adventurous in his conclusions, part of his work, in the first place his study *Motifs de chants cambodgiens* (1447) and his *Recherches de Géographie musicale en Indochine* (1448) – the latter illustrated with a wealth of excellent construction-drawings of complicated bamboo instruments – is worthy of our full attention.

[3] Some other articles and books in this field, not yet mentioned on p. 45, are (in chronological sequence): PAUL DEMIÉVILLE, *La Musique Came au Japon* (850); J. KUNST and C. J. A. KUNST-VAN WELY, *De Toonkunst van Bali* (2360), especially par. 13; HERBERT HÜBNER, *Die Musik im Bismarck-Archipel* (1987); J. KUNST, *De l'origine des échelles musicales javano-balinaises* (2365); CURT SACHS, *Geist und Werden der Musikinstrumente* (3553); ERICH VON HORNBOSTEL and ROBERT LACHMANN, *Asiatische Parallelen zur Berbermusik* (1956); HANS WIESCHHOFF, *Die afrikanischen Trommeln und ihre ausserafrikanischen Beziehungen* (4373); J. KUNST, *Oude Westersche liederen uit Oostersche landen* (2369); id., *Ein musikologischer Beweis für Kulturzusammenhänge zwischen Indonesien – vermutlich Java – und Zentral Afrika*; id., *A musicological Argument for cultural Relationship between Indonesia – probably the isle of Java – and Central Africa* (2372); WERNER DANCKERT, *Wandernde Liedweisen* (795); CURT SACHS, *Les Instruments de musique de Madagascar* (3561); HENRY GEORGE FARMER, *Reciprocal Influences in Music 'twixt the Far and Middle East* (1185A); SHIGEO KISHIBE, *On the origin of the P'i-p'a* (2238); CURT SACHS, *The History of Musical Instruments* (3564); FRITZ BOSE, *Klangstile als Rassenmerkmale* (424); J. KUNST, *A hypothesis about the origin of the gong* (2395); WALTER WIORA, *Alpenländische Liedweisen der Frühzeit und des Mittelalters im Lichte vergleichender Forschung* (4400); id., *Zur Frühgeschichte der Musik in den Alpenländern* (4398); id., *Europäischer Volksgesang* (4405); J. KUNST, *Kulturhistorische Beziehungen zwischen dem Balkan und Indonesien* (Engl. ed.: *Cultural relations between the Balkans and Indonesia*) (2408 and 2412).

treatise *Der Ursprung der Musik* (3394). The latter author gives the more detailed and extensive survey of the theories put forward. [1]

(1) There is, first of all, the hypothesis, which originated under the influence of Darwinian thought, that singing is an expression whose origin is purely sexual, just as the singing of birds is supposed to be closely related to their sex life. This assumption, however, is contradicted (*a*) by the fact that many birds sing quite as lustily outside the mating season, and (*b*) by the absence of any reason why human call-notes should precisely have to adopt the form of a melody with fixed and transposable intervals. (Recent animal-psychologic investigations, for that matter, have rendered plausible the theory that the purpose of the bird's song is to mark the boundaries of each individual bird's 'power-domain').

(2) Another theory is that of 'imitation', i.e. the imitation of the bird's song. Against this it may argued that nowhere in the world do we find any primitive people singing in the manner of any species of bird (although many primitive peoples, especially hunting tribes, intermix their songs with bird cries)(1905). And further, that the very nature of the bird's song completely differs from that of human singing, i.e. it represents purely 'unmittelbare und zwangsmässig entstandene Reaktionen biologischer Zustände des Tierindividuums' (i.e. direct, compulsively originating reactions to certain biological states of the individual animal) [2]. It is 'ein vererbtes, entwicklungsunfähiges, unveränderliches, starres Ausdrucksmittel' (i.e. an inherited, rigid, unchangeable means of expression, incapable of development) [3], invariably sounded by the same individuals at the same pitch. (Professor RÉVÉSZ, in common with STUMPF, considers the transposability of music one of its typical and fundamental characteristics, the two others being, according to him, the existence of fixed intervals and their use in all sorts of tone-combinations in different rhythmic patterns. [4]

(3) A third hypothesis is the so-called 'rhythm-theory', which holds that music generated from rhythmic movements, especially from those performed while working [5]. The great protagonist of this theory is CARL BÜCHER, the author of the well-known book *Arbeit und Rhythmus* (530). Both STUMPF and RÉVÉSZ reject this theory; the latter, among other things, on the ground that music could hardly have generated from actions which

---

[1] Cf. also J. HANDSCHIN, *Musikgeschichte* (1589), p. 29 ff.; CH. S. MYERS (2950), and SIEGFRIED NADEL (2955).

[2] RÉVÉSZ, *op. cit.*, p. 70.

[3] RÉVÉSZ, *op. cit.*, p. 70.

[4] See also ALEX. V. ARLTON, *Songs and other sounds of birds* (131); GARSTANG, *Songs of the birds* (1366); ERICH M. VON HORNBOSTEL, *Musikpsychologische Bermerkungen über Vogelsang* (1905); ROBERT LACH, *Eine Studie über Vogelgesang* (2464); id., *Der Ursprung der Musik im Lichte des Tiergesanges* (2471); F. SCHUYLER MATTHEWS, *Field book of wild birds and their music* (2790); W. B. OLDS, *Bird-music* (3060); HEINZ TIESSEN, *Musik der Natur* (4092). The last named author makes an exception for the 'amsel' (black bird), who, according to him, is a real creative artist.

[5] STUMPF, *op. cit.*, p. 20; RÉVÉSZ, *op. cit.*, p. 72.

47

themselves are soundless. It is, of course, certain, that music proved capable of lightening communal labour once it had come into existence; as it happens, however, really primitive peoples do not know any such common labour necessitating rhythmic movements that might lead to the production of working songs. And even at present the number of such working songs is only small among more primitive peoples; much smaller, for instance, than that of their magico-religious songs and dance melodies.

(4) A fourth hypothesis derives music from sounds uttered under the stress of emotion. [1] These sounds, however, are too spontaneous, too instinctive; they are too much in the nature of unchangeable reflex-expressions of affective states to be able to lead to the creation of vocal music, which precisely presupposes a psychic state that has risen above the primary affects.

(5) Professor RÉVÉSZ also rejects the theory according to which vocal music arose from the lulling of an infant. [1] This 'singing' is either produced quite unconsciously and instinctively, or – even at an early stage – melodic; in that case, however, it is undoubtedly pre-influenced by the singing of older persons, or by the child's hearing instrumental music. [2]

(6) Finally, there is the theory of 'the melody of speech'. [3] This hypothesis, too, according to both STUMPF and RÉVÉSZ, is untenable. The laws of sound governing speech are completely different from those of music. Speech – and this surely is the main contra-argument – knows no fixed intervals; the movement of its tones depends exclusively on the person's mood prevailing at the moment of speaking. In contradistinction to this point of view, see sub (8)).

(7) Both the authors cited above, as well as Father SCHMIDT, conclude as the most plausible explanation, that it is the *call* from the distance, of one human being to another, which should be regarded as the origin of vocal music [4]. I am fully inclined to agree with this hypothesis; indeed, as early as 1922, and without being aware of the content of the existing treatises at the time, I myself (in a paper on *Het Volkslied*, published in the Flemish periodical 'De Muziekwarande') mentioned, more or less in passing, the call as being the 'germinal cell' of folk-song.

(8) However, one more hypothesis, recently suggested by MARIUS SCHNEIDER (3768, p. 6/7), must be mentioned here, i.e. a common origin

---

[1] RÉVÉSZ, *op. cit.*, p. 73.

[2] See on children's singing also HEINZ WERNER, *Die melodische Erfindung im frühen Kindesalter* (4359), FRITZ BREHMER, *Melodieauffassung und melodische Begabung des Kindes* (498); BRUNO NETTL, *Notes on infant musical development* (2995); id., *Infant musical development and primitive music* (2996), and W. PLATT, *Child Music* (3197).

[3] STUMPF, *op. cit.*, p. 14 ff.; RÉVÉSZ, *op. ci*, p. 74; *vide* also WILHELM SCHMIDT, S.V.D., *Ueber WUNDT's Völkerpsychologie* ('Mitteilungen der anthropologischen Gesellschaft in Wien', vol. 33, p. 356 ff.).

[4] STUMPF, *op. cit.*, p. 26; WILHELM SCHMIDT, *op. cit.*; RÉVÉSZ, *op. cit.*, p. 75.

of speech and music from ancient sound-languages (typical, for instance, for many Negro tribes and for the Chinese) [1].

Whatever may have been the origin of vocal music, once we come to the now existing, most primitive, purely vocal melodics, we find that it obeys certain human, physiologically and psychologically explainable laws, while, on the other hand, there is not yet any question of real tonal systems. Such systems do not come into being until a people's culture has at its disposal musical instruments on which tonal *sequences* can be produced; these, however, do not make their appearance until a relatively late stage of development. It is true that prehistoric flutes, made of bone, have been excavated here and there in Europe, with fingerholes or stops, on which tones of different pitch can be played; but these stops appear to have been placed more or less arbitrarily; the intention of the makers evidently did not go further than to try to produce *different* tones, *not* tones having a pitch intentionally determined beforehand. But even supposing that it had been possible to play a consciously intended scale on these prehistoric flutes, this would not amount to much, since, notwithstanding their relatively great age, these flutes are already the products of a fairly high form of civilization, developed some hundreds of thousands of years later than the period at which we may assume that the first 'music' was heard on earth.

There is no doubt that vocal music is infinitely more ancient than instrumental music (although, according to some Africa explorers, the mountain gorilla's are in the habit of beating with sticks on (?hollow) trees) [2].

. As regards the origin of *instrumental* music, there exists a thought-provoking article entitled *Anfänge der Musik* by CURT SACHS (3549) [3], the great scholar on musical organology, one-time professor at Berlin, now at New York.

Professor SACHS points out that vocal and instrumental music originated from two totally different spheres, and must have existed side by side

---

[1] See also KUTTNER, *Die verborgenen Beziehungen zwischen Sprache und Musik* (2442), and on tone languages in general: KENNETH L. PIKE (3187).

[2] We may assume that BONNET-BOURDELOT's communication in his *Histoire de la Musique* (1715), to the effect that 'the monkeys in New Guinea play the flute', is not based on the author's own observation (there being no monkeys at all in New Guinea) – unless it was meant as a hardly flattering appreciation of the personality of the Papuas. – In regard to musical capabilities of monkeys see also J. A. BIERENS DE HAAN, *Discrimination of musical tempi by a young chimpanzee* ('Archives Néerlandaises de Zoölogie' VIII, p. 393 ff.), Leyden, 1951, from which article it appears that a chimpanzee can be made to discriminate between tempi as close to each other as Andante and Adagio, and H. MUNRO FOX, *The personality of animals* (American Pelican Books edition), April 1947, where we read on p. 52 about playing chimpanzees: 'At first a pair, then the others of the apes joined and circled round a tree, marching in orderly fashion. Then they trotted, stamping with one foot and putting the other down lightly, thus beating a rhythm. Sometimes their heads bobbed up and down in time with the stamping feet.' – See further also GEORGE HERZOG, *Do animals have music?* (1736).

[3] The same subjectmatter is also dealt with in the Introduction of the same author's *Geist und Werden der Musikinstrumente* (3553).

for a very long time, with hardly any mutual connexion. For, as is convincingly evident from customs and traditions still found today all over the world, instrumental music, taken as a whole, derives from the world of magic ritual; vocal music, although in later periods certainly also used for magical purposes (incantation!), originating as we suppose, from the *call*, will have been, in the first instance, discharge of affects.

We modern Westerners are able to imagine ourselves in the emotional world of the primitive mind only to a small degree; most readily, maybe, during our dreams. In the waking state, we are too analytically-minded; we have become too intellectual. Being, thinking, experiencing, feeling: these are categories which we shall not easily confuse. But the primitive hardly, if at all, makes these distinctions. He lives far more subconsciously, and infinitely more from an inner unity of being. His distinction between Ego and the outer world, too, is more vague; macrocosmos and microcosmos do not, as in our own case, confront him with analogies and parallelisms; they rather appear to him as identical.

On this level of consciousness, the aim of all actions is the preservation of life.

SACHS, in a masterly and fascinating pericope, has explained this in a convincing manner; he supports his argument with a wealth of documentary evidence, mainly derived from the history of the development of two musical instruments; the drum and the flute.

These two instruments, for that matter, are not by any means the most ancient that man learned to fabricate when he awoke to consciousness – however early in the history of human development they may have appeared on the scene. The oldest instruments were found by man on his own body; stamping and clapping of hands must have provided the first 'instrumental' accompaniment to the dance. [1] Also beating on one's buttocks – an illustration of which may still be seen on an ancient Greek vase (3553, Table I, fig. 3) – will have provided the rhythmic background to certain dances (fig. 45).

We may remark in this connexion that primitive man has the greatest difficulty – nay, often finds it totally impossible – when singing, to refrain from making other physical movements. I have repeatedly noticed this during my fieldwork in New Guinea. But even we, cultured as we are, sometimes catch ourselves gently moving our head to and fro when hearing certain melodies, or find, when playing ourselves, that we cannot keep our torso still. This, surely, is the last – evidently ineradicable – rest of the irrepressible inclination of the primitive (who, thank God, still slumbers in everyone of us!), to let himself go when hearing rhythmic sounds, and join in with them with his whole being.

[1] VIDE also 3680.

50

Even when a people has already reached a high level of culture, this inclination may still be present to a marked degree. We can see this, for instance, on some ancient Egyptian sepulchral paintings which have come down to us, and on which the singers are invariably depicted as gesticulating; the basic signification of the ancient Egyptian word for *singing* is *playing with the hand*, and is represented by a hieroglyph in the form of a lower arm with a hand (see fig. 45). From these, at first quite involuntary, movements there later grew a kind of sign-language, in which a given gesture expressed a certain interval, or, at any rate, the direction in which the melody was expected to move. This is the famous *cheironomy* of the ancient Egyptians, which served to replace, in this way, a probably non-existing musical script that thus remained unnecessary, and from which, it seems, the early Christian neum-notation ultimately developed in later centuries (3544, p. 9). The Vedic recitations, too, it appears, used to have a cheironomic accompaniment.

The musical instruments – apart from those directly placed at man's disposal by nature, such as rattles made from the outer shells of fruits – which we have sound reason to regard as the most ancient, represent, as it were, the objectivation and intensification of the clapping hands, stamping feet, beating of rolls on the performer's buttocks; in brief, of the 'music' produced by the body; technically put, they are extensions of bodily organs, just as, in another field of human activity, the fork is an extension of the hand and fingers, the spoon of the scoping hand, and the hammer of the fist. They are the instruments which we class as beating-sticks, stamping tubes, clappers etc. From these, in the course of untold thousands of years, there originated those countless instrumental forms we know today, the majority, of course, not for the purpose of serving the cause of Beauty, but with the aim of obtaining possession of instruments charged with magical power; others, also, as accompaniment to the (originally magico-religious) dance.

It was once again SACHS who gave us a concise and striking account of this development in his book *Die Musikinstrumente* (3529, p. 9). He puts forward the plausible theory that man learned how to increase the sound of stamping by performing it on a flat piece of wood, a rudimentary plank, instead of on the bare soil, and suggests how the result was found to be still further improved by digging a cavity underneath the plank. (An instrument of this kind is still found among the negritos (negroid pygmies) in the Andamans (Bay of Bengal); among some South-American Indian tribes, and among the North-Papuas). Or – another evolution – the stamping leg was replaced by a bamboo stamping tube (such instruments are still found, among other places, in the Indian archipelago, in East Africa, the Pacific, and in South-America).

From the clapping of hands there arose, by way of extension-forms of bodily organs, the countless different types of clappers, beating sticks, beating tubes, 'cymbals', and, finally, gongs; and from the 'snapping' of the fingers – ultimately, via many more primitive forms – the castanets. The beating of the player's buttocks was refined and the sound made louder by using a stick instead of the bare hand, and another stick, a tube, or a flat piece of wood in stead of the performer's body. It must then have become obvious that hollow objects make so much louder noises than solid ones, and further, that smaller and shorter objects produce higher tones than larger and longer ones. Gradually, the players must have taken pleasure in the alternation of high and low sounds; at first, however, without striving to obtain a particular pitch or tuning. This may have led to that peculiar subdivision into two or three groups, which were identified with the two sexes or the family relationships. The largest instrument, with the deepest sound, would then be designated as the 'man'; a smaller, higher-sounding one, as the 'woman', and the smallest and highest of all as the 'child'. Of this, too, the present time still provides many examples. As we already have noted above, the Chinese still know, *in musicalibus*, the contradistinction *yang* – *yin* = male – female. But also the Sundanese in West Java distinguish, in their panpipes, between *indung* = mother and *anak* = child; and all over Java and Bali we find 'male' and 'female' drums, gongs and kenongs. (A curious thing is that, in the latter islands, the instrument with the largest dimensions and the deepest sound is experienced by the people as female, and the smaller one with the higher pitch, as male).

In the beginning, instruments of different pitches were probably manipulated each by a different player; later on, as people learned how to combine them, a single player could handle the lot equally well, or even better.

The observation that a stamping plank sounds better when a hole is dug underneath, finally leads to the discovery that a beaten soundtube or -rod also sounds better when a calabash-gourd is placed under it. In this evolutionary direction lies the development of the later xylophones and metallophones, which either have a separate sound-body under each key or sound-kettle (as, for instance, on the Javanese and Balinese *gendèr* and the African *marimba*, derived from it), or a common sound-box under the entire range of keys (as in the case of the Javanese *saron*).

No doubt the wind instruments developed much later than the very simple instruments of the kinds discussed so far, as they do not constitute an extension of bodily organs.

Perhaps the most ancient form was a simple bamboo tube. The incidental discovery that it issued a tone, when the wind blew against it, may have been the incentive to produce the aircurrent by mouth. A combination

52

of such tubes of different lengths again produced the pleasant alternation of high and low tones. At first, each tube will probably have been blown by a separate individual (as is the case to this day with the West Florinese *hoi*, a set of loose pipes, but which belong together) (fig. 58); later on, these tubes were combined into a one-man instrument, and with this the pan-pipes were born (fig. 57).

The players further learned how to produce both high and low notes on one and the same tube, by the discovery of the 'stops' or fingerholes – an invention which, no doubt, was hailed at the time as a stroke of genius. And the difficulty of blowing into an uncut tube was overcome by fashioning some sort of mouth-piece, at first by a simple small notch in the upper edge of the tube (a modern example of this is the West-Javanese *chalintu*); afterwards by constructing, by some means or other, a slit which should drive the whole of the air blown into the tube against a sharp edge – which, as we know, is the origin of the sound produced by a flute.

A similar development may be observed in the case of the 'reed'-instruments or glottophones.

The most ancient and simplest example of this group of musical instruments is surely the blade of grass which is held tightly between the thumbs of both hands, as we all know from the days of our youth. Then follows a tube with a folded blade stuck in the top opening, or a pair of reedleaves, tied together and stuck on top of a tube; or, again, a tube into which, by means of a slightly oblique, either up- or downward cut, a so-called beating reed has been fashioned. (In the first case we are dealing with a 'free' aerophone, i.e. a so-called 'interruption'-aerophone; in the last case, with a clarinet; in the other cases, with simple types of the oboe family).

In the East (and for that matter also in Europe until the 17th century), the players of these oboe- and clarinet-forms manage to get a continuous sound out of these instruments, by taking the entire mouthpiece into their mouth. They breath through the nose, and feed the air into the tube by pressure of the cheeks, just enough to cause the instrumental 'reeds' to keep vibrating, also during inhalation. At a later stage, the mouth is replaced as air-reservoir by a calabash-gourd (we think here of the well-known snakecharmer's shawm of India Proper), and later still, by a flexible animal skin, sewn together in the form of a sack. This, then, leads to the development of the bagpipes, and, still later, to the church organ.

Of the trumpets – these are the instruments, in which the lips of the player function as a double reed – the oldest forms were also, without doubt, stout bamboo segments. Such bamboo trumpets are still to be found, for instance, in New-Guinea. The wooden ones, which presuppose a fairly well developed boring- and cauterizing-technique, must surely belong to a later period.

We see from all this how important was the rôle played by bamboo in the generation of the most ancient musical instruments; clappers, beating sticks, slit-drums, xylophones, flutes, clarinets, oboes, trumpets: they were all originally fabricated out of bamboo.

Of hardly lesser importance, it appears, was the calabash-gourd, which was especially used for all kinds of rattles, and as sound-intensifying body or as air-reserve.

The above considerations lead us to the assumption that the first musical instruments were invented and developed in tropical or subtropical regions.

The two materials mentioned must also have provided the means of producing the oldest types of drums; for the other materials: the hollowed out tree-trunk and the earthenware vessel – though already existing in ancient times – belong to a later cultural-historical period than those from which the drum originated. SACHS suggests that the drum was invented from calabash- or coconut-shells containing victuals, which were protected against dust, loss, decay, or insects by covering them with a tight-fitting bladder or skin.

But calabash and bamboo fulfilled their most important musical function in the creation – in a much later period – of the first string instruments. Probably the most ancient, but, especially in Indonesian cultural regions, to this day still perfectly vital form thereof, is the bamboo zither, with its string(s) 'lifted' out of the tube-wall. It was at first one-stringed and used alone; later – as in the case of the wooden or bamboo keys of the xylophone and of the flute (see above) – it was combined into series: the so-called raft-zithers (fig. 49).

In a later phase, the string lifted out of the tube-wall is replaced by a stretched string made of another material, at first – and here and there (for instance, in the Nicobar Islands) even today – of rattan; this turns it from an idiochord into a heterochord. A parallel development transforms this bamboo zither from a monochord into a polychord instrument i.e. one with more than one string. In order to lay the instrument down flat, it is cut in half along its longitudinal axis, a proceeding which, later on, leads to the long-drawn zither forms of China (*k'in*), Japan (*koto*) and Further India (*mi gyaung*, the crocodile zither of Burma and the Siamese *chaké*, which although closely akin, has lost its crocodile shape). This sliced bamboo zither still survives in a primitive, still idiochord, but already polychord form in Flores and Timor (fig. 48).

Another chain of development sees the fixing of a resonator – again, of course, a calabash – to the bamboo tube; and along this line there develop the instruments that culminate in the royal instrument which, in North India, is called *bin* (fig. 47), and in South India *vina*.

In addition to all these, a large number of stringed instruments are gradually developed from the hunter's bow, whose string, when the arrow is shot, produces a humming sound; this development proceeds, via different stages during which the mouth serves as sound-intensifier. Later on a calabash is added which evolves into the actual body of the instrument.

The primitive 'musical bow' (fig. 52), which is still found in the most unlikely corners of the world, and which has been the subject of a considerable literature, particularly the writings of HENRY BALFOUR (fig. 8) (210), TOBIAS NORLIND (fig. 5) (3039), PERCIVAL R. KIRBY (fig. 21) (2214, 2223, p. 171 ff., 2225), and CAMP and NETTL (fig. 42) (570), also survives in the mythology of many peoples: Apollo is an archer and at the same time the god of music; Shiwa, too, is both archer and Lord of the musical bow; the Japanese godhead Ameno Kamato constructs a string instrument from a number of hunter's bows (cf. the African *lu(n)komba*) (fig. 52) [1].

The musical bow with resonator is the common ancestor of all higher developed forms such as harps, lyres and lutes. Their manner of playing varies greatly; some are beaten with a small stick, others are plucked. Stroking the strings ('bowing') is the youngest playing method. There are some indications, that the use of the bow was first practized in Central Asia (Mongolia) and, if that is true, a long period must have elapsed [2] before the use of the bow reached West Europe.

Thus far our bird's eye view of the development of musical instruments.

* * *

Before proceeding now to give an exposition of the system of classification designed by SACHS in collaboration with his colleague VON HORNBOSTEL, following the Belgian musicologist VICTOR MAHILLON, which system constitutes a most succesful attempt to arrange in logical order all those instrumental forms, I will first give the reader a brief general survey of the subjectmatter.

One of the features of civilization in its later phases of development is a certain inclination to classify the available material and to construe some kind of system on the basis of this classification. As far as I am aware this has been done, in respect of musical instruments, three times: i.e. in China, in India and in modern Europe.

The Chinese classification is based on the material from which the instruments are chiefly fabricated. This classification includes eight groups:

---

[1] *Vide* also J. MAES, *Les Lukombe ou instruments de musique à cordes des populations du Kanai -Lac Léopold – Lukénie* (2702).

[2] See, however, our figure 50, on which apparently a bow is used. It is regrettable that no one knows in which period this prehistoric painting was made. It was found by G. W. STOW in the Maluti Mountains of Basutoland and copied *in situ*. Cf. PERCIVAL R. KIRBY, *The Musical Instruments of the Native Races of South Africa* (2223, p. 193 ff. and front picture). Perhaps it is very old; perhaps made by Bushmen only recently.

kin (metal), *che* (stone), *t'u* (earthenware), *ko* (skin), *hién* (strings), *p'o* (calabash), *chu* (bamboo), and *mu* (wood) (3895, p. 25; 750, p. 80). But however attractive, owing to its simplicity, this classification has never been adopted by Western scientists, because, after all, several instruments are made from a variety of materials, from the combination of which the instrument in question acquires its suitability to produce sound.

On the contrary, the old Indian classification in four groups: *ghana* (cymbals, gongs etc.), *avanaddha* (drums, tamburines etc.), *tata* (string instruments) and *çushira* (wind instruments), which is already to be found in the *Nâtya-çâstra*, – that large encyclopedic work, attributed to the great BHÂRATA and dating from before our era, – strongly appeals to the Western mind. When, as late as 1880, Europe at last arrives at a classification of its own, fulfilling all reasonable demands, it appears to base itself on exactly the same principles as this ancient Indian one.

Until that year, a hopeless confusion generally prevailed in this respect, also in professional circles. In that same year there appeared the extensive *Catalogue descriptif et analytique du Musée instrumental du Conservatoire de Bruxelles*, from the pen of the then Conservator of that museum, the musician and instrument-maker VICTOR MAHILLON (1841–1924). In this work, a logical system of classification, comprising all instruments housed in the Brussels museum, was for the first time put into practice (2707).

However, owing to the relatively small number of exotic instruments present in the said museum, the system, in the state it was published at the time, was still far too much concerned with European musical instruments alone, with the result that, on the one hand, certain features were given a relatively too important place in the subdivisions (e.g., whether or not they had a keyboard), while, on the other hand, distinct groups had been formed which, seen from a more general point of view, were not logically coördinated (as, for example, the division of aerophones into (a) reed-, (b) mouth-hole-, (c) polyphonous instruments with air-reservoir, and (d) funnel-mouthpiece-instruments). It further appeared, when more exotic instruments gradually became known, that several of them could find no place in this system.

With these facts in mind, VON HORNBOSTEL and SACHS proceeded, while preserving the main lines of the system, to extend it in such a way as to ensure that it would cover all instrumental forms known to them at the time, as well as any others which, although not yet discovered, might quite possibly be extant. VON HORNBOSTEL and SACHS, indeed, succeeded in bringing the task they had set themselves to a most felicitous conclusion, making use of the decimal system of DEWEY (1913).

But although we had, at last, an excellent system of classification at our disposal, there was still a long way to go before it was generally used in literature and in the existing museum catalogues. We still find, in many museums, completely unacceptable headings and subdivisions, in which, for instance, the mouth-organ (a wind-instrument) and the mouth-harp or jew's (= ? jaw's) harp (an instrument with vibrating lamella) are united in one and the same group, or in which the most dissimilar forms, such as drums and gongs, are classed together under the heading 'percussion-instruments'.

It is further usual to add, in addition to the group of Percussion-instruments, another two groups, viz. String-instruments and Wind-instruments. However, various other types of instruments cannot be brought under those headings and these are usually put collectively in a questionable fourth category 'Miscellaneous'!

In the subdivisions there prevails an even worse anarchy. A large number of curators and ethnologists do not know the difference between clarinets, oboes and flutes, while an oboe, if it happens to possess a 'bell' (soundfunnel) made of tin or other metal, is often listed as a 'trumpet'.

In connexion with this, it may be remarked that the indication of the native names is frequently anything but helpful, since the same names are used for different instruments in different places, and sometimes even in one and the same region. Thus, in a large of part Central Africa, the name *marimba* is given to a xylophone, while in the Congo-basin it is also frequently used to designate quite a different lamella-instrument, usually called *sanza*. The *chelempung* is, in West Java, a bamboo idiochord with either one or two strings; in Central Java it is a form of heterochord zither with 13 double strings. But in Siak (Central Sumatra) it is a metallophone consisting of a range of either 5 or 10 small horizontally placed gongs! In Siam, the name *klu'i* is given to wind instruments of the most divergent character, etc. etc.

But where musicologists were completely at a loss was in the case of the Aeolian harp – a stringed instrument played by the wind – and in that of the piano and the cembalo, which, although stringed instruments, are beaten by means of small hammers, and therefore perhaps ought to be filed with the percussion group.

A further point to be noted is the customary subdivision of orchestral wind instruments into the 'brass' and the 'wood-wind' groups, a most peculiar and, surely, equally unsatisfactory classification, since several instruments of the 'brass' group – particularly the more ancient ones – used to be made of wood (in some cases ivory), e.g. the 'Zinken' (a primitive type of cornet), the 'Serpents' and the Bass-horns, whereas, on the other hand, many of the 'wood-wind' group are often – or always – made of metal (flutes, saxophones, sarrusophones, etc.).

Not only in the museum catalogues, but also in the musicological literature, we find, even to this day, years after the creation of such a logical system of classification, the queerest subdivisions. As one of the most appalling examples we may mention STEPHEN CHAUVET's beautifully edited book *La Musique Négre* (629), in which this author follows a twofold classification, namely (a) 'les instruments de rhythme' (according to him, these are the drums, the horns ('trompes'), signalling whistles ('sifflets') and rattles ('hochets')), and (b) 'les instruments de musique proprement dits' (i.e. genuinely musical instruments). It would be hard to think of a more unsatisfactory classification.

However, the majority of musicologists today adhere to the system proposed by MAHILLON, SACHS and VON HORNBOSTEL. A few, who, for some reason or other, do not or only partly agree with this, apply a classification of their own, for example GEORGES MONTANDON in his *Généalogie des instruments de musique et les cycles de civilisation* (2907), and ANDRÉ SCHAEFFNER (3676–3692) the leader of the musicological department of the Musée de l'Homme at Paris, in his treatises *D'une nouvelle classification méthodique des instruments de musique* (3677) ; *Note sur la filiation des instruments à cordes* (3678) and in his book *Origine des instruments de musique* (3681). TOBIAS NORLIND, in his excellent *Systematik der Saiteninstrumente* (3039, 3040), has practically adopted in its entirety the classification of SACHS and VON HORNBOSTEL (without the decimal system), except for the fact, that he unites the idiophone and the membranophone groups [1] under the heading *autophones* (3041) and has carried the subdivisions much further. The above-mentioned, antiquated division into three classes – still followed at as late a date as 1904 by HENRY BALFOUR in his *Musical instruments from the Malay Peninsula* (214) and again, in 1929, in his *Music* (218) – is deficient not only in its failure to comprise all instrumental forms, but also in its lack of homogeneity: on the one hand it places the method of playing as the criterion (i.e. in regard to the percussion- and wind-instruments), and on the other the material which primarily is made to sound (i.e. as regards the group of stringed instruments).

MAHILLON's classification, on the contrary, puts forward only one single criterion for the division into the main groups, namely, the material which is made to sound in the first instance. This author distinguishes four main classes of instruments, i.e.:

(a) *Autophones*, whose material itself produces the sound, without being previously stretched in any way whatever;
(b) *Membranophones*, made to sound by means of a skin or membrane stretched over the instrument;
(c) *Chordophones*, made to sound by means of stretched strings;

---

[1] These terms will be discussed in the next alinea.

(d) *Aerophones,* in which it is not the material from which they are made, but, in the first instance, the air – in most cases the column of air inside the instrument – that is made to sound.

This main classification has been taken over by SACHS and VON HORN-BOSTEL. The only alteration they made in the above nomenclature was to replace the term *autophone* by *idiophone*, in view of the fact that we are accustomed, in our technical terminology, to associate the prefix *auto* with the concept of movement under a mechanism's 'own' power, i.e. automatic action.

Each of the above four main groups has naturally been subdivided. In this subdivision, however, there is not the same unity of criterion as seen in the main groups. The idiophones are classed and arranged according to the playing method; the membranophones, in the first instance, also according to the playing method, but further according to shape; the chordophones are first split into two groups, i.e. that of the simple, and that of the composite instruments, and they are further classified according to shape; in the case of the aerophones we first find a division into 'free' aerophones and wind instruments proper, after which the latter group is again subdivided according to the manner in which they are blown. In this subdivision, therefore, homogeneity of criterion is again conspicuous by its absence. VON HORNBOSTEL and SACHS, of course, intended this to be so; indeed, they say, in their Introduction: 'Da wir absichtlich die verschiedenen Gruppen nicht nach einem einheitlichen Prinzip unter-gestellt, sondern den Einteilungsgrund allemal der Eigenart der Gruppe angepasst haben, so sind Gruppen von gleicher Rangordnung im System durchaus nicht immer koordiniert'. (i.e. Since we purposely refrained from subjecting the various groups to some homogeneous principle, and, on the contrary, adapted the basis of our subdivisions in each case to the typical character of the group in question, certain sub-groups of the same order of precedence are not always coördinated in our system) (1913, p. 558).

None the less, MONTANDON rather frowned upon this inequality of criterion in the subdivisions, and, accordingly, in his own system sub-divided all groups according to one, the playing method.

ANDRÉ SCHAEFFNER finds that he cannot agree in every respect with either MAHILLON–VON HORNBOSTEL–SACHS' or MONTANDON's classifi-cation. As regards the former, he considers the group of the idiophones not homogeneous enough. Taking MONTANDON's definition as his starting point – which says that the idiophones include ...'tout corps, dont la vibration est le fait de leur carcasse et non de membrane, de corde ou primairement de l'air (2907, p. 47) (i.e. each instrument, in which the vibration is caused by the body, and not by a membrane, a string or, primarily, the air) – SCHAEFFNER points out that, in that case, instruments such as the African *sanza* have, in effect, been mistakenly classified with the idiophones. For here, it is the plucked metal or wooden tongues and not the body – a flat piece of wood or a sound-box – that constitute the primarily sounding material. (These instruments with 'hard' tongues also led Professor A. E. CHERBULIEZ, the Zürich musicologist, to distinguish, in addition to the four main groups, as classified by MAHILLON–SACHS–VON HORNBOSTEL, a fifth, which he calls the *linguaphone* group. With this group CHERBULIEZ classes, for instance, besides the sanza, the mouth-harps, and the imitation drum of the Javanese *kowangan* (2399, p. 200, and fig. 92)).

According to SCHAEFFNER the same applies – be it in a lesser degree – to many East-Asiatic and African xylophones and their family. Here also, it is not the body (a wooden box, a wooden frame with bamboo tubes, c.q. with calabash-gourds) that sounds in the first instance – although it does function secondarily – but another part of the instrument, *viz.* the keys.

As regards MONTANDON's system, SCHAEFFNER's special grievance is the use of the general criterion of the playing method all along the line. For, he says, if we do that, then we must class a plucked lute with a different group from that of a bowed lute, despite of the fact that the two are constructed exactly alike; one and the same instrument may quite well have started its career as a plucked one, and developed only centuries later into one played with a bow, for example the ancient Celtic *crwth* (Latin: *chrotta*). And what is one to do about the guitar, which, as occasion may demand, is made to sound in glissandi, by beating the sound-box, or plucking the strings? And what about the violin, which, though mostly played with a bow, is also plucked from time to time? And what are we to do with the bamboo idiochords, some of which are plucked, whereas others are beaten with a stick?

Taking all this into consideration, SCHAEFFNER finally preferred to design a classification system of his own. This – two-part – system distinguishes:

(a) instruments whose primarily vibrating material is a solid;
(b) instruments whose primarily vibrating material is a gas, namely, the air.

The first group, in its turn, is split into two, viz. (1) the sub-group characterized by ... vibration d'un corps solide, non susceptible de tension, et à intonations invariables ou indéterminables', and (2) the sub-group characterized by ... vibration d'un corps solide tendu, à intonation variable'.

In 1936 he made this subdivision threefold: from the first sub-group he detached as an independent one a sub-group 'corps solides flexibles', among which, he, for instance, classified the *sanzas* and the mouth-harps (3681, p. 371 ff).

There is certainly much to be said for this classification of SCHAEFFNER; it cannot be denied that it is logical. Nevertheless, in my opinion his objections to MAHILLON's system do not hold water; there is not the slightest reason, for instance, to take that definition of MONTANDON as a standard; after all, it is neither the sound-box of a xylophone nor that of a *sanza*, in short, not the body of those instruments, but the keys themselves which comply with the criterion of being able to produce a tone without having been previously stretched, as a string or a membrane is. And although a homogeneous criterion for the main groups is desirable, it is, in my opinion, a matter of complete indifference whether one waives this desire, purely from considerations of expediency, in the case of the subdivisions, providing always that they are consistent within the range of each subgroup, that is, neither overlap nor leave part of the field uncovered.

In 1948 a new, very detailed, classification system was proposed by HANS HEINZ DRÄGER in his brochure *Prinzip einer Systematik der Musikinstrumente* (1007). It is constructed on the foundations laid by MAHILLON, SACHS and VON HORNBOSTEL, but attempts to achieve a greater homogeneity in the criteria. The utility of this system will have to be proved in practice, but, personally, I think it is too detailed to be easily handled. The already existing systems are quite serviceable, and this new one will probably have difficulty in getting a foothold.

In my work, in common with WALTER KAUDERN in his *Musical Instruments in Celebes* (2178), K. G. IZIKOWITZ in his *Musical and other Sound-instruments of the South American Indians* (2044), CLAUDIE MARCEL-DUBOIS in her *Instruments de Musique de l'Inde ancienne* (2732), and HANS HICKMANN in his large Catalogue (1757), I have thought best to adhere to MAHILLON's system, as perfected by VON HORNBOSTEL and SACHS; my own experience being that only in extremely rare cases does it let the investigator down. Only, when dealing with modern European organology, one has to add a supplementary group, namely that of the *electrophones*, of which, during the last decades, many different types have been created (for instance, the *Trautonium*, MARTENOT's *Ondes sonores* e.t.q.). [1]

It was CURT SACHS who first made an attempt to order and classify the infinite variety of sound-instruments from the cultural-historical angle. In his book *Geist und Werden der Musikinstrumente* (3553), a masterly, authoritative and comprehensive work, he has succeeded in laying down the main lines of investigation, thus creating a firm basis for subsequent workers to build upon with confidence. In a later work, *The History of Musical Instruments* (3564), SACHS once again ordered and arranged the

---

[1] In his article *Musikinstrumentenkunde* (1009a), HANS HEINZ DRÄGER gives a clear survey of the classification problem as it now stands.

entire organological material, starting from a somewhat different stand-point, but with every sign of still deeper and more mature insight.

In the first-named work, the Berlin musicologist enumerates four ways along which we may come to a classification as intended by him, namely:

(a) the purely musicological way, in which the guiding principle is the greater or lesser development of an instrument. Here, however, we are faced with unsurmountable difficulties: where are we to look for the evidence of this higher development? In the volume of tone? In the reduction of the size of the intervals? In the greater purity and refinement of the tone-quality? In the increasing possibilities to produce rhythmic or dynamic variety? And again, is it possible to test the degree in which each of these elements is present in each particular case by trying an instrument found in a museum, and without the coöperation of a player who is familiar with its manipulation?

(b) the 'ergological' method, in which account is taken of the qualities showing the degree of craftsmanship needed to fabricate it;

(c) the classification according to the 'Kulturkreise' (i.e. cultural regions) in which the instrument is found, as FROBENIUS, GRAEBNER, FOY, ANKERMANN and Father WILHELM SCHMIDT have adopted;

(d) the theory that the further an instrument is found from its centre of origin, the older it is. One could call it the geographical method. This method can be applied only by the ethnomusicologist who, in the controversy 'Entlehnung oder Völkergedanke' (i.e. assimilation or plurigenesis) has voted for 'assimilation'. And, as SACHS rightly remarks, the evidence of migration, and adoption by other peoples, of different instrumental forms is so overwhelmingly convincing, that musicologists can hardly be expected to be other than adherents of the 'Entlehnung' theory. One of the primary reasons for rejecting the idea of plurigenesis (i.e. the independent appearance of the same instrument in different regions) is the presence, in so many cases, of perfectly identical, *non-essential* features of the instruments in question.

On the ground, therefore, of geographic diffusion, but also and unmistakably guided here and there by the 'Kulturkreislehre' (i.e. cultural regions-doctrine) of the Viennese ethnological school, as well as taking into account, where necessary, the structure and craftmanships shown by the various instruments, SACHS – aided by his phenomenal knowledge of facts, both in the field of the actual organology and that of comparative linguistics (he began his career as a man of letters and as historian of art) – was able to put some order into the instrumental chaos. He divides his subject-matter into three main parts, namely, the Stone Age, the Metal Age and the Middle Ages. The first period is again subdivided into no less than 12, the metal age into 7, and the middle ages into 4 periods.

What strikes one in this is that, generally speaking, the most ancient strata comprise a wider field than the later ones – resembling what happens when a stone is thrown, into water: the first circles – i.e. the outer ones – cover the greatest area. My late colleague J. S. BRANDTS BUYS (471–490), who made a most meritorious study of the music of Central Java and Madura, spoke of this phenomenon and the conclusions which were drawn from it, as the 'fairy circle theory'.

There are many things which point to the probability that this wealth of instrumental forms for the greater part owes its existence to two very ancient cultural centres, namely, the Egyptian-Mesopotamian centre and the ancient Chinese. Also there are a few indications which suggest that, behind these two civilizations, there must have been a still more ancient one from which they both originated, and which was probably located somewhere in Central Asia.

* * *

In this booklet many ethnomusicologists of great merit have not yet been mentioned, because it so happened that they did not fit into the scheme followed in its composition. For instance the Finnish musicologists OTTO ANDERSSON (83–94) and A. P. VÄISÄNEN (4167–4179a) ; the French investigators Father AMIOT (1779)!) (70), ALEXIS CHOTTIN (644–663, 1783), ALAIN DANIÉLOU (808–818a), RODOLPHE D'ERLANGER (1116–1119), JOANNY GROSSET (1534, 1535), RAOUL and MARGHÉRITE D'HARCOURT (98, 309, 1599–1607, 1929, 2489, 2490), Mrs. HUMBERT-SAUVAGEOT (1995, 1996, 4110), VICTOR LORET (2657–2660), LOUIS LALOY (2526–2531), A. MACHABEY (2678–2684), NOEL PÉRI (3158), GILBERT ROUGET (1524, 3498–3502), a.o.; the Mongol princess NIRGIDMA DE TORHOUT (4110) ; the Turkish musicologists ADNAN AHMED SAYGUN (3665–3668) and RAOUF YEKTA (4452, 4453) ; the Swiss SAMUEL BAUD-BOVY (fig. 13) (294–300) ; the Angelsaxon scholars PHYLLIS ACKERMAN (13), EDWIN G. BURROWS (547–552a), CHARLES RUSSELL DAY (834–838), HERBERT A. POPLEY (3217), HENRY GEORGE FARMER (1156–1210, 3456), EMANUEL WINTERNITZ (4393), COLIN MCPHEE (2803–2817), A. C. MOULE (2923–2926), FRANCIS PIGGOTT (3183–3185), LAURENCE PICKEN (3174–3181), and many others; the Danes ERIK DAL (fig. 33) (780–783a) and NILS SCHIØRRING (fig. 4) (136, 3703–3705) ; the Dutchmen J. A. VAN AALST (1), A. A. BAKE (fig. 22) (170–198c, 1289), J. P. N. LAND (487, 2533–2537) and CASPAR HÖWELER (1867) ; the African experts K. P. WACHSMANN (fig. 36) (4254–4262) and HERBERT PEPPER (3135–3152) ; the Indian scholars N.V. BHATKHANDE (353–355), ANANDA COOMARASWAMY (739–743), C. S. AIYAR (34–41), SRI PADA BANDOPADHYAYA (226–229), V. RAGHAVAN (3252–3308c), K. V. RAMACHANDRAN (3314–3320a),

Pandit RATANJANKAR (3348–3357), P. SAMBAMURTHY (3605–3623a) e.t.q.; the Japanese SHIGEO KISHIBE (2238–2241, 4138), GENJIRO MASU (2779, 2780), TARO OTA (3091), K. SUNAGA (4003), HIDEO TANABE (4041, 4042), KIYOSI TAKANO (4035, 4036), S. TANAKA (4046) a.o.; the Chinese EN SHAO WANG (4288) and KUANG CHI WANG (4289–4292); the Siamese PHRA CHEN DURYANGA (1026, 1027) and H. E. NAI V. VICHITR-VADAKARN (4229); the Burmese U KHIN ZAW (4477–4478a); the Bulgarians STOYAN DJOUDJEFF (985–990), IVAN KATSCHULEV (2150–2155), RAINA KATZAROVA (fig. 38) (2156–2176), VASIL (STOÏN 3958–3965) a.o.; the Yugoslavs VLADIMIR DJORDJEVIC (979–984), MIODRAG VASILJEVIC (fig. 41) (4198–4201), CVJETKO RIHTMAN (fig. 35) (3422–3424a), GIVKO FIRFOV (1245–1248a) a.o.; the Rumanian TIBERIU ALEXANDRU (51–54a); the Australian experts HAROLD E. DAVIES (830) and A. P. ELKIN (1063–1063b); the Maori specialist JOH. C. ANDERSSEN (77–80); the Hungarians ZOLTAN KODÁLY (fig. 10) (261, 265, 266, 283, 2267–2272) and LASZLO LAJTHA (fig. 40) (2520–2525); the Belgians OLGA BOONE (392, 393) and PAUL COLLAER (719–728a); the Korean scholar CHUNG SIK KEH (2186); the Cuban investigators FERNANDO ORTIZ (3073–3080) and EDUARDO SANCHEZ DE FUENTES (3627–3634); the Uruguayan LAURO AYESTARAN (155, 156); the Mexicans CARLOS CHAVEZ (633) and GABRIEL SALDIVAR (3591); the Brazilians LUIZ HEITOR CORRÊA DE AZEVEDO (157–161), Mrs. ONEYDA ALVARENGA (63–67) and RENATO ALMEIDA (60); the Argentine CARLOS VEGA (4207–3213); the German Japan-specialists ETA HARICH-SCHNEIDER (1612–1618a) and HANS ECKARDT (1044–1050a), and many others who, I hope, will not resent my omissions.

A variety of subjects, too, some of them most important, have been hardly, if at all, touched upon in the above. Thus, for example, the different tonal systems and scale systems in practical use in the world [1], the various melodic formulae and tonal patterns so characteristic of many non-European musical cultures (as in the ancient Greek *nomoi*, the Japanese *No*-music, the *raga's* of India Proper, the Hebrew *nigún*, the Javanese *patet*, and the Persian-Arab *maqamat*); the forms of multi-part music [2]; problems of metre and rhythm [3]; the cultural-historical currents in so far as they

---

[1] For the demonstration of the structure of exotic scales there has been developed at the Royal Tropical Institute, Amsterdam, a polychord, provided with 12 graduated scales, moveable bridges and tuning pegs, which can duplicate any kind of scale of known vibration numbers (fig. 60). It is available for any serious musicologist at a moderate price (address: Royal Tropical Institute, Department of Anthropology, Linnaeusstraat 2A, Amsterdam Oost).

[2] See, for instance: 113, 324, 405, 550, 1524, 1747, 1794, 1822, p. 97 ff., 1899, 1965, 2104, 2209, 2213, 2302, 2401, 2499, 2625, 2999, p. 77 ff., 3174, p. 239, 3176, 3327a, 3423, 3424, 3428a, 3551, 3635, 3730, 3731, 3734, 3739, 3757, 3954a, and 4123.

[3] In regard to rhythm, West-European musicians and musicologists are inclined to forget that the greater part of the white race is decidedly inferior to many non-European peoples, especially the African negro-peoples. Ample evidence of this may be found in 1384, 1432, 2093 II, 2104, 3523, and 4310. - For intricate (East-)European rhythmic structures, I may refer the reader to 120, 462, 464, 771, 985, 987, 2921, 3023, 4199, and 4200. - For problems of metre and rhythm in general, see: 75, 467, 645, 1504, 1868, 2008b, 2401, 2943, 2944, 3576, 3577, 3774a, 4033, 4274, 4372, and 4381.

found expression in music [1]; problems of style [2] and form [3]; the various exotic musical scripts [4]; music and magic [5]; music in its relation to work [6], music and philosophy [7], psychology of music [8], music as a sociological factor [9], music and religion [10], music and medicine [11], classification of melodies [12], music and mission [13], music and language [14], melodic typology [15], etc., etc.

For a more general and systematic exposition of the objects, technical means and subject-matter of ethnomusicology I may refer the reader to ROBERT LACH, *Die vergleichende Musikwissenschaft, ihre Methoden und Probleme* (2478); WILHELM HEINITZ, *Vergleichende Musikwissenschaft* (1659); ROBERT LACHMANN, *Musik des Orients* (2502); CURT SACHS, *Vergleichende Musikwissenschaft* (3554); BÉLA BARTÓK, *Pourquoi et comment receuille-t-on la musique populaire* (281); FRANK HOWES, *Man, Mind and Music* (1972); WILL G. GILBERT, *Buiten-Europese muziek* (1435); A. A. BAKE and MAUD KARPELES, *Manual for Folksong Collectors* (187); GLEN HAYDON, *Introduction to Musicology* (1632, p. 216 ff.); FRITZ BOSE, *Musikalische Völkerkunde* (432); BRUNO NETTL, *Music in primitive culture* (2999); the chapter 'Music' in 'Notes and Queries on Anthropology' (6th ed., p. 315 ff.) (3045), and, for a standard example, how an investigation into the music of a 'primitive' people should be made, for instance, to the

---

[1] See p. 46 note 3, and, for instance, 2238 and 2240.

[2] See 424, 793, 800, 1676, 1702, 1944, 1956, 1987, 2472, 2978, 2979, 3734, 3743, and 3745.

[3] See, for instance: 1703, 2288, 2602, and 3446.

[4] See for Babylonia: 3546, 3548, 3568, 3570a; for Sumeria: 1341, Chapter IV; for Egypt: 1812, 1822, p. 48 ff.; for Hellas: 1397a, p. 129 ff., 3545 and 3547; for Arabia: 2440a, 2534, 2537, 3491, p. 2733; for India: 41a, 641, 811 II, 1535, p. 300 ff. and 324, 3520, 3844, 3846; for Tibet: 3892; for Java: 2498 and 3184, p. 124 ff.; for Bali: 2360, par. 5 (p. 47 ff.); for Japan: 1050a (figs 2, 5, 6 and 15), 1617, 1919, 2255, 2603, 3174, p. 239 ff., 4000, 4011, 4144, 4146, 4290, 4549b; for Vietnam: 2519, p. 46 ff.; for Khwarizm: 318a; for Persia: 2534; for Byzantium: 1373, p. 547 and 553 ff., 4339; for the Hebrews: 3480a, 4358a, p. 6 25, and for the Mexican Aztecs: 3046. For a general survey see: 827, 1408, 3557a, 4085, 4430, and 4432.

[5] See, for instance: 128, 154a, 219, 285, p. 53 ff., 445, 529, 533, 730, 873, 891, 1062, 1225, 1459, 2119, 2419, 2421, 2422, 2425, 2545, 2571, p. 65, 2585, p. 91 ff., 2741, 2870, 2871, 2933, 3201, 3334a, 3446, p. 37, 3487, 3491, p. 2800, 3518, 3529, p. 21 ff., 3670, 3771, 3892, 4007, 4437, 4449, and 4498.

[6] See the famous book by CARL BÜCHER, *Arbeit und Rhythmus* (530), and, for instance: HEINITZ (1660), RAMON Y RIVERA (3327), and VARAGNAC (4190).

[7] See: 55, 507, 1532, 1972, 2531, 3170, 3510, 3769, 4144, 4265, and 4358.

[8] See: 46, 611, 1439, 1590, 1598, 1905, 1931, 1932, 1972, 2067, 2324, 2325, 2440, 2936, 3063, 3081, 3395, 3776, 3777, 3780, 3793, 3984, 3988, 3396, 4222, and 4312.

[9] See: 328, 375, 1972, 2056, 2275, 2406, 4319, and many others, for instance: 1038, 1478, 1532, 1478, 2274, 2473, 3836, 3871, 4130, 4286, 4287, and 4434.

[10] See, for instance: 445, 942, 1062, 1099, 1315, 1525, 1532, 1547, 1698, 1717, 2066, 2285, 2392, 2663, 2666, 2675, 2737a, 2860, 3114, 3487, 3517, 3820, 3898, and 4370.

[11] See, for instance: 119, 873, 890, 936, 937, 940, 943, 2421, 2422, 2683, 3005, 3081, 3780, 3859a, and 4007.

[12] The classification of European folk songs owes much to ILMARI KROHN (2332); see also: 267, 303, 1653, 1661, 2294, 2565, 2954, 3243, 3594, 4178, and 4497.

[13] See: 2392, 3517, and 4349.

[14] See, for instance: 1710, 2442, 2984, 3187, 3748, 3755, and 3925.

[15] See: 1053, 2289, 2603, 3744, 3747, 3749, 3751, 3760, 3872, and 3873.

excellent study by HELEN H. ROBERTS and MORRIS SWADESH on the songs of the Nootka Indians (3451).

As said above, SACHS gives a generously ample survey of the development of music and musical instruments in the course of the past millennia, in the two brilliant monographs, repeatedly cited in the foregoing pages: *Geist und Werden der Musikinstrumente* (3553) and *The History of Musical Instruments* (3564) and also in his book – no less recommendable – *The Rise of Music in the Ancient World, East and West* (3567), while for the nomenclature of musical instruments his *Reallexikon der Musikinstrumente* (3528) – published as early as 1913, but not by any means out of date – may be consulted with much benefit.

Most of the publications mentioned in these pages deal with problems and subjects of a general nature. But also for the study of the music of certain particular parts of the world, a large number of monographs are available to those interested. Most of them the reader will find listed alphabetically in the Bibliography, p. 79.

Index I gives the subjects treated and the instrumental names mentioned in this book; Index II the names of the countries, regions and peoples the music of which has been studied and/or recorded; Index III the names of authors, collectors and musicians; Index IV a list of periodicals, containing ethno-musicological publications. The numbers in brackets refer to the corresponding numbers of the publications found in the bibliography; the numbers in italics to the pages of this book.

ADDENDA

p. 25, sub *a*): KL. 5173 . Northern and Central Italy and the Albanians of Calabria (rec. and notes: ALAN LOMAX and DIEGO CARPITELLA);

KL. 5174. Southern Italy, Sicily, Sardinia (instr.: a.o. *launeddas*) (rec. and notes by id.);

p. 26, sub *f*): L.D. 333. Musique Polynésienne (islands: Society Islands (Maupiti, Moorea, Tahiti), Marquesas (= Tiki), Fatu Hiva) (instr.: guitar, beating sticks, handclapping) (rec. by FRANCIS MAZIÈRE);

L.D. 337. Musique d'Afghanistan (instr.: *daira, santur, tampura,* flute, *zerbevali, cetar, tabla, robab, delroba, tanbur, ritchak*) (rec. and notes: ALAIN DELAPRAZ);

p. 34, sub *ii*): MC 20.124 Gitans. Pélérinage aux Saintes Maries de la mer (rec. by DEBEN BHATTACHARYA, ass. by FRANCIS HÉRÉTIER);

p. 35, to add: *mm*) issued by the RADIODIFFUSION DE LA FRANCE D'OUTRE-MER: (46, rue d'Amsterdam, Paris IX) two L.P.-recordings 'Les Dogon' (instr.: gourd-drums, hourglass shaped drums, *guignerou* (small guitar with neck-bells), iron bells, trumpets, bull-roarers) (rec. by FRANCOIS DI DIO, notes by GERMAINE DIETERLEN).

nn) issued by the Yugoton firm (Ethnophilia): five 78-records of folk music from the Kroatian littoral and Istria (instr.: *sopele*) (rec. and notes by NEDJELJKO KARABAIĆ).

66

TRAINING POSSIBILITIES FOR ETHNOMUSICOLOGISTS

An inquiry into the training possibilities for students of ethnomusicology in different countries provided the following results:

BELGIUM

'En fait, les études ethnomusicologiques n'ont pas encore fait leur entrée, jusqu'ici, dans les Universités belges. La *musicologie* est, en somme, une branche relativement toute nouvelle dans ce domaine, et son enseignement s'attache principalement à l'histoire de la musique européenne de l'occident, telle qu'elle est exposée dans les manuels classiques (RIEMANN, ADLER, SMIJERS, Handbuch der Musikwissenschaft, etc.). Depuis que l'*ethno*musicologie a pris une place exceptionnellement importante dans le monde entier, on tend cependant à attirer l'attention des étudiants sur son existence et sur son intérêt. Mais cela ne se fait que d'une façon assez sporadique et superficielle, notamment quand le professeur se trouve dans la nécessité (*sic*) de s'occuper des origines de la musique ou plus spécialement, de la chanson populaire. Mais il est sans conteste qu'à l'avenir ces 'embryons' ne manqueront pas de se developper. Comment pourrait-il en être autrement, quand on est témoin de l'action d'un homme comme M. PAUL COLLAER, qui a si profondément pénétré dans ce domaine, et qui fait tant pour en faire comprendre l'importance par des conférences et par des colloques, comme ceux de Wégimont, si intelligemment organisés par Mme. CLERCX-LEJEUNE, mon ancienne élève, qui m'a succédé à la chair de musicologie de l'Université de Liège?

Le cycle ethnomusicologique, qui a eu lieu à l'Institut des Hautes Etudes de Belgique, est, de son côté, un témoignage significatif de l'intérêt croissant qui s'attache à cette nouvelle discipline. Mais vous le voyez, il n'y a encore, là, qu'une esquisse préparatoire. Ce qu'il faudrait, c'est pouvoir faire du travail de séminaire, sous la direction permanente d'un spécialiste comme PAUL COLLAER. J'ai le ferme espoir que son esprit d'entreprise l'amènera, un jour ou l'autre, à mettre sur pied un centre d'études de cette espèce. Mais encore faudra-t-il trouver, sur place, des élements assez sérieux pour poursuivre ces études en dehors de tout amateurisme. Les trouvera-t-on? – that is the question!'

CHARLES VAN DEN BORREN

CZECHOSLOVAKIA

'An den Universitäten der Tschechoslowakei wird Ethnomusicologie eigentlich nicht gepflegt, obwohl unser Land einen grossen Reichtum an Volksliedern und Volksmusik aufweist. Nur für die Hörer der Musikwissenschaft und der allgemeinen Volkskunde werden 1–2 Stunden wöchentlich (2 Semester) eine Einführung in die Ethnomusikologie mit praktischen Beispielen (hauptsächlich als gewisse Schulung für eventuelle Sammeltätigkeit) eingerichtet. Wenn die Hörer ein Thema aus dem Gebiete der Volksmusik für ihre Diplomarbeit wählen, dann beschränkt sich die Arbeit meistens auf musikhistorische oder volkskundliche Fragen des Landes'.

KAREL VETTERL

DENMARK

'At the University of Copenhagen it is possible to study ethnomusicology as a special subject for the Master of Arts degree (about the same as German Dr. Phil.) and for the candidatus magisterii-examination (teachers in music at the gymnasium and other highschools). I am lecturing this subject but only as a part of my other duties. Some people have already passed examination in ethnomusicology, e.g. in Kafir-music, Central-Asian music, Yugoslav music, Faerör-music a.s.o.

It is a pleasure for me to announce you that it has been possible to form a (small) institute or centre for ethnomusicology in connection with the Music Department of the Danish Folklore Archives. Address: Torvegade 47, Copenhagen. It will open about September 1958'.

NILS SCHIØRRING

FRANCE

'Il n'y a pas à la Sorbonne, pour l'instant, d'enseignement spécialisé de l'ethnomusicologie (j'espère que cela viendra un jour), mais l'ethnomusicologie tient depuis plusieurs années une place importante dans l'enseignement de l'histoire de la musique comme l'un des éléments essentiels de la discipline générale de 'philologie musicale' qui se développe chaque année davantage. Sous ce rapport il m'est permis de vous citer en référence la première partie (la seule polycopiée) de mon cours intitulé 'Formation et transformations du langage musical'.

Il y a en outre, à l'Institut de Musicologie, depuis cette année, un séminaire d'études d'ethnomusicologie qui groupe des étudiants déjà expérimentés. Il travaille à la mise au point d'une méthode d'analyse des enregistrements d'ethnomusicologie et à l'établissement d'une fichier analytique de ces enregistrements. Il est dirigé par moi-même et par M. BRAILOIU, en liaison avec le Musée de l'Homme, et se place dans le cadre du '3ième Cycle' actuellement en formation à la Sorbonne pour la préparation au Doctorat'.

Jacques Chailley

GERMANY I
(Cologne)

'Voraussetzung für das Studium der Ethnomusikologie ist das Abitur einer Realschule oder eines Gymnasiums. Die Studenten müssen einen kompletten Lehrgang in allgemeiner Musik*geschichte*, Akustik und vergleichender Musikwissenschaft hören (Naturvölker, Hochkulturen, Instrumentenkunde). Ferner müssen sie teilnehmen an drei Seminaren (je zwei Semester pro Seminar) und einem 'privatissime' Seminar (1–2 × wöchentlich) zum Abschreiben von Bandaufnahmen und Schallplatten während der ganzen Studienzeit. Jedes Jahr muss ein Referat abgehalten werden über ein von mir gestelltes Thema. Als Nebenfach muss Ethnologie studiert werden.

Man kann aber auch als Hauptfach Ethnologie nehmen und Musikethnologie im Nebenfach studieren. Dann braucht man keine allgemeine Musikgeschichte. Der Titel ist Dr. Phil.

Ich habe viele Hörer unter den Kandidaten für Kirchen- und Schulmusik, die an der Hochschule für Musik studieren, aber gleichzeitig 6 Semester an der Universität studieren müssen, um später an einem Gymnasium auch andere Nebenfächer unterrichten zu können'.

Marius Schneider

GERMANY II
(West-Berlin)

'Für die Freie Universität gelten dieselben Bedingungen wie für alle Universitäten in Westdeutschland. Nur die Universitäten im sowjetisch besetzten Teil Deutschlands und in Ost-Berlin haben eigene Regelungen des Studienganges, die von denen in Westdeutschland erheblich abweichen.

Das Studium der Musik-Ethnologie ist an der Freien Universität kein eigenes Studienfach, sondern ein Teilgebiet des Faches Musikwissenschaft. Der angehende Musikethnologe ist also verpflichtet, das gesamte Gebiet der Musikforschung zu studieren. Er muss sich zu diesem Zweck in der philosophischen Fakultät immatrikulieren lassen. Das Fach Musikwissenschaft gilt als ordentliches Studienfach und selbständiges Hauptfach. Der Ordinarius dieses Faches ist hier wohl überall ein Musikhistoriker. Der Dozent für Musikethnologie ist Professor Dr. Kurt Reinhard, zugleich Leiter des Phonogramm-Archivs beim Völkerkunde-Museum in Berlin-Dahlem.

Voraussetzung für die Zulassung zum Studium der Musik-Ethnologie:

zunächst dieselbe wie für das Studium aller Fächer der philosophischen Fakultät, nämlich ein Abschlusszeugnis (Abiturium) eines Gymnasiums, bezw. in Berlin Oberschule wissenschaftlichen Zweiges mit 13 Klassen. Dazu noch wie für alle Studierenden der Musikwissenschaft Nachweis ausreichender Kenntnisse in praktischer und theoretischer Musik.

Studiengang: im Hauptfach Musikwissenschaft Teilnahme an Vorlesungen und Übungen aller Teilgebiete. Für die Zulassung zu den Seminar-Übungen sind Aufnahmeprüfungen erforderlich:

a) in das Pro-Seminar, wobei vor allem Kenntnisse in den musikalischen Fertigkeiten geprüft werden, die zum Studium der Musikgeschichte notwendig sind, wie Harmonielehre und Kontrapunkt und das Spielen einfacher Partituren vokaler und instrumentaler Musik u.a.;

b) für das Hauptseminar, wobei bereits musikwissenschaftliche Kenntnisse und Fertigkeiten geprüft werden, wie z.B. musikgeschichtliche Daten und Zusammenhänge, das Übertragen von Musikdenkmälern aus alten Drucken und Handschriften u.a. Im Hauptseminar werden die Studierenden zu eigenen Forschungsarbeiten angehalten; es werden schriftliche Arbeiten und mündliche Referate verlangt. Das Teilgebiet Musikethnologie ist ein Pflichtfach für alle Studierenden der Musikwissenschaft. Diejenigen, die sich hierauf spezialisieren wollen, arbeiten intensiever in den Übungen des Phonogramm-Archivs mit und treten mit eigenen Versuchen der Übertragung von exotischer Musik usw. hervor.

Als Nebenfächer wählen die Studierenden der Musik-Ethnologie meist Völkerkunde, Philosophie und Psychologie. Das Studium ist zeitlich nicht begrenzt, doch wird es allgemein nicht weniger als 4 Jahre dauern können.

Der Abschluss kann erfolgen durch Erlangung des Titels eines Magisters der freien Künste (Mag. Art. libr.), der dem Namen mit den beiden Buchstaben M.A. nachgesetzt wird, oder durch Erlangung des Doktorsgrades (*Dr. phil.*) der dem Namen vorangestellt wird. Die Würde dieses M.A. wird nach mindestens 8 Semestern verliehen, wenn der Kandidat in einer schriftlichen Hausarbeit, die innerhalb von 3 Monaten angefertigt sein muss, die Fähigkeit zu selbständiger wissenschaftlicher Arbeit und in jeweils 4-stündlichen Klausurarbeiten sowie mündlichen Prüfungen im Hauptfach und in zwei gewählten Nebenfächern die Beherrschung des Stoffgebietes nachgewiesen hat. Für die Erlangung des Doktorsgrades ist eine umfassende wissenschaftliche Dissertation vorzulegen, die gedruckt werden muss, und es wird ein Examen im Hauptfach Musikethnologie und Musikgeschichte sowie in zwei Nebenfächern nach Wahl, z.B. Völkerkunde, Geographie, Anthropologie, Philosophie, Psychologie usw. verlangt'.

Fritz Bose

GERMANY III
(Hamburg)

'Um Musikethnologie in Deutschland zu studieren, muss man sich für allgemeine Musikwissenschaft einschreiben. Musikethnologie als Hauptfach gibt es nicht in Deutschland, sondern sie gilt als Teilgebiet der Musikwissenschaft. Um sich auf der Universität einzuschreiben gelten die üblichen Bestimmungen für die Zulassung zum Universitätsstudium, d.h. der Student muss das Reifezeugnis einer deutschen Oberschule vorweisen.

Der Student muss insgesamt mindestens 8 Semester studieren, und zwar allgemeine Musikwissenschaft, Systematik und vergleichende Musikwissenschaft, Seminararbeit einbegriffen. Will er sich für die Musikethnologie spezialisieren und auf diesem Teilgebiet promovieren, dann gilt für die Universität Hamburg ferner die Bestimmung, dass er als erstes Nebenfach obligatorisch Völkerkunde studieren muss. Die Wahl des zweiten Nebenfachs steht ihm frei.

Um zu promovieren reicht der Student, der vergleichende Musikwissenschaft als Arbeitsgebiet wählt, seine Dissertation der Fakultät ein. Die mündliche Prüfung erfolgt in Hamburg durch den Fachvertreter der Musikwissenschaft (Prof. Dr. HUSMANN), den Spezialisten der Musikethnographie (Dozent Dr. HICKMANN), den Völkerkundler für das erste Nebenfach (Prof. Dr. TERMER) und den Vertreter des zweiten Nebenfachs. Nach der Promotion erhält der Doktorand den Titel eines Dr. phil.'   HANS HICKMANN

HUNGARY

'A l'Université de Budapest, dès 1949 jusqu'à 1954, fonctionnait un cours de la musique populaire hongroise, attaché à la chaire de l'Ethnographie. Le but de ce cours facultatif était de faire connaître aux étudiants de l'ethnographie la musique populaire du pays, mais sans études approfondis, – en conséquence, sans aucun examen.

A l'Ecole Supérieure de Musique de Budapest on a créé en 1951 une Section de Musicologie. Cette section était divisée en trois sous-sections dont chacune était autonome et a donné des diplômes aux élèves qui ont passé l'examen du dit cours avec succès. Les trois sous-sections étaient les suivantes: a) cours d'histoire, b) cours de théorie et esthétique, c) cours de la musique populaire.

La sous-section 'musique populaire' a fonctionnée dès octobre 1951 jusqu'à juin 1956. La durée du cours était cinq ans. Il y avait un concours d'entrée et des examens à la fin des semestres et à la fin de l'année. Tout élève qui s'est présenté à ce cours a dû avoir l'oreille musicale et certain connaissance théorique. M. ZOLTAN KODALY a eu des cours théoriques et pratiques sur les problèmes de la musique populaire hongroise, moi-même j'ai eu la prati-

71

que de la notation musicale, systématologie et ethnomusicologie. En surplus, les étudiants ont dû suivre des cours de l'histoire de la musique, de l'harmonie et contrepoint analytiques, chant grégorien, paléologie et solfège. l'Ecole Supérieure de Musique a eu des cours, où les élèves pouvaient suivre des études préparatoires pour les trois cours de la musicologie'.

Laszlo Lajtha

NETHERLANDS

'The student at a Dutch University who wants to make ethnomusicology the ultimate aim of his studies, has the choice between two different ways of approach.

The most normal proceeding is to matriculate in the Department of Arts and Letters of a Gymnasium or Lyceum (the nearest equivalent of the English Grammarschool, take out one's leaving-certificate and then enter one of the four Universities including a chair of musicology (i.e. Amsterdam, Utrecht, Leyden, or Nijmegen) there to concentrate on the study of general musicology. After the B.A. examination (Dutch: candidaatsexamen) the student could take up ethnomusicology together with cultural anthropology by way of side-subjects, graduate and then take his doctor's degree by writing a thesis on an ethnomusicological subject. This degree (Dutch: Doctor in de Letteren en Wijsbegeerte) is comparable to the Ph. D. of English and American universities.

The Amsterdam Municipal University has since 1952 been entrusted with a lectureship in ethnomusicology. Moreover, the Department of Cultural and Physical Anthropology of the Royal Tropical Institute (2A, Linnaeus-straat, Amsterdam Oost) houses an ethnomusicological bureau with a comprehensive library and an all-compassing collection of sound-recordings.

An alternative procedure leads via the study of cultural anthropology, facilities for which are offered in the Universities of Amsterdam, Utrecht, Leyden and Nijmegen. Grammarschool education in both departments (Art and Letters, as well as Science) is the only prerequisite. After the relevant B.A. examination, graduation must cover the obligatory side-subject: Cultural anthropology of a non-European region, to be studied in conjunction with another side-subject, in the present instance of course ethnomusicology. Students are recommended also to taken up general musicology, though the subject is not listed in the curriculum as an obligatory item. Like in the first case, the thesis for the doctorate will deal with an ethnomusicological subject.

The degree to be conferred is, also in this case, that of *D. litt*. The Netherlands Academic Charter does not provide for a specific doctorate in Musicology, let alone in Ethnomusicology'.

Jaap Kunst

'Besondere Ausbildung für Ethnomusikologen gibt es bei den norwegischen Universitäten (Oslo und Bergen) nicht. Nur an der Osloer Universität gibt es zwei Möglichkeiten zur Musikausbildung: 1) 'Magistergrad' (Mag. Artium); 2) Musik als 'Bifag' (Nebenfach des 'Lektor'-Examens) für Philologen, das die Lehrberechtigung zum Musikunterricht an höheren Schulen gibt. Nun sind sowohl die 'Magistergrad'-Studierenden, wie auch die 'Bifag'-Studierenden zur Teilnahme an verschiedenen Kursen verpflichtet, darunter an einem zwei-Semester-Kurs (jede Woche drei Stunden) in norwegischer Musikgeschichte, (der mir anvertraut worden ist). Ein – zwar nicht unbedeutender – Teil dieses Kursus ist norwegischer *Volks*musik gewidmet, wodurch den Studenten eine Einführung in die verschiedenen vokalen und instrumentalen Typen gegeben wird. Nur wenig berührt wird primitive und orientalische Musik als Einleitung des Kursus in allgemeiner Musikgeschichte (Professor OLAV GURVIN). Es gibt also keine "training facilities' für die Ausbildung der Ethnomusikologen als solche, nur mehr oder weniger zufällige praktische Einführungen in volksmusikalische Typen (besonders einheimische).

Die Personen, die Volksmusik zu studieren wünschen, haben keine besonderen Ausbildungsmöglichkeiten. Dass wir, die wir uns mit Volksmusik beschäftigen, meistens an der Musikabteilung der Universität ausgebildet wurden, deren Unterricht sich auf die *kunst*musikalische west-europäische Tradition stützt, mag, meiner Meinung nach, eine verhängnisvolle Entwicklung der volksmusikalischen Forschung bedeuten, denn ich habe den Eindruck, dass das Verständnis für prinzipielle Erörterungen volksmusikalischer Fragen nicht bei den Musikologen, sondern eher bei den Ethnologen und Ethnographen zu finden ist. Die ethnologische Universitätsausbildung gibt aber ihrerseits keine besondere volks*musikalische* Orientierung'.

LIV GRENI

RUSSIA

'Folklore-musicologists are not trained in our Universities. In this country, the subjects concerning musical folklore and which are included in the specialized musicological curriculum, are taught as part of musical theory in a conservatory. Such conservatories admit the most gifted pupils who have passed through a college of music of the ten years course type. There are also schools with a seven years course; these schools give an elementary musical training, but do not prepare their pupils for admittance to a conservatory.

The folklore-musicologist who completes his training at a conservatory, must then matriculate. After this, the most gifted among them become aspirants for preparatory scientific research work for a period of three years. They are then required to write and defend a dissertation. If this is successfully accomplished, the aspirant receives the degree of Candidate (Bachelor) of Arts.

As you will see from the above, the system here differs considerably from that in use in your country'.

G. SCHNEERSON

SWEDEN

'Das Abitur an einem Gymnasium (sog. halb- oder ganz-klassische 'Linie') wird sowohl für das Studium der Musikwissenschaft als auch der Ethnologie vorausgesetzt. Der weitere Ausbildungsgang ist dann in grossen und sehr allgemeinen Zügen folgendermaszen:

Der junge Student hat zunächst einen Kandidatenaufsatz über ein bestimmtes, mit dem akademischen Lehrer zu vereinbarendem Thema zu schreiben, der eine gewisse Fähigkeit zu wissenschaftlichem Denken aufweisen soll und in einem Seminar zur Diskussion gestellt wird. Gleichzeitig muss sich der Kandidat in seinem Hauptfach und zwei wahlfreien Nebenfächern mündlichen Tentamina unterziehen.

Nach Ablegung des Kandidatenexamens mit dem Titel *fil. kand.* pflegt der Student einen grösseren Aufsatz, die sog. Lizentiaten-abhandlung zu schreiben, die ihn etwa 2 bis 4 Jahre kostet und die unter Beweis stellen soll, dass er zu selbständigem wissenschaftlichem Denken befähigt ist. Wird die Abhandlung angenommen, so erhält er den Titel philosophiae licentiatus (*fil. lic.*), einen Titel, der ungefähr dem deutschen Doktorgrad entsprechen dürfte. Viele begnügen sich mit demselben, sofern sie nicht die akademische Laufbahn ergreifen wollen. Diese setzt eine recht umfangreiche Dissertation voraus, eine Arbeit, die, trotz Stipendien, die bewilligt werden können, viele Jahre in Anspruch nimmt und die Aermsten oft in recht erhebliche Schulden zu versetzen pflegt. Die Abhandlung wird öffentlich zur Diskussion gestellt. Die Fakultät ernennt einen Hauptopponenten, der Doktorand seinerseits einen eigenen. Fernerhin kann jeder, der an der öffentlichen Doktorsdisputation teilnimmt, als Extra-opponent auftreten. Für die Beurteilung der Doktorarbeit, für die es verschiedene Gradierungen gibt, pflegt im allgemeinen das Gutachten des Fakultätsopponenten den Ausschlag zu geben. Fällt diese Begutachtung günstig aus, so kann der Doktorand unmittelbar zum Dozenten ernannt werden, und er erhält das Recht, an der Universität Vorlesungen zu halten. Andernfalls muss er sich mit dem Titel philosophiae doctor (*fil. dr.*) begnügen, und auf die akademische Laufbahn verzichten.

Dies ist – wie gesagt in grossen Zügen – der Gang der akademischen Ausbildung in Schweden. Besondere Forderungen an den Studenten der Musikethnologie haben sich noch nicht herauskristallisiert. Instrumentenkundliche Arbeiten setzen bekanntlich nicht notwendig das Studium der Musikwissenschaft voraus, hingegen aber das Studium der Ethnologie. Bei anderen Arbeiten empfiehlt sich naturgemäss die Kombination des Studium der Ethnologie mit demjenigen der Musikwissenschaft, gleichviel ob der Betreffende anfangs die Ethnologie oder die Musikwissenschaft als Hauptfach wählt.

Ich muss darauf aufmerksam machen, dass es hier bisher nur sehr sehr wenige gibt, die sich musikethnologisch spezialisiert haben. Sie lassen sich mit Hilfe einiger weniger Finger aufzählen'.

ERNST EMSHEIMER

UNITED KINGDOM I

'To my shame I have to tell you that there is no training of ethnomusicologists in any University in the United Kingdom. Furthermore, there is no training in any other institution either.

In Cambridge, for example, a distinguished visitor might be asked to give a public and popular lecture. But though the Faculty Board is just beginning to think of the possibility of including such a course in the distant future, it is unlikely to happen for another ten years.

So far as I am aware, Professor FARMER, for example, has never had the opportunity of teaching the field in which he was expert. I myself have never given even a single lecture at the invitation of the Music Faculty here.

It is deplorable, and the anthropologists look like doing something about the situation before the musicologists get round to doing so. The professor of Anthropology has considered the possibility of instituting a joint diploma in Ethnomusicology, combining instruction in the Music School and the Department of Anthropology. Perhaps now that Wachsmann is fixed in England, we shall see something of the kind.

I am sorry the survey turns out to be a void'.

LAURENCE PICKEN

UNITED KINGDOM II
(London)

'Although ethnomusicology is not yet officially recognized as a degree-subject, the School of Oriental and African Studies of the University of London takes an active interest in the matter as testified by the appointment of the Reverend A. M. JONES as a lecturer in African music and the existence of a section for musicological research in the Department of India, Pakistan and Ceylon under my supervision with the assistance of Mr. JAIRAZBHOY who has been specially appointed to further research in this subject.

The possibilities of making this a subject for degree studies are earnestly explored by the authorities of the School of Oriental and African Studies and the University.

The extra-mural department has arranged a series of six lectures on the history and scope of ethnomusicology scheduled for the beginning of session 1958–59' at the British Institute of Recorded Sound.'

A. A. BAKE

U.S.A. I

'Since I am more or less camped in the wild, I cannot give you all the data I could wish in answer to your question about requirements for ethnomusicologists. Courses offered you have, from Nettl's compilations in a couple of the past issues of 'Ethnomusicology' (No. 3, p. 5, No. 6, p. 10, No. 8, p. 6, No. 11, p. 18, vol. II No. 2, p. 88). [1] These courses are, in effect, the training facilities offered in this country. If you are thinking of opportunity to learn exotic instruments and equipment for accurate tuning to their scales etc., the only place I know of, that has this sort of thing, is U.C.L.A., where Hood is carrying on your own good work.

'Requirements for ethnomusicologists' suggests degrees specially in that field. Unless U.C.L.A. has such a degree I don't know of any institution that has one. The degrees amongst us, who are ethnomusicologists, are in anthropology and music with a specialty somehow developed in ethnomusicology. I don't know of a 'Department of Ethnomusicology' in this country.

The usual procedure is for a student in anthropology, who shows interest in this field, to get special training from a man in the department, if they have one, who can prepare him to do field work and write a dissertation in the subject. If the student is in music, he takes courses in anthropology. Rather than departments, we have individuals scattered about in a few institutions who encourage people to go into the field: MERRIAM (Northwestern), HERZOG (Bloomington), RHODES (Columbia), WATERMAN (Wayne), HOOD (U.C.L.A.). MERRIAM is compiling a bibliography on M.A. and Ph.D. dissertations in ethnomusicology. From this he could tell you what institutions are actually producing active workers in the vinyard.

As for Wesleyan University (really a small liberal arts college), the facilities and requirements are informal and adapted to the condition of the

---

[1] See hereafter p. 168. No. 2993 of the Bibliography.

student. For the course I give, there is an extensive record collection of folk and ethnic music, a museum of exotic instruments which the students can use and are expected to familiarize themselves with, and recording equipment. Some of the students have had an opportunity to learn techniques of recording in short field sessions. We haven't the equipment to go into the physics of scale and tuning, but are now building a laboratory where this can be done. We hope to obtain one of Seeger's melographs also'.

DAVID P. MCALLESTER

U.S.A. II
(University of California)

A. Los Angeles (U.C.L.A.)

'Training in ethnomusicology at the U.C.L.A., begins with a thourough education in the history, theory, and practice of western art music. An introduction to folk, primitive, and non-western art music along with the basic principles of ethnomusicology is given in a one year undergraduate course: *Musical Cultures of the World*. Through the interdepartmental folklore program under the direction of Dr. WAYLAND D. HAND additional undergraduate courses may be taken in *Folklore, Folk song, Research Methods and Field Collecting*, as well as studies in German, Italian, American, and Spanish folk materials.

The graduate program in ethnomusicology in the Department of Music is under the direction of Dr. MANTLE HOOD. Seminars in *ethnomusicology, ethnomusicological bibliography*, and graduate courses in *folklore* are available. Advanced students may do special research under the guidance of any of four music faculty members directly concerned with the field or specialists from other departments. There are performance study groups in Javanese and Balinese *gamelan*, and Japanese court-music (*gagaku*). Practical studies in other musics are encouraged whenever instruments and instructors are available. Native experts are invited to teach and study on the campus and field work in the environs or overseas is required of all researchers.

Special University facilities for ethnomusicological research include a world instrument museum, an expanding library of tapes, records, and oriental reference materials, and a special laboratory containing such equipments as a Stroboconn, a polychord, and a Seeger Melograph.

A more detailed discussion of the U.C.L.A. program may be seen in 'Ethnomusicology' No. 11 (Sept. 1957) pp. 2–8). [1]

WILLIAM MALM

---

[1] See hereafter p. 134. No. 1879 of the Bibliography.

B. Berkeley

'In view of the rapid development of facilities for ethnomusicology on the Los Angeles campus and in accordance with the general policy of the University of California not to duplicate special fields on each campus, the Berkeley campus is not attempting to develop an extensive program in, or comprehensive facilities for, ethnomusicology. However, there are a number of tape recording collections on campus: ALFRED L. KROEBER, Professor Emeritus of Anthropology. is working on a collection of California Indian music which he recorded on wax cylinders in the early 1900's; the Museum of Anthropology possesses a relatively large collection of tapes which it is expanding continually; Professor MARY HAAS in the Linguistics Department has access to some tapes of California Indian music. During the fall semester 1957, WILLIAM R. BASCOM, Director of the Museum of Anthropology, conducted a special studies course in ethnomusicology for several advanced undergraduates majoring in anthropology'.

HARRIET NICEWONGER

U.S.A. III
(University of Indiana, Bloomington)

'Courses are offered regularly in Folk Music, Primitive Music, Comparative Musicology, and Oriental Music. These courses are given by myself, except Oriental Music, which is given by Prof. WALTER KAUFMANN. All except Comparative Musicology and Oriental Music (which are given in the Music School) are offered in the Department of Anthropology, but are available to students of other Departments or schools of the University. Occasionally the Seminar of the Department of Anthropology is devoted to Ethnomusicology. The second semester this coming year I am introducing a new course, devoted to Transcription of Exotic Melodies. Students can also register for Research in Comparative Musicology in order to receive more attention and time in the guidance of their research projects. A student with a basic interest in Anthropology, Folklore, or Musicology, can receive an M.A. or a Ph.D. degree with a topic in Ethnomusicology.

Among the rich resources available at Indiana University to a student of Ethnomusicology may be mentioned the Archives of Folk and Primitive Music, with some 10.000 recordings; my own collection of recordings in Ethnomusicology, with some 3000 recordings, and my extensive bibliography and collection of manuscripts. There is also the collection of Musical Instruments in the Museum of Anthropology, which contains the collection of ERICH M. VON HORNBOSTEL and of myself.'

GEORGE HERZOG

BIBLIOGRAPHY

This bibliography contains two categories of books and articles:

a) works concerned with music and musical instruments of non-Western peoples;

b) many (but certainly not all) publications on ancient and early European music and musical instruments and on Western folk music. (Song collections without important commentary, for instance, are, as a rule, omitted.)

Publications of a more general character (e.g. reports of travels, ethnological expeditions and missionary activities) which often contain interesting data on music and musical instruments, musicians and the rôle of music in tribal life, are, as a rule, not included. These can easily be located by referring to the extensive bibliographies found in works marked by an asterisk. Nor are inserted publications in the Arabic, Hebrew, Chinese, Japanese, Indonesian, Javanese and Sundanese languages, and in the languages of the Indian subcontinent.

A capital **A** behind a title indicates, that the publication in question is included in the private library of the author (for the time being housed in the Royal Tropical Institute, 2A Linnaeusstraat, Amsterdam Oost), which, on request, is accessible to everybody interested in this field of study. Similarly

B. represents the Library of the Royal Tropical Institute;

C. the Music Library of the Municipal Museum, The Hague, 41 Stadhouderslaan;

D. the Institute of Musical Sciences, Utrecht, 5 Brigittenstraat;

D¹. the Library of Utrecht University;

E. the Institute of Musical Sciences, Amsterdam ⎱ both 59, 1ste Jacob

F. the Public Music Library, Amsterdam ⎰ v. Campenstr.;

G. the Library of Leyden University (incl. the Rijksmuseum voor Volkenkunde, the Africa Institute, the Institute-Kern, the Museum of Antiquities, the Department of 'Keel-, Neus- en Oorheelkunde' of the Academic Hospital, the Zoölogical Laboratory, the 'Prentenkabinet', the Museum of Natural History, the Institute of Theoretical Physics and the Laboratory of Anatomy);

H. the Library of Groningen University;

H¹. the Institute of Musical Sciences, 34 Oude Boteringestr., Groningen;

I. the Library of the British Museum, London;

J. the Library of the Horniman Museum, London SE 23, Forest Hill;

K. the Royal Library, Copenhagen;
L. the Institute of Musical Sciences
L¹. the Library of the University
L². the Library of the Ethnographical Museum (Rautenstrauch-Joest-Museum)
L³. the Seminary of Ethnographical Studies
L⁴. the Seminary of Oriental Studies
L⁵. the Library of the Museum of East-Asiatic Art
L⁶. the Library of the Institute of Prehistory
M. the Library of the Congo Museum, Tervueren (Belgium).

of Cologne University;

1. **Aalst, J. A. van**, *Chinese music* (1884, 2/1933). **ABCGI**
2. **Aarflot, Olav**, *Kinesisk Musikk* ('Hanbøken utgitt av Etnografisk Museum' No. 2), Oslo, 1948. **AIJ**
3. **Abas, S. P.**, *De muziek der Bataks* ('Caecilia-Muziekcollege'), May 1931. **ACD¹FGH**
4. **Abbasuddin Ahmed**, *Folksongs of East Pakistan* (July 1956). **AF**
5. **Abdu-l-wahab**, *Le développement de la musique arabe en Orient, Espagne et Tunisie* ('Revue Tunisienne' 1918). **K**
6. **Abel, M. S. C.**, Father, *Knabenspiele auf Neu-Mecklenburg* (Südsee) ('Anthropos' I, p. 818 ff.), 1906. **D¹GKL¹L²M**
7. **Abert, Hermann**, *Die Lehre vom Ethos in der griechischen Musik* (Leipzig, 1899). **ACHIK**
8. —— *Antike* (neu-bearbeitet von Curt Sachs) (in Guido Adler, 'Handbuch der Musikgeschichte' I, p. 35 ff.), 2/1929. **ACDEF**
9. **Abes, M.**, *Chansons d'amour chez les Berbères* ('France-Maroc' 1919). **D¹**
10. **Abrahamsen, Erik**, and H. Gruener Nielsen, *Danmarks gamle folkeviser* (Copenhagen, 1935 ff.). **K**
11. **Absolon, K.**, and **H. Kašlik**, *Die ältesten Musikinstrumente der Welt in Mähren entdeckt* ('Tagesbote' No. 184 d.d. 19th April 1936, p. 4 ff.), Brünn (Brno). **A**
12. **Acharya, B. T.**, *Haridasa sahitya, the Karnatic mystics and their songs* (Indian Inst. of Culture, Basavangudi, Bangalore), 1953.
13. **Ackerman, Phyllis**, *The character of Persian music* (in Pope and Ackerman, 'A Survey of Persian Art. From prehistoric times to the present', vol. III, p. 2805 ff.), Oxford, 1939. **A**
14. **Acquarone, F.**, *Historia da musica Brasileira* (Livraria Francisco Alves, Rio de Janeiro, undated), p. 99 ff.
15. **Adaiewsky, E.**, *Quelques chants tartares* ('Rivista Musicale Italiana' XXV), 1921. **CKL**

16. **Adalid y Gamero, Manuel**, *La música hondureña* ('Rev. del Archivo y Biblioteca Nacionales'), Tegucigalpa, 1938.
16a. **Adandé, A.**, *L'évolution de la musique africaine* ('Notes Africaines' No 54, p. 39 ff.), 1952. **M**
17. **Adler, Bruno**, *Pfeifende Pfeile und Pfeilspitzen in Sibirien* ('Globus' LXXXI), 1902. **D¹L²M**
18. **Adler, Cyrus**, *The shofar, its use and origin* (Smithsonian Report for 1892, p.437 ff.). **J**
19. **Adler, Guido**, *Ueber Heterophonie* ('Jahrbuch der Musikbibl. Peters' XV, p. 17 ff.), 1909. **CGKLL¹**
20. **Adolf, Helen**, *The ass and the harp* ('Speculum' XXV, p. 49 ff.), 1950. **D¹KL¹**

Adriani, N., see No. 2343.

21. **Advielle, V.**, *La musique chez les Persans* (Paris, 1885). **CI**
22. **Affelen van Saemsfoort, C. A. van**, *Feestvreugde* ('De Indische Gids' XXXIX, p. 477 ff.), Amsterdam, 1917. **ABD¹H**
22a. **Agbayani, A. T.**, *Philippine music* ('Asiana' I, No. 2, p. 49 ff.), 1957.
23. *African Music, Gramophone Records of,* ('African Music Transcription Library'), Catalogue July 1951 (Johannesburg, 1951). **A**
24. **Agnew, R. Gorden**, *The Music of the Ch'uan Miao* ('Journal of the West China Border Research Soc.' XI, p. 9 ff.), 1939.
25. **Agrawala, V. S.**, *Some early references to musical ragas and instruments* ('The Journal of the Music Academy, Madras' XXIII, p. 113 ff.), 1952. **AC**
26. **Aguero, Gaspar**, *El aporte africano a la música popular cubana* ('Estudios afrocubanos' V), Habana, 1940/46.
27. **Aguero, Salvador García**, *Presencia Africana en la música nacional* ('Ultra', Habana, Dec. 1936), p. 519.
28. **Aguilar y Tejera, Augustin**, *De musica marroqui* ('Revista de la Raza' 1928).
29. **Ahlbrinck, W.**, *Encyclopaedie der Karaiben* (Kon. Ned. Akad. v. Wetenschappen, Amsterdam, 1931), passim. **BD¹GH**

30. Ahlström, 300 nordiska folkvisor, harmoniskt behandlade (1855).

31. Ahmed, Nazir, The Luhjat-i-Sikendar Shahi, a unique book on Indian music of the time of Sikandar Shah ('Islamic Culture' XXVIII), July 1954. **G**

32. Aima, M. L., Musical instruments ('Kashmir'. May and June 1955).

33. —— The folk music of Kashmir ('Marg' VIII, p. 154 ff.), 1955. **J**

34. Aiyar, C. Subrahmania, Quartertones in South Indian (Carnatic) Music ('The Journal of the Music Academy, Madras' XI, p. 95 ff.), 1940. **A**

35. —— Comparative music, European and Indian (ibid. XII, p. 36 ff.), 1941. **A**

36. —— Some leading music systems (ibid. XIII, p. 21 ff., XVII, p. 97 ff.), 1942 and 1946. **AC (xvii)**

37. —— The Clarinet and classical Carnatic Music (ibid. XIX, p. 51 ff.), 1948. **A**

38. —— A Study of the Microtonal Variations in Frequencies in Karnatic Music with an Oscillograph (ibid. XX, p. 114 ff. 1949, and XXV, p. 49 ff., 1954). **AC(xxv)I**

39. —— Musical research and frequency ratios (ibid. XXI, p. 64 ff.), 1950. **AC**

40. —— Physics and Aesthetics of Hindusthani Music (ibid. XXII, p. 86 ff.), 1951. **AC**

41. —— The Grammar of South Indian (Karnatic) Music (Madras, 2/1951). **AI**

41a. —— 108 kritis in Devanagari script with gamaka signs (Madras, 1955).

42. Aiyar, M. S. Ramaswami, Thiagaraja, a great Musician Saint (Madras, 1927).

•43. —— Bibliography of Indian music ('Journal of the R. Asiatic Soc.'), 1941. **D¹GIKL¹**

44. Alba, Gregorio Hernandez de, De la música indígena en Colombia ('Bol. Lat.-Amer. de Música' IV. p. 721 ff.), Bogotá, 1938.

45. —— La música en las esculturas prehistóricas de San Agustin (ibid., p. 733 ff.), Bogotá, 1938.

46. Albersheim, G., Zur Psychologie der Ton- und Klangeigenschaften (1939).

47. Albini, Eugenio, La musica in China ('Rivista musicale Italiana' XLII, fasc. 1), 1938. **CDKL**

48. —— Instrumenti musicali degli Etruchi e loro origini ('L'Illustrazione Vaticana' VIII, p. 667 ff.), 1937.

49. —— La musica in China ('Riv. Mus. Ital.' 1942). **CKL**

50. Alden Mason, J., The ancient civilizations of Peru ('Pelican-book' No. A 395, London, 1957), pp. 72, 192, 194, 230. **B**

51. Alexandru, Tiberiu, Muzica populara banateana (i.e. Folk music of the Banat) (Bucarest, 1942).

52. —— Tilinca, ein uraltes rumänisches Volksinstrument ('Studia Memoriae Belae Bartók Sacra', p. 107 ff.), Budapest, 1956. **AC**

53. —— Instrumentele muzicale ale poporului Romin (Bucarest, 1956). **J**

54. Béla Bartók si folclorul Rominesc (i.e. Béla Bartók and the Rumanian folklore) ('Revista de Folclor' I, No. 1–2, p. 262 ff. Bucarest, 1956. **A**

54a. —— Vioara ca instrument muzical popular ('Revista de Folclor' II, No. 3, p. 29 ff.), Bucarest, 1957. **A**

54b. Algernon, Rose, Primitive African instruments ('Proc. of the Musical Association' Session XXX, p. 91 ff.), London, 1904.

55. Allawerdi, M., The philosophy of oriental music (Damascus, 2/1949).

56. Allende, Umberto, La musique populaire chilienne ('Art populaire' II, p. 118 ff.), Paris, 1931. **A**

57. —— Chilian Folk Music ('Bull. of the Pan American Union' LXV, No. 9, p. 917 ff.), Sept. 1941. **K**

58. —— Los origenes de la música popular chilena ('Antárctica' No. 2, Oct. 1944, p. 77 ff.) .

59. All-India Music Conference, Report of the second, (Delhi, 1919).

60. Almeida, Renato, Historia da Musica Brasileira (Rio de Janeiro, 2/1942).

61. Alport, C. J. M., Kenya's answer to the Maumau challenge ('African Music' I, p. 75 ff.), 1954. **ACJLM**

62. Alvad, Thomas, The Kafir harp (Man" LIV, p. 151, art. 233), Oct. 1954. **BD¹GJKL²M**

63. Alvarenga, Oneyda, A influencia negra na música brasileira ('Boletin Latino-Americano de Música' VI, p. 357 ff.), Rio de Janeiro, 1946. **AGL**

64. —— Musica popular brasileira (Porte Alegre, 1950).

65. —— Tambor-de-Mina e Tambor-crioulo (Sao Paulo, 1948).

66. —— Música popular brasileira (Rio de Janeiro, 1950).

67. —— Chgança de Marujos (Sao Paulo, 1955).

68. Alvina, Leandra, La musica Incaica ('Rev. Universitaria' XVIII, vol. II, p. 299 ff.), Cuzco, 1929.

69. Amezquita Borja, Francisco, Música y Danza (Puebla, 1943).

70. Amiot, Father, Mémoires concernant les Chinois, vol. VI, De la musique des Chinois, tant anciens que modernes (Paris, 1780). **C**

71. Amrouche, J., Chants berbères de Kabylie (Paris, 1946).

72. Amu, E., How to study African rhythm ('Teacher's Journal', Gold Coast, VI, p. 121 ff.), 1933/'34.

81

73. —— Twenty-five African songs in the Twi language (Sheldon Press, 1932).
74. Anadolu halk sarkilari (= Anatolian folk songs), Istanbul, 1925.   K
75. Andersen, A. O., Geography and Rhythm ('Univ. of Arizona Fine Arts Bull.' No. 2), Tucson, Arizona, 1935.
76. Anderson, Arthur J. O., Aztek music ('The Western Humanities Review' VIII, p. 131 ff.), 1954.
77. Anderssen, Johannes C., Maori Music ('Transactions of the New Zealand Inst.' LIV, p. 743 ff., LV, p. 689 ff.), 1923–'24. A
78. —— Maori musical instruments ('Art in New Zealand' II, p. 91 ff.), 1929.
79. —— An Introduction to Maori Music ('Transactions of the New Zealand Inst.') 1926.
80. —— Maori Music with its Polynesian background (New Plymouth, New Zealand, 1934).
81. Andersson, Nils, Skånska melodier, Musiken i Skåne ('Svenska Landsmål' XIV).   D¹G
82. —— and Olof Andersson, Svenska låtar I–XXIV (Stockholm, 1923 sqq.).
83. Andersson, Otto, Ueber schwedische Volkslieder und Volkstänze in Finnland ('Brage' III, p. 145 ff.), Åbo, 1908 (1909).
84. —— Altertümliche Tonarten in der Volksmusik ('Kongressber. Wien 1909', p. 259 ff.).   C
*85. —— Stråkharpan ('Föreningen för Svensk Kulturhistoria' IV). Stockholm, 1923.   A
86. —— Violinists and dancetunes among the Swedish population of Finland towards the middle of the nineteenth century ('Report of the 4th Congress of the Intern. Music Soc., London 1911', p. 159 ff.), London, 1911.   CF
87. —— The Bowed Harp (transl. by Kathleen Schlesinger), London, 1930.   CIJ
88. —— Musik och Musikinstrument ('Nordisk Kultur' XXV), Stockholm/Oslo/Kopenhagen, 1933.   AI
89. —— Nordisk musikkultur i äldsta tider ('Nordisk Kultur Musikk og Musikkinstrumenter', p. 3 ff.), Stockholm/Oslo/Kopenhagen, 1934.   A
90. —— Nordisk folksmusik i Finland (ibid., p. 113, ff.), 1934.   A
91. —— Folksmusiken i Svenskestland (ibid., p. 159 ff.), 1934.   A
92. On Gaelic Folk Music from the Isle of Lewis ('Budkavlen' XXXI, p. 1 ff.), Åbo, 1952.   AK
93. —— Altnordische Streichinstrumente (Kongressber. des 4. Kongress der Intern. Musikges', Vienna, 25–29 May, 1909). C.
94. —— Finlands svenska folkdiktning. V. Folkvisor. 1. Den äldre folkvisan (Helsingfors, 1934).

95. Andrade, Mario de, Popular music and song in Brazil (1936; Engl. transl. by L. V. le Cocq d'Oliveira), Rio de Janeiro, 1943.   K
95a. —— As danças dramáticas do Brasil ('Bol. Latino-Americano' VI, vol. I, p. 49 ff.), Rio de Janeiro, 1946.   AGL
96. Andree, R., Die Nasenflöte und ihre Verbreitung ('Globus' LXXV, No. 9, p. 150 ff.), Braunschweig, 1899.   D¹M
97. —— Signale bei Naturvolker ('Z.f. Ethnologie', XX, p. 410 ff.), 1888.   BD¹GHKL¹L²M
97a. Angles, Higino, Die Bedeutung des Volksliedes für die Musikgeschichte Europas ('Kongressbericht Bamberg 1953' p. 181 ff.), Kassel/Basel, 1954.   CDEFL
98. Angulo, Jaime de, and M. Béclard d' Harcourt, La musique des Indiens de la Californie du nord ('J. de la Soc. des Américanistes', N.S. XXIII), Paris, 1931.   GL²
99. Ankermann, Bernard, Die afrikanischen Musikinstrumente ('Ethnologisches Notizblatt' III, p. 1 ff.), 1901.   CGIJKL
100. —— L'Ethnographie actuel de l'Afrique méridionale. VII. La musique ('Anthropos' I, p. 926 ff.), 1906.   D¹GKL¹L²M
100a. Anki, F., De notre musique ('Voix du Congolais' 1952, p. 683 ff.)'   M
101. Annales du Musée du Congo. Ethnographie et anthropologie. Série III. Notes analytiques sur les collections ethnographiques du Musée du Congo. Tome I, fasc. 1. Les Arts: Instruments de musique. Musique-chant-dance (Brussels, 1902).   CM
102. Anonymous (George Grove?), Notes on Siamese musical instruments (London, 1885).
103. Anonymous, Les instruments de musique en usage à Zanzibar ('Revue Musicale' VI, p. 165 ff.), 1906.   K
104. —— Spielleute und Märchenerzähler Innerafrikas ('Westermanns Monatshefte' CXV, p. 573 ff.), Brunsvik, 1913.   L¹
105. —— Music in Trinidad (British Information Services, Reference Division, III, p. 45 ff.), May 1950.
106. —— La musique Ethiopienne ('Schweizer Zeitung f. Instrumentalmusik' XXIV pp. 294 ff., 519 ff., 544 ff., 567 ff., ibid. XXV, pp. 15, 41, 63 ff., 207 ff., 303).
107. —— The Music of the Swazis ('African Musik Society Newsletter' I, No. 5, June 1952, p. 14).   ACJM
108. —— The Arbatsky Collection ('Newberry Library Bulletin' III, p. 170 ff.), 1954.   AK
109. —— African music ('Lantern' V, vol. 5 No. 1, p. 35 ff.), Pretoria, Juli/Sept. 1955.   BG
110. —— Memorandum on cataloguing and

classification of sound recordings of folk music (London, no date). **A**

111. —— *De wassching van de heilige gong te Lodojo* ('Weekblad v. Ned.-Indië' IX, p. 202), 1912/'13. **A**

112. —— *Ancient musical instruments* ('People's China' 1957, No. 16, p. 39), Aug. 1957. **A**

112a. —— *Spevy nasho l'udu* (Bratislava, 1953).

112b. —— *Selected Ancient bronze drums found in China and Southeast Asia* (Peking n.d.)

112c. —— *Art musical indigène au Soudan* ('Brousse' 1946, Nos. 1–2, p. 28), 1946. **M**

112d. —— *Musiciens indigènes* ('Rayons' 1945, No. 1, p. 8 ff.). **M**

113. Antonowytsch, Miroslav, *Die Mehrstimmigkeit in den ukrainischen Volksliedern* ('Kongressber. Intern. Ges. f. Musikw., Utrecht 1952', p. 55 ff.), 1953. **ACD**

113a. —— *Oekraine* ('Elsevier's Encyclopedie van de Muziek' II, p. 407). **ACDEFH**[1]

113b. Apkalns, L., *Die lettische Volksmusik aus der Sicht der kulturhistorischen Gegebenheiten des baltischen Raumes* ('Anthropos' 195., p. xxx ff.), in preparation. **ABD**[1]**GHKL**[1]**L**[2]**M**

113c. Apti, V. M., *Some problems regarding Samagana that await investigation: a statement* ('Bull. of the Deccan College Research Institute' IV, p. 281 ff.), 1943.

113d. —— *Sound records of Sāmagāna, a prospect and retrospect* (ibid., p. 296 ff.), 1943.

114. Araujo, Alceo Maynard, *Instrumentos musicais e implementos* ('Revista de Arquivo' No. 157, p. 147 ff.), Sao Paulo, 1954.

115. Aravamuthan, T. G., *Pianos in Stones* ('The Journal of the Music Academy, Madras' XIV, p. 109 ff.), 1943.

116. Arbatsky, Yury, *Albanien* ('Die Musik in Geschichte und Gegenwart' I, col. 282 ff.), 1951. **ACDEFGH**[1]**KL**

117. —— *Balticum* (ibid. I, col. 1187 ff.), 1951. **ACDEFGH**[1]**KL**

118. —— *Communication on the chromatic Balkan-scale* ('Journal of the Amer. Musicol. Soc.' V, p. 150 ff.), 1952. **ACFKL**

119. —— *The Roga, a Balkan bagpipe, and its medico-magical conjurations* (Paper read at the Annual Meeting of the Amer. Musicol. Soc., in Chapel Hill, N.C.), Dec. 1953 (stencilled). **A**

120. —— *Beating the Tupan in the Central Balkans* (Newberry Library, Chicago, 1953). **ACFJ**

121. —— *A Triptych from the Arbatsky Collection at the Newberry Library* (Chicago, 1954), ed. by Walter G. Nau. **A**

122. Arbatsky, Yury, Jaap Kunst and J. H. Hanford, *Hellenic influence in folk music of the modern Balkans* ('Athene', autumn 1955, p. 3 ff.). **A**

122a. Arbatsky, Yury, *Das Verkürzen der Volkslieder bei den mazedonischen Gusluren vom musikalischen Standpunkte aus* ('Südostforschungen' IX, No. 10, p. 402 ff.), 1944/ '45.

123. *Archives of recorded music. Collection of the Phonetèque National, Paris* (1952) **B**

124. Aretz-Thielle, Isabel, *El folklore musical argentino* (Buenos Aires, 1952).

124a. —— *Musica tradicional Argentina. Tucuman historia y folklore.* (Buenos Aires, 1946).

125. —— *El canto popular* ('Boletin del Instituto de Folklore' I, No. 3, p. 43 ff.), 1954.

126. —— *Manéras typicas del cantar Venezolana* (ibid. No. 7, p. 171 ff.), 1954.

127. —— *Musicas pentatonicas en Sudamerika* ('Archivos venezolanos de folklore' I, No. 2, p. 1 ff.), Caracas July/Dec. 1952.

127a. —— and Luis Felipe Ramon y Rivera, *Resumen de un estudio sobre las expresiones negras en el folklore musical y coreográfico de Venezuela* ('Archivos Venezolanos de Folklore' IV/V, vol. III, No. 4, p. 65 ff.), Caracas, 1955/'56.

128. Arguedas, José Maria, *Cuentos mágico-realistas y canciones de fiesta tradicionales* ('Folklore Americano' I, p. 101 ff.), Lima, 1953.

128a. —— *Songs of the Quechuas* ('Americas' IX, No. 8, p. 30 ff.), August 1957. **B**

128b. —— *The singing mountaineers: songs and tales of the Quechua people* (ed. by Ruth Stephan), Edinburgh/London, 1958.

129. Arian Emile, *Preuve irréfutable de la division de l'échelle musicale orientale en 24 quarts de ton* ('Bull. de l'Egypte' VI, p. 159 ff.), Cairo, 1934.

130. Arima, D., *Japanische Musikgeschichte auf Grund der Quellenkunde* (diss. Vienna, 1933).

131. Arlton, Alexander V., *Songs and other sounds of birds* (Washington, 1949).

132. Armstrong, Robert Bruce, *Musical instruments. I. The Irish and Highland harps. II. English and Irish instruments* (Edinburgh, 1904/'10), **J**

133. Armstrong, Robert G., *Talking instruments in West Africa* ('Exploration' IV, p. 140 ff.), 1955.

134. —— *Talking drums in the Benue-Cross River Region of Nigeria* ('Phylon' XV, p. 355 ff.), 1954. **M**

134a. Arnaud, M., *Kangombiyo* ('Présence Africaine' 1948, No. 3, p. 470 ff.). **M**

135. Arnaudin, Félix, *Chants populaires de la grande Lande et des régions voisines* (Labouheyre, 1912), vol. I.

136. Arnholtz, A., Nils Schiørring and Finn Viderø, *Gamle danske Viser* (5 vols.), 1942/ '43.

137. **Arro, E.,** *Zum Problem der Kannel* ('Proc. Gelehrte Estnische Ges.', Tartu, 1931).

138. —— *Geschichte der estnischen Musik* (Tartu, 1933).

139. **Arsunar, Ferruh,** *Kisdzsiai török pentaton dallamok* (*Des mélodies pentatones des Turcs d'Asie Mineure*) (in 'Mélanges offerts à Zoltan Kodály à l'occasion de son 60ième anniversaire', p. 322 ff.), Budapest, 1943. **ACK**

140. **Artemides, Cleobulos,** *From the Folksongs of Cyprus* ('Folkloristic Suppl. of Cypriot Studies' XVI), Nicosia, 1953.

141. **Arvey, Verna,** *Ancient Music and Dance in Modern Ceylon* ('Etude' LX, p. 656 ff.), 1942.

142. **Arwidsson, Adolf Iwar,** *Svenska fornsånger* (Stockholm, 1834–'42).

143. **Arzeno, Julio,** *Del folklore musical dominicano* (Santo Domingo, 1927).

*144. **Askew, Gilbert,** *A bibliography of the bagpipe* (Newcastle-on-Tyne, 1932).

145. **Asturias, Miguel Angel,** *Marimba tocada por Indios* ('Repertorio Americano' XLIV, No. 4), Costa Rica, Aug. 10th, 1948.

145a. **Atangana, T.,** *Le cantique en langue indigène* ('Grands Lacs' LXII, p. 122 ff.), 1946/'47. **M**

146. **Aubry, Pierre,** *Au Turkestan, notes sur quelques habitudes musicales chez les Tadjiks et chez les Sartes* ('Mercure Musical', Paris, 1905).

147. —— *Essais de musicologie comparée* (Paris, 1903).

148. **Audisio, G.,** *Les soirées de Bagdad* ('Revue musicale' XI, No. 102), March 1930. **CD¹GKL**

149. **Augusta, Fr. Felix,** *Zehn Araukanerlieder* ('Anthropos' VI, p. 684 ff.),1911. **D¹GKL¹L²M**
Ausserdeutsche Volksmusik, see Pauli, F. W.

150. **Avasi, Béla,** *Tonsysteme aus Intervall-Permutationen* ('Studia Memoriae Belae Bartók Sacra', p. 249 ff.), Budapest, 1956. **AC**

151. —— *Ötfokúságbol hétfokúság* (i.e. The development of pentatonic scales into diatonic scales) ('Ethnographia, a Magyar néprajzi társaság folyóirata' LXVII, p. 262 ff.), Budapest, 1956. **B**

152. —— *Die Harmoniegestaltung eines ungarischen Volksmusikorchesters* ('Acta Ethnographica' IV, p. 479 ff.), Budapest, 1955. **A**

153. **Avelot,** *La musique chez les Pahouins, les Ba-Kalai, les Eshira, les Iveïa et les Bavili* (*Congo Français*) (L'Anthropologie' XVI, p. 287 ff.), 1905. **D¹GHL¹L²**

154. **Avenary, Hanoch,** *Abu'l-Salt's treatise on Music* ('Musica Disciplina' VI, p. 27

ff.), Amer. Inst. of Musicology, Rome, 1952. **CKLL¹**

154a. —— *Magic, symbolism and allegory of the old-Hebrew sound-instruments* ('Collectanea Historiae Musicae' II), Florence, 1956.

154b. —— *Jüdische Musik* ('Die Musik in Geschichte und Gegenwart' VII, col. 224 ff.), 1958. **ACDEFGH¹KL**

154c. **Avermaet, E. van,** *Les tons en kilubasamba et le tambour-téléphone* ('Aequatoria' VIII, p. 1 ff.), 1945. **L²M**

155. **Ayestaran, Lauro,** *Fuentes para el estudio de la musica colonial Uruguaya* (Montevideo, 1947).

156. —— *La música indígena en el Uruguay* (Montevideo, 1949, 2/1953 (vol. I)).

157. **Azevedo, Luiz Heitor Corrêa de,** *Escala, ritmo e melodia na musica dos indios brasileiros* (diss.), Rio de Janeiro, 1938.

*158. —— *Brazilian Folk Music* ('Grove's Dictionary' 5th ed., vol. III, p. 198 ff.), 1954. **ACFH¹K**

159. —— *Tupynamba melodies in Jean de Léry's Histoire d'un voyage faict en la terre du Brésil* ('Papers of the American Musicol. Soc.', Annual meeting 1941, p. 85 ff.).

160. —— *La guitare archaïque au Brésil* ('Studia Memoriae Belae Bartók Sacra', p. 123 ff.), Budapest, 1956. **AC**

161. —— *A música brasileira e seus fundamentos* (Washington, 1948). **K**

162. **Azzawi, Abbas Al-,** *Iraqian music under the Mogols and the Turkmans 1258–1534* (Bagdad, 1951).

163. **B.** *Musica e danza nella Tripolitania* ('Musica' 1911).

164. **Baas, F.,** *The Central Eskimo* ('Ann. Report Bur. Amer. Ethnol.' VI), Smithsonian Inst., Washington, 1888 (with music). **GKL²**

165. **Bachman, W.,** *Die Verbreitung des Quintierens im europäischen Volksgesang des späten Mittelalters* ('Festschrift-Max Schneider' p. 25 ff.), 1955. **C**

165a. **Bagatti, B.,** *Arpa e arpisti* (1932).

166. **Baglioni, S.,** *Ein Beitrag zur Kentnnis der natürlichen Musik* ('Globus' XCVIII, pp. 232, 249, 264), 1910. **D¹L²M**

167. **Bahadhurji, K. N.,** *Ein indisches Saiteninstrument, genannt Taus* (Z. f. Ethnol.' XIX, p. 418 ff.), 1887. **BD¹GHKL¹L²M**

168. **Baillet, Auguste and Jules,** *La chanson chez les Egyptiens* ('Mémoires de l'Inst. Français d'Archéologie orientale' 1934).

169. **Baines, Anthony,** *Recordings and the study of musical instruments* ('Bull. of the British Inst. of Recorded Sound' I, p. 6 ff.), 1956. **I**

169a. —— *Woodwind instruments and their history* (London, 1957). **CJ**

170. **Bake, Arnold A.,** *A talk on folk-music*

('The Visva-Bharati Quarterly' V, p. 144 ff.), Calcutta, July 1927.

171. —— *Bijdrage tot de kennis der Voor-Indische muziek* (Paris, 1930). **AG**

172. —— *Indische muziek en de composities van Rabindranath Tagore* ('De Gids', 1930). **AD[1]GHK**

173. —— *Over de muziek van Tagore* ('Muziek en Religie' 1929, p. 9 ff.), 1930. **A**

174. —— *Indian Music and Rabindranath Tagore* ('Indian Art & Letters' V), 1931. **AGIK**

175. —— *Die Bedeutung Rabindranath Tagores für die indische Musik* ('Wiener Beiträge zur Kunst- und Kulturgeschichte Asiens' VI, p. 60 ff.), 1931. **G**

176. —— *Indian Music* (London, The India Soc., 1932). **A**

177. —— *Researches in Indian Music* ('Indian Art and Letters', New Series VII, p. 10 ff.), 1933. **GIK**

178. —— *Lectures on Indian music* (Baroda, 1933). **G**

178a. —— *The practice of Samaveda* ('Proc. of the 7th All India Oriental Congress, 1933').

179. —— *Different Aspects of Indian Music* ('Indian Art and Letters', VIII, p. 60 ff.), 1934. **GIK**

180. —— *26 Chansons de Rabindranath Tagore* ('Bibl. musicale du Musée Guimet', 1st series, vol. II), Paris, 1935. **AKL**

181. —— *Indian Folk Music* ('Proc. of the Musical Association' LXIII, p. 65 ff.), 1936/'37.

182. —— *Some Folkdances in South India* ('Asiatic Review' N.S. XXXV, p. 525 ff.) 1939. **AD[1]**

183. —— *Çri Chaitanya Mahaprabhu* ('Meded. Kon. Ned. Akad. v. W., Afd. Letterk., N.S. XI, No. 8), Amsterdam, 1948. **GHI**

184. —— *Kirtan in Bengal* ('Indian Art and Letters' N.S. XXI, p. 34 ff.), 1947. **GIK**

185. —— *Indian Folk Dances* ('Journal of the Intern. Folk Music Council' I, p. 47 ff.), 1949. **ACKL**

186. —— *Der Begriff Nâda in der indischen Musik* ('Kongressber. I.M.G., Bâle, 1949', p. 55). **ACDEFL**

187. —— (in collab. with **Maud Karpeles**), *Manual for Folk Music Collectors* (1951). **A**

188. —— *A Javanese musicological puzzle* ('Bingkisan Budi', p. 24 ff.), 1950. **A**

189. —— *Some aspects of the development of Indian Music* ('Proc. R. Mus. Ass.', Session LXXVI, p. 23 ff.), 1950. **A**

190. —— *Die beide Tongeschlechter bei Bharata* ('Kongressber. D.G.M., Lüneburg 1950', p. 158 ff.). **ACDEFKL**

191. —— *The Impact of Western Music on the Indian Musical System* ('Journal of the Intern. Folk Music. Council' V, p. 57 ff.). 1953. **ACJKL**

192. —— *Bemerkungen zur Entstehungsgeschichte eines Modus* ('Kongress-ber. Bamberg 1953' p., 184 ff.), Kassel, 1954. **ACEF**

193. —— Review of Mantle Hood, 'The nuclear theme as a determinant of paṭet in Javanese music' ('Music & Letters', May 1955). **AFKL[1]**

194. —— Review of Mantle Hood, 'The nuclear theme as a determinant of paṭet in Javanese music' ('Indonesia' VIII, p. 354 ff.), 1955. **AD[1]GL[2]**

195. —— *Indonesian Music* ('Grove's Dictionary' 5th ed., vol. IV, p. 460 ff.), 1954. **ACFH[1]K**

*196. —— *Indian Music* ('The New Oxford History of Music', 3rd ed., vol. I; p. 195 ff.), 1957. **ABCD[1]FGH[1]JK**

197. —— *India* ('Encyclopedie van de Muziek' I, p. 52 ff.), Amsterdam 1956. **ACDEFGH[1]**

198. —— *India* (ibid. II, p. 171 ff.), Amsterdam, 1957. **ACDEFGH[1]**

*198a. —— *Indische Musik* ('Die Musik in Geschichte u. Gegenwart' VI, col. 1150 ff.), 1957. **ABCDEFH[1]KL**

198b. —— *Bharata's experiment with the two vinas* ('Bull. of the School of Oriental and African Studies' XX, p. 61 ff.), London, 1957. **ABM**

199. **Baker, St. B. R.,** *Africa drums* (London, 1943). **I**

200. **Baker, Theodore,** *Ueber die Musik der Nordamerikanische Wilden* (Leipzig, 1882). **CG**

200a. **Baková-Paulovovičova, Luba:** *Spevy od Hrona* (Bratislava, 1956).

201. **Balaci, Emanuela** and **Andrei Bucsan,** *Folclorul coreografic din Sibiel* ('Revista de folclor' I, Nos. 1–2, p. 213 ff.), Bucarest, 1956. **A**

202. *Balade populare* (Editura de Stat pentru literatura si Artã), Bukarest, 1954.

202a. **Balanchivadze, V., Donadze, V.,** and **Tsutsua, P.,** *Grousinskaia muzikalnaia kultura* (= The musical culture of the Georgians), Moscow, 1957.

203. **Balandier, Georges,** *Femmes 'possédées' et leurs chants* ('Présence Africaine V, p. 749 ff.), 1948.

204. **Balasubrahmaniam, G. N.,** *Give and take in music* ('Silver Jubilee Souvenir of the Marris College of Hindustani music, Lucknow, Nov. 1952'), Lucknow, 1953.

205. **Baldus, Herbert,** *Indianer Studien im nordöstlichen Chaco* (Leipzig, 1931), p. 102 ff. **AB**

206. **Balfoort, Dirk J.,** *Indonesische muziekinstrumenten in het muziekhistorische museum-Scheurleer te 's Gravenhage* ('Ne-

derlandsch Indië Oud & Nieuw' XV, p. 2 ff.), 1930/'31. **ABD[1]FGHL[2]**

207. —— *Eigenartige Musikinstrumente* (The Hague, Kruseman, und.). **AC**

207a. —— *Oostersche oorsprong van Westersche muziekinstrumenten* ('Kroniek van hedendaagsche Kunst en Kultuur' II, No. 7, p. 209 ff.), Amsterdam, May 1937.

208. Balfour, Henry, *The Old British 'Pibcorn' or 'Hornpipe' and its Affinities* ('Journal of the Royal Anthrop. Inst. of Gr. Britain and Ireland' XX, p. 142 ff.), 1890. **ACKL[1]L[2]M**

209. —— *A primitive musical instrument (the whit-horn)* ('Reliquary and Illustr. Archaeologist', N.S. II, p. 221 ff.), 1896. **K**

210. —— *The Natural History if the Musical Bow* (1899). **ACIJL[2]M**

211. —— *Three bambu Trumpets from Northern Territory, South Australia* ('Man' I, Nos. 28, 33–34), 1901. **BD[1]GKL[2]M**

212. —— *The goura, a stringed wind musical instrument of the Bushmen and Hottentots* ('Journal of the Royal Anthrop. Inst.' XXXII, p. 156 ff.), 1902. **ACGIJKL[1]L[2]M**

213. —— Review of C. W. Mead, 'The musical instruments of the Incas' (New York, 1903), ('Man' III, Nos. 112, 191–192), 1903. **BD[1]GKL[2]M**

214. —— *Report on a collection of musical instruments from the Siamese Malay States and Perak* ('Fasciculi Malayenses', Anthropology, Part II), Liverpool, 1904. **J**

215. —— *Musical Instruments from the Malay Peninsula* ('Fasc. Malayenses' 1901–'02, Part. II), Liverpool, 1904. **AC**

216. —— *Musical Instruments of South Africa* ('Report of the British Association, South African Meeting, 1905'), p. 528 ff.

217. —— *The Friction Drum* ('Journal of the R. Anthrop. Inst. of Gr. Britain and Ireland', XXXVII, p. 67 ff.), 1907. **AGIJKL[1]L[2]M**

218. —— Musical Section in 'Notes and Queries on Anthropology', publ. by the R. Anthrop. Inst., p. 295 ff., (5/1929). **A**

219. —— *Ritual and secular uses of vibrating membranes as voice disguisers* ('J. Royal Anthrop. Inst. of Great Britain and Ireland' XXXVIII), London, 1951. **GIKL[1]L[2]M**

220. Bali, Roy Umanath, Tribhuvana Nath Sinha and Ratanjankar, *Silver Jubilee Souvenir of the Marris College of Hindustani music, Lucknow, Nov. 1952* (Lucknow, 1953).

221. Ballanta, Nicholas George Julius, *An African scale* ('Musical Courier' 84/26, p. 6 ff.), 1922.

222. —— *Gathering folk tunes in the African country* ('Musical America' 44/23, p. 3 and 11), New York, 1926.

223. —— *Music of the African races* ('West Africa' XIV, p. 752 ff.), 1930.

223a. Banaitis, W., *Kanonformen in der Lithauischen Volksmusik* ('Pro Musica' 1958 I, p. 4 ff.). **A**

224. Bañas y Castillo Raymundo, *The Music and Theater of the Philipino People* (Manilla, 1924).

225. Bandar, Mahawala, *Kandyan Music* ('Journal of the R. Historical Soc. of Ceylon' XXI, p. 129 ff.), 1909. **K**

226. Bandopadhyaya, Sri Pada, *The Music of India* (D. B. Taraporevala Sons & Co., Bombay, und.). **CKLL[2]**

227. —— *The Origin of Raga (a short historical sketch of Indian Music)*. Delhi, 1946.

228. Bandopadhyaya, S., *The music of India. A popular handbook of Hindostani music* (Bombay, c. 1947). **G**

229. —— *Tantuvidya* ('Lakshya Sangeet' I), Delhi, 1954/'55.

230. Bank, J. A., *Hellas* ('Encyclopedie van de Muziek' I, p. 66 ff.), 1956. **ACDEFGH[1]**

231. —— *Rome* (ibid. I, p. 75), 1956. **ACDEFGH[1]**

232. Baratta, Maria de, *Ensayo sobre musica indigena de el Salvador* ('Revista de Estudios musicales' I, No. 3, p. 61 ff.), Mendoza, Argentina, 1950. **AEKL**

233. Barbeau, Marius, *Veillées du Bon Vieux Temps* (Montreal, 1919).

234. —— *Folksongs of French Canada* (in collab. with Edward Sapir) (Yale Univ. Press, 1925).

235. —— *Songs of the Northwest* ('The Musical Quarterly' XIX), 1933. **C**

236. —— *Folk Songs of Old Quebec* (Nat. Mus. of Canada, 1935). **A**

237. —— *Asiatic survivals in Indian Songs* ('The Musical Quarterly' XX, p. 107 ff.) 1934, **(C)** = 'The Scientific Monthly', Washington, April 1942. **DG**

238. —— *Alouette* (Montreal, 1946).

239. —— 'Archives de Folklore' I, II, III (Montreal, 1946, '47, '48).

240. —— *Come a Singing* (in collab. with Arthur Bourinot and Arthur Lismer) (Nat. Mus. of Canada, 1947). **AG**

241. —— *The Dragon Myths and ritual songs of the Iroquoians* ('Journal of the Intern. Folk Music Council' III, p. 81 ff.), 1951. **ACJKL**

242. —— *Folkmusic* (in Canada) (in Ernst Macmillan, 'Music in Canada'), Univ. of Toronto Press, 1955.

243. Barbès, L. L., *La musique musulmane en Algérie* ('Information coloniale' No. 33), 1947.

244. Barbier, Pierre, and France Vernillat, *Histoire de France par les chansons* I. *Des croisades à Richelieu*. II. *Mazarin et*

Louis IV. III. *Du Jansenisme au Siècle des Lumières*, IV. *La Révolution* (Paris, Gallimard, resp. 7/1956, 7/1956, 3/1957. 8/1957). **AC**

244a. **Barblan, Guglielmo,** *Musiche e strumenti musicali d'ell Africa Orientale Italiana* (Naples, 1941). **L**

245. **Bárdos, Lajos,** *Natürliche Tonsysteme* ('Studia Memoriae Belae Bartók Sacra', p. 209 ff.), Budapest, 1956. **AC**

246. —— *Gyöngyvirág. 92 Magyar népdal* (Budapest, 1952). **K**

247. **Barkechli, Mehdi,** *La gamme persane et ses rapports avec la gamme occidentale* ('Olympia' I, p. 53 ff.), 1950. **G**

248. —— *La gamme de la musique iranienne* ('Annales des Télécommunications' V, p. 5 ff.), May, 1950.

249. —— *L'art Sassanide, base de la musique arabe* (Teheran, 1947).

250. **Barlow, Roberto,** and **Henri Lehmann,** *Statuettes-grelots aztèques de la vallée de Mexico* ('Tribus' IV/V, p. 157 ff.), Stuttgart, 1956. **BGL¹**

251. **Barriuso, P. G.,** *La música hispano musulmana en Marruedos* (Inst. de Estud. Africanos, Madrid, 1950).

252. **Barrow, John,** *Voyage en Chine* (traduit de l'anglais par J. Castera), Paris, 1805. **C**

252a. **Barry, Phillips,** *La música del pueblo estadounidense* ('Bol. Latino-Americano' V, p. 369 ff.), Montevideo, 1941. **AGL**

*252b. —— *Folk music in America* (with an introductory essay by George Herzog) (National Service Bureau Publ. No. 80-S), June 1939. **A**

*253. **Bartha, Dénes von,** *Neue ungarische Literatur zur vergleichenden Melodieforschung* ('Acta Musicologica' VIII, p. 38 ff.), 1936. **CDEH¹KLL¹**

254. —— *Untersuchungen zur ungarischen Volksmusik* ('Archiv f. Musikforschung' VI, fasc. 1 and 4), 1941. **CH¹KL**

254a. —— *Avarische Doppelschalmei von Janoshida* (Budapest, 1934). **L**

255. **Bartholomew, Wilmer T.,** *Acoustics of Music* (New York, 1946).

256. **Bartók, Béla,¹** *Cântece populare românesti din Comitatul Bihor* (Chansons populaires roumaines du Département Bihor), Bukarest, 1913.

257. —— *A hunyadi román nép zenedialektusa* ('Ethnographia' 1914, p. 108 ff.). German transl.: *Der Musikdialekt des rumänischen Volkes in Hunyad* ('Z. f. Musikw.' II, p. 352 ff.), 1920. **CDH¹KL**

258. —— *Die Volksmusik der Araber von Biskra und Umgebung* ('Z. f. Musikw.' II, p. 489 ff.), 1920. **CDH¹KL**

259. —— *The relation of folk-song to the deve-*

lopment of the art music of our time ('The Sackbut' II, No. 1, p. 5 ff.), June, 1921.

260. —— *La musique populaire hongroise* ('Revue musicale' II, No. 1), 1st Nov., 1921. **CD¹FGHKL**

261. —— and **Zoltan Kodály,** *Chansons populaires de Transylvanie* (Budapest, 1921).

262. —— *Rumanian folkdances* (Vienna, 1922).

263. —— *Volksmusik der Rumänen von Maramures* ('Sammelb. f. vergl. Musikw.,' IV), München, 1923. **CGIKLL¹**

264. —— *Vier slovakische Volkslieder* (Copenhagen, Atelier Electra, no date). **K**

265. —— and **Zoltan Kodály,** *Erdélyi magyarsdg Népdalok* (150 Hung. Folksongs from Siebenbürgen), Budapest, 1923.

266. —— and **Zoltan Kodály,** *Transsylvanian Hungarian Folksongs* (1923).

267. —— *A magyar népdal* (Budapest, 1924). German transl.: *Das ungarische Volkslied. Versuch einer Systematisierung der ungarischen Bauernmelodien* ('Ung. Bibl.' vols. I and II), Berlin, 1925. **KL** Engl. transl.: *Hungarian Folk Music* (London, 1931).

268. —— *Hungarian Folktunes* (New York, 1927).

269. —— *Slovakische Volkslieder* (1928/'29).

270. —— *Les recherches sur le folklore musical en Hongrie* ('Art populaire' II, p. 127 ff.), 1931. **A**

271. —— *Hungarian peasant music* ('The Musical Quarterly' XIX, p. 267 ff.), July 1933. **C**

272. —— *Vom Einfluss der Bauernmusik auf die Musik unserer Zeit* (1921) (repr. in 'Musik der Zeit' III, p. 18 ff.), 1953. **A**

273. —— *Népzenénk és a szomszéd népek népzenéje* (Budapest, 1934). – German transl.: *Die Volksmusik der Magyaren und der benachbarten Völker* ('Ung. Jahrbüchlein' XV, p. 194 ff.), Berlin, 1935. **(I)** – French transl.: *La musique populaire des Hongrois et des peuples voisins* ('Archivum Europae Centro-Orientalis' II), Budapest, 1937. **D¹K**

274. —— *Melodien der rumänischen Kolinde* (i.e. Christmas songs), Vienna, 1935. **ACKL**

275. —— *Auf Volkslied-Forschungsfahrt in der Türkei* (1937) (repr. in 'Musik der Zeit' III, p. 23 ff.), 1953. **A**

276. —— *Musique et chanson populaires* ('Acta Musicologica, VIII, p. 97 ff.), 1936. **CDEH¹KLL¹**

277. —— *Fifteen Hungarian Peasant Songs* (New York, 1939).

278. —— *Rassenreinheit in der Musik* (1942) (repr. in 'Musik der Zeit' III, p. 27 ff.), 1953. **A**

---

¹) See also No. 4021c.

87

279. —— *Ueber die alte ungarische Bauern-musik* ('Mélanges offertes à Zoltan Kodály à l'occasion de son 6oième anniversaire', p. 5 ff.), 1943. **ACK**

280. —— *Gypsy music or Hungarian music?* ('The Musical Quarterly' XXXIII, p. 240 ff.), 1947. **CDFK**

281. —— *Pourquoi et comment receuille-t-on la musique populaire?* (Genova, 1948). **AF**

282. —— and Albert B. Lord, *Serbo-Croatian Folk Songs. Texts and transcriptions of 75 folk songs from the Milman Parry collection and a morphology of Serbo-Croatian Folk melodies* (New York, 1951). **DL**

283. —— and Zoltan Kodály, *Magyar népzene tára* (Corpus musicae popularis Hungaricae). I. *Gyermekjátékok* (Children's songs) Budapest, 1951) **ACDFL**; II. *Jeles napok* (ibid. 1953) **CDF**; III. *Lakodalom* (ibid., 1955) **CDFL** (I and II ed. by György Kerényi; III by Lajos Kiss).

283a. —— *Népdalkutatás Keleteurópában* (= the study of folk song in Eastern Europe) ('Emlékkönyv Kodály Zoltán 70. születésnapjára' p. 73 ff.), Budapest, 1953. **A**

283b. Bartók, János, *Az ötfokúság formái nép-zenénkben* (= The pentatonic form in our folk music) ('Emlékkönyv Kodály Zoltán 70. születésnapjára', p. 733 ff.), Budapest, 1953. **A**

284. Bartsch, Christian, *Dainu Balsai, Melodien lithauischer Volkslieder* (2 vols.), Heidelberg, 1886–'89. **AKL**

285. Barzaga, Margarita Blanco, *La música di Haiti* (Habana, 1953).

286. Bascom, William R., *Folklore and Anthropology* ('J. of Amer. Folklore' LXVI, p. 283 ff.), 1953. **GK**

287. Basden, G. T., *Niger Ibos* (London, 1938), Chapter XVII. *Music* (p. 356 ff.). **J**

288. Basedow, Herbert, *The Australian aboriginal* (Adelaide, 1925), Chapter XXX. *Music and Dance* (p. 371 ff.). **J**

289. Basile, P., *Aux rythmes des tambours* (Montreal, 1950). **K**

289a. Basoski, Cornelis, some articles in 'Elsevier's Encyclopedie van de Muziek', vol. II: *Joegoslavië* (p. 204), *Rusland. Volksmuziek* (p. 536), *Tsjechoslowakije. Volksmuziek* (p. 647), Amsterdam, 1957. **ACDEFGH[1]**

290. Basset, René, *L'insurrection algérienne de 1871 dans les chansons populaires Kabyles* (Louvain, 1892).

291. Bastos, Maria Henriqueta Calçada, *Tres cançôes dos Maputo* ('Moçambique' II, p. 29 ff.), Lorenzo Marques, 1935.

292. —— and C. Montez, *Cançôes Djongas* (*Magude*) ('Moçambique' III, p. 17 ff.), Lorenzo Marques, 1935.

293. Batra, Rai Bahadur R. L., *Science and Art of Indian Music* (Lahore, 1945). **K**

294. Baud-Bovy, Samuel, *La chanson populaire grecque du Dodécanèse* (2 vols.) (Paris, 1935 and 1938). **L**

295. —— *La chanson clephtique* ('Journal of the Intern. Folk Music Council' I, p. 44 ff.), 1949. **ACKL**

296. —— *Sur la prosodie des chansons clephtiques* ('Dēmosieumata etaireias Makedonikoon spoudoon' 1953, p. 95 ff.), Tessalonica, 1953. **A**

297. —— *Chansons du Dodécanèse* (2 vols.) (Athens, 1955).

298. —— *Sur la chanson grecque antique et moderne* ('Schweizerische Musikzeitung' XCIII, p. 418 ff.), 1953. **C**

299. —— *La strophe de distiques rimés dans la chanson grecque* ('Studia Memoriae Belae Bartók Sacra', p. 365 ff.), 1956. **AC**

300. —— *Enregistrements en Crète* ('Les Colloques de Wégimont' I, p. 206 ff.), Brussels, 1956. **ACL**

*300a. —— *Etudes sur la chanson cleftique* (avec 17 chansons cleftiques de Roumélie transcrites d'après les disques des Archives musicales de folklore)(Introduction de Mad. Melpo Merlier) (Coll. de l'Inst. Français d'Athènes), Athens, 1958. **A**

301. Bauer, Marion, *The primitive art instinct* ('The Musical Quarterly' IX, p. 157 ff.), 1923. **AC**

302. Bayard, Samuel Preston, *Ballad tunes and the Hustvedt indexing method* ('J. of Amer. Folklore' LIV, p. 248 ff.), 1942. **K**

303. —— *Aspects of melodic kinship and variation in British-American folk-tunes* ('Papers Intern. Congress of Musicology, New York 1939', p. 122 ff.), New York, 1944. **AC**

304. —— *Decline and Revival of Anglo-American folk music* ('Midwest Folklore' V, No. 2), 1955.

304a. —— *Prolegomena to a study of the principal melodic families of British-American folk song* ('J. of American Folklore' LV, p. 248 ff.), 1942. **K**

305. Beart, Charles, *Contribution à l'étude des langages tambourinés, sifflés, musicaux* ('Notes Africaines' No. 57, p. 11 ff.), Jan. 1953. **AL[2]M**

306. —— *Jeux et jouets de l'ouest Africain* II, Chapter 29: *La musique* ('Mémoires de l'Inst. Français d'Afrique noire' No. 42), Dakar, 1955. **GL[2]**

307. Beaver, W. N., *A further Note on the Use of the Wooden Trumpet in Papua* ('Man' XVI, p. 23 ff.), 1916. **BD[1]GJKL[2]M**

308. Becking, Gustav, *Der musikalische Bau des Montenegrinischen Volksepos* ('Proc. of the Intern. Congress of Phonetic Sciences, 1932', p. 53 ff.), 1933.

309. Béclard-d'Harcourt, Marghérite, *La musique indienne chez les anciens civilisés d'Amérique*. II. *Le folklore musical de la région andine. Équateur, Pérou, Bolivie* (1920) (in Lavignac, 'Hist. de la Mus.' p. 3353 ff.), 1922. **ACDEFHJK**

310. Behn, Friedrich, *Die Musik im römischen Heere* ('Mainzer Zeitschrift' VII), 1912. **GK**

311. —— *Eine antike Syrinx aus dem Rheinland* ('Die Musik' XII), 1913. **CDFKL**

312. —— *Die Laute im Altertum und frühen Mittelalter* ('Z. f. Musikw.' I, p. 89 ff.), 1918. **CDH¹KL**

313. —— *Die Musik des Altertums* (Mainz, 1925). **G**

314. —— *Musikleben im Altertum und frühen Mittelalter* (Stuttgart, 1954). **C**

315. Beichert, E. A., *Die Wissenschaft der Musik bei Al Farabi* (diss. Berlin, 1936). **G**

316. Beier, H. Ulli, *Yoruba folk operas* ('African Music' I, p. 32 ff.), 1954. **ACJLM**

317. —— *The talking drums of the Yoruba* (ibid. p. 29 ff.), 1954. **ACJLM**

318. —— *Yoruba vocal music* ('African Music' I N°. 3, p. 23 ff.), 1956. **ACJLM**

318a. Belayev, Viktor, *Khoresmian notation* ('The Sackbut' 1924).

319. —— *Turkomanian Music* ('Pro Musica Quarterly' V, No. 1, p. 4 ff.), 1927; (ibid. V, No. 2, p. 9 ff.), 1927.

320. —— *The Longitudinal Open Flutes of Central Asia* ('Musical Quarterly' XIX, p. 84 ff.), 1933. **C**

321. —— *Turkish Music* ('Musical Quarterly' XXI, p. 356 ff.), 1935 (transl. from the Russian by S. W. Pring). **CD**

322. —— *Muzykalnye instrumenty Uzbekistana* (i.e. Musical instruments of Uzbekistan), Moscow, 1933.

323. —— *Istoriya razvitiya s drevneishikh vremen* (i.e. The history of musical development since ancient times).

324. —— *Early Russian Polyphony* ('Studia Memoriae Belae Bartók Sacra', p. 307 ff.), Budapest, 1956. **AC**

325. —— *The folk-music of Georgia* ('The Musical Quarterly' XIX, p. 417 ff.), 1933. **C**

325a. —— *A népi harmóniarendszer* (= The harmonic system of the folk) ('Emlékkönyv Kodály Zoltán 70. születésnapjára', p. 75 ff.), Budapest, 1953. **A**

326. Belden, H. M., *Ballads and songs, collected by the Missouri Folklore Society* (1/1940, 2/1953).

327. Belik, Vratislav, *Horacky zpevnik* (1954).

*328. Belvianes, Marcel, *Sociologie de la Musique* (Paris, 1951). **A**

329. Benet, Sula, *Song, dance and customs of peasant Poland* (London/New York, 1951).

329a. Bennet-Clark, M. A., *Iron gongs from the Congo* ('Man' LV, p. 176, No. 196), 1955. **BD¹GKL¹L²M**

330. Ben Smail, *Sur la musique et les musiciens arabes* ('France-Maroc' 1919).

331. Bentoiu, Pascal, *Citeva consideratiuni asupra ritmului si notatiei melodiilor de joc Rominesti* (i.e. The rhythm in the Rumania folk tunes and dances) ('Revista de Folclor' I, No. 1–2, p. 36 ff.), Bucarest, 1956. **A**

331a. Berendt, Joachim Ernst, *Blues* (München, 1957).

332. Bérenger-Féraud, L. J. B., *Etude sur les griots des peuplades de la Sénégambie* ('Revue d'Ethnographie' V, p. 266 ff.), Paris, 1882. **KL²**

333. Berggreen, A. P., *Folkesange og Melodier, faedrelandske og fremmede* I–XI), Copenhagen, 1/1842–'55, 2/1860.

334. Bergstrásser, Gotthelf, *Ramadan-Kinderlieder aus Kairo* ('Z. f. Semistik' VIII, p. 149 ff.), 1932. **KL⁴**

335. Bernard, R., *Congrès de musique marocaine à Fès* ('Revue musicale' 1939). **DGKL**

336. Bernatzik, Hugo Adolf, *Afrikanische Musikinstrumente* ('Atlantis' VI, p. 645 ff.), Leipzig, 1934. **D¹L¹L²**

336a. —— *Afrika, Handbuch der angewandten Völkerkunde* (Vienna, 1947), Index s.v. Musik. **B**

337. Berner, Alfred, *Studien zur arabischen Musik auf Grund der gegenwärtigen Theorie und Praxis in Egypten* ('Schriftenreihe des Stl. Inst. f. deutsche Musikforschung', Heft 2), Leipzig, 1937. **ACGIKL**

338. —— *Neue Bestrebungen der arabischen Musik in Aegypten* ('Allgemeine Musikalische Zeitung' 1942). **D¹KL**

338a. Bersa, Vladoje, *Zbirka narodnih popievaka in Dalmacije* (Zagreb, 1944).

339. Bertho, Jacques, *Instruments de musique des rois de Nikki, au Dahomey* ('Notes Africaines de l'Institut Français d'Afrique Noire LII, p. 99 ff.), 1951. **L²M**

339a. —— *Personification d'instruments de musique à percussion au Dahomey* ('Notes Africaines' XXV, p. 1 ff.), Dakar, 1945. **M**

340. Bertholon, L. and E. Chantre, *Recherches anthropologiques dans la Berberie Orientale* (Lyon, 1913), Chapter VI. *La musique et la danse* (p. 495 ff.). **J**

341. Bessa, Bento, Antonio Mourinho and Santos Júnior, *Coreografia popular trasmontana* IV. *O Pingacho* ('Douro Litoral' 8th series, p. 1 ff.), Porto, 1957. **M**

342. Bessaraboff, Nicholas, *Ancient European Musical Instruments* (Cambridge, Mass, Harvard Univ. Press, 1941). **J**

343. Besseler, Heinrich, *Cobla* ('Die Musik in

Geschichte und Gegenwart' II col. 1517 ff.), Kassel/Basel, 1952. **ACDEFGH¹KL**

344. —— *Katalanische Cobla und Alta-Tanz-kapelle* ('Kongress-Bericht d. Intern. Ges. f. Musikwiss., Basel 1949', p. 59 ff.), Basel 1950. **ACDEFL**

344a. —— *La cobla catalana* ('Anuario musical' IV), 1949. **CL**

345. Best, Elsdon, *Maori Songs* ('New Zealand Official Yearbook' 1918, p. 739). **G**

346. —— *The Maori* (Wellington, N.Z., 1924). II, Chapter XII. *Vocal and instrumental music* (p. 135 ff.). **J**

347. Betz, R., *Die Trommelsprache der Duala* ('Mitteil. aus den deutschen Schütz-gebieten' XI, p. 1 ff.), 1898. **GKL²**

348. Bevan, P., *Harmonies in Japanese music* (London, 1898).

349. —— *Japanese music* ('Transactions and Proceedings of the Japan Soc.' V, p. 312 ff.), 1901. **J**

350. Beyer, Herman, *Mexican bone rattles* (Mari publication, No. V-7), Tulane Univ. New Orleans.

351. Bhandankar, Rao P. R., *Contribution to the study of ancient Hindu music* ('Indian Antiquary' 1912). **GK**

352. Bhanu, Dharma, *Promotion of music by the Turko-Afghan rulers of India* ('Islamic Culture' XXIX), Jan. 1955. **G**

353. Bhatkande, N. V., *A short historical survey of the music of Upper India*(Bombay,1934).

354. —— *A Comparative Study of some of the Leading Music Systems of 15th, 16th, 17th and 18th Centuries* (Madras, 2/1949).

355. —— *Short historical survey of the music of Upper India* (Bombay, 1934). **I**

355a. Bielawski, Ludwik, and Jan Steszewski, *Le folklore musical* ('Feuilles Musicales' XI, Nos. 2 and 3, Numéro spécial sur la vie musicale en Pologne), 1958.

356. Bielenstein, J., *Lettische Volkslieder* (Riga, 1918).

357. Bigoshak, *Music, light or classical?* ('Jankar music circle 1953 souvenir'), Calcutta, 1953.

358. Birket-Smith, Kaj, *The Eskimos* (transl. from the Danish by W. E. Calvert), London, 1936. **BK**

359. Birnbaum, Martin, *The long-headed Mangbetus* ('Natural History' XLIII, p. 73 ff.), Febr. 1939.

360. Biro, Ludwig, *Beschreibender Katalog der ethnographischen Sammlung aus Deutsch-Neu-Guinea (Astrolabe-Bai)*, Budapest, 1901 (p. 176 ff.). **J**

361. —— *Magyarische Sprach- und Gesangsaufnahmen* (1913).

362. Bishop, Marcia Brown, *Hawaiian life of the Pre-European period* (publ. by the Peabody Museum, Salem, 1940), p. 52 ff.: *Ancient Hawaiian music and musical instruments*. **J**

363. Bjørndal, Arne, *The Hardanger fiddle* ('J. of the Intern. Folk Music Council' VIII, p. 13 ff.), 1956. **ACJKL**

364. —— *Norsk Folkemusikk* (Bergen, 1952).

365. —— *Norske slåttar* (Oslo, 1911).

366. —— *Gamle slåttar* (Oslo, 1929). **A**

367. —— *Dei gamle Spelemennene. Martinus Gjelsvik, 1826–1886* (Årbok for Nord- og Midthordland sogelag'), 1948. **A**

368. —— *Då ein høyrde "underjordisk musikk" på Kyrkje-Byrkjeland i Fana* ('Bergens Museums Årbok, 1945, Historiskantik-varisk rekke, No. 1), Bergen, 1946. **A**

369. Blacking, John A. R., *Some notes on a theory of African rhythm advanced by Erich von Hornbostel* ('African Music' 1, No. 2, p. 12 ff.), 1955. **ACJLM**

370. —— *Eight flute tunes from Butembo* (ibid., p. 24 ff.), 1955. **ACJLM**

371. —— *Musical instruments of the Malayan aborigines. A short description of the collections in the Perak Museum, Taiping, the Selangor Museum, Kuala Lumpur, and the Raffles Museum, Singapore* ('Federation Museums Journal' N.S. vols. I and II, p. 35 ff.), 1954/'55.

372. Blackwood, Beatrice, *Both sides of Buka passage* (Oxford, 1935), p. 52 ff.: *Musical instruments*. **J**

373. Blaes, Jacob, *Die Kinder-Singspiele auf der Insel Ali, nordöst Neu-Guinea* ('Anthropos' XLI–XLIV, p. 119 ff.), 1946–'49). **BD¹GHJKL¹L²M**

373a. Blaho, Jonas, *Zahoråcké pjesničky* (vols. I and II), Bratislava 1952 and 1954.

373b. Blainville, de, *Histoire générale, critique et philologique de la musique* (Pissot, Paris, 1767): chapters on Turkish and Hebrew music with pictures and musical examples. **C**

374. Blanco, Pedro, *La musique populaire portugaise* ('Revue musicale Bull. française de la Société Intern. de la Mus.', p. 41 ff.), 19..? **AD¹K**

374a. Blankenburg, Walter, *Kirchenlied und Volksliedweise* (Gütersloh, 1953). **L**

375. Blaukopf, K., *Musiksoziologie* (1950). **ACG**

375a. Block, Edward A., *Chaucer's Millers and their Bagpipes* ('Speculum' XXIX, p. 239), 1954.

376. Blockmann, H., *The Naqqarahkhanah and the imperial musicians* (in Surindro Mohun Tagore, 'Hindu music from various authors', p. 209 ff.), Calcutta, 1882. **CFIKL²**

377. Blume, Friedrich, *Das Rasseproblem in der Musik* (Wolfenbüttel, 1938).

378. Boas, Franz, *Chinook Songs* ('Journal of American Folklore' I, p. 220 ff.), 1888. **GK**

379. —— *Songs and Dances of the Kwakiutl*

('Journal of American Folklore' I), 1888.
GK
380. —— The Central Eskimo (1884), p. 648ff.
381. Boden Closs, C., Malayan musical instruments ('Journal of the Royal Asiatic Society Malayan Branch' XLV, p. 285 ff.), 1906. D¹KL⁵
382. Bodrogi, Tibor, Yabim drums in the Biro collection (Orszagos Neprajzi Museum, Budapest, 1950). J
383. Boehme, Franz Magnus, Deutsches Kinderlied und Kinderspiel (Leipzig, 1924).
383a. —— Altdeutsches Liederbuch (Leipzig, 1925). L
384. Boelaert, E., De zwarte telefoon ('Congo' 1933, p. 356 ff.), Brussels. GKL¹L²
385. —— and G. Hulstaert, La musique et la danse chez les Nkundo ('Brousse', 1939, IV, p. 13 ff.). M
385a. Boerens, H., La musique indigène au Katanga ('Revue Congolaise Illustrée' XXII, No. 10, p. 25 ff.), 1950. M
385b. Börnstein, Ethnographische Beiträge aus dem Bismarcharchipel I: Trommelsprache und Musik ('Baessler Archiv' V), 1916. BD¹GKL²
385c. Böttger, Walter, Einige Bemerkungen zur kultischen Verwendung menschlicher Hirnschalen in Zentralasien ('Jahrbuch des Museums für Völkerkunde zu Leipzig' XV, p. 16 ff.), Berlin, 1957. B
385d. Boggs, Ralph S., La recolección de la música folklórica en el Nuevo Mundo ('Bol. Latino-Americano' V, p. 221 ff.), Montevideo, 1941. AGL
386. Bohlin, Karl, Folktoner från Jämtland ('Svenska Landsmål' II, p. 10 ff.), Stockholm, 1883. D¹G
386a. Bois, F. du, The gekkin musical scale ('Transactions of the Asiatic Soc. of Japan' XIX), 1891.
387. Bojanus, Wilhelm, Ueber die Musik auf Java ('Z. f. Musik' XCV, p. 271 ff.),1928. L
388. Bolinder, Gustaf, Busintana – Indianernas Musikbåge ('Ymer' XXXVII, p. 300 ff.), Stockholm, 1917. GK
389. Bomos, J., Musik in Südafrika (Brugge, Uitg. Voorland, 1946).
*390. Bonaccorsi, Alfredo, Italian Folk Music ('Grove's Dictionary' 5th ed., vol. III, p. 299 ff.), 1854. ACFH¹K
*390a. —— Italien. Volksmusik ('Die Musik in Geschichte u. Gegenwart' VI, col. 1552 ff.), 1958. ACDEFGH¹KL
391. Bonvin, L., On Syrian liturgical chant ('The Musical Quarterly' IV, p. 593 ff.), 1918.
392. Boone, Olga, Les Xylophones du Congo Belge (Annales du Musée du Congo Belge, Ethnographie, Série III, Notes analytiques sur les Collections du Musée du Congo Belge, vol. III, fasc. 2, p. 69 ff.), Tervueren, 1936. ABCJM

393. —— Les Tambours du Congo Belge et du Ruanda-Urundi (ibid., N.S. Sciences de l'Homme. Ethnographie, vol. I), Tervueren, 1951. ACIJM
393a. Boots, Mrs. J. L., Korean musical instruments and an introduction to Korean music ('Transactions of the Korean Branche of the R. Asiatic Soc.' XXX, p. 1 ff.), Seoul, 1940.
394. Borchart, L., Die Rahmentrommel im Museum zu Kairo ('Mélanges Maspéro' I, 'Orient ancien'), Cairo, 1934.
395. Borde, Jean Benjamin de la, Essai sur la musique ancienne et moderne (4 vols.), Paris, 1780. Vol. I, chapter XV: 'De la Musique des Chinois'.
396. Bordes, Charles, La musique populaire des Basques (Paris, 1899).
397. —— Cent chansons populaires basques (Paris, 1894).
398. —— 12 Noëls basques anciens (Paris,1897).
399. —— 12 Chansons amoureuses du pays basque français (Paris, 1910).
400. Borisoff, Boris, Der Norwegische Langeleik ('Pro Musica' IV, p. 115 ff.), Trossingen/Wolfenbüttel, 1957. A
401. Bormida, Marcelo, Pampidos y Australoides; Coherencias ergologicas y miticas ('Archivos Ethnos' I, fasc. 2, p. 51 ff.), Buenos Aires, Sept. 1952.
402. Born, Einige Bemerkungen über Musik, Dichtkunst und Tanz der Yapleute ('Z. f. Ethnologie' XXXV, p. 134 ff.), 1903. ABD¹GHKL¹L²M
403. Bornemann, Ernest, Les racines de la musique américaine noire ('Présence Africaine' IV, p. 576 ff.), 1948.
404. Bornemann, Fritz, H. E. Kaufmanns Songs of the Naga Hills ('Anthropos' XLVIII, p. 613 ff.), 1953. BD¹GHJKL¹L²M
405. Borrel, E., La question de la polyphonie en Orient ('Tribune de St. Gervais' XXII, p. 57 ff.), 1921.
406. —— La Musique turque ('Revue de Musicologie' III, p. 149 ff.; IV, p. 26 ff. and 60 ff.), 1922/'23. CD¹LL¹
*407. —— Contribution à la bibliographie de la musique turque au XX siècle ('Revue des Etudes Islamiques' II, p. 513 ff.), Paris, 1928. CGKL¹
*408. —— Publications musicologiques turques ('Revue de Musicologie' XIV, p. 235 ff.), 1933. CD¹EKLL¹
409. —— Sur la musique secrète des tribus turques Alévi ('Revue des Etudes Islamiques' VIII, p. 241 ff.), 1934. CGKL¹
410. —— Le crise de la musique en Orient ('Guide musical', Paris, 1934).
411. —— La musique turque (in Norbert Dufourc, 'La Musique des origines à nos jours', ed. Larousse, p. 433 ff.), 1946. ACDEFHJK

412. —— *Les poètes Kizil Bach et leur musique* ('Revue des Etudes Islamiques' XV, p. 157 ff.), 1947. **GKL[1]**

412a. Borris, S., *Einfluss und Einbruch primitiver Musik in die Musik des Abendlandes* ('Sociologus' II, p. 52 ff.), 1952. **L[2]**

413. Borsy, Istvan, and Ernö Rossa, *Tiszan innen, dunan tul, 150 magyar népdal IV, javitott kiadds* (Budapest, 1954). **K**

414. Bosanquet, R. H. M., *On the Hindoo Division of the Octave, with some additions to the Theory of Systems of Higher Orders* ('Proc. of the R. Soc. of London' XXVI, p. 372), 1877 (D[1]HL[1]); reprinted in S. M. Tagore, 'Hindu Music from various authors' (Calcutta, 1882), p. 317 ff. **CFIKL[2]**

415. Bose, Fritz, *Die Musik der Uitoto* ('Z. f. vergl. Musikw.' II, p. 1 ff.), 1934. **ACK**

416. —— *Lieder der Völker. Die Musikplatten des Instituts für Lautforschung. Katalog und Einführung.* (Berlin, 1935). **L**

417. —— *Musik der aussereuropäischen Völker* ('Atlantisbuch der Musik' 1/1937, 8/1953), p. 789 ff. **CEF**

418. —— *Typen der Volksmusik in Karelien* ('Archiv f. Musikforschung' III, p. 96 ff.), 1938. **CDH[1]KL**

419. —— *Musik und Musikinstrumente des Balkan* ('Atlantis' 1938, fasc. 11). **D[1]L[1]L[2]**

420. —— *Klangprobleme in der Musik aussereuropäischer Völker* ('Z. f. Instrumentenbau' LVII, p. 214, 217), 1938. **D[1]L**

421. —— Introduction and some chapters in Elsa Ziehm, 'Rumänische Volksmusik' (Berlin, 1939). **I**

422. —— *Einfluss der Musikerziehung auf Begabung und Leistung* ('Der Erzieher' No. 37, 1940, p. 3 ff.).

423. —— *Musikpolitische Aufgaben in Afrika* ('Koloniale Rundschau' 1941). **L[2]M**

424. —— *Klangstile als Rassenmerkmale* ('Z. f. Rassenkunde' XIV, p. 78 ff. and p. 208 ff.), 1943/'44. **GHL[2]**

425. —— *Rassentheorie und Rassenforschung in der vergleichenden Musikwissenschaft* ('Musikblätter' No. 16, 1948, p. 5 ff.).

426. —— *Vergleichende Musikwissenschaft heute* ('Musica' III, p. 255 ff.), 1949. **CDKLL[1]**

427. —— *Das Verstehen exotischer Musik* ('Melos' XVII, p. 244 ff.), 1950. **KL**

428. —— *Das Sprache-Musik-Problem* ('Musica' V, p. 82 ff.), 1951. **CDKLL[1]**

429. —— *Messbare Rassenunterschiede in der Musik* ('Homo' II. Heft 4, p. 147 ff.), Göttingen, 1952. **D[1]GHM**

430. —— *Ein Hilfsmittel zur Bestimmung der Schrittgrösse beliebiger Intervalle* ('Die Musikforschung' V, p. 205 ff.), 1952. **ACEIKLL[1]**

431. —— *Die finnische Kantele, die aelteste*

Zither Europas ('Atlantis' XXIV, p. 328 ff.), 1952. **D[1]**

*432. —— *Musikalische Völkerkunde* (Freiburg i/Isr., 1953). **AJL**

433. —— *Die Tonqualitäten.* Erich M. von Hornbostel zum Gedächtnis (1877–1935) ('Z. f. Phonetik u. allgem. Sprachwissenschaft' VII, p. 283 ff.), 1953. **AGHKL[1]**

434. —— *Volksmusik in Indien* ('Musica' VIII, p. 178 ff.), 1954. **ACDKLL[1]**

435. —— *Instrumentalstile in primitiver Musik* ('Kongressbericht Bamberg 1953', p. 212 ff.), 1954. **ACDEFL**

436. —— *Indische Musik* ('Atlantis' XXVI, p. 17 ff.), 1954. **D[1]**

437. —— *Musik und Folklore in Amerika* ('Atlantis' XXVII, p. 319 ff.), July 1955. **D[1]**

438. —— *Folk music research and the cultivation of folk music* ('J. of the Intern. Folk Music Council' IX, p. 20 ff.), 1957. **ACJKL**

438a. —— *Law and freedom in the interpretation of European folk epics* ('J. of the Intern. Folk Music Council' X, p. 29 ff.), 1958. **ACIJKL**

438b. Bose, Narendra Kumar, *Melodic types of Hindustan, a scientific survey of the Raga system of Northern India* ('The J. of the Music Academy Madras' XXVII, p. 151 ff.), Madras, 1957. **A**

439. Bose, S., *The Theory of Melodies; Some Aspects of Indian Music* ('Perspective' II, p. 47 ff.), Sept. 1947.

440. Boshoff, S. P. E., and L. J. du Plessis, *Afrikaanse volksliedjes. Piekniekliedjes (Ballade-Poësie)* vol. I. *Woorde met Toeligtinge;* vol. II. *Woorde met Wijsiemusiek* (Pretoria/Amsterdam, 1918). **AF**

440a. Bossche, A. van den, *Art Bakuba* ('Brousse' N.S. I, p. 11 ff.), 1952. **M**

441. Boucheman, A. de, *Quartorze chansons de l'Arabie du Nord accompagnées à la rabâba* ('Bull. d'Etudes Orientales' 1945/'46). **KL[4]**

442. Bouisset, Max, *La Musique au Viêt-Nam* ('Sud-Est' Dec. 1950, p. 48 ff.). **A**

443. Boulton, Laura C., *West African music* ('Man' XXXVII, p. 130 ff.), Aug. 1937. **BD[1]GKL[1]L[2]**

444. —— *Bronze artists of West Africa* ('Natural History' XXXVI, p. 17 ff.), New York, 1935. **G**

445. Bouteiller, Marcelle, *Chamanisme et guérison magique* (Paris, 1950).

446. Bouveignes, Olivier de, *La musique indigène au Congo Belge* ('African Music Society Newsletter' I, No. 3, p. 19 ff.), 1950. **ACJM**

447. —— *Les danses nègres* (ibid. I No. 5, June 1952, p. 21 ff.). **ACJM**

448. —— *Le rythme dans la musique nègre*

('Revue nationale' XXI, p. 193 ff.), Brussels, 1949.

448a. —— *De inheemse muziek in Belgisch-Kongo* ('Band' X, p. 95 ff.), 1951. M

448b. —— *La musique indigène au Congo Belge* ('Trait d'Union' XXI, p. 13 ff.), 1953. M

448c. —— *De inheemse muziek in Belgisch Kongo* ('Kengele' XXI, p. 13 ff.), 1953. M

448d. —— *Musica indigena nel Congo Belga* 'Affrica' VI, p. 323 ff.), 1951. M

448e. —— *La musique indigène au Congo Belge* ('Les arts au Congo Belge et au Ruanda-Urundi' 1950, p. 72 ff.). M

449. Bouws, Jan, *Zuid-Afrikaanse volksmuziek* ('Mens en Melodie' V, p. 125 ff.), 1950. AC

450. —— *Afrikaanse volksmuziek* ('Die Tijdskrif vir Wetenskap en Kuns', April 1951, p. 123 ff.). AD¹FGM

451. —— *Musiek in Suid-Afrika* (Brugge, 1946). K

452. —— *In die voetspore van die Afrikaanse volkslied* ('Tijdskrif vir Wetenskap en Kuns', April 1956), p. 51 ff. ABD¹G

453. Bowers, Faubion, *Theatre in the East. Asian dance and drama* (Thomas Nelson, London/Edinburgh/Paris/Melbourne/Toronto/New York, 1956).

454. —— *Japanese theatre* (London, no date). C

455. Bowles, E. A., *Haut and Bas: the grouping of musical instruments in the middleages* (Massachusetts Institute of Technology Publ. No. 13). AC

456. Bowles, Paul, *Calypso-music of the Antilles* ('Modern Music' XVII, p. 154 ff.), Jan./Febr. 1940.

457. Boys, R. S., *Music in Toowoomba (Queensland)* ('The Canon' IV, p. 300 ff.), 1951.

458. Brailoiu, Constantin, *Cântece bătrânești din Oltenia, Muntenia, Moldova si Bucovina* ('Publ. of the Folklore Archives', Bukarest, 1932). I

459. —— *Esquisse d'une méthode de folklore musical* ('La Revue de Musicologie' No. 40), 1932. CD¹EKLL¹

460. —— *Die rumänische Volksmusik* ('Mélanges offertes à Zoltan Kodály' p. 300 ff.), 1943. ACK

461. —— *Le Folklore musicale* ('Musica Aeterna', French edition, vol. II, p. 277 ff.), 1948. A

462. —— *Le rhytme Aksak* (Abbeville, 1952). AL

463. —— *A propos du jodel* ('Kongressber. Intern. Musikges., Basel 1949', p. 69). ACDEFL

464. —— *Le giusto syllabique bichrone* ('Polyphonie' 1948, No. 2, p. 26 ff. (K) and 'Anuario musical' VII, 1952). CL

465. —— *Sur une mélodie russe* (in Pierre Souvtchinsky, 'Musique Russe' vol. II, p. 329 ff.), Paris, 1953.

466. —— *Le vers populaire Roumain chanté* ('Revue des études roumaines' 1950, p. 7 ff.). AK

467. —— *Le rythme enfantin* ('Les Colloques de Wégimont' I, p. 64 ff.), Brussels, 1956. ACL

*467a. —— *l'Ethnomusicologie* (in: Jacques Chailley, 'Précis de Musicologie'), Paris, 1958 (Chapter IV, p. 41 ff.). A

468. Brandel, Rose, *Sounds from the equator* (New York Univ., master's thesis, 1950).

469. —— *Music of the Giants and Pygmies of the Belgian Congo (Watusi, Bahutu, Batwa)* ('Journal of the Amer. Musicol. Soc.' V, p. 16 ff.), 1952. ACFKL

470. —— *The music of African circumcision rituals* (ibid. VII, p. 52 ff.), 1954. ACFK

470a. —— Review of Sukehiro Shiba, 'Score of Gagaku, Japanese classical court music' vol. I: Kangen-orchestra in Haya-gaku and Haya-tada-byôshi' ('J. of the American Musicological Soc.' X, No. 1, p. 39 ff.), 1957. A

471. Brandts Buys, J. S., *Over het onderzoek der Javaansche en daarmee verwante muziek* ('Koloniale Studiën' IV, no. 3, p. 455 ff.), 1920. ABD¹DGH

472. —— *Over de ontwikkelingsmogelijkheden van de muziek op Java* ('Djawa' I, Preliminary Advices, vol. II, p. 1 ff.), 1921. ABD¹G

473. —— (in collab. with A. Brandts Buys-Van Zijp) *Snorrepijperijen* ('Djawa' IV (1924), p. 18 ff.; ibid. VI (1926), p. 318 ff.; ibid. XI (1931), p. 133 ff.; ibid. XII (1932), p. 50 ff.; ibid. XIII (1933), p. 205 ff. and 341 ff.). ABD¹G

474. —— *Uitslag van de prijsvraag inzake een Javaans muziekschrift* ('Djawa' IV, p. 1 ff.), 1924. ABD¹G

475. —— (in collab. with A. Brandts Buys-Van Zijp), *Oude klanken* (ibid. V, p. 10 ff.), 1925. ABD¹G

476. —— (in collab. with id.), *Toeters en piepers* (ibid. V (1925), p. 311 ff.; ibid. VI (1926), p. 27 ff., 76 ff. and 318 ff.). ABD¹G

477. —— (in collab. with id.), *Over muziek in het Banjoewangische* (ibid. VI, p. 205 ff.), 1926. ABD¹G

478. —— (in collab. with id.), *Over fluiten* ('Ned.-Indië Oud & Nieuw' XI, p. 57 ff. and 155 ff.), 1926/'27. ABD¹GH

479. —— (in collab. with id.), *Over spleettromorkestjes* ('De Muziek' II, p. 389 ff. and 437 ff.), 1928. ACDEFH

480. —— (in collab. with id.), *De toonkunst bij de Madoereezen* ('Djawa' VIII, p. 1 ff.), 1928. ABD¹GJ

481. —— (in collab. with id.), *Een en ander*

over Javaansche muziek ('Program of the Java-Congress, held on 27–29 Dec. 1929 at Solo, on the occasion of the 10th anniversary of the Java-Institute' p. 45 ff.), 1929. **A**

482. —— (in collab. with id.), *Inlandsche dans en muziek* ('Timboel' III, nrs. 13, 15, 16, 17 and 18), 1929.

483. —— *Tooverklanken. Muzikale pikoelans* ('Djawa' XII, p. 341 ff.), 1932. **ABD¹G**

484. —— *De tjuntang baloeng's* (ibid. XIII, p. 258 ff.), 1933. **ABD¹G**

485. —— *De muziek van de Sekatèn-gamelans* (ibid. XIV, p. 243 ff.), 1934. **ABD¹G**

486. —— (in collab. with **A. Brandts Buys-Van Zijp**), *Omtrent notaties en transcripties en over de constructie van gamelanstukken* (ibid. XIV, p. 127 ff.), 1934. **ABD¹G**

487. —— (in collab. with id.), *Lands transcripties van gendings* (ibid. XV (1935), p. 174 ff.; ibid. XVI (1936), p. 230 ff.; ibid. XVIII (1938), p. 182 ff.). **ABD¹G**

488. —— (in collab. with id.), *Omtrent de rebab* (ibid. XIX, p. 308 ff.), 1939. **ABD¹G**

489. —— *Het gewone Javaansche tooncijferschrift (het Solosche kepatihan-schrift)* (ibid. XX, p. 87 ff.), 1940. **ABD¹**

490. —— *Roneographieën van de gereconstrueerde gending-transcripties van Prof. Dr. J. P. N. Land* (Jogjakarta, 1939). **AC**

491. **Braschowanow, St.**, *Das bulgarische Volkslied als Brauchtum und Kunst* ('Jahrbuch des Auslandamtes der deutschen Dozentenschaft', Leipzig, 1942).

492. —— *Bulgarische Musik* ('Die Musik in Geschichte und Gegenwart' II, col. 453 ff.), 1952. **ACEFGH¹KL**

493. **Brasseur de Bourbourg, Charles Etienne**, *Gramática de la lengua quiché. Grammaire de la langue Quichée-espagnole-française ... servant d'introduction au Rabinal Achi drame indigène avec sa musique originale* etc. (Paris, 1862).

493a. **Brauns, D.**, *Traditions japonaises sur la chanson, la musique et la danse* (Paris, 1890).

493b. **Braunwieser, Martin**, *O Cabaçal* ('Bol. Latino-Americano' VI, vol. I, p. 601 ff.), Rio de Janeiro, 1946. **AGL**

494. **Brazys, Th.**, *Die Singweisen der litauischen Daina* (in 'Tauta ir Žodis' IV), Kaunas, 1918.

495. **Breazul, G.**, (= G. Georges Cu-Breazul), *Patrium carmen. Contributie la studiul muzicii Rominesti* (Craiova, 1941).

496. **Bredicianu, Tiberius**, *Historique et état actuel des recherches sur la musique populaire roumaine* ('Art populaire' II, p. 133 ff.), Paris 1931. **A**

497. —— *Muzica populara din Banat. Cercetatorii si cultivatorii ei* (in vol. 'Banatul.

Contributii la cunoasterea unei provincii), Bucarest, 1943.

498. **Brehmer, Fritz**, *Melodieauffassung und melodische Begabung des Kindes* ('Z. f. angewandte Psychologie' 1927, Beiheft 36). **D¹HKL¹**

499. **Breloer, Bernhard**, *Die Grundelemente der altindischen Musik nach dem Bharatiya-natya-śāstra* (Bonn, 1922). **G**

500. **Brenecke, Ernest**, *The 'Country Cryes' of Richard Deering* ('The Musical Quarterly' XLII, p. 366 ff.), 1956. **CDFKL¹**

501. **Briceño, Olga**, *Música folklórica venezolana* ('Bol. de la Union Panamericana' LXXXII), Washington, 1948.

502. **Bricqueville, Eugène H. de**, *Notice sur la vielle* (Paris, 2/1911). **A**

503. —— *Les musettes* (Paris, 1894).

504. **Brinton, G.**, *Native stringed musical instruments* ('American Antiquarian' 1897).

505. **Bris, E. le**, *Musique annamite: Airs traditionnels.* ('Bull. des Amis du Vieux Hué' IX, p. 255 ff.), 1922.

506. —— *Musique annamite: les musiciens aveugles de Hué* (ibid. XIV, p. 137 ff.), 1927.

507. **Briton, H. H.**, *Philosophy of Music* (1911).

508. **Broadwood, Lucy, and J. A. Fuller Maitland**, *English county songs* (London, 1893). **K**

509. **Broholm, H. C., J. P. Larsen and G. Skjerne**, *The Lures of the Bronze Age* (Copenhagen, 1949). **ACGL**

510. **Brömse, Peter**, *Flöten, Schalmeien und Sackpfeifen Südslawiens* ('Veröffentl. des Musikw. Inst. der deutschen Univ. in Prag'), Brünn, 1937. **CL**

511. —— *Von südslawischer Volksmusik* ('Musikblätter der Sudetendeutschen' II).

512. **Bronson, Bertrand Harris**, *Mechanical help in the study of folk song* ('J. of Amer. Folklore' LXII, p. 81 ff.), 1949. **GK**

513. —— *Melodic stability in oral transmission* ('J. of the Intern. Folk Music Council' IX, p. 50 ff.), 1951. **AC**

514. —— *Folksong and the modes* ('The Musical Quarterly' XXXII No. 1, p. 37 ff.), Jan. 1956. **CDFKL¹**

515. —— *About the commonest Biritsh ballads* ('J. of the Intern. Folk Music Council' IX, p. 22 ff.), 1957. **ACKL**

516. **Bruce-Mitford, R. L. S.**, *The Sutton Hoo Ship Burial* ('Comm. of the R. Inst. of Great Britain', 21th Oct. 1949). **A**

517. **Brücker, Fritz**, *Die Blasinstrumente in der altfranzösischen Literatur* (Giessen, 1926).

518. **Bruning, Father Elis.**, *Nederlandse volksmuziek* ('Elsevier's Encyclopedie van de

Muziek' II, p. 388 ff.), Amsterdam, 1957. **ACDEFH¹**

518a. —— *Volkslied* (ibid. II, p. 678), Amsterdam, 1957. **ACDEFH¹**

518b. —— *Het Nederlandse Kerstlied* (Tilburg, 1941). **ACL**

519. Bryan, Charles Faulkner, *American folk instruments. I. The Appalachian mountain dulcimer* ('Tennessee Folklore Society Bulletin' XVIII), March 1952. **C**

520. —— *American folk instruments. II. The hammered dulcimer* (ibid. XVIII), June 1952. **C**

521. —— *American folk instruments. III. Improvised instruments* (ibid. XVIII), Sept. 1952. **C**

522. Buchanan, Annabel Morris, *Modal and melodic structure in Anglo-American folk music – a neutral mode* ('Papers read at the Intern. Congress of Musicology, held at New York, Sept. 1939', p. 84 ff.), Richmond, 1944. **AC**

523. Buchner, Alexander, *Musikinstrumente im Wandel der Zeiten* (Artia, Prague, 1956). **CL**

524. —— *Musical instruments through the ages* (London, 195. ?). **J**

525. Buck, Peter H., (= Te Rangi Hiroa) *The material culture of the Cook Islands* (New Plymouth, N.Z., 1927), p. 354 ff.: *Musical instruments*. **J**

526. —— *Samoan material culture* (Honolulu, 1930), p. 575 ff.: *Musical instruments*. **J**

527. —— *Pan-pipes in Polynesia* ('Journal of the Polynesian Soc.' L, p. 173 ff.), 1941. **ABGL²**

528. —— *The coming of the Maori* (Wellington, N.Z., 1950), Chapter X, p. 252 ff.: *Musical instruments*. **J**

528a. —— *Arts and crafts of Hawaii* (Publ. No. 45 of the Bernice P. Bishop Mus.), Honolulu, 1957 (p. 387 ff.). **AB**

529. Budde, Karl, *Das Schwirrholz Werkzeug der alttestamentlichen Totenbeschwörung?* ('Z. f. d. Alttest. Wiss.' XLVI, p. 75 ff.), 1928. **D¹GHKL¹**

530. Bücher, Karl, *Arbeit und Rhythmus* (1896, 5/1918). **CJL²**

531. Bürchner, L., *Griechische Volksweisen* ('Sammelb. d. Intern. Musikges.' III), 1901/'02. **CDFH¹L**

532. Buhle, E., *Die musikalischen Instrumente in den Miniaturen des frühen Mittelalters* (Leipzig, 1903). **C**

533. Bukofzer, Manfred, *Magie und Technik in der Alpenmusik* ('Schweizer Annalen' 1926, Heft III, p. 205).

534. —— *Präzisionsmessungen an primitiven Musikinstrumenten* ('Z. f. Physik' vol. 99, p. 643 ff.), 1936. **CD¹GHL¹**

535. —— *Kann die Blasquintentheorie zur Erklärung exotischer Tonsysteme beitragen?* ('Anthropos' XXXII, p. 402 ff.), 1937. **AD¹GHKL¹L²M**

536. —— *The Evolution of Javanese Tonesystems* ('Papers read at the Intern. Congress of Musicology, held at New York, Sept. 11th to 16th, 1939', p. 241 ff.), New York, 1944. **AC**

537. —— *Blasquinte* (in 'Die Musik in Geschichte und Gegenwart' I, col. 1918 ff.), 1951. **ACDEFGH¹KL**

538. —— *Observations on the study of non-western music* ('Les Colloques de Wégimont' I, p. 33 ff.), Brussels, 1956. **ACL**

539. Bukoreschliev, A., Vasil Stoin and Raina Katzarova, *Rodopski pesni* (coll. of 1252 songs) ('Sbornik za narodni umotvoreniya' XXXIX), Sofia, 1934.

540. Bunting, Edward, *Ancient music of Ireland* (Dublin, 1796).

541. —— *Ancient music of Ireland* (Dublin, 1809).

542. —— *Ancient Irish music* (London, 1840).

543. Burlin, Nathalie, *The Indian's Book* (New York/London, 1907, 3/1935). **I**

544. —— *Songs and tales from the Dark Continent* (New York, Schirmer, 1920), p. 81 ff.

545. —— *American Indian cradle-songs* ('The Musical Quarterly' VII, p. 549 ff.), 1921.

546. Burnier, Th., *Chants zambéziens* (Paris, undated).

546a. —— *Notes d'ethnographie zambésienne* ('Arch. Suisses d'Anthropologie générale' XII, p. 92 ff.), 1946. **M**

547. Burrows, Edwin G., *Some Paumotu chants* ('Journal of the Polynesian Soc.' XII, p. 221 ff.), 1903. **BGL**

548. —— *Native music of the Tuamotus* ('Bull. No. 109 of the Ber. F. Bishop Mus.'), Honolulu, 1933. **IL**

549. —— *Music of the Tahaki chants* (in J. F. Stimson, 'The legends of Mani and Tahaki') (Bull. No. 127 of the Ber. F. Bishop Mus.), Honolulu, 1934.

550. —— *Polynesian part singing* ('Z. f. vergl. Musikw.' II, p. 69 ff.), 1934. **ACK**

*551. —— *Polynesian music and dancing* ('Journal of the Polynesian Soc.' XLIX, p. 331 ff.), 1940. **ABGL**

552. —— *Songs of Uvea and Futuna* ('Bull. No. 183 of the Ber. F. Bishop Museum'), Honolulu, 1945. **ABL**

552a. —— *Music on Ifaluk atoll in the Caroline islands* ('Ethnomusicology' II, No. 1, p. 9 ff.), Jan. 1958. **AGL**

553. Burssens, A., *Le Luba, langue à intonation et le tambour-signal* ('Proc. of the Third Intern. Congress of Phonetic Sciences, Ghent, 1938', p. 503 ff.).

554. Burton, Frederick R., *American primitive music, with especial attention to the songs of the Ojibways* (New York, 1909). **I**

555. Buttree, Julia M., *The rhytm of the*

95

red man: in song, dance and decoration (Barnes, 1930).

556. **Buvarp, Hans,** *Studiet av Folkemusikken. Problemer verdrørende det melodiske Grunnlag* ('Norveg' II, p. 133 ff.), Oslo, 1952. **AK**

557. —— Review of Christian Leden, 'Ueber die Musik der Smith Sund Eskimos und ihre Verwandtschaft mit der Musik der amerikanischen Indianer' ('Norveg' III, p. 233 ff.), Oslo, 1953. **K**

558. **Cabral, Jorge,** *La música incaica* (Buenos Aires, 1915).

559. **Cabussi-Kabusch, N.,** *Bulgarische Volksmusik* ('Die Musik' 1931). **CDFKL**

560. **Cadilla de Martínez, María,** *La música popular en Puerto Rico* (San Juan, 194.?).

561. **Cadman, Charles W.,** *The 'idealization' of Indian music* ('The Musical Quarterly' I, p. 387 ff.), 1915.

562. **Cadwell, Helen,** *Hawaiian music* ('Hawaiian Annual' 1916, p. 71 ff.).

563. **Caferoğlu, Ahmed,** *75 azerbayğanische Lieder 'Bayaty' in der Mundart von Gänğä nebst einer sprachlichen Einleitung* ('Mitt. d. Seminars f. Orientalischen Sprachen zu Berlin' XXXII, 2 Abt. p. 55 ff. (1929), p. 105 ff. (1930). **D¹L³**

564. **Cahen, Abraham,** *Hébreux* (undated, but before 1913) (in Lavignac, 'Hist. de la Mus.' I, p. 67 ff.), 1922. **ACDEFHJK**

564a. **Calame-Griaule, Geneviève,** *Note complémentaire sur le symbolisme du tambour kunyu (Soudan français)* ('Notes africaines' Oct. 1956, p. 62 ff.). **GL²M**

564b. —— and **Blaise Calame,** *Le problème des langages tambourinés* ('La Revue Française' Jan. 1956, p. 68 ff.).

564c. —— and id. *Symbolisme de la musique africaine* ('Essec', Reflets d'une promotion, 1956, p. 73 ff.).

564d. —— and id. *Introduction à l'étude de la musique africaine* ('La Revue Musicale' 1957, No. spécial No. 238). **AD¹GK**

565. **Calleja, R.,** *Colección de canciones populares de la provincia de Santander* (Madrid, 1901).

566. **Callenfels, P. V. van Stein,** *The age of bronze kettledrums* ('Bull. of the Raffles Mus.' Series B, vol. I no. 3, p. 150 ff.), 1937. **D¹**

567. **Calmet, Augustin,** *Dissertations sur la poésie et la musique des anciens en général et des Hébreux en particulier. Avec les figures des instruments de musique* (Amsterdam, 1723). **C**

568. **Caluza, Reuben Tolakele,** *African music* ('Southern Workman' LX, p. 152 ff.), Hampton, 1931.

569. —— *Three Zulu songs* (in 'Negro anthology' ed. by Nancy Cunard, p. 415 ff.), Wishart., 1934.

570. **Camp, Ch. M.,** and **Bruno Nettl,** *The musical bow in Southern Africa* ('Anthropos' L, p. 65 ff.), 1955. **BD¹GHJKL¹L²M**

571. **Campbell,** *Notes on the musical instruments of the Nepalese* (in S. M. Tagore, 'Hindu Music from various authors'), Calcutta, 1882 (*vide* below No. 4031). **CFIKL³**

572. **Campbell, A.,** *Herdman's songs and yoik in northern Sweden* ('J. of the Intern. Folk Music Council' III, p. 64 ff.), 1951. **AC**

573. **Campbell, J. L.,** *Gaelic folksongs from the Isle of Barra* (ed. by the Folklore Institute of Scotland), undated. **G**

574. **Campen, C. F. H.,** *Eenige mededeelingen over de Alfoeren van Hale-Ma-Héra* ('Bijdragen tot de Taal-, Land- en Volkenk. van Ned.-Indië' 4th series, VIII, p. 187 ff.), The Hague, 1884. **ABD¹GL²**

575. **Campos, Rubén M.,** *El folklore y la musica mexicana* (Publ. of the Secr. of Publ. Educ.), Mexico, 1928. **I**

576. —— *El folklore musical de Mexico* ('Estudios Latino-americanos' III, p. 137 ff.), 1937.

577. —— *La música popular de Mexico* ('Revista de estudios musicales' I, p. 81 ff.), Mendoza, Argentina, 1949. **AKL**

577a. **Candied, Fr.,** *Muziek en zang in Kongo* ('Toren', Sept. 1951, p. 23 ff., Oct. 1951, p. 37 ff.). **M**

578. **Cano, D. M.,** *Fiesta en un poblado Bubi* ('Africa' (Madrid), No. 114, p. 23 ff.), 1951. **M**

579. **Canteloube, J.,** *Anthologie de chants populaires français groupés et présentés par pays ou provinces* (4 vols.) (Paris, 1951). **L**

580. *Canto popular, El, – Documentos para el etudio del folk-lore argentino*, vol. I. *Música precolombiana* (Buenos Aires, 1923). **K**

581. **Canziani, Estella,** *Costumes, traditions and songs of Savoy* (London, 1911).

581a. **Canzoneri, V.,** *A theory of the modes in Japanese popular traditional music* ('Tôyô-ongaku-kenkyû' I), 1938.

582. **Capitan,** *L'omichicahuatzli mexicain et son ancêtre de l'époque du renne en Gaule* ('Proc. Congress of Americanists' XVI), Vienna, 1908.

583. **Capmañy, A.,** *Cançoner popular* (3 series), Barcelona.

584. **Cappelle, H. van,** *De binnenlanden van het district Nickerie (Suriname)* (Baarn, 1903), p. 39 and 217/8. **A**

585. **Capus, M. G.,** *La musique chez les Khirgizes et les Sartes de l'Asie Centrale* ('Revue d'Ethnographie' III), 1884. **G**

586. **Carámbula, Rubén,** *Negro y tambor. Poemas, pregones, danzas y leyendas sobre motivos del folklore afrorioplatense. Melodias y anotaciones sobre el candome* etc.

(Buenos Aires, Folklórica Americana, 1952).

587. **Carlheim-Gyllenskiöld**, *Visor ock melodier* ('Svenska Landsmål' VII, p. 7 ff.), Stockholm, 1892. **D¹G**

588. **Carp, Paula**, *Citeva cintece de ieri si de azi din comuna Batrini* ('Revista de folclor' II, Nos. 1–2, p. 7 ff.), Bucarest, 1957. **AC**

589. **Carpentier, Alejo**, *La musica en Cuba* ('Colección Tierra Firme' No. 19), Mexico, 1946.

590. **Carr, Andrew T.**, *A Rada community in Trinidad* ('Carribbean Quarterly' III, No. 1, p. 35 ff.), 1953. **B**

591. **Carra de Vaux**, *Le traité des rapports musicaux ou l'épître à Scharaf ed-Din, par Safi Ed-Din Abd El-Munin* (Paris, 1891).

592. **Carrington, J. F.**, *A comparative study of some Central African Gong-languages* ('Mém. Inst. Royal Col. Belge', Brussels, and Carey Kingsgate Press Ltd., London), 1949. **AM**

593. —— *The drum language of the Lokele tribe* ('African Studies' III, p. 75 ff.), June 1944. **KM**

594. —— *Notes on an idiophone used in 'kabile' initiation rites by the Mbae* ('African Music' I, p. 27 ff.), 1954. **ACJLM**

595. —— *Talking drums of Africa* (Carey Kingsgate Press Ltd., London, 1949). **CIJM**

596. —— *African music in Christian worship* ('Intern. Review of Missions' XXXVII, p. 198 ff.), April 1948.

597. —— *Individual names given to talking gongs in the Yalemba area of Belgian Congo* ('African Music' I, No. 3, p. 10 ff.), 1956. **ACJLM**

597a. —— *Four-toned announcements on Mbele talking gongs* ('African Music' I No. 4, p. 23 ff.), 1957. **ACJLM**

598. **Carroll**, Father **K.**, *Yoruba religious music* ('African Music' I, No. 3, p. 45 ff.), 1956. **ACJLM**

599. **Carybé**, *O jogo da capoeira* (Bahia, 1955).

600. **Castagné, J.**, *Chants et danses populaires folkloriques de quelques Orientaux de l'U.R.S.S.* ('l'Ethnographie' N.S. No. 51, p. 62 ff.), Paris, 1957. **ABD¹GK**

601. **Castañeda, Daniel**, *Las flautas en las civilizaciones azteca y tarasca* ('Musica, Revista Mexicana' II, Nos. 2–4), Mexico, 1930 and '31.

602. —— and **V. T. Mendoza**, *Los percutores precortesianos* ('Anales del Museo Nacional de Arqueología' VIII), 1933.

603. —— and —— *Los teponaztlis en las civilizaciones precortesianas* (ibid.), 1933.

603a. **Casteele, J. M. van de**, *La place du cantique dans la musique religieuse indigène*

('Revue du Clergé Africain' IX, p. 158 ff.), 1954. **M**

603b. —— *Musique religieuse africaine et negro-spirituals* (ibid. IX, p. 396 ff.), 1954. **M**

603c. —— *Een ontroerend klaaglied* ('Jezuieten-Missies' 1947, No. 44, p. 72 ff.). **M**

603d. —— *Musique indigène – musique religieuse* ('Revue du Clergé africain' (Mayidi) III, No. 5, p. 392 ff.), 1948. **M**

603e. —— *L'avvenire della musica africana* ('La Nigrizia' LXIX, No. 5, p. 96 ff.), 1950. **M**

604. **Castellanos, Israel**, *Instrumentos musicales de los Afrocubanos* ('Archivos del Folklore Cubano' II, p. 193 ff.), Havana, 1926.

605. **Castillo, Jesus**, *La música autóctona* ('Anales de la Soc. de Geografia e Historia' IV), Guatemala, 1927.

606. **Castro, José**, *Sistema pentafónico en la música precolonial del Peru* ('Bol. Lat.-Amer. de Música' IV, p. 835 ff.), Bogotá, 1938.

606a. **Caughie, Catherine**, *The scales of some Central Australian songs* ('J. of the Intern. Folk Music Council' X, p. 57 ff.), 1958. **ACIJKL**

607. **Caussin de Perceval, A.**, *Notices anecdotiques sur les principaux musiciens arabes des trois premiers siècles de l'Islamisme* ('J. Asiatique'), Dec. 1873. **CD¹GHKL¹**

608. **Cavazzi, P.**, *Relation historique de l'Ethiopie occidentale* (Paris, 1732), p. 48 ff.

609. **Cesky, Lid**, *Sbornik venovaný studiu lidu českého v čechách na morave, ve slezsku a na slovensku* (vol. I), Prague, 1892.

610. **Chailley, Jacques**, *La notation musicale* (in Dufourcq, 'La musique des origines à nos jours', Paris, ed. Larousse, p. 515 ff.), 1946. **ACDEFHJK**

610a. —— *Formation et transformations du langage musical. I. Intervalles et échelles* (Centre de Documentation Universitaire, 5, Place de la Sorbonne, Paris n.d.). **AC**

611. **Chaitanya Deva, B.**, *The emergence of the drone in Indian music, a psychological approach* ('The Journal of the Music Academy, Madras' XXIII, p. 126 ff.), 1952. **AC**

611a. —— *Tonal structure of tambura* ('The J. of the Music Academy Madras' XXVII, p. 89 ff.), Madras, 1957. **A**

611b. —— *Psychology of the drone in melodic music* ('Bull. of the Deccan College Research Inst.' XI), 1950.

612. **Chakravarthi, Suresh Chandra**, *India in Music* ('Jhankar music circle 1953 Souvenir'), Calcutta, 1953.

613. —— *The folk music of Bengal* ('Sangeet Natak Akadami Bull.' No. 2), 1954.

614. —— *A cultural survey of Rajasthan folk entertainment* (ibid.), 1954.

615. Chambers, G. B., *Folksong-Plainsong. A study in origins and musical relationship* (Merlin Press, London, 1956).

616. Chandra Vedi, Pandit R. Dilip, *Compositions and the six fundamental Ragas of Hindusthani Music* ('The Journal of the Music Academy, Madras' XX, p. 104 ff.), 1949. **A**

617. Chao, Mei-Ba, *La cloche jaune* (Brussels, 1932) (English translation: Baltimore, 1934). **I**

618. Chao, Wei-Pang, *Modern Chinese Folklore Investigation* ('Folklore Studies of the Museum of Oriental Ethnology, Catholic Univ. of Peking' I, p. 55 ff. and III, p. 79 ff.), 1942 and '43. **G**

619. —— *Yang-ko: the Rural Theatre in Tinghsien, Hopei* (ibid. III, p. 1 ff.), 1944. **G**

620. Chao, Y. R., *Singing in Chinese* ('Le Maître phonétique' XXXIX), 1924.

620a. —— *A note on Chinese scales and modes* ('Oriens' X, p. 140 ff.), 1957.

621. —— *Music* (in Sophia Chen Zen, 'Symposium on Chinese Culture'), Shanghai, 1931.

621a. Chapin, James P., *The travels of a talking drum* ('Natural History' L), New-York, Sept. 1942.

622. Chappel, Louis W., *Folk songs of Roanoke and the Albemarle* ('Southern Folklore Quarterly' V, p. 202 ff.), 1941.

623. Charlton, George V. B., *The Northumbrian bagpipe* (Newcastle-upon-Tyne, 1930). **J**

624. Chase, Gilbert, *The music of Spain* (New York, 1941). **K**

625. —— *America's music* (New York/Toronto/London, 1955), Chapter XX. *Indian tribal music* (p. 403 ff.). **A**

*626. —— *Bibliography of American folk music* (Washington, 1942). **K**

627. —— *A guide to Latin American music* (Washington, 1943). **K**

628. Chaubey, S. K., *The art and the personality of ustad Faiyaz Khan* ('Silver Jubilee Souvenir of the Marris College of Hindustani music, Lucknow, Nov. 1952'), Lucknow, 1953.

629. Chauvet, Stephen, *La musique nègre* (Paris, 1929). **CFIJKLL²M**

629a. —— *La musique nègre* ('Encycl. Col. et Maritime', Afrique Occidentale Française vol. II, p. 371 ff.), Paris, 1949. **M**

630. Chavannes, Edouard, *Les chants du bureau de la musique: des rapports de la musique grecque avec la musique chinoise. Les Mémoires historiques de Sema Ts'ien* (Paris, 1895), vol. III, part II, App. 1 and 2.

631. —— *Sur la musique chinoise* ('Indian Antiquary' XII), Bombay, 1912. **GK**

632. —— *Chinese and Japanese music compared* ('China Review' V), Hongkong, 1877. **G**

633. Chavez, Carlos, *La Musica. Part I. La música en las culturas Indias* ('Mexico y la Cultura', p. 475 ff.), Mexico, 1946.

634. Chavez, Franco M., *La marimba. Visitas al Museo de Guayaquil* ('Revista Municipal de Guayaquil', Sept. 1927).

635. —— *El tundy y la marimba* (ibid.?, 1929?).

636. Chengalavarayan, N., *Music and musical instruments of the ancient Tamils* ('Quarterly Journal of the Mythic Soc.' XXVI), 1935. **G**

*637. Cherbuliez, Antoine E., *Swiss Folk Music* ('Grove's Dictionary' 5th ed. vol. III, p. 376 ff.), 1954. **ACFH¹K**

638. Child, F. J., *The English and Scottish popular ballads* I–V (Boston, 1882–1908), reprinted in 3 vols. by B. H. Bronson (New York, 1956).

639. Chilesotti, O., *Le scale arabico-persana e indù* ('Sammelb. der Intern. Musikges.' III, p. 595 ff.), 1901/'02. **CDFH¹L**

640. Chinchore, Prabhakar, and Imogen Holst, *Ten Indian Folktunes for Solo Descant Recorder* (Soc. of Recorder Players, No. 19, Schott & Co., London), undated.

641. Chinnaswamy Mudaliar, A. H., *Oriental Music in Staff Notation* (Madras, 1892). **A**

642. Chinnery, E. W. P., *Further Notes on the Wooden Kipi Trumpet and Conch Shell by the Natives of Papua* ('Man' XVII, p. 73, No. 55), 1917. **BD¹GJKL²M**

643. Choleau, Jean and Marie Drouart, *Chansons et danses populaires de Haute Bretagne* (Paris, 1938).

644. Chottin, Alexis, *Airs populaires receuillis à Fès* ('Hespéris' III, p. 275 ff.; IV. p. 225 ff.), 1923/'24. **D¹ (IV only) GKL²**

645. —— *Note sur le rhythme à cinq temps* ('Hespéris' 1928). **D¹GKL²**

646. —— *La musique marocaine* ('France-Outre-Mer' March 1929).

648. —— *Les genres dans la musique marocaine* ('Revue musicale du Maroc' 1930).

649. —— *Les visages de la musique marocaine* ('Le Ménestrel' vol. 93, p. 217 and 230), 1931. **K**

650. —— *Corpus de musique marocaine*, fasc. 1: *Nouba de Ochchak* (Paris, 1931).

651. —— *Airs populaires marocains* ('Le Ménestrel' vol. 94, p. 351, 359, 367), 1932. **K**

652. —— *Chants et danses berbères au Maroc* (ibid., vol. 95, p. 359), 1933. **K**

653. —— *Instruments, musique et danse chleuhs* ('Z. f. vergl. Musikw.' I, p. 11 ff.), 1933. **ACK**

654. —— *La pratique du chant chez les musi-*

ciens marocains (ibid. I, p. 52 ff.), 1933.
ACK
655. ——— *Corpus de musique marocaine*, fasc.
2: *Musique et danses berbères du pays
chleuh* (Paris, 1933).
656. ——— *Bsat* ('Revue de Musicologie'
XVIII, p. 66 ff.), 1934. CD¹EKLL¹
657. ——— *Yâ Asafâ, complainte arabe sur la
perte de l'Andalousie* ('Z. f. vergl. Musikw.' III, p. 83 ff.), 1935. ACK
658. ——— *Chants et danses berbères* ('Revue de
Musicologie' XX), Paris, 1936.
CD¹EKLL¹
659. ——— *Le chant et la danse berbères dans le
folklore européen* ('Proc. 1st Intern.
Congress of Folklore, Tours, 1938'), p.
154 ff.
*660. ——— *Tableau de la musique marocaine*
(Paris, 1939). ACGL
661. ——— *La musique musulmane* (in Dufourcq, 'La Musique des origines à nos
jours', ed. Larousse, p. 74 ff.), Paris,
1946. ACDEFHJK
*662. ——— (in collab. with **Hans Hickmann**)
Arabische Musik ('Die Musik in Geschichte und Gegenwart' I, col. 577 ff.),
1951. ACDEFGH¹KL
*663. ——— *Visages de la musique marocaine*
('Encycl. coloniale et maritime', vol. IV,
Maroc: Fasc. 14), Paris, 1949. AM
664. *Chou king, Le*, traduit et enrichi de
notes par feu le P. Gaubil, missionnaire
à la Chine. Revue et corrigé par De
Guignes (Paris, 1770). C
665. **Chowdhuri, B. K. Roy**, *Tan Sen,
brightest gem of Akbar's court* ('Silver
Jubilee Souvenir of the Marris College of
Hindustani music, Lucknow, Nov. 1952'),
Lucknow, 1953.
666. ——— *Jod and Bols* ('Lakshya Sangeet'
I), Delhi, 1954/'55.
667. **Christensen, A.**, *La vie musicale dans
la civilisation des Sassanides* ('Bull.
de l'Association Française des Amies de
l'Orient', Paris, 1926, p. 24).
667a. **Christensen, Dieter**, *Die Musik der Kate
und Sialum* (diss.), Berlin, 1957. A
668. **Christian, Geoffrey**, *A new musical
instrument from Papua* ('Man' XXXII,
p. 70, No. 83), 1932. ABD¹GKL¹L²M
669. **Christianowitsch, Alexandre**, *Esquisse
historique de la musique arabe aux temps
anciens* (Cologne, 1863). CG
670. **Christiansen, L.**, *Sowremenojé narodnojé
pjessennojé tworotsjestwo Swerdlowskoj ob-
lasti* (i.e. The creation today of folk songs
in the district of Swerdlow), Moscow,
1954.
671. **Christov, Dobri**, *Ritmitchnite osnovi na
narodnata ni musica* ('Sbornik za narodni
umotvoreniya' XXVII). Sofia, 1913.
672. ——— *Bulgarskata narodna musika* (Sofia,
19. . ?).

673. ——— *Tekhnitcheskiyat stroëzh na bulgarskata narodna musika* (Sofia, 1928).
674. ——— *66 chansons populaires des Bulgares
macédoniens* (Sofia, 1931).
675. **Chrysander, Friedrich**, *Ueber die alt-
indische Opfermusik* ('Vierteljahrschrift
f. Musikwiss.' I), 1885. CFKL
676. **Cibot, Father**, *Essai sur les pierres sonores de Chine* ('Mémoires concernant
l'histoire, les sciences, les arts etc. des
Chinois' par les missionnaires de Pékin,
VI), Paris, 1780.
676a. **Ciger, Anton**, *Sto sarisskych piesni*
(Bratislava, 1956).
677. *Cîntece si Doine, 200*, (Bukarest, 1955).
678. *Cîntese și jocuri, pentru orchestra populare*, vol. I (Bukarest, 1954), vol. II
(Bukarest, 1955).
679. **Ciobanu, Gh.**, *Despre factorii care in-
lesnesc evolutia muzicii populare* (i.e.
The essential factors present in the
evolution of folk music) ('Revista de
Folclor' I, No. 1–2, p. 68 ff.), Bucarest,
1956. A
680. ——— *Contributii la cîntecului nostru popular* ('Revista de folclor' II, Nos. 1–2,
p. 149 ff.), Bucarest, 1957. AC
680a. ——— *Un cîntec al lui Dimitrie Cantemir
in colectia lui Anton Pann* ('Revista de
Folclor' II, No. 3, p. 81 ff.), Bucarest,
1957. A
681. **Ciortea, Vera Proca**, *Jocuri populare
Rominesti* (Bukarest, 1954).
682. **Ciurlionyte, J.**, *Lithuanian Folk Melodies*
('Tautosakos Darbai' V), Kaunas, 1938.
683. **Clapham, John**, *Dvorák, Irokézové a
Kickapúové* (i.e. Dvorák, the Iroquois
and the Kickapoos), ('Hudebni, Rozhledy' X, No. 23, p. 983 ff.), Prague, 1956.
684. ——— *The power of primitive music*
('Musical Opinion' LXXVII, p. 525 ff.),
June 1954.
685. **Claridge, G. Cyrill**, *Wild bush tribes of
tropical Africa*. Chapter XX (p. 221 ff.):
Native music; Chapter XXI (p. 233 ff.):
Musical instruments (London, 1922).
686. **Clark, E. A.**, *Negro folk music in
America* ('Journal of American Folklore,
LXIV, No. 253, p. 281 ff.), 1951. GK
687. **Clarke, Roger T.**, *The drum language of
the Tumba people* ('Amer. J. of Sociology'
XL, p. 34 ff.), Chicago, 1934. GK
688. **Classe, A.**, *The Silbo Gomero* ('Scientific
American' 1956). D¹
688a. ——— *Phonetics of the Silbo Gomero*
('Archivum Linguisticum' IX, p. 44 ff.),
Glasgow, Sept. 1957. A
688b. ——— *The unusual whistle language of
the Canary islanders* ('The Unesco
Courier' X, Nov. 1957, p. 30 ff.). ABD¹K
689. **Cleather, Gabriel G.**, *The musical aspects
of drums* ('J. of the Royal Soc. of Arts'
LVII), London, 1909.

690. Clemens, W. M., *Songs of the South Sea islanders* ('Munsey's Magazine' Febr. 1901).

691. Clements, E., *Introduction to the Study of Indian Music (an attempt to reconcile modern Hindostani music with ancient musical theory and to propound an accurate and comprehensive method of treatment of the subject of Indian musical intonation)* (London/New York/Bombay/Calcutta, 1913). **AI**

692. —— *Lectures on Indian music* (Bombay, 1927). **GI**

692a. —— *The ragas of Hindustan* (The philharmonic Soc. of Western India, Poona, 1917).

692b. —— *The rāgas of Tanjore. Songs and hymns from the repertoire of the Karnatic singer Natrajan* (London, 1920).

693. Closson, Ernest, *L'instrument de musique comme document ethnographique* ('Guide Musical', p. 2 ff., Bruxelles, 1902).

693a. —— *Notes sur l'onomatopée dans la terminologie organologique* ('J. of the Intern. Music Soc.' VII, p. 16 ff.), 1911. **K**

694. —— *Les conques sonores dans la préhistoire* ('Le Guide musical', Bruxelles, 1912).

695. —— *Notes sur la chanson populaire en Belgique* (Brussels, 1913).

696. —— *M. von Hornbostel et l'ethnographie musicale* ('Guide Musical' LX, p. 335 ff.), Bruxelles, 1914.

697. —— *A propos de la Zambumbia colombienne* ('Acta Musicologica' II, p. 122 ff.), 1930. **CDLL[1]**

698. —— *Une nouvelle série de hautbois égyptiens antiques* ('Festschrift-Guido Adler', p. 17 ff., Berlin, 1930). **C**

699. —— *Un principe exotique inconnu d'organologie musicale* ('La Revue musicale' XIII, p. 200 ff.), 1932. **ACDFGHKL**

700. —— *La flûte égyptienne antique de Fétis* ('Acta Musicologica' IV, p. 145 ff.), 1932. **CDEKLL[1]**

701. —— *Questionnaire d'Ethnographie. Musique* ('Bull. de la Soc. Royale Belge de Géographie' XLIX, p. 132 ff.), 1925. **CD[1]**

702. —— *Les mélodies lithurgiques syriennes et chaldéennes* ('La vie et les arts lithurgiques' No. 134, p. 178 ff.), Paris, Febr. 1926.

703. —— *La musique Chinoise* ('Le Flambeau', undated). **C**

704. —— *Le folklore* (in: 'La musique en Belgique du moyen âge à nos jours', p. 301 ff.), 1950. **C**

705. —— *La chanson populaire en Belgique* ('J. of the Intern. Folk Music Council' II, p. 50 ff.), 1950. **ACJKL**

705a. —— *Le Lied Néerlandais ancien dans ses accointances avec le Lied populaire allemand* ('Annuaire de la Commission de la vieille chanson populaire' 1939), p. 100 ff. (Antwerp, 1939). **A**

706. Clyne, Anthony, *The skirl of the bagpipe* ('The Sackbut' VII, p. 43 ff.), 1926.

707. Coart, E., and A. de Haulleville, *La musique* ('Annales du Musée du Congo belge' III, tome I, fasc. 1, p. 145 ff.), Brussels, 1906. **GKM**

708. Cocchiari, G., and F. B. Pratella, *L'anima del popolo italiano nei suoi canti* (Milan, 1929).

709. Cocisiu, Ilarion, *Despre armonia tonala si armonia modala in cintecul popular* (i.e. Tonal and modal harmonies in folk music) ('Flacara' 1948, No. 49, p. 4).

710. —— *Un strǎin (anonim) despre muzica Romîneascǎ la începutul secolului al XIX-Lea* (i.e. Commentary of a (anonymous) stranger about the Rumanian music at the beginning of the 19th century) ('Revista de Folclor' I, No. 1–2, p. 271 ff.), Bucarest, 1957. **A**

*711. Cocks, William A., *Bagpipe* ('Grove's Dictionary' 5th ed., vol. I, p. 344), 1954. **ACFH[1]K**

712. Coello Ramos, Rafael, *La cultura musical del pueblo hondureño* ('Bol. Lat. Amer. de Musica' IV), Bogotá, 1938.

713. Coeuroy, André, *Le folklore et la chanson populaire en Europe* (in: Dufourcq, 'La Musique des origines à nos jours', ed. Larousse, p. 83 ff.), Paris, 1946. **ACDEFHJK**

*714. —— and André Schaeffner, *Le Jazz* (Paris, 1926).

715. Cohn-Antenorid, W., *Chinesische Musikaesthetik* ('Monatshefte f. Musikgesch.' XXXV, p. 1 ff. and 30 ff.), 1903. **CKL**

716. Coirault, Patrice, *Notre chanson folklorique* (Picard, Paris, 1942). **C**

717. —— *Formation de nos chansons folkloriques* (ed. du Scarabée, Paris, vol. I, 1953, vol. II, 1955). **CF**

717a. —— *Recherches sur notre ancienne chanson populaire traditionnelle. Exposés I–V* (Paris, 1933).

718. Coliac, *Chansons berbéres de la région d'Azilal* ('France-Maroc' 1920).

719. Collaer, Paul, *Importance des musiques ethniques dans la culture musicale contemporaine* ('Journal of the Intern. Folk Music Council' IV, p. 56 ff.), 1952. **ACJKL**

720. —— *Notes sur la musique d'Afrique centrale* ('Problèmes d'Afrique Centrale' No. 26, p. 267 ff.), 1954. **AGJKM**

722. —— *Les phénomènes primitifs de l'invention musicale* ('Acta Oto-Rhino-Laryngologica Belgica' 1954, fasc. 1, p. 9 ff.). **AH**

723. —— *Musique caraïbe et maya* ('Studia Memoriae Bélae Bartók Sacra', p. 125 ff.), Budapest, 1956. **AC**

724. —— *Notes concernant certains chants Espagnols, Hongrois, Bulgares et Géorgiens* ('Anuario Musical del Inst. Español de Musicología' IX, p. 153 ff.), Barcelona, 1954. **ACL**

725. —— *État actuel des connaissances relatives à la perception auditive, l'émission vocale et la mémoire musicale. Conclusions au sujet de la mesure des fréquences vibratoires et des rythmes* ('Les Colloques de Wégimont' I, p. 37 ff.), Brussels, 1956. **ACL**

726. —— *Le tambour à friction (Rommelpot) en Flandre* ('Les Colloques de Wégimont' I, p. 188 ff.), Brussels, 1956. **ACL**

727. —— *Les colloques de Wégimont. Cercle International d'Etudes Ethno-Musicologiques* vol. I (Brussels, 1956). **ACJL**

728. —— *A series of articles in 'Elsevier's Encyclopedie van de Muziek':* vol. I. *Achter-Indië* (p. 232), *Albanië* (p. 239), *Arabië* (p. 255), *Armenië* (p. 262), *Australië. Volksmuziek* (p. 272), *Basken* (p. 296), *Ceylon* (p. 404), *China* (p. 411), *Denemarken. Volksmuziek* (p. 464), *Duitsland. Volksmuziek* (p. 497), *Egypte* (p. 508), *Ethiopië* (p. 522), *Finland. Volksmuziek* (p. 542), *Frankrijk. Volksmuziek* (p. 566), *Griekenland. Volksmuziek* (p. 622), *Groot-Brittannië. Volksmuziek* (p. 629); vol. II. *Italië. Volksmuziek* (p. 192), *Japan* (p. 198), *Kelten* (p. 219), *Madagascar* (p. 307), *Melanesië* (p. 331), *Mexico* (p. 341), *Noorwegen. Volksmuziek* (p. 400), *Polynesië* (p. 471), *Tibet* (p. 631), *Ysland* (p. 706), *Zigeuners* (p. 712), *Zwitserland. Volksmuziek* (p. 717) (Amsterdam, 1957). **ACDEFGH[1]**

728a. —— *Similitudes entre des chants espagnols, hongrois, bulgares et géorgiens (addendum)* ('Anuario Musical' X), 1955. **CL**

728b. —— *Muziek* ('Kunst in Kongo', Chapter 3), Brussels, 1958. **BM**

728c. —— *Cartography and ethnomusicology* ('Ethnomusicology' II No. 2, p. 66 ff.), May, 1958. **AGL**

729. Collangettes, Father, *Etude sur la musique arabe* ('Journal Asiatique' 1904, p. 6 ff.). **D[1]GHKL[1]**

730. Combarieu, Jules, *La musique et la magie. Etude sur les origines populaires de l'art musical, son influence et sa fonction dans les sociétés* (Paris, 1909). **AIKL[2]**

731. —— *Histoire de la Musique* (Paris, 1913), vol. I. **AC**

732. Comettant, Oscar, *La musique, les musiciens et les instruments de musique chez les différents peuples du monde* (Paris, 1869). **J**

732a. Comhaire-Sylvain, S., *La chanson haïtienne* ('Présence Africaine' XII, p. 61 ff.), 1951. **M**

732b. —— *Les danses Nkundu du Territoire d'Oshwe au Congo Belge* ('African Studies' VI, p. 124 ff.), 1947. **KL[2]M**

733. Comisel, Emilia, *La ballade populaire roumaine* ('Studia Memoriae Bélae Bartók Sacra' p. 27 ff.), Budapest, 1956. **AC**

734. Comvalius, Theod. A. C., *Het Surinaamse negerlied: de banja en de doe* ('West-Indische Gids' XVII, p. 213 ff.), 1935. **BD[1]G**

735. —— *Een der vormen van het Surinaamse lied na 1863* (ibid. XXI, p. 355 ff.), 1939. **ABD[1]G**

736. Condominas, G., *Le lithophone préhistorique de Ndut Lieng Krak* ('Bull. de l'École Française d'Extrême Orient' XLV, p. 359 ff.), Hanoi 1952 (written in 1950). **AGK**

737. Conklin, Harold C., and William C. Sturtevant, *Seneca Indian Singing Tools at Coldspring Longhouse* ('Proc. Amer. Philos. Soc.' XCVII, p. 262 ff.), June 1953. **CG**

738. Conklin, Harold C., and José Maceda, *Hanunóo music from the Philippines* (commentary to Ethnic Folkways Library Album P. 466), 1955. **A**

739. Coomaraswami, Ananda K., *Thirty songs from the Punjab and Kashmir* (1913). **I**

740. —— *Indian Music* ('The Musical Quarterly' III, p. 163 ff.), 1917. **C**

741. —— *The parts of a Vinā* ('Journal of the Amer. Oriental Soc.' L, p. 238 ff.), 1930. **ADK**

742. —— *The old Indian Vinā* ('Journal of the Amer. Oriental Soc.' LI, p. 47 ff.), 1931. **AD[1]GKL[1]**

743. —— *A passage on Vinā-playing* ('Z. f. vergl. Musikw.' III, p. 88), 1935. **ACK**

744. Coopersmith, J. M., *Music and musicians of the Dominican Republic* (Música e músicos de la República Dominicana), Pan American Union publ., Washington D.C., 1949. **F**

745. *Copyright in folk music, Statement on.* ('Bull. of the Intern. Folk Music Council' XII, p. 25 ff.), Sept. 1957. **ACJ**

*746. Corbet, August L., *Netherlandish Folk Music* ('Grove's Dictionary' 5th. ed. vol. III, p. 317 ff.), 1954. **ACFH[1]K**

747. Cornell, C. H., *Music in the Old Testament* (Chicago, 1909). **I**

747a. Cornevin, R., *Note documentaire sur les arts, la musique et la toponymie* ('Encycl. Africaine Française' s.v. Cameroun-Togo, p. 564 ff.), Paris, 1951. **M**

748. Costello, Edith, *Amhrain mhuighe séola* (Folk-songs of Galway and Mayo), Dublin, 1916. **I**

749. Costermans, B., *Muziekinstrumenten van*

Watsa-Gombari en omstreken ('Zaire' I, p. 514 ff. and 629 ff.), 1947. **D¹GL¹L²M**

749a. —— *Termieten-larvenoogst bij de Logo* ('Kongo-Overzee' XVI, No. 4, p. 185 ff.), 1950. **D¹GKL²M**

*750. **Courant, Maurice**, *Essai historique sur la musique classique des Chinois, avec un appendice relatif à la musique coréenne* (1912) (in Lavignac, 'Hist. de la Mus.', vol. I, p. 77 ff.), 1922. **ACDEFHJK**

751. —— *Japon, notice historique* (1912) (ibid., p. 242 ff.), 1922. **ACDEFHJK**

752. **Courlander, Harold**, *Notes from a Abyssinian diary* ('The Musical Quarterly' XXX, p. 345 ff.), 1944. **C**

753. —— *Haiti singing* (Chapel Hill, Univ. of N. Carolina Press, 1939). **I**

754. —— *Musical instruments of Haiti* ('The Musical Quarterly' XXVII, No. 3), 1941. **H¹**

755. —— *Musical instruments of Cuba* (ibid. XXVIII, p. 227 ff.), 1942. **CH¹**

756. **Cousins, Margaret, E.** *The music of Orient and Occident* (Madras, 1935).

757. **Coussemaker, E. de**, *Chants populaires des Flamands de France* (Gent, 1856). **D¹HL**

757a. **Coutts, P. G.**, *Some musical instruments of Usuku* ('Uganda Journal' XIV, No. 2, p. 160 ff.), 1950. **M**

758. **Couvreur, J.**, *Over krontjongmuziek en nog wat* ('Onze Stem' 1930, p. 737 ff.). **B**

759. **Cowell, Henry**, *Dos estudios: la música entre los pueblos primitivos* ('Bol. Lat. Amer. de Música' V, p. 105 ff.), Montevideo, 1941. **AGL**

759a. —— *Orientalische Musik* ('Encycl. of Social Sciences' XL, p. 152 ff.), New York, 1950. **L²**

759b. **Cox, John Harrington**, *Folk songs mainly from West Virginia* (with an introductory essay and supplementary references by Herbert Halpert) (National Service Bureau Publ. No. 81-S), June 1939. **A**

759.c **Coyne, A. E.**, *Visual indication of pitch* ('African Music Soc. Newsletter' I, No. 4, p. 19 ff.), 1951. **ACJM**

760. **Crampton, H. E.**, *The songs of Tahiti* ('American Museum Journal' XII, p. 141 ff.), 1912.

761. **Crawfurd, Music and dancing** (in Surendro Mohun Tagore, 'Hindu music from various authors', p. 295 ff.), Calcutta, 1882. **CFIKL²**

761a. **Creighton, Helen**, *Songs and Ballads from Nova Scotia* (Toronto, 1932).

761b. **Cresson, H. T.**, *Aztec music* ('Proc. Acad. of Natural Sciences of Philadelphia' XXXV (1883), p. 86 ff.), Philadelphia, 1884.

762. **Cringan, Alexander T.**, *Iroquois Folk Songs* ('Archeological Report, Appendix

to Report of Minister of Education', Toronto, 1902, p. 137 ff.).

763. —— *Music of the pagan Iroquois* (Archeological Report, Appendix), Toronto, 1899.

764. **Crossley-Holland, P.**, *Chinese music* ('Grove's Dictionary of Music and Musicians' 5th ed., vol. II, p. 219 ff.), 1954. **ACFH¹K**

*765. —— *Tibetan Music* ('Grove's Diction ary' 5th ed. vol. VII, p. 456 ff.), 1954. **ACFH¹K**

*766. —— *Welsh Folk Music* ('Grove's Dictionary' 5th ed., vol. III, p. 398 ff.), 1954. **ACFH¹K**

767. **Crowley, Daniel J.**, *Festivals of the calendar in St. Lucia* ('Caribbean Quarterly' IV, p. 99 ff.), Dec. 1955. **B**

768. —— *Song and dance in St. Lucia* ('Ethnomusicology Newsletter' No. 9, p. 4 ff.), Jan. 1957. **AGL**

769. **Cruz, Clément da**, *Les instruments de musique dans le Bas-Dahomey* (populations Fon, Adja, Katafon, Péda, Aïzo) ('Etudes dahomiennes' XII), Porto Novo, 1954. **GL²M**

770. **Csenki, Imre** and **Sándor**, *Népdalgyüjtés a magyarországi cigányok között* (*A collection of folkmusic among the gypsies in Hungary*) (in 'Mélanges offerts à Zoltan Kodály à l'occasion de son 60ième anniversaire', p. 343 ff.), Budapest, 1943. **ACK**

771. **Cučkov, Emanuil**, *Contenue idéologique et proces rhythmique de la danse populaire macédonienne* ('Journal of the Intern. Folk Music Council' IV, p. 39 ff.), 1952. **ACJKL**

771a. **Cudjoe, S. D.**, *Art in Africa* ('West African Revue' XXIV, p. 434), 1953.

772. —— *The techniques of Ewe drumming and the social importance of music in Africa* ('Phylon' XIV, p. 280 ff.), 1953.

772a. **Cuisinier, Jeanne**, *Le théâtre d'ombres à Kelantan* (Paris, 1957), Chapter II. *L'orchestre* (p. 59 ff.). **A**

773. **Cultrera, G.**, *I canti di Libia* (Catania, 1936).

774. **Culwick, A. T.**, *A Pogoro flute* ('Man' XXXV, p. 40 (No. 39)), 1935. **BD¹GKL¹L²M**

775. **Culwick, G. M.**, *Degeneration of a wind instrument* ('Man' XXXIV, p. 112, (No. 138)), July 1934. **BD¹GKL¹L²M**

776. **Cummings, Charles Gordon**, *The Assyrian and Hebrew Hymns of Praise* (New York, 1934).

777. **Cuney-Hare, Maud**, *Negro musicians and their music* (Washington, 1934). **K**

778. **Cunningham, Eloise**, *The Japanese Kouta and Ha-uta, the 'little songs' of the 17th century* ('The Musical Quarterly' XXXIV, p. 68 ff.), 1948. **CDFKL¹**

778a. Cunnison, I., *Central African chronology* ('Man' LV, p. 143, No. 157), 1955.
BD[1]GKL[1]L[2]M

779. Čurčin, M., *Das serbische Volkslied* (Leipzig, 1905).

Curtis, Natalie, see Burlin.

780. Dal, Erik, *Scandinavian Folk Music* ('J. of the Intern. Folk Music Council' VIII, p. 6 ff.), 1956.   ACJKL

781. —— *Glimt af international folkemusikforskning* ('Nordisk Musikkultur' I, p. 340 ff.), 1952.   AK

*782. —— *Nordisk folkeviseforskning siden 1800* (Copenhagen, 1956).   ACK

783. —— *Opgaver og muligheder i folkemusikforskningen belyst gennem anmeldelser af ny udenlandsk litteratur* (= Problems and possibilities in folk music research, illustrated by reviews of recent foreign literature) ('Dansk Musiktidsskrift' XXXII, p. 69 ff.), Copenhagen, 1957.   AK

783a. —— *The Faroese folk-song chain dance* ('The Folklorist' IV, No. 4, p. 106 ff.), Manchester, Winter 1957/'58.   A

783b. —— *The linked stanza in Danish ballads: its age and its analogues* ('J. of the Intern. Folk Music Council' X, p. 35 ff.), 1958.   ACIJKL

784. Dalal, Navinkumar, *Die Pflege der indischen Kunstmusik* ('Musica' VIII, p. 182 ff.), 1954.   CKLL[1]

785. Dalberg, F. H. von, *Ueber die Musik der Indier* (ein Abhandlung des Sir William Jones), translated from the English, with additions by ——), Erfurt, 1802. C

786. Dalman, G., *Arabische Gesänge* ('Palästina-Jahrbuch' 1924, p. 77 ff.).   D[1]K

787. —— *Nachlese arabischer Lieder aus Palästina* ('Beiträge zur alttestamentischen Wissenschaft' 1920, p. 43 ff.).

787a. Dalyell, John, *Musical memoirs of Scotland, with historical notes and annotations* (Edinburgh, 1849).

788. Dam, Theodore van, *The influence of the West African songs of derision in the New World* ('African Music' I, p. 53 ff.), 1954.   AC

789. Damais, E., *Chants Africains notés* (in Hubert Caron, 'Rybani'), Le Havre, 1936.

790. Dam Bo, *The music of the Pemsians* ('The Journal of the Music Academy, Madras' XXI, p. 139 ff.), 1950.   AC

791. Danckert, Werner, *Ursymbole melodischer Gestaltung* (Kassel, 1932).   A

792. —— *Ostasiatische Musikästhetik* ('Ostasiatische Zeitschrift' N.S. VII), 1931.
D[1]GKL[5]

793. —— *Musikwissenschaft und Kulturkreislehre* ('Anthropos' XXXII, p. 1 ff.), 1937.
BD[1]GHKL[1]L[2]M

794. —— *Musikethnologische Erschliessung der Kulturkreise* ('Mitteil. d. Anthrop.

Ges. Wien' LXVII, p. 53 ff.), 1937.
D[1]GHL[2]

795. —— *Wandernde Liedweisen, eine Grundfrage volkskundlicher Musikforschung* ('Archiv f. Musikforschung' II, p. 101 ff.), 1937.   CDH[1]KL

796. —— *Grundriss der Volksliedkunde* (Berlin, 1938).   IL

797. —— *Das europäische Volkslied* (Berlin, 1939).   DFHIJL

798. —— *Die ältesten Spuren germanischer Volksmusik* ('Z. f. Volkskunde' XLVIII, p. 137 ff.), 1939.   AD[1]KL[1]

799. —— *A félhang nélküli pentatonica eredete* (*The origin of anhemitonic pentatonic scales*) in 'Mélanges offerts à Zoltan Kodály à l'occasion de son 60ième anniversaire', p. 9 ff.), Budapest, 1943.
ACK

800. —— *Älteste Musikstile und Kulturschichten in Ozeanien und Indonesien* ('Z. f. Ethnologie' vol. 77, p. 198 ff.), 1952.
ABD[1]GHJKL[1]L[2]M

801. —— *Wesen und Ursprung der Tonwelt im Mythos* ('Archiv f. Musikw.' XII, p. 97 ff.), 1955.   ACDFGKLL[1]

802. —— *Melodiestile der finnisch-ugrischen Hirtenvölker* ('Studia Memoriae Belae Bartók Sacra', p. 175 ff.), Budapest, 1956.   AC

803. —— *Tonmalerei und Tonsymbolik in der Musik der Lappen* ('Die Musikforschung' IX, p. 286 ff.), 1956.   ACEFIKLL[1]

804. —— *Hirtenmusik* ('Archiv f. Musikwiss.' XIII, p. 97 ff.), 1956.   DFGKLL[1]

805. —— *Melodiestile der Ob-Ugrier* ('Acta Musicologica' XXVIII, p. 122 ff.), Basel, 1956.   ACDGH[1]KLL[1]

806. Daniel, F., *Note on a gong of bronze from Katsina, Nigeria* ('Man' XXIX, No. 113, p. 157 ff.), 1929.   BD[1]GKL[2]M

807. Daniel, Gaston, *La musique au Congo* ('J. de la Soc. Intern. de Musique' VIII, p. 56 ff.), Paris, 1911.

808. Daniélou, Alain, *Introduction to the Study of Musical Scales* (London, 1943).
ACJ

809. —— *The categories of intervals or Sruti Jatis* ('The Journal of the Music Academy Madras' XVII, p. 74 ff.), 1946. C

810. —— *The different schools of Indian Music* (ibid. XIX, p. 165 ff.), 1948.

*811. —— *Northern Indian Music* (2 vols.): I. *History, Theory and Technique* (London/Calcutta, 1950); II. *The main Ragas. An analysis and notation* (London, 1953).
ACD (1 only), G (id.) IKL

812. —— *A Commentary on the Mahesvara Sutra* ('The Journal of the Music Academy, Madras' XXII, p. 119 ff.), 1951. AC

813. —— *Notes on the Sangita Damodara* (ibid. XXII, p. 129 ff.), 1951.   AC

814. —— *Some Problems facing research on*

Indian Literatures on Music (ibid. XXIII p. 117 ff.), 1952. **AC**

815. —— *Catalogue of Indian Music* (Unesco, Paris, 1952). **ACGJL**

816. —— *Research on Indian Music* ('The Journal of the Music Academy, Madras' XXIV, p. 57 ff.), 1953. **AC**

817. —— *Les arts traditionels et leur place dans la culture de l'Inde* ('L'originalité des cultures', p. 200 ff.), Paris (Unesco), 1953, 2/1954.

818. —— *Can harmony be introduced in Indian music?* ('Silver Jubilee Souvenir of the Marris College of Hindustani music, Lucknow, Nov. 1952'), Lucknow, 1953.

818a. —— *Ethno-musicology* ('The J. of the Music Academy Madras' XXVII, p. 47 ff.), Madras, 1957. **A**

818b. —— *La musique du Cambodge et du Laos* (Publ. of the Institut Français d'Indologie No. 9), Pondichery, 1957. **A**

819. Darmsteter, James, *Chants populaires des Afghans* ('Soc. asiatique, Collection d'ouvrages orientaux', 2nd series), Paris, 1880–1890 (2 vols.).

820. —— *Afghan Songs* ('Selected Essays' p. 105 ff.), Boston, 1895.

821. Das, K. N., *The Music of Assam* ('The Journal of the Music Academy, Madras' XXI, p. 143 ff.), 1950. **AC**

822. —— *Time Theory of the Ragas* (ibid. XXII, p. 69 ff.), 1951. **AC**

822a. Das, J. Srinivasa, *Music phonography* ('The J. of the Music Academy, Madras' XVII, p. 41 ff.), 1946. **C**

*823. Daugherty, D. N., *A bibliography of periodical literature in musicology and allied fields and a record of graduate theses accepted* (American Council of Learned Societies, Washington, 1940).

824. Daumas, G., *L'Afrique qui chante* ('Revue Grégorienne' XXI, p. 165), 1938.

825. Davenson, Henri, *Le livre des chansons* (Neuchâtel, 1946).

825a. —— *Introduction à la chanson populaire française* (Paris, 1944). **L**

826. David, Ernst, *La musique chez les Juifs* (Paris, 1873). **C**

827. —— and M. Lussy, *Histoire de la notation musicale depuis ses origines* (Paris, 1882).

*828. David, Paul, *Basque Folk Music* ('Grove's Dictionary' 5th ed. vol. III, p. 193 ff.), 1954. **ACFH¹K**

829. Davidson, H. G., *Recent musical progress in Egypt* ('Musical Courier', New York, 1932).

830. Davies, Harold E., *Aboriginal Songs of Central- and South-Australia* ('Oceania' II, p. 454 ff.), 1932. **BD¹GJL²**

831. Davy, J., *Music of Ceylon* (in: S. M. Tagore, 'Hindu Music from various authors'), Calcutta, 1882. **CFIKL²**

832. Dawes, F., *Six essays on the ancients, their music and instruments.* I. *Chinese, Japanese, Hindoos* (Oxford, 1893). **C**

833. Dawson, Warrington, *Le caractère spécial de la musique nègre en Amérique* ('Journal de la Soc. des Américanistes' XXIV, p. 273 ff.), Paris, 1932. **GL³**

834. Day, Charles Russell, *The Music and Musical Instruments of Southern India and the Deccan* (New York/London, 1891). **CL**

835. —— *Music and musical instruments of Southern India* (London, 1891). **I**

836. —— *Native musical instruments* (in: A. F. M. Ferryman, 'Up the Niger', Philip, 1892), p. 264 ff. **I**

837. —— *Notes on Indian Music* ('Proc. of the Mus. Ass.' XX, p. 45 ff.), 1893/'94.

338. —— *Denkmäler der japanischen Tonkunst* (Tokyo, 1930).

839. Deacon, A. Bernard, *Malekula, a vanishing people in the New Hebrides* (London, 1934), p. 41 ff., 391 ff. and 498 ff. **B**

*840. Dean-Smith, Margaret, *A guide to English folk song collections 1822–1952* (Liverpool, 1954).

841. —— *Hornpipe* ('Die Musik in Geschichte u. Gegenwart' VI, col. 756 ff.), 1957. **ACDEFGH¹KL**

842. Dechevrens, S. J., *Etudes de science musicale* (Paris, 1898), 4 vols, containing a.o.: *Système model de Pythagore et des Grecs postérieurs; La musique gréco-romaine et l'octoechos; Chants liturgiques chez les Juifs et les Orientaux; Mélodies arméniennes, etc.*

843. —— *Etude sur le système musical chinois* ('Sammelb. d. Intern. Musikges.' II, p. 485 ff.), 1901. **CDFH¹L**

843a. Degani, Mario, *La musica nella preistoria e nelle antiche civilta* (no place, 1939). **L**

844. Dejardin, A., *Alain Gheerbrant aux sources de l'homme* ('Synthèses' VII, No. 78, p. 50 ff.), 1952.

844a. Delachaux, Théodore, *Omakola (ekola), instrument de musique du Sud-Ouest de l'Angola* ('Anthropos' XXXV–XXXVI, p. 341 ff.), 1940/'41. **BD¹GHJKL¹L²M**

845. Delavignette, Robert, *Du tam-tam à l'imprimé* ('La Revue de Paris' LXII, Dec. 1955, p. 64 ff.). **GHK**

846. Delgadillo, Luis A., *La Musica Indigena y Colonial en Nicaragua* ('Estudios Musicales' I, No. 3, p. 43 ff.), Mendoza, Argentina, 1950. **A**

847. Deliz, Monserate, *Renadió. Del cantar folklórico de Puerto Rico* (Madrid, 2nd ed. 1952).

848. Delmas, Siméon, *Ami hune (chant de cannibales)* ('Bull. de la Soc. d'Etudes Océaniennes' III, p. 254 ff.), 1929.

849. Delphin, H., and L. Guin, *Notes sur la*

poésie et la musique arabes dans le Maghreb algérien (Paris, 1886).

850. Deniéville, Paul, *La Musique Çame au Japon* ('Etudes Asiatiques', vol. I, p. 199 ff.), 1925.　　　　　　**ABG**

851. Dénes, Bartha, and Kiss, József, *Ötödfélszáz énekek* (Budapest, 1953).

852. Denis, Valentin, *De muziekinstrumenten in de Nederlanden en in Italië naar hun afbeelding in de 15de eeuwsche kunst* (Leuven, 1944).　　　　**AGL**

852a. —— *Het volkslied in Vlaanderen tot omstreeks 1600* (Brussels, 1942).　　**L**

853. Denny, S. R., *Some Zambesi boat songs* ('Nada' XIV, p. 35 ff.), 1936/'37.　**M**

854. Dennys, N., *Short notes on Chinese instruments of music* ('J. of the R. Asiatic Soc., North-China branch' VIII, p. 93 ff.).　　　　　　　　　　**CKL⁵**

855. Densmore, Frances, *The Music of the Philippinos* ('Amer. Anthrop.' VIII No. 4, p. 611 ff.), 1906.　　　**GL²**

856. —— *Scale formation in primitive music* (ibid. N.S. XI, p. 1 ff.), 1909.　**GL³**

857. —— *Chippewa Music* ('Bull. of the Bureau of American Ethnology' Nos. 45 and 53), 1910 and 1913. **ACD¹GHIJKL³**

858. —— *The study of Indian music* ('The Musical Quarterly' I, p. 187 ff.), 1915.

859. —— *Preservation of Indian music* ('Exploration and Fieldwork Smithsonian Inst. in 1915', p. 81 ff.), 1916.

860. —— *Study of Indian music* ('The Musical Quarterly' II, p. 108 ff.), 1917.

861. —— *Music in its relation to the religious thought of the Teton Sioux* (in: 'Anthropological essays presented to William Henry Holmes') ('Holmes Anniversary Volume'), p. 67 ff. (1916).

862. —— *Study of Indian music* ('Exploration and Fieldwork Smithsonian Inst. in 1916', p. 108 ff.), 1917.

863. —— *Recent developments in the study of Indian music* ('Proc. 19th Intern. Congress of Americanists, Washington 1915'), 1917.

864. —— *The rhythm of Indian songs* ('Music correspondence Bureau, Theosophical Soc., Amer. Section', June/July Letter, 1917).

865. —— *Teton Sioux Music* ('Bull. of the Bureau of Amer. Ethnology' No. 61), 1918.　　　　**CD¹HIJKL²**

866. —— *The study of Indian music* ('Scientific American' Suppl. 2207), April 20th, 1918.

867. —— *Indian action songs. A collection of descriptive songs of the Chippewa Indians, with directions for pantomimic representation in schools and community ensembles* (Boston, 1921).

868. —— *Recent developments in the study of Indian music* ('Proc. of the 19th Intern.

Congress of Americanists', Washington 1915. (Reprinted in 'Scientific Amer. Supplement', April 20, 1918).

869. —— *The rhythm of Sioux and Chippewa music* ('Art and Archaeology' IX, p. 59 ff.), 1920.　　　　　　**G**

870. —— *Music of the Papago and Pawnee* ('Exploration and Fieldwork Smithsonian Inst. in 1920', pl 102 ff.), 1921.

871. —— *Northern Ute Music* ('Bull. of the Bureau of American Ethnology' No. 75), 1922.　　　　　　**CD¹HIJKL²**

872. —— *Mandan and Hidatsa Music* (ibid. No. 80), 1923.　　　**CD¹HIJKL²**

873. —— *Music in the treatment of the sick by American Indians* ('Hygeia' April, 1923, p. 29 ff.).　　　　**H**

874. —— *Field studies of Indian music* ('Exploration and Fieldwork Smithsonian Inst. in 1923', p. 119 ff.), 1924.

875. —— *Rhythm in the music of the American Indian* ('Annales XX Congress International de Americanistas' Rio de Janeiro, 1924, p. 85 ff.).

876. —— *Field studies of Indian music* ('Exploration and Fieldwork Smithsonian Inst. 1923, p. 119 ff.), 1924.

877. —— *Study of Tule Indian music* ('Exploration and Fieldwork Smithsonian Inst. in 1924', p. 115 ff.), 1925.

879. —— *The music of the American Indians* ('Science' LXII, p. 565 ff.), 1925.　　　　　　　**D¹GHL¹**

880. —— *Music of the Tule Indians of Panama* ('Smithsonian Miscellaneous Collections' vol. 77, No. 11, publ. No. 2864), 1926.　　　　**I**

881. —— *Studies of Indian music among the Menominee of Wisconsin* ('Exploration and Fieldwork Smithsonian Inst. in 1925', p. 119 ff.), 1926.

882. —— *The songs of the Indians* ('The American Mercury', Jan. 1926, p. 65 ff.).　　　　　　　　　　　**K**

883. —— *'Sep', an Indian song-game* ('Music and Youth', May 1926).

884. —— *The American Indians and their Music* (New York, 1926, 2/1936).

885. —— *The Study of Indian Music in the 19th century* ('American Anthropologist' XXIX, p. 77 ff.), 1927.　**GL²**

886. —— *Field studies of Indian music* ('Exploration and Fieldwork Smithsonian Inst. in 1926', p. 247 ff.), 1927. **D¹**

887. —— *Handbook of the collection of musical instruments in the U.S.A. National museum* (Washington, 1927).　**CGIJL²**

888. —— *The study of Indian music in the nineteenth century* ('Amer. Anthropologist' XXIX, p. 77 ff.), 1927.　　**GL²**

889. —— *Musical composition among the American Indians* ('Amer. Speech' II, p. 393 ff.), 1927.　　　　**K**

105

890. —— *The use of music in the treatment of the sick by American Indians* ('The Musical Quarterly' XIII, p. 555 ff.), 1927.

891. —— *How the Indian seeks power through dream music* ('Musical America', Jan. 11th, 1927).

892. —— *Some results of the Study of American Indian Music* ('Journal of the Washington Acad. of Science' XVIII). 1928. **H**

893. —— *Music of the Winnebago Indians* ('Exploration and Fieldwork Smithsonian Inst. in 1927', p. 183 ff.), 1928. **D¹**

894. —— *The melodic formation of Indian songs* ('Journal of the Washington Acad. of Sciences' XVIII, p. 16 ff.), 1928. **H**

895. —— *Some results of the study of Indian music* ('J. of the Washington Acad. of Sciences' XVIII, p. 395 ff.), 1928. **H**

896. —— *Papago Music* ('Bull. of the Bureau of American Ethnology' No. 90), 1929. **ABCD¹HIJKL²**

897. —— *Pawnee Music* (ibid. No. 93), 1929. **ABCD¹HIJKL²**

898. —— *Music of the Winnebago and Menominee Indians of Wisconsin* ('Exploration and Fieldwork Smithsonian Inst. in 1928', p. 189 ff.), 1929. **D¹**

899. —— *What intervals do Indians sing?* ('Amer. Anthropol.' XXXI, p. 271 ff.), 1929. **GJL²**

900. —— *The music of the American Indians at public gatherings* ('The Musical Quarterly' XVII, p. 464 ff.), 1931. **C**

901. —— *Pecularities in the singing of the American Indians* ('Amer. Anthropol.' XXXII, p. 651 ff.), 1930. **GJL²**

902. —— *Music of the Winnebago, Chippewa and Pueblo Indians* ('Explor. and Fieldwork of the Smithsonian Inst. in 1930', Publ. 3111, p. 217 ff.), 1931.

904. —— *Recording Indian music* ('Explor. and Fieldwork Smithsonian Inst. in 1931', p. 183 ff.), 1932. **D¹**

905. —— *The native music of American Samoa* ('Amer. Anthropologist' XXXIV, p. 415 ff. and 694 ff.), 1932. **GL²**

906. —— *Menominee Music* ('Bull. of the Bureau of Amer. Ethnology', No. 102), 1932. **ABCD¹GHIJKL²**

907. —— *Yuman and Yaqui Music* (ibid. No. 110), 1932. **ABD¹HIJKL²**

908. —— *The music of the North American Indians* ('Proc. of the XXV Congress of Americanists, 1932', p. 119 ff.), 1932.

909. —— *A resemblance between Yuman and Pueblo Songs* ('Amer. Anthropologist' XXXIV, p. 694 ff.), 1932. **GL²**

910. —— *Recording Seminole songs in Florida* ('Explor. and Fieldwork Smithsonian Inst. in 1932', p. 93 ff.), 1933. **D¹**

911. —— *The songs of Indian soldiers during the world war* ('The Musical Quarterly' XX, p. 419 ff.), 1934. **CD**

912. —— *A Study of Indian Music in the Gulf States* ('Amer. Anthropologist' XXXVI, p. 386 ff.), 1934. **GL²**

913. —— *On 'expression' in Indian singing* (ibid., p. 487 ff.), 1934. **GL²**

914. —— *'Four Saints' and some American Indian music* ('Musical America' Aug. 12th, 1934).

915. —— *Studying Indian music in the Gulf States* ('Explor. and Fieldwork Smithsonian Inst. in 1933), 1934. **D¹**

916. —— *A study of Cheyenne and Arapaho music* ('The Masterkey' IX, No. 6, p. 187 ff.), Southwest Mus., Los Angeles, 1935. **L²**

917. —— *Cheyenne and Arapaho Music* (Publ. of the S. W. Museum, No. 10), 1936.

918. —— *The Alabama Indians and their music* ('Straight Texas', No. 13, p. 270 ff.), Austin, 1937.

919. —— *Music of Santo Domingo Pueblo, New Mexico* (Publ. of the S. W. Museum, No. 12), 1938.

920. —— *The influence of hymns on the form of Indian songs* ('Amer. Anthropol.' XL, p. 175 ff.), 1938. **GL²**

921. —— *Musical instruments of the Maidu Indians* ('Amer. Anthropol.' XLI, p. 113 ff.), 1939. **GL²**

922. —— *The use of the term 'tetrachord' in musicology* ('Journal of Musicol.' I, p. 16 ff.), 1940.

923. —— *Nootka and Quileute Music* ('Bull. of the Bureau of American Ethnology' No. 124), 1939. **ABCD¹HIJKL²**

924. —— *Native songs of two hybrid ceremonies among the American Indians* ('Amer. Anthropol.' XLIII, p. 77 ff.), 1941. **BGL²**

925. —— *Music of the Indians of British Columbia* ('Anthropol. Papers' No. 27, Bull. No. 136 of the Bureau of American Ethnology' p. 1 ff.), 1943. **ABD¹HIJKL²**

926. —— *Choctaw Music* ('Anthropol. Papers, No. 28, Bull. No. 136 of the Bureau of American Ethnology', p. 101 ff.), 1943. **AD¹HIJKL²**

927. —— *La música de los indios norteamericanos* ('Boletin Latino-Americano de Música' V, p. 363 ff.), 1941. **ABL**

928. —— *The study of Indian music* ('Annual Report, Smithsonian Inst. for 1941', p. 527 ff.), 1942. **D¹JL²**

929. —— *The use of meaningless syllables in Indian songs* ('Amer. Anthropol.' XLV, p. 160 ff.), 1943. **GL²**

930. —— *Traces of foreign influences in the music of the American Indians* ('Amer. Anthropol.' XLVI, p. 106 ff.), 1944. **G**

931. —— *The survival of Omaha songs* ('Amer. Anthropol.' XLVI), 1944). **BG**

932. —— *A search for songs among the Chitimacha Indians of Louisiana* ('Bur. Amer. Ethnol. Bull. No. 133, Anthropol. Papers No. 19, p. 1 ff.), 1944. **ABD¹KL²**

933. —— *The origin of a Siwah song* ('Amer. Anthropol.' XLVII, p. 173 ff.), 1945. **BG**

934. —— *Prelude to the study of Indian music in Minnesota* ('The Minnesota Archeologist' XL, p. 27 ff.), 1945.

935. —— *The importance of recordings of Indian songs* ('Amer. Anthropol.' XLVII p. 4), 1945. **G**

936. —— *The uses of music in the treatment of the sick by American Indians* ('Music and Medicine' p. 25 ff.), New York, 1947.

937. —— *What the Indians knew about musical therapy* ('Musical Courier', March 15th, 1948). **K**

938. —— *The music of the Sioux Indians* ('Program National Folk Festival St. Louis', April, 1948).

939. —— *Folk songs of the American* ('The Masterkey' XXIV, No. 1), Los Angeles, 1950. **GL²**

940. —— *The use of music in the treatment of the sick by American Indians* ('Annual Report of the Smithsonian Inst. for 1952', p. 439 ff.), 1953. **D¹HJL²**

941. —— *Technique in the music of the American Indians* ('Anthropol. Papers' Bull. No. 151, p. 213 ff.), 1953. **AJ**

942. —— *The belief of the Indians in a connection between song and the supernatural* ('Anthropological Papers' Bull. No. 151, p. 219 ff.), 1953.

943. —— *Importance of rhythm in songs for the treatment of the sick by American Indians* ('Scientific Monthly' LXXIX, p. 109 ff.), 1954. **G**

944. —— *The music of the American Indians* ('Southern Folklore Quarterly', Sept. 1954).

945. —— *For the sake of Indian songs* ('The Masterkey' XXIX, No. 1, p. 27 ff.), Los Angeles, 1955. **GL²**

946. —— *Music of the Maidu Indians of Northern California* (in preparation).

947. —— *Seminole music* ('Bull .of the Bureau of American Ethnology', No. 161), 1956. **B**

947a. —— *Music of Acoma, Isleta, Cochiti and Zuñi Pueblos* ('Bur. Amer. Ethnol. Bull.' No. 165), 1957. **BCJL²**

948. —— *Songs of the Chippewa* (notes for the album XXII and the L.P. record L 22 issued by the Library of Congress), Washington, undated. **B**

949. —— *Songs of the Sioux* (notes for the L.P. record L 23, issued by the Library of Congress), Washington, undated. **B**

950. Denys, Pierre, *Discographie du Congo Belge* ('Les Colloques de Wégimont' I, p. 222 ff.), Brussels, 1956. **AC**

951. —— Derwil, G., and Essafi, *Chansons marocaines* ('Revue Méditerranée', June 1932).

952. Desai, Vibhukumar S., *Hazrat Inayat Khan, the Sufi musician of Baroda* ('J. of the Oriental Inst., Baroda' III, p. 28s ff.), 1953/'54. **D¹**

953. —— *Ragatattvavibodha of Srinivasa* (Gaekwad's Oriental series, No. CXXVI, Oriental Institute Baroda, 1956). **A**

954. Desprez, Adrien, *La musique dramatique en Perse* ('Revue et Gazette musicale de Paris' XL, p. 236 ff.), 1873. **C**

955. Desvallons, Gilbert, *Musique et danse du Gabon* ('La Revue Musicale' XXX, p. 215 ff.), Paris. **DGK**

956. Deuber, Arnold, *Musikinstrumente und Musik der Arapai* (in Felix Speiser, 'Im Düster des Brasilianischen Urwaldes'), Stuttgart, 1926.

957. Deubner, Ludwig, *Die viersaitige Leier* ('Mitt. d. Deutschen Archäologischen Inst., Athenische Abt.' LIV, p. 194 ff.), 1929. **GL¹**

958. *Deutsches Jahrbuch für Volkskunde* (Berlin, 1955 – in progress). **A**

959. *Deutsche Volkslieder mit ihren Melodien* (herausg. vom Deutschen Volksliedarchiv). vols. I (1935), II¹ (1937), II² (1939), III¹ (1939), III² (1954). **H**

960. Dev, G., *Essai nouveau sur la musique chez les Chinois* ('Magasin pittoresque' 1885, tome 3 etc.). **CK**

961. Deval, K. B., *Music East and West compared* (Poona, 1908).

962. —— *The Hindu musical scale and the 22 shrutees* (Poona, 1910). **I**

962a. —— *Theory of Indian music as expounded by Somanatha* (Poona, 1916).

963. Devéria, Charlotte, *Essai nouveau sur la musique chez les Chinois* ('Magasin pittoresque' pp. 234 ff., 287 ff., 327 ff., 390 ff.), 1885. **CK**

964. Devi, Ratan, *Thirty Indian songs with texts and translations by A. K. Coomaraswamy* (London, 1913).

965. Dévigne, Roger, *Rapport sur les Phonothèques et leur rôle dans la culture musicale mondiale* ('Orphée I, 4th quarter, p. 30 ff.), 1953. **A**

966. —— *L'Indochine folklorique. Chants et musique du Laos, du Cambodge et de l'Annam* ('Orphée' I, 4th quarter, 1953, p. 11 ff.). **A**

967. —— *Ethnographie sonore. Musiques africaines, mélanésiennes, malaises, islamiques, hindoues* ('Revue de Psychologie des Peuples' XI, p. 425 ff.), 1956. **AB**

968. Deydier, H., *Notes sur un tambour de bronze au Musée de Batavia* ('Bull. Soc. Etudes Indochinoises' 1943). **L³**

969. Dharma, P. C., *Musical Culture in the Ramayana* ('Indian Culture' IV, p. 447 ff.), 1937. **D¹G**

969a. Dieterlen, Germaine, *La morphologie et la symbolique de deux instruments de musique bambara: la guitare du Sema et le tambour royal* (Proc. of the 'Séances de l'Inst. Français d'Anthropol.' L, 3rd fasc., p. 13 ff.), 1947/'49. **M**

970. Dincsér, Oszkar, *Wogulische und ostjakische Melodien* ('A Neprajzi Muzeum Értesitöje' 1938, No. 1).

971. —— *Két Csíki hangszer mozsika és gardon* (i.e. Two musical instruments from the district Csík), Budapest, 1943. **A**

972. —— *Die Probleme der Varianten in der Musikforschung* (Geneva, 1947).

973. *Din folclorul nostru. Culegere de Texte si Melodii* (prefată de M. Beniuc), Bukarest, 1953.

974. Dirr, A., *25 Georgische Volkslieder* ('Anthropos' V), 1910.

975. Dittmer, Kunz, *Musikinstrumente der Völker. Einführung in die Musikinstrumentenkunde der aussereuropaischen Völker* (Hamburg, 1947). **A**

976. —— *Zur Entstehung der Kernspaltflöte* ('Z. f. Ethnol.' LXXV, p. 83 ff.), 1950. **BD¹GHJL¹L²M**

977. Dixon, Roland B., *The musical bow in California* ('Science' N.S. XIII, p. 274 ff.), 1901. **AL¹**

978. Djarwo, S., and M. M. Daroesman, *Krontjongmuziek* ('Contact' IV, p. 152 ff.), 1937. **AB**

979. Djordjevic, Vladimir R., *Skopke gaidardjie i njihovi musički instrumenti* (Skopje, 1926). **A**

980. —— *Nekoji dečji narodni muzički instrumenti* ('Svete Cecilije' XXII), 1928. **A**

981. —— *Mélodies populaires serbes (Serbie du sud)* (Skoplje, 1928). **A**

982. —— *Mélodies populaires serbes* (Beograd, 1931). **A**

983. —— *Collection of 125 serbian folk songs* (Beograd, 1933). **A**

984. —— *55 Serbian folkdance melodies harmonized for small orchestra* (Beograd, 1934). **A**

985. Djoudjeff, Stoyan, *Rythme et Mesure dans la Musique populaire Bulgare* (Paris, 1931). **AHIL**

986. —— *Bulgarska narodna horéografia* (Sofia, 1945).

987. —— *Teoria na Bulgarskata musika.* vol. I. *Ritmika i metrika* (*Bulgarsko durtavno izdatelstvo*), Sofia, 1950.

988. —— *Teoria na Bulgarskata musika*, vol. II. *Melodica* (ibid., 1954).

988a. —— *Ritmul şi mâsura in muzica populară bulgară* (*Rhythm and measure in*

Bulgarian folk music) (with an English summary) ('Revista de Folclor' III No. 2, p. 7 ff.), Bucarest, 1958. **A**

989. —— *Le folklore musical en Bulgarie* ('Revue Intern. des Etudes Balkaniques' IV), Beograd, 1936.

990. —— *Melodies Bulgares de l'Albanie du sud* (Beograd, 1936).

990a. Djurić-Klajn, Stana, *Yugoslawien*. II. *Die Volksmusik.* 3b. *Montenegro* ('Die Musik in Geschichte u. Gegenwart' VII, col. 304), 1958. **ACDEFGH¹KL**

991. Dobronić, Anton, *A study of Jugoslav music* ('The Musical Quarterly' XII, p. 56 ff.), 1926. **C**

992. Dodge, Ernest, and Edwin T. Brewster, *The acoustics of three Maori flutes* ('Journal of the Polynesian Soc.' LXIV, p. 39 ff.), 1945. **BGL²**

993. *Doine, Cîntece, Strigaturi* (Bukarest, 1955).

994. Doke, Clement M., *Games, plays and dances of the ≠ Khomani Bushmen* ('Bantu Studies' X, p. 461 ff.), 1936. **KL²M**

995. —— *The Lambas of Northern Rhodesia* (London, 1931), Chapter XXII, p. 352: *Folklore and music*. **J**

995a. Dolanská, Vera, *Volkslieder aus der Tschechoslowakei* (Prague, 1955).

996. Dominguez, Francisco, *Músico Yaqui* ('Mexican Folkways'), Mexico, July 1937.

997. Domòkos Pál, Péter, and Benjamin Rajeczky, *Csángó népzene* vol. I (coll. of folksongs of Hungarians, who have been immigrated from the Moldau to Hungary) (Budapest, 1956).

998. Donington, Robert, *Instruments* ('Grove's Dictionary' 5th ed., vol. IV, p. 487 ff.), 1954. **ACFH¹K**

999. Donostia, Father José Antonio de, *Basken* ('Die Musik in Geschichte und Gegenwart' I, col. 1366 ff.), 1949. **ACDEFGH¹KL**

1000. —— *Instrumentos musicales del pueblo vasco* ('Anuario Musical' VII, p. 3 ff.), Barcelona, 1952. **CL**

1001. —— *Les instruments des danses populaires espagnoles* ('Journal of the Intern. Folk Music Council' VI, p. 26 ff.), 1954. **ACJKL**

1002. —— *La musica popular vasca* (Bilbao, 1918).

1003. —— and J. Tomás, *Instrumentos de música popular española. Terminología general. Ensayo de clusificación* ('Anuario Musical' II, p. 105 ff.), 1947. **CL**

1004. —— *Notas acerca de las canciones de trabajo en el pais vasco* ('Anuario musical' III, p. 163 ff.), 1948. **CL**

1005. —— *Tipología musical y literaria de la canción de cuna en España* (ibid. III, p. 3 ff.), 1948. **CL**

1005a. —— *El modo de mi en la canción popular española* ('Anuario musical' I), 1946. **CL**

1005b. —— *Historia de las danzas de Guipúzcoa con sus melodías antiguas* (ibid. IX), 1954. **CL**

1006. **Dounias, Minos E.**, *Griechenland. C. Volksmusik und neuere Musik* ('Die Musik in Geschichte und Gegenwart' V, col. 882 ff.), 1956. **ACDEFGH¹KL**

1007. **Dräger, Hans Heinz**, *Prinzip einer Systematik der Musikinstrumente* (Kassel, 1948). **ACI**

1008. —— *Das Instrument als Träger und Ausdruck des musikalischen Bewusstseins* ('Kongress-Bericht Bamberg 1953' p. 67 ff.), 1954. **C**

1009. —— *Hackbrett* ('Die Musik in Geschichte und Gegenwart' V, col. 1210 ff.), 1956. **ACDEFGH¹KL**

*1009a. —— *Musikinstrumentenkunde* ('Die Musik in Geschichte u. Gegenwart' VI, col. 1288 ff.), 1957. **ABCDEFGH¹KL**

1010. **Drăgoi, Sabin**, *Musical folklore research in Rumania and Béla Bartók's contribution to it* ('Studia Memoriae Bélae Bartók Sacra', p. 9 ff.), Budapest, 1956. **AC**

1010a. —— *20 colinde din comuna Zam-Hunedoara* ('Revista de Folclor' II, No. 3, p. 55 ff.), Bucarest, 1957. **A**

1011. **Draws-Tychsen, Hellmut**, *Siamsänge* (Leyden, 1955).

1012. **Driver, Harold E.**, *The Spatial and Temporal Distribution of the Musical Rasp in the New World* ('Anthropos' LVIII, p. 578 ff.), 1953. **BD¹GHJKL¹L²M**

1013. **Drost, Dietrich**, *Tönerne Trommeln in Afrika* ('Jahrbuch des Museums f. Völkerkunde, Leipzig' XIV, p. 31 ff.), 1955. **GKL²**

1014. **Drucker, Philip**, *Indians of the Northwest Coast* (New York/Toronto/London, 1955.) **AB**

1015. **Dubois, Henri**, *Le répertoire africain* (Rome, St. Claver Soc., 1932).

1016. **Dubois, H. M.**, *Monographie des Betsileo (Madagascar)* ('Travaux et mémoires de l'Institut d'Ethnologie' XXXIV, p. 1156 ff.: *Instruments de musique*, etc. **ABJ**

1016a. **Duchemin, G. J.**, *Autour d'un arc musical du Saloum oriental* ('Proc. of the 1st. Intern. Conf. of the Africanists of the West' vol. II, p. 248 ff.), 1951. **M**

1017. **Duchenet, Edouard**, *Le chant dans le folklore Somali* ('Revue de folklore Français' IX, p. 72 ff.), 1939.

1018. **Duchesne, J.** and **Marcelle Guillemin**, *La harpe en Asie occidentale ancienne* ('Revue d'Assyriologie' XXXIV), 1937. **GHKL¹**

1019. **Duesel, Jakob**, *Der Jodel und das Jodellied in der Schweiz* ('Heimatleben' XXVIII, No. 2), 1955.

1020. **Dufays, Felix**, *Lied und Gesang bei Brautwerbung und Hochzeit in Mulera-Ruanda* ('Anthropos' IV, p. 847 ff.), 1909. **D¹GKL¹L²M**

1021. **Dufourcq, Norbert**, *La musique des origines à nos jours* (Paris, ed. Larousse, 1946, 2/1957). **ACDEFHJK**

1022. **Duhamel, M.**, *Les 15 modes de la musique bretonne* ('Annales de Bretagne' XXVI No. 4), 1911. **I**

1023. **Dumont, Louis**, *Une sous-caste de l'Inde du Sud. Organisation sociale et religion des Pramalai Kallar* (The Hague, 1957), p. 33, 47, 49, 217 ff., 239, 246 ff., 349, 354, 381, 386–7, 394. **B**

1023a. **Dumoutier, G.**, *Les chants et les traditions populaires des Annamites* (Paris, 1890). **C**

1024. **Duncan, T.**, *South African songs and Negro Spirituals* ('Music Journal' VIII), May/June 1950.

1025. **Duran, Sixto M.**, *La musique aborigène et populaire de l'Equateur* ('Art populaire' II, p. 117 ff.), Paris, 1931. **A**

1026. **Duriyanga, Phra Chen**, *A Talk on the Technic of Siamese Music in relation to Western Music* ('Newsletter of the African Music Soc.' I, No. 4, p. 2 ff.), 1951. **AC**

1027. —— *Thai Music* (3rd ed., Bangkok, 1954) = Siamese music in theory and practice as compared with the West and a description of the piphat band (Bangkok, undated). **AGL**

1028. **Dutt, Benoy Krishna**, *Music, a vital democratic art* ('Entally Cultural Conference, 8th session, Jan. 1955'), Calcutta, 1955.

1029. **Duyse, Florimond van**, *De melodie van het Nederlandsche volkslied en haar rhythmische vormen* (The Hague, 1902). **DHIL**

*1030. —— *Het oude Nederlandsche lied* (Den Haag, 1903–'05). **ACDFH**

1031. **Dworakowska, Maria**, *The origin of bell and drum* ('Prace Ethnologizne' 1938).

1032. **Dybeck, Richard**, *Svenska folkmelodier* (Stockholm, 1853–'56). **K**

1033. **Dyer Ball, J.**, and **E. Chalmers Werner**, *Things Chinese, or notes connected with China* (Shanghai, 1925), pp. 26, 28, 68, 69, 114, 404, 406, 408–413, 658, 659, 674, 715.

1034. **Dygacz, Adolf**, *Piesni ludowe slaska opolskigo* (Krakau, 1954).

1035. **Dzambul**, *Mein Leben* ('Intern. Litteratur' VII, No. 12, p. 77 ff.), Moscow, 1939.

1036. **Eastlake, F. W.**, *The "sho" or Chinese*

reed organ ('China Review' XI, p. 33
ff.), Hongkong, 1882/'83. **G**

1037. Ebding, F., and J. Ittmann, *Religiöse
Gesänge aus dem nördlichen Waldland
von Kamerun* ('Afrika und Uebersee'
XXXIX, p. 169 ff., XL, p. 39 ff.), Nov.
and Dec. 1955. **GKM**

1038. Eberhard, W., *Chinas Geschichte* (Bern,
1948) (Transl. of "History of China"),
pp. 123, 194, 196, 294.

1038a. Eberhardt, Ch. C., *Sound signalling by
Indians of tropical South America* (in:
Smithsonian Miscellaneous Collection'
LII, vol. 2, No. 1823), Washington,
1928. **L²**

1039. Eberlein, P. J., *Die Trommelsprache
auf der Gazelle-Halbinsel (Neu-Pom-
mern)* ('Anthropos' V, p. 635 ff.), 1910.
D¹GKL¹L²M

1040. Ebner, Carlos Borromeu, *Beiträge zur
Musikgeschichte am Amazonas* ('Anais
missionarios do preciosissimo sangue'),
Belem, 1950.

1041. Eboué, Félix, *The Banda, their music
and language* ('Revue du Monde Noir'
April 1932.

1041a. —— *La clef musicale des langages
tambourinés et sifflés* ('Bull. de la Société des Recherches Congolaises'
XXVIII, p. 89 ff.), Brazzaville, 1941.

1042. Echegaray, Carlos González, *La música
indígena en la Guinea Española* ('Archivos del Instituto de Estudios Africanos' No. 38), 1957. **B**

1043. Eckardt, Andreas, *Koreanische Musik*
('Mitteil. d. deutsche Ges. f. Natur- u.
Völkerk. Ost-asiens' XXIV, B), Tokyo,
1930. **AGI**

1044. Eckardt, Hans, *Die Ei und Saezuri,
verschollene melismatische Gesangsfor-
men im japanischen Tanz* ('Kongressber. D.G.M., Lüneburg 1950', p. 170
ff.), 1951. **ACDEFKL**

1045. —— *Ryówó* ('Sinologica' III No. 2, p.
110 ff.), 1952. **AD¹GKL¹**

1046. —— *Asiatische Musik* ('Die Musik
in Geschichte und Gegenwart' I, col.
750 ff.), 1949/'51. **ACDEFGH¹KL**

*1047. —— *Chinesische Musik* ('Die Musik in
Geschichte und Gegenwart' II, col. 1205
ff.), 1952. **ACDEFGH¹KL**

1048. —— *Somakusa* ('Sinologica' III No. 3,
p. 174 ff.), 1953. **AD¹GKL¹**

1049. —— *Die geistige Umwelt des Tachibana
Narisue* ('Nachrichten der ost-asiati-
schen Ges.' No. 34), Hamburg, 1953. **A**

1050. —— *Das Kokonchomonshū des Tachibana Narisue als musikgeschichtliche
Quelle* (Wiesbaden, 1956), **CL**

*1050a. —— *Japanische Musik* ('Die Musik
in Geschichte u. Gegenwart' VI, col.
1720 ff.), 1958. **ACDEFGH¹KL**

1051. Ecker, L. E., *Arabischer, provenzalischer

und deutscher Minnesang: ein motiv-
geschichtliche Untersuchung* (Bern/Leip-
zig, 1934).

1052. Edelman, Albert, *Toggenburger Lieder*
(Basel, 1/1945, 2/1955).

1052a. Edge-Partington, J., *A new Zealand
flageolet* ('Man' III), 1903. **BD¹GKL²M**

1053. Edwards, Arthur C., *The art of melody*
(New York, 1956). **AE**

1053a. Edwards, E. D., *Principles of whistling
- Hsiao chih - anonymous* ('Bull. of
the School of Oriental and African
Studies' XX, p. 217 ff.), London, 1957.
BM

1054. Edwards, L. F., *Notes on the oriental
scale system* ('The Sackbut' II, No. 11,
p. 14 ff.), June 1922.

1055. Edwards, S. Hylton, *Music in Africa*
('J. of the R. Soc. of Arts' CIII, p. 704
ff.), 19 Aug. 1955.

1056. Eggen, Erik, *Skalastudier* (Oslo, 1923).

1056a. Egorova, V., *Muzikalnaia kultura
Avtonomnii Respublik* (= The musical
culture of the Autonomous Republics),
Moscow, 1957.

1057. Ehrenreich, Paul, *Der Flötentanz der
Moki* ('Z. f. Ethnol.' XXXII, p. 494 ff.),
1900. **BD¹GHKL¹L²M**

1058. Eichenauer, *Musik und Rasse* (Munich,
1932). **I**

1059. Elbert, Johannes, *Die Sunda-Expedi-
tion des Ver. f. Geogr. u. Stat. zu Frank-
furt a/M. Festschrift*, vol. II, p. 70 ff.
*Die Insel Sumbawa. I. Das Sultanat
Bima. Religion und Gebräuche der
Donggos* (Frankfurt a/M. 1912). **AB**

1060. Elbert, Samuel H., *Chants and love
songs of the Marquesas Islands, French
Oceania* ('The J. of the Polynesian Soc.'
L, p. 53 ff.), Wellington N.Z., 1941.
ABGL²

1061. Elia, Piero, *La canzone napolitana*
(Rome, 1952).

1062. Eliade, Mircea, *Le chamanisme et les
techniques archaïques de l'extase* (Paris,
1951).

1063. Elkin, A. P., *Arnhemland Music*
('Oceania' XXIV, p. 81 ff., XXV, p. 74
ff., XXVI, p. 59 ff., p. 127 ff., p. 214 ff.,
252ff., resp. Dec. 1953, Dec. 1954,
Sept. 1955, Dec. 1955, March 1956,
June 1956). **ABD¹GL²**

1063a. —— *Australian and New Guinea
musical records* ('Oceania' XXVII,
No. 4, p. 313 ff.), Sydney, June 1957. **B**

1063b. —— and Trevor A. Jones, *Arnhem-
land Music* (Oceania Monograph No. 9),
Sydney, 1957. (being a combination of
Nos. 1063 and 2106).

1063c. —— *The Australian aboriginals* (Syd-
ney/London/Melbourne/Wellington,
1938, 3/1956), Chapter X. *Music and
dancing*. **D¹**

1064. Elkin, Clarence, *Maori Melodies* (Sydney, 1923).
1065. Elling, Catharinus, *Vore Folkemelodier* ('Videnskabsselskabets Skrifter' II, Hist.-fil. Klasse, Oslo, 1909, p. 5 ff.).
1066. —— *Vore Kjaempeviser fra musikalsk synspunkt* (ibid. 1913, p. 4 ff.).
1067. —— *Norsk Folkemusik* (Oslo, 1922).
1068. —— *Vore Slaatter* ('Videnskabsselskabets Skrifter', Oslo, 1915, p. 4 ff.).
1069. —— *Vore religiøse folketoner* (Oslo, 1927).
1070. Ellis, Alexander J., *On the Conditions of a Perfect Musical Scale on Instruments with Fixed Tones* (Publ. of the Royal Society, 1864). D¹
1071. —— *On the Physical Conditions and Relations of Musical Chords* (Publ. of id. 1864). D¹
1072. —— *On the Temperament of Instruments with Fixed Tones* (Publ. of id., 1864). D¹
1073. —— *On Musical Duodenes (Theory of Constructing Instruments with Fixed Tones in just or practically just Intonation)* (Publ. of id., 1874). AD¹
1074. —— Translation of and Commentary on Helmholtz, 'Lehre von den Tonempfindungen' (1875).
1075. —— Translation of and commentary on Preyer, 'Ueber die Grenzen der Tonwahrnehmung' (1876/'77).
1076. —— *On the Measurement and Settlement of Musical Pitch* (Publ. of the Musical Association, 1877).
1077. —— *The Basis of Music* (Publ. of id., 1877).
1078. —— *Pronunciation for Singers* (Publ. of id., 1877).
1079. —— *Speech in Song* (Publ. of id., 1878). C
1080. —— *The History of Musical Pitch* (1880/'81). AI
1081. —— *Tonometrical Observations on some existing non-harmonic Scales* ('Proc. of the R. Soc.', 1884). D¹HIL¹
1082. —— *On the Musical Scales of Various Nations* ('Journal of the Soc. of Arts', 1885) (Cf. No. 1924). BCI
1083. Elwin, Verrier, *Folksong of the Maikal hills* (1944).
1084. —— *Folksongs of Chhattisgarh* (1946).
1085. —— *Musical instruments of tribal India* ('Ill. Weekly of India' 27 Nov. 1955, p. 26 ff. and 4 Dec. 1955, p. 48 ff.)
1086. —— *The Muria and their Ghotul* (Oxford Univ. Press, 1947), Chapter XX, p. 521: *Musical instruments.* J
1087. Emerson, Joseph, S., *Music of the Hawaiians. Singing, musical instruments* ('Mid-Pacific Magazine' XII, p. 579 ff., XIII, p. 249 ff.), 1916 and '17.
1088. Emerson, Nathaniel H., *Unwritten Literature of Hawaii. The sacred songs of the Hula* ('Bull. of the Bureau of American Ethnology' No. 38), Washington, 1909.
1089. Emmanuel, Maurice, *Grèce (Art Gréco-Romain)* (1911) (in Lavignac, 'Hist. de la Musique' I, p. 377 ff.), 1922. ACDEFHJK
1090. Emrich, Duncan, *Folk Music of the United States and Latin America (combined catalogue of phonograph records)* (The Library of Congress, Washington D.C., 1948). A
1091. Emsheimer, Ernst, *Drei Tanzgesänge der Akamba* ('Ethnos' 1937). L²M
*1092. —— *Ueber das Vorkommen und die Anwendungsart der Maultrommel in Sibirien und Zentralasien* ('Ethnos' 1941, p. 109 ff.). AL²M
1093. —— *The Music of the Mongols. Music of-Eastern Mongolia* ('Reports from the scientific expedition to the NW provinces of China under the leadership of Dr. Sven Hedin', publ. 21, p. 69 ff.), Stockholm, 1943. ACIK
*1094. —— *Musikethnographische Bibliographie der nichtslavische Völker in Russland* ('Acta musicologica' XV, p. 34 ff.), 1943. ACEKLL¹
1095. —— *Zur Ideologie der lappischen Zaubertrommel* ('Ethnos' 1944, p. 141 ff.). AL²M
1096. —— *Schamanentrommel und Trommelbaum* (ibid. 1946, p. 166 ff.). AL²M
1097. —— *Eine sibirische Parallele zur lappischen Zaubertrommel?* (ibid. 1948, p. 17 ff.). AGL²M
1098. —— *A Lapp musical instrument* (ibid. 1947, p. 86 ff.). AGL²M
1099. —— *Lappischer Kultgesang* ('Kongressbericht Deutsche Ges. f. Musikforschung, Lüneburg, 1950', p. 153 ff.) Kassel/Basel, 1951. ACDEFKL
1100. —— *Schallaufnahmen georgischer Mehrstimmigkeit* (ibid. p. 172 ff.), Kassel/Basel, 1951. ACDEFKL
1101. —— *Singing contests in Central Asia* ('J. of the Intern. Folk Music Council' VIII, p. 26 ff.), 1956. ACJKL
1102. Ende, A. von, *Die Musik der amerikanischen Neger* ('Die Musik' V, fasc. 24), 1905/'06. CDFKL
1103. —— *Die Musik der nordamerikanischen Indianen* ('Die Musik' II, fasc. 10), 1903. CDFKL
*1104. Endo, Hirosi, *Bibliography of Oriental and Primitive Music* (Tokyo, The Nanki Music Library, 1929). K
1105. Engel, Carl, *The music of the most ancient nations, particularly of the Hebrews, with special reference to recent discoveries in Western Asia and in Egypt* (London, 1864). JLL²

1106. —— *Musical myths and facts* (London, 1876).

1107. —— *Musical instruments* (London, 1875). **CJ**

1108. —— *Researches into the early history of the violin family* (London, 1883). **CJ**

1109. —— *Musical instruments* (Handbook Victoria & Albert Museum), London, 1908. **J**

1110. Engel, Hans, *Ueber indische Musik* ('Arch. f. Musikforschung' IV, p. 202 ff.), 1939. **CDH¹KL**

1111. *English Folk Dance and Song Society, Journal of the*, (London, 1932 – in progress). **A**

1112. Enright, D. J., *Arab music* ('Music & Letters' XXXIII, p. 27 ff.), 1952. **KL¹**

1112a. Erdélyi, János, c.s., *Magyar Népköltési Gyüjteményi* (Budapest, 1846–1941).

1113. Erdmann, Hans, *Zur musikalischen Praxis des mechlenburgischen Volkstanzes* ('Deutsches Jahrbuch für Volkskunde' II, p. 212 ff.), Berlin, 1956. **A**

1114. Erk, Ludwig, and Father M. Böhme, *Deutscher Liederhort* (Leipzig, 1893–'94), 3 vols. **D¹H**

1115. Erkmann, R., *Der Einfluss der arabisch-spanischen Kultur auf die Entwicklung des Minnesangs* ('Deutsche Vierteljahrschrift f. Literatur' 1931, p. 240 ff.). **D¹KL¹**

1116. Erlanger, Rodolphe d', *La musique arabe* ('Revue musicale' XIII, No. 128), July/Aug. 1932. **CD¹GKL**

1117. —— *La musique arabe* (5 vols.), Paris, 1930/'49.
A (vol. 1 only) **CD** (1–4 only), **GIKL**

1118. —— *L'Archéologie musicale. Un vaste champ d'investigations pour les musiciens de la jeune génération* ('Revue Musicale' XI, part 2, p. 45 ff.), 1930. **CDGKL**

1119. —— *Mélodies tunésiennes (Hispano-arabes, arabo-berbères, juive, nègre)* (Paris, 1937). **K**

1120. Erzakovitsch, B., *Narodnya pesni Kazakhstana* (i.e. Folksongs of Kazakhstan), ...

1121. —— *Istoritsheskiye sviazi russkoi i kazakhkoi muzyki* (i.e. Historical connections between Russian and Kazakh music), ...

1122. Espinet, Charles S., and Harry Pitts, *Land of the Calypso: the origin and development of Trinidad's folk song* (Port of Spain, Guardian Commercial Printery, 1944).

1122a. Esser, J., *Musique de l'Afrique noire* ('Revue Congolaise Illustrée' XXVI, No. 3, p. 17 ff.), 1954. **M**

1123. Estella, Pe. H. Olazaran de, *Txistu. Tratado de flauta Vasca* (Ediciones

musicales ordorico, Bilbao, 2/1951).

1124. Estreicher, Zygmunt, *The Music of the Caribou-Eskimos* ('Encl. Arctica' II: Anthropology), New York, 1931.

1125. —— *Zur Polyrhythmik in der Musik der Eskimos* ('Schw. Musikzeitung' LXXXVII, p. 411 ff.), 1947. **A**

1126. —— *La musique des Esquimaux-Caribous* ('Bull. de la Soc. neuchâteloise de Géographie' LIV, p. 1 ff.), 1948. **AG**

1127. —— *Teoria dwytonowych melodii* ('Kwartalnik Muzycky' VI, p. 208 ff.), Warschau, 1948. **A**

1128. —— *La polyphonie chez les Esquimaux* ('J. de Soc. des Américanistes' XXXVII, p. 259 ff.), 1948. **AGL²**

1129. —— *Die Musik der Eskimos* ('Anthropos' XLV, p. 659 ff.), 1950.
ABD¹GHIJKLL¹L²M

1130. —— *Eskimo-Musik* ('Die Musik in Geschichte und Gegenwart' III, col. 1526 ff.), 1954. **ACDEFGH¹KL**

1131. —— *Chants et rhythmes de la danse d'hommes Bororo* ('Bull. de la Soc. Neuchâteloise de Géographie' LI, fasc. 5, p. 57 ff.), 1954/'55. **ABM**

1132. —— *Cinq chants des Esquimaux Ahearmiut* (in Geert van den Steenhoven, 'Research-report on Caribou Eskimo law'), The Hague, Aug. 1956. **AB**

1133. —— *Une technique de transcription de la musique exotique (expériences pratiques)* ('Rapport des Bibliothèques et Musées de la Ville de Neuchâtel, 1956'), Neuchâtel, 1957. **AL**

*1134. *Ethnomusicology*, Newsletters No. 1 (Dec. 1953), 2 (Aug. 1954), 3 (Dec. 1954) 4 (Apr. 1955), 5 (Sept. 1955), 6 (Jan. 1956), 7 (April 1956), 8 (Sept. 1956), 9 (Jan. 1957), 10 (May 1957), 11 (Sept. 1957), 12 (Jan. 1958) (= *Ethnomusicology* II No. 1), (in progress) issued bij Alan P. Merriam c.s., c/o Dept. of Anthropology, Northwestern Univ., Evanston (Ill.), U.S.A. **AL**

1135. Evans, Ivor H. N., *A brass drum from Borneo* ('Man' XVIII), 1918.
BD¹GKL²M

1136. —— *Among primitive peoples in Borneo* (London, 1922), Chapter XIV, p. 130 ff., *Musical instruments, music and dancing*. **BJ**

1137. —— *The Negritos of Malaya* (Cambridge Univ. Press, 1937), Chapter XII, p. 114 ff.: *Musical instruments, singing, dancing*. **J**

1138. Evrard, W., *Sur les xylophones africains* ('Brousse' 1940), II). **M**

1139. Exner, F., and R. Pöch, *Phonographische Aufnahmen in Indien und Neu-guinea* (1905).

1140. Ezgi, Suphi, *Amêlî ve Nazarî Türk Musikisi* (i.e. Practice and Theory of

Turkish Music), vols. I and II (1953), III (undated), IV (1940), V (1953).

1141. Faber, E., *The Chinese theory of music* ('China Review' 1873).

1142. Faber, G. H. von, *Van krontjonglied tot 'lagoe modern'* ('Cultureel Nieuws' 1951, No. 9, p. 23 ff.). **AB**

1143. Fabó, Bertalan, *A magyar népdal zenei fejlödése* (i.e. The development of Hungarian folksong), Budapest, 1908.

1144. Faddegon, Barend, *Studies on the Samaveda*, Part I. ('Verhand. Kon. Akad. v. Wetensch.' Afd. Letterk. N.S. LVII, No. 1), Amsterdam 1951. AD¹EGHKL¹

1145. Fagg, Bernard E. B., *The cave paintings and rock gongs of Birnin Kudu* ('Proc. 3rd Pan-African Congress of Prehistory' 1955), in the press.

1146. —— *The discovery of multiple rock gongs in Nigeria* ('Man' LVI, p. 17 ff., No. 23), Febr. 1956. BD¹GKL¹L²M repr. in 'African Music' I No. 3, p. 5 ff.), 1956. **ACJL**

1147. —— *Rock gongs and rock slides* ('Man' LVII, p. 30 ff., No. 32, and p. 112, No. 142), 1957. BD¹GKL¹L²M

1148. Fagg, William, *A Yoruba xylophone of musical type* ('Man' L, p. 145, No. 234), 1950. BD¹GKL¹L²M

1148a. —— *A drum probably from the Ivory Coast* ('British Museum Quarterly' XV, p. 109 ff.), 1941/'50. **IM**

1149. Falconi, Gerardo, *Geografía y paisaje del ritmo* ('Anales Universidad Central del Ecuador' LXXXII, No. 337, p. 195 ff.), 1954.

1150. Falla, Manuel de, *El canto jondo: canto primitivo andaluz* (Granada, 1922); (French translation in 'Revue musicale' IV, p. 256 ff.), 1923. CDFGHKL

1151. Falls, J. C. E., *Beduinenlieder der libyschen Wüste* (Cairo, 1908).

1151a. Faly, I., *Musique indigène, musique religieuse* ('Revue du Clergé Africain' IV, No. 1, p. 34 ff.), 1949.

1152. Fara, Giulio, *Su uno strumento musicale sardo* (Turino, 1913).

1153. —— *Giocattoli di musica rudimentale in Sardegna* (Cagliari, 1916).

*1154. —— *L'anima della Sardegna. La musica tradizionale* (Udine, 1940).

1155. Faragó, József, and János Jagamas, *Moldvai csángó népdalok és népballadék* (Bukarest, 1954).

1156. Farmer, Henry George, *The music and musical instruments of the Arab, by F. Salvador-Daniel* (London, 1915). **I**

1157. —— *The Arab Influence on Music in the Western Sudan, including References to Modern Jazz* ('Musical Standard' N.S. XXIV, p. 158 ff.), 1924. D¹I

1158. —— *Clues for the Arabian Influence on European Musical Theory* ('The Journal of the R. Asiatic Soc. of Gr. Britain and Ireland' 1925). D¹GIKL¹

1159. —— *Byzantine Musical Instruments in the Ninth Century* ('ibid. 1925, p. 299 ff.). CD¹GIKL¹

1160. —— *The Arabian influence on musical theory* (London, 1925). **GI**

*1161. —— *The Arabic musical MSS. in the Bodleian Library* (London, 1925). **K**

1162. —— *Facts concerning the Arabian musical influence* ('Musical Standard' XXVI, p. 215 ff.; XXVII, p. 9 ff., 29 ff., 43 ff., 61 ff., 75 ff., 98 ff., 113 ff., 132 ff., 161 ff., 175, and 196 ff.), 1925 and '26. D¹

1163. —— *The influence of music: from Arabic sources*. Lecture delivered before the Musical Association (London, 1926). **I**

1164. —— *The Canon and Eschaquiel of the Arabs* ('Journal of the Royal Asiatic Soc.' 1926, p. 239 ff.). AD¹GIKL¹

1165. —— *The old Persian musical modes* ('J. of the R. Asiatic Soc.' 1926, p. 93 ff.). D¹GIKL¹

1166. —— *Ibn Kurdadhbih on Musical Instruments* ('Journal of the Royal Asiatic Soc.' 1928, p. 509 ff.). D¹GIKL¹

1167. —— *A North African folk instrument (guenvri)* ('J. of the R. Asiatic Soc.', Jan. 1928). D¹GIKL¹

*1168. —— *A History of Arabian Music* (London, 1929). **ABCGIKL**

1169. —— *The evolution of the tambur or pandore* ('Transactions of the Glasgow Univ. Oriental Soc.' V), 1930.

1170. —— *Greek Theorists of Music in Arabic Translation* ('Isis' XIV, p. 325 ff.), 1930. GL¹

1171. —— *Historical facts for the Arabian musical influence* (London, 1930). GIL

1172. —— *Studies in Oriental musical Instruments* (1st series), London, 1931, containing:
A. *The Medieval Psaltery in the Orient*
B. *The Origin of the Eschaquiel*
C. *Two Eastern Organs*
D. *A North African Folk Instrumen*
E. *Ninth Century Musical Instrumetnts*
F. *A Note on the Mizmār and Nāy*
G. *Meccan Musical Instruments*
H. *The Origin of the Arabian Lute and Rebec* **ACGIJ**

1173. —— *The Organ of the Ancients: from Eastern sources (Hebrew, Syriac and Arabic)* (London, 1931). **CI**

1174. —— *Music* (in Arnold and Guillaume, 'The Legacy of Islam'), London, 1931.

1175. —— *The influence of Al-Farabi's 'Ihsā 'al-'ulum' (De Scientiis) on the writers on music in Western Europe* ('Journal of the R. Asiatic Soc.' 1931, p. 349 ff.; ibid. 1932, p. 99 ff. and 379 ff.). D¹GIKL¹

1176. —— The 'Ihsa 'al- 'ulum' ('Journal of the R. Asiatic Soc.' 1933, p. 906 ff.). D¹GIKL¹
1177. —— Maimonides on listening to music (ibid. 1933, p. 867 ff.). D¹GIKL¹
1178. —— A further Arabic-Latin writing on Music ('Journal of the Royal Asiatic Soc.' 1933, p. 307 ff.). D¹GIKL¹
1179. —— Al-Farabi's Arabic-Latin Writings on Music (Glasgow, 1934). A
1180. —— Ancient Egyptian instruments of music ('Transactions Glasgow Univ. Oriental Soc.' VI), 1934.
1181. —— Sa'adyah Gaon on the Influence of Music (Glasgow, 1934, London 1943). CHK
1182. —— Turkish Instruments of Music in the Seventeenth Century, as described in the Siyahat Nama of Ewliya Chelebi (Glasgow, 1937). CGJ
1183. —— Outline History of Music (in Arthur Upham Pope, 'Survey of Persian Art'), London, 1938.
1184. —— Ancient Arabian musical instruments (translation of the 'Kitab al-malahi' by James Robson; Notes on the instruments by Farmer), Glasgow, 1938. ACG
1185. —— Studies in Oriental musical instruments (2nd series), Glasgow, 1939, containing:
    A. Reciprocal Influences in Music 'Twixt the Far and Middle East
    B. A Maghribi Work on Musical Instruments
    C. An Old Moorish Lute Tutor AG
    D. The Lute Scale of Avicenna
    E. Was the Arabian and Persian Lute fretted?
    F. The Instruments of Music on the Tāq-i-Bustān Bas Reliefs
    G. The Structure of the Arabian and Persian Lute in the Middle Ages ABC
1186. —— The music of the Sumerians ('J. of the R. Asiatic Soc.' 1939). ACD¹GIKL¹
1187. —— Early References to Music in the Western Sudan ('Journal of the Royal Asiatic Soc.' 1939, p. 569 ff.). D¹GIKL¹
1188. —— Turkish Instruments of Music in the Fifteenth Century ('Journal of the Royal Asiatic Soc.' 1940, p. 195 ff.). D¹GIKL¹
*1189. —— The Sources of Arabian Music, an Annotated Bibliography (Bearsden, 1940). GHIK
1190. —— The Jewish Debt to Arabic Writers on Music ('Islamic Culture' XV, p. 59 ff.), 1941. G
1191. —— Music: The Priceless Jewel (from the 'Kitab al-iqd al-farid' of Ibn 'Abd Rabbihi (d. 940)), Bearsden, 1942. A

1192. —— Wechselwirkungen mittel- und ost-asiatischer Musik ('Mélanges offerts à Zoltan Kodaly' p. 32 ff.), 1943. ACK
1193. —— The Music of the Arabian Nights ('Journal of the R. Asiatic Soc.' 1944, p. 172 ff.; ibid. 1945, p. 39 ff.). D¹GIKL¹
1194. —— The Minstrelsy of the Arabian Nights (Bearsden, 1945). IK
1195. —— 'Ghosts'; an Excursus on Arabic Musical Bibliographies ('Isis' XXXVI, p. 123 ff.), 1945/'46. GL¹
1197. —— Oriental Studies, mainly musical (London, 1953):
    A. What is Arabian Music?
    B. Arabian Musical Instruments on a Thirteenth Century Bronze Bowl
    C. Turkish Musical Instruments in the Fifteenth Century
    D. The Importance of Ethnological Studies
    E. Early References to Music in the Western Sudan
    F. The Musical Instruments of the Sumerians and Assyrians
    G. An early Greek Pandore ACIL
*1198. —— Arabian Music ('Grove's Dictionary' 5th ed., vol. I, p. 179 ff.), 1954. ACFH¹K
*1199. —— Berber Music (ibid. vol. I, p. 632 ff.), 1954. ACFH¹K
*1200. —— Egyptian Music (ibid. vol. II, p. 891 ff.), 1954. ACFH¹K
*1201. —— Iraquian and Mesopotamian Music (ibid. vol. IV, p. 529 ff.), 1954. ACFH¹K
*1202. —— Maghribi Music (ibid. vol. V, p. 504 ff.), 1954. ACFH¹K
*1203. —— Moorish Music (ibid. vol. V, p. 868 ff.), 1954. ACFH¹K
*1204. —— Persian Music (ibid. vol. VI, p. 676 ff.), 1954. ACFH¹K
*1205. —— Syrian Music (ibid. vol. VIII, p. 251 ff.), 1954. ACFH¹K
*1205a. —— Turkestani music (ibid., vol. VIII, p. 610 ff.), 1954. ACFH¹K
*1206. —— The Music of Ancient Mesopotamia ('The New Oxford History of Music', 3rd ed., vol. I, p. 228 ff.), 1957. ABCD¹FGH¹JK
*1207. —— The Music of Ancient Egypt (ibid., vol. I, p. 255 ff.), 1957. ABCD¹FGH¹JK
*1208. —— The Music of Islam (ibid., vol. I, p. 421 ff.), 1957. ABCD¹FGH¹JK
1209. —— Pundur or Pantur ('Grove's Dictionary of Music and Musicians' 5th ed., vol. VI, p. 535), 1954. ACFH¹K
1210. —— Pandoura (ibid. vol. VI, p. 534), 1954. ACFH¹K
1211. Farnsworth, P. R., J. C. Trembley, and C. E. Dutton, Masculinity and Femininity of musical phenomena ('Jour-

nal Aesth. Art. crit.' IX, No. 3, p. 257
ff.), 1951. **K**

1212. **Faroughy, A.,** *A concise Persian
Grammar* (New York, Orientalia Inc.,
1944), p. 174 ff.

1212a. **Faublée, J.,** *L'ethnographie de Madagascar* (with the collaboration of R.
Falck, R. Hartweg, G. Rouget), Paris,
1946. **JM**

1212b. **Faulkner, Maurice,** *Korean music and
American military government* ('Korean
Survey' V, p. 10 ff.), Jan. 1956.

1213. **Favari, Alberto,** *Corpus di musiche
popolari siciliane, a cura di Ottavio Tiby*
('Acad. di Scienze, lettere e arti' I,
p. 172 ff., II, p. 582 ff.), Palermo, 1957.
L

*1214. **Feather, Leonard,** *The encyclopedia of
jazz* (New York, Horizon, 1955).

1215. **Fedeli, Vito,** *Zampogne Calabrese* ('Sammelb. der Intern. Musikges.' XIII, p.
433 ff.), 1911/'12. **CDFH¹L**

*1216. **Feilberg, C. G.,** *Les Papis (tribu persane
de nomades montagnards du sudouest de
l'Iran* ('Nationalmuseets Skrifter', Eth-
nografisk Raekke IV, p. 156 ff.), Copenhagen, 1952. **AK**

1217. **Felber, Erwin,** *Die Musik in den
Märchen und Mythen der verschiedenen
Völker* ('Report of the 4th Congress of
the Intern. Musicol. Soc., London 1911',
p. 167 ff.), London, 1912. **CF**

1218. —— *Das Gesetz der Zahlenverschiebung
im Märchen und Mythos und sein
Einfluss auf die Skalenbildung* ('Report
of the 4th Congress of the Intern.
Music Soc. London, 1912', p. 178 ff.),
London, 1911. **CF**

1219. —— *Die indische Musik der vedischen
und der klassischen Zeit* ('Sitzungsber. d.
Kais. Akad. d. Wiss., Wien', Phil.-hist.
Kl. vol. 170 No. 7), 1912. **ACD¹GIL¹**

1220. —— *Oost en West in de muziek* ('De
Muziek' III, p. 398 ff.), 1929. **ACDEFH**

1221. —— *Der Gesang im Orient und bei den
Naturvölken* ('Die Musik' XXII, p. 828
ff.), 1930. **CDFKL**

1222. —— *New approaches to primitive music*
('The Musical Quarterly' XIX, p. 288
ff.), 1933. **C**

1223. **Feline, Pierre,** *Le plaisir musical chez
l'Européen et chez l'Arabe* ('Mercure de
France', 15th Febr. 1937). **D¹**

1224. **Fellerer, Karl Gustav,** *Die Musik im
Wandel der Zeiten und Kulturen* (Re-
gensberg/Münster, 1948). **A**

1225. **Fenton, William N.,** and **Gertrude P.
Kurath,** *The Feast of the Dead, or
Ghost Dance at Six Nations Reserve,
Canada* (Bureau of Amer. Ethnol.,
Smithsonian Inst., Bull. 149, No. 7),
Washington, 1951. **B**

1226. —— and —— *The Iroquois Eagle Dance*

('Bureau of Amer. Ethnology, Smithsonian Inst., Bull. No. 156'), 1953. **BF**

1227. —— *Songs from the Iroquois longhouse:
program notes for an album of American
Indian music from the Eastern wood-
lands* (Washington, Smithsonian Inst.,
1942). **AK**

1227a. **Fenwick Jones, G.,** *Wittenwiler's Becki
and the medieval bagpipe* ('J. of English
and Germanic philology' XLVIII, pp.
209 ff. and 219 ff.), 1949.

1228. **Ferand, Ernst Th.,** *The 'howling in
seconds' of the Lombards* ('Musical
Quarterly' XXV, p. 313 ff.), 1939. **ACD**

1229. —— *Die Improvisation in der Musik*
(Zürich, 1939), Chapter II. *Die Primitive, der Orient und das alte Hellas.* **C**

1230. **Ferguson, John,** *Two bronze drums* (Peiping, 1932).

1231. **Fernald, Helen E.,** *Ancient Chinese
Musical Instruments* ('Journal of the
Univ. of Pennsylvania Museum' XVII,
p. 325 ff.), 1926. **GJ**

1232. —— *Ancient Chinese musical instruments as depicted on some early monu-
ments* (in Hsiao Ch'ien, 'A harp with a
thousand strings: a Chinese anthology')
London, 1944.

1233. —— *A selection of Chinese music and
songs* (ibid., p. 515 ff.).

1234. **Ferreira, Ascenso,** *O Bumba-Meu-Boi*
('Arquinos' I/II, p. 121 ff.), Recife,
1944.

1235. **Ferrero, F.** *La musica dei negri ame-
ricani* ('Rivista musicale Italiana'
XIII), 1906. **CKL**

1236. **Fewkes, J. W.,** *On the use of the phonograph among the Zuñi Indians* ('Amer.
Naturalist' XXIV, p. 687 ff.), 1890.

1237. **Ficker, Rudolf von,** *Primäre Klang-
formen* ('Jahrbuch-Peters' XXXV),
1929. **CGKL¹**

1238. **Fiedler, Hermann,** *Die Insel Timor*
(1929), III. *Sitten und Gebräuche bei
Atoni und Belu. o. Musikinstrumente*
(p. 53 ff.). **AB**

1239. **Fillmore, John Comfort,** *The harmonic
structure of Indian Music* ('Archiv f.
Anthropologie' I, Fasc. 2), 1899.
D¹GKL²

1240. —— *What do Indians mean when they
sing and how far do they succeed?* ('J. of
Amer. Folklore' VIII, p. 138 ff.), 1895.
GK

1241. —— *The harmonic structure of Indian
music* ('Amer. Anthropol.' I, p. 297 ff.),
1888. **GL²**

1242. —— *A woman's song of the Kwakiutl
Indians* (ibid. VI, p. 285 ff.), 1893. **GL²**

1243. **Finesinger, Sol Baruch,** *Musical Instruments in the Old Testament* (Baltimore,
1926).

1244. **Fink, Gottfried Wilhelm,** *Notizen über*

Musik und Gesänge der malaiischen Eingebornen auf den sundischen und molukkischen Inseln (Ost-Indien). Von einem Ohrenzeugen ('Allgem. Musikal. Zeitung' XLII, p. 1057 ff.), 1840. CD¹K

1245. Firfov, Givko, *Makedonski musichi folklore* (Macedonian Music Folklore), Skopje, 1953.

1246. —— *Les caractères métriques dans la musique populaire macédonienne* ('Journal of the Intern. Folk Music Council' IV, p. 49 ff.), 1952.   ACJKL

1247. —— *Makedonski narodni pesni* vols. I-IV (Skopje, 1956).

1248. —— and Paitonjiev, Gancho, *Makedonski narodni ora* (Macedonian Folk Dances) vol. I (Skopje, 1953).   A

1248a. —— *Yugoslawien. II. Die Volksmusik. 4. Mazedonien* ('Die Musik in Geschichte u. Gegenwart' VII, col. 364 ff.), 1958.   ACDEFGH¹KL

1249. Fischer, Adolf, *Die Herkunft der Shantrommeln* ('Z. f. Ethnologie' XXXV, p. 668 ff.), 1903.   BD¹GHKL¹L²M

1250. Fischer, E., *Patagonische Musik* ('Anthropos' III), 1908.   D¹GKL¹L²M

1251. —— *Beiträge zur Erforschung der chinesischen Musik* ('Sammelb. d. Intern. Musikges.' XII, p. 153 ff.), 1910/'11.   CDFH¹L

1252. Fischer, Hans, *Zwei einfache Musikinstrumente aus Blatt in Ozeanien* ('Jahrbuch des Museums f. Völkerkunde zu Leipzig' XIV, p. 67 ff.), 1956.   GKL²

1253. —— *Ueber stehende Schlitztrommeln auf den Neuen Hebriden und am Sepik* ('Z. f. Ethnol.' LXXXII, p. 58 ff.), 1957.   ABD¹GHKL¹L²M

*1253a. —— *Schallgeräte in Ozeanien. Bau und Spieltechnik; Verbreitung und Funktion* (Baden-Baden, 1958).   AC

1254. Fischer, H. W., *Een rammelaar als hulpmiddel bij de vischvangst* ('Intern. Archiv f. Ethnogr.' XVIII, p. 179 ff.), 1908.   BD¹GKL²

1255. Fisher, Miles Mark, *Negro slave songs in the United States* (with a foreword by Ray Allan Billington), Ithaca, Cornell Univ. Press, 1953.

1256. Flanders, Helen Hartness, and Margherite Olney, *Ballads migrant in New England* (with an introduction by Robert Frost), New York, Farrar, Straus and Young, 1953.

1257. Fleischer, Oskar, *Ein Kapitel vergleichender Musikwissenschaft* ('Sammelb. d. Intern. Mus. Ges.' I), 1900.   CDFH¹L

1258. —— *Zur vergleichenden Musikforschung* (ibid. III), 1902.   ACDFH¹L

1259. Flesche, Francis la, *The Osage tribe* ('Annual Report of the Bur. of Amer.

Ethnology' No. 45, p. 529 ff.), 1927/'28, publ. in 1930.   BGKL²

1261. Fletcher, Alice Cunninham, *A Study of Ohama Indian music* (Harvard Univ. Cambridge Mass., 1893).   IL

1262. —— *Indian Story and Song from North America* (1900).

1263. —— *The Hako* ('Annual Report of the Bureau of Amer. Ethnol.' No. 22, part 2), Washington D.C., 1904.

1264. —— *Music and musical instruments* (in: Fred. Webb Hodge, 'Handbook of American Indians north of Mexico' part 1), Washington D.C., 1907.

1265. —— *The Osage Tribe* ('Annual Report of the Bureau of American Ethnology', No. 36, p. 37 ff.), 1914-'15.   GKL²

1266. —— and Francis la Flesche, *The Onaha Tribe* ('Annual Report of the Bur. of Amer. Ethnology' No. 27), 1906, publ. in 1911.   GKL²

1267. —— *Indian games and dances* (Boston, 1915).

1268. Flood, William H. Grattan, *The story of the bagpipe* (London, 1911).   ACJ

1269. —— *The story of the harp* (London, 1905).   CJ

1270. Focke, H. C., *De Surinaamsche negermuzijk* ('Bijdr. tot de bevord. v. d. kennis der Ned. West-Ind. koloniën', Haarlem, 1858, p. 93 ff.).   C

1271. Fökövi, *Die Zigeunermusik in Ungarn* ('Monatshefte f. Musikgesch.' XXX, No. 12), 1898.   CKL

1272. Foldes, A., *Impressions of a musical journey to Africa* ('Etude' LXXI), 1953.

1273. Foley, Rolla, *Song of the Arab. The Religious Ceremonies, Shrines, and Folk Music of the Holy Land Christian Arab* (New York, 1953).

1274. *Folklore musicale* (ed. by the Intern. Inst. f. Intellectual Co-öperation), Paris, 1939.

1275. *Folk-Song Society, Journal of the,* (London, 1899-1931 – 35 Nos.).   A (partly)

1276. Förde, F. von der, *Die Musik bei den Eingeborenen auf den Südsee-Inseln* ('Der Erdball' IV, p. 47 ff.), 1930.   D¹

1277. Foucart, F., *La musique dans l'ancienne Egypte* ('Musica' 1933).   K

1278. Fourneau, J., *Des transmissions acoustiques chez les indigènes du Sud-Cameroun* ('Togo-Cameroun' 1930, p. 387 ff.), Paris.

1279. Fowke, Edith Fulton, and Richard Johnston, *Folk songs of Canada* (Waterloo, Ontario, 2/1955).

1280. Fowke, Francis, *On the vina or Indian lyre* (in Surindro Mohun Tagore, 'Hindu music from various authors', p. 191 ff.), Calcutta, 1882.   CFIKL²

1281. Fox, C., *Annals of the Irish harpers* (London, 1911).

1282. Fox Strangways, A. H., *The Hindu Scale* ('Sammelb. d. Intern. Musikges.' IX), 1908. CDFH¹IL

*1283. —— *The Music of Hindostan* (Oxford, 1914). ACFGJK

1284. —— *Exotic Music* ('Music and Letters' VI, p. 119 ff.), 1925. KL¹

1285. —— *The Pipes of Pan* ('Music and Letters' X, p. 57 ff.), 1929. KL¹

1286. —— *East and West* ('Z. f. vergl. Musikw.' I, p. 2 ff.), 1933. ACK

1287. —— *The Gandhara Grama* ('Journal R. Asiatic Soc.' 1935, p. 689 ff.). D¹GIKL¹

1288. —— *Music* (in G. T. Garratt, 'The Legacy of India', p. 305 ff.), Oxford, 1937.

1289. —— *Indian Music* (rev. by A. A. Bake) ('Grove's Dictionary' 5th ed., vol. IV, p. 456 ff.), 1954. ACFH¹K

1290. —— *Indian music* ('Encycl. Brittannica' XII, p. 241 ff.), 1951. B

1291. Foy, Wilhelm, *Zur Verbreitung der Nasenflöte* ('Ethnologica' I, p. 239 ff.), 1909. GJKL²

1292. —— *Zu den Bronzepauken aus südost-Asien* ('Abhandl. u. Berichte des kgl. Zoöl. u. Anthrop.-Ethnogr. Museums zu Dresden' IX No. 6, Ethnogr. Miscell. I von A. B. Meyer und W. Foy und O. Richter), p. 145 ff.), 1900/'01.

1293. Fraknoi, Karoly, *Jewish folk chorusses* ('Goldmark Music School Libr.' I), Budapest, 1948.

1294. Francke, A. H., *La musique au Thibet* (1906) (in Lavignac, 'Hist. de la Mus.' V, p. 3084 ff.), 1922. ACDEFHJ

1295. —— *Musikalische Studien in West-Tibet* ('Z. d. Deutschen Musikges.' LIX) 1905.

1296. François, A., *Musique indigène* (Commémoration du cinquantième anniversaire du Comité spécialisé du Katanga) ('Report of the Congress of Science, Elisabethville, Aug. 1950', VI, p. 169 ff.). M

1297. Fraser, A. D., *Some Reminiscenses and the Bagpipe* (Edinburgh, 1907). AJ

1298. Fraser, Norman, *International Catalogue of recorded Folk Music* (ed. for Unesco and the Intern. Folk Music Council), London, Oxford Univ. Press, 1954. AL

1299. —— *South American (except Brazilian) Folk Music* ('Grove's Dictionary' 5th ed. vol. III, p. 361 ff.), 1954. ACFH¹K

1300. Fraser, S., *The airs and melodies peculiar to the Highlands of Scotland and the isles* (Edinburgh, und.).

1301. Frédéric, Louis, *La danse sacrée de l'Inde* (Paris, 1957). B

1302. Fredéricq, Paul, *Onze historische volksliederen van vóór de godsdienstige beroeringen der 16de eeuw* (Gent/The Hague, 1894). DF

1303. Fredin, August, *Gotlandstoner* ('Svenska Landsmål' 1909–1933). D¹G

1304. Freeman, Linton C., and Alan P. Merriam, *Statistical Classification in Anthropology: an Application to Ethnomusicology* ('American Anthropologist' LVIII, p. 464 ff.), 1956. ABGL²M

1304a. Freeman, Linton C., *The changing functions of a folksong* ('J. of American Folklore' LXX, p. 215 ff.), July/Sept. 1957. GK

1305. French, P. T., *Catalogue of Indian Musical Instruments* (in: S. M. Tagore, 'Hindu Music from various authors'). Calcutta, 1882. CFIKL²

1306. Friedenthal, Albert, *Der Gehörsinn der Chinesen* ('Allgem. Musikzeitung' XXXIV), 1907. D¹L

1307. —— *Musik, Tanz und Dichtung bei den Kreolen Amerikas* (Berlin, 1913).

1307a. Friedländer, Max, *German Folk-songs with reference to English and American Folk-songs* ('Report of the 4th Congress of the Intern. Musical Soc.', p. 59), London, 1911. CF

1308. Frobenius, Leo, *Die Saiteninstrumente der Naturvölker* ('Prometheus' XII, p. 648 ff.), Berlin, 1901. G

1309. —— *Atlas Africanus*. Heft 3, Blatt 17, No. 8 (München, 1922).

1310. Fryklund, Daniel, *Etymologische Studien über geige-gigue-jig* ('Studier i modern Sprakvetenskap' VI, p. 101 ff.), 1917. C

1311. —— *Studien über die Pochette* (Sundsvall, 1917). C

1312. —— *Studier över Marintrumpeten* ('Svensk Tidskrift för Musikforskning' I, p. 40 ff.), 1919. CK

1313. Fürer-Haimendorf, Christoph von, *Folk music of India: primitive instruments of primitive peoples* ('The Ill. London News' 19th April 1952, p. 668 ff.). AJ

1314. Fürst, H., *Musiques persanes* ('Revue musicale' VII, No. 5), 1st March 1926. CD¹GHKL

1314a. Fuhrmann, Ernst, *Die Garamut oder Signaltrommel der Papuas* ('Steyler Missionsbote' XLI), 1913/'14.

1315. Fujii, Seishin, *A buddhismus és a zene* (*Der Buddhismus und die Musik*) (in 'Mélanges offerts à Zoltan Kodaly à l'occasion de son 60ième anniversaire', p. 139 ff.), Budapest, 1943. ACK

1316. Furlong, Guillermo, *Músicos argentinos* (Buenos Aires, 1944).

1317. Furness, Clifton Joseph, *Communal Music among Arabians and Negroes* ('The Musical Quarterly' XVI, p. 38 ff.), 1930. C

1318. Fyzee-Rahamin, Atiya Begum, *The music of India* (London, 1925). GIKL

1319. Gabus, Jean, *Vie et coutumes des Esqui-maux Caribou* (Lausanne, 1944).

1320. Gadzekpo, Sinedzi, *Making music in Eweland* ('West African Review' XXIII, p. 817 ff.), 1952. **G**

1321. Gagnon, E., *Chansons populaires du Canada, receuillis et publiées avec annotations* (Québec, 1880).

1322. Gailhard, A., *Théâtre et musique modernes en Chine* (Paris, 1926).

1323. Gairdner, W. H. T., *Oriental hymntunes, Egyptian and Syrian* (London, 1930).

1324. Gale, Albert, *Music* (in Fay Cooper Cole, 'The Tinguian', p. 443 ff.), 1922. **A**

1324a. Galis, K. W., *Papua's van de Humboldt baai. Bijdrage tot een ethnografie* (diss.), Den Haag, 1955 (p. 150 ff.).

1325. Gallop, Rodney, *Music of the Southern Slavs* ('The Musical Quarterly' XXIII), 1937. **CD**

1326. —— *Basque wassailing songs* ('Music & Letters' XI, p. 324 ff.), 1930. **KL¹**

1327. —— *The development of folksong in Portugal and the Basque country* ('Proc. of the Musical Association' LXI), 1935.

1328. —— *Folksongs of modern Greece* ('The Musical Quarterly' XXI, No. 1), Jan. 1935. **CD**

1329. —— *The folk-music of Eastern Portugal* ('The Musical Quarterly' XX, p. 96 ff.), 1934. **CD**

1330. —— *Basque songs from Soule* ('The Musical Quarterly' XXII, p. 458 ff.), 1936. **CD**

1331. —— *The music of Indian Mexiko* ('The Musical Quarterly' XXV, p. 210 ff.), 1939. **CD**

1332. —— *Otomi Indian music from Mexiko* ('The Musical Quarterly' XXVI, p. 87 ff.), 1940. **CDH¹**

1332a. —— *Mexican Mosaic* (London, 1939).

1332b. Galmés, Antonio, *Mallorca, Menorca, Ibiza Folklore* (Mallorca, 1950). **L**

1333. Galpin, Francis W., *Aztec Influence on American Indian Instruments* ('Sammelb. d. Intern. Musikges.' IV, p. 661 ff.), 1902/'03. **CDFH¹L**

1334. —— *The Whistles and Reed Instruments of the American Indians of North-West Coast* ('Proceedings of the Musical Association' XXIX), 1903. **C**

1335. —— *Notes on a Hydraulis* ('The Reliquary and Illustr., Archaeologist', 1904). **CK**

1336. —— *The Sackbut* ('Proc. of the Musical Association' XXXIII, p. 1 ff.), 1907.

1337. —— *Old English Instruments of Music* (London, 1910). **CIJ**

1338. —— *The origin of the clarsech or Irish harp* ('Report of the Congress of the Intern. Mus. Soc., May/June 1911'). **C**

1339. —— *The Sumerian Harp of Ur* ('Music and Letters' X, p. 108 ff.), 1929. **AKL¹**

1340. —— *Monsieur Prin and His Trumpet Marine* ('Music and Letters' XIV, p. 18 ff.), 1933. **KL¹**

1341. —— *The Music of the Sumerians and their immediate successors, the Babylonians and Assyrians* (Cambridge, 1937). **ABCGK**

1342. —— *A Textbook of European Musical Instruments* (London, 1939). **CJ**

1343. —— Review of Kathleen Schlesinger 'The Greek Aulos' ('Music & Letters' XX, p. 325 ff.), 1939. **KL¹**

1344. —— *Babylonian Music* ('Grove's Dictionary' 5th ed. vol. I, p. 282 ff.), 1954. **ACFH¹K**

1345. —— *Hurdy-gurdy* (ibid. vol. IV, p. 415 ff.), 1954. **ACFH¹K**

1346. —— *Hydraulis* (ibid. vol. IV, p. 423 ff.), 1954. **ACFH¹K**

1347. —— *Jew's harp* (ibid. vol. IV, p. 636 ff.), 1954. **ACFH¹K**

1348. Ganay, Solange de, *Le xylophone chez les Sara du Moyen Chari* ('J. de la Soc. des Africanistes' XII, p. 203 ff.), Paris, 1942. **GL³M**

1348a. Gand, Hanns in der, *Volkstümliche Musikinstrumente in der Schweiz* (Basel, 1937). **JL**

1349. Gangadhara, *Theory and practice of Hindu music and the vina tutor* (Madras, 1914). **I**

1350. Gangoly, Ordhendra Coomar, *Ragas and raginis, a pictorial and iconographic study of Indian musical modes, based on original sources* (2 vols)., Calcutta, 1934. **G**

1351. —— *The Birth of Melodies: an Indian View* ('Aryan Path' VIII, p. 14 ff.), 1937.

1352. —— *Non-Aryan Contribution to Indian Music* ('Annals of the Bhandarkar Oriental Research Inst.' XIX, p. 263 ff.), 1938.

1353. —— *Visual aspects of Hindu melodies* ('Entally Cultural Conference, 8th Annual session, Jan. 1955'), Calcutta, 1955.

1353a. —— *The manner of 'applause' in ancient Indian stage* ('The J. of the Music Academy, Madras' XVII, p. 141 ff.), 1946. **C**

1354. Gangopadhyaya, Ardhendra Kumara, *Ragas and Raginis. A pictorial iconographic study of Indian musical modes based on original sources* (Nalanda publications, Bombay, 1948). **I**

1354a. Gani, O., *Notes sur les coutumes funéraires des Pila* ('Etudes Dahoméennes' IV, p. 13 ff.), 1950. **M**

1355. Garay, Narciso, *Tradiciones y cantares de Panama* (1930). **A**

1356. Garcia, Angelica de Rezende, *Nossos*

118

Avo's contavam e cantavam. Ensaios folcloricos e tradiçoes brasileiras (Belo Horizonte, 1949).

1357. **Garcia Barriuso, Patrocinio,** *La Musica hispano-musulmana en Marruecos* (Publ. del Inst. General Franco para la investigación hispano-arabe, Ser. VI, No. 4, 1941 = Inst. de Estud. Africanos, Madrid, 1950). **IL**

1358. **Garcia, Juan Francisco,** *Panorama de la música dominicana* (Ciudad Trujillo, 1917). **K**

1359. **Gárdonyi, Zoltan,** *Népzenénk és a Zenei Forma Elemei* (i.e. our popular music and the elements of musical form) (in 'Emlékkonyv Kodály. I, 70 Zsulétesnapjára' p. 405 ff.), Budapest, 1953. **A**

1360. **Garfield, Viola E., Paul S. Wingert** and **Marius Barbeau,** *The Tsimshian: their arts and music* (New York, 1952).

1361. **Garms, J. H.,** *Over straatuitroepen en primitieve muziek* ('T. v. Nederl. Muziekgeschiedenis' IX, p. 1 ff.), Amsterdam, 1909. **ACFH[1]**

1362. —— *"Suid-Afrikaanse volkspoësie"* ('Caecilia en het Muziekcollege' Nov. 1928, p. 21 ff.). **ACD[1]F**

1363. **Garnault, Paul,** *La trompette marine* (Nice, 1926).

1364. **Garner, F. H., and Alan P. Merriam,** *Jazz (a definition),* 1955. **A**

1365. **Garnot, Jean Sainte-Fare,** *L'offrande musicale dans l'Ancienne Egypte* ('Mélanges d'histoire et d'esthétique musicales, offerts à Paul-Marie Masson', p. 89 ff.), Paris, 1955. **F**

1366. **Garstang,** *Songs of the birds* (1912).

1367. **Gascué, F.,** *Origen de la musica popular vascongada* ('Rev. intern. de Estud. vascos', 1913).

1367a. **Gaspar, D.,** *Quand l'Afrique chante et danse* ('Revue Coloniale Belge' VII, p. 170 ff.), 1952. **M**

1368. **Gassmann, A. L.,** *Das Volkslied im Luzerner Wiggertal und Hinterland* (Basel, 1906).

1369. —— *Naturjodel des Josef Felder am Entlebuch* (Zürich, 1908).

1370. **Gaster, Theodor Herzl,** *Thespis; ritual, myth and drama in the ancient near east* (New York, 1950).

1371. **Gastoué, Amédée,** *L'Arménie et son art traditionnel* ('Revue de Musicologie' XIII, p. 194 ff.), 1929. **CD[1]EKLL[1]**

1372. —— *La musique byzantine* (in Dufourcq, 'La Musique des origines à nos jours', ed. Larousse, p. 69 ff.), Paris, 1946. **ACDEFHJK**

1373. —— *La musique byzantine* (1912) (in Lavignac, 'Histoire de la Musique' I, p. 547 ff.), Paris, 1922. **ACDEFHJ**

1374. **Gaudefroy-Demombynes, J.,** *Musiques européennes. Le peuple arabe* ('Revue de Psychologie des Peuples' XI, p. 379 ff.), 1956. **AB**

*1375. **Gaukstad, Østein,** *Norsk folkemusikk. Ein bibliografi* (Oslo, 1951).

1376. **Gavazzi, Milovan,** *Jadranska 'Lira – 'Lirica'* (Zagreb, 1930). **A**

1377. **Gay, R.,** *Les 'constantes nègres' dans la musique américaine* ('Problèmes d'Afrique' No. 26, p. 316 ff.), 1954. **AGJKM**

1378. —— *Essai de discographie nègre africaine* (ibid., p. 345 ff.), 1954. **AGJKM**

1379. **Gazimihâl, Mahmut R.,** *Aperçus préliminaires sur l'origine asiatique de quelques instruments turcs* (Uvodni pogledi na azijsko porijeklo nekih Turskih muzičkih instrumenata) ('Bilten Inst. za proučavanje folklora Sarajevo' III, p. 125 ff.), Sarajevo, 1955. **A**

1380. **Gbeho, Phillip,** *Africa's Drums Are More than Tom-Toms* ('West African Review' XXII, p. 1150 ff.), Oct. 1951. **G**

1381. —— *Beat of the Master Drum* (ibid. XXII, p. 1263 ff.), Nov. 1951. **G**

1382. —— *African Music Deserves Generous Recognition* (ibid. XXII, p. 910 ff.), Aug. 1951. **G**

1383. —— *The Indigenous Gold Coast Music* ('United Empire' XLII, p. 121 ff.), May-June 1951 = African Music Soc. Newsletter I No. 5, p. 30 ff.), 1952. **CM**

1384. —— *Cross Rhythm in African Music* ('West African Review' XXIII, p. 11 ff.), Jan. 1952. **G**

1385. —— *Music of the Gold Coast* ('African Music' I, No. 1, p. 62 ff.), 1954. **ACILM**

1386. **Gebik, Wladislaw,** *Piosenki Mazurski* (Krakau, 1955).

1387. **Geering, Arnold,** *Quelques problèmes touchants la chanson populaire en Suisse* ('J. of the Intern. Folk Music Council' II, p. 37 ff.), 1950. **ACJ**

1388. **Geiger, P.,** *Volksliedinteresse und Volksliedforschung in der Schweiz bis zum Jahre 1830* (Bern, 1912).

1389. **Geiringer, Karl,** *Vorgeschichte und Geschichte der europäischen Laute* ('Z. f. Musikw.' X), 1928. **CDH[1]KL**

1390. —— *Musical Instruments. Their history from the stone age to the present day* (New York, Oxford Univ. Press, 1945). **J**

1391. **Gelats, Joan Amades,** *Ritos primitivos de Siembra* ('Miscelanea de Estudios dedicados al Dr. Fernando Ortiz' vol. I, p. 63 ff.), La Habana, 1956.

1392. **Geller, H.,** *I pifferari* (Leipzig, 1954). **AC**

1393. **Genin, Auguste,** *Notes sur les danses, la musique et les chants des Mexicains anciens et modernes* (Paris, 1913). **C**

1394. —— *Notes on the Dances, Music, and Songs of the Ancient and Modern Mexicans* (Publ. Smithsonian Inst., Report for 1920) p. 657 ff.), Washington D.C., 1922. **CD¹JK**

1395. —— *The Musical Instruments of the Ancient Mexicans* ('Mexican Magazine' III, p. 355 ff.), 1927.

*1396. George, Zelma Watson, *A guide to Negro music. An annotated bibliography of Negro folk music and art music by Negro composers or based on Negro thematic material* (Ann Arbor Univ. Microfilms, Publ. No. 8021), 1953.

1397. Georgiades, Thrasybulos, *Der griechische Rhythmus. Musik, Reigen, Vers und Sprache* (Hamburg, 1949).

1397a. —— *Greek music, verse and dance* (Merlin Music Books vol. V), New York, 1958.

*1397b. —— *Musik und Rhythmus bei den Griechen. Zum Ursprung der abendländischen Musik* (Rowohlts deutsche Enzyklopädie, Hamburg, 1958). **A**

1397c. Germann, P., *Zwei Trommeln aus Dahomey im Leipziger Museum für Völkerkunde* ('Jahrb. d. Museums f. Völkerk.' XI, p. 101 ff.), 1953. **M**

1398. Gerson-Kiwi, Edith, *The transcription of Oriental Music* ('Communities' III, p. 181 ff.), 1947/'48, (A) = 'Edoth' III, p. 17 ff. (1947/'48). **AK**

1399. —— *Wedding Dances and Songs of the Jews of Bokhara* ('Journal of the Intern. Folk Music Council' II, p. 17 ff.), 1950. **ACJKL**

1400. —— *Migrations and Mutations of Oriental Folk Instruments* ('Journal of the Intern. Folk Music Council' IV, p. 16 ff.), 1952. **ACJKL**

1401. —— *Towards an exact Transcription of Tone-Relations* ('Acta Musicologica' XXV, p. 80 ff.), 1953. ACDEFGH¹KLL¹

*1402. —— *Jewish Folk Music* ('Grove's Dictionary' 5th ed., vol. III, p. 304 ff.), 1954. **ACFH¹K**

*1402a. —— *Jüdische Volksmusik* ('Die Musik in Geschichte und Gegenwart' VII, col. 261 ff.), 1958. **ACDEFGH¹KL**

1402b. —— *Musicology in Israel* ('Acta Musicologica' XXX, p. 17 ff.), 1958. **ACDEFGH¹KLL¹**

1402c. —— *The musicians of the Orient* ('Edoth' I), Jerusalem, 1945. **K**

1402d. —— *Musique dans la Bible* ('Dictionnaire de la Bible', Suppl. vol. V), Paris, 1957.

1403. Gersoni, C., *I canti popolari lettoni* (Rome, 1933).

1404. Gesemann, Gerhard, *Ueber jugoslawische Volksmusik oder zur Wahrung des kulturellen Ansehens vor der Welt* ('Slawische Rundschau' III, p. 5 ff.), 1931. **GK**

1405. Geijer, E. G., and A. A. Afzelius, *Svenska folk-visor från forntiden* I–III (Stockholm, 1814–'16).

1406. —— and —— *Svenska folkvisor, ny, betydligt tillökad upplaga ved R. Bergström & L. Hoijer* (Stockholm, 1880). **K**

1407. Geurtjens, Father H., *Het leven en streven der Inlanders op de Kei-eilanden* ('s Hertogenbosch, 1921), Chapter XI. *Spel en dans* (p. 69 ff.). **AB**

1408. Ghose, Loknath, *The music and musical notation of various nations* (Calcutta, 1874). **K**

1409. Gibling, R. Styx, *Notes on the Latin American national dances* ('African Music Society Newsletter' I, No. 4, p. 32 ff.), 1951. **ACJM**

1410. Gibson, H. E., *Music and musical instruments of the Shang* ('J. of the R. Asiatic Soc., North-China Branch' LXVIII, p. 8 ff.), Shanghai 1937. **KL⁶**

1411. Gide, André, *Musiques et danses au Tchad* ('Revue musicale' IX, p. 97 ff.), 1927. **CDFGHKL**

1412. Gigliolo, Enrico R., *La kpwen, tromba de guerra delle Amazzoni del Dahomii* ('Archivio per l'Antropologia e la Ethnologia' XXVI, p. 106 ff.), Florence, 1896. **L³**

1413. Gil Garcia, Bonifacio, *Cancionero popular de Extremadura* (I (1931); II (Badajoz, 1956).

1414. —— *Romances populares de Extremadura* (Badajoz, 1944).

1415. —— *Folklore musical extremeño. Principales rasgos de su origen y riqueza tonal* ('Revista del Centro de Estudios Extremeños' IX), 1935.

1416. —— *Folklore musical Extremeño. La cancion extremeña en el folklore español. Comparaciones textuales e influencias reciprocas* (ibid. X), 1936.

1417. —— *Folklore extremeño. Extremadura y la posible "regionalización" de su música popular. La tradición en la canción extremeña y su evolución* (ibid. XI), 1937.

1418. —— *El canto de relación en el folklore infantil de Extremadura* (ibid. XVI), 1942.

1419. —— *Cancionero infantil universal* (in preparation).

1420. —— *Folklore infantil* (in preparation).

1421. —— *Madrid en la tradición popular* (in preparation).

1422. —— *Mosaico folklorico de Extremadura* ('Estudios musicales' I, No. 3, p. 197 ff.), 1950.

1423. Gilbert, Dorothy R., *The lukumbi, a sixtoned slit drum of the Batetela* ('African Music' I, No. 2, p. 21 ff.), 1955. **ACJLM**

1424. Gilbert, Henry F., *Folk-music in Art music, a discussion and a theory* ('The Musical Quarterly' III, p. 577 ff.), 1912. **C**

1425. **Gilbert, Will G.**, *Een en ander over negroide muziek van Suriname* (Meded. van het Kon. Inst. voor de Tropen No. LV), Amsterdam, 1940. **ABCFGHLM**

1426. —— *Gewijde trommen op Haiti en in Suriname* ('N. Rotterdamsche Crt.' 31th Dec. 1939).

1427. —— *Authentieke Negro-Spirituals* ('Studiën' LXXII), 1940. **AC**

1428. —— *Negermuziek uit de Nederlandsche West* ('N. Rotterdamsche Crt.' 10th Febr. 1940).

1429. —— *Onderzoek naar het ontstaan van de anhemitonische pentatonische toonladder in verband met de spraakmelodie* ('De Wereld der Muziek' VIII, No. 9, p. 277 ff.), Juni 1942. **ACDEFGH**

1430. —— *Muziek uit Oost en West* (The Hague, 1942). **ACFI**

1432. —— *Negerrhythmen* (ibid. IX, p. 131 ff.), Jan. 1943. **ADEFGH**

1433. —— *De cultuurhistorische beteekenis van de marimba* ('De wereld der muziek' IX, p. 344 ff.), 1943. **ACDEFGH**

1434. —— *Rumbamuziek* (The Hague, 1945). **AC**

1435. —— *Inleiding tot de buiten-Europese muziek* (The Hague, 1950). **ACFH**

1436. —— *Zuid-zuidoost van Marakesch* ('Luister' No. 44, p. 219), Amersfoort, 15th May 1956. **A**

1437. —— *Langs de oude karavaanwegen van Marco Polo* (ibid. No. 48, blz. 306 vv.), Sept. 1956. **A**

1437a. **Gille, A.**, *L'Umuganuro ou fête du sorgho en Urundi* ('Bull. Jurid. Indig.' XIV, No. 11, p. 368 ff.), 1946. **M**

1438. **Gilman, B. I.**, *Zuñi Melodies* ('Journal of Amer. Archaeol. and Ethnol.' I), 1891.

1439. —— *On some psychological aspects of the Chinese musical system* ('Philosophical Review' I), reprinted with notes in 1892.

1440. —— *Hopi Songs* ('Journal of Amer. Archaeol. and Ethnol.' V), 1908.

1441. —— *The Science of Exotic Music* ('Science' N.S. XXX), 1909. **L[1]**

1442. **Gil-Marchex, Henri**, *La musique au Japon* ('Revue musicale' XII, No. 120), Nov. 1931. **CD[1]GKL**

1443. **Giorgetti, Filiberto**, *Note di musica Zande (con transcrizioni musicali di uccelli, tamburi, xilofoni e canti Zande)*, Verona, 1951. **M**

1443a. —— *Musica e tamburi fra gli Azande* ('Nigrizia' LXX, p. 15 ff.), 1951. **M**

1443b. —— *Musica e tamburi fra gli Azande. Hanno la musica nel sangue* ('Africana' II, p. 12 ff.), 1955. **M**

1443c. —— *African music (with special reference to the Zande tribe)* ('Sudan Notes & Records' XXXIII, p. 216 ff.), 1952. **M**

1444. **Girard, Rafael**, *Ein Mythos aus Guatmala über den Ursprung der Kalebussenrassel* ('Paideuma' VI, Heft 4, p. 235 ff.), Nov. 1956. **B**

1445. **Gironcourt, Georges de**, *La Géographie musicale* (Nancy, 1932). **AI**

1446. —— *Recherche de géographie musicale dans le Sud tunésien* ('La Géographie' I, No. 2, p. 65 ff.), 1939. **CD[1]GKL[1]**

1447. —— *Motifs de chant cambodgiens* ('Bull. de la Soc. des Etudes Indochinoises', N.S. XVI no. 1), 1941. **ABL[8]**

1448. —— *Recherches de Géographie musicale en Indochine* (ibid. XVII no. 4), 1942. **ABCL[8]**

1449. —— *Recherches de Géographie musicale au Cambodge et à Java* (ibid. XIX no. 3), 1944. **ABCL[8]**

1450. —— *Enquête de géographie musicale aux îles Marquises et aux Samoa* ('Bull. de la Soc. des études océaniennes' IX, No. 106, p. 212 ff.), Papeete, 1954.

1451. —— *Enquête de géographie musicale aux îles Sous-le-Vent. Epei de Maupiti. Patio de Tahaa.* (ibid. IX, No. 107, p. 231 ff.), Papeete, 1954.

1451a. **Giurchescu, A.**, *Jocurile din Vrancea* ('Revista de Folclor' II, No. 4, p. 55 ff.), Bucarest, 1957.

1452. **Gladwin, Frances**, *An Essay on Persian Music* ('New Asiatic Miscellany' I, p. 261 ff.), 1789.

1453. —— *Sungeet* (in Surindro Mohun Tagore, 'Hindu music from various authors', p. 199 ff.), Calcutta, 1882. **CFIKL[2]**

1453a. **Goddard, P. E.**, *A graphic method of recording songs* ('Anthropological Papers' p. 137 ff.), 19...

1454. **Goeie, C. H. de**, *De Wiri-wiri, een muziekinstrument van Curaçao* ('West-Indische Gids' XXIX, p. 15 ff.), 1948. **ABD[1]G**

1455. —— *Verwanten van de Curaçaose Wiri-wiri* (ibid. XXXI, p. 180 ff.), 1950. **ABD[1]G**

1456. **Goethem, L. van**, *Lokole of Tam-Tam bij de Nkundo-negers* ('Congo' 1927, p. 711 ff.), Brussels. **D[1]GKL[1]L[2]**

1457. **Goetz, L. K.**, *Volkslied und Volksleben der Kroaten und Serben* (2 vols.) (Heidelberg, 1937). **L**

1457a. **Gojkovic, Andrijana**, *The main characteristics of folk-music in Yugoslavia* ('The Folklorist' IV, No. 3, p. 79 ff., No. 4, p. 114 ff.), 1957. **A**

1457b. —— *Characteristic folk instruments of Yugoslavia* ('ibid. IV, No. 5, p. 139 ff.) (to be continued), Spring 1958. **A**

1458. **Goldstein, Walter**, *The natural harmonic and rhythmic sense of the Negro* ('Proc. of the Music Teacher's National Association' 1917, p. 29 ff.).

1459. Goloubew, Victor, *Les tambours magiques en Mongolie* ('Bull. de l'École Française de l'Extrême Orient' XXIII, p. 407 ff.), 1923. **BK**

1460. —— *Report on the making and diffusion of metallic drums through Tonking and Northern Annam* ('Proc. of the 4th Pacific Science Congress, Java, 1929').

1461. —— *Sur l'origine et la diffusion des tambours métalliques* ('Pre-historica Asiae Orientalis' I, p. 137 ff.), 1932. **G**

1462. —— *L'archéologie du Tonkin et les fouilles de Dong-So'n* (Hanoi, 1937).

1463. —— *Le tambour métallique de Hoang-Ha* ('Bull. de l'École Française de l'Extrême Orient' XL, p. 383 ff.), 1941. **BK**

1464. Gombosi, Otto, *Tonarten und Stimmungen der antiken Musik* (Copenhagen, 1939). **C**

1465. —— *The melody of Pindar's 'Golden Lyre'* ('The Musical Quarterly' XXVI, p. 381 ff.), 1940. **CDH¹**

1466. —— *Studien zur Tonartenlehre des frühen Mittelalters* ('Acta Musicologica' X, p. 149 ff., XI, p. 28 ff. and 128 ff., XII, p. 21 ff. and 29 ff.), 1938/'40. **CDEKLL¹**

1467. —— *Music in ancient Crete and Mycenae* ('Bull. of the Amer. Musicol. Soc.' VI, p. 25 ff.), 1942.

1468. —— *New Light on Ancient Greek Music* ('Papers Intern. Congr. of Musicol., New York 1939', p. 168 ff.), New York, 1944. **AC**

1469. —— *Key, Mode, Species* ('Kongressber. der Intern. Ges. f. Musikwiss., Basel, 1949', p. 133 ff.), Basel 1950) ('Journal of the Amer. Musicol. Soc.' IV, p. 20 ff.). 1951. **ACFKL**

1469a. Gomes, A., *Notas sobre a musica indigena da Guiné* ('Boletin Cultural Guiné Port.' V, No. 19, p. 411 ff.), 1950. **M**

1470. Gomes, Edwin H., *Seventeen years among the Sea Dyaks of Borneo* (London, 1911), Chapter XVIII, p. 225 ff.: *Song and music.* **J**

1471. Gonzales Bravo, A., *Kenas, pincollos y tarkas* ('Estudios Latino-americanos' III, p. 25 ff.), La Paz, 1937.

1472. —— *Trompeta, flauto traversa, tambor y charango* ('Bol. Latino-Americano' IV), Bogotá, 1938.

1472a. Good, A. I., *Drum talk is the 'African's wireless'* ('Natural History' L, p. 69 ff.), 1942.

1473. Goodwin, A. J. H., *Rock gongs, chutes, paintings and fertility* ('The South African Archaeological Bulletin' VII, No. 45, p. 37 ff.), Capetown, March 1957. **B**

1474. Goodrich, L. C., *The Chinese sheng and western musical instruments* ('China Magazin' XVII, p. 10 ff.), New York, 1941.

1475. Goossens, Han, *De draailier, een vergeten instrument* ('t Getouw' XIV, No. 5, p. 12 ff.), 1957.

1476. Gosh, Juan Prakash, *Indian orchestra with a reference to All India Radio* ('Jhankar music circle 1953 souvenir'), Calcutta, 1953.

1477. Goswami, G. N., *An epoch in classical music* ('Silver jubilee souvenir of the Marris College of Hindusthani music, Lucknow, Nov. 1952'), Lucknow, 1953.

1478. Goswami, Kanai Lal, *Music and society* ('Jhankar music circle 1954 souvenir'), Calcutta, 1954.

1478a. Gosvami, O., *The story of Indian music* (Bombay, 1958). **AB**

1478b. Gover, Charles, *Badaga songs* ('Orient Review' XL, p. 19 ff.), Aug. 1956.

1479. Governor of Lagos, *On the melodies of the Wolof, Mandingo, Ewe, Yoruba, and Hausa people of West Africa* ('J. of the Manchester Geographical Soc.' V, Nos. 7–9), March 1890.

*1480. Graça, Fernando do Lopez, *Portuguese Folk Music* ('Grove's Dictionary' 5th ed. vol. III, p. 339 ff.), 1954. **ACFH¹K**

1481. Grace, C. W., *Songs and poems from Aotearoa* (Wellington, 1924).

1482. Gradenwitz, Peter, *The Music of Israel; its Rise and Growth through 5000 years* (New York, 1949). **CL**

1483. Graebner, F., *Holztrommeln des Ramu-Distriktes auf Neu-Guinea* ('Globus' LXXXIV, p. 299 ff.), 1902. **D¹L²M**

1484. Graf, Walter, *Das estnische Volkslied* (Vienna, 1933).

1485. —— *Ueber den deutschen Einfluss auf den estnischen Volksgesang* (diss.), Vienna, 1933.

1486. —— *Zur Spieltechnik und Spielweise von Zeremonialflöten von der Nordküste Neuguineas* ('Archiv f. Völkerk.' II, p. 87 ff.), 1947. **AGKL¹L²**

1487. —— *Ein deduktiver Ansatz musikethnologischer Forschung* ('Anzeiger der phil.-hist. Klasse d. Oesterr. Akad. d. Wissenschaften' 1948, No. 46, p. 211 ff.). **AK**

1488. —— *Die musikwissenschaftlichen Phonogramme Rudolf Pöchs von der Nordküste Neuguineas* (Vienna, 1950). **AC**

1489. —— *Einige Bemerkungen zur Schlitztrommel-Verständigung in Neu-Guinea* ('Anthropos' XL, p. 861 ff.), 1950. **ABD¹GHJKL¹L²M**

1490. —— *Zur Individualforschung in der Musik-Ethnologie* ('Kultur und Sprache', Festschrift, p. 218 ff.), 1952. **AB**

1491. —— *Repräsentant der vergleichenden Musikwissenschaft* (in: Robert Lach, Persönlichkeit und Werk, zum 80. Geburtstag, p. 13 ff.), Vienna, 1954.

122

1492. —— *Oesterreichs Anteil an der musik-ethnologischen Forschung* ('Wiener völkerkundige Mitteilungen' II, No. 2, p. 200 ff.), 1954.　　　**AGL²**

1493. —— *Sind paläoanthropologische Hinweise seitens der Musikwissenschaft möglich?* ('Mitteilungen d. Anthrop. Ges. in Wien' LXXXIII, p. 205 ff.), 1954.　　　**AD¹GHL²**

1494. —— *Musikethnologie und Quellenkritik* ('Die Wiener Schule der Völkerkunde, Festschrift zum 25jährigen Bestand 1929–1954', p. 111 ff.).　　　**A**

1495. —— *Die Tanzschrift als wissenschaftliches Hilfsmittel* ('Mitteil. d. Anthrop. Ges. in Wien' LXXXIV/LXXXV, p. 83 ff.), Vienna, 1955.　　**AD¹GHL²**

1496. —— *Musikethnologische Notizen zum Orpheus von Enns-Lorch* ('Anthropos' LI, p. 735 ff.), Fribourg, 1956.　　　**ABD¹GHJKL¹L²M**

1497. **Graff, Ragnwald,** *Music of Norwegian Lapland* ('Journal of the Intern. Folk Music Council' VI, p. 29 ff.), 1954.　　　**ACJKL**

1498. **Graham, David Crockett,** *Songs and stories of the Ch'uan Miao* ("Smithsonian miscellaneous collections', vol. 123 No. 1), Washington, 1954.　　**F**

1499. **Graham, W. A.,** *Siam* (London, 1924), p. 195 ff.: *Music, dancing and the drama.*　　　**J**

1500. **Grainger, Percy,** *The impress of personality in unwritten music* ('The Musical Quarterly' I, p. 416 ff.), 1915.

1501. **Granet, Marcel,** *Fêtes et chansons anciennes de la Chine* (Paris, 1919); = *Festivals and Songs of Ancient China* (transl. by E. D. Edwards), New York, 1932.

1502. **Granner, Erwin,** *Ein afrikanisches Musikinstrument* ('Kosmos' X, p. 269 ff.), Stuttgart, 1913.

1503. **Grant, John,** *Piobaireachd: its origin and construction* (Edinburgh, 1915).

1504. **Grasserie, R. de la,** *Rhythmics of the Arabian and Mussulman nations* ('Babylonian and Oriental record' 1891, p. 253 ff.; ibid. 1892, p. 62 ff., 78 ff., 110 ff., and 133 ff.).　　　**GK**

1505. **Grattan, C. Hartley,** *The Australian bushsongs* ('The Musical Quarterly' XV, p. 426 ff.), 1929.　　　**C**

Grattan Flood, William H., see: Flood, William H. Grattan.

1506. **Gray, H. St. George,** *A Maori flageolet* ('Man' IV), 1904.　　**BD¹GKL²M**

1507. **Grébert, M. F.,** *L'Art musical chez les Fang du Gabon* ('Archives suisses d'Anthropologie générale' V, p. 75 ff.), Geneva, 1928.　　　**H**

1508. —— *Au Gabon* (Paris, Soc. des Missions Evangéliques' 1922), p. 89 ff.

1509. **Green, G. P.,** *Some aspects of Chinese music* (London, 1913).　　　**I**

1509a. **Greenleaf, Elizabeth, and Grace Y. Mansfield,** *Ballads and Sea Songs of Newfoundland* (Cambridge, Mass., 1933).

1510. **Greenway, John,** *American folk songs of protest* (Philadelphia and London, 1953).

1511. **Greig, Gavin,** *Last Leaves of Traditional Ballads and Ballad Airs* (Aberdeen, 1925).

1512. **Grenet, Emilio,** *Popular Cuban music* (Habana, 1939).

1513. **Greni, Liv,** *Ueber Vokaltradition in norwegischer Volksmusik* ('Les Colloques de Wégimont' I, p. 154 ff.), Brussels, 1956.　　　**ACL**

1514. **Gressmann, H.,** *Musik und Musikinstrumente im Alten Testament* ('Religionsgeschichtliche Versuche und Vorarbeiten' II), Giessen, 1903.　**CIK**

1515. **Greyerz, O. von,** *Das Volkslied der deutschen Schweiz* (Frauenfeld/Leipzig, 1927).

1516. **Griaule, Marcel,** *Symbolisme des tambours soudanais* ('Mélanges d'histoire et d'esthetique musicales, offerts à Paul-Marie Masson', p. 79 ff.), Paris, 1955.　　　**FM**

1517. —— and G. Dieterlen, *La harpe-luth des Dogon* ('Journal de la Soc. des Africanistes' XX, p. 222), 1950.　　**GL²M**

1518. —— *Nouvelles remarques sur la harpe-luth des Dogon* ('J. de la Soc. des Africanistes' XXIV, p. 119 ff.), 1954. **GL²M**

1519. **Griffith, Charles E.,** *Folk Music in the Philippines* ('Music Supervisors' Journal' X, p. 26 ff. and 62 ff.), 1924.

1520. **Griffith, John,** *The Ajanta cavepaintings* ('J. of Indian Art and Industry' VIII, No. 61), London, Jan. 1898.　　**C**

1521. **Griffith, W. J.,** *On the appreciation of African music* ('Nigerian Field' XVI, p. 88 ff.), 1951.　　　**M**

1522. **Grigson, W. V.,** *The Muria Gonds of Bastar* (London, 1938), p. 181 ff.: *Musical instruments.*　　　**J**

1523. **Grimaud, Yvette, and Gilbert Rouget,** *Notes on the Music of the Bushmen compared to that of the Babinga pygmies* (issued as L.P. record L.D. 9 by the Peabody Museum, Harvard Univ., Cambridge (Mass.) and by the Musée de l'Homme, Dept. of Ethnomusicology, Paris).　　　**A**

1525. **Groeger, H.,** *Die Musikinstrumente im Kult der Afrikaner* (Vienna, 1946).

1526. **Grolimund, S.,** *Volkslieder aus dem Kanton Solothurn* (Basel, 1910).　　**L**

1527. —— *Volkslieder aus dem Kanton Aargau* (Basel, 1911).

1528. **Groneman, J.,** *De gamelan te Jogjakarta* (1890).　　　**ABCHIJ**

1529. —— *In den kedaton te Jogjakarta* (Leiden, 1888). **BC**
1530. —— *De garebeg's te Ngajogyakarta* (The Hague, 1895). **AB**
1531. Groot, J. J. M. de, *De antieke keteltrommen in den Oost-Indischen archipel en op het vasteland van Zuidoost-Azië* ('Versl. en Meded. der Kon. Akad. v. Wetensch., afd. Letterk.', 4de reeks, 2de dl., p. 330 ff.), 1898. **D¹GH**
1532. —— *Universismus. Die Grundlage der Religion und Ethik, des Staatswesens und der Wissenschaften Chinas* (Berlin, 1918), pp. 78 ff., 154 ff., 165, 169, 179, 240, 343.
1532a. Grootaert, J. E. A., *Pensées autour d'un tam-tam 'lokombe'* (*Mutetela*) '(Brousse', 1946, Nos. 3–4, p. 20 ff.). **M**
1533. Groslier, George, *Recherches sur les Cambodgiens* (Paris, 1921), p. 125 ff. **A**
1534. Grosset, Joanny, *Contribution à l'étude de la musique hindoue* ('Bibliothèque de la Fac. des Lettres de Lyon' VI), 1888.
1535. —— *Inde. Histoire de la musique depuis l'origine jusqu'à nos jours* (1907) (in Lavignac, 'Hist. de la Mus.', I, p. 257 ff.), 1922. **ACDEFHJ**
1536. Grottanelli, Vinigi L., *Asiatic influences on Somali culture* ('Ethnos' XII, p. 153 ff. (espec. sub VI, p. 172 ff.)), 1947. **AGL²M**
1537. Groven, Eivind, *Naturskalaen* (Skien, 1927). **I**
1538. —— *Eskimomelodier fra Alaska. Studier over tonesystemer og rytmer* (Oslo?). Stencilled.
1539. Gruener Nielsen, H., *Vore aeldste folkedanse, langdans og polskdans* (Copenhagen, 1917). **K**
1540. —— *Folkelig Vals* (Copenhagen, 1920). **K**
1541. —— *Nyindsamling af faerøsk folkemusik* ('Musikhistorisk Arkiv' 1932, p. 137 ff.) **K**
*1542. —— *Folkemusik i Danmark* ('Nordisk Kultur. Musikk och Musikkinstrumenter', p. 81 ff.), 1934. **AK**
1543. —— *Faerøske Folkemelodier* (ibid., p. 152 ff.), 1934. **AK**
1544. —— *De faerøske Kvadmelodiers Tonalitet i Middelalderen* (Copenhagen, 1945) (with an English summary). **K**
1545. Grundtvig, Svend, Axel Olrik and H. Grüner-Nielsen, *Danmarks gamle Folkeviser* (1853–1923). **K**
1546. Gudenian, Haig, *The call of the ancient East. A few suggestions for the understanding of it through pure oriental music* (und., 1930?). **I**
1547. Guebels, L., *African Music and the Christian outlook*: I. R. P. Peeters, P.B., *Native Music and the Catholic religion;* II. Idohou, *Indigenous and sacred music* III. N.N., *Reflections of a missionary* ('African Music Society Newsletter' I, No. 2, p. 9 ff.), 1949. **ACM**
1548. Guenther, E., *Die schlesische Volksliedforschung* (Breslau).
1549. Guerrero, Raúl G., *La música zapoteca* ('Neza' IV, No. 1), Mexico, 1939.
1550. —— *Música de Chiapas* ('Revista de Estudios musicales' I, No. 2, p. 129 ff.), Mendoza (Arg.), Dec. 1949. **A**
1550a. —— *Consideraciones sobre la música turasca* ('Bol. Latino-Americano' V, p. 477 ff.), Montevideo, 1941. **AGL**
1551. Gugitz, Gustav, *Lieder der Strasse. Die Bänkelsänger im josephinischen Wien* (Vienna, 1954).
1551a. Guiart, Jean, *Notes sur les tambours d'Ambrym* ('J. de la Soc. des Océanistes' XII, p. 334 ff.), 1956. **BGL²**
1552. Guillemin, M., and J. Duchesne, *Sur l'origine asiatique de la cithare grecque* ('L'Antiquité Classique' IV), 1935. **D¹HK**
1553. Guillemin, L., *Le tambour d'appel des Ewondó* ('Etudes Camerounaires' I), 1948. **G**
1554. Gulik, R. H. van, *On three antique lutes* ('Transactions of the Asiatic Soc. of Japan' XVII, p. 153 ff.), Dec. 1938. **CGKL⁵**
*1555. —— *The Lore of the Chinese Lute* (Tokyo, 1940). **A**
1556. —— *Hsi K'ang and his poetical Essay on the Lute* (Tokyo, 1941). **A**
1557. —— *Brief Note on the Cheng, the Chinese Small Cither* ('Journal of the Soc. for Research in Asiat. Mus.' No. 9, p. 10 ff.), 1951. **A**
1558. —— *The Lore of the Chinese Lute. Addenda et Corrigenda* (Tokyo, 1951). **A**
1559. Gulliver, Pamela, *Dancing clubs of the Nyasa* ('Tanganyika Notes and Records' XLI, p. 58 ff.), Dec. 1955. **M**
1560. Gurvin, Olav, *Photography as an aid in folkmusic research* ('Norveg' III), 1955. **AK**
1560a. —— ass. by Eivind Groven, Truls Ørpen and Arne Bjørndal, *Norwegian Folk Music. Harding fiddle music* (6 vols. of which the 1st. will appear in autumn 1958) (Norwegian and English text), Univ. Press, Oslo. **A**
1561. Gustaver, B., *On a peculiar type of whistle found in ancient American Indian graves* ('American Anthropologist' XXIII, p. 307 ff.), 1923. **GJL²**
1562. Gwynn Williams, W. S., *Welsh National Music and Dance* (London, 1952).
1562a. Gyai, F., *Ueber indische Musikauffassung* ('Schweizerische Musikzeitung' 1924, p. 341 ff.).
1563. Gysi, Fritz, *Herkunft und Verbreitung des Alphorns* ('Heimatleben' XXVIII, No. 2), 1955.

1564. **Haase, R.,** *Musik und Astrologie* ('Musica' XII), 1951. **C**
1565. **Habig, J. M.,** *La valeur du rythme dans la musique bantoue* ('Problèmes d'Afrique Centrale' No. 26, p. 278 ff.), 1954. **AGJKM**
1565a. —— *Le rythme dans la vie indigène* ('Bull. de l'Union des Femmes coloniales' XVIII, No. 199, p. 6 ff.), 1947. **M**
1566. **Haddon, A. C.,** *Sound-producing Instruments* ('Reports of the Cambridge Anthropol. Exped. to Torres Straits' IV (Arts and Crafts), p. 270 ff.), 1912. **B**
1567. —— *Songs* (ibid., p. 284 ff.), 1912. **B**
1568. —— *Notes on Wooden Trumpets in New Guinea* (Man' XVII, p. 77 ff., No. 56), 1917. **BD¹GKL²M**
1569. **Haden, R.** Allen, *Dance Music of the Temiar* ('Asia Magazine' XXXIX, p. 114 ff.), 1939.
1570. **Hadži Manov, Vasil,** *Makedonski narodni pesni* vols. I–IV (Skopje, 1956).
1571. **Hagen, Karl,** *Ueber die Musik einiger Naturvölker (Australier, Melanesier, Polynesier)* (Diss.), Hamburg, 1892. **L²**
1572. **Hague, Eleanor,** *Eskimo songs* ('J. of Amer. Folklore' XXVIII, p. 96 ff.), 1915. **GK**
1573. —— *Latin American Folk music* (in Thompson, 'The intern. Cyclopedia of music and musicians' (1939), p. 575 ff. **C**
1574. —— *Latin American music, past and present* (Santa Ana, Cal., 1934).
1575. —— *Music in ancient Arabia and Spain,* being 'La Musica de las Cantigas' by Julian Ribera, transl. and abridged by —— and Marion Leffingwell (Stanford Univ. Press, Cal., 1929). (Cf. No. 3408). **D**
1575a. **Hahn, Kurt,** *Verzeichnis der wissenschaftlichen Arbeiten von Curt Sachs* ('Acta Musicologica' XXIX, p. 105 ff.), 1957. **ACDEH¹KLL¹**
1576. **Hajek, L.,** *Das Phonogramm-Archiv der Akademie der Wissenschaften* ('Z. f. vergl. Musikw.' I, p. 15 ff.), 1933. **ACK**
1577. **Halde, Jean Baptiste du,** *Description . . . de l'Empire de la Chine . . .* (5 vols.), Paris, 1735. Vol. III, p. 264 ff., vol. V (musical examples).
1577a. **Halim, A.,** *Music and musicians of Shah Jahan's court* ('Islamic Culture' XIX No. 4), Haiderabad, Oct. 1945.
1578. **Hall, Henry Usher,** *A drum from Benin* ('Mus. Journ. Philadelphia' XIX, p. 130 ff.), 1928. **JL²**
1579. **Hall, Jody,** and **Bruno Nettl,** *Musical style of the Modoc* ('Southwestern Journal of Anthropology' XL, p. 58 ff.), 1955. **D¹GL²**
1580. **Hall, Leland,** *What price harmony?* ('Atlantic Monthly' CLIV, p. 511 ff.), Oct. 1929.

1580a. **Halpert, Herbert,** *La técnica para la grabación de canciones folklóricas* ('Bol. Latino-Americano de Música' V, p. 177 ff.), 1941. **A**
*1581. **Halski, Czeslaw R.,** *Polish Folk Music* ('Grove's Dictionary' 5th ed. vol. III, p. 326 ff.), 1954. **ACFH¹K**
1581a. **Hambruch, Paul,** *Ueber Trommelsprache* (in: Thilenius/Meinhof/Heinitz, 'Die Trommelsprache') ('Vox' XXVI), 1916. **G**
1582. **Hamilton, I.,** *Listening for the drums* (London, Faber & Faber, 1944).
1583. **Hammerich, Angul,** *Studien über isländische Musik* ('Sammelb. d. intern. Musikges.' I, p. 333 ff.), 1899–1900. **CDFH¹L**
1584. —— *Les lurs de l'âge de bronze au musée national de Copenhague* ('Mémoires de la Soc. Royal des Antiquairs du Nord' N.S., 1892), p. 137 ff. C
1585. —— *Studier over islandisk Musik* ('Aarbøger for nordisk Oldkyndighed og Historie' 1899, p. 1 ff.).
1586. **Handschin, Jacques,** *Mennyiség és minőség a zenében (Quantité et qualité dans la musique)* (in 'Mélanges offerts à Zoltan Kodaly à l'occasion de son 60ième anniversaire', p. 55 ff.), Budapest, 1943. **ACK**
1587. —— *Indische Musik* ('Neue Zürcher Z.' No. 2040), 1932; reprinted in 'Gedenkschrift Jacques Handschin' (Bern, 1957), p. 306 ff. **AD**
1588. —— *Erich M. von Hornbostel* ('Neue Zürcher Z.' No. 2209), 1936; reprinted in 'Gedenkschrift Jacques Handschin' (Bern, 1957), p. 385 ff. **AD**
1589. —— *Musikgeschichte* (Basel, 1948). **A**
1590. —— *Der Toncharacter* (Zürich, 1948). **A**
1591. —— *La musique exotique* (in 'Musica Aeterna', vol. I, French ed., p. 129 ff.), 1948. **A**
1592. —— Review of Kathleen Schlesinger, 'The Greek Aulos' ('Acta Musicologica' XX, p. 60 ff.), 1948. **ACEFH¹KLL¹**
1593. —— Review of J. Kunst, 'Music in Java' ('Acta Musicologica' XXII, p. 156 ff.), 1951. **ACDEFH¹KLL¹**
1594. —— *La musique paysanne russe* ('Schweizerische Musikzeitung' XCII, p. 289 ff.), 1952. **CL**
1595. **Handy, E. S. Craighill,** *The native culture in the Marquesas* ('Bull. Bernice P. Bishop Museum' IX, p. 310 ff.: *Musical instruments*), Honolulu, 1923. **J**
1596. **Handy, E. S. Craighill,** and **J. L. Winne,** *Music in the Marquesas Islands* (Ber. P. Bishop Nus. Bull. XVII), Honolulu, 1925. **AGK**
1597. **Hannagan, M.,** and **S. Clandillon,** *Songs of the Irish Gaels with the music and*

125

English metrical translation. 3 vols. (London, 1927).

1598 .Harap, Louis, Some Hellenic Ideas on Music and Character ('Musical Quarterly' XXIV, p. 153 ff.), 1938. **CD**

1598a. Haraszti, Emile, La question Tzigane-Hongroise au point de vue de l'histoire de la musique ('Kongressbericht Lüneburg 1950', p. 140 ff.). **ACDEFKL**

1599. Harcourt, Raoul D', La musique indienne chez les anciens civilisés d'Amérique. I. Les instruments de musique des Mexicains et des Péruviens. (1920) (in Lavignac, 'Hist. de la Mus.' V, p. 3337 ff.), 1922. **ACDEFHJ**

1600. —— (with the collab. of Mrs. Margherite d'Harcourt) La musique des Incas et ses survivances (Paris, 1925). **CIK**

1601. Harcourt, Raoul, and Margherite d', La fabrication de certains grelots métalliques chez les Yunka ('Atti del XXII congresso intern. degli Americanisti' I), Rome, 1928.

1602. —— and —— Chants populaires du Pérou ('Revue musicale' VI, No. 7), 1st May 1925. **CD¹GHKL**

1603. —— L'ocarina à cinq sons dans l'Amérique préhispanique ('Journal de la Soc. des Américanistes' XXIII, p. 189 ff.), 1931. **GL²**

1604. —— Sifflets et ocarinas du Nicaragua et du Mexique ('J. de la Soc. des Américanistes', Paris, 1941). **GL²**

1605. —— La musique en Amérique (in Dufourcq, 'La Musique, des origines à nos jours', ed.-Larousse, p. 465 ff.), Paris, 1946. **ACDEFHJK**

1606. —— Les formes du tambour à membrane dans l'ancien Pérou ('J. de la Soc. des Américanistes' XLIII), 1954. **BGL²**

1607. —— and Margherite d', Chansons folkloriques françaises au Canada. Leur langue musicale (Quebec, Presses universitaires de France, 1956). **C**

1607a. —— La musique chez les Maya ('Bull. de la Soc. Suisse des Américanistes' III, p. 1 ff.), Geneva, 1951.

1608. Hardiment, Melville, A master of Indian music ('Eastern World' X, No. 12, p. 38), Dec. 1956. **B**

1609. Hare, Maud Cuney, Negro musicians and their music (Washington, 1936).

1610. —— History and song in the Virgin Islands ('Crisis' XL, p. 83 ff.), New York, 1933.

1611. —— Negro music in Porto Rico (in 'Negro Anthology' ed. by Nancy Cunard, p. 400 ff.), Wishart, 1934.

1612. Harich-Schneider, Eta, Japanische Impressionen I-III ('Musica' No. 3, p. 85 ff., No. 4, p. 129 ff., No. 6, p. 205 ff.), Kassel, 1949. **CKLL¹**

1613. —— A survey of the remains of Japanese

Court Music ('Ethnos' 1951, p. 105 ff.). **ABJL²M**

1614. —— Die Gagaku in der Musikabteilung des japanischen Kaiserhofes ('Kongressber. D.M.G., Lüneburg 1950', p. 168 ff.), 1951. **ACDEFKL**

1615. —— Koromogae, one of the Saibara of Japanese Court Music ('Monumenta Nipponica' VIII, no. 1/2, p. 398 ff.), Tokyo, 1952. **AGL¹L⁶**

1616. —— The present Condition of Japanese Court Music ('The Musical Quarterly' XXXIX No. 1, p. 49 ff.), 1953. **ACDFKL¹**

1617. —— The rhythmical Patterns in Gagaku and Bugaku (Leyden, 1954). **AC**

1618. —— The earliest sources of Chinese music and their survival in Japan ('Monumenta Nipponica' XI, No. 2, p. 85 ff.), 1955. **AGL¹L⁶**

1618a. —— Ueber die Gilden blinder Musiker in Japan ('Kongressbericht Ges. f. Musikforschung, Hamburg 1956', p. 107 ff.). **CEL**

1619. Harlez, C. de, Deux traités de la musique ('Giorn. de la Soc. Asiatica Italiana' VI, p. 161 ff.), 1892. **GH**

1619a. Harper, F. J., Nigerian music ('Nigerian Field' XVII, p. 91 ff.), 1952. **M**

1620. Harrington, J. P., and Helen H. Roberts, Picuris children's stories with texts and songs ('Annual Report of the Bur. of Amer. Ethnology' No. 43 (1925–'26), p. 289 ff.), Washington D.C. 1928. **BHI**

1621. Harris, P. G., Notes on Drums and Musical Instruments seen in Sokoto Province, Nigeria ('Journal of the Royal Anthropol. Inst. of Gr. Britain and Ireland', 1932). **BGIJKL¹L²M**

1622. Hartmann, Arthur, The Czimbalom, Hungarys national instrument ('The Musical Quarterly' II, p. 590 ff.), 1916.

1623. Hartmann, M., Arabische Lieder aus Syrien ('Z. der Deutschen Morgenl. Ges.' 1897, p. 177 ff.). **D¹GHL⁴**

1624. Hasan Husni 'Abd Al-Wahhab, Le développement de la musique arabe en Orient, Espagne et Tunisie (Tunis, 1918).

1625. Haslund-Christensen, H., On the trail of ancient Mongol tunes ('Reports from the scientific expedition to the Northwestern provinces of China under the leadership of Dr. Sven Hedin. Publ. 21 VIII. Ethnography. 4. The music of the Mongols. Part I. Eastern Mongolia. **AC**

1626. Hasselt, A. L. van, Volksbeschrijving van Midden-Sumatra (Leiden, 1882), vol. III, Chapter IV, p. 99 ff. **B**

1627. Haupt, Leopold, and Johann Ernst Schmaler, Volkslieder der Sorben in der Ober- und Nieder-Lausitz (Anastatic reprint of the edition of 1841), Berlin, 1953. **L**

1628. **Hause, H. E.**, *Terms for Musical Instruments in the Sudanic Languages* ('Suppl. 7 to the Journal of the Amer. Oriental Soc.', LXVIII, No. 1), Jan./March 1948. **AD¹GKL¹**

1629. **Hawkes, E. W.**, *The dance festivals of the Alaskan Eskimo* ('Univ. of Pennsylvania Anthropol. Public.' VI), Philadelphia, 1914.

1630. **Hawley, E. H.**, *Distribution of the notched rattle* ('American Anthropologist' XI, p. 344 ff.), 1898.

1631. —— *An inverted double reed* ('Amer. Anthropol.' I, p. 587 ff.), 1899. **GL²**

*1632. **Haydon, Glen**, *Introduction to Musicology* (New York, 1941, 4/1950). **A**

1632a. **Hayes, Gerald R.**, *Notes on the crwth* ('Y Cerddor', 2nd series, p. 417 ff., 451 ff.), March/April, 1931.

1633. **Hayward, Richard**, *The story of the Irish harp* (London, 1954).

*1634. **Haywood, Charles**, *A Bibliography of North American Folklore and Folksong* (New York, 1951).

1635. **Hazeu, G. A. J.**, *Eine Metalltrommel aus Java* ('Intern. Archiv f. Ethnogr.' XIX, p. 82 ff.), 1910. **BD¹GKL²**

1636. **Heekeren, H. R. van**, *Bronzen keteltrommen* ('Orientatie' No. 46, p. 615 ff.), Jan. 1954. **AD¹GH**

1637. **Heepe, M.**, *Trommelsprache der Jaunde in Kamerun* ('Z. f. Eingeborenensprachen' X, p. 43 ff.), 1920. **GKL¹**

1638. **Heerkens, A.**, *Musical instruments* ('Picture Encyclopedia' No. 20), Alkmaar, und. (prob. 1956).

1639. **Heerkens, S. V. D., Father P.**, *Lieder der Florinesen, Sammlung 140 Florinesischer Lieder und 162 Texte mit Uebersetzung aus dem Sprachgebiete der Lionesen, Sikanesen, Ngada's und Manggaraier* (Supplement to vol. XLVI of the 'Intern. Arch. of Ethnogr.'), Leyden, 1953. **ABCD¹GHLL²M**

1640. **Hefny, Mahmoud El**, *Ibn Sin'as Musiklehre* (Berlin, 1931). **G**

1641. —— *Music in Egypt* ('Egypt in 1945', p. 218 ff.), Calcutta, 1946.

1641a. —— *Aegyptische Musik von einst bis heute* (Cairo, 1956). **L**

1642. **Heger, Franz**, *Alte Metalltrommeln aus südost-Asien* (Leipzig, 1902).

1643. **Heilfurth, Gerhard**, *Das Bergmannslied: Wesen, Leben, Funktion; ein Beitrag zur Erhellung von Bestand und Wandlung der sozial-kulturellen Elemente im Aufbau der industriellen Gesellschaft* (Kassel/Basel, Bärenreiter Verlag, 1954). **L**

1644. **Heine-Geldern, Robert von**, *Bedeutung und Herkunft der ältesten hinter-indi-*

schen Metalltrommeln (Kesselgonge) ('Asia Major' VIII, fasc. 3, p. 519 ff.), 1932. **D¹GL¹**

1645. —— *Tambours en métal au Cambodge* ('Asia Major' VIII, p. 519 ff.), 1932. **D¹GL¹**

1646. —— *Trommelsprachen ohne Trommeln* ('Anthropos' XXVIII, p. 485), 1933. **AD¹GHKL¹L²M**

1647. —— *Prehistoric research in the Netherlands Indies* ('Science and Scientists in the Netherlands Indies' New York, 1945, p. 129 ff.), p. 145 ff. **A**

1648. —— *The drum named Makalamau* ('India Antiqua', a vol. of oriental studies presented to J. Ph. Vogel), 1947, p. 167 ff. **A**

1649. **Heinitz, Wilhelm**, *Die Trommelsprache in Afrika und in der Südsee* (in collab. with Prof. Thilenius and Prof. Meinhof) ('Vox' 1916, p. 179 ff.). **G**

1650. —— *Musikinstrumente und Phonogramme des Ost-Mbam-Landes* (in F. und M. Thorbecke, 'Im Hochland von Mittelkamerun' vol. III), 1919. **JM**

1651. —— *Ueber die Musik der Somali* ('Z. f. Musikw.' II, p. 257 ff.), 1920. **CDH¹KL**

1652. —— *Transkription zweier Lieder aus Nil-Nubien* ('Z. f. Musikw.' II, p. 733 ff.), 1920. **CDH¹KL**

1653. —— *Eine lexikalische Ordnung für die vergleichende Betrachtung von Melodien* ('Archiv f. Musikwis.' III, p. 247 ff.), 1921. **CDFH¹KLL¹**

1654. —— *Sechs Zigeunerlieder mit untergelegten Texten* ('Vox' 1921, p. 187 ff.). **G**

1655. —— *Ein Materialbeitrag zur Kenntnis der arabischen Musik* ('Z. f. Musikw.' IV, p. 193 ff.), 1922. **CDH¹KL**

1656. —— *Musikalisch-dynamische Textauslese in faeröischen und faeröisch-dänischen Reigentänzen* ('Festschrift-Pipping', p. 160 ff.), Helsingfors, 1924. **L**

1657. —— *Grammophonaufnahmen im Dienste der Musikwissenschaft* ('Z. f. Musikw.' VI, p. 332 ff.), 1924. **CDH¹KL**

1658. —— *Lieder aus Ost-Neumecklenburg* ('Z. f. Musikw.' VII, p. 257 ff.), 1924. **CDH¹KL**

1659. —— *Vergleichende Musikwissenschaft* ('Z. f. Musik' XCII), 1925. **L**

1660. —— *Musik und Arbeit* (ibid.), 1925. **L**

1661. —— *Statistik und Experiment bei der musikalischen Melodievergleichung* ('Z. f. Musikw.' VII, p. 221 ff.), 1925. **CDH¹KL**

1662. —— *Vier Lieder aus Ost-Neu-Mecklenburg* ('Z. f. Musikwiss.' VIII, p. 257 ff.), 1926. **CDH¹KL**

1663. —— *Analyse eines abessinischen Harfenliedes* ('Festschrift-Meinhof', p. 263), 1927.

127

1664. —— *Ein Beitrag zum Problem der Trommelsprache* ('Vox' 1927, p. 29 ff.). **G**

1665. —— *Die vergleichende Musikwissenschaft im Dienste der Völkerkunde* ('Ber. d. Deutschen Anthropol. Ges. über ihre 50. Vers. zu Hamburg'), 1928.

1666. —— *Analyse eines Mende-Liedes* ('Vox' IX, p. 40 ff.), Hamburg, 1928. **G**

1667. —— *Instrumentenkunde* (in Ernst Bücken, 'Handbuch der Musikwissenschaft' vol. II, p. 1 ff.), 1929. **CDEFGH¹JKLL²**

1668. —— *Versuch einer Analyse des Berliner Notenpapyrus P. 6870* ('Z. f. Musikw.' XI, p. 222 ff.), 1929. **ACDEH¹KL**

1669. —— *Analytische Betrachtung eines mongolischen Liedes* ('Vox' XVII, p. 65 ff.), 1931.

1670. —— *Eine Melodieprobe von den Sara-Kaba* (ibid., p. 69 ff.), 1931.

1671. —— *Strukturprobleme in primitiver Musik* (Hamburg, 1931). **AIJL²**

1672. —— *Die Erfassung des subjektiv-motorischen Elements in der musikalischen Produktion Primitiver* ('Kongressber. der Intern. Ges. f. Musikw., Lütich 1930', p. 148 ff.), 1931.

1674. —— *Organologische Studie an den Varianten eines Dronning Dagmar-Liedes* ('Acta Musicologica' III, p. 156 ff.), 1932. **CDEKLL¹**

1675. —— *Chirimia- und Tambór-Phonogramme aus Nordwest-Guatemala* ('Vox' XIX, p. 4 ff.), 1933.

1676. —— *Die vergleichende Musikwissenschaft als Instrument der Stil- und Rassenkunde* ('Forschungen und Fortschritte' XI No. 3, p. 30 ff.), 1935.

1677. —— *Musikwissenschaftliche Vergleiche an vier afrikanischen (Djarma- Ewe- und Yefe-) Gesängen* ('Vox' 1935, p. 23 ff.).

1678. —— *Was kann die vergleichende Musikwissenschaft zur Indogermanenfrage beitragen?* ('Festschrift-Herman Hirt' 1935, p. 125 ff.).

1679. —— *Neue Wege der Volksmusikforschung* (Hamburg, 1937). **I**

1680. —— *Musikwissenschaft und Völkerkunde* ('Mitteilungsblatt der Gesellschaft f. Völkerkunde', No. 8, p. 43), Hamburg, 1938.

1681. —— *Die Erforschung rassischer Merkmale aus der Volksmusik* (Hansischer Gildenverlag, Hamburg, 1938). **I**

1682. —— *Zum Problem der afrikanischen Trommelsprache* ('Afrika-Rundschau' VII, p. 142 ff.), 1941. **M**

1683. —— *Rassische Merkmale an afrikanischem Musikgut* ('Z. f. Rassenkunde' XII, p. 9 ff.), 1941. **GH**

1684. —— *Probleme der afrikanischen Trommelsprache* ('Beiträge zur Kolonialforschung' IV, p. 69 ff.), 1943. **D¹G**

1685. Heintze, R., *Ueber Batakmusik* (in W. Volz, 'Die Batakländer', p. 373 ff.), 1919. **AB**

1685a. Helffer, Mireille, *La musique classique de l'Inde et un de ses plus grands interprètes actuels: Ravi Shankar* ('Arts Asiatiques' IV, No. 4, p. 311 ff.), Paris, 1957. **B**

1686. Helfritz, Hans, *Muziek en Muziekbeoefening in Arabië* ('De Muziek' V, p. 145 ff.), 1931. **ACDEFH**

*1686a. Helgason, Hallgrimur, *Island* ('Die Musik in Geschichte u. Gegenwart' VI, col. 1438 ff.), 1957. **ACDEFGH¹KL**

1687. Hemsi, A., *La musique de la Torah* (Alexandria, 1929).

1688. Hen, F. J. de, *Tamtams in Belgisch Congo* (Licentiaatsverhandeling, Universitair Inst. voor de Overzeese gebieden), 1954–'55. **CM**

*1689. Henderson, Isobel, *Ancient Greek Music* ('The New Oxford History of Music', 3rd ed., vol. I, p. 336 ff.), 1957. **ABCD¹FGH¹JK**

1690. Henriques-Ureña, Pedro, *Musica popular de America* ('Conferencias' I), La Plata, 1930.

1691. Herbig, Reinhard, *Griechische Harfen* ('Mitt. des Deutschen Archäologischen Inst. Athenische Abt.' LIV, p. 164 ff.), 1929. **GL¹**

1692. Hermann, Eduard, *Schallsignalsprachen in Melanesien und Afrika* ('Nachrichten d. Akad. d. Wiss. in Göttingen' 1943). **AD¹GHL¹**

Hernandez de Alba, Gregorio, see Alba, Gregorio Hernandez de.

1693. Herscher-Clément, Mad. J., *Chants d'Abyssinie* ('Z. f. vergl. Musikw.' II, p. 51 ff.), 1934. **ACK**

1694. —— *Notes musicologiques. Chants indigènes de la Nouvelle Guinée* ('La Revue Musicale' No. 173, p. 223), 1937. **DGKL**

1695. —— *Quelques mots sur la musique indigène en Nouvelle Guinée* ('L'Ethnographie' No. 35/6, p. 51 ff.), 1938. **D¹GK**

1696. Herskovits, Melville J., *El estudio de la música negra en el hemisferio occidental* ('Bol. Latino-Americano de Música' V), Montevideo, 1941. **AGL**

1697. —— *Dahomey* (New York, 1938), p. 31g ff.

1698. —— *Drums and Drummers in Afro-Brazilian Cult-life* ('The Musical Quarterly' XXX, No. 4, p. 477 ff.), 1944. **ACH¹**

1699. —— *Tambores y tamborileiros no culto afrobrasileiro* ('Bol. Latino-Americano de Música', VI, p. 99 ff.), Rio de Janeiro, 1946. **AEL**

1700. —— *Patterns of Negro music* (undated).

1701. —— and Richard A. Waterman, *Mu-*

128

1769. —— *Abrégé de l'histoire de la musique en Egypte* ('Revue de Musicologie' XXXII Nos. 93-94), Paris, 1950. **ACD¹EFKL¹**

1770. —— *Ein unbekanntes ägyptisches Saiteninstrument aus koptischer Zeit* ('Die Musikforschung' III), 1950. **ACEIKLL¹**

1771. —— *Fabrikationsmarken an altägyptischen Blasinstrumenten* (ibid. III, p. 241 ff.), 1950. **ACEIKLL¹**

1772. —— *Abrégé de l'histoire de la musique en Egypte* ('Revue de Musicologie' XXXII p. 93 ff.), 1950; transl. in Spanish in: 'Boletin cultural, Departamento de la Prensa, Cairo', (Cairo, 1950).

1773. —— id. transl. in English (Cairo, 1950).

1774. —— *Quelques observations sur la musique lithurgique des Coptes* (Communication au Congrès de Musique Sacrée, Rome 1950). **A**

1775. —— *Miscellanea musicologica* ('Annales du Service des Antiquités de l'Egypte' L, p. 523 ff.), Cairo 1950: VII. *Les harpes de la tombe de Ramses III;* VIII. *Deux vases siffleurs de l'Egypte ancienne;* IX. *Le fragment d'un instrument à cordes.* **AGJL**

1776. —— *Miscellanea egyptologica* ('Journal of the Galpin Soc.' I, p. 25 ff.), London, 1951. **CJ**

1777. —— *Ueber den Stand der musikwissenschaftlichen Forschung in Aegypten* ('Kongressber. des IV. Kongress der Intern. Ges. f. Musikw., Basel' p. 150 ff), Basel 1951. **AC**

1778. —— *Miscellanea musicologica* ('Annales du Service des Antiquités de l'Egypte' LI, p. 317 ff.) (Cairo 1951): X. *Le tambourin rectangulaire du Nouvel Empire.* **AG**

1779. —— *Die ältesten Musikernamen* ('Musica' V, p. 89 ff.), 1951. **CDKLL¹**

1780. —— *Classement et classification des flûtes, clarinettes et hautbois de l'Egypte ancienne* ('Chronique d'Egypte' XXVI, No. 51, p. 17 ff.), 1951. **ADG¹HK**

1781. —— *Note on an Egyptian wind instrument* ('Journal of the Intern. Folk Music Council' III, p. 108 ff.), 1951. **ACJKL**

1782. —— *La castagnette égyptienne* ('Annales du Service des Antiquités de l'Egypte' LI), Cairo 1951. **G**

1783. —— *Arabische Musik* (in collab. with Alexis Chottin) ('Die Musik in Geschichte und Gegenwart' I, col. 577), 1951. **ACDEFGH¹KL**

1784. —— *Aegyptische Musik* (ibid., col. 92 ff.), 1951. **ACDEFGH¹KL**

1785. —— *Aethiopische Musik* (ibid., col. 105 ff.), 1951. **ACDEFGH¹KL**

1786. —— *Afrikanische Musik* (ibid., col. 123 ff.), 1951. **ACDEFGH¹KL**

1787. —— *Armenische Musik* (ibid. col. 654 ff.), 1951. **ACDEFGH¹KL**

1788. —— *Le métier de musicien au temps des Pharaons* ('Cahiers d'histoire égyptiennes' IV, 2), Cairo, 1952, 2/1954 (ibid. VI, 5/6). **AG**

1789. —— *Miscellanea musicologica* ('Annales du Service des Antiquités de l'Egypte' LII, p. 161 ff.), Cairo, 1952: XI. *Les luths aux frettes du Nouvel Empire.* **ACGL**

1790. —— *Das Harfenspiel im alten Egypten* ('Die Musikforschung' V, p. 21 ff.), 1952. **ACDEGKLL¹**

1791. —— *The antique cross-flute* ('Acta Musicologica' XXIV, p. 108 ff.), 1952. **ACDEFH¹KLL¹**

1792. —— *Quelques observations sur la musique lithurgique des Coptes d'Egypte* ('Atti del Congresso Intern. di Musica Sacra, Roma 1950'), Tournay, 1952. **A**

1793. —— *La daraboukah* ('Bull. de l'Inst. d'Egypte' XXXIII, p. 229 ff.), Cairo, 1952. **ACGL**

1794. —— *La musique polyphonique dans l'Egypte ancienne* (ibid. XXXIV, p. 229 ff.), 1953. **AGL**

1795. —— *Le jeu de la harpe dans l'Egypte ancienne* ('Archiv Orientalni,' XX Nos. 3-4, p. 449 ff.), Prague, 1952. **ABGK**

1796. —— *The Egyptian 'Uffatah' Flute* ('Journal of the R. Asiatic Soc.' Oct. 1952). **D¹GIKL¹**

1797. —— *Quelques nouveaux documents concernant le jeu de la harpe et l'emploi de la chironomie dans l'Egypte pharaonique* ('Kongressber. Intern. Mus. Ges. 1952', p. 263 ff.), Amsterdam, 1953. **ACDEF**

1798. —— *Die Anfänge eines geordneten Musiklebens im Aegypten der Pharaonen* (Communication Intern. Congress, Vienna 17-24th May, 1952), Vienna, 1953. **AB**

1799. —— *Quelques considérations sur la danse et la musique de danse dans l'Egypte pharaonique* ('Cahiers d'histoire égyptiennes' V, p. 161 ff.), Cairo, 1953. **AG**

1800. —— *Les harpes de l'Egypte pharaonique (Essai d'une nouvelle classification)* ('Bull. de l'Institut d'Egypte', XXXV, p. 309 ff.), Cairo, 1954. **AGL**

1801. —— *Miscellanea musicologica* ('Annales du Service des Antiquités de l'Egypte' LIII), Cairo, 1953: XII. *La scène musicale d'une tombe de la VIième dynastie à Guizah (Idou)* (**A**); XIII. *Note sur un objet en forme d'instrument de percussion;* XIV. *Une nouvelle cymbalette à manche?* **G**

1802. —— Review of Max Wegner, 'Die Musikinstrumente des Alten Orient' (1950) ('Orientalische Literaturzeitung' 1954, Nos. 1/2, p. 34). **AD¹HKL¹**

1803. —— *Aegyptische Volksinstrumente* ('Musica' VIII), Kassel, 1954. **CDKLL¹**

1804. —— *Dieux et déesses de la musique* ('Cahiers d'Histoire Egyptienne' VI, p. 31 ff.), March 1954. **AG**

1805. —— *Fidel I. Orientalische Vorläufer und Verwandte* ('Die Musik in Geschichte und Gegenwart' IV, col. 156 ff.), 1954. **ACDEFGH¹KL**

1807. —— *Unbekannte ägyptische Klangwerkzeuge. I. Schwirrholz und Schwirrscheibe* ('Die Musikforschung' VIII p. 151 ff.); *II. Muschelpfeifen und Gefässflöten* (ibid. p. 314 ff.); *III/VI. Knochenpfeifen; Blockflöten; Sackpfeife; Querflöte* (ibid. p. 398 ff.), 1955. **ACEFIKLL¹**

1808. —— *A new type of Egyptian harp* ('Acta Musicologica' XXVI, p. 127 ff.), 1954. **ACDEFGH¹KLL¹**

1809. —— *Die altaegyptische Rassel* ('Z. f. Aegypt. Sprache und Altertumskunde' LXXIX, vol. II, p. 116 ff.), Berlin, 1954. **AD¹GHK**

1810. —— *Usage et signification des frettes dans l'Egypte pharaonique* ('Kemi' XIII), Paris, 1954. **GK**

1811. —— *La menat* (ibid.), Paris, 1954. **GK**

1812. —— *Le problème de la notation musicale dans l'Egypte ancienne* ('Bull. de l'Inst. d'Egypte' XXXVI, p. 489 ff.), Cairo, 1955. **AGJ**

1813. —— *Terminologie musicale de l'Egypte ancienne* (ibid. XXXVI, p. 583 ff.), Cairo, 1955. **AGJ**

1814. —— Compte rendu du livre de F. Behn, 'Musikleben im Altertum und fruehen Mittelalter' ('Cahiers d'Histoire Egyptienne' Série VII, fasc. 3), Cairo, 1955. **AG**

1815. —— *Flöteninstrumente. Flötencharacter und Form* ('Die Musik in Geschichte und Gegenwart' IV, col. 319 ff.), 1956. **ACDEFGH¹KL**

1816. —— *Flöteninstrumente. Altertum: Orient und Antike* (ibid. col. 323 ff.), 1956. **ACDEFGH¹KL**

1817. —— *Gitarre. Vorgeschichte und aussereuropäische Formen* (ibid. V, col. 17 ff.), 1956. **ACDEFGH¹KL**

1818. —— *Glocken. Altertum und aussereuropäische Glocken* (ibid. V, col. 267 ff.), 1956. **ACDEFGH¹KL**

1819. —— *Musique et vie musicale sous les Pharaons. Etude historique, systématique et descriptive des instruments et de l'évolution de l'art musical dans l'Egypte ancienne* (3 vols.), Richard-Masse, Paris (in preparation).

1820. —— *Randbemerkungen zu A. Berners Besprechung* ('Die Musikforschung' IX, p. 200 ff.), 1956. **ACEFIKLL¹**

1821. —— *Les problèmes et l'état des recherches musicologiques en Egypte* ('Acta Musicologica' XXVIII, p. 59 ff.), 1956. **ACDEFGH¹KLL¹**

1822. —— *Musicologie pharaonique. Etudes sur l'évolution de l'art musical dans l'Egypte ancienne* (Kehl, 1956). **AK**

1823. —— *Handzeichen. I. Altertum und ausser-europäische Musik* ('Die Musik in Geschichte und Gegenwart' V, col. 1443 ff.), 1956. **ACDEFGH¹KL**

●1824. —— *Harfe* ('ibid. V, col. 1507 ff.), 1956. **ACDEFGH¹KL**

1824a. —— *Une scène de musique pharaonique (analyse iconographique)* ('Revue de la Soc. belge de Musicol.' X), 1956. **C**

1825. —— *La flûte de Pan* ('Chronique d'Egypte' XXX, p. 217 ff.), 1955. **AD¹GHKL**

1826. —— *Une scène de musique pharaonique (analyse iconographique)* ('Revue de la Soc. belge de Musicologie' X), 1956. **C**

1827. —— *L'essor de la musique sous l'Ancien Empire de l'Egypte pharaonique (2778–2423 av. J.C.)* ('Memorial pour F. Ortiz'), Havana, 1956.

1828. —— *La chironomie dans l'Egypte ancienne (????)*.

1829. —— *La danse au miroirs. Essai de reconstruction d'une danse pharaonique de l'Ancien Empire* ('Bull. de l'Inst. d'Egypte' XXXVII, p. 151 ff.), Cairo, 1956. **AL**

1829a. —— *Du battement des mains aux planchettes entrechoquées* ('Bull. de l'Inst. d'Egypte' XXXVII, p. 67 ff.), Cairo, 1954/'55. **G**

1830. —— *Rapport préliminaire sur la campagne d'enregistrements de musique folklorique egyptienne sous le patronage de S. A. le Duc de Mecklembourg (été 1955)* ('Bull. de l'Inst. d'Egypte' p. . . .), Cairo, 1958. **G**

1831. —— *Klingendes Pharaonenland* (M. Hesse, Berlin, 195.).

1832. —— *Aegyptische Musikgeschichte in Bildern* (Breitkopf, 195.).

1833. —— *45 siècles de musique dans l'Egypte ancienne* (Paris, 1956). **AC**

1834. —— *Musik, Musiker -namen und -instrumente* ('Handwörterbuch der Aegyptologie'), Wiesbaden, 1956.

1834a. —— Articles on Music, Musicians, Musical instruments (in: W. Helck and E. Otto, 'Kleines Wörterbuch der Aegyptologie'), Wiesbaden, 1956.

1834b. —— *Die Gefässtrommeln der Aegypter* ('Mitteilungen des Deutschen Archaeologischen Instituts', Abt. Kairo, vol. XIV 'Festschrift-H. Kees'), Wiesbaden, 1956.

1835. —— *The instruments of music in the Antique Oriental Civilisation* (Pinguin Books), 1957.

1836. —— *Un zikr dans le mastaba de Debhen Gutzah (4th dynastie)* ('J. of the Intern. Folk Music Council' IX, p. 59 ff.), 1957. **ACJKL**

1837. —— *Miscellania musicologica* ('Annales du Service des Antiquités de l'Egypte' LVII, p. .... ff.), Cairo, 1958: XV. *Le grelot dans l'Egypte ancienne.* **G**

1838. —— *La castagnette dans l'Egypte ancienne* ('Bull. de la Soc. des amis de l'art copte'), 1958.

1839. —— *Horninstrumente.* **B.** *Frühgeschichte, Orient und Altertum* ('Die Musik in Geschichte und Gegenwart' VI, col. 733 ff.), 1957. **ACDEFGH¹KL**

1839a. —— *Die altaegyptischen Becken* ('Z. f. Instrumentenbau' XII, p. 2 ff.), Siegburg, 1957. **AD¹**

1840. —— *Hufu-anh und andere ägyptische Musiker* ('Die Musik in Geschichte u. Gegenwart' VI, col. 852 ff.), 1957. **ACDEFGH¹KL**

1840a. —— *Musikerziehung im alten Aegypten* ('Musikerkenntnis und Musikerziehung' (Festschrift-Mersmann), p. 55 ff.), Kassel/Basel, 1957. **A**

1840b. —— *Neues Musikleben in Aegypten* ('Mitteilungen des Instituts für Auslandsbeziehungen' II), Stuttgart, 1957.

1840c. —— *Ein Beitrag "zum Problem des Ursprungs der mittelalterlichen Solmisation"* ('Die Musikforschung' X, p. 403 ff.), 1957. **ACEFIKLL¹**

1840d. Hillelson, S., *Weekend Caravan* (London/Edinburgh/Glasgow, 1937, 2/1947), p. 89 ff.: *Songs of Araby (Sudan, Egypt, Palestine).*

1841. Hipkins, Alfred James, *Old Keyboard Instruments* (1887).

1842. —— *Musical Instruments, historic, rare and unique* (London, 1888, 2/1945). **ACI**

1843. —— *A Description and History of the Pianoforte and Older Keybord Stringed Instruments* (1896). **CI**

1844. —— *Dorian and Phrygian* (1903). **I**
Hiroa, Te Rangi, see: Buck, Peter H.

1844a. Hirschberg, Walter, *Der Ahnencharakter des Schwirrholzes* ('Ethnos' V, p. 112 ff.), 1940. **M**

1845. Hirth, F., *Ueber hinterindische Bronzetrommeln* ('T'oung-pao' I, p. 137 ff.), 1890. **GK**

1846. —— *Chinesische Ansichten über Bronzetrommeln* ('Mitt. d. Seminars f. Orientalische Sprachen' VII, Part I, p. 200 ff.), 1904. **D¹L²**

1846a. Ho Lu-Ting, *What kind of music for China* ('China reconstructs' Dec. 1956; repr. in 'China in transition' p. 377 ff.), Peking, 1957. **C**

1847. Hobbs, Cecil C., *Burmese musical recordings* ('Quarterly Journal of current acquisitions' X, p. 3 ff.), 1952. **AD¹**

1848. Hoboken, P. C. J. van, *De vertolkers van het Indiase lied* ('Gramofoon voor kenner en liefhebber', Sept. 1955, p. 24 ff.), Amsterdam, Charles' gramofoonplatenhandel N.V. **A**

1849. —— *Indiase muziekinstrumenten en musici* (ibid. Oct. 1955, p. 18 ff.). **A**

1850. —— *Indiase muziekopnamen van Deben Bhattacharya* (ibid. April 1956, p. 28 ff.). **A**

1851. —— *Yehudi Menuhin introduceert Ali Akbar Khan* (ibid. May 1956, p. 22 ff.). **A**

1852. —— *De Bhajans van Mirabai* (ibid. Jan. 1956, p. 16 ff.). **A**

1853. —— *Anthologie de la musique classique de l'Inde* (ibid., Juni 1956, p. 20 ff.). **A**

1854. —— *Tibetaanse muziek uit Sikkim* (ibid., Juli 1956, p. 16 ff.). **A**

1855. —— *Introduction to the classical music of India* (publ. by the Indian Embassy, The Hague, 1957). **A**

1856. Hodeir, A., *Prolongements de la musique africaine* ('Problèmes d'Afrique Centrale' VII, p. 286 ff.), 1954. **AGJK**

1856a. —— *Jazz: its evolution and essence* (New York, 1956).

1857. *Hoe de krontjong hier geboren werd* ('De Vrije Pers' 12th Jan. 1951, reprinted in 'Indonesische Documentatie' 16th Febr. 1951, p. 382 ff.).

1858. Hoerburger, Felix, *Katalog der Europäischen Volksmusik im Schall-archiv des Institutes für Musikforschung, Regensburg* (Regensburg, 1952). **AL**

1859. —— *Correspondence between eastern and western folk epics* ('J. of the Intern. Folk Music Council' IV, p. 23 ff.), 1952. **AC**

1859a. —— *Der Tanz mit der Trommel* (Regensburg, 1954). **JL**

1860. —— *Schwert und Trommel als Tanzgeräte* ('Deutsches Jahrbuch f. Volkskunde' I, p. 240 ff.), Berlin, 1955. **AL¹**

1861. —— *'Die Zwiefachen'. Gestaltung und Umgestaltung der Tanzmelodien im nördlichen Altbayern* ('Veröffentl. d. Inst. f. Deutsche Volkskunde der Deutschen Akademie der Wiss. zu Berlin' V), Berlin, 1956. **AL**

1862. —— *Westöstliche Entsprechungen im Volksepos* ('Die Musikforschung' V, p. 354 ff.), 1954. **ACDEGKLL¹**

1863. Hoëvell, G. W. W. C., baron van, *De Kei-eilanden* ('Tijdschr. v. h. Bat. Gen.' XXXIII, p. 127 ff.), Batavia/'s Hage, 1890. **ABD¹GH**

1864. —— *De Aroe-eilanden, geographisch, ethnographisch en commerciëel* ('Tijdschr. v. h. Bat. Gen.' XXXIII, p. 82 and 85), 1890. **ABD¹GH**

1865. —— *Mitteilungen über die Kesseltrommel zu Bonto Bangun (Insel Saleier)*

('Intern. Archiv. f Ethnogr.' XVI, p. 158 ff.), 1904. **ABD¹GKL²**

1866. —— *Die Kesseltrommel zu Pedjeng, Gianjar* (ibid. XVIII, p. 3 ff.), Leiden, 1906. **BD¹GKL²**

1867. Hoëvell, W. R. van, *Beschrijving van de muzijk en zang bij de Badoeïnen in het zuiden van de residentie Bantam* ('Tijdschr. v. Ned.-Indië' VII, vol. IV, p. 428 ff.), 1845. **B**

1868. Höweler, Casper, *Rhythme in Vers en Muziek* (Den Haag, 1952). **A**

1869. Hoffmann, A., *Die Lieder des Li Yü* (Cologne, 1950). **A**

1870. Hofwijk, J. W., *Er zit nog muziek in de Antillen* ('De Katholieke Illustratie' XC, 11th Febr. 1956, p. 12 ff.). **AG**

1871. Hohenemser, H., *Ueber die Volksmusik in den deutschen Alpenländern* ('Sammelb. der Intern. Musikges.' XI, p. 324 ff.), 1909/'10. **CDFH¹L**

1872. Holiday, Geoffrey, *The Tuareg of the Ahaggar* ('African Music' I, No. 3, p. 48 ff.), 1956. **ACJLM**

1873. Holmes, William H., *Ancient art of the province of Chiriqui, Columbia* (Washington, 1888), p. 156 ff.

1874. Holzknecht, K., *Die Musikinstrumente der Azera* ('Z. f. Ethnologie' LXXXI, p. 64 ff.), 1956. **BD¹GHL¹L²M**

1875. —— *Ueber Töpferei und Tontrommeln der Azera in Ost-Neuguinea* ibid. LXXXII, p. 97 ff.), 1957. **ABD¹GHL¹L²M**

1876. Honda Yasuji, *The Nembutu-melody of the Traditional Songs* ('Journal of the Soc. for Research in Asiatic Music', No. 12–13, English Section, p. 8 ff.), Tokyo, Sept. 1954.

*1877. Hood, Mantle, *The Nuclear Theme as a Determinant of Patet in Javanese Music* (diss., Groningen, 1954). **ABCDEFGHL**

1878. —— *Indonesië* ('Encycl. van de Muziek' II, p. 181 ff.), Amsterdam, 1957. **ACDEFGH¹**

1879. —— *Training and research methods in ethnomusicology* ('Ethnomusicology' Newsletter No. 11, p. 2 ff.), Sept. 1957. **AGL**

1880. Hoogt, I. M. van der, *The Vedic Chant studied in its textual and melodic forms* (Wageningen, 1929).

1881. Hoose, Harned Pettus, *Peking Pigeons and Pigeon-Flutes* (Peiping, Coll. of Chin. Studies, California Coll. in China, 1938).

1882. Hornbostel, Erich M. von, and Abraham, Otto, *Tonsystem und Musik der Japaner* ('Sammelbände der Intern. Musikgesellschaft' IV), 1903, **(CDFH¹ L)**, reprinted in 'Sammelbände für vergleichende Musikwissenschaft' I, p. 179 ff.), 1922. **ABCDFGH¹IKLL¹**

1883. —— and —— *Ueber die Bedeutung des Phonographen für vergleichende Musikwissenschaft* ('Zeitschrift f. Ethnologie' vol. 36, p. 222 ff.), 1904. **ABD¹GHIKL¹L²M**

1884. —— and —— *Phonographierte Türkische Melodien* (ibid. vol. 36), 1904, **(BD¹GHKL¹L²M)**, reprinted in 'Sammelb. f. vergl. Musikw.' I, p. 233 ff., (1922). **ABCDFGH¹IKLL¹**

1885. —— and —— *Phonographierte Indische Melodien* ('Sammelb. der Intern. Musikges.' V), 1904 **(CDFH¹L)**, reprinted in 'Sammelb. f. vergl. Musikw.' I, p. 251 ff.), 1922. **ABCDFGH¹IKLL¹**

1886. Hornbostel, Erich M. von, *Melodischer Tanz* ('Z. d. Intern. Musikgesellschaft' V, fasc. 12), 1904. **ABCDFH¹IKL**

1887. —— *Die Probleme der vergleichenden Musikwissenschaft* ('Z. der Intern. Musikg.' 1905, fasc. 3). **ABCDFH¹IKL**

1888. —— *Ueber den gegenwärtigen Stand der vergleichenden Musikwissenschaft* ('Kongressbericht der Intern. Musikges., Basel 1906'). **ABCI**

1889. —— and Abraham, Otto, *Ueber die Harmonisierbarkeit exotischer Melodien* ('Sammelb. der Intern. Mus. Ges.' VII), 1906. **ABCDFH¹IL**

1890. —— and —— *Phonographierte Indianermelodien aus Britisch-Columbia* ('Boas Anniversary Vol.' New York, 1906), reprinted in 'Sammelb. f. vergl. Musikw.' I, p. 291 ff. (1922). **ABCDFGH¹IKLL¹**

1891. Hornbostel, Erich M. von, *Phonographierte Tunesische Melodien* ('Sammelb. der Intern. Mus. Ges.' VIII **(CDFH¹L)**, 1907), reprinted in 'Sammelb. f. vergl. Musikw.' I, p. 311 ff. (1922). **ABCDFGH¹IKLL¹**

1892. —— *Notiz über die Musik der Bewohner von Süd-Neu-Mecklenburg* (in E. Stephan und F. Graebner, 'Neu-Mecklenburg', Berlin, 1907), reprinted in 'Sammelb. f. vergl. Musikw.' I, p. 349 ff. (1922). **ABCDFGH¹IKLL¹**

1893. —— *Ueber das Tonsystem und die Musik der Melanesier* ('Kongressber. der Intern. Musikges., Basel 1906', p. 60), 1907. **ABCI**

1894. —— *Ueber die Musik der Kubu* (in B. Hagen, 'Die Orang-Kubu auf Sumatra', Frankfurt a/M,. 1908), reprinted in 'Sammelb. f. vergl. Musikw.' I, p. 359 ff. (1922). **ABCDFGH¹IJKLL¹**

1895. —— and Abraham, Otto, *Vorschläge zur Transkription exotischer Melodien* ('Sammelb. der Intern. Mus. Ges.' XI), 1909. **ABCDFH¹IL**

1896. Hornbostel, Erich M. von, *Phonographierte Melodien aus Madagaskar und Indonesien* (in 'Forschungsreise S.M.S.

'Planet' 1906–1907' vol. V, Anthropologie und Ethnographie), 1909. **ABI**

1897. —— *Wanyamwezi-Gesänge* ('Anthropos' IV), 1909. **ABD¹GIKL¹L²M**

1898. —— and Stumpf, Carl, *Ueber vergleichende akustische und musikpsychologische Untersuchungen* (in C. Stumpf, 'Beiträge zur Akustik und Musikwissenschaft', vol. IV–VI, p. 147 ff.), 1910. **ABI**

1899. Hornbostel, Erich M. von, *Ueber Mehrstimmigkeit in der aussereuropäischen Musik* (in 'Kongressbericht der Intern. Mus. Ges., Wien 1910'). **ABCI**

1900. —— *Wasukuma-Melodie* ('Extrait du Bull. de l'Académie des Sciences de Cracovie, Classe des Sciences mathématiques et naturelles', Série B. Sciences naturelles), 1910. **ABD¹I**

1901. —— *Ueber einige Panpfeifen aus nordwest Brasilien* (in Theodor Koch-Grünberg, 'Zwei Jahre unter den Indianern', vol. II, Berlin 1910). **ABIL²**

1902. —— and Stumpf, Carl, *Ueber die Bedeutung ethnologischer Untersuchungen für die Psychologie und Aesthetik der Tonkunst* (in 'Bericht über den 4. Kongress f. experimentelle Psychologie' Innsbruck, 1910, vol. IV, p. 256 ff.), 1911. **ABI**

1903. Hornbostel, Erich M. von, *Ueber ein akustisches Kriterium für Kulturzusammenhänge* ('Z. f. Ethnologie' 1910, p. 601 ff.). **ABD¹GHIKL¹L²M**

*1904. —— *Notizen über kirgisische Musikinstrumente und Melodien* (in R. Karutz, 'Unter Kirgisen und Turkmenen', Leipzig 1911). **ABHI**

1905. —— *Musikpsychologische Bemerkungen über Vogelgesang* ('Z. d. Intern. Mus. Ges.' XII), 1911. **ABCDFH¹IKL**

1906. —— *U.S.A. National Music* ('Z. der Intern. Mus. Ges.' XII), 1911 **ABCDFH¹IKL**

1907. —— Review of Allessandro Kraus figlio, 'Appunti sulla Musica dei Popoli Nordici', 1907 ('Anthropos' VI, p. 231), 1911. **ABD¹GIKL¹L²M**

1908. —— *Musik der Naturvölker* ('Meyer's Grosses Konversationslexikon', 1912. **ABI**

1909. —— *Arbeit und Musik* ('Z. d. Intern. Mus. Ges.' XIII, p. 341 ff.), 1912. **ABCDFH¹IKL**

1910. —— and Karl Theodor Preuss, *Zwei Gesänge der Cora Indianer* (in K. Th. Preuss, 'Die Nayarit-Expedition' vol. I, p. 367 ff.), 1912. **ABI**

1911. Hornbostel, Erich M. von, *Die Musik auf den nordwestlichen Salomo-Inseln* (in R. Thurnwald, 'Forschungen auf den Salomo-Inseln und Bismarck-Archipel' vol. I, p. 461 ff.), 1912. **ABCI**

1912. —— *Melodie und Skala* ('Jahrbuch der Musikbibl. Peters' XX, p. 11 ff.), 1912. **ABCGIKLL¹**

1913. —— and Curt Sachs, *Systematik der Musikinstrumente* ('Z. f. Ethnologie' XLVI, p. 553 ff.), 1914. **ABCD¹GHIKL¹L²M**

1914. —— *Die Musik der Pangwe* (in G. Tessmann, 'Die Pangwe', vol. II, p. 320 ff.), 1914. **ABIJ**

1915. —— *Bemerkungen über einige Lieder aus Bougainville* (in Frizzi, 'Ein Beitrag zur Ethnologie von Bougainville und Buka', 1914). **ABI**

1916. —— *Gesänge aus Ruanda* (in 'Wissenschaftl. Ergebnisse der deutschen Zentral-Afrika-Expedition 1907–1908', vol. VI, 1st. Part, Ethnographie und Anthropologie I, edited by Jan Czekanowski), 1917. **ABHI**

1917. —— *Musik und Musikinstrumente* ('Deutsches Kolonial-Lexikon' vol. II), 1919. **ABI**

1918. —— First communication about the Theory of blown fifths ('Anthropos' XIV–XV, p. 569 ff.), 1919. **ABD¹GIKL¹L²M**

1919. —— *Ch'ao-t'ien-tze, eine chinesische Notation und ihre Ausführungen* ('Festschrift-Stumpf' p. 477 ff.), 1919. **ABI**

1920. —— *Formanalysen an siamesischen Orchesterstücken* ('Archiv f. Musikw.' II, p. 306 ff.), 1920. **ABCDFIKLL¹**

1921. —— *Musikalischer Exotismus* ('Melos' 1921, fasc. 9). **AIK**

1922. —— *Das Erotische in der modernen Musik* ('Z. f. Aesthetik und allgemeine Kunstwissenschaft' XIX), 1925. **ABD¹GIKL**

1923. —— *Eine Tafel zur Logarithmischen Darstellung von Zahlenverhältnissen* ('Z. f. Physik' VI, p. 29 ff.), 1921. **ABD¹GHIL¹**

1924. —— Translation of A. J. Ellis, 'On the Musical Scales of Various Nations' ('Sammelbände f. vergl. Musikwiss.' I p. 1 ff.), München, 1922. **ABCGH¹IKLL¹**

1925. —— *Musik der Makuschi, Taulipang und Yekuana* (in Theodor Koch-Grünberg, 'Vom Roroima zum Orinoco', vol. III, p. 395 ff.), 1923. **ABIJ**

1926. —— Review of Kurt Huber, 'Der Ausdruck musikalischer Elementarmotive', Leipzig, 1923) ('Deutsche Literaturzeitung' XLVII), 1926. **ABD¹GIK**

1927. —— *Die Entstehung des Jodelns* ('Bericht Musikw. Kongress, Basel 1924'), p. 203 ff. **ABI**

1928. —— *Geschichte des Phonogramm-Archivs der Staatlichen Hochschule für Musik in Berlin* (1925). **ABI**

1929. —— Review of R. et M. d'Harcourt,

'La musique des Incas et ses survivances' Paris, 1925) ('Anthropos' XXII), 1927. **ABD¹GIKL¹L²M**

1930. —— *Die Musik der Semai auf Malakka* ('Anthropos' XXI, p. 277), 1926. **ABD¹GIKL¹L²M**

1931. —— and Otto Abraham, *Zur Psychologie der Tondistanz* ('Z. f. Psychologie und Physiologie der Sinnesorgane' vol. 98), 1926. **ABCD¹GHI**

1932. Hornbostel, Erich M. von, *Psychologie der Gehörserscheinungen* ('Handbuch der Physiologie' XI, p. 701 ff.), 1926. **ABI**

1933. —— *American Negro Songs* (review), ('The Intern. Review of Missions' XV, No. 60), 1926. **ABI**

1934. —— *Laut und Sinn* ('Festschrift-Meinhof'), 1927. **ABI**

1935. —— *Musikalische Tonsysteme* (in Geiger und Scheel, 'Handbuch der Physik', vol. VIII, p. 425 ff.), 1927. **ABI**

1936. —— *Ethnologisches zu Jazz* ('Melos' VI), 1927. **ABIK**

1937. —— Review of Walter Kaudern, 'Musical Instruments in Celebes', Göteborg, 1927 ('Ethnologische Anzeiger II), 1927. **ABGIKL²**

1938. —— Review of Fritz Brehmer, 'Melodieauffassung und melodische Begabung des Kindes' ('Z. f. angewandte Psychologie' 1927, Beiheft 36) (L¹) ('Deutsche Literaturzeitung' XLVIII, p. 220 ff.), 1927. **ABD¹GHIK**

1939. —— *African Negro Music* ('Africa' vol. I no. 1), 1928. **ABCIK**

1940. —— *Musik des Orients* (Commentary to an album of exotic records, edited by Carl Lindström A.G.), 1928. **ABCI**

1941. —— *Die Maassnorm als kulturhistorisches Forschungsmittel* ('Festschrift-Wilhelm Schmidt', p. 303 ff.), 1928. **ABIL²**

1942. —— *Tonart und Ethos* ('Festschrift-Johannes Wolf' p. 73 ff.), 1929. **ABI**

1943. —— Review of Charles W. Mead, 'The Musical Instruments of the Incas' ('Ethnol. Anzeiger' II, p. 72 ff.), 1929/'30. **ABGIKL²**

1944. —— *Gestaltpsychologisches zur Stilkritik* ('Festschrift-Guido Adler'), 1930. **ABCI**

1945. —— *Musik des Orients auf der Schallplatte* ('Kultur und Schallplatte', Berlin, 1931 and 'Die Musik' XXIII, p. 829 ff.), 1931. **ABCDFIKL**

1946. —— *Ueber Verschiebung der Tonhöhe* ('Z. f. Laryngologie' XXI, p. 100 ff.), 1931. **ABD¹GIL¹**

1947. —— Review of Walter König-Beyer, 'Völkerkunde im Lichte vergleichender Musikwissenschaft', (Reichenberg,

1931) ('Baessler Archiv' XV, p. 55 ff.), 1932. **ABD¹GIKL²**

1948. —— Review of Andreas Eckardt, 'Koreanische Musik' (Leipzig 1930) ('Orientalische Literaturzeitung' 1931, No. 9/10). **ABD¹HIK**

1949. —— Review of Kanetune-Kiyosuke and Syioti Tudi, 'Die geschichtliche Denkmäler der japanischen Tonkunst', Abt. I, Hofmusik, Heft 1, Saibara ('Z. f. Musikwiss.' XIV, p. 235 ff.), 1932. **ABCEH¹IKL**

1950. —— *Zum Kongress für arabische Musik, Kairo 1932* ('Z. f. vergl. Musikw.' I, p. 16 ff.), 1933. **ABCIK**

1951. —— *Carl Stumpf und die vergleichende Musikwissenschaft* ('Z. f. vergl. Musikw.' I, p. 25 ff.), 1933. **ABCIK**

1952. —— Review of P. G. Harris, 'Notes on Drums and Musical Instruments seen in Sokoto Province, Nigeria' ('Journal of the Royal Anthropological Inst. of Gr. Britain and Ireland' 1932) ('Z. f. vergl. Musikw.' I, p. 63 ff.), 1933. **ABCIK**

1953. —— *The Ethnology of African Sound Instruments* ('Africa' VI, p. 129 ff. and 277 ff.), London, 1933. **ABCGIKL¹L²M**

1954. —— *Das Berliner Phonogrammarchiv* ('Z. f. vergl. Musikw.' I, p. 40 ff.), 1933. **ABCIK**

1955. —— *Phonographierte isländische Zwiegesänge* ('Deutsche Islandforschung 1930', p. 300 ff.), Breslau, 1933. **ABI**

1956. —— and Robert Lachmann, *Asiatische Parallelen zur Berbermusik* ('Z. f. vergl. Musikw.' I, p. 4 ff.), 1933. **ABCIK**

1957. —— and —— *Das indische Tonsystem bei Bharata und sein Ursprung* ('Z. f. vergl. Musikw.' I, p. 73 ff.), 1933. **ABCIK**

1958. Hornbostel, Erich M. von, Review of Helen H. Roberts, 'Form in Primitive Music' (New York, 1933) ('Z. f. vergl. Musikw.' II, p. 60 ff. and 39), 1934. **ABCIK**

1959. —— Review of Heinz Wieschhoff, 'Die afrikanischen Trommeln und ihre ausser-afrikanischen Beziehungen' (in 'Studien zur Kulturkunde' ed. by L. Frobenius, vol. II), 1933 ('Z. f. vergl. Musikw.' III, p. 88 ff.), 1935. **ABCIK**

1960. —— Review of Percival R. Kirby, 'The musical instruments of the native races of South Africa' ('Nature' CXXXVI, p. 3 ff.), 1935. **ABD¹GHL¹**

1961. —— *Fuegian Songs* ('American Anthropologist', New Series, vol. 38, p. 357 ff.), 1936. **ABGIJL¹**

1962. —— *The Music of the Fuegians* ('Ethnos' 1948, p. 61 ff.). **ACGIL²M**

1963. —— *La musica de los Makuschi, Tauli-*

pang y Yekuana ('Archivos venezolanos de Folklore' IV/V, vol. III No. 41, p. 137 ff.), Caracas, 1955/'56. (Translation of No. 1925).

1964. Hornburg, Friedrich, *Die Musik der Tiv* ('Die Musikforschung' I, p. 47 ff.), 1948.   ACKLL[1]

1965. —— *Phonographierte afrikanische Mehrstimmigkeit* (ibid. III, p. 120 ff.), 1950.   ACEIKLL[1]

1966. Houston, John, *Aotea (chants and songs)* ('Journal of the Polynesian Soc.' XLIV, p. 36 ff.), 1935.   BGL[2]

1967. Houston-Péret, Elsie, *Chants populaires du Brésil* ('Bibl. mus. du Musée de la Parole et du Musée Guimet', 1st series, vol. I), Paris, 1930.   KL

1968. Howard, Albert H., *The aulos or tibia* ('Harvard Studies of Philology' IV), 1893.

1969. Howard, Walter, *Chinesische und europäische Musik* (in: Richard Wilhelm, 'Chinesische Musik'), Frankfurt, 1927. G

1970. Hough, Walter, *The Hopi Indian collection in the United States National Museum* (Washington D.C.), 1918, p. 291 ff.: *Musical instruments.*   J

1971. Howes, Frank, *Anthropology and Music* ('Man' XLV, p. 107 ff. (no. 83)), Sept./Oct. 1945.   ABD[1]GKL[1]L[2]M

1972. —— *Man, Mind and Music, Studies in the philosophy of music and in the relations of the art to anthropology, psychology and sociology* (London, 1948).   A

1973. Howitt, A. W., *Songs and songmakers of some Australian tribes* ('Anthrop. Journal' XVI, p. 327).

1973a. Howland Rowe, John, *An ethnographic sketch of Guambia, Colombia* ('Tribus' N.S. IV/V, p. 48 ff.), Stuttgart, 1956.   BGL[1]

1974. Hrovatin, Radoslav, *Les rapports réciproques du folklore et de la création musicale artistique en Slovénie* ('J. of the Intern. Folk Music Council' IV, p. 35 ff.), 1952.   ACJKL

1975. Hsiao Shu Hsien, *A Harp with a thousand Strings* (London, 1944).

1976. —— *La chanson populaire chinoise* ('Sinologica' I, p. 65 ff.), 1947. D[1]GKL[1]

1977. Hsing Chi, *China's klassieke opera* (Publ. of the Exotic Music Soc.), Amsterdam, 1957.   A

1978. Huard, Paul, *Les instruments de musique chez les Unong* ('Bull. et travaux de l'Inst. indochin. pour l'étude de l'homme' II, fasc. 1, p. 135 ff.), 1939.   K

1979. Huart, Cl., *Etude biographique sur trois musiciens arabes* ('Journal Asiatique' 8th series, No. 3, p. 141 ff.), 1884.   D[1]GHKL[1]

1980. —— *Musique persane* (in Lavignac,

'Hist. de la Mus.' V, p. 3065 ff.), 1922   AC

1981. Huber, Kurt, *Frauengesänge aus Birma* (in Lucian und Christine Scherman, 'Im Stromgebiet des Irawaddi, Birma und seine Frauenwelt'), München-Neubiberg, 1922.

1982. —— *Ponnakultlied aus Mandalay* ('Asia major' I, p. 453 ff.).   D[1]GL[1]

1983. Hubers, Father Hubert, *Kleine musikethnologische Beiträge von der Insel Karkar in Neu-Guinea* ('Anthropos' XXXVII, p. 122 ff.), 1942/'45.   BD[1]GHJKL[1]L[2]M

1984. Huchzermeyer, Helmut, *Aulos und Kithara* (Diss., Münster, 1931).

*1985. Hudec, Konstantin, *Slovak Folk Music* ('Grove's Dictionary' 5th ed. vol. III, p. 355 ff.), 1954.   ACFH[1]K

1986. Hübner, Herbert, *Studien zur Musik im Bismarck-Archipel* ('Anthropos' XXX, p. 669 ff.),1935. ABD[1]GHKL[1]L[2]M

1987. —— *Die Musik im Bismarck-Archipel* (Berlin, 1938).   BCIK

1988. —— *Melodiestile und Kulturschichten im Bismarckarchipel* ('Archiv f. Musikforschung' IV, fasc. 4), 1939. CDH[1]KL

1989. Huettner, Johann Christian, *Ein Ruderliedchen aus China mit Melodie* ('J. des Luxus und der Moden' XI), 1796.   K

1990. Huggler, Rudolf, *Das Alphorn im Berner Ober-Land* ('Heimatleben' XXVIII, No. 2), 1955.

1991. Hulbert, Homer B., *The passing of Korea* (London, 1906), Chapter XXIV, p. 314 ff.: *Music and poetry.*   J

1992. Hulstaert, G., *Note sur les instruments de musique à l'Equateur* ('Congo' Oct. 1935, p. 356 ff.).   GKL[1]L[3]

1992a. —— *Musique indigène et musique sacrée* ('Aequatoria' XII, p. 86 ff.), 1949.   L[2]M

1993. —— *De telefoon der Nkundo* ('Anthropos' XXX, p. 655 ff.), 1935.   ABD[1]GHKL[1]L[2]M

1993a. Hulstijn, P. van, *Soela-eilanden* ('Meded. v. h. Encycl. Bureau' XV, p. 87 ff.), Weltevreden, 1918.   B

1994. Hultkrantz, Ake, *Some Notes on the Arapaho Sun Dance* ('Ethnos' XVII, p. 24 ff.), 1952.   BJL[2]M

1995. Humbert Sauvageot, Mrs. M., *La musique à travers la vie laotienne* ('Z. f. vergl. Musikw.' II, p. 14 ff.), 1934. ACK

1996. —— *Quelques aspects de la vie et de la musique dahoméennes* (ibid. II, p. 76 ff.), 1934.   ACK

1996a. Hunter, G., *Hidden drums in Singida district* ('Tanganyika Notes and Records' 1953, p. 28 ff.).   M

1997. Huntington, Mary, *Man and Music* ('Natural History' XLIV, p. 107 ff.), New York, 1939.   BJ

137

1998. Hurston, Zora, *Dance songs and games from the Bahamas* ('Journal of Amer. Folklore' XLIII, p. 294 ff.), 1930. GKL³

1999. Hurt, Ambra H., *The music of the Congo* ('Etude' LIII, p. 402 ff.), July 1935.

2000. Husmann, Heinrich, *Marimba und Sansa der Sambesikultur* ('Z. f. Ethnologie' vol. 68, p. 14 ff.), 1936. ABD¹GHKL¹L³M

2001. —— *Sieben afrikanische Tonleitern* ('Jahrbuch der Musikbibliothek Peters', 1937). ACGKL¹

2002. —— *Olympos, die Anfänge der griechischen Enharmonik* ('Jahrb. der Musikbibl. Peters' 1937, p. 29 ff.). ACGKL¹

2003. —— *Fünf- und siebenstellige Centstafeln zur Berechnung musikalischer Intervalle* (Leyden, 1951). ACIL

2004. —— *Afghanistan* ('Die Musik in Geschichte und Gegenwart' I, col. 121 ff.), 1951. ACDEFGH¹KL

2005. —— *Das neuentdeckte Steinzeitlithophon* ('Die Musikforschung' V, p. 47 ff.), 1952. ACEIKLL¹

2006. —— *Zu Kurt Reinhards 'Tonmessungen an fünf ostafrikanischen Klimpern'* ('Die Musikforschung' V, p. 218 ff.), 1952. ACEIKLL¹

2007. —— *Nochmals die Mwera-Sansen* (ibid. VI, p. 49 ff.), 1953. ACEIKLL¹

2008. —— *Ursprung und Entwicklung der Tonsysteme* (in preparation).

2008a. —— *Antike und Orient in ihren Bedeutung für die europäische Musik* ('Kongressbericht Ges. f. Musikforschung, Hamburg 1956', p. 24 ff.). CEL

2008b. —— *Zur Grundlegung der musikalischen Rhythmik* ('Archiv f. Musikw.' IX, p. 2 ff.), 1952. CDEKL

2008c. —— *Eine neue Konsonanztheorie* (ibid. X, p. 219 ff.), 1953. CDEKL

2009. Hustvedt, Sigurd Bernhard, *Ballad books and ballad men. Raids and rescues in Britain, America and the Scandinavian north since 1800* (Cambridge Mass., 1930).

2010. Hutchings, Arthur, *Music in Bengal* ('Music and Letters' XXVII, p. 26 ff.), 1946. KL¹

2011. —— *Indian traditions, classical and popular* ('Music & Letters' XXVII, p. 29 ff.), 1946. KL¹

2012. Huth, Arno, *Die Musikinstrumente Ost-Turkestans* (Diss., Berlin, 1928).

2012a. —— *Instruments of Eastern Turkestan* ('Grove's Dictionary of Music and Musicians' vol. VIII, p. 608 ff.), 1954. ACFH¹K

2012b. Huth, E. von, *Gesänge und Märchen aus Ponape* ('Globus' XCV), 1909. D¹GL²M

2013. Huxley, H. M., *Syrian songs, proverbs and stories* ('J. of the Amer. Oriental Soc.' 1902, p. 175 ff.). D¹GKL¹

2014. Huyser, J. G., *Mokko's* ('Ned.-Indië Oud & Nieuw' XVI, p. 225 ff., 279 ff., 309 ff. and 337 ff.), 1931. ACD¹GHL³

*2015. Hwei, Li, *A comparative study of the Jew's harp among the aborigines of Formosa and East Asia* (in Chinese with Engl. summary) ('Bull. of the Inst. of Ethnol. of the Academia Sinica' I, p. 85 ff.), March 1956. AB

2016. Hyslop, Graham H., *The choice of music for festivals in Africa* ('African Music' I, No. 2, p. 53 ff.), 1955. ACJLM

2016a. Ibarrola, R., *La música y el baile en los territorios del Golfo de Guinea* ('Africa' (Madrid) XXVII, vol. I, p. 254 ff.), 1953. M

2017. Idelsohn, A. Z., *Die Maqamen der arabischen Musik* ('Sammelbände der Intern. Mus. Ges.' XV, p. 11 ff.), 1913. CDFH¹L

2019. —— *Hebräisch-Orientalischer Melodienschatz* (Leipzig, 1914 and following years). C

2020. —— *Phonographierte Gesänge und Aussprachsproben des Hebräischen der jemenitischen, persischen und syrischen Juden* (Vienna, 1917).

2021. —— *Parallelen zwischen gregorianischen und hebräisch-orientalischen Sangesweisen* ('Z. f. Musikw.' 1921). CDH¹KL

2022. —— *Musical characteristics of Eastern European Jewish folksong* ('The Musical Quarterly' XVIII, p. 634 ff.), 1932. C

2023. —— *Jewish music in its historical development* (New York, 1929, 2/1948). ACGL

2024. —— *Der jüdische Tempelgesang* (in Guido Adler, 'Handbuch der Musikgesch.' I, p. 149 ff.), 2/1929. ACDEF

2025. —— *Die Maqamen in der hebräischen Poesie der orientalischen Juden* ('Monatschr. f. d. Wissenschaft des Judentums' LVII, p. 314 ff.). CG

2026. —— *The Features of the Jewish Sacred Folk Song in Eastern Europe* ('Acta Musicologica' IV, p. 17 ff.), 1932. CDEKLL¹

2027. —— *Der Volksgesang der osteuropäischen Juden* (Leipzig, 1932).

2028. —— *Parallels between the Old-French and the Jewish Song* ('Acta Musicologica' V, p. 26 ff. and VI, p. 15 ff.), 1933/'34. CDEH¹KLL¹

2029. Ilyin, A., *Muzikalnoye tvortshestvo altaitsev* (i.e. Musical creativity among Altai peoples) ('Sovetskaya muzyka' 1950, No. 8, p. 63 ff.).

2030. International Folk Music Council, *Journal of the*, (edited by Maud Karpeles), London, 1949–in progress. ACJKL

2031. Irish Folk Song Society, *Journal of the*, (London, 1904 ff.).

2032. Isamitt, Carlos, *Cuatro instrumentos musicales araucanos* ('Estudios Latinoamericanos' III, p. 55 ff.), 1937.

2033. —— *Los instrumentos araucanos* ('Bol. Latino-Americano de Música' IV, p. 310 ff.), Bogotá, 1938.

2034. Isawa, Sh., *Collection of Koto Music* (Tokyo, 1888 and 1913).

2035. Ito, S., *Comparison of the Japanese folk-song and the Occidental* ('Univ. of California Publications in Psychology' vol. II No. 5), 1916. **I**

2036. Ivens, W. G., *Melanesians of the Southeast Solomon Islands* (London, 1927), Chapter VII. *Feasts, dances, gongs, pipes.* **B**

2037. Iyengar, R. **Rangaramanuja**, *Kriti Mani Mala*, vols. V and VI (Madras, 1953).

2038. Iyengar, V. V. Srinivasa, *Masters of music in South India* ('J. of the Music Acad.' XXIV), Madras, 1953. **AC**

2039. Iyer, E. Krishna, *Personalities in present day music* (Madras, 1933).

2040. —— *Misconceptions about Bharata Natya* ('Annual Music Festival Souvenir, Madras, 1953').

2040a. Iyer, K. Bharatha, *Kathakali, the sacred dance-drama of Malabar* (London, 195.).

2040b. Iyer, Mudikondan C. Venkatarama, Review of Sri B. Subba Rao, 'Raga Nidhi' ('The J. of the Music Academy Madras' XXVII, p. 172 ff.), Madras, 1957. **A**

2041. Iyer, S. Venkatasubramania, *The ragamalikas of Svati Tirunal* ('J. of the Music Acad.' XXIV), Madras, 1953. **AC**

2042. —— *Some composers of Malayalam music* ('J. of the Music Academy, Madras' XXV, p. 101 ff.), Madras, 1954. **AC**

2043. Iyer, T. L. Venkatarama, *The scheme of 72 melas in Carnatic Music* ('The Journal of the Music Academy' XI, p. 80 ff.), Madras 1940.

2043a. —— *The padas of Sri Svati Tirunal* ('The J. of the Music Academy, Madras' XVII, p 157 ff.), 1946. **C**

2043b. —— *The personality of Sri Muthuswami Dikshitar* ('Annual Music Festival Souvenir, Madras 1953').

2043c. Iyer, Vina Vidvan A. Sundaram, *Sri Muthuswami Dikshitar's Kritis* ('J. of the Music Academy, Madras' XXV, p. 76 ff.), Madras, 1954. **AC**

*2044. Izikowitz, Karl Gustav, *Musical and other Sound-instruments of the South American Indians* (Göteborg, 1927). **ACGIJL²**

2045. —— *Le tambour à membrane au Pérou* ('Journal de la Soc. des Américanistes' XXIII, p. 163 ff.), Paris, 1931. **GL²**

2046. —— *Les instruments de musique des Indiens Uro-Chipaya* ('Revista de Inst. de Etnología' II, p. 263 ff.), 1932. **GL¹**

2046a. J., *Musica indigena da Lunda* ('Estudos Coloniais' II, No. 1, p. 99 ff.), 1950. **M**

2046b. Jabavu, D. D. T., *The origin of 'Nkosi Sikelel'i Afrika* ('Nada' 1949, No. 26, p. 56 ff.). **M**

2047. Jackson, G. Pullen, *Some enemies of folk-music in America* ('Papers read at the Intern. Congress of Musicology, New York, 1939, p. 77 ff.), New York, 1944. **AC**

2048. Jackson, Wilfrid, *Shell-trumpets and their distribution in the Old and New world* ('Memoirs of the Manchester Literary Soc.' LX, fasc. 8), 1916. **G**

2049. Jacobs, J., *Signaaltrommeltaal bij de Tetela* ('Kongo-Overzee' XX, fasc. 4–5), 1954. **D¹GKL²M**

2050. —— *Nkumi-zang, Tetela* ('ibid.' XXI, p. 42 ff.), 1955. **D¹GKL²M**

2051. Jacobson, E., and J. H. van Hasselt, *De gongfabrikatie te Semarang* (Leiden, 1907). **ABCHL²**

2052. Jacovleff, A., and Tchou-Kia-Kien, *Le théatre Chinois* (Paris, 1922). **C**

2053. Jadot, M. Pj., *Literature and music in Belgian Congo* ('Native Arts and Craftmanship in Belgian Congo', p. 23 ff.), place and date unknown. **C**

2054. Jagamas, Ioan, *Cîntecul satului* ('Revista de folclor' II, Nos. 1–2, p. 93 ff.), Bucarest, 1957. **AC**

2055. Jagamas, János, *Beiträge zur Dialektfrage der ungarischen Volksmusik in Rumänien* ('Studia Memoriae Belae Bartók Sacra', p. 469 ff.), Budapest, 1956. **AC**

2056. Jager, H. de, *De sociologische benaderingswijze van de muziekgeschiedenis* ('Mens en Maatschappij' XXXII, p. 22 ff.), 1957. **BD¹HL¹**

2056a. Jairazbhoy, Nazir Ali, *Bharata's concept of sadharana* ('Bull. of the School of Oriental and African studies' 1958, p. 54 ff.). **ABM**

2057. Jaina data about musical instruments ('J. of the Oriental Inst. Baroda' II, p. 276 ff. and 377 ff.), 1952/'53. **D¹**

2058. Janáček, Leoš, *O lidové pisni a lidové hudbě* (Prague, 1955).

2058a. —— and P. Vasa, *Moravske písně milostné*, vol. I (Prague, 1930).

2059. Jankovic, Danica S., 40 Serbian dance melodies (Beograd, 1937). **A**

2060. —— and Ljubica Jankovic, *Narodne igre (Dances populaires)*, vol. I–VI (Beograd, 1934–1951), with a summary in French. **A**

2061. —— and —— *Melodije narodnih igara*

(i.e. Melodies of folk dances) (Beograd, 1937).

2062. —— and —— *Narodne Igre*, vol. VII (Beograd, 1949). **AL**

2063. —— and —— *Pravilno u Nepravilnome* (i.e. Regularity in irregularity) ('Zvuk, Jugoslovenska muzička revija', June/July 1955, p. 65 ff.). **A**

2064. —— and —— *Narodne igre*, vol. VIII (Beograd, 195.).

2065. —— and —— *Prilog prouchavaniju ostataka orskih obrednik igara u Yugoslavije* (A contribution to the study of the survival of ritual dances in Yugoslavia), Beograd, 1957. **A**

2066. Jans, P., *Essai de la musique religieuse pour indigènes dans le Vicariat apostolique de Coquilhatville* ('Aequatoria' XIX, No. 1), Coquilhatville, 1956. **GL²M**

2067. Jansky, Herbert, *Vergleichende Volksliederkunde als Hilfsmittel der Völkerpsychologie* ('Proc. Anthropol. Congress, Vienna, 1–8 Sept. 1952' II. Ethnologica, 1st vol., p. 79 ff.), Vienna, 1955. **AB**

2068. Janus, Carolus, *Musici scriptores Graeci. Supplementum, melodiarum reliquiae* (Leipzig, 1899). **A**

2069. Japanese Radio Institute, *Sixteen Ainu songs, recorded in Karafuto (Saghalien) and Hokkaido (1947–1951)* ('Colloques de Wégimont' I, p. 195 ff.), Brussels, 1956. **AC**

2070. Járdanyi, Pál, *A kidei magyarság világi zenéje* (i.e. The wordly music of the Hungarians of the village Kide), Kolozsvár, 1943. **A**

2071. —— *The determining of scales and solmization in Hungarian musical folklore* ('Studia Memoriae Belae Bartók Sacra', p. 301 ff.), Budapest, 1956. **AC**

2072. —— *Hangnem-típusok a Magyar Népzenében* (i.e. The typical tonalities of the Hungarian folk music) (in 'Emlékkonyv Kodály. I. 70 Zsulétes napjára' p. 255 ff.), Budapest, 1953. **A**

2073. —— *The significance of folk music in present-day Hungarian musicology and musical art* ('J. Intern. Folk Music Council' IX, p. 40 ff.), 1957. **ACJKL**

2074. Jasim Uddin, *Folk Music of East Pakistan* ('Journal of the Intern. Folk Music Council' III, p. 41 ff.), 1951. **ACJKL**

2075. —— *Folksongs of East Bengal* (Dacca, U.S. Information Service), 1957.

2076. *Jaunimo saviveiklos scena* No. 11 and No. 14 (Wilna, 1955).

2077. Jeannin, Dom J., *Mélodies lithurgiques syriennes et chaldéennes* (2 vols.) (1926 and '28).

2078. —— *L'Octoechos syrien* ('Oriens Christianus' new series, III, p. 82 ff. and 277 f.). **D¹GHKL¹**

2079. —— *Le chant lithurgique syrien* ('Journal asiatique' 1912, p. 295 ff.; 1913, p. 65 ff.). **D¹GHKL¹**

2080. Jeffreys, M. D., *A musical pot from Southern Nigeria* ('Man' XL, p. 186 (No. 215 ff.)), 1940. **BD¹GKL¹L²M**

2080a. —— *The bull-roarer among the Ibo* ('African Studies' VIII, p. 23 ff.), 1949. **KL³M**

2081. Jenkins, B., *Notions of ancient Chinese music* ('J. of the R. Asiatic Soc., North-China Branch' 1868). **KL⁵**

2082. Jenkinson, N. H., and E. Morris, *Bells and gongs of old Japan* ('Apollo', Nov. 1939). **C**

2083. Jenness, D., *Eskimo music in Northern Alaska* ('The Musical Quarterly' VIII, p. 377 ff.), 1922. **C**

2083a. Jensen, A. E., *Hainuwele, Volkserzählungen von der Molukken-Insel Ceram* (s.v. Flaute, Gong, Gesang, Muscheltrompete (tahuri)), Frankfurt a/M, 1939. **B**

2083b. Jhering, H. von, *Nasenflöte* ('Globus' LXXV), 1899. **D¹GM**

2084. Jiránek, Jaroslav, *Volkschina in der Musik* (Dresden, 1955).

2085. Joest, W., *Malayische Lieder und Tänze aus Ambon und den Uliase (Molukken)* ('Intern. Archiv f. Ethnogr.' V, p. 1 ff.), 1892. **BD¹GHKL³**

2086. John-Laugnitz, A., *Neue Beiträge zur chinesischen Musikaesthetik* ('Allgem. Musikzeitung' XXXII), 1905. **D¹L**

2087. John, J. T., *Village music of Sierra Leone* ('West African Review' XXIII, p. 1043 ff.), 1952. **G**

2088. Johnson, Guy Benton, *The Negro spiritual: a problem in anthropology* ('Amer. Anthrop.' XXXIII, p. 151 ff.), 1931. **GL²**

2089. Johnson, Orme, *Musical instruments of ancient Hawaii* ('The Musical Quarterly' XXV, p. 498 ff.), 1939. **CDH¹**

2090. Johnsson, Bengt, *Om folkeviseoptegnelse i äldre tider* ('Dansk Musiktidsskrift' XXV, p. 224 ff.), Copenhagen, 1950. **K**

2091. Jones, Arthur Morris, *African drumming* ('Bantu Studies' VIII, p. 1 ff.), 1934. **KL²M**

2092. —— *The study of African musical rhythm* ('Bantu Studies' XI, p. 295 ff.), 1937. **KL²M**

2093. —— *African Music in Northern Rhodesia and some other places* (Rhodes-Livingstone Museum Occasional Paper No. II, combined with a previous Essay on African Music in 'African Studies' VIII), 1949. **AIKL²M**

2094. —— *African music* (Rhodes-Livingstone Museum, Occasional Papers, N.S. No. 4, O.S. No. 2).

2095. —— *The music makers* (London, 1948, s.l.). **IM**

2096. —— *African Music: the Mganda Dance* ('African Studies' Dec. 1945, p. 180 ff.). **AKM**

2097. —— *The Xalimba of the Lala tribe, Northern Rhodesia* ('Africa' XX, p. 324 ff.), London, 1950. **BGJKL¹L²M**

2098. —— *What in a smile?* (in 'Newsletter of the African Music Soc.' I no. 3, p. 13 ff.), 1950. **ACJM**

2099. —— Report on a lecture on 'African Music' given to the Bulawayo Music Club in Sept. 1950 (ibid. I no. 3, p. 16 ff.), 1950. **ACJM**

2100. —— *Hymns for the African* (ibid. I no. 3, p. 8 ff.), 1950. **ACJM**

2101. —— *Blue Notes and Hot Rhythm* (ibid. I no. 4, p. 9 ff.), 1951. **ACJM**

2102. —— (in collab. with **L. Kombe**) *The Icila Dance Old Style* (publ. by the African Music Soc., 1952). **AFIJLM**

2103. —— *Folk Music in Africa* ('Journal of the Intern. Folk Music Council' V, p. 36 ff.), 1953. **ACJKL**

2104. —— *African Rhythm* ('Africa' XXIV, p. 26 ff.), 1954. **ABGIJKL¹L²M**

2105. —— *East and West, North and South* ('African Music' I, No. 1, p. 57 ff.), 1954. **ACJLM**

2105a. —— *European and African music. Differences of scale and rhythm* (*Broadcast talk from the Lusaka station*) ('East Africa and Rhodesia' XXIII, No. 1164, p. 515), London, 1947.

2105b. —— *Drums down the centuries* ('African Music' 1 No. 4, p. 4 ff.), 1957. **ACJLM**

2106. **Jones, Trevor A.**, *Arnhem land music. Part II. A musical survey* ('Oceania' XXVI, p. 252 ff. XXVIII, p. 1 ff.), 1956 and 1957. **ABD¹G**

2107. **Jones, William**, *On the musical modes of the Hindus* ('Asiatic Researches' III, p. 55 ff.), 1792 (reprinted in S. M. Tagore, 'Hindu Music from various authors', p. 123 ff.), Calcutta, 1882, (*vide* below No. 4031). **CFIKL²**

2108. —— *Ueber die Musik der Indier* (transl. from the English), Erfurt, 1802. **C**

2109. **Jong Lsn., J. L. de**, *De Noordske Balke* (Assen, 1942). **ACH**

2110. —— *De Noordse balk* ('Mens en Melodie' XII, p. 174 ff.), June 1957. **AC**

2111. **Jorge, Tomás**, *As aptidões musicais dos indigenas de Moçambique* ('Bol. da Sociedade de Estudos da Colonia de Moçambique' III, p. 163 ff.), Lorenzo Marques, 1934.

2112. **Jourdain, M.**, *Un instrument du pays Bobo (Haute Volta)* ('L'Anthropologie' XLII, p. 676), Paris, 1932. **D¹GH**

2113. **Joyce, Patrick Weston**, *Ancient Irish music* (Dublin, 1873).

2114. —— *Old Irish folk music and songs* (Dublin/London, 1909).

2114a. **Joyce, T. A.**, *The pottery whistle-figurines of Lubaantum* ('J. of the R. Anthrop. Inst.' LXIII, p. xv ff.), 1933. **BGIJKL¹L²M**

2115. **Joyeux, Charles**, *Notes sur quelques manifestations musicales observées en Haute Guinée* ('Revue musicale' X, p. 49 ff.; XI, p. 103 ff.), 1910/'11. **D¹GK**

2116. —— *Etudes sur quelques manifestations musicales observées en Haute-Guinée Française* ('Revue d'Ethnographie et des traditions populaires', Paris, 1924, p. 183 ff.). **G**

2117. **Judd, Neil M.**, *The material culture of Pueblo Bonito* ('Smithsonian Miscellaneous Collections' vol. 124, Washington D.C., 1954), p. 304 ff.: *Musical instruments*. **J**

*2118. **Jungbauer, G.**, *Bibliographie des deutschen Volksliedes in Böhmen* (Prag, 1913).

2119. **Jungblut, Magic Songs of the Bhils of Jhabua State C. I.** ('Intern. Archiv f. Ethnogr.' XLIII, p. 1 ff.), 1943. **BD¹GHKL²M**

2120. **Júnior, Santos**, *Nota de coreografia popular trasmontana I. A dança dos pretos (Moncorvo)* ('Trabalhos da Sociedade Portuguesa de Antropologia e Etnologia' VI, p. 33 ff.), Porto, 1935.

2121. —— *Nota de coreografia popular trasmontana II. A dança dos pretos (Carviçais)* (ibid. VIII, p. 95 ff.), Porto, 1937.

2122. **Junod, Henri A.**, *The mbila or native piano of the Tsopi tribe* ('Bantu Studies' III, p. 275 ff.), Johannesburg, 1929. **KL²M**

2123. —— *Les chants et les contes des Ba-Ronga* (Lausanne, Bridel, 1897).

2124. —— *The life of a South African tribe* (Macmillan, 2/1928), vol. I, p. 431; vol. II, pp. 276 ff., 423 and 484.

2125. **Jurjans, A.**, *Lettische Volkslieder* (Riga, 1885).

2125a. **Juszkiewicz, A.**, *Melodje ludowe litewskie*, vol. I (Cracow, 1900).

2126. **Juškos, Antano**, *Lietuviškos svotbinés dainos* (Vilnius, 1955).

2127. **Kadman, G.**, *Yemenite dances and their influence on the new Israeli folkdances* ('J. of the Intern. Folk Music Council' IV, p. 27 ff.), 1952. **ACJKL**

2127a. **Kahan, Y. L.**, *Yidishe folkslider mit melodyes*. Reissued by M. Vaynraykh (New York, 1957).

2128. **Kalff, G.**, *Het lied in de Middeleeuwen* (Leiden, 1884). **ADGH**

2128a. **Kallenberg, S.**, *Indische Musik* ('Z. f. Musik' 1927). **L**

141

2129. **Kamburov, Ivan,** *Chants de Noël bulgares* (Paris, 1929).

2130. —— *Bulgarskata musica* (Sofia, undated).

2131. —— *Bulgarski narodni pesni* (Sofia, 1941).

2132. —— *Suschtnost, znatchenie i zapisvane na naschia musikalen folklore* ('Izvestia narodnija etnografski musey' V, fasc. l–IV), Sofia, 1925.

2133. —— *Nuschite narodni napevi i teoriite na Riemanna* (Sofia, 1926).

2134. **Kamel El-Kholay,** *Kitabu 'l-musiqi* (Cairo, 1905).

2134a. **Kamitin, F. R.,** *The rongo* ('Sudan Notes & Records' XXVIII, p. 179 ff.), 1947. **M**

2135. **Kanai, Kikuko,** *Ryūkyū no Minyō* (*Folksongs of the Ryukyu Islands*) (Tokyo 1954).

2136. —— *The folk music of the Ryūkyūs* ('J. of the Intern. Folk Music Council' VII, p. 17 ff.), 1955. **AC**

2136a. **Kaneko, Nobori,** *Zum Problem der ältesten japanišchen Musik* ('Wiener Volkenkundl. Mitt.' II, p. 144 ff.), 1954. **L¹**

2136b. **Kanetune-Kyosuke and Syoti Tudi,** *Die geschichtlichen Denkmäler der japanischen Tonkunst.* Abt. I. *Hofmusik,* I. *Saibara* (Tokyo, 1930).

2136c. —— *Japanese music, past and present* ('Oriental Economist' XXIV, p. 186 ff.), April 1956.

2137. **Kantor, S. A.,** and **S. Ladižinský,** *Piesne SSSR pre tenské a detske spevokoly* (Bratislava, 1949).

2138. **Kao Tung Chia,** *Le Pi-pa-ki ou l'histoire de luth* (French translation by Bazin Ainé), Paris, 1841.

2138a. **Kappe, Gustav,** *Tanz und Trommel der Neger* (Festschrift-Prof. Schauinsland), Bremen, 1927.

*2138b. **Karabaić, Nedjeljko,** *Muzički folklor Hrvatskog Primorja i Istre* (Rijeka, 1956). **A**

2139. **Karabey, Lâika,** and fellow-workers, *Musiki Mecmuasi* (i.e. Music Magazine), a monthly periodical, published since 1948, containing exclusive studies and articles on theory, application, history etc. of Turkish music.

2140. **Karastoyanov, A.,** *Melodichni i harmonichni osnovi na bulgarskata narodna pessen* (Sofia, 1950).

2140a. **Karpeles, Maud,** *Folk songs from Newfoundland,* 2 vols. (1934).

2141. —— and **Arnold A. Bake,** *Manual for Folk Music Collectors* (1951). **A**

*2142. —— *English Folk Music* ('Grove's Dictionary of Music and Musicians', 5th ed. vol. III, p. 227 ff.), 1954. **ACFH¹K**

2143. —— *Cecil Sharp, collector of English folk music* ('Studia Memoriae Belae Bartók Sacra', p. 445 ff.), Budapest, 1956. **AC**

2144. —— *Folk songs of Europe* (London, 1956). **AL**

2144a. —— *The collecting of folk music and other ethnomusicological material. A manual for field workers* (considerably enlarged and partly rewritten ed. of No. 2141, issued by the I.F.M.C. and the R. Anthrop. Inst. of Gr. Br. and Ireland), London, 1958. **A**

2145. *Kashmiri Mūsiqi* (*sa, ri, ga, ma*), vol. I (Teacher's Training College, Srinagar, undated).

2146. **Kastaljskij, A.,** *Osobĕnosti russkoj narodnoj muzykalnoj sistemy* (Moscow/Petrograd, 1923.)

2147. **Kataoka, Gidō,** *On Shakujo* ('Journal of the Soc. for Research in Asiatic Music', No. 12–13, English Section, p. 6 ff.), Tokyo, Sept. 1954.

2148. **Kate, H. ten,** *Geographical distribution of the musical bow* ('Amer. Anthrop.' O.S. XI, p. 93 ff.), 1898. **GL³**

2149. —— *The musical bow in Formosa* ('American Anthropologist' V, p. 581 ff.), 1903.

2150. **Katschulev, Ivan,** *Bulgarski narodni musikalni instrumenti-tamburite v Razlotko* ('Izvestia na Instituta za musica' I, publ. by the Bulgarska Akademia na Naukite), Sofia, 1952.

2151. —— *Svirkarstvoto v selo schipka* (ibid. II–III), Sofia, 1956.

2152. —— *Ovtscharski zvuntsi v grad gotse deltschev* (ibid. II–III), Sofia, 1956.

2153. —— *Bulgarski narodni pesni za rusia* (publ. by the Bulgarska Akademia na Naukite), Sofia, 1953.

2154. —— *Sustoyanieto na narodnata musika v Rodopite* (Report of the Rodopska Ekspeditia 1953, publ. by the Bulgarska Akademia na Naukite), Sofia, 1955.

2155. —— *Narodni musikalni instrumenti v Dobrudta* (Report of the Dobrudžanska Expeditia 1954, publ. by the Bulgarska Akademia na Naukite), Sofia, 1956.

2155a. —— *Instruments de musique anciens* ('La Bulgarie d'Aujourd'hui' April 1958, No. 7, p. 24 ff.).

2156. **Katzarova, Raina,** *Gaydite na edin schumenski maystor* ('Izvestia na narodniya etnografski musey' XII), Sofia, 1936.

2157. —— *Koprischki gaydi i gàydari* ('Vjesnik etnographskog museija u Zagrebu' III), Beograd, 1937.

2158. —— *Dneschnoto systoyanie na epitschniya retsitativ v Bulgaria* ('Izvestia na narodnia etnografski musey' XIII), Sofia, 1939.

142

2159. —— *Koledarski pesni* (Sofia, 1934).
2160. —— *Trois générations de chanteuses bulgares* (in 'Mélanges offerts à Zoltan Kodaly à l'occasion de son 60ième anniversaire'), Budapest, 1943. **ACK**
2161. —— *Tri pokolenija narodni pevitzi* (Izvestia Institut za Musika I, Bulgarska Akademia na Naukite), Sofia, 1952 (2nd enlarged edition of No. 2160).
2162. —— *Méthodes de préservation et de renaissance du folklore musical* ('J. of the Intern. Folk Music Council' I, p. 49 ff.), 1949. **AC**
2163. —— *Bulgarische Tänze und Tanzrhythmen* ('Festschrift-Dr. Erich Müller von Assow), Berlin, 1942.
2164. —— *Dances of Bulgaria* (Parrisch and Coy., London, 1951).
2165. —— *Canti populari Bulgari. Motivi primaverili. Le vie del Oriente* (Montanina Magio, 1932).
2166. —— *Dva otlitschitelni beleg na Bulgaromohamedanskite narodni napevi* ('Sbornik na slvyanskite geografi i etnografi'), Sofia, 1936.
2167. —— *Gherghyovdenski obitchai v selo gorni pasarel, samokovsko* ('Bulgarski narod' I, fasc. I), Sofia, 1941.
2168. —— *Dneschnoto systoyanie na narodnara pesen i Tantsovia folklore v Dobrudzha* ('Sbornik Dobrudzhanska Ekspeditsia 1954').
2169. —— *Bulgarski narodni instrumenti* ('Biblioteka hudožestvena samodeynost' I, fasc. 9), 1955.
2170. —— *Detski igri s pesni v Trakija,* ('Bulgarski narod' I, fasc. III).
2171. —— *Ugartschinska pentatonika* ('Izvestia na narodnia etnografski musey' XIV).
2172. —— *Narodnia pevetz Christo Gheorghiev* ('Revue Bulgarska Muzika' V, fasc. IV, I), Sofia, 1954.
*2173. —— *Bulgarian Folk Music* ('Grove's Dictionary' 5th ed. vol. III, p. 201 ff.), 1954. **ACFH¹K**
2174. —— *Verbreitung und Varianten eines bulgarischen Volkstanzes* ('Studia Memoriae Belae Bartók Sacra', p. 69 ff.), Budapest, 1956. **AC**
2175. —— *Bulgarski tantzof folklore* (i.e. Bulgarian folkloristic dances), Sofia, 1955.
2176. —— *Narodni chora i igre ot cèlo Chlévéné Lovesko* (i.e. Folkloristic rondes and dances from the village of Chl. district Lovetch), Sofia, 1956. **A**
2177. **Katzenellenbogen, U.,** *Anthology of Lithuanian and Latvian Folksongs* (Chicago, 1935).
2178. **Kaudern, Walter,** *Musical Instruments in Celebes* ('Ethnographical Studies in Celebes' III), Göteborg, 1927. **ABCJ**

2179. **Kaufmann, F. M.,** *Die schönste Lieder der Ostjuden* (Berlin, 1920).
2180. **Kaufmann, Nikolay,** *Narodni pesni na edin glas* (Biblioteka hudozestvena samodejnost, I, vol. XI), Sofia, 1955.
2181. —— *Trivremennia takt v horovodnite pesni v Pirinskia kray* ('Revue Bulgarska Musika' VIII), Sofia, 1956.
2182. **Kaufmann, Walter,** *Folksongs of the Gond and Baiga* ('Musical Quarterly' XXVII, p. 280 ff.), 1941. **H¹**
2184. **Kavi, M. Ramakrishna,** *Bharata Kosa, a dictionary of technical terms with definitions from the works on music and dramaturgy by Bharata and others* (Sri Venkatasvara Oriental Inst., Tirupati, 1951).
2185. **Keel, Frederick,** *Some characteristics of British folksong* ('Report of the 4th Congress of the Intern. Music Soc., London 1911', p. 179 ff.), London, 1911. **CF**
2186. **Keh, Chung Sik,** *Die koreanische Musik* ('Samml. musikw. Abhandl., Strassburg', 1935). **AIJ**
2187. **Keldis, Juri,** *Geschichte der russischen Musik* (transl. from the Russian by Dieter Lehman), Leipzig, 1956 ff. **C**
2188. **Keller, Gustav,** *Tanz und Gesang bei den alten Germanen* (Bern, 1927). **H**
2189. **Kennedy, Keith,** *The ancient four-note musical scale of the Maoris* ('Mankind' I, p. 11 ff.), 1931. **L²**
2190. —— *The music system of the Fijians* (ibid. I, p. 37 ff.), 1931. **L²**
2191. —— *The drums of Mbau* (ibid. IV, p. 219 ff.), 1934. **L²**
2192. **Kenny, E. C.,** *Chinese gongs* ('Man' XXVII, p. 165 ff., (No. 113)), 1927. **BD¹GKL²M**
2193. **Kerényi, György,** *The system of publishing the collection of Hungarian folksongs: Corpus Musicae Popularis Hungaricae* ('Studia Memoriae Belae Bartók Sacra', p. 453 ff.), Budapest, 1956. **AC**
2194. —— *A Regös-ének magje* (i.e. The kernel of the singing of the Regös, the folk bards) (in 'Emlékkonyv Kodály. I. 70 Zsulétesnapjára' p. 241 ff.), Budapest, 1953. **A**
2195. **Kertész, Gyula,** *A Népdal Gépi Felvétele* (i.e. The recording of folk songs) (in 'Emlékkonyv Kodály. I. 70 Zsulétesnapjára' p. 659 ff.), Budapest, 1953. **A**
2196. **Keyser, P. de,** *Enkele losse beschouwingen over volksliedkunde* ('Miscellanea musicologica' dedicated to Floris van der Mueren, p. 85 ff.), 1950. **C**
2197. **Khokar, Mohan,** *Bharata-natya in Baroda* ('Souvenir of the 8th South Indian Natyakala Conf., Dec. 1953-Jan. 1954') Madras, The Indian Inst. of Fine Arts, 1954.

2198. Kidson, Frank, *Traditional Tunes* (Oxford, 1931).

2199. —— *Manx Folk Music* ('Grove's Dictionary' 5th ed. vol. III, p. 314), 1954. **ACFH¹K**

2200. —— *Hurdy-gurdy* (ibid. vol. IV, p. 415 ff.), 1954. **ACFH¹K**

2201. Kiesewetter, R. G., *Die Musik der Araber* (Leipzig, 1842). **FGK**

2202. Kimotsuki, Kanekazu, *The Analysis of Sound-wave* ('Journal of the Soc. for Research in Asiatic Music', No. 12–13, English Section, p. 11 ff.), Tokyo, Sept. 1954. **A**

2202a. Kin, Maung Tha, *The cant of the musicians of Burma* ('J. of the Burma Research Soc.' XIV, p. 51 ff.), 1924. **G**

2203. Kingslake, Brian, *The Art of the Yoruba* ('African Music Society Newsletter' I, No. 4, p. 13 ff.), 1951. **ACJM**

2203a. —— *Musical memories of Nigeria* ('African Music' I No. 4, p. 17 ff.), 1957. **ACJLM**

2204. Kingsley, Victoria, *Further Notes of the Illustrated Talk on Folk Music of the West* ('The Journal of the Music Academy, Madras' XXII, p. 83 ff.), 1951. **AC**

2205. Kingsmill, Thomas, W. *The music of China* ('J. of the R. Asiatic Soc., North China Branch' XLI, p. 26 ff.), 1910. **KL⁶**

2206. Kinkeldey, Otto, *Changing relations within the field of musicology* ('Proc. Music Teacher's National Ass.' LX, p. 246 ff.).

2207. —— *Chinese music* ('Encycl. Brittannica' V). **BD¹GH**

2208. Kirby, Percival R., *Oldtime chants of the Mpumuza chiefs* ('Bantu Studies' II, p. 23 ff.), 1923. **KM**

2209. —— *Some problems of primitive harmony and polyphony, with special reference to Bantu practice* ('South African Journal of Science' XXIII), 1926. **M**

2211. —— *Primitive and exotic music* ('S. African Journal of Science' XXV, p. 507 ff.), Cape Town, 1928. **M**

2212. —— *Study of South African native music* ('S. African Railways Mag.' 2001 ff.), 1928.

2213. —— *A Study of Negro harmony* ('Musical Quarterly' XVI, p. 404 ff.), New York 1930. **C**

2214. —— *The Gora and its Bantu successors* ('Bantu Studies' V), 1931. **AKL²M**

2215. —— *The mystery of the great Gomgom* ('South African Journal of Science' XXVIII), 1931. **M**

2216. —— *The recognition and practical use of the harmonics of stretched strings by the Bantu of South Africa* ('Bantu Studies' VI, p. 31 ff.), 1932. **KL²M**

2217. —— *The music and musical instruments of the Korana* (ibid. p. 163 ff.), 1932. **AKL²M**

2218. —— *The drums of the Zulu* ('South African Journal of Science' XXIX, p. 655 ff.), 1932. **M**

2219. —— *The reed-flute ensembles of South Africa* ('Journal of the R. Anthrop. Inst. of Great Britain and Ireland' XIII), 1933. **BGIKL¹L³M**

2220. —— *Musical origins in the light of the musical practices of the Bushmen, Hottentot and Bantu* ('Proc. of the Mus. Association'), Leeds, 1933.

2221. —— *The ethnology of African sound instruments. A communication on the early history of the mbila in Africa.* ('Bantu Studies' VII), 1934. **BKL²M**

2222. —— *The effect of Western civilization upon Bantu music* (in: I. Schapera, 'Western civilization and the Natives of South Africa'), London, 1934.

2223. —— *The Musical Instruments of the Native Races of South Africa* (Oxford/London, 1934, 2/1953). **ABCIJLL³**

2224. —— *The principle of stratification as applied to South African native music* ('South African Journal of Science' XXXII, p. 72 ff.), 1935. **ACD¹M**

2225. —— *A further note on the Gora and its Bantu successors* ('Bantu Studies' IX), 1935. **AKL²M**

2227. —— *The musical practices of the /ʔAuni and ≠Khomani Bushmen* ('Bantu Studies' X p. 373), 1936. **AKL²M**

2228. —— *A Study of Bushman Music* ('Bantu Studies' X, p. 205 ff.), 1936. **AKL²M**

2229. —— *Musical instruments of the Cape Malays* ('South African Journal of Science' XXXVI, p. 477 ff.), Dec. 1939. **M**

2230. —— *African Music* (Chapter XXIX of Ellen Hellman, assisted by Leah Abrahams, 'Handbook of Race Relations in South Africa'), 1949. **A**

2231. —— *A note on the shipalapala of the Tonga* ('South African Journal of Science' XXXV, p. 361 ff.), 1938. **AD¹M**

2232. —— *The Trumpets of Tut-Ankh-Amen and their successors* ('Journ. of the R. Anthrop. Inst. of Great Britain and Ireland' 1950, p. 33). **AGIKL¹L²M**

2233. —— *A secret musical instrument: the ekola of the Ovakuanyana of Ovamboland* ('South African Journal of Science' XXXVIII, p. 345 ff.), 1942. **AM**

2234. —— *Bantu* ('Die Musik in Geschichte und Gegenwart' I, col. 1219 ff.), 1951. **ACDEFGH¹KL**

2235. —— *Buschmann- und Hottentottenmusik* (ibid. II, col. 501 ff.), 1952. **ACDEFGH¹KL**

2236. —— *Science and Music* ('South-African Journal of Science' LI, p. 67 ff.), Oct. 1954. **AGM**

2237. —— *Primitive Music* ('Grove's Dictionary' 5th ed., vol. VI, p. 921 ff.), 1954. **ACFH¹K**

2238. Kishibe, Shigeo, *On the Origin of the P'i-p'a* ('Transactions of the Asiatic Soc. of Japan', 2nd ser. vol. XIX, p. 259 ff.), 1940. **GKL⁵**

2239. —— *The Character of the Shi-pu-chi, 'the Ten Kinds of Music' of the T'ang Dynasty* ('Journal of the Soc. for Research in Asiatic Music', No. 9, p. 8 vv.), 1951. **A**

2240. —— *Emigration of Musicians from Central Asia to China and Diffusion of Western Music in China* ('Annales of the Inst. of History, Faculty of General Culture, Tokyo Univ.' No. 1), 1953. **A**

2241. —— *The society for research in Asiatic music; its aims, functions, and achievements* ('Ethnomusicology' X, p. 12 ff.), May 1957. **AGL**

2241a. Kirtikar, Padmavati, *The theory of Indian music* (Santa Cruz, Bombay, 1933).

2241b. Klausmeier, Friedrich, *Kleine Europäische Melodienkunde, eine musikalische Reisebeschreibung fremder Länder in Volksliedern* (Suppl. to the Unesco-Liederbuch), Berlin, 1957. **A**

2242. Klier, Karl, *Die volkstümliche Querpfeife* ('Das Deutsche Volkslied' XXV), 1923.

2243. —— *Volkstümliche Querflöten und die Maultrommel* ('Kongressber. der Beethoven-Zentenarfeier' Vienna, 1927, p. 375 ff.). **C**

2244. —— *250 Jahre Maultrommelmacherzunft zu Molin* ('Tagespost', Linz, No. 226), 29/IX, 1929.

2245. —— *Neue Anleitung zum Schwegeln* (Vienna, 1931). **L**

*2246. —— *Volkstümliche Musikinstrumente in den Alpen* (Kassel/Basel, 1956). **CJL**

2247. Klose, H., *Musik, Tanz und Spiel in Togo* ('Globus' 89), 1911.

2248. Klusen, Ernst, *Der Stammescharakter in den Weisen neuerer deutscher Volkslieder* (Bad Godesberg, 1953). **CL**

2248a. —— *Die rheinische Fassungen des Liedes von den 12 heiligen Zahlen im Zusammenhang der europäischen Ueberlieferung* (Cologne, 1956). **L**

2248b. —— *Deutsch-niederländische Beziehungen im Volkslied* (Cologne, 1956). **L**

2248c. Knosp, Gaston, *Les chants d'amour dans la musique orientale* ('Mercure Musical' IV, p. 785 ff.), 1908.

2249. —— *Annamitische Melodien* ('Die Musik' III, fasc. 24), 1903/'04. **CDFKL**

2250. —— *La Birmanie* (1906) (in Lavignac,

'Hist. de la Musique' V, p. 3094 ff.), 1922. **ACDEFHJ**

2251. —— *Histoire de la musique dans l'Indo-Chine* (1907) (ibid., p. 3100 ff.), 1922. **ACDEFHJ**

2252. —— *Ueber annamitische Musik* ('Sammelb. der Intern. Musikges.' VIII, p. 137 ff.), 1906–'07. **CDFH¹L**

2253. —— *Les iles Canaries* (1908) (in Lavignac, 'Hist. de la Musique', p. 3234 ff.), 1922. **ACDEFH**

2254. —— *Les Chants d'amour dans la musique orientale* ('Mercure Musical', IV, p. 768 ff.), 1908.

2255. —— *Notes sur la tablature chinoise* ('Revue Musicale de Lyon' VI, p. 785 ff.), 1909.

2256. —— *Le Eulk-Ya et la musique Chinoise* ('Le Guide Musical' IV, p. 571 ff., 591 ff.), 1908. **D¹**

2257. —— *Notes sur la musique persane* ('Le Guide Musical' IV, p. 283 ff., 307 ff., 327 ff. and 347 ff.), 1909. **D¹**

2258. —— *Notes sur la musique indo-chinoise* ('Rivista musicale Italiana' XVI, p. 833 ff. and XVII, p. 415 ff., 428 ff.), 1909 and 1910. **CKL**

2259. —— *La Musique dans l'éducation chinoise* ('Mercure de France' LXXXIII, p. 757 ff.), 1910. **D¹**

2260. —— *Rapport sur une mission officielle d'étude musicale en Indochine* (Leyden, 1911). **CL**

*2261. —— *Bibliographia musicae exotica* (Brussels, 2/1914).

2262. *La musique des Indiens de l'Amérique du Nord* (in Lavignac, 'Histoire de la Musique' V, p. 3333 ff.), 1922. **ACDEFHJ**

2263. —— *Les Tziganes* (ibid., p. 2646 ff.), 1922. **ACDEFHJ**

2264. —— *Le gamelan* ('Rivista musicale Italiana' XXXI and XXXIII), resp. 1924 and 1926. **CKL**

2265. —— *Le problème de la musique exotique* ('Rivista Musicale Italiana' XXXII, p. 566 ff.), 1925. **CKL**

2265a. Knott, C. G., *Remarks on Japanese musical scales* ('Transactions of the Asiatic Soc. of Japan' XIX), 1891.

2266. Knudsen, Thorkild, *Praemodal og pseudo-gregoriansk struktur i danske folkevisemelodier* ('Dansk Musiktidsskrift' XXXII, p. 63 ff.), Copenhagen, 1957. **A**

2266a. —— *Structures premodales et pseudogrégoriennes dans les mélodies des ballades danoises* ('J. of the Intern. Folk Music Council' X, p. 4 ff.), 1958. **ACIJKL**

2266b. Kochnitzky, L., *D'un carnet de route musical* ('Jeune Afrique' VI, p. 27 ff.), 1952. **M**

2267. Kodály, Zoltan, *Kelemen kőmies balla-*

dája. Egy dallam 38 változatban (i.e. A ballad-melody with all its variation in 38 stanzas) ('Zenei Szemle' II, p. 37 ff.), 1926.

2268. —— *Néprajz és zenetörténet* (i.e. Folclore and Musical history) ('Ethnographia' 1933, p. 4 ff.).

2269. —— *Ötfokú zene I–IV* (i.e. Pentatonic music), Budapest, 1943/'47. **A**

2270. —— *A magyar népzene* (i.e. The Hungarian folk music), Budapest, 3/ 1952. **AK**

2271. —— *Eine Vorbedingung der vergleichende Liedforschung* ('Studia Memoriae Belae Bartók Sacra', p. 7 ff.), Budapest, 1956. **AC**

2272. —— *Die Ungarische Volksmusik*(transl. by Bence Szabolsci from the Hungarian) (No. 2270), Budapest, 1956. **ACFL**

2273. Kodikar, Mukta, *Role of classical music in Indian films* ('Lakshya Sangeet' I), Delhi, 1954/'55.

2274. Kohl, Louis von, *Tönende Amtsembleme. Zur Entwicklungsgeschichte der chinesischen Musik* ('Sinica' VII, p. 5 ff.), 1932. **GK**

2275. —— *Die Grundlagen des altchinesischen Staates und die Bedeutung der Riten und der Musik* ('Baessler Archiv' XVII), 1934. **D¹GKL²**

2276. Kohlbach, B., *Das Widderhorn* ('Z. des Ver. f. Volksk.' XV, p. 113 ff.), 1916. **D¹GHK**

2277. Kolari, Eino, *Musikinstrumente und ihre Verwendung im alten Testament. Ein lexikalische und kulturgeschichtliche Untersuchung* (Helsinki, 1947). **G**

2277a. Kolberg, O., *Lud* (29 vols.), 1865/'90.

2278. Kolessa, Philaret, *Phonographierte Melodien der ukrainischen rezitierenden Gesänge* ('Dumy') (vol. XIII of the 'Beiträge zur Ukrainischen Ethnologie') Lemberg, 1910.

2279. —— *Ueber den rhythmischen Aufbau der ukrainischen (klein-russischen) Volkslieder* ('Report 4th Congress I.M.S., 1911', p. 184 ff.), London, 1911. **CF**

2280. —— *Volkslieder aus dem galizischen Lemkengebiete* ('Beiträge zur Ukrainischen Ethnologie' vol. XXXIX), Lemberg, 1929.

2280a. —— *Das ukrainische Volkslied, sein melodischer und rhythmischer Aufbau* ('Oesterreichische Monatschrift für die Orient' XLII), 1916.

2281. Kolff, D. H., *Reize door den weinig bekenden Zuidelijken Molukschen Archipel en langs de geheel onbekende Zuidwestkust van Nieuw-Guinea, gedaan in de jaren 1825 en 1826* (Amsterdam, 1828), p. 176, 178, 181 and 208. **AB**

2282. Kolinski, Mieczyslaw, *Die Musik der Primitivstämme auf Malakka und ihre Beziehungen zur samoanischen Musik* ('Anthropos' XXV, p. 588 ff.), 1930. **AD¹GKL¹L²M**

*2283. —— *Suriname Music* (in M. J. and F. S. Herskovits, 'Suriname Folklore', New York, 1936). **BI**

2284. —— *Suriname music* (Columbia Univ. contributions to Anthropology XXVII) New York, 1936. **IJ**

2285. —— *Música de Culto Afrobahiano* ('Revista de Estudios Musicales' I, No. 2, p. 65 ff.), Mendoza, Argentina, Dec. 1949. **AKL**

2286. —— *La música del Oeste Africano. Musica Europea y extraeuropea* ('Revista de Estudios Musicales' I, No. 2, p. 191 ff.), Mendoza, Argentina, 1949. **AKL**

2287. —— *Die Musik Westafrikas* (deposited at the Dept. of Anthropology of Northwestern University). **A**

2290. —— *Ethnomusicology, its problems and methods* ('Ethnomusicology' Newsletter X, p. 1 ff.), May 1957. **AGL**

2291. —— *The structure of melodic movement, a new method of analysis* (in 'Miscelanea de estudios dedicados al Dr. Fernando Ortiz', vol. II, p. 881 ff.), La Habana, 1956. **A**

2292. —— *The determinants of tonal construction in tribal music* ('The Musical Quarterly' XLIII, p. 50 ff.), 1957. **CDEFKL¹**

2293. Koller, Oswald, *Die Musik im Lichte der Darwinschen Theorie* ('Jahrb. der musikbibl. Peters' VII, p. 35 ff.), 1901. **CGKLL¹**

2294. —— *Die beste Methode, Volks- und volksmässige Lieder nach ihrer melodischen (nicht textlichen) Beschaffenheit lexikalisch zu ordnen?* ('Sammelbände der intern. Musikges.' IV), Leipzig, 1902/'03. **CDFH¹L**

2295. Kollmann, Paul, *Flöten und Pfeifen aus Alt-Mexico* ('Bastian Festschrift'), Berlin, 1896.

2296. —— *The Victoria Nyanza* (London, 1899). Music: p. 37 ff., 60 ff., 94 ff., 116 ff., 161 ff., 205 ff. **J**

2297. Komitas, *La musique rustique arménienne* ('Revue Musicale Mensuelle' 1907, p. 472 ff.). **D¹K**

2298. —— *Armenische Dorflieder* (Leipzig, 1913) (2 vols.).

2299. König-Beyer, Walter, *Völkerkunde im Lichte vergleichender Musikwissenschaft* (Reichenberg, 1931). **L**

2299a. Kono, Tama, *Utsuhomonogatari as a glorification of the music of kin* ('Ochanomizu Joshi Daigaku Jombun kagaku kiyô' VIII, p. 283 ff. (in Japanese), p. 149 ff. (Engl. summary), March 1956.

2300. Koole, Arend, *Report on an inquiry*

into the music and instruments of the Basutos in Basutoland ('Kongressbericht Intern. Ges. f. Musikwissenschaft, Utrecht 1952', p. 263 ff.), 1953. **ACDEF**

2301. —— *The history, study, aims and problems of comparative musicology* ('South African Journal of Science' LI No. 8, p. 227 ff.), March 1955. **AGM**

2302. **Korda, Viktor,** *Genuine folk polyphony in the Austrian Alps* ('J. of the Intern. Folk Music Council' IX, p. 9 ff.), 1957. **ACJKL**

2303. **Koritschöner, H.,** *Some East African native songs* ('Tanganyika Notes and Records' IV, p. 51 ff.), 1937.

2304. **Kornfeld, Fritz,** *Die tonale Struktur Chinesischer Musik* (Mödling bei Wien, Skt. Gabrieler Studien, vol. XVI), 1955. **L**

2305. **Kortshmarov, K.,** *Notation of over 200 traditional melodies* (Place and date unknown).

2305a. **Koutev, Philip,** and **Maria Kouteva,** *Folk dance instruments. Kaval* ('The Folklorist' IV No. 1, p. 12 ff.), Manchester, 1957. **A**

2305b. —— and —— *Folk dance instruments: Gadulka* ('The Folklorist' IV, No. 4, p. 111), Manchester, Winter 1957/'58. **A**

2306. **Kozáky, St.,** *A haldltáncok története (Geschichte der Totentänze)* vols. I–III (Budapest, 1936–'44). **C**

*2307. **Kraeling, Carl H.,** and **Lucetta Mowry,** *Music in the Bible* ('The New Oxford History of Music', 3rd ed., vol. I, p. 283 ff.), 1957. **ABCD¹FGH¹JK**

2308. **Krämer, Augustin,** *Die Malanggane von Tombara* (München, 1925), pp. 54 and 56 ff. **AB**

2309. **Kraus, Alex.,** *La musique au Japon* (Florence, 1878). **C**

2310. **Kraus, Al.,** *Di alguni strumenti musicali della Micronesia e della Melanesia regalati al Museo Nazionale d'antropologia e di etnologia dal dott. Otto Finsch* ('Archivio per l'Anthropologia e la Etnologia' XVII, p. 35 ff.), Florence, 1887. **L²**

2311. **Krause, Eduard,** *Trommeln aus vorgeschichtlicher Zeit* ('Z. f. Ethnologie' XXIV, p. (97) ff.), 1892. **BD¹GHKL¹L²M**

2312. —— *Die ältesten Pauken* ('Globus' LXXVIII, p. 193 ff.), Brunsvik, 1900. **D¹M**

2313. **Krauss, H.,** *Altchinesische Militärmusik und Militärsignale* ('Deutsche Militär-Musiker-Zeitung' 1907).

2314. **Krawc, Bjarnat** (= Bernard Schneider), *Dreiunddreissig Wendische Lieder* (Leipzig, 1925).

2315. **Kreemer, J.,** *Atjèh* (Leyden, 1922), vol. I, p. 391 ff. **AB**

2316. —— *Javaansche kinderspelen met zang* ('Mededeelingen vanwege het Nederl. Zendelinggenootschap' XLII, p. 229 ff.), 1898. **B**

2317. **Krehbiel, H. E.,** *Afro-American Folk songs* (G. Schirmer, New York, 1913). **F**

2318. —— *Afro-American folksongs. A study in racial and national music* (New York/London, 1914). **K**

2319. **Kremenliev, Boris A.,** *Bulgarian-Macedonian Folk Music* (Berkeley/Los Angeles, 1952). **ACIL**

2320. —— *Some social aspects of Bulgarian folksongs* ('J. of American Folklore' LXIX, p. 310 ff.), July/Sept. 1957. **GK**

2320a. **Krenn, Ernst,** *Fároyische Spiele, Tanze und anderer Zeitvertreib* ('Wörter und Sachen' XXII, p. 217 ff.), 1942.

2321. **Kresánek, Jozef,** *Slovenská l'udová pieseň so stanoviska hudobného* (Bratislava, 1951). **A**

2321a. —— *Bartók's Sammlung slowakischer Volkslieder* ('Studia Memoriae Belae Bartók Sacra', p. 51 ff.), Budapest, 1956. **AC**

2322. **Krieg, Hans,** *Palestina* ('Encycl. v. d. Muziek' I, p. 64 ff.), 1956. **ACDEFGH¹**

2323. **Krieger, Herbert W.,** *Material culture of the people of South-Eastern Panama* ('Bull. of the Smithsonian Inst.' No. 134), Washington D.C., 1926, p. 115 ff.: *Musical instruments.* **J**

2323a. **Krishnacharya, Vidvan Hulugur,** *Fretting musical instruments* ('The J. of the Music Academy, Madras' XVI, p. 85 ff.), 1945. **C**

2323b. —— *The intonation of Karnataka Raga Melas* ('The J. of the Music Academy, Madras' XVII, p. 51 ff.), 1946. **C**

2324. **Krishna Rao, H. P.,** *The Psychology of Music* (Mysore, 1916).

2325. —— *The Psychology of Music* (Bangalore, 1923). **I**

2326. **Kristensen, Evald Tang,** *Jy(d)ske Folkeminder. I. Jydske Folkeviser og Toner, samlede af Folkemunde, isaer i Hammerum-Herred* (1868–'71); II. *Gamle Jyske Folkeviser* (1874–'76); X. *100 gamle jyske Folkeviser* (1889); XI. *Gamle Viser i Folkemunde* (1891). **K**

2327. **Kristić, Augustin,** *Alat majstora tambura iz kreševa* ('Bilten Inst. za proucavanje folklora Sarajevo' III, p. 153 ff.), Sarajevo, 1955. **A**

2328. **Krohn, Ilmari,** *Geistliche Melodien* ('Suomen Kansan Sävelmiä' I), 1898.

2329. —— *Ueber die Art und Entstehung der geistlichen Volksmelodien in Finland* (1899).

2330. —— *De la mesure à 5 temps dans la mu-*

147

sique populaire finnoise ('Sammelb. der
Intern. Musikges.' II), 1901/'02.
CDFH¹L

2331. —— Ueber die chinesischen Melodien
von P. du Halde ('Allgem. Musikzeitung'
1900–'01). D¹L

2332. —— Welches ist die beste Methode, um
Volks- und volksmässige Lieder nach
ihrer melodischen Beschaffenheit lexikalisch zu ordnen ('Sammelbände d.
Intern. Musikges.' IV, p. 1 ff.), 1902/
'03. CDFH¹L

2333. —— Weltliche Melodien ('Suomen Kansan Sävelmiä' II), 1904. I

2334. —— Tanzmelodien (ibid. III), 1905.

2335. —— Mongolische Melodien ('Z. f. Musikw.' III, p. 65 ff.), 1920. CDH¹KL

2336. —— Melodien der Permier ('Mém. de
la Soc. Finno-Ugrienne' LVIII), Helsinki, 1929. G

2337. —— Die finnische Volksmusik ('Ber.
a.d. Inst. f. Finnlandkunde', Greifs-
wald, 1935). IL

2338. —— Merkmale der finnischen Volksmusik ('Allgemeine Musikzeitung' 1938,
No. 11). D¹L

2339. —— Módszertani kérdések az összehasonlító népdalkutatásban (Zur Methode
der vergleichenden Volksmelodienfor-
schung) (in 'Mélanges offerts à Zoltan
Kodály à l'occasion de son 60ième
anniversaire', p. 97 ff.), Budapest, 1943.
ACK

2339a. Krojer, P. S. M., Het Chineesch tooneel
(Antwerp, Brussels, Ghent, 1946). C

2340. Krumscheid, A., Die Alalás aus Galicia
('Pro Musica' 1955, p. 7 ff.). A

2341. Kruyt, Albert C., Huwelijk en geboorte
in den Banggai-archipel ('T. v. h. Kon.
Bataviaasch Genootschap' LXXII, p.
13 ff. (p. 52 ff.)), 1932. ABD¹GH

2342. —— De fluit in Indonesië ('Tijdschrift
van het Bataviaasch Gen.' LXXVIII,
p. 246 ff.), 1938. ABD¹GH

2343. —— and N. Adriani, De Bare'e spreken-
de Toradjas van Midden-Celebes ('Verh.
Kon. Ned. Akad. v. Wetensch., Afd.
Letterk., N.S., vol. LVI, No. 1), Am-
sterdam, 2/1951. Vol. III, Chapter
XXV. Dans en Muziek. AB

2344. —— Verslag van een reis over het eiland
Soemba ('Tijdschr. v. h. Kon. Ned.
Aardrijksk. Gen.' 2nd series, XXXVIII,
p. 533, 538), 1921. ABD¹GHL²

2345. —— De Soembaneezen ('Bijdr. t. d.
Taal-, Land- en Volkenk. v. Ned-
Indië' LXXVIII (The Hague, 1922),
p. 488, 538, 561, 563, 590, 591, 601.
ABD¹GL²

2346. —— Verslag van een reis door Timor
('Tijdschr. v. h. Kon. Aardrijksk. Gen.'
2nd series, XXXVIII, p. 769 ff.), 1921
(p. 773, 803). ABD¹GHL²

2347. Kuba, Ludvik, The folksongs of White-
Russia ('Music', Chicago, 1898).

2347a. —— Česká muzika na Domašlicku
(Prague, 1894, 2/1947).

2348. —— Slovanstvo ve svych zpeveck (16
vols.) (= The Slavs and their songs)
(Prague, 1884–1929).

2349. —— Pjesmei napjevi iz Bosne i Hercegovine ('Glasnik Zemaljskog Muzeja u
Bosni i Hercegovine' XVIII, 183 ff.,
354 ff., 499 ff.; ibid. XIX, p. 103 ff.,
273 ff., 405 ff., 629 ff.; ibid. XXI, p. 303
ff., 581 ff.; XXII, p. 513 ff.), Sarajevo,
resp. 1906, 1907, 1909 and 1910.

2350. —— Einiges über das istro-dalmatini-
sche Lied ('Ber. 3. Kongress d. Intern.
Musikges.' 1909, p. 271 ff.). C

2351. —— Pisen Jihoslovanska (Prague,
1923).

2352. —— Cesty za Slovanskou Písní. II.
Le Midi slave (Prague, 1935).

2353. Kuhač, F., Južnoslavenske narodne popijevke (5 vols.) (Zagreb, 1878–1919,
and 1941).

2354. —— Das türkische Element in der Volksmusik der Croaten, Serben und Bulgaren
(Vienna, 1899).

2355. Kühnert, F., Zur Kenntniss der chinesischen Musik ('Wiener Zeitschr. für die
Kunde des Morgenlandes' XIV, p. 126
ff.), 1900. HD¹GKL¹

2356. —— Bestehen Beziehungen zwischen chinesischer und ungarischer Musik? ('Keleti Szemle' III, p. 1 ff.), 1902. GKL²

*2356a. Kumer, Zmaga, Yugoslawien. II. Die
Volksmusik. I. Slowenien ('Die Musik
in Geschichte u. Gegenwart' VII, col.
336 ff.), 1958. ACDEFGH¹KL

2357. Kunike, Musikinstrumente aus dem
alten Michoacan ('Baessler Archiv' II,
p. 282 ff.), 1911. BD¹GKL²

*2358. Kunst, Jaap, Terschellinger Volks-
leven (1st. ed. 1914; 2nd and 3rd. ed.
The Hague, 1938 and 1950). AFGHI

2359. —— Het levende lied van Nederland
(1st. ed. 1918/'19; 4th. ed. Amsterdam,
1948). ACGH

2359a. —— Open brief naar aanleiding van de
gestelde vragen omtrent de ontwikkelingsmogelijkheden van de muziek op Java
('Djawa', Prae-adviezen II, p. 123 ff.),
1921. ABD¹G

2359b. —— and R. T. Wiranatakusuma, Een
en ander over Soendaneesche muziek
('Djawa' I, p. 235 ff.), 1921. ABD¹G

2359c. —— and C. A. J. Kunst-Van Wely,
Over toonschalen en instrumenten van
West-Java ('Djawa' III, p. 26 ff.), 1923.
ABD¹G

2359d. —— De muziek in den Mangkoe Na-
garan ('Djawa' IV, Mangkoe Nagara-
Jubilee-number, p. 24 ff.), 1924.
ABD¹G

*2360. —— and C. J. A., Kunst-van Wely, *De toonkunst van Bali* (Weltevreden, 1925). **ABCDGHIJKL**

2361. —— and —— *De toonkunst van Bali II* ('Tijdschrift v.h. Kon. Bataviaasch Genootschap' LXV, p. 369 vv.), 1925. **ABCDEGHL**

*2362. Kunst, Jaap, (in collab. with R. Goris), *Hindoe-Javaansche muziekinstrumenten* (Weltevreden, 1927). **ABCDEFGHIJK**

2363. —— *Over eenige Hindoe-Javaansche muziekinstrumenten* ('Tijdschrift v.h. Kon. Bataviaasch Genootschap' LXVIII, p. 347 ff.), 1929. **ABCD¹GH**

2364. —— *Een overwalsche bloedverwant van den Javaanschen gamelan* ('Ned.-Indië Oud & Nieuw' XIV, p. 79 ff.), 1929. **ABD¹GHL²**

2365. —— *De l'origine des échelles musicales javano-balinaises* ('Journal of the Siam Soc.' XXIII, p. 111 ff.), 1929. **ABDFGK**

*2366. —— *A Study on Papuan Music* (Bandung, 1930). **ABCDFGHK**

2367. —— *Songs of North New-Guinea* (Publ. No. 2 of the Neth.-Indian Musicological Archives), 1931. **ABCDEGHJK**

2368. —— *Verslagen van den ambtenaar voor het systematisch musicologisch onderzoek in den Nederlandsch-Indischen Archipel omtrent de door hem verrichte werkzaamheden, Januari 1930–December 1933; benevens een voorlopige catalogus van de zich in het N.I. Musicologisch Archief .... bevindende inheemsche muziekinstrumenten* (with 8 supplements). **ABCFG**

2369. —— *Oude Westersche liederen uit Oostersche landen* (Bandung, 1934). **ABCEFGH**

*2370. —— *De toonkunst van Java* (2 vols), The Hague, 1934. **ABCGIKL**

2371. —— *Musicological Exploration in the Indian Archipelago* ('The Asiatic Review' October 1936). **ABD¹**

2372. —— *A musicological argument for cultural relationship between Indonesia – probably the Isle of Java – and Central Africa* ('Proc. of the Musical Association', Session LXII), 1936. **(ABC)** ± = *Ein musikologischer Beweis für Kulturzusammenhänge zwischen Indonesien – vermutlich Java – und Zentral-Afrika* ('Anthropos' XXXI, p. 131 ff.), 1936. **ABD¹GHKL¹L²M**

2373. —— *Bij den dood van Erich von Hornbostel* ('Orgaan der Federatie van Ned. Toonkunstenaarsvereenigingen', Jan. 1936) **(ABCFGH)** = *Zum Tode Erich von Hornbostels* ('Anthropos' XXXII, p. 239 ff.), 1937. **ABD¹GHL¹L²M**

2374. —— *John Hazedel Levis' 'Foundations*

of Chinese musical art' ('T'oung Pao' XXXIII, p. 184 ff.), 1937. **ABGK**

2375. —— *New Light on the early History of the Malay Archipelago* ('Indian Art and Letters' XII, p. 99 ff.), 1938. **ABGK**

2376. —— *Music in Nias* (Leyden, 1938). **ABCFIL**

2377. —— *In Memoriam Robert Lachmann* ('Cultureel Indië' I, p. 298), 1939. **ABD¹GHLL²**

2378. —— *Een onbekend Javaansch muziekinstrument* ('Cultureel Indië' I, p. 140 ff.), 1939. **ABD¹GHL¹**

2378a. —— *In contact met Jogja's grootsten nog levenden kunstenaar* ('Djawa' XIX, p. 238 ff.), 1939. **ABD¹**

2379. —— *Een merkwaardig blaasinstrument: de Maleische duivenlokfluit* ('Cultureel Indië' II, p. 47 ff.), 1940. **ABCD¹GHL²**

2380. —— *Indonesische muziek en Gouvernementszorg* ('Kroniek van Kunst en Kultuur' V, p. 243 ff.), 1940. **A**

2381. —— Review of Claudie Marcel-Dubois, 'Les instruments de musique de l'Inde ancienne' ('Cultureel Indië' IV, p. 226 ff.), 1942. **ABCD¹EFGHL²**

*2382. —— *De waardeering van exotische muziek in den loop der eeuwen* (inaugural oration) (The Hague, 1942). **ABCDEFGHK**

2383. —— *Music in Flores, a Study of the vocal and instrumental Music among the Tribes living in Flores* (Leyden, 1942). **ABCEFGIJKL**

2384. —— *Barabuḍur-luiten met stemmen* ('Cultureel Indië' V, p. 30), 1943. **ABD¹GHL²**

*2384a. —— *Een en ander over de Javaansche wajang* (Publ. No. LIII of the R. Tropical Inst., Amsterdam), Amsterdam, 4/1945. **ABCDGHJ**

*2385. —— *Een en ander over de muziek en den dans op de Kei-eilanden* (Public. LXIV of the Royal Tropical Institute, Amsterdam), 1945. **ABCDEGHJL**

2386. —— *Het lot der Javaansche gamelans* ('Indonesia' 8th Sept. 1945). **A**

2387. —— Review of F. Baltazard Solvijns, 'Les Hindous' ('Cultureel Indië' VII, p. 197 ff.), 1945. **ABD¹GHL²**

2388. —— *Muziek en Dans in de Buitengewesten* (Publ. LXVII of the R. Tropical Inst., Amsterdam), 1946. **ABCDEFGHJLL²**

2389. —— *Een novum op Indonesisch muziekgebied* ('Cultureel Indië' VII, p. 200 ff.), 1945 **(ABD¹GHL²)** = 'Mensch en Melodie' I, p. 23 ff., (1946). **ABCDF**

2390. —— *Teylers muzikale prijsvraag* ('Mensch & Melodie' I, p. 19 ff.), 1946. **ABCDF**

2391. —— *Walter Spies als musicus* ('Cultureel Indië' VIII, p. 25 ff.), 1946. **ABD¹GHL²**

2392. —— *De Inheemsche muziek en de Zending* (Publ. LXXII of the R. Tropical Inst.), 1947. **ABCDEFGHJLL²M**

2393. —— *Musicology* ('Report on the Scientific Work done in the Netherlands on behalf of the Dutch Overseas Territories during the period between approximately 1918 and 1943', publ. by the Werkgemeenschap van Wetensch. organisaties in Nederland, and compiled by Dr. B. J. O. Schrieke), p. 194 ff. (1948). **AB**

2394. —— *Around Von Hornbostel's theory of the cycle of blown fifths* (Publ. LXXVI of the R. Tropical Inst.), 1948. **ABCEGH**

2395. —— *A hypothesis about the origin of the gong* ('Ethnos' 1947, p. 79 ff. and 147). (ABCFGL²M) (also in: 'Mélanges offerts à Zoltán Kodály à l'occasion de son 60ième anniversaire, p. 84 ff.). **ACK**

2396. —— *The Music of Bali and its emotional appeal* ('Britain and Holland' 1949). **AB**

2397. —— *Sundanese Music* ('Art and Letters': India and Pakistan' New Series vol. XXII no. 2, p. 54 ff.), 1949. **AGK**

2398. —— *The cultural background of Indonesian Music* (Publ. LXXXII of the R. Tropical Inst., Amsterdam), 1949. **ABCDEFGHL**

*2399. —— *Music in Java, its History, its Theory and its Technique* (2 vols.), The Hague, 1949. **ABCDHIJK**

2400. —— *La Musique indonésienne* ('Revue du Monde Nouveau' 1950, No. 1, p. 86 ff.). **A**

2401. —— *Metre, Rhythm and Multipart Music* (also in a French and a Dutch edition) (Leyden, 1950). **ABCDGJ**

2402. —— *De Inheemse muziek in Westelijk Nieuw-Guinea* (Publ. XCIII of the R. Tropical Inst., Amsterdam), 1950. **ABCDEFGHJL**

2403. —— *Die 2000-jährige Geschichte Süd-Sumatras gespiegelt in ihrer Musik* ('Kongress-Bericht, Lüneburg 1950'), 1951. **ABCDEFKL**

2404. —— *In Memoriam Dr. Ernest Diamant* ('Mens en Melodie' VII, p. 60 ff.), 1952. **ACF**

2405. —— *Nederlandse Volksdansen* ('Program of the National Folkloristic Festival, Hengelo, 17th Aug. 1952'), p. 18 ff. **A**

2406. —— *Sociologische bindingen in de muziek* (inaugural oration) (The Hague, 1953). **ABCEIJL**

2407. —— *Begdja the gamelan boy, a story of the Isle of Java* with musical illustrations by the Study Group for Gamelan Music 'Barbar Layar' (L. P. record No. 00165 L, made by Philips), 1953. **ABFL**

2408. —— *Kulturhistorische Beziehungen zwischen dem Balkan und Indonesien* (Publ. CIII of the R. Tropical Inst., Amsterdam), 1953. **ABGHIL**

2409. —— *Gamelan Music* ('Kongressbericht Intern. Mus. Ges., Utrecht 1952', p. 271 ff.), 1953. **ACDEF**

2410. —— *Een en ander over auteursrecht op volksliederen* ('Mens en Melodie' IX, p. 15 ff.), 1954. **ACF**

2411. —— *Alexander John Ellis* ('Die Musik in Geschichte und Gegenwart' vol. III, col. 1284 ff.), 1954. **ABCDEFGH¹KL**

2412. —— *Cultural Relations between the Balkans and Indonesia* (Publ. CVII of the Royal Tropical Inst., Amsterdam), 1954. **ABCDEFGHJ**

2413. —— *Flores* ('M.G.G.' vol. IV, col. 415 ff.), 1954. **ACDEFGH¹KL**

*2414. —— *Gamelan* (ibid. vol. IV, col. 1351 ff.), 1955. **ABCDEFGH¹KL**

*2415. —— *Gong* (ibid. vol. V, col. 517 ff.), 1956. **ABCDEFGH¹KL**

*2416. —— *Hindu-Javanische Musik* (ibid. vol. VI, col. 451 ff.), 1957. **ABCDEFGH¹KL**

*2417. —— *Indonesische Musik* (ibid. vol. VI, col. 1185 ff.), 1957. **ABCDEFGH¹KL**

*2418. —— *Javanische Musik* (ibid. vol. VI, col. 1784 ff.), 1958. **ABCDEFGH¹KL**

2418b. Kuong-Hong-Sen, *Note additionelle à l'étude du M. Nguyen-dinh-Lai sur la musique sino-viêtnumienne et les chants populaires du Viêt-Nam* ('Bull. de la Soc. des Etudes Indo-chinoises' N.S. XXXI, p. 87 ff.), 1956. **ABL³**

2419. Kurath, Gertrude P., *Iroquois midwinter medicine rites* ('Journal of the Intern. Folk Music Council' III, p. 96 ff.), 1951. **ACJKL**

2420. —— *Local Diversity in Iroquois Music and Dance* (in William Fenton, 'Symposium on Local Diversity in Iroquois Cultus') ('Bull. of the Bureau of Amer. Ethnology' No. 149, p. 109 ff.), 1951. **BCD¹KL²**

2421. —— *Syncopated Therapy* ('Midwest Folklore' I, p. 179 ff.), 1951.

2422. —— *Therapeutic Dance Rhythms* ('Dance Observer', Oct. 1952, p. 117 ff.).

2423. —— *An Analysis of the Iroquois Eagle Dance and Songs* ('Bull. of the Bureau of Amer. Ethnology' No. 156, p. 223 ff.), 1953. **BD¹KL³**

2424. —— *The Tutelo Harvest Rite: a musical and choreographic analysis* ('Scientific Monthly' LXXVI, p. 153 ff.), 1953. **G**

2425. —— *The Tutelo Fourth Night Spirit Release Singing* ('Midwest Folklore' IV, p. 87 ff.), Bloomington, Indiana Univ., 1954. **A**

2426. —— *Rhythms of Work and Play*

('Journal of Health, Phys. Education and Recreation' IX, p. 5 ff.), 1938.

2427. —— Los Concheros ('Journal American Folklore' LIX, p. 234 ff.), 1946. **GK**

2428. —— Los Arrieros of Acapulco ('Western Folklore' VI, p. 3 ff.), 1947.

2429. —— Bronze Ceremonials ('Journal of Health, Phys. Education and Recreation' XIX, p. 4 ff.), 1948.

2430. —— Mexican Moriscas (ibid. LXII, p. 244 ff.), 1949. **A**

2431. —— The Feast of the Dead ('Bull. of the Bureau of Amer. Ethnology' No. 149), 1951. **B**

2432. —— Matriarchal Dances of the Iroquois ('Proc. Intern. Congress of Americanists' 1952).

2433. —— Chippewa Sacred Songs in Religious Metamorphosis ('Scientific Monthly' LXXIX, p. 5 ff.), 1954. **G**

2434. —— Modern Ottawa Dancers ('Midwest Folklore' V, p. 1 ff.), 1955.

2435. —— Ceremonies, songs and dances of Michigan Indians ('Michigan History' XXXIX, No. 4, p. 566 ff.), 1955.

2436. —— Songs of the Wigwam (Coöperative Recreation Service, Delaware, Ohio, 1955).

2437. —— Antiphonal songs of Eastern Woodland Indians ('The Musical Quarterly' XLII, p. 520 ff.), Oct. 1956. **ACDFKL¹**

2438. —— Dance-Music interdependence ('Ethnomusicology' Newsletter X, p. 8 ff.), May 1957. **AGL**

2438a. —— Local diversity in Iroquois music and dance ('Bull. of the Bureau of American Ethnol.' No. 149, p. 109 ff.), Washington D.C., 1951. **KL³**

2438b. —— A new method in dance notation ('American Anthropologist' LII, p. 120 ff.), 1950. **BGHL²**

2438c. —— Memorial to Francis Densmore ('Ethnomusicology' II No. 2, p. 70 ff.), May 1958. **AGL**

2438d. —— Rhapsodies of salvation: Negro-responsory hymns ('Southern Folklore Quarterly' XX, p. 178 ff.), 1956. **A**

2439. Kurosawa, Takatomo, The Musical Bow of the Bunun Tribe in Formosa and suggestion as to the Origin of the Pentatonic Scale ('Journal of the Soc. f. Research in Asiatic Music' No. 10–11, p. 2 ff.), Dec. 1952. **A**

2440. Kurth, E., Musikpsychologie (1931).

2440a. Kutahialian, Jean Onnik, Ecriture musicale arabe moderne (1957).

2441. Kutter, Wilhelm, Radio as the destroyer, collector and restorer of folk music ('J. of the Intern. Folk Music Council' IX, p. 34 ff.), 1957. **ACJKL**

2442. Kuttner, Fritz A., Die verborgenen

Beziehungen zwischen Sprache und Musik, (dargestellt am Beispiel Chinas) ('Musica' V, p. 13 ff.), 1951. **CDKLL¹**

2443. —— The Musical Significance of archaic Chinese Jades of the Pi Disc Type ('Artibus Asiae' XVI fasc. 1–2, p. 25 ff.), 1953. **BGL⁵**

2444. —— Nochmals: die Steinzeit-Lithophone von Annam ('Die Musikforschung' VI, p. 1 ff.), 1953. **ACEIKLL¹**

2445. —— Der stroboskopische Frequenzmesser (ibid. VI, p. 235 ff.), 1953. **ACEIKLL¹**

2446. Kutz, Adalbert, Musikgeschichte und Tonsystematik (Berlin, 1943).

2447. Kuusisto, Taneli, Kansansävelmätoisinto jen osoittaminen säkeittäisen vertailun avulla (Feststellung von Volksmelodievarianten durch Vergleichung der einzelnen Melodiezeilen) (Juhlakirja Ilmari Krohnille), Helsinki, 1927.

2448. Kuypers, John M., Music of the West and the classical music of India; a study in values ('The Viswabharati Quarterly' XIX, p. 272 ff.), Santiniketan, 1953/'54. **G**

2449. Kvitka, Melodies populaires ukrainiennes (Kiev, 1922). **K**

2450. Kyagambiddwa, Joseph, African music from the source of the Nile (New York, Fred. A. Praeger, 1955). **ACJLL²M**

2450a. Kyōkai, Nihon Hōsō, Nihon Minyō Taikan, Chūbu-hen (= A comprehensive treatise on Japanese folk songs: Chubu region, Hokuriku district), Tokyo, 1955.

2450b. —— Tōhoku Minyōshu, Aomori-ken (= Folk songs of the Tohoku area, Aomori prefecture), Tokyo, 1956.

2451. Labat, J. B., Relation historique de l'Ethiopie Occidentale, vol. II, Chapter IV. De la musique des Nègres et de leurs danses (Paris, 1732). Transl. from a work by P. Cavazzi.

*2452. Labouret, Henri, Langage tambouriné et sifflé ('Bull. du Comité d'études hist. et scientifiques de l'A.O.F.' VI, p. 120 ff.), 1923.

2453. —— Un grand tambour de bois ébrié ('Bull. du Musée d'Ethnographie du Trocadéro' II, p. 48 ff.), Paris, 1931.

2454. —— Les tribus du rameau Lobi (Publ. of the Institut d'Ethnologie, Paris, 1931). Chapter III, p. 192 ff.: Musique, chants, danses. **J**

2455. —— and Moussa Travele, Le théâtre mandingue (Soudan français) ('Africa' I, p. 73 ff.), London, 1928. **BGKL¹L²M**

2456. Lach, Robert, Natur- und orientalische Kulturvölker ('Studien zur Entwicklungsgeschichte der ornamentalen Melopoie. Beiträge zur Geschichte der Melodie', p. 93 ff.), Leipzig, 1913. **C**

2457. —— *Der Einfluss des Orients auf die Musik des Abendlandes* ('Oesterr. Monatschrift für den Orient' XL, p. 327 ff.), 1914.

2458. —— *Orientalistik und vergleichende Musikwissenschaft* ('Wiener Zeitschrift für die Kunde des Morgenlandes' XXIX, p. 463 ff.), Vienna, 1916. D[1]GHKL[1]

2459. —— *Das Kadenz- und Klauselproblem in der vergleichenden Musikwissenschaft* ('Z. f. d. oesterr. Gymn.', LXVII, p. 601 ff.), 1916. D[1]GK

2460. —— *Vorläufiger Bericht über die im Auftrage der kais. Akad. d. Wiss. erfolgte Aufnahme der Gesänge russischer Kriegsgefangener im August und September 1916* (Akad. d. Wiss. in Wien, Phil.-hist. kl., Sitzungsber. No. 183, Abh. 4 = 46. Mitteilung der Phonogramm-archiv-Kommission), 1917. D[1]GIKL[1]

2461. —— *id. im August bis Oktober 1917* (Akad. d. Wiss. in Wien, Phil.-hist. kl., Sitzungsber. No. 189. Abh. 3 = 47. Mitteilung der Phonogramm-archiv-Kommission), 1918. D[1]GIKL[1]

2462. —— *Die Musik der turk-tatarischen, finnisch-ugrischen und Kaukasusvölker in ihrer entwicklungsgeschichtlichen und psychologischen Bedeutung für die Entstehung der musikalischen Formen* ('Mitteil. der Anthropol. Ges., Wien', vol. 50, p. 23 ff.), 1920.

2463. —— *Das Phonationsproblem in der vergleichenden Musikwissenschaft* ('Wiener Medizinische Wochenschrift', 1920, Nos. 16, 18 and 19: pp. 749–752, 738–840 and 881–884). D[1]HL[1]

2464. —— *Eine Studie über Vogelgesang* ('Musikalischer Kurier' II, p. 22 ff.), Vienna, 1920.

2465. —— *Musik im Islam* ('Der Auftakt' I, p. 282 ff.), Prag, 1920/'21.

2466. —— *Das Problem des Sprachmelos* ('Wiener Medizinische Wochenschrift', 1922, No. 27, p. 1173 ff.). D[1]HL[1]

2467. —— *Musik in China* ('Der Auftakt' III p. 35 ff.), Prag, 1922.

2468. —— *Musik der Japaner* (ibid. II, p. 107 ff.), Prag, 1922.

2469. —— *Die Musik Ostasiens* ('Faust', vol. 1922, fasc. 8, p. 26 ff.). K

2471. —— *Der Ursprung der Musik im Lichte des Tiergesanges* ('Wiener Medizinische Wochenschrift', 1923, Nos. 28 and 30/31, p. 1307–1310 and 1401–1406). D[1]HL[1]

2472. —— *Das Rassenproblem in der vergleichenden Musikwissenschaft* ('Berichte des Forschungsinstitutes für Osten und Orient' III, p. 107–122), Vienna 1923. GK

2473. —— *Zur Geschichte des musikalischen*

Zunftwesens (Akad. d. Wiss. zu Wien, Phil.-hist. Klasse, Sitzungsber., vol. 199), 1923. AD[1]GIKL[1]

2474. —— *Der Orient in der ältesten abendländischen Musikgeschichte* ('Ber. d. Forschungsinst. f. Osten u. Orient' III, p. 162 ff.), Vienna, 1923. GK

2475. —— *Die Musik der Natur- und orientalischen Kulturvölker* (in Guido Adler, 'Handbuch der Musikgeschichte' vol. I), 1924, 2/1930. ACEF

2476. —— *Das Konstruktionsprinzip der Wiederholung in Musik, Sprache und Literatur* (Akad. d. Wiss. in Wien, Phil.-hist. Kl. Sitzungsber. No. 201, Bd. 2), 1925. D[1]GIKL[1]

2477. —— *Das musikalische Konstruktionsprinzip der altmexikanischen Tempelgesänge* ('Johannes Wolf-Festschrift' 1929), p. 88 ff.

2478. —— *Die vergleichende Musikwissenschaft, ihre Methoden und Probleme* (Akad. d. Wiss. in Wien, Phil.-hist. Klasse, Sitzungsber., vol. 200), 1924. AD[1]GIKLL[1]

2479. —— *Vergleichende Kunst- und Musikwissenschaft* (ibid. vol. 201), 1925. AD[1]GKLL[1]

2480. —— *Gesänge russischer Kriegsgefangener*, part I, *Finnisch-ugrische Völker*, 1st section: *Wotjakische, syrjanische und permiakische Gesänge* (transcr. and transl. by Bernard Munkacsi and Raphael Fuchs) (ibid. vol. 203), 1926; id. part III, *Kaukasusvölker*, 1st section: *Georgische Gesänge* (transcr. and transl. by A. Dirr) (ibid. vol. 204), 1928; id. part I, *Finnisch-ugrische Völker*, 3rd section: *Tscheremissische Gesänge* (transcr. and transl. by Beke Oedoen) (ibid. vol. 204), 1929; id. part II, *Turktatarische Völker*, 1st section: *Krimtatarische Gesänge* (transcr. and transl. by Herbert Jansky) (ibid. vol. 211), 1930; id. part III, *Kaukasusvölker*, 2nd section: *Mingrelische, abchasische, svanische und ossetische Gesänge* (transcr. and transl. by Robert Bleichsteiner) (ibid. vol. 205), 1931. AD[1]GIKLL[1]

2481. —— part I, *Finnisch-ugrische Völker*, 2nd section: *Mordwinische Gesänge* (transcr. and transl. by Ernst Lewy) (ibid. vol. 205), 1933; id. part II, *Turktatarische Völker*, 2nd section: *Baschkirische Gesänge* (transcr. and transl. by Herbert Jansky; transl. by Tagan Galimdschan) (ibid. vol. 218), 1939; id. part I *Finnisch-ugrische Völker*, 4th section: *Tschuwaschische Gesänge* (transcr. and transl. by Kaare Grønbeck) (ibid. vol. 218), 1940. AI

2482. —— *Georgische Gesänge* ('Anzeiger der phil.-hist. Klasse der Akad. d. Wis-

sensch. in Wien' vol. LXIII, p. 13 ff.),
1926. **L¹**
2483. —— *Tscheremissische Gesänge* (ibid.
vol. LXIII, p. 138 ff.), 1926. **L¹**
2484. —— *Mingrelische, abchasische, svanische und ossetische Gesänge* (ibid., vol.
LXIII, p. 140 ff.), 1926. **L¹**
2485. —— *Mordwinische Gesänge* (ibid., vol.
LXIII, p. 145 ff.), 1926. **L¹**
2486. —— *Vergleichende Sprach- und Musikwissenschaft* ('Paul Kretschmer-Fest-
schrift', p. 128 ff.), 1926.
2487. —— *Die Musik der Inkas* ('Der Auftakt' VI, p. 124 ff.), Prag, 1926.
2488. —— *Die Musik der Inkas* ('Der Zuschauer' 1925/26, fasc. 8, p. 6 ff.).
2489. —— Review of R. et M. d' Harcourt,
'La musique des Incas et ses survivances' ('Mitteil. der Anthropol. Ges. in
Wien' LVII, p. 73 ff.), 1926/'27.
D¹GHL²
2490. —— Review of R. et M. d'Harcourt,
'La musique des Incas et ses survivances' ('Z. f. Musikw.' IX, p. 240 ff.),
Leipzig, 1926/'27. **CDH¹KL**
2491. —— *Die physiologischen Urtypen der
musikalischen Formen* ('Wiener Medizinische Wochenschrift' LXXVII, col.
15 ff.), 1927. **D¹HL¹**
2492. —— *Die vergleichende Musikwissenschaft* ('Forschungen und Fortschritte'
III, p. 210 ff.), Berlin, 1927. **D¹G**
2493. —— *Kaukasische Volksgesänge* (ibid.
IV, p. 43 ff.), 1928. **D¹G**
2494. —— *Musikalische Ethnographie* ('Mitteil. der Anthrop. Ges in Wien' LX,
p. 356 ff.), 1930. **D¹GHL²**
2495. —— *Volksgesänge von Völkern Russ-
lands* (Akad. d. Wiss. in Wien, Phil.-
hist. Klasse, Sitzungsber., vol. 227,
4th section), Vienna, 1952. Part II.
*Turktatarische Völker. Kasantatarische,
mischärische, westsibirisch-tatarische, no-
gai-tatarische, turkmenische, kirgische
und tscherkessisch-tatarische Gesänge*
(transcr. and transl. by Herbert Jansky). **AD¹GIKL¹**
2496. **Lachmann, Robert,** *Die Musik in den
tunesischen Städten* ('Archiv f. Musikw.'
V), 1923. **ACFH¹KLL¹**
2497. —— *Ein grundlegendes Werk über die
Musik Indiens* ('Archiv f. Musikw.' VI,
p. 484 ff.), 1924. **ACDFH¹KLL¹**
2498. —— *Musik und Tonschrift der No*
('Proc. Musicol. Congress, Leipzig, June
1925', p. 80 ff.), 1925. **AC**
2499. —— *Zur aussereuropäischen Mehrstimmigkeit* (Beethoven Festival, Vienna
1927; Kongressbericht, p. 321 ff.).
2500. —— *Ostturkestanische Gesänge* (in A.
von Lecoq, 'Von Land und Leuten in
Ostturkestan'), 1928.
2501. —— *Die Weise vom Löwen und der*

pythische Nomos ('Festschrift-Johannes Wolf', p. 97 ff.), 1929. **A**
2502. —— *Musik des Orients* (Breslau, Jedermann's Bücherei, 1929). **AKL**
2503. —— *Die Musik der aussereuropäischen
Natur- und Kulturvölker* (in Bücken,
'Handbuch der Musikwissenschaft'),
1929. **ACDEFGH¹IKL²**
2504. —— *Musikalische Forschungsaufgaben
im Vorderen Orient* ('Bericht über die
1. Sitzung der Ges. zur Erforschung der
Musik des Orients am 27. April 1930'
p. 3 ff.), Berlin, 1930. **A**
2505. —— *Musikwissenschaftliche Forschungen in Tunesien* ('Forschungen und
Fortschritte' VI), 1930. **AD¹GL²**
2507. —— and Mahmud El-Hefny, *Ja'qūb Is-
hāk al-Kindī Risāla fī hubr ta' līf al-
alhan* (i.e. About the composition of
melodies), Leipzig, 1931. **AI**
2508. —— *Von der Kunstmusik des vorderen
Orients* ('Kultur und Schallplatte' II,
p. 164 ff.), 1931. **A**
2509. —— *Asiatische Parallelen zur Berbermusik* (in collab. with E. von Hornbostel) ('Z. f. vergl. Musikw.' I, p. 4
ff.), 1933. **ACK**
2510. —— *Das indische Tonsystem bei Bharata und sein Ursprung* (in collab. with
E. von Hornbostel) (ibid., I, p. 73 ff.),
1933. **ACK**
2511. —— *Die Vina und das indische Tonsystem bei Bharata* (ibid. II, p. 57 ff.),
1934. **ACK**
2512. —— *Musiksysteme und Musikauffassung* (ibid. III, p. 1 ff.), 1935. **ACK**
2513. —— *Mustaqbil al-mūsiqa l-'arabijja*
('Al Kullijja l-'arabijja' XVI, vol. 1 p.
17 ff.), 1935.
2514. —— *Jewish Cantilation and Song in the
Isle of Djerba* ('Archives of Oriental
Music', The Hebrew Univ., Jerusalem,
1940). **A**
2515. —— and A. H. Fox Strangways *Mu-
hammedan Music* ('Grove's Dictionary of Music' 4th ed., vol. III, p. 575
ff.), London, 1940. **F**
2516. **Lacouperie, Terrien de,** *On antique and
sacred bronze drums of Non-China*
('Babylonian and Oriental Record' VII,
p. 193 ff., p. 217 ff.; VIII, p. 1 ff.),
1894 and 1895. **CGK**
2517. **Laforest, Franz,** *Une boîte à musique
unique au monde* ('Le Courier de
l'Unesco' IX, p. 12 ff.), Paris, July/
Aug. 1956. **ABD¹K**
2518. **Lagus, Ernst,** *Nyländska folkvisor I—
II = Nyland, samlingar utgifna af nyländska afdelningen* III, Va-b (Helsingfors, 1887–1900).
2519. **Lai, Nguyen-Dinh,** *Etude sur la musique
Sino-Viêtnamienne et les chants populaires du Viêt-Nam* ('Bull. de la Soc.

des Etudes Indochinoises' N.S. XXXI, p. 1 ff.), Saigon, 1956.   ABL³

2520. Lajtha, Laszlo, *A tárogató utja Persziából Európába* (i.e. Migration of the tárogató from Persia to Europe), Budapest, 1923.

2520a. —— *Bártok Béla zenefolklorisztikai munkái* (i.e. Bela Bartok's works on music folklore) ('Ethnographia' XXXVI, Nos. 7–12), Budapest, 1925.

2520b. —— *Két régi lantról* (i.e. Of two lutes) ('Zenei Szemle' XI, Nos. 3–5), Budapest, 1927.

2520c. —— *A magyar népzene kora* (i.e. The age of Hungarian folkmusic) ('Debreceni Szemle' I, No. 9), Debrecen, 1929.

2520d. —— *Disszitett hangszerek* (i.e. Decorated instruments) ('Magyar Müvészet' V, No. 3), Budapest, 1929.

2520e. —— *Magyar hangszerábrázolásokról* (i.e. Hungarian drawings of instruments) ('Muzsika' I, No. 10), Budapest, 1929.

2520f. —— *Népzenei formaproblémák* (i.e. Form problems in folk music) ('Muzsika' I, No. 3), Budapest, 1929.

2520g. —— *Az 1930 évi népzenei gyüjtések* (i.e. Folk music collected in the year 1930) ('Ethnographia' XLII, No. 2), Budapest, 1931.

2520h. —— *A népzeneről* (i.e. Of folk music) ('Nyugat' XXVI, No. 1), Budapest, 1933.

2520i. —— *Kuruc eredetü dallam a magyar népdalgyüjtésben* (i.e. Melody of Kuruc origin in the Hungarian folk music collection) ('Ethnographia' XLVII, Nos. 1–2,) Budapest, 1936.

2520j. —— and **Sándor Veress**, *Népdal, népdalgyüjtés* (i.e. Folksong, folksong-collecting) ('Magyar Muzsika Könyve'), Budapest, 1936.

2520k. —— and **Sándor Gönyei**, *A magyar néptánc* (i.e. The Hungarian folkdance) ('A Magyarság Néprajza' IV), Budapest, 1937.

2520l. —— and **Oszkar Dincsér**, *A tekerő* (i.e. The hurdy-gurdy) ('A Néprajzi Muzeum Ertesitöje' Nos. 2–4), Budapest, 1939.

2520m. —— *La musica d'oggi e il pubblico* ('Proc. of the Intern. Congress of Music, Florence, 1940').

2520n. —— *Erdélyi népköltés* (i.e. Transylvanian folk poetry) ('Pasztortüz' XXVII, Nos. 3–9), Kolozsvár, 1941.

2520o. —— *Les origines de l'art populaire* ('Nouvelle Revue de Hongrie' Budapest, 1941).   D¹K

2520p. —— *Ujra megtalált magyar népdalstílus* (i.e. Discovery of an ancient type of folk song) (in 'Melanges offerts à Zoltan Kodály à l'occasion de son

2520q. —— *Egy magyar ráolvasó énekelt töredéke* (i.e. A song fragment) ('Ethnographia' LVIII, Nos. 1–2), Budapest, 1947.

2521. —— *Széki gyüjtés* (i.e. The collection of Szék), Budapest, 1954.

2522. —— *Körispataki gyüjtés* (i.e. The collection of Körispatak), Budapest, 1955.

2523. —— *Szépkenyerüszentmártoni gyüjtés* (i.e. The collection from Szépkenyerüszentmárton), Budapest, 1955.

2524. —— *Ugor réteg a magyar népzenében* (i.e. The Ugrian elements in the Hungarian folk music) (in: 'Emlékkonyv Kodály. Zenetudományi tanulmányok' I, p. 611 ff.), Budapest, 1953.   AC

2525. —— *A propos de 'l'intonation fausse' dans la musique populaire* ('Les Colloques de Wégimont' I, p. 145 ff.), Brussels, 1956.   ACL

2525a. Lakatos, Istvan, *A román népdal és irodalma* (i.e. The Rumanian folksong and its literature) (diss.), Budapest, 1939.

2526. Laloy, Louis, *Musique et danses cambodgiennes* ('Mercure Musical' 1906, p. 98 ff.).

2527. —— *Notes sur la musique cambodgienne* ('Ber. über den 2. Kongress der Intern. Musikges. zu Basel'), Leipzig, 1907, p. 61 ff.   C

2528. —— *La musique chinoise* (Paris, 1910).   ACFGIKL

2529. —— *Hoat-Nân Tzĕ et la musique* ('T'oung Pao' XV, p. 501 ff.), 1914.   GK

2530. —— *Les principes de la danse cambodgienne* ('Revue musicale' III, No. 9), 1st July 1922.   CD¹FGHKL

2531. —— *La Musique et les philosophes chinois* ('Revue Musicale' VI, p. 132 ff.), 1925.   CDGHKL

2531a. Lambert, H. E., *Some songs from the Northern Kenya coast* ('J. of the East African Swahili Committee' XXVI, p. 49 ff.), June 1956.

2532. Lamson, Roy, *English Broadside Ballad tunes of the 16th and 17th centuries* ('Proc. Intern. Congress of Musicology, New York 1939' p. 112 ff.), Richmond, 1944.   AC

2532a. Lamsweerde, Felix van, many descriptions of exotic instruments in 'Elsevier's Encyclopedie van de Muziek' I and II, and small articles on gamelan (I, p. 518 ff.), *Krontjong* (II, p. 254), *Luit* (II, p. 298), and *Trom* (II, p. 640), Amsterdam, 1956/'57.   ACDEFGH¹

2532b. Land, J. P. N., *Over de toonladders der Arabische muziek* ('Verslagen en Mededelingen der Kon. Akademie v. Wetenschappen', Afd. Letterkunde, 2de reeks, vol. IX, p. 246 ff.), 1880. **AD¹GH**

2533. —— *Recherches sur l'histoire de la gamme arabe* ('Proc. of the 6th Intern. Congress of Orientalists, Leyden 1883', vol. II, 1st section, p. 35 ff.), Leyden, 1884. **C**

2534. —— *Essais de notation musicale chez les arabes et les persans* ('Etudes archéologiques, linguistiques et historiques dédiées à M. le Dr. C. Leemans', p. 315 ff.), Leyden, 1885. **AC**

2535. —— *Remarks on the Earliest Development of Arabic Music* ('Proc. of the 9th Intern. Congress of Orientalists, London 1892' vol. II, p. 155 ff.), London 1893.

2536. —— *Over onze kennis der Javaansche muziek* (Introduction to J. Groneman, 'De gamelan te Jogjakarta'), 1890. **ABCHIJ**

2537. —— *Tonschriftversuche und Melodienproben aus dem muhammedanischen Mittelalter* ('Vierteljahrschr. f. Musikw.' vol. 2), 1886 (CFKL), reprinted in 'Sammelbände f. vergl. Musikw.' I, p. 77 ff., (1922). **ACGH¹IKLL¹**

2538. **Landstad, M. B.,** *Norske Folkeviser* (1853).

2539. **Landtman, Gunnar,** *Ethnographical collection from the Kiwai district of British New Guinea* (Helsingfors, 1933), VI, p. 68 ff.: *Sound producing instruments.* **J**

2540. **Landtmanson, Samuel,** *Folkmusik i Västergötland* I (...?..., 1911-'15).

2541. **Lane, E. W.,** *Manners and customs of the modern Egyptians* (London, 1860, reprinted 1908, lastly 1954), pp. 330 ff., 359 ff., 400, 452, 454 ff., and 481 ff.

2542. **Lane, M. G. M.,** *The music of Tiv* ('African Music' I, No. 1, p. 12 ff.), 1954. **ACJLM**

2543. —— *The music of the Tiv* ('Nigerian Field' XX, p. 177 ff.), Oct. 1955. **M**

2544. —— *The origin of present-day musical taste in Nigeria* ('African Music' I, No. 3, p. 18 ff.), 1956. **ACJLM**

2545. **Lang, Andrew,** *Bull-roarer* (in Hastings, 'Encyclopedia of Religion and Ethics' II, p. 889), London, 1909. **D¹GH**

2546. **Langdon, Stephen,** *Babylonian musical terms* ('J. of the R. Asiatic Soc. of Britain and Ireland' 1921). **D¹GIKL¹**

2547. **Lange, Daniel de,** *De collectie Indische muziekinstrumenten, boekwerken over muziek en schilderijen in het Rijks Ethnographisch Museum te Leiden* (Amsterdam, 1881). **C**

2548. —— and Joh. F. Snelleman, *La musique et les instruments de musique dans les Indes Orientales Néerlandaises* (in Lavignac, 'Hist. de la Musique' V, p. 3147 ff.), Paris, 1922. **ACDEFH**

2549. **Laoye, I. H. H.,** *Time of Ede. Yoruba drums* ('Nigeria' XLV, p. 4 ff.), 1952. **GL²M**

2550. **Laparra, R.,** *La musique et la danse populaires en Espagne* (1920) (in Lavignac, 'Histoire de la musique'), Paris, 1922. **C**

2551. **Lara, M. de,** and Escobar, M. L., *Ritmo y melodia nativos de Venezuela* ('Estudios Latino-americanos' III, p. 121 ff.), 1937.

2552. —— and —— *Los instrumentos musicales aborigenes y criollos de la Argentina* (Buenos Aires, undated).

2552a. **Larrea Palicin,** Arcadio de, *Preliminares al estudio de la jota aragonesa* ('Anuario musical' 1), 1946. **CL**

2553. —— *La saeta* ('Anuario musical' IV, p. 105 ff.), 1949. **CL**

2554. —— *Organografia de Ifni* ('Africa' No. 187), Madrid, July 1957. **BM**

*2555. —— *Cancionero del Africa Occidental Española. I. Canciones Joglarescas de Ifni* ('Idea', Madrid, 1955); II. *Canciones populares de Ifni* (ibid., 1957).

2555a. —— *Canciones de Ifni* ('Africa' (Madrid) XIII, p. 18 ff.), Oct. 1956.

2556. **Larsson, Karl-Erik,** *Snäcktrumpeterna på Fiji* ('Etnografiska Museet, Göteborg, Arstryck 1953-1955', p. 13 ff.), Göteborg, 1956.

La Rue, Jan, see: Rue, Jan la.

2557. **Laub, Th.,** and Axel Olrik, *Danske folkeviser med gamle melodier* (Copenhagen, 2/1930). **K**

2558. **Laubenstein, Paul Fritz,** *Race values in Afro-American music* ('The Musical Quarterly' XVI, p. 378 ff.), 1930. **C**

2559. **Launis, Armas,** *Lappische Juoikosmelodien* (Helsinki, 1908). **L²**

2560. —— *Ueber Art, Entstehung und Verbreitung der estnisch-finnischen Runenmelodien* (Helsinki, 1910). **I**

2561. —— *Ueber die Notwendigkeit einer einheitlichen Untersuchungsmethode der Volksmelodien* ('Report of the 4th Congress of the Intern. Music Soc., London 1911', p. 185 ff.), London, 1911. **CF**

2562. —— *Runen* ('Suomen Kansan Sävelmiä' VI), 1910 and 1930. **L**

2562a. —— *Estnisch-finnische Runenmelodien* (Helsinki, 1913). **L**

2563. —— *Eesti runoviisid* (*Estnische Runenmelodien*), Tartu, 1930.

2564. —— *Pentatonik in den Melodien der Lappen* ('Kongressber. III. Kongress d. Intern. Musikges., Wien, 1909'). **C**

2566. **Lavauden, Thérèse,** *African orchestics* ('Chesterian' X, p. 127 ff.), 1929.

2567. —— *Orchestique africaine* ('Le Guide musical' III, p. 230 ff.), 1930.

2567a. **Laveda, L.,** *Les Mandingues dans le*

Cercle de Tambacounda ('Sénégal' II, No. 50, p. 109 ff., No. 51, p. 143 ff.), 1943. **M**

2568. Lavin, Ch., *La musique des Araucans* ('Revue musicale' VI, No. 5), 1st March 1925. **CD¹GHKL**

2569. Lawirdi, Mikha'il Khalil Al-, *Falsafat al-musiqi aš-šarqiyya fi asrar al-jasin al-Arabi* (Damascus, 1948). **G**

2570. Lawrance, J. C. D., *The Iteso. Fifty years of change in a Nilo-Hamitic tribe of Uganda* (London, Oxford Univ. Press 1957), Part V. *Culture*, Chapter I. *Music and dancing.* **AB**

2571. Laxton, P. B., and Te Kautu Kamoriki, *'Ruoia', a Gilbertese Dance* ('The Journal of the Polynesian Soc.' LXII, p. 57 ff.), March 1953. **ABGL²**

*2571a. Lazarević, Stojan, *Yugoslawien.* II. *Die Volksmusik.* 3a. *Serbien* ('Die Musik in Geschichte u. Gegenwart' VII, col. 359 ff.), 1958. **ACDEFGH¹KL**

2571b. Leach, MacEdward, *Folksong and ballad. A new emphasis* ('J. of American Folklore' LXX, p. 205 ff.), July/Sept. 1957.

2572. Leaky, L. S. B., *The religious element in Mau-mau* ('African Music' I, No. 1, p. 77 ff.), 1954. **ACJLM**

2572a. Lebesque, Ph., *Les chants féminins serbes* (mus. suppl. by M. Miloiévic), 1920.

2573. Leblond, Marius-Ary, *Lettre sur la musique malgache* ('J. de la Soc. Intern. de Musicologie' IV, p. 877 ff.), Paris, 1908.

2573a. —— *La grande île de Madagascar* (Paris, 1946).

2574. Leden, Christian, *Musik und Tänze der grönländischen Eskimos* ('Z. f. Ethnologie' XLIII), 1911. **BD¹GHJKL¹L²M**

2575. —— *Musikethnologische Grönlandexpedition* ('Z. der Intern. Musikges.' XII, p. 370 ff.), 1910. **CDFH¹KL**

2576. —— *Ueber Kiwatins Eisfelder* (Leipzig, 1927) (with music).

2577. —— *Ueber die Musik der Smith Sund Eskimos und ihre Verwandtschaft mit der Musik der amerikanischen Indianer* ('Meddelelser om Grønland', CLII No. 3), Copenhagen, 1952. **L²**

2577a. —— *Ueber die Musik der Ostgrönländer* ('Meddelelser om Grønland' CLII, No. 4), Copenhagen, 1954. **L²**

2577b. Lee, Hyeku, *Studies in Korean music* (in the Korean language, with a Table of contents in English) (publ. by the National Music Research Soc. of Korea) Seoul, 1957. **A**

2577c. Lee, Kang Nyum, *Korean folk songs* (authentic songs, but with piano-accompaniment), with pictures of Korean instruments with English commentary) (publ. by the National Music Research Soc. of Korea), Seoul, 1957. **A**

2578. Lehmann, Johannes, *Beiträge zur Musikinstrumental-Forschung* ('Festschrift zur Feier d. 25. jähr. Best. d. Frankfurter Ges. f. Anthrop., Ethnol. u. Urgesch.'), Frankfurt a/M, 1925.

2579. Lehmann-Nitsche, Robert, *Patagonische Gesänge und Musikbogen* ('Anthropos' III, p. 916 ff.), 1908. **D¹GJKL¹L²M**

2580. Lehtisalo, T., *Beobachtungen über die Jodler* ('Suomalais-Ugrilaisen Seura Aikakausk' XLVIII, No. 2, p. 1 ff.), 1937. **K**

2581. Lehuraux, Léon, *Chants et chansons de l'armée d'Afrique* (Société générale d'imprimerie, Paris, 1935).

2582. Leifs, Jon, *Isländische Volksmusik und germanische Empfindungsart* ('Die Musik' XVI, fasc. 1), 1923/'24. **CDFKL**

2582a. —— *Isländische Volkslieder* ('Z.f. Musikw.'. XI, p. 365 ff.), '29. **ACDH¹KL**

2583. Leiris, Michel, *Rhombes dogon et dogon pignari* ('Bull. du Musée d'Ethnographie du Trocadéro' No. 7, p. 3 ff.), 1934.

2584. Lekkerkerker, C., *Mededeeling over het Kéblai der Rotineezen* ('Bijdr. t. d. Taal-, Land- en Volkenk. v. Ned.-Indië' LXIII, p. 111 ff.), The Hague, 1910. **ABD¹GL²**

2584a. Lemm, F. H., *Musique et arts nègres. Lettres du Soudan* ('Bull. des recherches soudanaises' No. 36), Koulouba, Sept. 1936.

2585. Lennep, Jkvr. Henriette van, *De muziek der volkeren* (Gouda, 1956). **AC**

2586. —— *De Twentse midwinterhoorn en verwante instrumenten* ('Nehalennia' I, p. 116 ff.), 1956. **AC**

2587. —— *Musique Proto-Indochinoise* ('Gramofoon voor kenner en liefhebber' April 1957, p. 14 ff.). **AC**

2588. —— *Musique Indienne du Brésil, vol. I* ('Gramofoon voor kenner en liefhebber' Sept. 1957, p. 16 ff.). **AC**

2588a. —— *Fragmenten van laat-Romeinse auloi uit Zuid-Limburg* ('Honderd eeuwen Nederland' p. ... ff.), The Hague, 1958. **A**

2588b. —— *De midwinterhoorn* (ibid., p. ... ff.), The Hague, 1958. **A**

2589. Lenoir, Raymond, *La musique comme institution sociale* ('L'Anthropologie' XLIII, p. 47 ff.), 1933. **D¹G**

2590. Lens, Thérèse de, *Ce que nous savons de la musique du Maroc* ('Bull. de l'Inst. des Hautes Etudes Marocaines' 1920).

2591. —— *Sur le chant des moueddin et sur les chants chez les femmes à Meknis* ('Revue de musicologie' VIII No. 12), Nov. 1924. **C**

2592. Leon, Argeliers, *Lecciones del curso de música folklórica en Cuba* (Habana, 1948).

2593. —— *El patrimonio folklórico musical cubano* (Habana, 1952).

2593a. Leport, J. M., *Vervlogen tijden* ('Nieuw Afrika' LXVIII, p. 200 ff.), 1952. **M**

2594. Leriche, A., *Instruments de musique maure et griots* ('Bull. de l'Inst. Francais de l'Afrique Noire' XII, p. 744 ff.), Dakar, 1950. **BGL²M**

2594a. —— *Poésie et musique maure* (ibid. p. 710 ff.), Dakar 1950. **B**

2595. Leroux, A., *Rapports entre la musique bretonne et la musique orientale* (Vannes, 1891). **I**

2596. Leroux, Ch., *La musique classique japonaise* (1911). **I**

2597. Leslau, Wolf, *Chansons Harari* ('Rassegna di studi Etiolici' VI, p. 130 ff.), 1947. (Notes on music by George Herzog).

2598. Lethbridge, H. O., *Australian aboriginal songs* (Melbourne, 1937).

2599. Levi, Leo, *On the tape recording project of 500 Jewish melodies in Italy* ('Yeda-Am' III, p. 58 ff.), 1955.

2600. Lévi-Provençal, E., *Un chant populaire religieux du Djebel Marocain* ('Revue Africaine' 1918, p. 215 ff.). **G**

2601. Levis, John Hazedel, *The Musical Art of Ancient China* ('T'ien Hsia Monthly' I, p. 404 ff.), 1935.

2602. —— *Fundamentals of Chinese melody, rhythm and form as seen through the music poems of Ancient China* (Peiping, 1933).

*2603. —— *Foundations of Chinese Musical Art* (Peiping, 1936). **ACGIJK**

2604. —— *Chinese Music* ('Asia' XXXVII p. 863 ff.), 1937. **AD¹**

2605. Levy, J., *Die Signalinstrumente in den altfranzösischen Texten* (Diss., Halle, 1910).

2606. Lhote, Henri, *La documentation sonore (chant, musique et poésie) établie chez les Touareg du Hoggar en 1948* ('Cahiers Charles de Foucauld' XXVII, p. 114 ff.), 1952.

Li, Hwei, see: Hwei, Li (2015).

Li, Yuang-Ching, see: Yuan-Ching Li (4458).

*2606a. Libiez, Albert, *Chansons populaires de l'ancien Hainaut* vol. I (Brussels, 1939), vol. II (ibid. 1941), vols. III and (with collab. of Roger Pinon) (ibid. 1951 and 1957). **A**

2607. Lichtheim, J., *The songs of the harpers* ('J. of Near Eastern Studies' IV), 1945. **D¹GHKL¹**

2608. Lichtveld, Lou, *De muziek der Roodhuiden* ('Leven en Werken' IV, N.S., No. 1, p. 3 ff.), Januari 1940. **AD¹**

2609. —— *Muziek* ('Ons Koninkrijk in Amerika', p. 84 ff.), 1947. **B**

2610. Ligeti, György, *Egy Arademegyi Román Együttes* (i.e. A Rumanian ensemble from the Comitat of Arad), (in 'Emlékkonyv Kodály. I. 70 Zsulétesnapjára', p. 399 ff.), Budapest, 1953. **A**

2611. Ligtvoet, A. W., *Exotische en oude europese muziekinstrumenten* (Den Haag, 1956). **AC**

2612. —— *An interesting musical instrument from New-Ireland* ('Antiquity and Survival' No. 4, p. 299 ff.), 1955. **ABCD¹GHJK**

2613. Lieutenant R. N., A, *The boatswain's call, as it was, and as it should still be, used in H.M. Navy* ('The Mariner's Mirror' I, p. 9 ff.), 1911.

2614. Lima, Emirto de, *La musique Colombienne* ('Acta Musicologica' II, p. 92 ff.), 1930. **CDLL¹**

2615. —— *La chanson populaire en Colombie* (ibid. IV, p. 128 ff.), 1932. **CDEKLL¹**

2616. —— *Las flautas indigenas colombianas* ('Estudios Latino-americanos' III, p. 67 ff.), 1937.

2617. —— *Diverses manifestations folkloriques sur la côte des Antilles en Colombie* ('Acta Musicologica' VII, p. 107 ff.), 1935. **CDEH¹KLL¹**

2618. Limbert, Francis L., *Beitrag zur Kenntnis der volkstümlichen Musik, insbesondere der Balladenkomposition in England* (Diss.), Strassburg, 1895. **L**

2619. Lindblom, Gerhard, *Die Stosstrommel, insbesondere in Afrika* ('Ethnos' 1945, p. 17 ff.). **ACL²M**

2620. —— *The Akamba in British East Africa* (Archives d'Etudes orientales XVII), Uppsala ,1920, p. 398 ff.: *Music and dancing.* **J**

2621. Lindeman, L. M., *Aeldre og nyere norske Fjeldmelodier* I–XIII (1853–'67), (cf. No. 3887).

2622. Linder, Sven, *Palästinische Volksgesänge* (aus dem Nachlass herausgeg. und mit Anmerkungen versehen von Helmer Ringgren), Uppsala/Wiesbaden, 1952 = 'Uppsala Universtets Arsskrift' 1952, fasc. 5, p. 1 ff.

*2623. Lindsay, Maurice, *Scottish Folk Music* ('Grove's Dictionary' 5th ed., vol. III, p. 346 ff.), 1954. **AC**

2624. Lineff, Eugenie, *Peasant songs of Great Russia as they are in the folk's harmonization* I (Moscow, 1905), II (Moscow, 1911).

2625. —— *A musical tour in the Caucasus* ('Sammelb. der Intern. Musikges.' XIII, p. 552 ff.), 1911/'12. **CDFH¹L**

2625a. —— *Psalms and religious songs of Russian sectarians in the Caucasus* ('Report of the 4th Congress of the

Intern. Musical Soc.', p. 187 ff.), London, 1911. **CF**

2626. **Lineman, W.**, *Traces of a bronze age culture associated with Iron age implements in the regions of Klang, Selangor* ('J. of the Malayan branche of the R. Asiatic Soc.' XXIV, part 3, p. 1 ff.), Oct. 1951: I. *The bronze drum of Klang, Selangor.* **BD¹GKL²L⁵**

2627. **Linné, S.**, *Zapotecan antiquities and the Paulson collection in the Ethnographical Museum of Sweden* (publ. of the said Museum, N.S. No. 4), Stockholm, 1938 (p. 66). **B**

2628. **Linton, Ralph**, *The material culture of the Marquesas Islands* ('Memoirs of the Berenice P. Bishop Museum' VIII No. 5), Honolulu, 1923, p. 403 ff.: *Musical instruments.* **J**

2629. **Liscano, Juan**, *Baile de tambor* ('Bol. de la Soc. Venezolana de Ciencias Naturales' VIII), Caracas, 1943. **D¹**

2629a. **List, George**, *An ideal marriage of ballad text and tune* ('Midwest Folklore' VII, No. 2, p. 95 ff.), Summer 1957. **A**

2630. **Little, K. L.**, *A Mende musician sings of his adventures* ('Man' XLVIII, p. 27/8), 1948. **BD¹GKL¹L²M**

2631. **Liu, Charles**, *On the Jew's Harps from Hainan Island* ('Journal of the Science Soc. of China' XX, p. 12 ff.), 1938.

2632. **Liu, Chungshee Hsien**, *Sur un instrument musical à anches libres en usage chez les Miao dans la Chine du Sud-Ouest* ('L'Ethnographie' N.S. XXVIII, p. 27 ff.), 1934. **D¹GK**

2633. **Liu Fu**, *Etude expérimentale sur les tons du Chinois* (Paris, 1925).

2634. —— *Five tones to three hundred and sixty tones* (1930).

2635. **Livshitz, A.**, *Dva narodnykh muzykanta* (i.e. Two folk musicians) ('Sovetskaya muzyka' 1950, No. 5, p. 51 ff.).

2636. **Llanos, C. A.**, *Ethnographica tibetanos en el museo etnográfico de Buenos Aires* ('Acta Asiatica' I No. 1, p. 54 ff. (p. 73 ff.): *Rag-dun.* **A**

2637. **Lloyd, A. L.**, *Recent developments in the folk song of Hunedoara* ('J. of the Intern. Folk Music Council' IX, p. 67 ff.), 1957. **ACJKL**

2638. **Lloyd, Llewelyn S.**, *The Myth of Equal-Stepped Scales in Primitive Music* ('Music and Letters' XXVII, p. 73 ff.), 1946. **KL¹**

2639. —— *Hornbostel's Theory of Blown Fifths* ('Monthly musical record', London, 1946, Jan. and Febr.).

2640. —— *Pitch notation* ('Grove's Dictionary' 5th ed. vol. VI, p. 785 ff.), 1954. **ACFH¹K**

2641. —— *Pitch, standard*, ('Grove's Dictionary 5th ed., VI, p. 788 ff.), 1954. **ACFH¹K**

2642. —— *Trumpet marine* ('Grove's Dictionary of music and musicians' 5th ed., vol. VIII, p. 572 ff.), 1954. **AC**

2643. —— *The bagpipe scale* ('Monthly Musical Record' LXXX, No. 921).

2644. **Lloyd, Theodosia**, *Sunday morning at Randfontein* ('New Statesman' XVI, p. 218 ff.), 6 Aug. 1938. **D¹**

2645. **Lo Liang Chu**, *Hauptwerke chinesischer Musik* (in: Richard Wilhelm, 'Chinesische Musik'), Frankfurt, 1927. **G**

2646. **Lods, Adolphe**, *Les idées des anciens Israélites sur la musique* ('Journal de Psychologie' 1926).

2646a. **Loesche, E. Pechuel**, *Volkskunde von Loango* (Stuttgart, 1907), p. 111 ff.

2647. **Lomax, John A.** and **Alan Lomax**, *Folk Song: U.S.A. The 111 Best American Ballads* (New York, 1947). **AK**

2648. **Long, Kenneth R.**, *African Folk-Song. Some notes on the Music of the Bantu Tribes of Southern Africa* (in 'Hinrichsen's Musical Yearbook' VII, p. 577 ff.), 1952. **K**

2648a. —— *The future of African music* ('Nada' 1946, No. 23, p. 24 ff.).

2649. **Longmore, L.**, *Music and Song among the Bantu People in urban areas on the Witwatersrand* ('African Music Society Newsletter' I No. 6, p. 15 ff.), 1953. **ACJM**

2650. **Loorits, Oskar**, *Volkslieder der Liven* ('Opetatud Eesti Seltsi toimetused' XXVIII), Tartu, 1936. **G**

2651. **Lopez Chavarri, E.**, *Música popular española* (Barcelona, 1927). **FH**

2652. **López Chiñas, Gabriel**, *La música aborigen de Juchitán* ('Neza' IV, No. 1), Mexico, 1939.

2652a. **Lopez Cruz, Francisco**, *El aguinaldo y el villancico en el folklore Puertorriqueno* (Puerto Rico, Inst. de Cultura Puertorriquena, 1956).

2653. **Lord, Albert Bate**, *Yugoslav epic songs*, vol. I (Harvard Univ. Press, 1954).

2654. —— *Serbo-croatian heroic songs collected by Milman Parry.* Vols. I and II: *Novi Pazar* (Harvard Univ. Press, Serbian Acad. of Sciences, Belgrade and Geoffry Cumberlege, London, 1953 and '54). **L**

2655. —— *Avdo Mededovic, Guslar* ('J. of American Folklore' LXIX, p. 320 ff.), July/Sept. 1956. **GK**

2656. **Lorenc, Antoni**, *Folklori muzikuer shqiptar* (Pristina, 1956).

2657. **Loret, Victor**, *Quelques documents relatifs à la litterature et à la musique populaires du Haute-Egypte* ('Mémoires de la Mission Archéologique Française au Caire' I, p. 305 ff.), 1881/'84.

2658. —— Les flûtes égyptiennes antiques ('Journal Asiatique' LXIV, p. 133 ff.), 1889. CD¹GHKL¹

2659. —— Egypte. Note sur les instruments de musique de l'Egypte ancienne (1910) (in Lavignac, 'Hist. de la Mus.' I, p. 1 ff.), 1922. ACDEFHJ

2660. —— Les cymbales égyptiennes ('Sphynx' V), 1902. K

2661. Lorimer Y Paul, Le sacrifice du tambor Assoto (Port-au-Prince, 1942).

2662. —— Essai d'organographie Haitienne (Port-au-Prince, 194.).

2663. Louw, J. K., The use of African music in the church ('African Music' I, No. 3, p. 43 ff.), 1956. ACJLM

2664. Lübke, Anton, Der Himmel der Chinesen (Leipzig, 1931), p. 68 ff. ('Glocken und Trommeln als Zeitkünder in China'), p. 126 ff. ('Astronomie und Chinesische Musik').

2665. Lugossy, Emma, 77 léanytánc (Budapest, 1952).

2666. Lury, E. E., Music in East African churches ('African Music' I, No. 3, p. 34 ff.), 1956. ACJLM

2667. Lush, Allan J., Kiganda drums ('Uganda Journal' III, p. 7 ff.), 1925. L²

2667a. Lussy, K., Some aspects of work and recreation among the Wapogoro of Southern Tanganyika ('Anthropol. Quarterly' XXVI, p. 109 ff.), 1953. M

2668. Lutter, E., Les Wasamba et leur usage dans la circoncision ('Minotaure' II), 1933.

2669. Lyle, Robert, The music of the ancient Egyptians: a conjectural sketch ('Musical Monthly Record' LXXVIII), 1948.

2670. Maas, Chr. J., Mesopotamië ('Encyclopedie van de Muziek' I, p. 56 ff.), Amsterdam 1956. ACH¹

2671. —— Perzië (ibid. I, p. 59 ff.), Amsterdam 1956. ACH¹

2672. —— Egypte (ibid. I, p. 60 ff.), Amsterdam 1956. ACH¹

2673. Mac Culloch, J. A., Horns (in: Hastings, 'Encyclopedia of Religion and Ethics' VI), London, 1909.

2674. —— Primitive and savage music (ibid. IX), London, 1909.

2675 Macdonald, D. B., Emotional religion in Islam as affected by music and singing ('J. of the Royal Asiatic Soc.' 1901, p. 2 ff.). D¹GIKL¹

2676. —— Irish music and Irish scales (Breitkopf & Härtel, Leipzig, 1910). I

2677. Maceda, José, Philippine music and contemporary aesthetics (in: Herbert Passin, 'Cultural Freedom in Asia' (Vermont/Tokyo, 1956), p. 116 ff. A

2677a. —— Chants from Sagada mountain province Philippines (Part I), ('Ethnomusicology' II No. 2, p. 45 ff.), May 1958. AGL

2678. Machabey, A., La musique des Hittites ('Revue de Musicologie' XXIII, p. 1 ff.), 1944. CD¹KL¹

2679. —— La musique suméro-chaldéenne et égyptienne (in Dufourcq, 'La musique des origines à nos jours', ed. Larousse, p. 59 ff.), Paris, 1946. ACDEFHJK

2680. —— La musique hébraique (ibid., p. 63 ff.), 1946. ACDEFHJK

2681. —— La musique grècque (ibid., p. 64 ff.), 1946. ACDEFHJK

2682. —— La musique latine (ibid., p. 67 ff.), 1946. ACDEFHJK

2683. —— La musique et la médecine ('Polyphonie' 1950, Nos. 7–8, p. 40 ff.). K

2684. —— La notation musicale (Paris, 1952).

2685. Machida, Kasho, The musical meaning of 'kataru' (narration) and 'utau' (singing) in Japanese vocal music accompanied by the shamisen ('J. of the Soc. f. Research in Asiatic Music' No. 10–11, p. 1 ff.), Tokyo, Dec. 1952. A

2686. —— Notes on Japanese Music (Japan, 1953). A

2687. Mackay, Mercedes, The traditional musical instruments of Nigeria ('The Nigerian Field' XV, No. 3, p. 112 ff.), 1950. JM

2688. —— The Shantu music of the Harims of Nigeria ('African Music' I, No. 2, p. 56 ff.), 1955. ACJLM

2688a. —— Nigerian folk musical instruments ('Nigeria' 1949, No. 30, p. 337 ff.). GL²M

2688b. —— and Augustine Ene, The Atilogwu dance ('African Music' I No. 4, p. 20 ff.), 1957. ACJLM

2689. Mackensen, Lutz, Der singende Knochen ('F.F. Communications' No. 49, p. 160 ff.), Helsinki, 1923.

2689a. Mackenzie, Roy, Ballads and Sea Songs from Nova Scotia (Harvard Univ. Press, 1928).

2690. Maclaud, Note sur un instrument de musique employé au Fouta-Dialon ('L'Anthropologie' XIX, p. 271 ff.), Paris, 1908. D¹G

2691. Maclean, Charles, The Principle of the Hydraulic Organ ('Sammelb. der Intern. Musikges.' VI, p. 183 ff.), 1905. CDFH¹L

2692. Macleod, afterwards Lady A. C. Wilson, Short account of the Hindu system of music (Lahore, 1904). I

2693. Macler, Frédéric, La musique en Arménie (Paris, 1917). I

2694. Madhi, Barkashli, La gamme de la musique iranienne ('Annales des Télécommunications' V, p. 5 ff.), May 1950.

2695. Madumere, Adèle, Ibo village music ('African Affairs' LII, Jan. 1953, p. 63 ff.). BKL¹L²M

2696. Madrid, Esther Samonte, *The structure of Philippine music* ('Diliman Review' Quezon City, II, No. 4, p. 373 ff.), 1954.

2697. —— *What is Philippine folk music?* (ibid. No. 2, p. 114 ff.), 1954.

2698. Maes, Joseph, *On xylophones of Bakuba* ('Man' XII, p. 90 ff. (No. 46)), 1912.
BD¹GKL²M

2699. —— *Xylophones du Congo belge* ('Revue Congolaise' III, p. 116 ff.), 1912.
AL²

2700. —— *Les tams-tams du Congo Belge* (Louvain, 1912). A

2701. —— *La sanza du Congo Belge* ('Congo, revue générale de la colonie belge', 1921). AKM

2702. —— *Les Lukombe ou instruments de musique à cordes des populations du Kanai – Lac Léopold – Lukénie* ('Z. f. Ethnologie' LXX, p. 240 ff.), 1939.
BD¹CGHKL¹L²M

2703. —— *Un tamtam d'initiation du Haut-Kwilu* ('Man' XXIX No. 128 (p. 167), 1929. BD¹GKL²M

2704. Maeyens, L., *Het inlandsch lied en het muzikaal accent met semantische functie bij de Babera* ('Kongo-Overzee' IV, p. 250 ff.), Dec. 1938. D¹GL²M

2704a. Maheswari Devi, N., *A first book of Indian music* (Indian music series, vol. I), Jaffna, Ceylon, 1930.

2704b. —— *Veena tutor* (Indian music series, vol. II), Jaffna, Ceylon, 1935.

2705. Ma Hiao-Ts'iun, *La musique chinoise de style européen* (Paris, 1941). G

2706. —— *La musique chinoise* (in Dufourcq, 'La musique des origines à nos jours', ed. Larousse, p. 438 ff.), Paris, 1946.
ACDEFHJK

2707. Mahillon, Victor, *Catalogue descriptif et analytique du Musée instrumental du Conservatoire de Bruxelles* (5 vols.), Bruxelles/Gand 2/1893–1922. A (ed. in one vol., 1880) CD (ed. in one vol.) J

2708. Mahler, Elsa, *Altrussische Volkslieder aus dem Pécoryland* (Basel, 1951). AL

2709. Maissen, Alfons, and Werner Wehrli, *Rätoromanische Volkslieder. I. Die Lieder des Consolaziun dell'olma devoziusa* (Basel, 1945). A

2710. Maitra, Radhika Mohan, *Some recent trends of instrumental music* ('Jhankar music circle 1953 souvenir'), Calcutta, 1953.

2711. —— *Technique of musical art* ('Jhankar music circle 1954 souvenir'), Calcutta, 1954.

2711a. Makiling, Juan, *Music of the Philippines* ('Larawan' series 1, Nov. 4th, p. 1 ff.), 1955.

2712. Makin, William J., *The Zulus dance at Eshowe* ('Travel' LVIII, p. 30 ff.), Dec. 1931.

2713. Ma, Ko, *Chinese folk song* ('People's China', March 1957, p. 1014 ff.). A

2714. Mammery, A., *La musique andalouse à Marrakech* ('Nord-sud' No. 5), Casablanca.

2715. —— *La musique et le théâtre populaires à Marrakech* ('l'Atlas', special issue, 1939).

2716. Manga, János, *A török háborúk emlékei a magyarországi szlovák népdalokban* (i.e. Reminiscences of the Turkish wars in the slovak folksongs of Hungary) ('Ethnographia, a Magyar néprajzi társaság folyóirata' LXVII, p. 241 ff.), Budapest, 1956. B

2717. —— *Nógrádi dudasok* (i.e. The bagpipe players from Nógrád), Budapest, 1950.

2717a. Mangahas, Ruby K., *Philippine music* ('Philippine Life' 1957(?)).

2718. Manizer, H. H., *Music and musical instruments among some Brasilian tribes* ('Sbornik muzei antropol. i. etnogr. pri ross. akad. nauk.' V), Petrograd, 1918.

2719. Manker, Ernst, *Die Lappische Zaubertrommel. I. Die Trommel als Denkmal materieller Kultur* ('Acta Lapponica' I), Stockholm, 1938. GK

2720. Manoylović, K. P., (*Narodne melodije iz intotzne Serbije* (*Mélodies populaires de l'est de la Serbie*) (Monographies of the Serbian Academy of Sciences, vol. CCXII), Beograd, 1953.

2721. Manrato, A., *Musica ed instrumenti indiani* ('Rivista musicale Italiana' XXX), 1923. CKL

2722. Mansoor Uddin, M., *Folksongs. Their uses in Pakistan* (Dacca, 1952). A

2723. —— *Folk Songs in East Pakistan* ('Journal of the Intern. Folk Music Council' V, p. 51), 1953. ACJKL

2724. Manusama, A. Th., *Krontjong als muziekinstrument, als melodie en als gezang* (Batavia, 1919). A

2725. Manwaring, G. E., *The whistle as a naval instrument* ('The Mariner's Mirror' V, p. 72 ff.), 1919.

2726. Maquet, J. N., *La musique chez les Bupende* ('Problèmes d'Afrique Centrale' No. 26, p. 299 ff.), 1954.
AGJKM

2727. —— *Initiation à la musique congolaise* ('Jeunesses Musicales' No. 21, Dec. 1953, p. 3 ff., repr. in 'African Music' I No. 1, p. 64 ff.), 1954. AM

2728. —— *Musiciens Bapende* ('Bulletin de l'Union des Femmes Coloniales', Jan. 1954, p. 31 ff.). M

2729. —— *La musique chez les Pende et les Tschokwe* ('Les Colloques de Wégimont' I, p. 169 ff.), Brussels, 1956. **ACL**

2730. —— *Les instruments à vent du Congo belge* ('J. mensuel de la Féd. nationale des Jeunesses musicales de Belgique', March, 1956).

*2731. —— *Note sur les instruments de musique congolais* (Brussels, 1956). **AB**

2731a. —— *Initiation à la musique congolaise* ('Micro Magazine' X, Nos. 462, p. 11 ff.; 463, p. 9 ff. and 26; 464, p. 11; 465, p. 9; 466, p. 8 ff. and 14; 467, p. 8 ff., 468, p. 8 ff.; 469, p. 9; 470, p. 9 ff.; 471, p. 10 ff.; 472, p. 9 ff.; 473, p. 9; 474, p. 12 and 14), 1954. **M**

2731b. —— *Musiques nègres* ('Cahiers Musicaux' I, No. 3, p. 25 ff.), 1955.

*2732. Marcel-Dubois, Claudie, *Instruments de Musique de l'Inde ancienne* (Paris, 1941). **ACDIJL**

2733. —— *Les instruments de musique populaires* (in Dufourcq, 'La Musique des origines à nos jours', ed. Larousse, p. 53 ff.), Paris, 1946. **ACDEFHJK**

2734. —— *La musique de l'Inde* (ibid., p. 454 ff.), 1946. **ACDEFHJK**

*2735. —— *French Folk Music* ('Grove's Dictionary' 5th ed. vol. III, p. 239 ff.), 1954. **ACFH[1]K**

2736. —— *Extensions du domaine d'observations directes en ethnographie musicale française* ('Les Colloques de Wégimont' I, p. 97 ff.), Brussels, 1956. **ACL**

2737. —— *Une pratique instrumentale: 'Tirer les joncs'* ('Arts et traditions populaires' P.U.F. No. 2), Paris, 1953. **AHK**

2737a. —— *La 'Saint-Marcel' de Barjols* ('Arts et traditions populaires' Jan./March 1957, p. 3 ff.). **AK**

2738. —— and Maguy Andral, *Musique populaire vocale de l'île de Batz* ('Arts et Traditions populaires' July/Sept. 1954), p. 13 ff. **AHK**

2739. Marchal, H., *Orchestre cambodgien* ('Sud-Est', Saigon, Dec. 1950, p. 27 ff.). **A**

2740. Marchal, Sappho, *Danses Cambodgiennes* (Saigon, 1926), p. 30: *Instruments*. **B**

2740a. Marchesseau, G., *Quelques éléments d'ethnographie sur les Mofu du massif de Durum* ('Bull. de la Soc. des Etudes Camerounaises' No. 10, p. 7 ff.), 1945. **M**

2740b. Marcu, G., *Cîntecele polifonice aromîne* (*The Arumanian polyphonic songs*) (with an English summary) ('Revista de Folclor' III No. 2, p. 79 ff.), Bucarest, 1958. **A**

2741. Marett, R. R., *Savage supreme beings and the bull-roarer* (in 'The Threshold of Religion'), London, 1914.

2741a. Marfurt, Luitfrid, *Musik in Afrika* (München, 1957). **ABC**

2742. Mariano, P. A., *Burmese Music and Musical Instruments* (in J. G. Scott, 'Burma, a Handbook of Practical Information', London, 3/1921), p. 360 ff.

2743. —— *Samples of Burmese music* (in: Max and Bertha Ferrars, 'Burma'), London, 1900.

2743a. Marie-Elisabeth, Mother, *La musique et l'éducation sociale dans l'Urundi* ('XXIe Semaine de Missiologie', p. 128 ff.), 1951 (publ. 1953). **M**

2744. Marijic, Father Branko, *Die Volksmusik Bosniens und der Herzegovina* (1936).

2745. —— *Hercegovačke svirale* (Sarajevo, 1938).

2746. —— *Pentatonika u Bosansko-Hercegovačkoj Pučkoj Muzici* ('Svete Cecilije'), Zagreb, 1938. **A**

2747. Marinus, Albert, *Le folklore des instruments de musique* ('Le Folklore brabançon' XIII, Nos. 73–74), Brussels, 1933. **AGL[1]**

2748. —— *Chanson populaire – chanson folklorique* ('J. of the Intern. Folk Music Council' VI, p. 21 ff.), 1954. **ACJKL**

2749. —— *Tradition, evolution, adaptation* ('J. of the Intern. Folk Music Council' IX, p. 15 ff.), 1957. **ACJKL**

2751. Marks, R. W., *The Music and Musical Instruments of Ancient China* ('The Musical Quarterly' XVIII, p. 593 ff.), 1932. **C**

2752. Marolt, France, *Slovene folk dance and folk music* ('J. of the Intern. Folk Music Council' IV, p. 4 ff.), 1954. **ACJKL**

2753. Marques, A., *Ancient Hawaiian music* ('Hawaiian Annual' 1914, p. 97 ff.).

2754. —— *Music in Hawaii Nei* (ibid. 1886, p. 51 ff.).

2755. Marques, Belo, *Musica Negra* (Edicão da Agencia Geral das Colonias, Lisbon, 1943).

2756. Marr, John, *Oriental influence on Western music* ('J. of the Music Academy, Madras' XXV, p. 62 ff.), Madras, 1954. **AC**

2756a. —— Review of C. S. Ayyar, '108 kritis of Sri Tyagaraja' ('Bull. of the School of Oriental and African Studies' XIX, p. 595 ff.), London, 1957. **BM**

2757. Marsden, William, *The History of Sumatra* (3rd. ed., London, 1811), p. 195 ff. **AB**

2758. Marshall, Harry Ignatius, *Karèn bronze drums* ('J. of the Burma Research Soc.' XIX, p. 1 ff.), Rangoon 1929. **GJ**

2759. —— *The use of the bronze drum in Siam* (ibid. XXII), 1932. **G**

2761. Martens, Frederick H., *Music in the life of the Aztecs* ('The Musical Quarterly' XIV, p. 413 ff.), 1928.

2762. —— *Mahomet and music* (ibid. XII, p. 376 ff.), 1926.

2763. —— *The influence of music in world history* (ibid. XI, p. 196 ff.), 1925. **CF**

2764. —— *Music in Chinese fairytale and legend* (ibid. VIII, p. 528 ff.), 1922. **CH¹**

2765. —— *The musical observations of a Maroccan ambassador (1690–1691)* ('The Musical Quarterly' XV, No. 4), Oct. 1929. **C**

2766. Marti, Samuel, *Precortesian music* ('Ethnos' XIX, p. 69 ff.), 1954. **ABJL²M**

*2767. —— *Instrumentos musicales precortesianos* (Mexico, 1955). **A**

2768. —— *Música de las Américas* ('Cuadernos Americanos' LII, No. 4), Mexico, 1950.

2769. —— *Organografía Precolumbina* (ibid. LVI, No. 2), Mexico, 1951.

2770. —— *Flautilla de la Penitencia* (ibid. LXXII, No. 6), Mexico, 1953.

2771. —— *Música Precortesiana* (ibid. LXXVI, No. 4), Mexico, 1954.

2772. Martin, E., *Trois documents de musique grecque. Transcriptions commentées de Deuxième hymne delphique à Apollon, Epitaphe de Seikilos (Ile s. ap. J.-C.) et fragment d'un Choeur d'Oreste d'Euripide* (1953).

2773. Martin, Rudolf, *Die Inlandstämme der Malayischen Halbinsel* (Jena, 1905), p. 913. **A**

2773a. Martinengo-Ceraresco, E., *Essays in the study of folk songs* (London, 1936).

2774. Marx, B. L., *The Hawaiian mele from a musical standpoint* ('Hawaiian Annual' 1904, p. 154 ff.).

2775. Mašek, N., *Tambours énéolitiques en Bohème et en Moravie* ('Archeologické rozhledy' VI, fasc. 5), 1954.

2776. Mason, Otis T., *Music in Honduras* ('Amer. Anthropol.' II (O.S.), p. 158 ff.), 1889. **GL²**

2777. —— *Geographical distribution of the musical bow* (ibid. X (O.S.), p. 377 ff.), 1897. **GL²**

2778. Maspéro, Gaston C. C., *Chansons populaires receuillies dans la Haute-Egypte de 1900 à 1914* ('Annales du Service des Antiquités de l'Egypte', 1914). **D¹G**

2779. Masu, Genjiro, *The place of folk music in the cultural life of the present day in Japan* ('Journal of the Intern. Folk Music Council' V, p. 64 ff.), 1953. **ACJKL**

2780. —— *Japanese Music and Japanese Life* ('Japanese Music'), Tokyo, 1953. **A**

2781. Matchinsky, A., *A propos de la gamme musicale égyptienne* ('Publ. du Musée de l'Hermitage' II, p. 9), 1935.

2782. Mátlová-Uhrová, Ludmila, *Hanácké tance z Tovačovska* ('Orbis' 1954).

2783. Matos, Manuel Garcia, *Lirica popular de la Alta Extremadura (folklore coreografico y costumbrista) (436 documentos musicales ineditos)*, Madrid, undated (after 1931). **AL**

2784. —— *Cante flamenco. Algunas de sus presuntos origenes* ('Anuario Musical de l'Instituto de Musicología' V, p. 97 ff.), Barcelona, 1950. **ACL**

2785. —— *Cancionero popular de la Provincia de Madrid*, vol. I. Edicion critica por Marius Schneider y José Romeu Figueras (Barcelona/Madrid, 1951). **A**

2786. —— *Folklore en Falla* ('Musica' Madrid, 1953, Nos. 3–4, p. 41 ff. and No. 6, p. 3 ff.).

2787. —— *Instrumentos musicales folkloricos de España. I. Las 'Xeremies' de la Isla de Ibiza* ('Anuario Musical' IX, p. 161 ff.), 1954. **CL**

2788. Matsunaga, Susumo, *The evolution of sumisen music* ('Contemporary Japan' III, p. 105 ff.), 1934. **D¹**

2788a. Mattfeld, Julius, *The folk music of the Western hemisphere; a list of references in the New York Public Library* ('Bulletin of the New York Public Library' XXVIII, No. 11, p. 799 ff., No. 12, p. 864 ff.), resp. Nov. and Dec. 1924.

2789. Matthews, Basil, *Calypso and Pan America* ('The Commonweal' XXXVII, p. 91 ff.), 13 Nov. 1942.

2790. Matthews, F. Schuyler, *Field book of wild birds and their music: a description of the character and music of birds, ... with songs reproduced in musical notation* (New York, 1904).

2790a. Matthews, W., *The basket drum* ('American Anthropologist' VII, p. 202 ff.), 1894. **L²**

2791. Matthieu, G., *Le Système musical* ('T'oung Pao' XV (1915); p. 339 ff.; XVII (1917), p. 489 ff.; XVIII (1918), p. 31 ff.; XIX (1819/'19), p. 41 ff.; XX (1920/'21), p. 40 ff. and p. 355 ff.). **GK**

2792. Maures, N. G., *Contribution à l'étude de la chanson populaire égyptienne* (Alexandrie, 1931).

2793. Maybon, A., *Le théâtre japonais* (Paris, 1925). **C**

2794. Maynard Araujo, Alceo, *Instrumentos muscicais e implementos* ('Revista do Arquivo' 157, p. 147 ff.), Sao Paulo, 1954.

2795. Mayr, Franz, *Short study on Zulu music* ('Annals of the Natal Museum' I, p. 241 ff.), Pietermaritz, 1908.

2796. Mazzini, G., *Etnofonia sud-americana (del Cili e del Perú)* ('Rivista musicale Italiana' XLVII, fasc. 5–6), 1943. **CKL**

2796a. Mbiye, B., *Kasala des Mulumba (ntiite)* ('Kongo-Overzee' XXI, p. 160 ff.), 1955. **M**

2797. McAllester, David P., *Peyote Music*

162

('Viking Fund Publ. in Anthrop.' XIII), New York, 1949.   **ACFGHK**

2798. —— *Menomini Peyote Music* (in J. S. Slotkin, 'Menomini Peyotism') (Philadelphia, Transactions of the Amer. Phil. Soc.' XLII, part 4, p. 681 ff.), 1952.

2799. —— *Notes on the Music of the Navajo Creation Chants* (in Record album 'Navajo Creation Chants', issued by Peabody Museum, Harvard Univ., p. 33 ff.), 1952.   **A**

2800. —— *Enemy Way Music. A Study of Social and Esthetic Values as seen in Navaho Music* ('Papers of the Peabody Museum of American Archaeology and Ethnography' XLI, No. 3), 1954.
BGJL²

2801. —— *American Indian songs and pantribalism* ('Midwest Folklore' V, p. 132 ff.), Summer 1955.

2802. —— *An Apache fiddle* ('Ethnomusicology' Newsletter No. 8, p. 1 ff.), Sept. 1956.   **AGL**

2803. McPhee, Colin, *The 'absolute' music in Bali* ('Modern Music' XII, no. 4, p. 163 ff.), 1935.

2804. —— *Figuration in Balinese Music* ('Peabody Bull.', May 1935).

2805. —— *The Balinese Wajang koelit and its music* ('Djawa' XVI, p. 1 ff.), 1936.
BD¹G

2806. —— *Angkloeng gamelans in Bali* ('Djawa' XVII, p. 322 ff.), 1937.   **BD¹G**

2807. —— *Children and Music* (ibid. XVIII, p. 309 ff.), 1938.   **BD¹GJ**

2808. —— *Musical Exploration in Bali* ('Musical America' LX, No. 3, p. 12, 263), 10 Febr. 1940.

2809. —— *The Music of Bali*, recorded by Colin McPhee, Benjamin Britten and Georges Barrère (Schirmer's Library of recorded music' No. 17), New York, 1940.

2810. —— *Balinese Ceremonial Music, transcribed for two pianos, four-hands* (New York, 1940).   **A**

2811. —— *The technique of Balinese Music* ('Bull. of the Amer. Musicol. Soc.' No. 6, p. 4 ff.), 1942.

2812. —— *Eight to the bar* ('Modern Music' XX, p. 235 ff.), 1943.   **A**

2812a. —— *A house in Bali* (New York, 1944).
AB

2813. —— *Dance in Bali* (in Marian Eames and Lincoln Kırstein, 'Dance Index' VII, Nos. 7/8, p. 156 ff.), 1948.

2814. —— *The five-tone Gamelan Music of Bali* ('The Musical Quarterly' XXXV, no. 2, p. 250 ff.), 1949.   **ACDFK**

2815. —— *A club of small Men* (1947).

2816. —— *Children and Music in Bali* (in: Margaret Mead and Martha Wolfen-

stein, 'Childhood in contemporary cultures' Univ. of Chicago Press, 1955), p. 79 ff.   **B**

2817. —— *Music in Bali 1931–1939* (in preparation).

2818. Mead, Charles W., *The Musical Instruments of the Incas* ('Anthrop. Papers of the Amer. Mus. of Natural Hist.' XV, part III), New York, 1924.   **GL³**

2819. Meadows, Capt. Taylor, *Catalogue of Indian musical instruments presented by Colonel French* ('Proc. of the R. Irish Acad.' IX, vol. I).

2820. Meeteren, N. van, *Volkskunde van Curaçao* (Willemstad, Curaçao, 1947), Chapter II, p. 37 ff.: *Muziek en zang;* p. 241 ff.: *Musical examples.*   **B**

2820a. Meeus, F. de, *Musique africaine* ('L'art nègre du Congo Belge' Brussels, 1950, p. 55 ff.).   **M**

2821. Mehta, Manharram H., *Twenty-two shrutis and two gramas of Indian music* (Bombay, 1938).   **I**

2821a. Meier, John, *Deutsche Volkslieder. Balladen* (4 vols.), Berlin, 1935, 1939, 1954/'57, 1957.   **L**

2822. Meijer, D. H., *De spleettrom* ('Tijdschr. v. h. Batav. Gen.' LXXIX, p. 415 ff.), 1917.   **ABD¹GH**

2823. Meinhof, Carl, *Die Geheimsprachen Afrikas* ('Globus' LXVI, p. 117 ff.), Aug. 1894.   **D¹M**

2824. Meinhof, Carl, Thilenius and Wilhelm Heinitz, *Die Trommelsprache in Afrika und in der Südsee* ('Vox' IV, p. 179 ff.), 1916.   **G**

2824a. Mello Carvalho, Irene da Silva, *O Fado. Um problema de aculturação musical luso-brasileiro* ('Bol. Latino-Americano' VI, vol. I, p. 225 ff.), Rio de Janeiro, 1946.   **AGL**

2825. Melo, Guilherme, T. P. de, *A Música Brasil* (Rio de Janeiro, 1947).   **A**

2826. Melo, Vérissimo de, *Rondas infantis brasileiras* ('Revista do Arquivo' CLV, p. 227 ff.), Sao Paulo, 1953.   **A**

2827. Mendizabel, Miguel Othón de, *La poesía indígena y las canciones populares* ('Boletin del Museo Nacional de Arqueología, Hist. y Ethnogr.' II, 4th period, No. 4), Mexico, 1923.

2828. —— *Los cantares y la música indígena* ('Mexican Folkways' II, p. 109 ff.), Mexico, 1929.

2829. Mendoza, Vicente T., *Los percutores precortesianos* ('Anales del Museo Nacional de Arqueología'), 1933.

2830. —— *Los teponazlis en las civilizaciones precortesianas* (ibid.), 1933.

2831. —— *Música indígena Otomi* vol. I ('Revista de Estudios Musicales' V/VI, p. 351 ff.; II (ibid. VII, p. 221 ff.),

Mendoza, Argentina, 1951 and 1954. **AEKL**

2832. —— *Música precolombiana de America* ('Bol. Latino-Americano de Música' IV), Bogotá, 1938.

2833. —— *Tres instrumentos musicales prehispanicos* ('Anales del Inst. de Investigaciones estéticas' No. 7), Mexico, 1947.

2834. —— *Supervivencias de la cultura Azteca. La canción y baile del música indígena de Mexico* ('Rev. Mexico en el Arte' IX), Mexico, 1950.

2835. —— *Música indígena de Mexico* (ibid. IX), 1950.

2836. —— *Folklore y Música tradicional de la Baja California* ('Anuario de la Soc. Folklórica de Mexico' X, p. 53 ff.), 1955.

2836a. —— *La canción de Mayo en Mexico* ('Bol. Latino-Americano' V, p. 491 ff.), Montevideo, 1941. **AGL**

2836b. —— *Panorama de la musica tradicional de Mexico* ('Estudios y Fuentes del Arte in Mexico' VII), Mexico, 1956.

2837. Meng Chih, *Remarks on Chinese Music and Musical Instruments* (China Institute, New York, 1932).

2837a. Mengrelis, Th., *La voix des 'niamou' chez les Guerzé de Guinée Française* ('Notes Africaines' 1948, No. 38, p. 8). **M**

2838. Menon, Narayana, *Music of India and its role in Indian dance* ('Atlantic Monthly' CXCII, p. 152 ff.), 1953. **A**

2839. —— *Gustav Holst's 'Savitri'* ('J. of the Music Academy, Madras' XXV, p. 60 ff.), Madras, 1954. **C**

2840. —— *The musical instruments of India* ('Curtain Call', Dec. 1954).

2841. Meny de Marangue, *La musique Marocaine (analyses des modes; vues sur la musique populaire)*, Imprimerie Dauphinoise, Nyons (undated).

2842. Merian, W., *Das schweizerische Volkslied in musikalischer Beziehung* ('Garbe' Nos. 4–6), Basel, 1918.

2843. Merlier, Melpo, *Essai d'un tableau du folklore musical grec* (Athens, 1935). **L**

2844. —— Τραγουδια της Ρουμελης (Tragoudia tès Roumelès), Athens, 1931.

2845. Merriam, Alan P., *Instruments and instrumental usages in the history of jazz* (diss.) (Evanston, Ill., 1948).

2846. —— *Notes on Cheyenne Songs* ('Journal of the American Musicol. Soc.' III, p. 289 ff.), 1950. **CFK**

*2847. —— *A bibliography of Jazz* (unpublished MS, 1950).

2848. —— *Flathead Indian Instruments and their Music* ('Musical Quarterly' XXXVII, p. 368 ff.), July 1951. **CDFK**

2849. —— *African Music Reexamined in the*

Light of New Materials from the Belgian Congo and Ruanda-Urundi ('Zaire' VII, p. 245 ff.), March 1953. **AGD¹KL¹L³M**

2850. —— *Les Styles Vocaux dans la Musique du Ruanda-Urundi* ('Jeune Afrique' VII, p. 12 ff.), 1953. **M**

2851. —— *Recording in the Belgian Congo* ('African Music Society Newsletter' I, No. 5, June 1952, p. 15 ff.). **ACJM**

2852. —— *Song text of the Bashi* ('Zaire' VIII, p. 27 ff.), 1954. **(AD¹GKL¹L³M)** = 'African Music' I, No. 1, p. 44 ff. (1954)). **ACM**

*2853. —— *An annotated bibliography of African and African-derived music since 1936* ('Africa' XXI, p. 319 ff.), London, Oct. 1951. **AGBJKL¹L³M**

2854. —— *The selection of recording equipment for field use* (in: Kroeber, 'Anthropological Soc. Papers' X, p. 5 ff.), Berkeley, 1954. **A**

2855. —— *The use of music in the study of a problem of acculturation* ('Amer. Anthropol'. LVII, p. 28 ff.), 1955. **ABGL²M**

2856. —— *Musical instruments and techniques of performance among the Bashi* ('Zaire' IX, p. 123 ff.), 1955. **AD¹GKL¹L²M**

2857. —— and Barbara W. Merriam, *Flathead Indian Music. Report on Field Research* (Evanston, 1950), re-issued, in enlarged form, in 1955 ('Western Anthropology' No. 2). **AF**

2858. —— *Music in American culture* ('Amer. Anthropol.' LVII, p. 1173 ff.), 1955. **AGL²M**

2859. Merriam, Alan P., Sara Whinery and B. G. Fred, *Songs of a Rada Community in Trinidad* ('Anthropos' LI, p. 157 ff.), 1956. **BD¹GHJKL¹L²M**

2860. —— *Songs of the Ketu cult of Bahia* ('African Music' I, No. 3, p. 53 ff. and No. 4, p. 73 ff.), 1956 and 1957. **ACJLM**

2860a. —— *The African background* ('Record Changer' XI, p. 7 ff.), 1952.

2861. Mersmann, H., *Grundlagen einer musikalischen Volksliedforschung* (Leipzig, 1930). **A**

2861a. —— *Volkslied und Gegenwart* (Potsdam, 1937). **L**

2862. —— *Das deutsche Volkslied* (undated). **D**

2863. —— c.s., *Europäische Lieder in den Urspruchen* (im Auftrage der Deutschen Unesco Kommission herausgegeben von Josef Gregor, Friedrich Klausmeier und Egon Kraus), Berlin, 1957.

2864. Merton, Hugo, *Forschungsreise in den süd-östlichen Molukken (Aru- und Kei-Inseln)*, (Frankfurt, 1910), p. 198 ff. **AB**

2865. Merwin, B. W., *A vodoo drum* ('The Museum Journal' VIII), Philadelphia. **L²**

2866. Metfessel, Milton E., *Phonophotography in Folk Music* (Univ. of North Carolina Press, 1928). **IK**

2867. —— *The Strobophotography* ('Journal of Gen. Psychology' II, p. 135 ff.), 1929. **D¹H**

2868. Métraux, Alfred, *Le bâton de rhytme. Contribution à l'étude de la distribution géographique des éléments de culture d'origine mélanésienne en Amérique du Sud* ('Journal de la Soc. des Américanistes', N.S. XIX, p. 117 ff.), Paris, 1927. **GL²**

2869. —— *La civilisation matérielle des tribus Tupi-Guarani* (Paris, 1928), Chapter XXVII. *Instruments de musique.* **AB**

2870. —— *La causa y el tratamiento magico de las enfermedados entre los Indios de la region tropical Sud-Americana* ('Americana indigena' IV, p. 157 ff.), April 1944.

2871. —— *Le shamanisme chez les Indiens de l'Amerique sud-tropicale* ('Acta Americana' II, No. 3, p. 197 ff.; No. 4, p. 320 ff.), 1944.

2871a. Meulen, R. van der, *Die Naturvergleiche in den Liedern und Totenklagen der Lithauer* (Leyden, 1907). **L**

2872. Meyer, A. B., *Die Nasenflöte im Ostindischen Archipel* ('Globus' LXXV, No. 12, p. 195 ff.), Braunschweig, 1899. **D¹M**

2873. Meyer, A. B., and W. Foy, *Bronzepauken aus Süd-ost-Asien* (1897).

2874. —— and —— *Bronzepauken aus dem ostindischen Archipel* (Dresden 1898)

2875. Meyer, Gustav William, *Tonale Verhältnisse und Melodiestruktur im ostslavischen Volkslied* (Leipzig, Breitkopf und Härtel, 1956). **L**

2875a. Meyer, Leonard B., *Emotion and Meaning in Music* (Chicago, 1956).

2876. Meyer, Max, *The musician's arithmetic* ('Univ. of Missouri Studies' IV, app. VI, p. 115 ff.), 1929.

2876a. —— *Zur Theorie japanischer Musik* ('Z. f. Psychologie u. Physiologie der Sinnesorgane' XXXIII), 1903.

2877. Michaelides, Solon, *The Neohellenic Folk Music* (Limassol, Cyprus, 1948). **A**

2878. —— *Greek Folk Music, its preservation and traditional practice* ('Journal of the Intern. Folk Music Council' I, p. 21 ff.), 1949. **ACKL**

•2879. —— *Greek (Neo-Hellenic) Folk Music* ('Grove's Dictionary' 5th ed. vol. III, p. 268 ff.), 1954. **ACFH¹K**

2880. —— *Greek song-dance* ('J. of the Intern. Folk Music Council' VIII, p. 37 ff.), 1956. **ACJKL**

2881. Migeod, F. W. H., *Mendi drum signals* ('Man' XX, p. 40 ff.), 1920. **BD¹GKL²M**

2882. Miles, C., *Aboriginal musical instruments in North America* ('Hobbies' LVII, p. 134 ff.), 1953.

2882a. Miller, Philip L., *The record archive in the New York Public Library* ('Bull. of the British Inst. of Recorded Sound' V, p. 20 ff.), summer 1957. **I**

2883. Millet, Ll., *De la canço popular catalana* (Barcelona, 1917).

2884. Milošević, Vlado, *Bosanske narodne pjesme* (i.e. folk songs of Bosnia), vol. I (red. of the texts by Ljubomir Trivić), Banja Luka, 1954. **A**

2885. —— *Bosanske narodne pjesme* (i.e. folk songs of Bosnia) vol. II (red. of the texts by Ljubomir Trivić, transcription by Branislav Golubović), the textes by Ljubomir Trivic; musical transcription by Branislav Golubović), Banja Luka, 1956. **A**

2886. Mincoff-Marriage, Elizabeth, *Souterliedekens* (The Hague, 1922). **FL**

2886a. Minderovic, C., *Yugoslav folk poetry* ('The Indo-Asian Culture' VI, No. 1, p. 63 ff.), New Delhi, July 1957. **AB**

2887. Mingote, Angel, *Cancionero musical de la provincia de Zaragoza* (Zaragoza, 1950). **KL**

2888. Mirinov, N. N., *Tadshikskaya muzyka* (i.e. Tadshik music), 1932.

2889. Misra, Sushila, *Music, the panacea* ('Silver Jubilee Souvenir of the Marris College of Hindustani music, Lucknow, Nov. 1952'), Lucknow, 1953.

2890. —— *Music profiles* (Pioneer Press, Lucknow, 1954)

2891. Mitchison, William, *Handbook of the songs of Scotland, with music and descriptive and historical notes* (London/Glasgow, no date). **K**

2892. Moberg, Karl-Allan, *Tvd kapitel om svensk folkmusik.* 1. *Tonalitetsproblem i svensk folkmusik.* 2. *Ro, ro till fiskeskär* ('Svensk tidskrift för musikforskning' XXXII, p. 5 ff.), 1950. **K**

2893. —— *Swedish Folk Music* ('Grove's Dictionary' 5th ed. vol. III, p. 372 ff.), 1954. **ACFH¹K**

2894. —— *En studie i de svenska fäbodarnas musikaliska organisation* (Ueber Kuhreigen, eine musikalische Organisation der schwedischen Sennhütten) ('Svensk Tidskrift för Musikforskning' XXXVII, p. 7 ff.), 1955. **K**

2895. Moeck, Hermann, *Ursprung und Tradition der Kernspaltflöten der Europäischen Folklore und die Herkunft der musikgeschichtlichen Kernspaltflöten-Typen* (Diss. Göttingen, 1951). **C**

2896. —— *Die skandinavischen Kernspaltflöten in Vorzeit und Tradition der Folklore* ('Svensk Tidskrift för Musikforskning' XXXVI, p. 56 ff.), 1954. **ACK**

2897. Möhler, A., *Gedanken über die Musik*

der alten Hebräer und der vorklassischen Antike ('Die Musik' I, No. 4), 1902. **CEF**

2898. **Möller, H.**, Spanische, katalanische, portugiesische und baskische Volkslieder (Mainz, 1924).

2899. **Mohan, B. S.**, Revival of Indian music ('Lakshya Sangeet' I), Delhi, 1954/'55.

2900. **Moheyeddin, K.**, Muslim contribution to Indian music ('Pakistan Review', March 1955).

2901. **Mojzisek, Sebral Josef**, Lidové pisne z Tešinska (Ostrave, 1956).

2902. **Mokri, M.**, Kurdish songs with transliteration, Persian translation and glossary (Teheran, 1951).

2903. **Molitor, H.**, La musique chez les nègres du Tanganyika ('Anthropos' VIII, p. 714 ff.), Vienna, 1913. **D¹GKL¹L²M**

2904. **Molnár, Antal**, A Népzenekutatás Kérdéseiből (i.e. Problems of musical ethnography) (in 'Emlékkonyv Kodály. I. 70 Zsulétesnapjára' p. 331 ff.), Budapest, 1953. **A**

2905. **Moloney, C. Alfred**, On the melodies of Ewe people of West Africa ('J. of the Manchester Geogr. Soc.' V, p. 277 ff.), 1889. **K**

2906. **Mondon-Vidailhet, M.**, La musique Éthiopienne (before 1910) (in Lavignac, 'Hist. de la Mus.' V, p. 3179 ff.), 1922. **ACDEFHJ**

2907. **Montandon, Georges**, Généalogie des instruments de musique et les cycles de civilisation ('Archives suisses d'Anthropologie générale' III, fasc. 1), 1919. **C**

2908. —— La musique en Roumanie (in Lavignac, 'Hist. de la Musique' V, p. 2656 ff.), Paris, 1914. **ACDEFH**

2909. —— Nouveaux exemplaires africains de la cithare en radeau ('L'Anthropologie' XLII, p. 676 ff.), 1932. **D¹GH**

2910. **Mooney, James**, The Ghost-dance religion and the Sioux outbreak of 1890 ('Annual Report of the Bur. of Amer. Ethnol.' No. 14, part 2), Washington D.C., 1896. **GKL²**

2911. **Moor, Arthur Prichard**, Oriental Music (in Oscar Thompson, 'Intern. Cyclopedia of Music and Musicians' 4th ed., p. 1322 ff.), 1946. **CK**

2912. **Moore, George F.**, Symphonia not a Bagpipe ('Journal of Biblical Literature' XXIV, p. 166 ff.), 1905. **K**

2913. **Moreño, Segundo Luis**, Musica y danzas autoctonas del Ecuador (Indigenous music and dances of Ecuador), Quito, 1949. **A**

2913a. —— La música de los Incas. Rectificación a la obra intitulada 'La musique des Incas et ses survivances' par R. y M. d'Harcourt (Quito, Casa de la Cultura ecuatoriana, 1957).

2914. **Moreux, Serge**, La musique japonaise (in Dufourcq, 'La musique des origines à nos jours', ed. Larousse, p. 446 ff.), Paris, 1946. **ACDEFHJK**

2915. **Morici, G.**, Canti popolari lituani (Rome, 1925).

2916. **Morris, E.**, Bells and gongs of old Japan ('Apollo', Sept. 1938). **C**

2917. **Morris, Frances**, Catalogue of the musical instruments of Oceania and America (The Metropolitan Museum of Art, Catalogue of the Crosby Brown Collection of musical instruments (4 vols.), New York, 1914. **CI**

2917a. **Morton-Williams, P.**, A cave painting, rock gong and rock slide in Yorubaland ('Man' LVII, p. 170, No. 213), Nov. 1957. **BD¹GKL¹L²M**

2918. **Moseley, A. B.**, More about music ('Central Africa' LII, p. 54 ff.), 1934.

2918a. **Moser, Hans Joachim**, Tönende Volksaltertümer (Berlin, 1935). **L**

2919. **Mosharrafa, M. M.**, Music Eastern and Western (Egyptian Institute, London, 1946). **I**

2920. **Moss, Claude Russell** and **A. L. Kroeber**, Nabaloi Songs ('Univ. of California Publ. in Amer. Archeol. and Ethnol.' XV, p. 187 ff.), Univ. of Cal. Press, May 1919. **A**

2921. **Motzev, Aleksandre**, Ritm i takt v Bulgarskata narodna musika (Publ. of the Bulgarska Akademia na Naukite), Sofia, 1949.

2922. —— Bulgarskata narodna pesen (publ. by Nauka i izkustvo), Sofia, 1954.

2923. **Moule, A. C.**, A List of the Musical Instruments of the Chinese ('Journal of the North-China Branch of the Royal Asiatic Soc.' XXXIX), 1908. **BCIJKL⁵**

2925. —— and **F. W. Galpin**, A western organ in medieval China ('J. of the R. Asiatic Soc. of Gr. Britain and Ireland' 1926, p. 193 ff.). **AD¹GIJKL¹**

2926. **Moule, G. E.**, Notes on the Ting-chi, or half-yearly sacrifice to Confucius (with an appendix on the music by A. C. Moule) ('Journal of the North China Branch of the R. Asiatic Soc.' XXXIII, p. 37 ff.), Shanghai, 1901. **CKL⁵**

Mudaliar, A. H. Chinnaswamy, see: Chinnaswamy, Mudaliar, A. H.

2927. **Müller, H.**, Einige Notizen über die japanische Musik ('Mitt. der Deutschen Ges. f. die Natur- und Völkerk. Ostasiens' I, fasc. 6), 1876. **G**

2927a. **Müller, Salomon**, Land- en Volkenkunde. Bijdragen tot de kennis van Timor. Tweede afdeling: Ethnographische berigten ('Verhandelingen over de Natuurlijke Geschiedenis der Nederlandsche overzeesche gebieden' ...

uitgeg. op last van den Koning door C. J. Temminck), p. 256, 265, 269, 270, 271), Leiden, 1839-'44. **AB**

2928. **Mukerji, D. P.,** *Indian Culture and Music* (in 'The Cultural Heritage of India' III, p. 601 ff.), Calcutta, 1939.

2929. ——— *Indian Music* (Bombay, 1945). **BG**

2930. **Mukhopadhyaya, Debabrata,** *Musical instruments of ancient India* ('Entally Cult. Conference, 8th Annual Session, Jan. 1955'), Calcutta, 1955.

2931. **Munkácsi, Bernhard,** *Volksbräuche und Volksdichtung der Wotjaken* (Aus dem Nachlass herausgeg. von D. R. Fuchs), Helsinki, 'Suomalais-Ugrilaisen Seura' XXXVI), 1952 = 'Suomalais-Ugrilaisen toimituksia (i.e. Mémoires de la Soc. finno-ougrienne'), No. 102. **K**

2932. **Munoz Sanz,** *La música ecuatoriana* (Quito, 1938).

2933. **Murdoch, John,** *The whizzing-stick or bull-roarer on the Westcoast of Africa* ('Amer. Anthropol.' (O.S.) III, p. 258), 1890. **GL²**

2934. **Murko, M.,** *Phonographische Aufnahmen epischer, meist mohammedanischer Volkslieder im nordwestlichen Bosnien* (1912).

2935. ——— *Phonographische Aufnahmen epischer Volkslieder im mittleren Bosnien und der Herzegowina* (1915).

2935a. **Murray, K. C.,** *Music and dancing in Nigeria* ('African Music Soc. Newsletter' I, No. 5, p. 44 ff.), 1952. **ACJM**

2936. **Mursell, James L.,** *Psychology and the problem of the scale* ('The Musical Quarterly' XXXII, p. 564 ff.), 1946. **CDFK**

*2936a. *Music of Latin America* (Club and Study Fine Art Series), Pan American Union, Washington D.C., 3/1953. **A**

2937. *Musique et chansons populaires* (ed. by the Intern. Inst. f. Intellectual Cooperation), Paris, 1934. **A**

2938. **Mutatkar, Mrs. Sumati,** *Alap in Hindusthani music* ('The Journal of the Music Academy, Madras' XXIV, p. 77 ff.), 1953. **AC**

2939. ——— *A short account of the development of Islamic music* ('Lakshya Sangeet' I), Delhi, 1954/'55.

2940. ——— *The basic pattern of Indian music* (ibid. I), Delhi, 1954/'55.

2941. ——— *Indian music: the classical tradition* ('Roopa-Lekha' XXVI, No. 1), 1955. **G**

2942. *Muziek uit Olievaten* ('Terpsichore' VII, p. 52 ff.), May, 1954. **A**

2943. **Myers, Ch. S.,** *The Rhythm-Sense of Primitive Peoples* ('Transactions 5th Intern. Psychol. Congress in Rome 1904').

2944. ——— *A Study of Rhythm in Primitive*

Music ('British Journal of Psychology' I, p. 397 ff.), 1905. **D¹GHK**

2945. ——— *Traces of African melody in Jamaica* (in Walter Jekyll, 'Jamaica song and story', Publ. of the Folk Lore Soc. LV, p. 278 ff.), 1907.

2946. ——— *The ethnological study of music* (in 'Anthropological essays presented to Edward Tylor'), Oxford, 1907. **JL¹**

2947. ——— *Music of the Veddas* (in Seligmann, 'The Veddas'), Cambridge, 1911. **J**

2948. ——— *The Study of Primitive Music* ('Musical Antiquary' III, p. 121 ff.), 1912. **D¹**

2949. ——— *Music* (in 'Reports of the Cambridge Anthrop. Exped. to Torres Straits' IV), 1912. **J**

2950. ——— *The beginnings of music* (in 'Essays and Studies presented to William Ridgeway', p. 561 ff.), 1913. **JL¹**

2951. ——— *A Study of Sarawak Music* ('Sammelbände der Intern. Musikges.' XV, p. 296 ff.), 1913/'14. **CDFH¹L**

2952. *Naar een nationale Indonesische muziek* ('De Vrije Pers' 18th Jan., 1951, reprinted in 'Indonesische Documentatie' March 1951, p. 405 ff.). **B**

2953. **Nabaraoui, Ceza,** *Le conservatoire de musique orientale* ('l'Egyptienne' 1930).

2954. **Nadel, Siegfried,** *Gesänge der jemenitischen Juden; Versuch einer neuen Einteilungsweise für alte Melodien* ('Die Musik' XIV, No. 4), 1914/'15. **CEF**

2955. ——— *The Origins of Music* ('The Musical Quarterly' XVI, p. 531 ff.), 1930. **C**

2956. ——— *Marimba-Musik* ('Sitzungsber. der phil.-hist. Klasse der Akad. d. Wiss. zu Wien' CCXII), 1931. **AM**

2957. ——— *Sur la structure des systèmes de gammes et le problème du 'cycle' dans la musique primitive* ('Art populaire' vol. II, p. 102 ff.), 1931. **A**

2958. ——— *Musikalische Astrologie* ('Der Erdball' V, p. 441 ff.), 1931. **D¹**

2959. ——— *Zur Ethnographie des afrikanischen Xylophons* ('Forschungen und Fortschritte' VIII, p. 444 ff.), 1932. **AD¹GL²**

2960. ——— *Georgische Gesänge* (Berlin, 1933).

2961. ——— *Messungen an kaukasischen Grifflochpfeifen* ('Anthropos' XXIX, p. 469 ff.), 1934. **D¹GHKL¹L²M**

2961a. **Nakaseko, Kazu,** *Symbolism in ancient Chinese music theory* ('J. of Music Theory', a publ. of the Yale school of music, I No. 2, p. 147 ff.), Nov. 1957. **ABC**

2962. **Narasimhan, V. M.,** *Temple Curiosities. Some strange musical objects* ('The March of India' VI, No. 3, p. 41 ff.), Jan./Febr. 1954. **A**

167

2963. **Nasto, L.**, *Die Volkslieder der Litauer* (1893).

*2964. **Nataletti, Giorgio**, *El folklore musical en Italia desde 1918 hasta 1948. Ensayo bibliografico* ('Revista de Estudios musicales' I, No. 2, p. 153 ff.), Mendoza (Arg.), Dec. 1949. **AKL**

2964a. —— *Il folklore musicale in Italia dal 1918 ad oggi* (Rome, 1948).

2965. **Nathan, J.**, *Music of the Hindus* (in Surindro Mohun Tagore, 'Hindu music from various authors', p. 229 ff.), Calcutta, 1882. **CFIKL²**

2966. **Nathan, M. Montague**, *Armenian Folk Music* ('Grove's Dictionary' 5th ed. vol. III, p. 184 ff.), 1954. **ACFH¹K**

2967. **Nau, Walter G.**, *A triptych from the Arbatsky collection at the Newberry Library, Chicago (Ill.)* (Chicago, 1954). **A**

2968. **Nayudu, B. Chitti Babu**, *A key to Hindu music* (Madras, 1925). **I**

2968a. **N'Doye, M. C.**, *Le son du tabala dans le Rip (Sénégal)* ('Notes Africaines' 1948, No. 38, p. 9 ff.). **M**

2969. **Needham, Joseph**, *Science and civilisation in China*, vol. IV, Chapter h (in collab. with **Kenneth Robinson**): *Sound (Acoustics)* (University Press, Cambridge, England) (in preparation). **A**

2970. **Neefe, Konrad**, *Die Kriegsmusik der Chinesen im vorchristlichen Zeitalter* ('Allgemeine Musikzeitung' 1890). **D¹L**

2971. —— *Die Tonkunst der Babylonier und Assyrer* ('Monatshefte für Musikgeschichte' XXII No. 1), 1890. **C**

2972. **Nekes, Hermann**, *Trommelsprache und Fernruf bei den Jaunde und Duala in Süd Kamerun* ('Mitteil. d. Seminars f. Orientalische Sprachen: Afrikanische Studien' XV, p. 1 ff., 69 ff.), Berlin, 1912.

2973. **Neog, Sri Maheswar**, *An old Assamese work on timing in music* ('The Journal of the Music Academy, Madras' XXII, p. 147 ff.), 1951. **AC**

2974. —— *Sankarananda and his predecessors* (Lawyers Bookstall, Gauhati (Assam), 1953.

2974a. —— *Medieval Assamese dramas and contemporary dance-dramas of other parts of India* ('J. of the University of Gauhati' VI, p. 151 ff.), 1955.

2975. **Nesselmann, G.H. F.**, *Lithauische Volkslieder* (Berlin, 1853).

2976. **Nettel, Reginald**, *Sing a song of England. A social history of traditional song* (Denver, Col., 1954).

2977. —— *Seven centuries of popular song; a social history of urban ditties* (London, 1956). **F**

2978. **Nettl, Bruno**, *Historical Perspective in Primitive Music: the Shawnee Musical Style* ('Journal of the Amer. Musicol. Soc.' V, p. 144 ff.), 1952. **CFKLL²**

2979. —— *Stylistic Variety in North American Indian Music* ('Journal of the American Musicol. Soc.' VI, p. 160 ff.), 1953. **CFKL**

2980. —— *The Shawnee musical style* ('Southwestern J. of Anthropology' IX, p. 277 ff.), 1953. **D¹GL²**

2981. —— *Observations on meaningless Peyote song texts* ('J. of Amer. Folklore' LXVI, p. 161 ff.), 1953. **GK**

2982. —— *Notes on Musical Composition in Primitive Culture* ('Anthropological Quarterly' XXVII (N.S. II), p. 81 ff.), July 1954.

2983. —— *Ibo Songs from Nigeria, Native and Hybridized* ('Midwest Folklore' III, p. 237 ff.), 1954.

2984. —— *Text-music relationships in Arapaho songs* ('Southwestern Journal of Anthropology' X, p. 192 ff.), 1954. **D¹GL²**

2985. —— *Stylistic change in folk music* ('Southern Folklore Quarterly' XVII, p. 216 ff.), 1953.

2986. —— *North American Indian Musical Styles* ('Journal of American Folklore' LXVII, p. 45 ff., p. 297 ff. and p. 351 ff.), 1954 = Memoir 45 of the American Folklore Soc. (Philadelphia, 1954). **FGKL²**

2987. —— *Ukrainian polyphonic choral songs* ('The Ukrainian Trend' VI, p. 18 ff.), 1954.

2988. —— *Recording primitive and folk music in the field* ('American Anthropol.' LVI, p. 110 ff.), 1954. **BGL²M**

2989. —— *Musical culture of the Arapaho* ('Musical Quarterly' XLI, p. 325 ff.), 1955. **CDFH¹KL¹**

2990. —— and **Ivo Moravcik**, *Czech and Slovak songs collected in Detroit* ('Midwest Folklore' V, No. 1, p. 37 ff.), 1955.

*2991. —— *Musicological studies in American ethnological journals* ('Notes of the Music Library Association' XIII, p. 205 ff.), 1955. **DKL**

2992. —— *Ukrainian polyphonic folksongs* ('J. of the Amer. Musicol. Soc.' VII), 1954. **CK**

2993. —— *A survey of courses on ethnomusicology and related fields* ('Ethnomusicoly', Newsletter vol. I No. 3, p. 5, No. 6 p. 10, No. 8 p. 6, No. 11 p. 18, vol. II No. 2 p. 88), resp. Dec. 1954, Jan. '56, Sept. '56, Sept. '57, June '58. **AL**

2994. —— *La musica folklorica* ('Folklore Americas' XIV), 1954.

2995. —— *Notes on infant musical development* ('The Musical Quarterly' XLII, p. 28 ff.), 1956. **ACDFKL¹**

168

2996. —— *Infant musical development and primitive music* ('Southwestern Journal of Anthrop.' XII, p. 87 ff.), 1956. **D¹GL²**

2997. —— *Change in folk and primitive music: a survey of methods* ('J. of the Amer. Musicol. Soc.' VIII), 1955. **ACFKL**

2998. —— *Folk hymns of the Amish in Indiana* ('J. of the Amer. Folklore' LXIX), 1956. **GK**

2999. —— *Music in primitive culture* (Harvard Univ. Press, Cambridge Mass., 1956). **ABCL**

3000. —— *Musikalische Völkerkunde in Amerika* ('Die Musikforschung' IX, p. 303 ff.), 1956. **ACEFIKLL¹**

3001. —— *Michigan Indian music* ('Michigan History' XXXIX, p. 471 ff.), Dec. 1955.

3002. —— *The musical style of English Ballads collected in Indiana* ('Acta Musicologica' XXVII, p. 77 ff.), 1955. **ACDEFGH¹KLL¹**

3003. —— *Relaciones entre la lengua y la musica en el folklore* ('Folklore Americas' XVI, p. 1 ff.), June 1956.

3005. —— *Aspects of primitive and folk music relevant to music therapy* ('Music Therapy' 1955, p. 36 ff.). **A**

*3005a. —— *Indianermusik* ('Die Musik in Geschichte u. Gegenwart' VI, col. 1140 ff.), 1957. **ACDEFGH¹KL**

3005b. —— *Some linguistic approaches to musical analysis* ('J. of the Intern. Folk Music Council' X, p. 37 ff.), 1958. **ACIJKL**

3005c. —— *Transposition as a composition technique in folk and primitive music* ('Ethnomusicology' II No. 2, p. 56 ff.), May 1958. **AGL**

3006. Neus, H., *Esthnische Volkslieder* (Reval, 1850).

3007. Nevermann, Hans, *Hawaii. Musik* ('Die Musik' XX, p. 818 ff.), 1928. **CDFKL**

3008. Neves e Mello, Adelino A. Das, *Musicas e cançoes populares colligidas da tradiçao* (Lisbon, 1872).

3008a. Neves, Victor, *Música folklórica do Rio Grande do Sul* ('Bol. Latino-Americano' VI, vol. II), Rio de Janeiro, 19...

3009. Nevin, Arthur, *Two summers with the Blackfeet Indians of Montana* ('The Musical Quarterly' II, p. 258 ff.), 1916.

3010. Newman, A. K., and W. H. Warren, *On the musical notes and other features of the long Maori trumpet* ('Transactions of the New Zealand Inst.' XXXVIII, p. 134 ff.), 1906.

3011. Newmarch, Rosa, *Rumanian Folk Music* ('Grove's Dictionary' 5th ed. vol. III, p. 342 ff.), 1954. **ACFH¹K**

3012. —— *Russian Folk Music* (ibid., vol. III, p. 343 ff.), 1954. **ACFH¹K**

Nguyen-Dinh Lai, see Lai, Nguyen-Dinh,

3013. Nguyen Van Huyen, *Les Chants alternés des garçons et des filles en Annam* (Paris, 1934). **I**

3013a. N.H.D.S., *Mutivi* ('Nada' 1950, No. 27, p. 56 ff.). **M**

3014. Nielson, A. C., *Folkvisor* ('Studium Generale' II, p. 75 ff.), Leyden, March 1956. **A**

3015. Niemeyer, Wilhelm, *Flöteninstrumente. Vor- und Frühgeschichte* ('Die Musik in Geschichte und Gegenwart' IV, col. 330 ff.), 1956. **ACDEFGH¹KL**

3016. —— *Germanische Musik* (ibid. IV, col. 1809 ff.), 1956. **ACDEFGH¹KL**

3017. Nieuwenkamp, W. O. J., *De trom met de hoofden te Pedjeng op Bali* ('Bijdr. Kon. Inst. v. Taal-, Land- en Volkenk.' LXI, p. 319 ff.), 1908. **BD¹GL²**

3018. —— *Drie keteltrommen op Leti* ('T. Kon. Aardr.k. Gen.' 2nd series, XXXV, No. 6, p. 818 ff.), 1918. **ABCD¹GHL²**

3019. —— *Iets over een Mokko poeng Djawa noerah van Alor* (ibid. XXXVI, p. 220 ff.), 1919. **ABD¹GHL²**

3020. —— *Over de verschillende soorten van mokko's van Alor* (ibid. XXXVI, p. 222 ff.), 1919. **BCD¹GHL²**

3021. —— *Mokko's* (ibid. XXXVI, p. 332 ff.), 1919. **BCD¹GHL²**

3022. —— *Een kort bezoek aan de eilanden Kisar, Leti en Roma* ('Ned.-Indië Oud & Nieuw' VIII, p. 104 ff.), Aug. 1923. **ABD¹GHL²**

3022a. Niggemeyer, H., *Trommelsprachen ohne Trommeln* ('Paideuma' I, p. 191 ff.), 1958. **B**

3023. Nikolov, Kosla, *Beiträge zum Studium des bulgarischen Volksliedes. Metrik, Rhythmik, Tonalität* (Berlin, 1942).

3023a. Nikolskji, N. W., *Uebersicht über die Geschichte der Volksmusik bei den Wolgavölkern* (Kazan, 1920).

3023b. Nimuendajú, Curt, *Die Palikur-Indianer und ihre Nachbarn* (Göteborg, 1926), Chapter 17 (p. 54 ff.): *Musikinstrumente*. **B**

3024. Nketia, J. H., *The role of the drummer in Akan society* ('African Music' I, No. 1, p. 34 ff.), 1954. **ACJLM**

3025. —— *Funeral dirges of the Akan people* (Achimota Press, Goldcoast, 1955). **L**

3025a. —— *Modern trends in Ghana music* ('African Music' I No. 4, p. 13 ff.), 1957. **ACJLM**

3026. Noguera, A., *Memoria sobre los cantos bailes y tocatas populares de la Isla de Majorca* (Palma, 1893).

3027. Nolasco, Florida de, *La música en Santo Domingo y otros ensayos* (Ciudad Trujillo, 1939).

3028. Nordenskjold, Erland, *Ist die sogenannte Schlitztrommel in der neuen sowohl wie in der alten Welt selbständig erfunden worden?* ('Ethnologische Studien', Leipzig, 1929).

3029. —— *An ethno-geographical analysis of the material culture of two Indian tribes in the Gran Chaco* (Göteborg, 1919), p. 164 ff.: *Signals and musical instruments.* **J**

3030. Noreen, Erik, Herbert Gustavson and Nils Dencker, *Gotländska visor samlade av P. A. Säve* (Kungl. Gustav Adolfs Akad., Svenska visor I), 3 vols. (Uppsala/Stockholm, 1949/'55).

3031. Norlind, Tobias, *Bidrag till Marintrumpetens historia* ('Svensk Tidskrift för Musikforskning' IV, p. 97 ff.), 1922. **CK**

3032. —— *Bidrag till kantelens historia* (ibid., V, p. 37 ff.), 1923. **CK**

3033. —— *Musikinstrumentensystematik* (ibid. XIV, p. 95 ff.), 1932. **KL²**

3034. —— *Lyra und Kithara in der Antike* (ibid. XVI, 1934). **K**

3035. —— *Beiträge zur chinesischen Instrumentengeschichte* (ibid. XV, p. 48 ff.), 1933. **AK**

3036. —— *Svensk folkmusik och folkdans* (Stockholm, 1930).

3037. —— *Den svenska folkmusiken under medeltiden* ('Nordisk Kultur. Musikk og Musikkinstrumenter' p. 98 ff.), Oslo, 1934. **A**

3038. —— *Melodier till Svenska folkvisor och folkdanser, upptecknade före år 1800* ('Svenska Landsmål' 1906, p. 67 ff.). **D¹G**

*3039. —— *Systematik der Saiteninstrumente,* vol. I. *Geschichte der Zither* (1936). **ACIJKL**

*3040. —— *Systematik der Saiteninstrumente,* vol. II. *Geschichte des Klaviers* (1939). **ACIJL**

*3041. —— *Musikinstrumentens Historia* (Stockholm, 1941). **ACIJK**

3042. —— *Die indonesischen Gambus-Instrumente* ('Ethnos' XVIII, p. 143 ff.), 1953. **ABJL²M**

3042a. —— *Die polnischen Tänze ausserhalb Polens* ('Report of the 4th Congress of the Intern. Musical Soc.', p. 201 ff.), London, 1911. **CF**

3043. Norton, William Alfred, *African native melodies* ('Report of the S. African Association for the Advancement of Science' XII, p. 619 ff.), Cape Town, 1916.

3044. *Notation of Folk Music. Recommandations of the Committee of Experts, convened by the Intern. Archives of Folk Music, Geneva 4–9 July 1949 and Paris 12–15 December 1950* (issued in 1952 with the assistance of Unesco). **A**

3045. *Notes and Queries on Anthropology* (6th ed., revised and rewritten by a committee of the R. Anthrop. Inst. of Great Britain and Ireland), London, 1954. Chapter on Music on p. 315 ff.

3046. Nowotny, Karl Anton, *Die Notation des 'Tono' in den Aztekischen Cantares* ('Baessler Archiv' N.S. IV, p. 185 ff.), 1956. **BD¹GKL³**

3047. Ntahokaja, J. B., *La musique des Barundi* ('Grands Lacs' 1948–'49). **M**

3048. Nuez Caballero, Sebastian de la, *Instrumentos musicales populares en las Islas Canarias* ('Miscelanea de Estudios Dedicados al Dr. Fernando Ortiz por sus discipulos, colegas y amigos' vol. II, p. 1143 ff.), La Habana, 1956.

*3048a. Nuñez, Julio Espejo, *Bibliografia basica de arqueologia Andina. V. Musica precolombina* ('Bol. Bibliografico, Universidad Nacional Mayor de San Marcos' XXIX Nos. 1–4, p. 70 ff.), Dec. 1956.

3049. Nyerup, R., and K. L. Rahbek, *Udvalgte Danske Viser fra Middelalderen efter A. S. Bedelog P. Syvs* (Copenhagen, 1813 ff.). **K**

3049a. Obata, J., *Acoustical investigations of some Japanese musical instruments: syakuhati, syamisen, tudumi and koto* (Tokyo, 1930).

*3049b. O'Boyle, Jean, *Irische Musik* ('Die Musik in Geschichte u. Gegenwart' VI, col. 1405 ff.), 1957. **ACDEFGH¹KL**

3050. Obreschkoff, Christo, *Das bulgarische Volkslied* ('Berner Veröff. z. Musikforschung' IX), 1937. **AFL**

3051. O'brien, F., *Minstrels of the tropics* (the *Arioi*) ('Century' C, p. 714 ff.), 1920.

3052. Ocón, E., *Cantos españoles con notas esplicativas y biográficas* (Malaga, 1874, 2/1906).

*3053. Oderigo, Nestor R. Ortiz, *Panorama de la musica Afro-americana* (Buenos Aires, 1944). **AK**

3054. —— *Strumenti musicali degli Afro-Americani* ('Rivista di Etnografia' VII, p. 1 ff.), 1953. **M**

3055. —— *El 'Calypso', expresión musical de los Negros de Trinidad* ('Miscelanea de estudios dedicados al Dr. Fernando Ortiz', vol. II, p. 1163 ff.), La Habana, 1956.

3056. —— *Negro rhythm in the Americas* ('African Music' I, No. 3, p. 68 ff.), 1956. **ACJLM**

3057. Oesau, Wanda, *'Und Jan Mayen der alte Flegel ...' Alte deutsche Walfanglieder* (Wolfenbüttel/Berlin, undated).

3058. Olbrechts, Fr. M., *De studie van de inheemse muziek van Belgisch Congo* ('Miscellanea musicologica' dedicated to Floris van der Mueren, p. 147 ff.), 1950. **CM**

3059. **Oldenberg, Andreas,** *Vallhorn, herde-pipor och lurar* ('Värmland förr och nu' XLVIII), 1950. **K**

3060. **Olds, W. B.,** *Bird-music* ('The Musical Quarterly' VIII, p. 242 ff.), 1922.

3060a. **Oliveira, J. O. de,** *Uma acçao cultural em Africa* (Lisboa, 1954).

3061. **Oliver, D. L.,** *The relation between slit-gongs and reknown in a Solomon Islands culture* (in Kroeber, 'Anthropological Society Papers' (Berkeley) Nos. 8 and 9, p. 69 ff.), 1953.

3062. —— *A Solomon island society* (Cambridge, 1955), s. v. composers, dirges, flutes, music, singing and slitgongs. **B**

3063. **Oliver, Richard A. C.,** *The musical talent of natives of East Africa* ('Brit. J. of Psychology' gen. section, XXII, p. 333 ff.), 1932. **D¹GH**

3064. **Olmeda, F.,** *Cancioneiro popular de Burgos* (Sevilla, 1903).

3065. **Olrog, Ulf Peder,** *Svensk visarkiv, en orientering om en ny institution* ('Arv' IX (1953), p. 129 ff.), 1954.

3065a. **Ombredane, A.,** *Les techniques de fortune dans le travail coutumier des noirs* ('Présence Africaine' XIII, p. 58 ff.), 1952. **M**

3065b. **Onyido, U.,** *The Nigerian Institute of Music* ('Rhodes-Livingstone Journal' 1955, No. 19, p. 46 ff.). **M**

3066. **Oost, P. J. van,** *Chansons populaires de la région des Ortos* ('Anthropos' VII) 1912. **D¹GKL¹L²M**

3067. —— *La musique chez les Mongols des Urdus* (ibid., X and XI), 1915/'16. **D¹GKL¹L²M**

3068. —— *Chansons populaires chinoises* 190?).

3069. —— *Receuil de chansons mongoles* ('Anthropos' III, p. 219 ff.), 1908. **D¹GKL¹L²M**

3070. **Oransay, Gültekin,** *Das Tonsystem der türkei-türkischen Kunstmusik* ('Die Musikforschung' X, p. 250 ff.), 1957. **ACEFIKLL¹**

3071. **Orden, Burt,** *Fi Man's Fancy* (on recordings of steelband, calypso and jawbone of an ass) ('High Fidelity' VII No. 2, p. 88 ff.), Febr. 1957.

3072. **O'reilly, Patrick,** *Autour de la musique des Néo-Calédoniens* ('Journal de la Soc. des Océanistes' II, p. 93 ff.), 1946. **BGKL²**

3073. **Ortiz, Fernando,** *La música sagrada de los negros Yorubas en Cuba* ('Estudios Afro-cubanos' II, p. 89 ff.), Habana, 1938.

*3074. —— *Les Instrumentos de la Música Afrocubana.* vol. I. *Los Instrumentos Anatómicos y los Palos Percusivos;* vol. II. *Los Instrumentos Sacuditivos, los Frotativos y los Hierros;* vol. III. *Los tambores xilofonicos y los membranófonos abiertos* (Habana, 1952); vol. IV, *Los Membranóforos abiertos N-Z, Los bimembranóforos y otros tambores especiales* (Habana, 1954); vol. V. *Los pulsativos, los fricativos, los insuflativos y los aeritivos* (Habana, 1955). **ACJLM**

3075. —— *Afro-Cuban music* ('Quarterly Journal of Inter-American relations' I, p. 66 ff.), July 1939.

3076. —— *La clave xilofónica de la música Cubana* (Habana, 1935) (also in 'Estudios Afro-cubanos' V), 1945/'46.

3077. —— *La música religiosa de los Yorubas entre los negros Cubanos* ('Estudios Afro-cubanos' V), 1945/'46.

3078. —— *Las músicas Africanas en Cuba* ('Rev. de Arqueo- y Etnologia' II, p. 235 ff.), 1947.

3079. —— *La Africanía de la música folklórica de Cuba* (Habana, 1950).

3080. —— *Los bailes y el teatro de los negros en el folklore de Cuba* (La Habana, 1951). **L**

Ortiz Oderigo, Nestor R., see: **Oderigo, Nestor R. Ortiz.**

3081. **Ortman, Otto,** *Visual, kinaesthetic, olfactory, and gustatory effects of music* (in: Max Schoen, 'The effects of music', p. 244 ff.), London, 1927. **A**

3081a. **Ortutay, Gyula,** *Az 'európai' ballada kérdéséhez* (= The problem of the 'European' ballad) ('Emlékkönyv Kodály Zoltán 70. születésnapjára', p. 125 ff.), Budapest, 1953. **A**

3082. **Osa, Sigbjørn B.,** *Hardang Fela, the Hardangar Fiddle* (Oslo, 1952). **A**

3082a. **Osafo, F. Onwona,** *An African orchestra in Ghana music* ('African Music' I No. 4, p. 11 ff.), 1957. **ACJLM**

3083. **Osanai, Tadao,** *Twice intermediate tuning* ('Journal of the Soc. for Research in Asiatic music' 10/11, p. 5 ff.), 1952. **A**

3084. **Osburn, Mary Hubbell,** *Some prehistoric musical instruments of North-America* ('Hinrichsen's Musical Yearbook' VII, p. 243 ff.), 1952. **K**

3085. **Ostrowskich, P.,** *Ueber die Musikinstrumente der Katschinzen* ('Z. f. Ethnol. XXVII, p. (616) ff.), 1895. **ABD¹GHKL¹L²M**

3086. **O'Sullivan, Donal J.,** *Folk music and songs I–VI* (Irish Folk Song Soc., London, 1927–1939).

*3087. —— *Irish Folk Music* ('Grove's Dictionary' 5th ed. vol. III, p. 289 ff.), 1954. **ACFH¹K**

3088. —— *Irish folk music* (publ. by the Cultural Relations Committee of the Dept. of External Affairs, Dublin, 1952).

3089. —— *Songs of the Irish* (Dublin, 1957).

3090. —— *The music of Carolan* (London, 1957).

3091. Ota, Taro, *Wind instruments of the Ainu* ('Journal of the Soc. f. Research in Asiatic Music' IX, p. 5 ff.), March 1951. **A**

3092. Otaño, N., *El canto popular montañés* (Santander, 1915).

*3093. Oxford Academy. *The Arabic musical manuscripts in the Bodleian library* (1925). **I**

3093a. Pausonen, H., *Tatarische Lieder* (Surgut, 1900). **L**

3093b. Paduano, Luigi, *La musica folkloristica nella vita culturale italiana* (Edizione Enal, 1952).

3094. Pages, P., *Des joueurs de flûte et de cithare* ('Brousse' 1940, III, p. 6).
Palacin, Arcadion de Larrea, see **Larrea Palacin, Arcadion de.**

3094a. Paladian, S., *Armenian folksongs* (Californian Univ. Press, Berkeley/Los Angeles), 19...

3095. Palavicino, Enrique, *Una ocarina pentafónico del N.O. Argentina* (Univ. de la Plata, 'Antropología' No. 55), La Plata, 1949. **G**

3096. Pálinkás, Jozsef, *Gyermekdalok* (Budapest, 1951).

3097. Panditar, M. Abraham, *Karunamirtha sagaram.* Extract from the first book of srutis (Part 3. Extract from the first book on staff notation for Indian music. An essay by **Maragathavalla Ammal**), Tanjore, 1916. **I**

3098. —— *The system of srutis and some important points that are in use in the music of ancient South Tamil country* (Tanjore, 1916). **I**

3099. —— *The system of Dwavimsati srutis according to Sarnga Dev and the opinions of different writers who determine the Dwavimsati srutis in an octave by taking Sa-Pa as* ²/₃ (Tanjore, 1916). **I**

3100. Panhuys, L. C. van, *Mitteilungen über surinamische Ethnographie und Kolonisationsgeschichte: Trommelsprache, etc.* ('Verh. d. XVI. Intern. Amerikanisten-Kongr.', p. 521 ff.), Vienna, 1909. **B**

3101. —— *Les chansons et la musique de la Guyane Neerlandaise* ('J. de la Soc. des Américanistes de Paris', N.S. IX, p. 27 ff.), 1912. **GL**

3102. —— *Surinaamsche folklore* (Liederenverzameling Van Vliet) ('De West-Ind. Gids' XVII, p. 282 ff.), 1931/'32. **ABD¹G**

3103. —— *Aard en karakter van Surinaamsche liederen* (ibid. XVIII, p. 1 ff.), Mei 1936. **ABD¹G**

3104. Pann, Anton, *Cintece de Lume, transcrise din psaltica in notatia moderna, cu un studiu introductiv de Gh. Ciobanu* (Bukarest, 1955). **J**

3105. Panoff, Peter, *Phonographierte wotjakische, permjakische und tatarische Lieder* ('Z. f. Musikw.' XI, p. 609 ff.), 1929. **ACDEH¹KL**

3106. —— *Die altslawische Volks- und Kirchenmusik* (in Bücken, 'Handbuch der Musikwissenschaft'), 1929. **CDEFH¹IKL**

3107. Panum, Hortense, *Middelalderens Strenge-instrumenter og deres Forløbere i Oldtiden* (Copenhagen, 1915). **I**

3108. —— *The stringed instruments of the Middle Ages* (London, undated, but published after 1921). **AJ**

3109. —— *Middelalderens Musikinstrumenter* ('Nordisk Kultur. Musikk og Musikk-Instrumenter', 1934, p. 50 ff.). **A**

3109a. Pâques, V., *Bouffons sacrés du Cercle de Bougouni* (Soudan français) ('J. de la Soc. d. Africanistes' XXIV, p. 63 ff.), 1954. **M**

3110. Parisot, J., *Rapport sur une mission scientifique en Turquie d'Asie* (chants orientaux), Paris, 1899. **I**

3111. Parker, D. C., *Some aspects of Gypsy music* (London, 1913). **I**

3112. Parmentier, H., *Anciens tambours de bronze* ('Bull. de l'Ecole Française d'Extrême Orient' XVIII, p. 1 ff.), 1918. **K**

3113. —— *Notes d'archéologie indochinoise. IX. Nouveaux tambours de bronze* (ibid. XXXII, p. 171 ff.), 1932. **BK**

3114. Parrinder, E. G., *Music in West African churches* ('African Music' I, No. 3, p. 37 ff.), 1956. **ACJLM**

3115. Parsons, Elsie Clews, *Folklore of the Antilles, French and English* (publ. XXVI, part II of the Amer. Folklore Soc.), New York, 1933. **B**

3116. Parthasarathi, S., *A study of Sri Tyagaraja* ('J. of the Music Acad.' XXIV, p. 90 ff.), 1953. **AC**

3117. Pasini, Fr., *Prolegomènes à une étude sur les sources de l'histoire musicale de l'ancienne Egypte* ('Sammelb. d. Intern. Musikges.' IX), 1907/'08. **CF**

3118. Pastor, Willy, *The music of primitive peoples and the beginning of European music* ('Annual Report Smithsonian Inst.', Washington, 1912), p. 679 ff. **D¹JL²**

3119. Paterson, A., *Old Lithuanian Songs* (Kaunas, 1939).

3120. Paterson, J. D., *On the gramas or musical scales of the Hindus* (in Surindro Mohun Tagore, 'Hindu music from various authors', p. 173 ff.), Calcutta, 1882. **CI**

3121. Patterson, Annie, *The folk-music of Ireland* ('The Musical Quarterly' VI, p. 455 ff.), 1920. **C**

3122. Paucitis, K., *Latvian Folk Music* ('Grove's Dictionary' 5th ed. vol. III, p. 313 ff.), 1954. **ACFH¹K**

3123. **Pauli, F. W.,** *Ausserdeutsche Volks-musik. Erster Katalog mit volkskund-lichen Erläuterungen* (publ. by the Lautarchiv des deutschen Rundfunks), Frankfurt a/M., March 1956.　**F**

3124. —— *Ausserdeutsche Volksmusik. Zwei-ter Katalog. Volksmusik der U.S.A.* (publ. by id.), Frankfurt a/M., Septem-ber 1956.　**F**

3125. **Pauwels, P. M.,** *Les métiers et les objets au Rwanda.* Chapter IV. *Instruments de musique* ('Annali Lateranensi' 1955, p. 185 (217 ff.)).　**BGKL²**

3125a. **Parry, M.,** and **A. B. Lord,** *Serbo-croatian heroic songs* (2 vols.), Cam-bridge/Beograd, 1953/'54).　**L**

3126. **Payer,** *Ein am Amazonenstrom ge-bräuchlicher Trommelapparat* ('Z. f. Ethnologie' XXXV), 1903.
　　　　　　　　　BD¹GHKL¹L²M

3127. **Peabody, Ch.,** *A prehistoric wind-instru-ment from Pecos, New Mexico* ('Amer. Anthropologist' N.S. XIX), 1917. **GL²**

3127a. **Pearse, Andrew** (arranged and ed. by), *Mitto Sampson on calypso legends of the 19th century* ('Caribbean Quarterly' IV, p. 250 ff.), March/June 1956.　**B**

3128. —— *Aspects of change in Carribean folk music* ('Journal of the Intern. Folk Music Council' VII, p. 29 ff.), 1955.　**ACJKL**

3128a. **Peate, Iorwerth,** *Welsh musical instru-ments* ('Man' XLVII, p. 21, No. 17), Febr. 1947.　**ABD¹GKL²M**

3128b. **Péczely, A.,** *Hochzeitstrinklieder aus dem südlichen Teil des Komitates Zala* (Hung. text) ('Néprajzi Közlemények' II, p. 135 ff.), Budapest, 1957.

3129. **Pedrell, Felipe,** *Cancionero Musical Popular Español* (3 vols.), Valls, Cata-lonia, undated.　**AFIL**

3130. **Pedrosa, Mario,** *Brazilian music* ('Thea-tre Arts Monthly' XXIII, p. 363 ff.), May 1939.

3130a. **Peeters, Theophiel,** *Oudkempische volksliederen en dansen* (Brussel, 1952).

3131. **Pekker, Ian,** *V. A. Uspenskij* (his work as an ethnographer-musicologist and composer in Uzbekistan and Turkme-nistan), Gvnt. Music Publication, Mos-cow, 1953.

3132. **Pélagaud, Fernand,** *Syriens et Phry-giens* (1910) (in Lavignac, 'Hist. de la Mus.' I, p. 49 ff.), 1922.　**ACDEFHJ**

3133. **Pelay Briz,** *Cançons de la terra* (5 vols.) (Barcelona, 1866–'74).　**L**

3134. **Pelliot, Paul,** *Le k'ong-heou et le qobuz* ('Mélanges Naitô'), Kyoto, 1926.

3135. **Pepper, Herbert,** *Chant d'adultère* ('Le mois de l'Afrique Equatoriale Fran-çaise', Jan. 1945), p. 22 ff.

3136. —— *Musique et pensée africaines* ('Pre-sence Africaine' I, p. 149 ff.), 1947.　**M**

3137. —— *Trois danses chantées avec accom-pagnement de linga* ('Etudes Came-rounaises' Douala, No. 21–22, p. 85 ff.), June–Sept. 1949.　**G**

3138. —— *Le sanzi compagnon dans la soli-tude* ('Tropiques' No. 316), Dec. 1949.

3139. —— *Histoire contée sur un vieux tam-bours de bois* ('Jeune Afrique', Elisa-bethville, June 1949), p. 13 ff.

3140. —— *A la recherche des traditions musi-cales en pays Vili* ('Bull. d'information et documentation du Haut-Commissa-riat de la République Française en A.E.F.' No. 69), 1950.

3141. —— *Traditional music at the Vali* ('Africa' XL, p. 1 ff.), London, 1951.
　　　　　　　　　BGJKL¹L²M

3142. —— *Les problèmes généraux de la musi-que populaire en Afrique noire* ('Journal of the Intern. Folk Music Council' II, p. 22 ff. and 'Newsletter of the African Music Soc.' I No. 3, p. 4 ff.), 1950.
　　　　　　　　　ACJKLM

3143. —— *Images musicales équatoriales* ('Tropiques' XLVIII, p. 47 ff.), Dec. 1950.　**A**

3144. —— *Musique centre-africaine* ('Encycl. coloniale et maritime'), 1950.　**AM**

3146. —— *Sur un Xylophone Ibo* ('Newsletter of the African Music Soc.' I, No. 5, p. 35 ff.), 1952.　**ACJM**

3147. —— *Classification méthodique d'une oeuvre musicale ethnique et de ses élé-ments techniques* ('Rapport Annuel de l'Inst. d'Etudes Centre-africaines', Brazzaville, 1952), p. 33 ff.

3148. —— *Enquête sur le contenu verbal de 21 disques Ngoma* (Brazzaville, Inst. d'Etu-des Centre-africaines, 1952).

3149. —— *Réflexions sur l'art musical en Af-rique Equatoriale* ('L'Afrique Fran-çaise' XXVIII, p. 82 ff.), 1952.　**M**

3150. —— *L'enregistrement du son et l'art mu-sical ethnique* ('Bull. Inst. Et. centrafr.', new series, 1952, p. 143 ff.).　**M**

3151. —— *Textes de chants Matsouanistes et des Mfoumou Mpou* (chefs traditionels Lari du Moyen-Congo), 1951.

3151a. —— *Considérations sur le langage tam-bouriné et autres langages musicaux d'Afrique Centrale, sur la pensée musi-cale africaine* (in (4a) Conferencia … 1954, p. 165 ff.).　**M**

3152. —— *Essai de définition d'une gram-maire musicale noire* ('Problèmes d'Af-rique Centrale' VII, p. 289 ff.), 1954.
　　　　　　　　　AGJKM

3152a. **Pépratx-Saisset, Henry,** *La sardane. La danse des Catalans. Son symbole, sa magie, ses énigmes* (Perpignan, 1956).

3153. **Percival, Caussin de,** *Les musiciens ara-bes* ('Journal Asiatique' 1873, p. 397 ff.).　**D¹GHKL¹**

3154. Perdomo Escobar, José Ignacio, *Esbozo histórico sobre la música colombiana* ('Bol. Lat.-Amer. de Música' IV, p. 387 ff.), Bogotá, 1938.

3155. —— *Historia de la Música en Colombia* (Bogotá, 1945).

3156. —— *El vilancico en Colombia* ('Hojas de cultura popular Colombiana' No. 12), Bogotá, 1951.   D¹

*3157. Pereira Salas, Eugenio, *Guía bibliográfica para el estudio del folklore chileno* (Chile, 1952).   A

3157a. —— *La música de la Isla de Pascua* (Santiago de Chile, Inst. de investigaciones musicales, colleccion de ensayos No. 1), n.d.   A

3158. Péri, Noël, *Essai sur les Gammes Japonaises* (Paris, 1934).   AGIJKL

3159. Peristeres, Spuros D., Δημοτικα τραγουδια Επειρου και Μωρηα (Dèmotica tragoudia Epirou kai Morèa), Athens, 1950.

3160. Pernot, H., *L'Ile de Chios* (Paris, 1903).

3161. Perron, Michel, *Chants populaires de la Sénégambie et du Niger* ('Bull. de l'Agence Générale des Colonies' XXIII, p. 803 ff.), Paris, 1930.

3162. Petit, Raymond, *Exotic and contemporary music* ('The Musical Antiquary' XI, p. 200 ff.), 1934.

3163. Petneki, Jenő, *Das ungarische Volkslied* (Budapest/Leipzig/Milano/Danubia, 1943).

3164. Petri, George, *Ancient music of Ireland* (Dublin, 1855).

3165. —— *Music of Ireland* (Dublin, 1882).

3166. Pettazzoni, Raffaele, *Mythologie australienne du rhombe* ('Revue de l'Histoire des Religions' XXXIII, vol. 65), Paris, 1912.   D¹HL¹

3167. Pfister, G. A., *La música Ashanti* ('Revista Musicale Italiana', Turino, 1925).   CKL

3168. —— *Les chansons historiques et le 'Timpam' des Achantis* ('La Revue Musicale' IV, p. 230 ff.), Paris, 1923. CDFGHKL¹

3169. Pfrogner, H., *Die zwölfordnung der Töne* (Zürich, 1953).   C

3170. Phelps, D. L., *The plan of music in the Platonic and Confucian system of moral education* ('J. of the R. Asiatic Soc. of Great Britain and Ireland' 1928).   D¹GIKL¹

3171. Philharmonic Society of Western India, The, *The Ragas of Hindustan* (with an introduction on the theory of Indian music by E. C. Clements), Poona, 1918.

3172. Phillips, Ekundayo, *Yoruba Music* (Johannesburg, 1953).   ALM

3173. Phillips, W. J., *Maori bird calls or whistles* ('Ethnos' XV, p. 201 ff.), 1950.   BJL²M

*3174. Picken, Laurence, *Chinese Music*

('Grove's Dictionary of Music and Musicians', 5th ed., vol. II, p. 219 ff.), 1954.   ACFH¹K

3175. —— *Japanese Music* (ibid., vol. IV, p. 589 ff.), 1954.   ACFH¹K

3176. —— *Instrumental Polyphonic Folk Music in Asia Minor* ('Proc. R. Musical Ass.' LXXX, p. 73 ff.), 1954.   A

*3177. —— *The Music of Far-Eastern Asia* ('The New Oxford History of Music', 3rd ed., vol. I, p. 83 ff.), 1957.
          ABCD¹FGH¹JK

3178. —— *Review of 'Kashmiri Musiqi (sa, ri, ga, ma)'* ('Journal of the Intern. Folk Music Council' VII, p. 62 ff.), 1955.
          ACJKL

3179. —— *The origin of the short lute* ('J. of the Galpin Soc.' VIII, p. 32 ff.), London, 1955.   AC

3180. —— *Twelve ritual melodies of the T'ang dynasty* ('Studia Memoriae Belae Bartók Sacra', p. 147 ff.), Budapest, 1956.   AC

3181. —— *Chiang K'uei's Nine songs for Yüeh* ('The Musical Quarterly' XLIII, p. 201 ff.), 1957.   ACDEFKL¹

3182. Pigeaud, Th., *Over den huidigen stand van de tooneel- en danskunst en de muziekbeoefening op Java* ('Djawa' XII, p. 155 ff.), 1932.   ABD¹G

3183. Piggott, Francis T., *The Japanese musical scale* ('Transactions and Proceedings of the Japan Soc.' III, p. 33 ff.), 1893. J

3184. —— *The music and musical instruments of Japan* (London, 1909).
          ABCGIJK

3185. —— and A. H. Fox Strangways, *Japanese music* ('Grove's Dictionary of Music and Musicians', 5th ed. vol. IV, p. 589 ff.), 1955.   ACFH¹K

3186. Pike, Kenneth L., *The flea: melody types and pertubations in a Mixtec song* ('Tlalocan' II, p. 128 ff.), 1946.

3187. —— *Tone languages* (Ann Arbor, 1948).

3188. Pilet, Raymond, *Rapport sur une mission en Islande et aux Iles Féroe* ('Nouvelles archives des missions scientifiques' VII), Paris, 1896.

3189. Pillai, Vidvan Palani Subramania, *Vidvan Munpoondiya Pillai* ('J. of the Music Academy, Madras' XXV, p. 73 ff.), Madras, 1954.   AC

3190. Pinches, T. G., *Babylonian and Assyrian music* ('Hasting's Encycl. of Religion and Ethics'), Edinburgh, 1917.   D¹GH

3191. Pinck, Louis, *Verklingende Weisen* I–IV (Heidelberg 1920–1939). A (III only).

3192. Pingle, Bhavanrao A., *Indian music* (Byculla, 2/1898).

3193. Pinon, Roger, *La nouvelle Lyre Malmédienne ou la vie en Wallonie malmédienne reflétée dans la chanson folklori-

que ('Folklore Stavelot-Malmédy' vol.
XIII, p. 35 ff. (1949), XIV, p. 77 ff.
(1950), XV, p. 65 ff. (1951), XVI, p. 3
ff. (1952), XVII, p. 53 ff. (1953), XVIII,
p. 81 ff. (1954), XIX, p. 59 ff. (1955)). A

3194. Piobaireachd, edited by the Piobaireachd Society (several volumes),
Glasgow 192?–193?.

3195. Pischner, Hans, Musik in China (Berlin, 1955). ACL

3196. Plath, Joh. Heinrich, Die Religion und
der Cultus der alten Chinesen ('Abhandl.
d. k. bayer. Akad. d. W.' I. Klasse,
Bd. IX, Section III), München, 1862
(Part II. Der Cultus der alten Chinesen,
p. 70 ff.: Von der Musik und den Tän-
zen bei den Opfern der Kaiser).

3197. Platt, W., Child music. A study of
tunes made up by young children (London, 1905). I

3198. Plessis, I. D. du, Die bijdrae van die
Kaapse Maleiers tot die Afrikaanse
volkslied (Nasionale Pers, Capetown,
1935).

3199. —— Die Maleise samenlewing aan die
Kaap (Nasionale Pers, Capetown,
1939).

3200. Plička, Karel, Songs of the Slovak
mountains ('J. of the Intern. Folk
Music Council' VIII, p. 30 ff.), 1956.
ACJKL

3201. Plischke, Hans, Geistertrompeten und
Geisterflöten aus Bambus vom Sepik,
Neuguinea ('Jahrbuch des Mus. f.
Völkerk. zu Leipzig' VIII, p. 57), 1922.
GL[1]

3202. Poduval, R. V., The music of Kerala
and other essays (Gemini Studios, Madras, 1954).

3203. —— Music and the Muslim courts of
India ('The Madras Music Acad. Annual Conf. Souvenir, Dec. 1953'), 1954.

3204. —— The imperial city of music (ibid.,
Dec. 1954), 1955.

3205. Poensen, C., De wajang ('Mededeelingen
vanwege het Nederl. Zendelinggenootschap' XVI, p. 59 ff, 204 ff., 233 ff.,
and 253 ff.), 1872. B

3206. Polácek, Jan, Slovácke pěsničky (2 vols.)
Prague, 1950.

3207. Poladian, Sirvart, Armenian Folk Songs
(Publ. in Music of the Univ. of California, II, no. 1), Berkeley/Los Angeles,
1942. GH

3208. —— The problem of melodic variation in
folk song ('J. of Amer. Folklore' LV,
p. 204 ff.), 1942. GK

3209. —— Armenian Folksongs (1942).

3210. Polak, A. J., Die Harmonisierung
indischer, türkischer und japanischer
Melodien (Leipzig, 1905). AFI

3211. Polin, Claire C. J., Music of the ancient
Near East (New York, 1955).

3212. Pollmann, J., Ons eigen volkslied (Amsterdam, 1936). C

3213. Poloczek, František, Slovenské Ludové
Piesne ('Academiae Scientiarum Slo-
vacae Corpus musicae popularis' I–III),
Bratislava 1950 [1], 1952 and 1956. AK

3214. —— Slovakian folk song and folk dance
in the present day ('J. of the Intern.
Folk Music Council' IX, p. 13 ff.), 1957.
ACJKL

3215. Ponce, M. M., Apuntes sobre musica
mexicana ('Estudios Latino-americanos'
III, p. 37 ff.), 1937.

3216. Poona Academy, Philharmonic Society
of Western India, The ragas of Hindostan. Skeleton melodies collected and
arranged by the executive committee
(Poona, 1918). I

3216a. Pop, M., Nunta din Seliste (Wedding in
S.) (with an English summary) ('Re-
vista de Folclor' III No. 2, p. 47 ff.),
Bucarest, 1958. A

*3217. Popley, Herbert A., The Music of
India (Calcutta/London, 1921, 2/1950).
ACFHJ

3218. Porée-Maspéro, Eveline, Mythes du Dé-
luge et tambours de bronze ('Actes du
IVe Congrès intern. des sciences anthropologiques et ethnologiques, Vienne,
1–8 Sept. 1952', Tome II, Ethnologica,
1re partie, p. 246 ff.), Vienna, 1955. B

3219. Portmann, M. V., Andamanese Music
('Journal of the R. Asiat. Soc.' XX, p.
181 ff.), 1888. D[1]GIKL[1]

3219a. Possoz, E., Negermuziek ('Band' IX,
p. 190 ff.), 1950. M

3220. Pott, A. F., Namen musikalischer Instrumente bei den Kurden (no place,
no date). C

3221. Pott, P. H., Musique tibétaine du Sikkim
('Gramofoon voor kenner en liefhebber'
Amsterdam, Juli 1956, p. 14 ff.). A

3222. Poueigh, J., Chansons populaires des
Pyrénées Françaises. Traditions,
moeurs, usages. Rapport à M. le Mi-
nistre de l'Instruction publique et des
Beaux-Arts (Paris, 1926).

3223. Pound, Ezra, 'Noh' plays ('The translations of Ezra Pound', p. 211 ff.), London, Faber & Faber, undated.

3224. Pradines, Emerante de, Instruments of
Rhythm ('To Morrow' III No. 1, p. 123
ff.), 1954.

3225. Prajnanananda, Swami, Music of Hin-
du and Buddhist India ('Entally Cult.
Conf., 8th Annual Session, Jan. 1955),
Calcutta, 1955.

3226. Pratella, F. B., La musica nelle nostre
colonie d'Africa ('Musica d'ogni', 1927).

---

[1]) Vol. I appeared under the editorship of K. Hudec.

175

3226a. Price, E. W., *Native melody and christian hymns* ('Congo Mission News' No. 135, p. 14), 1946. **M**

3227. Prichici, Constantin Gh., *125 melodii de jocuri din Moldova* (Bucarest, 1955).

3228. —— *Metodă de tambal* (Bucarest, 1956). **J**

3228a. —— *Geneza melodica a baladei lui Pintea Viteazul* ('Revista de Folclor' II, No. 4, p. 7 ff.), Bucarest, 1957. **A**

3229. Prick van Wely, Max, *Het bloeitijdperk van het Nederlandse volkslied van het ontstaan tot de zeventiende eeuw* (Heemstede, 1949). **AF**

3230. Prietze, Rudolf, *Haussa Sänger* (Göttingen, 1916).

3231. —— *Lieder des Haussavolkes* ('Mitt. d. Seminars f. Orientalische Sprachen' XXX, p. 5 ff.), 1927. **D¹L²**

3232. Prin, J. B., *Mémoire sur la trompette marine* (1742), publ. by L. Vallas ('Sammelb. d. Intern. Musikges.' IV, p. 1176 ff.), 1908. **CDFH¹L**

3233. Prince, J. D., *Muhammadan music* (in: Hasting, 'Encycl. of Religion and Ethics' IX, p. 53 ff.), Edinburgh, 1917. **D¹GH**

3234. Pringsheim, Klaus, *Music of Thailand* ('Contemporary Japan' XIII, p. 745 ff.), 1944. **G**

3235. —— *Musik in Siam* ('Stimmen' I, p. 46 ff.), 1947/'48. **L**

3236. —— *Siamesische Opern* ('Stimmen' 1950, fasc. 18, p. 520 ff.). **L**

3237. Pritchard, W., *The music and musical instruments of Wales, and its bards and minstrels* (und., 1880?). **I**

3238. Proca, Vera, *Despre notarea dansului popular Rominesc* ('Revista de folclor' I, Nos. 1–2, p. 135 ff.), Bucarest, 1956. **A**

3239. —— *Despre notarea dansului popular Rominesc* ('Revista de folclor' II, Nos. 1–2, p. 65 ff.), Bucarest, 1957. **AC**

3239a. Procope, Bruce, *The Dragon band or Devil band* ('Caribbean Quarterly' IV, p. 275 ff.), March/June 1956. **B**

3240. Psachos, C. A., *Le chant populaire hellénique de l'antiquité à nos jours* ('Art populaire' II, p. 126), 1931. **A**

3241. —— 50 Δημώδη ἄσματα πελοποννησου και Κρητης (50 Demode asmata Peloponnesou kai Kretes), Athens, 1930.

3242. Pujol, F., *L'oeuvre du chansonnier populaire de la Catalogne* (Barcelona, 1927).

3243. —— *Clasificación de las canciones populares. Metodología* ('Anuario musical' I, p. 19 ff.), 1946. **C**

3244. Pulestone, F., *African drums* (London, 1930). **C**

3245. Pulver, Jeffry, *Israel's music-lesson in Egypt* ('Musical Times' LVI), 1915.

3246. —— *The music of ancient Egypt* ('Proc. of the Musical Association', London, 1921/'22). **I**
Quaritsch Wales, H. G., see: Wales, H. G. Quaritsch.

3247. Quasten, Johannes, *Musik und Gesang in den Kulten der heidnischen Antike und christlichen Frühzeit* (Münster, 1930).

3248. Quénum, Maximilien, *Au pays des Fons: la musique* ('Bull. du Com. d'Etudes Histor. et Scientif. de l'Afrique Occidentale Française' XVIII, p. 323 ff.), Paris, 1935.

3249. Querino, Manuel, *Costumes africanos no Brasil* (Rio de Janeiro, Civilizaçao Brasileira).

3249a. Rabesahala, E., *Evolution de l'art malgache et culture française* ('Encycl. Mens. Outre-Mer' VI, vol. V, No. 64, p. 517 ff.), 1955. **M**

3250. Rabinovitch, M. G., *Les instruments de musique chez les troupes de l'ancienne Russie et les instruments populaires de musique* ('Sovetskaia Etnografiia', 1956, p. 142 ff.). **D¹KM**

3250a. Raemsdonck, M. van, *Jazz et musique Bantoue* ('Jeune Afrique' VI, p. 7 ff.), 1952. **M**

3251. Raffles, Thomas Stamford, *The History of Java* (1817), p. 469 ff. **B**

3252. Raghavan, V., *Some names in early Sangita literature* ('J. Music Acad. III, p. 11 ff. and 154), Madras, 1932.

3253. —— *Some more names in early Sangita literature* (ibid. III, p. 94 ff.), Madras, 1932.

3254. —— *Later Sangita literature* (ibid. IV, p. 10 ff. and 50 ff.), Madras, 1933.

3255. —— *The Rasaratnakosa, the Nataratnakosa and the Sangitaraja* ('Annals of the Bhandarkar Oriental Research Inst., Poona' XIV, p. 258 ff.), 1932/'33.

3256. —— (under the pseudonym 'Bhavuka'): *Papanasam Sivan: Sound and Shadow* (Madras, 1933), p. 59 ff.

3257. —— *Sanskrit music manuscripts in the B.O.R.I., Poona* ('J. Music Acad. V, p. 89 ff.), Madras, 1934.

3258. —— *The Alankaracandrika of king Narayana* ('Annals of the Bhandarkar Oriental Research Inst., Poona' XVI, p. 129 ff.), 1934/'35.

3259. —— *Life of Sri Muthusvami Diksitar* (publ. by the Triplicane Club, Madras), 1935.

3260. —— *Music in the Brhaddharma-Purana* ('J. Music Acad.' IX, p. 37 ff.), 1938.

3261. —— *Music in Jain works* (ibid. IX, p. 40 ff.), 1938.

3262. —— *Music in the Hamsavilasa* (ibid. IX, p. 42 ff.), 1938.

3263. —— *Daksina Citra* ('J. of the Indian

Soc. of Oriental Art' VI, p. 195 ff.), 1938.

3264. —— *Sangitasudha of king Raghunatha of Tanjore* (publ. by the Music Acad., Madras, Series 1), 1940.

3265. —— *The so-called Akalanka of the Sangitasara-Sangrahamu* ('J. Music Acad.' XII, p. 38 ff.), 1941.

3266. —— *Venkatamakhin and the 72 Melas* (ibid. XII, p. 67 ff.), 1941.

3267. —— *Nati's songs in the Abhjnana Sakuntala* (ibid. XLL, p. 92 ff.), 1941.

3268. —— *Music contributions in other journals* (ibid. XX, p. 96 ff.), 1941.

3269. —— *Sangita-Saramrta of king Tulaja of Tanjore* (publ. by the Music Acad., Madras, Series 5), 1942.

3270. —— *Merattur Kasintha, a composer of sabdus of the 18th century A.D.* ('J. Music Acad.' XIV, p. 130 ff.), 1943.

3271. —— *Ragas in Kerala* (ibid. XIV, p. 135 ff.), 1943.

3272. —— *Music in Palikuriki Somanatha's works* (ibid., XIV, p. 140 ff.), 1943.

3273. —— *Soma raga* (ibid. XIV, p. 145 ff.), 1943.

3274. —— *Two new sabdas on Sri Maharaja Svati Tirunal* (ibid. XV, p. 22), 1944.

3275. —— *Music in the Adbhuta-Ramayana* (ibid. XVI, p. 65 ff.), 1945.   **C**

3276. —— *Some musicians and their patrons about 1800 A.D. in Madras city* (ibid. XVI, p. 127 ff.), 1945.   **C**

3277. —— *Hyderabad as a centre of Sangita* (in: 'Krishnagana Sabha Souvenir', repr. in 'J. Music Acad.' XVI, p. 116 ff.), 1945.   **C**

3278. —— *A note on 'Applause in ancient India'* (ibid. XVII, p. 144 ff.), 1946. **C**

3279. —— *The Useni svarajati* (ibid. XVII, p. 149 ff.), 1946.   **C**

3280. —— *Tyagaraja* ('Tyagaraja Centenary Conf. Souvenir'), 1946.

3281. —— *The vina* (ibid.), 1946.

3282. —— *Two manuscripts of Tyagaraja songs* ('J. Music Acad.' XVIII, p. 133 ff.), 1947.

3283. —— *Saint Tyagaraja* ('Vedanta Kesari' XXXIV and XXXV, p. 291 ff.), Madras, 1947/'48 and 1948/'49.

3284. —— *Music in the Lingapurana* ('J. Music Acad.' XIX, p. 203 ff.), 1948.

3285. —— *Chunguru, a rare musical instrument* (ibid. XIX p. 206), 1948.

3286. —— *The Indian origin of the violin* (ibid. XIX, p. 65 ff.), 1948.

3287. —— *Nagasvara* (ibid. XX, p. 155ff.), 1949.   **AC**

3288. —— *Some non-musical works of some leading music writers* (ibid. XX, p. 152 ff.; ibid. XXI, p. 182 ff.), 1949 and 1950.   **AC**

3289. —— *Music in ancient literature* ('Music

Acad. 24th Conf. Souvenir 1950', p. 5 ff.).

3290. —— *Sri Tyagaraja* (Calcutta, 1950).

3291. —— *The music works of Samunnu Suri* ('J. Music Acad.' XXI, p. 190 ff.), 1950.   **AC**

3292. —— *Papanasam Sivan* ('Papanasam Sivan Shastiabdapurti Souvenir'), Madras, 1950, p. 7 ff.

3293. —— *Tyagaraja songs in manuscript* ('J. Music Acad.' XXII, p. 161 ff.), 1951.   **AC**

3294. —— *An Outline Literary History of Indian Music* (ibid. XXIII, p. 64 ff.), 1952.   **AC**

3295. —— *Sabdas* (ibid. XX, p. 160 ff.), 1949.   **AC**

3296. —— *Some early references to Musical Ragas and Instruments* (ibid. XXIII, p. 115 ff.), 1952.   **AC**

3297. —— *Syama Sastri* ('The Mylapore Fine Arts Club Souvenir 1952', p. 25 ff.).

3298. —— *Why is the mrdangga so called?* ('J. Music Acad.' XXIV, p. 135 ff.), 1953.   **AC**

3299. *Another rare composition of Merattur Veerabdhadrayya* (ibid., XXIV, p. 151 ff.), 1953.   **AC**

3300. —— *The so-called Svararnava* ('Suppl. to the J. Music Acad.' XXIV), 1953. **AC**

3301. —— *The Music Academy, Madras Silver Jubilee and Festival* ('Indian Review' LIV, p. 54 ff.), 1953.

3302. —— *The present state of music education in the Asiatic continent (India)* ('Music Acad. 27th Conf. Souvenir'), 1953, repr. as 'Music in Education' by Unesco, Paris, 1955, p. 72 ff.

3303. —— *Music in ancient drama* ('Art & Letters' XXVIII), 1953.   **GK**

3305. —— *Music in ancient Indian drama* ('J. of the Music Academy, Madras' XXV, p 79 ff.), Madras, 1954.   **AC**

3306. —— *The multi-faced drum* (ibid. XXV, p. 107 ff.), Madras, 1954.   **AC**

3307. —— *The music of the Hebrews: resemblances to Samaveda chant* (ibid. XXV, p. 109 ff.), Madras, 1954.   **AC**

3308. —— *Music in ancient Indian drama* ('Sangeet Natak Akadami, Bull. No. 4, p. 5 ff.), New Delhi, March 1956.   **A**

3308a. —— *Upanishad Brahma Yogin, his life, works and contribution to Carnatic music* ('The J. of the Music Academy Madras' XXVII, p. 113 ff.), Madras, 1957.   **AC**

3308b. —— *Music in the Adbhuta Ramayana* ('The J. of the Music Academy, Madras' XVI, p. 65 ff.), 1945.   **C**

3309. **Rajagopalam, N.,** *Kirtana Ratnakaram. Vol. I: Tyagaraja Pancharatna Kirtanas* (Madras, 1955).

3310. **Rajagopalam, T. K.,** *The Music of the*

177

Sama-Veda Chants ('The Journal of the Music Academy, Madras' XX, p. 144 ff.), 1949. **A**

3311. Rajamannar, P. V., *Standards in music* ('Annual Music Festival Souvenir, Madras, 1953').

3312. Rajeczky, Benjamin, *Parallelen spät-gregorianischer Verzierungen im unga-rischen Volkslied* ('Studia Memoriae Belae Bartók Sacra', p. 337 ff.), Buda-pest, 1956. **AC**

3313. —— *Typen ungarischer Klagelieder* ('Deutsches Jahrbuch für Volkskunde' III, p. 31 ff.), 1957. **AL[1]**

3314. Ramachandran, K. V., *Carnatic Ragas from a new angle – Sankarabharana* ('Journal of the Music Academy, Madras', XXI, p. 88 ff.), 1950. **AC**

3315. —— *Carnatic Ragas and the textual Tradition* (Madras, 1950). **A**

3316. —— *Apurva Ragas of Tyagaraja's Songs* (Madras, 1950). **A**

3317. —— *Music and Dance in Kalidasa* (Madras, 1950). **A**

3318. —— *Subandhu's Overtones* ('Journal of the Music Academy, Madras', XXIII, p. 3 ff.), 1953. **AC**

3319. —— *Music in Subandhu* ('Silver Jubilee Souvenir of the Marris College of Hindustani music, Lucknow, 1953').

3320. —— *The grace-notes of dance* ('J. of the Music Academy, Madras' XXV, p. 93 ff.), Madras, 1954. **AC**

3320a. —— *Gopala Nayaka* ('The J. of the Music Academy, Madras' XVII, p. 66 ff.), 1946. **C**

3321. Ramachandran, N. S., *The evolution of the theory of music in the Vijaya-negara Empire* ('S. Krishnaswami Aiy-angar Commemoration Volume', 1936).

3322. —— *The Ragas of Karnatic Music* (Univ. Madras, 1938). **K**

3322a. Raman, C. V., *On some Indian stringed instruments* ('Proc. Indian Ass. of Cult. Sciences' VII, p. 29 ff.), 1921/'22.

3323. Ramanujachariar, A., *On music and on drama* ('Annual Music Festival Souve-nir, Madras, 1953').

3324. Ramaswami Aiyar, M. S., *The question of Grāmas* ('J. of the R. Asiatic Soc.' 1936, p. 629 ff.). **D[1]GIKL[1]**

3325. Ramirez, Aracelio, *Marimba* ('Revista Municipal de Guayaquil'), Guayaquil, 1929.

3326. Ramon y Rivera, Luis Felipe, *Politri-mia y melódica independiente* ('Archivos Venezolanos de Folklore' I), Caracas, 1952.

3327. —— *Cantos de trabajo del pueblo Vene-zolano* (Fundacion Eugenio Mendoza, Caracas, 1955).

3327a. —— *La polifonia popular de Venezuela* (Buenos Aires, 1949). **L**

3328. Ramos, Arthur, *O negro Brasileiro* (Sao Paulo, 2/1940), p. 223 ff.

3329. —— *The negro in Brazil* (Washington, Ass. Publishers, 1939), p. 107 ff.

3329a. *Ramwong (folk dance) songs* (Fine Arts Department, Bangkok, 1957). **AB**

3330. Ranade, G. H., *The Indian music of the Vedic and the classical period* ('The Journal of the Music Academy, Madras' XIX, p. 71 ff.), 1948. **A**

3331. —— *Hindusthani Music, an Outline of its Physics and Aesthetics* (Sangli, 1938, 2/1951, Luzac & Co. London). **I**

3332. —— *Hindusthani music* (Poona, 1939).

3333. —— *Hindusthani music* (publ. by the Univ. of Bombay).

3334. —— *The function of music* ('Silver Jubi-lee Souvenir of the Marris College of Hindusthani music, Lucknow, Nov. 1952'), Lucknow, 1953.

3334a. Rangeley, W. H. J., *Two Nyasaland rain shrines* ('Nyasaland Journal' V, No. 2, p. 31 ff.), 1952. **M**

3335. Ranki, György, *Indokinai dallamok* (= Indochinese melodies) (in 'Emlék-könyv Kodály Zoltán 70. születésnap-jára', p. 412 ff.), Budapest, 1953. **A**

3335a. Rao, Sri B. Subba, *Raga Nidhi, a comparative study of Hindustani and Karnatik ragas* (Poona, 1957).

3335b. Rao, Bahadur N. M. Adyantayya, *The therapeutic qualities of music* ('The J. of the Music Academy, Madras' XVII, p. 58 ff.), 1946. **C**

Rao, H. P. Krishna, see Krishna Rao, H. P.

3335c. Rao, Srinivasa, *Sri Tyagaraja* ('The J. of the Music Academy, Madras' XVI, p. 92 ff.), 1945. **C**

3336. Rao, T. V. Subba, *Modernity of Tyaraga* (J. Music Acad.' XXII, p. 138 ff.), Madras, 1951. **AC**

3337. —— *Desadi and Madhyadi Talas* (ibid. XXIII, p. 92 ff.), Madras, 1952. **AC**

3338. —— *The glory of music* ('Silver Jubilee Souvenir of the Marris College of Hin-dusthani music, Lucknow, Nov. 1952'), Lucknow, 1953.

3339. —— *'Vuchamagochara' and 'Banturiti'* (J. Music Acad.' XXV, p. 53 ff.), Madras, 1954. **AC**

3340. —— *Giripai of Tyagaraja* (ibid. XXIV, p. 98 ff.), 1953. **AC**

3340a. —— *Mukhari raga* ('The J. of the Music Academy Madras' XXVII, p. 168 ff.), Madras, 1957. **A**

3340b. —— *Teaching of music* ('J. of the Music Acad. ,Madras' XXVI, p. 76 ff.), 1955. **C**

3340c. —— *The ragas of the Sangita Saramrta* ('The J. of the Music Academy, Madras' XVI, p. 45 ff.; ibid. XVII, p. 104 ff.), 1945 and 1946. **C**

3340d. —— *A Hero as a composer: Sri Tya-garaja* ('Souvenir Volume of the Tya-garaja Mahotsava' 1945).

3340e. —— *Sri Muthia Bhagavatar* ('The J. of the Music Academy, Madras' XVII, p. 134 ff.), 1946. **C**

3341. Rao, Vissa Appa, *The Vizianagaram music manuscript* (J. Music Acad.' XXIII, p. 153 ff.), Madras, 1952. **AC**

3342. —— *Arohana and Avurohana kala sva-ras of 94 Carnatic ragas taken from the Vizianagaram manuscripts* (ibid. XXIV p. 125 ff.), Madras, 1953. **AC**

3342a. —— *The science of Music* ('J. of the Music Acad., Madras' XXVI, p. 81 ff.), 1955. **C**

3342b. —— *A note on a musical reference in the Lankavatara sutra – a Mahayana text of the first century A.D.* ('The J. of the Music Academy, Madras' XVI, p. 37 ff.), 1945. **C**

3342c. —— *A note on the Raga Tala Chinta-mani, an unpublished Telugu manu-script work written nearly 250 years back* (ibid. p. 39 ff.), 1945. **C**

3342d. —— *A note on the Sringara Rasaman-jari (an unpublished Telugu manuscript, containing 100 unpublished Muvva Go-pala Pada, composed by Kshetrajna* (ibid. p. 41 ff.), 1945. **C**

3343. Rasmussen, K., *Observations on the intellectual culture of the Caribou Eski-mos* ('Rep. 5th Thule Exp.' 17–2), Copenhagen, 1930 (with music).

3344. —— *The Netsilik Eskimos* (ibid. 8, 1–2), Copenhagen, 1931 (with music).

3345. —— *Intellectual culture of the Copper Eskimos* (ibid. 9), Copenhagen, 1932 (with music).

3346. Rasmussen, P., and R. Nyerup, *Udvalg af Danske Viser fra Midten af det 16de Aarhundrede til henimod Midten af det 18de, med Melodier* (Copenhagen, 1821). **K**

3347. Rason, Marie-Robert, *Étude sur la mu-sique malgache* ('Revue de Madagascar' I, p. 41 ff.), Antananarivo, 1933. **AB**

3348. Ratanjankar, S. N., *The closed Forms of Hindusthani Music* ('The Journal of the Musical Academy, Madras' XX, p. 78 ff.), 1949. **A**

3349. —— *Tana Sangraha* (Lucknow, und.).

3350. —— *Just Intonation in Hindusthani Raga Singing* ('The Journal of the Musical Academy, Madras' XX, p. 89 ff.), 1949. **A**

3351. —— *Points of Affinity between Hin-dusthani and Carnatic Music* (ibid. XXI, p. 73 ff.), 1950. **AC**

3352. —— *Ragas in Hindusthani Music* (ibid. XXII, p. 97 ff.), 1951. **AC**

3353. —— *Raga Expression in Hindusthani Music* (ibid. XXIII, p. 56 ff.), 1952. **AC**

3354. —— *The cultural aspect of Indian music* ('Lakshya Sangeet' I), Delhi, 1954/'55.

3355. —— *Music as a career or profession* (ibid.).

3356. —— *Raga, its meaning and purpose* (ibid.).

3357. —— *The two systems of Indian music* (ibid.).

3358. Rattray, R. S., *Ashanti* (Oxford Univ. Press, 2/1955), p. 242 ff. (*The drum language*).

3359. —— *The drum language of West Africa* ('J. of the African Soc.' XXII, p. 226 ff., 302 ff.), 1923. **J**

3360. —— *What the African believes, as re-vealed by the talking drums* ('West Afri-can Review' VI, p. 12 ff.), Liverpool, 1935.

3361. Raudkats, A., *Estnische Volkstänze und Kinderspiele* (Tartu, 1926/'27).

3362. Raven-Hart, Major R., *Musical accul-turation in Tonga* ('Oceania' XXVI, p. 110 ff.), 1955. **ABD[1]GJ**

3362a. —— *A village in the Yasawas (Fiji)* ('J. of the Polynesian Soc.' LV, p. 95 ff. (136 ff.)), June 1956. **BGL[2]**

3363. Read, F. W., *A new interpretation of the Phaestos disk: the oldest music in the world?* ('The Quarterly Statement, a journal of Palestine Research and Discovery' Jan. 1921, p. 29 ff.).

3364. Rebel, Juanita de, *Van Zamba tot Sam-ba, een zwerftocht door de Zuid-Ameri-kaanse volksmuziek en volksdansen* (Leyden, 1955). **A**

3365. *Receuil des traveaux du Congrès de mu-sique arabe, tenu au Caire en 1932* (Cairo, 1934).

3366. Reche, Otto, *Zur Ethnographie des ab-flusslosen Gebietes Deutsch-Ostafrikas* (Hamburg, 1914). **B**

3366a. Redinha, J., *Campanha etnográfica ao Tchiboc (Alto-Tchicupa)* ('Publicaçoes culturais, Museu do Dundo' 1953, p. 11 ff.). **JM**

3367. Regelsperger, Gustave, *Les instruments de musique dans le pays du Chari-Tchad* ('La Nature' XXXVII, p. 19 ff.), Paris, 1908. **L[1]**

3367a. Reignighaus, Fr. W., *Die Trommel-und Pfeifsprache* ('Archiv f. Völkerk.' V, p. 187 ff.), Vienna, 1950.

3368. Reinach, Théodore, *La musique Grecque* (Paris, 1926). **AK**

3369. Reiner, M., *The Music Rule* ('Expe-rientia' V, p. 441 ff.), Basel, Oct. 1949. **AD[1]GHL[1]**

3370. Reinhard, Kurt, *Die Verwendung der Shantrommeln* ('Ethnologischer Anzei-ger' IV, p. 95 ff.), Stuttgart, 1937. **GL[2]**

3371. —— *Die Musik Birmas* (Wurzburg-Aumühle, 1939). **ABCGIK**

179

3372. —— Die Musik exotischer Völker (Berlin, 1951.) ACJL
3373. —— Bedeutung, Wesen und Erforschungsmöglichkeiten primitiver Musik ('Sociologus' N.S. I, p. 81 ff.), 1951. D¹GHKL¹L³L³
3374. —— Exotismen in der abendländischen Gegenwartsmusik ('Melos' XVIII, p. 129 ff.), 1951. KL
3375. —— Zur Frage der Klimpernmessung ('Die Musikforschung' V, p. 373 ff.), 1952. ACEIKLL¹
3376. —— Das Berliner Phonogramm-Archiv ('Die Musikforschung' VI, p. 46 ff.), 1953. ACEIKLL¹
3377. —— Tonmessungen an fünf ostafrikanischen Klimpern ('Die Musikforschung' IV, p. 366 ff.), 1951. ACEIKLL¹
3378. —— Die Musik des mexikanischen Fliegerspiels ('Z. f. Ethnologie' LXXIX p. 59 ff.), 1954. ABD¹GHJLL¹L²M
3379. —— Angewandte Musikethnologie ('Z. f. Musik' 1954, p. 222 ff.). L
3380. —— Konsonanz und Dissonanz in japanischer Sicht ('Das Musikleben' VII, p. 171 ff.), 1954. CL
3381. —— Juwelenstrom (chinesisches Schattenspiel) ('Musikblätter' VIII, p. 195 ff.), 1954.
3382. —— Die Musik der Lolo ('Baessler Archiv' N.S. Fasc. 3), 1955. ACD¹GKL²
3383. —— Zur Quellensituation der Musikethnologie in Deutschland ('Die Musikforschung' IX, p. 196 ff.), 1956. ACEFIKLL¹
*3384. —— Chinesische Musik (Eisenach/ Kassel, 1956). ACJL
3385. —— Zustand und Wandel des bäuerlichen Musiklebens in der türkischen Provinz Adana ('Sociologus' N.S. VI, p. 68 ff.), Berlin, 1956. AD¹GHKL¹L³
3386. —— Acht Lieder sinisierter Lolo ('Baessler Archiv' N.S. IV, p. 105 ff.), 1956. ABGKL²
3387. —— Types of Turkmenian songs in Turkey ('J. of the Intern. Folk Music Council' IX, p. 49 ff.), 1957. ACJKL
3388. —— Review of Fritz Kornfeld, 'Die tonale Struktur Chinesischer Musik' ('Ethnomusicology' Newsletter No. 11, p. 34 ff.), Sept. 1957. ACGJL
3388a. —— On the problem of pre-pentatonic scales: particularly the third-second nucleus ('J. of the Intern. Folk Music Council' X, p. 15 ff.), 1958. ACIJKL
3388b. —— Tanzlieder der Turkmenen in der Süd-Türkei ('Kongressbericht Ges. f. Musikforschung, Hamburg 1956', p. 189 ff.). CEL
*3389. Reinholm, A., Finnish Folk Music ('Grove's Dictionary' 5th ed. vol. III, p. 237 ff.), 1954. ACFH¹K
*3390. Reisner, Robert George, The literature

of Jazz. A preliminary bibliography (New York, The N. Y. Public Library, 1954).
3391. Relação dos discos gravados no estado do Goiás (Publicações do Centro de pesquisas folklóricas, Escola nacional de música, Universidade do Brasil, No. 2), Rio de Janeiro, 1942. A
3392. Relação dos discos gravados no estado do Ceará (ibid. No. 3), Rio de Janeiro, 1943. A
3393. Relação dos discos gravados no estado do Minas Gerais (ibid. No. 4), Rio de Janeiro, 1956. A
3393a. Renou, L., Sanskrit et culture, p. 34 ff.: Récitation du Véda (Paris, 1950).
*3393b. Rensch, R., The harp. A history from the earliest times in Egypt. Its introduction and development in Europe. With details of instruments and advanced technique, bibliography and extensive lists of harp music (New York, 1950).
3393c. Requile, Ch., Quand l'Afrique chante et danse ('Messager de St. Joseph' XXII, p. 125 ff.), 1952. M
3394. Révész, Géza, Der Ursprung der Musik ('Intern. Archiv f. Ethnogr.' XL, p. 65 ff.), 1941. ABD¹GKL¹L²M
3395. —— Einführung in die Musikpsychologie (Bern, 1946). ACH
3396. Revue des traditions populaires I–VI (Paris, 1886/'91). C
3397. Rexroth, Kenneth, American Indian songs: the United States Bureau of Ethnology Collection ('Perspectives USA' XVI, p. 197 ff.), summer 1956.
3398. Rhesa, L., Betrachtung über die lithauischen Volkslieder (Kaunas, 1935).
3399. Rhodes, Willard, Acculturation in North American Indian Music ('Selected Papers of the XXIXth Intern. Congress of Americanists', p. 127 ff.), Chicago, 1952. A
*3400. —— North American Indian Music: a Bibliographical Survey of Anthropological Theory ('Notes' X, p. 33 ff.), 1952. DKL
3401. —— On the subject of Ethno-musicology ('Ethno-musicology' Newsletter No. 7, p. 1 ff.), April 1956. AGL
3402. —— Towards a definition of Ethnomusicology ('Amer. Anthropologist' LVIII, p. 457 ff.), June 1956. ABGL²M
3403. —— American Indian music ('Tomorrow' IV, p. 97 ff.), 1956.
3404. —— Music of the American Indian. Northwest (Puget Sound) (notes for an album of music of the Lummi, Makah, Quinault, Skokomish and Swinomish), Washington, Library of Congress, undated. A
3405. —— Music of the American Indian Kiowa (Washington, Library of Congress, undated). A

3405a. —— *A study of musical diffusion based on the wandering of the opening peyote song* ('J. of the Intern. Folk Music Council' X, p. 42 ff.), 1958. **ACIJKL**

3406. **Ribeiro, Darcy,** *Music of the American Indian* (10 vols.), Washington, Library of Congress, 1954-'55.

3407. —— *Noticia dos Ofaié-Chavante* ('Revista do Museu Paulista', N.S. V, p. 105 ff.), Sao Paulo, 1951. **GL²**

3408. **Ribera y Tarago, J.,** *Music in Ancient Arabia and Spain* (New York, 1950). **GHI**

3409. —— *La musica de las cantigas* (Madrid, 1922). English transl. by E. Hague and M. Leffingwell, as *Music in Ancient Arabia and Spain* (1927). **GI**

3410. —— *Historia de la musica arabe medieval y su influencia en la Española* (Madrid, 1927). **G**

3411. **Ricard, P.,** *Essai d'action sur la musique et le théâtre populaire marocain* (? Rabat, 1936).

3412. —— *La rénovation des arts musicaux au Maroc* ('Revue d'Afrique', 1936).

3413. —— *Le conservatoire de musique marocaine à Rabat* ('France-Outre-Mer' 1932).

3414. **Ricard, R.,** *A propos du langage sifflé des Canaris* ('Hespéris', 1932). **D¹GKL²**

3415. **Richard, Mrs. Timothy,** *Paper on Chinese Music* (Shanghai, 1899,²/1907). **I**

3416. **Ridgeway,** *Origin of the guitar and fiddle* ('Man' 1908, No. 7). **BD¹GJKL²M**

3417. **Riedel, J. G. F.,** *De sluik- en kroesharige rassen tusschen Selebes en Papua* (1886), p. 241 ff. **AB**

3418. **Riegler Dinu, Emil,** *Studien über das rumänische Volkslied* (1927).

3419. —— *La Hora, la Maquam et la chanson populaire de l'Orient européen* ('Art populaire' II, p. 140 ff.), Paris, 1931. **A**

3420. —— *Das rumänische Volkslied* (Berlin, 1942).

3420a. **Riemann, Hugo,** *Folkloristische Tonalitätsstudien* (Leipzig, 1916). **L**

3421. **Riemann, Ludwig,** *Über eigentümliche bei Natur- und orientalischen Kulturvölkern vorkommende Tonreihen und ihre Beziehungen zu den Gesetzen der Harmonie* (Essen, 1899).

3422. **Rihtman, Cvjetko,** *Polyphonic Forms in Bosnian and Hercegovinian Folkmusic* ('Bilten Inst. za proučavanje folklora u Sarajevo' I, p. 7 ff.), Sarajevo, 1951. **AK**

3423. —— *Les formes polyphoniques dans la musique populaire de Bosnie et d'Herzégovine* ('Journal of the Intern. Folk Music Council' IV, p. 30 ff.), 1952. **ACJKL**

*3424. —— *Yugoslav Folk Music* ('Grove's Dictionary' 5th ed. vol. III, p. 412 ff.), 1954. **ACFH¹K**

*3424a. —— *Yugoslawien. II. Die Volksmusik. 5. Bosnien und Herzegowina* ('Die Musik in Geschichte u. Gegenwart' VII, col. 371 ff.), 1958. **ACDEFGH¹KL**

3425. **Rio, João do,** *Fados, Canções e dunsas de Portugal* (Paris, 1909).

3425a. **Risari, P. M.,** *Musique congolaise de demain* ('Voix du Congolais' IX, p. 725 ff.), 1953. **M**

3426. **Ritter, Helmuth,** *Der Reigen der tanzenden Derwische* ('Z. f. vergl. Musikw.' I, p. 28 ff.), 1933. **ACK**

3427. —— *Mesopotamische Studien. II. Vierzig arabische Volkslieder* ('Der Islam' 1920, p. 120 ff.). **D¹GHKL¹**

3428. —— *Mesopotamische Studien. III. Arabische Kriegspoesie aus Mesopotamien und den Irak* (ibid. 1923, p. 268 ff.). **D¹GHKL¹**

3428a. **Riverson, I. D.,** *The growth of music in the Gold Coast* ('Transactions of the Gold Coast and Togoland Historical Soc.' I, part IV, p. 121 ff.), 1955. **M**

3429. **Robb, John Donald,** *Hispanic folk songs of New Mexico* (Albuquerque, 1954).

3430. **Roberts, Helen Heffron,** *Some songs of the Puget Sound Salish* (in collab. with H. K. Haeberlin) ('Journal of Amer. Folklore' XXXI), 1918. **GK**

3431. —— *Chakwena Songs of Zuñi and Laguna* (ibid. XXXVI), 1923. **GKL²**

3432. —— *Folksgames of Jamaica,* collected by Martha Warren Beckwith, with music recorded by Helen H. Roberts (Poughkeepsie, New York, Vassar College, 1922).

3433. —— *Christmas mumming in Jamaica* by Martha Warren Beckwith, with music recorded by Helen H. Roberts (Poughkeepsie, New York, Vassar College, 1923).

3434. —— *Some drums and drum rhythms in Jamaica* ('Natural History' XXIV, p. 241 ff.), 1924. **G**

3435. —— *Jamaica Anansi stories* by Martha Warren Beckwith, with music recorded in the field by Helen Roberts (publ. XVII of the Amer. Folklore Soc.), New York, 1924. **BH**

3436. —— *Songs of the Copper Eskimo* ('Report of the Canadian Arctic Exped. 1913/'18' XIV) (in collab. with D. Jenness), Ottawa, 1925. **I**

3437. —— *Ancient Hawaiian Music* ('Bull. No. 29 of the Ber. P. Bishop Mus.'), Honolulu, 1925.

3438. —— *A study of folk song variants based on field work in Jamaica* ('J. of the Amer. Folklore' XXXVIII, p. 149 ff.), 1925. **GKL²**

3439. —— *Possible survivals of African song*

in Jamaica ('Musical Quarterly' XII), 1926. **AD**

3440. —— *Variation in melodic renditions as an indicator of emotion* ('Psychological Review' XXXIV), 1927. **AD¹HL¹**

3441. —— *New Phases in the Study of Primitive Music* ('Amer. Anthrop.' N.S. XXIV, p. 144 ff.), 1928. **GL²**

3442. —— *Jamaica Folklore*, collected by Martha Warren Beckwith, with music recorded by Helen H. Roberts (New York, 1928). **I**

3443. —— *How the Hawaiian instrument, the Ukulele, received its name* ('Journal of the Polynesian Soc.' XL, p. 175 ff.), 1931. **BGL²**

3444. —— *Suggestions to field workers in collecting folk music and data about instruments* ('Journal of the Polynesian Soc.' XL, p. 103 ff.), 1931. **BGL²**

3445. —— *Melodic composition and scale foundations in primitive music* ('Amer. Anthrop.' N.S. XXXIV, p. 79 ff.), 1932. **AGJL²**

3446. —— *Form in Primitive Music* (New York, 1933). **ACI**

3447. —— *Modern Tahitian popular songs or ute, sung by Armstrong Sperry* (Inst. of Human Relations, Yale Univ., Publ. in Anthrop., 1932).

3448. —— *The pattern phenomenon in primitive music* ('Z. f. vergl. Musikw.' I, p. 49 ff.), 1933. **ACK**

3449. —— *Musical areas in aboriginal North America* ('Yale Univ., Publ. in Anthrop.' XII), 1936. **AHIJL**

3450. —— *The Viewpoint of Comparative Musicology* ('Proc. Music Teachers Nat. Ass.' XXXI, p. 233 ff.), 1936.

3451. —— and Morris Swadesh, *The Songs of the Nootka Indians of Western Vancouver Island* ('Transactions of the American Philosophical Soc.', Philadelphia, 1955). **AD¹FI**

3451a. —— *Primitive music* ('Encycl. of Social Sciences').

3451b. —— *Variation in melodic renditions as an indicator of emotion* ('Psychol. Review' XXXIV), 1927. **D¹HL¹**

3451c. —— *Indian music of the Southwest* ('Natural History' XXVII, p. 257 ff.), 1927. **B**

3452. Robertson, J. W. R., *Further notes on the Ingessana tribe* ('Sudan Notes and Records' XVII, Part. I, p. 118 ff.), 1934. **L²**

3453. Robins, R. H., and Norma McLeod, *Five Yurok Songs: a musical and textual analysis* ('Bull. of the School of Oriental and African Studies, Univ. of London' XVIII, p. 592 ff.), 1956. **BM**

3453a. —— and —— *A Yurok song without words* ('Bull. of the School of Oriental and African Studies' XX, p. 501 ff.), London, 1957. **BM**

3454. Robinson, Arthur E., *Sudan drums* ('Man' XXXII, p. 259 ff.), 1932. **ABD¹GJKL¹L²M**

3455. Robinson, Kenneth, *Chinesische Musik* ('Die Musik in Geschichte und Gegenwart' II, col. 1195 ff.), 1952. **ACDEFGHKL**

3456. Robson, James, *Ancient Arabian musical instruments as described by Al-Mufaddul ibn Salama (9th century)* (including notes on the instruments by H. G. Farmer), Glasgow, 1938. **I**

3457. —— *Tracts on listening to music* (London, 1938).

3458. Roche, Simone, *Collection Musée de l'Homme (Paris)*, Catalogue prepared by the Intern. Commission on Folk Arts and Folklore (C.I.A.P.), Unesco, Paris, 1952. **C**

3458a. Roda, Cecilio de, *Les instruments de musique en Espagne au XIIIe siècle* ('Report of the 4th Congress of the Intern. Musical Soc.', p. 322 ff.), London, 1911. **CF**

3459. Rodan-Kahane, Mariana, *Cîntece si jocuri de nuntă din tinutul Pădurenilor, regiunea Hunedoara* (i.e. Wedding songs and dances of the Padureni district, Hunedoara region) ('Revista de Folclore' I, No. 1–2, p. 172 ff.), Bucarest, 1956. **A**

3460. Rodger, George, *Ceremony in Bunyoro* ('Natural History' LXIV, No. 4, p. 184 ff.), 1955. **B**

3461. Rodrigues, J. Barbosa, *O canto e la dança selvicola* ('Revista Brazileira' III, vol. IX, p. 32 ff.), Rio de Janeiro, 1881.

3462. Rodriguez Valle, Flausino, *Elementos de folklore musical brasileiro* ('Archivo Municipal' LVII, p. 83 ff.), Sao Paulo, 1936.

3463. Rohrer, Ernst Friedrich, *Ein Tanztrommel der Goldküste* ('Jahrbuch des Bernischen Historischen Museums' XXV, p. 147 ff.), 1946. **G**

3464. Rojo, Casiano, and Germán Prado, *El canto mozarabe* (Barcelona, 1929). **G**

3465. Roman, Marcelino M., *América criolla. Canciones y poemas sobre motivos americanos* (Panamá, 1953).

3466. Romansky, L., *Die einfachen Koledo-Refrains der bulgarischen Weihnachtslieder* (Sofia, 1942).

3467. Romero, Fernando, *Instrumentos musicales de la Costa Zamba* ('Turismo' XIV, p. 137 ff.), Lima, 1939.

3468. Romero, Jesus, *Música precortesiana* ('Anales del Inst. Nacional de Antropología e Historia' II), Mexico, 1947. **KL²**

3469. **Romeu Figueras, José**, *El canto dia-logudo en la canción popular. Los can-tares a desafío* ('Anuario musical' III, p. 133 ff.), 1948. **C**

3470. —— *El cantar paralelístico en Cataluña; sus relaciones con el de Galicia y Portu-gal y el de Castilla* (ibid. IX, p. 3 ff.), 1954. **C**

3471. **Romualdez, Norberto**, *Filipino Mu-sical Instruments and Airs of long ago* ('Encycl. of the Philippines' IV, p. 86 ff.), Manilla, 1935.

3472. **Rookmaker, H. R.**, *Neger-volksmuziek* ('Gramofoon voor kenner en liefhebber', April 1956, p. 22 ff.), ed. Charles, Am-sterdam. **A**

3473. **Roo van Alderwerelt, J. de**, *Eenige me-dedeelingen over Soemba* ('Tijdschr. v. h. Kon. Bat. Gen.' XXXIII, p. 565 ff.), 1890 (p. 576 and 586). **ABD¹GH**

3474. **Roscoe, John**, *The Baganda* (Macmil-lan, 1911), p. 25 ff.

3475. **Rose, Algernon S.**, *African primitive instruments* ('Proc. Music Teachers' National Association' XXX, p. 91 ff.), 1904.

3476. —— *South African 'clickers'* ('Z. d. Intern. Musikges.' VI), 1904/'05. **CF**

3477. **Rosenthal, Ethel**, *Indian music and its instruments* (London, 1928). **C**

3478. —— *The story of Indian music and its instruments* (London, 1929). **CIJK**

3479. —— *Tyagaraja: a great South Indian Composer* ('Musical Quarterly' XVII, p. 14 ff.), 1931. **C**

3480. **Rosner, Victor**, *Tribal drums* ('The March of India' VII, No. 9, p. 16 ff.), July 1955. **B**

3480a. **Rosovsky, Solomon**, *The cantillation of the Bible: the five books of Moses* (New York, 1957).

3480b. **Ross, Uilleam**, *Pipe Music* (new edi-tion), 1875. **A**

3481. **Rossat, Arthur**, *Les chansons populaires de la Suisse romande* I. *Les chansons traditionelles* (Basel, 1917).

3483. —— and E. Piguet, *Les chansons popu-laires de la Suisse romande.* II, I. *Chan-sons des fêtes de l'année* (Basel, 1930).

3484. —— and —— *Les chansons populaires de la Suisse romande.* II, 2. *Vies et mi-racles de Jésus, de la Vierge et des Saints, Complaintes et Chansons de couvent* (Basel, 1931).

3485. **Roth, Henry Ling**, *The natives of Sara-wak and British North Borneo* (London, 1896), Chapter XXVI, p. 257 ff. **BJ**

3486. —— *The aborigines of Tasmania* (Hali-fax, 1899), p. 134 ff.: *Music.* **J**

3487. **Roth, Walter Edmund**, *An introductory study of the arts, crafts and customs of the Guyana Indians* ('Annual Report of the Bur. of Amer. Ethnology' No. 38

(1916–'17), p. 25 ff.) (p. 450 ff.: *Musi-cal and other sound instruments*), Washington D.C., 1924. **ABGKL²**

3488. **Rothmüller, A. M.**, *The music of the Jews. An historical appreciation* (Lon-don, 1953).

3489. **Rouanet, Jules**, *La chanson populaire arabe en Algérie* ('Revue Musicale' V, p. 161 ff.), 1905. **K**

3490. —— *Esquisse pour une histoire de la musique arabe en Algérie* ('Mercure Musicale' I, p. 553 ff.; II, p. 128 ff., 208 ff.), 1905/'06. **A**

3491. —— *La musique arabe* (in Lavignac, 'Hist. de la Mus.' vol. V, p. 2676 ff.), 1922. **ACDEFHJ**

3492. —— *La musique arabe dans le Maghreb* (in Lavignac, 'Hist. de la Musique' V, p. 2813 ff.), 1922. **ACDEFHJ**

3493. —— *Les visages de la musique musul-mane* ('Revue musicale' V, No. 1), 1st Nov. 1923. **KL**

3494. —— *La suite dans la musique musulmane* ('Revue musicale' VIII), 1927. **CDGHKL**

3495. —— and E. N. Yafil, *Répertoire de mu-sique arabe et maure* (1904).

3495a. **Rouche, J.**, *Culte des génies chez les Sonray* ('J. de la Soc. des Africanistes' XV, p. 15 ff.), 1945. **GL²M**

3495b. —— *La danse* ('Présence Africaine' 1950, Nos. 8/9, p. 219 ff.). **M**

3496. **Rouffaer, G. P.**, *Keteltrommen (bron-zen)* ('Encycl. v. Ned.-Indië' 2nd ed., vol. II, p. 305 ff.), 1917. **B**

3497. **Rouger, G.**, *Chansons berbères* ('France-Maroc' 1920).

3498. **Rouget, Gilbert**, *Anthologie de musique centro-africaine* ('Présence africaine' 1949, No. 7, p. 324 ff.).

3499. —— *A propos de la forme dans les musi-ques de tradition orale* ('Les Colloques de Wégimont' I, p. 132 ff.), Brussels, 1956. **ACL**

3500. —— *Chroniques musicales. Nouvelles des Griots* ('Présence Africaine' N.S. Nos. 1-2, p. 153 ff.), April/July 1955. **B**

3501. —— *La musique (du Sénégal, de Casa-mance et de Guinée)* ('Présence Afri-caine' N.S. No. 5, p. 108 ff.), Dec. 1955/Jan. 1956. **B**

3502. —— *La musique à Madagascar* (in: J. Faublée, 'Ethnographie de Madagas-car', Paris, 195.), p. 85 ff. **JM**

3502a. —— *Note sur les travaux d'ethnogra-phie musicale de la mission Ogooué-Congo* ('Proc. Conferencia Internacio-nal' V, p. 193 ff.), Bissau, 1947, Lisboa, 1952. **M**

3502b. —— *Les travaux d'ethnographie musi-cale de la mission Ogooué-Congo* ('Proc. of the 'Séances de l'Institut Français d'Anthropol.', XLIII, 3rd fasc., p. 4 ff.), 1947/'49. **M**

3502c. —— *La musique* ('Présence Africaine' 1955, p. 71 ff.). **BM**
3503. Roumain, Jacques, *Le sacrifice du tambour Assoto* (Port-au-Prince, 1943).
3503a. Rousseau, M., *La musique et la danse en Afrique Occidentale* ('Musée Vivant' XII, Nos. 36–37, p. 21 ff.), 1948. **M**
3504. Routledge, W. S. and K., *With a prehistoric people: the Akikuyu of British East Africa* (London, 1910), p. 111 ff.: *Music*. **J**
3505. Roy, Carmen, *La littérature orale en Gaspésie. Les chansons* (Bull. No. 134 du Musée National du Canada', p. 235 ff.), 1955.
3506. Roy, Dilip Kumar, *Music* ('The March of India' VII No. 3, p. 55 ff.), 1955. **B**
3507. Roy, Hemendralal, *Problems of Hindostani Music* (Calcutta/London, 1937). **A**
3508. Roy, Robindralal, *Hindusthani Ragas* ('Musical Quarterly' XX, p. 320 ff.), 1934. **CD**
3509. —— *North Indian Ragas and Melas* ('The Journal of the Music Academy, Madras' XIII, p. 1 ff., XIV, p. 51 ff.), 1942–'43.
3510. —— *Philosophy of Music: number in sensation, feeling, and thought* ('The Journal of the Music Academy, Madras' XXII, p. 106 ff., XXIII, p. 75 ff., XXIV, p. 104 ff., XXV, p. 112 ff., XXVI, p. 113 ff.), 1951–'55. **AC**
3511. —— *On Transformation of Sthayas by Alteration of Sruti and Consequent Importance of 32 Melakartas as Specially Suited to Musical Composition* (ibid. XXIV, p. 70 ff.), 1953. **AC**
3511a. Roy, Trina, *Outlines of Tagore's music* ('Festschrift-Schmidt-Görg' p. 235 ff.), Bonn, 1957. **E**
3512. Rubec, A., *Collection of Ukraine folk songs* (Moscow, 1872). **K**
3513. Rubin, R., *Nineteenth-century yiddish love songs of East Europe* ('J. of the Intern. Folk Music Council' VII, p. 44 ff.), 1955. **ACJKL**
3514. Rudyar, D., *The rebirth of Indian music* (Adyar, 1928). **I**
3515. Rue, Jan la, *Native Music on Okinawa* ('The Musical Quarterly' XXXII, p. 157 ff.), 1946. **CDFK**
3516. —— *The Okinawan notation system* ('Journal of the American Musicol. Soc.' IV, p. 27 ff.), 1951. **ACFKL**
3517. Ruehl S.V.D., Theodor, *Die missionarische Akkomodation im gottesdienstlichen Volksgesang* ('Z. f. Missionswissenschaft' XVII, p. 113 ff.), 1927. **KL[1]**
3518. Ruelle, C. E., *Le Chant gnosticomagique des sept voyelles grecques* ('Proc.

Intern. Congress of Musicol.', Paris, 1914). **C**
3519. Rullins, Vera, *Latvians and their folklore* ('The Folkdancer' III, p. 88 ff.), Sept./Oct. 1956. **A**
3520. Runge, Paul, *Die Notation des Somanatha* ('Monatshefte f. Musikgeschichte' XXXVI, p. 56 ff.), 1904. **CKL**
3521. Rusič, Branislav, *Prilepski guslar Apostol (Prilozi proučavanju narodne poezije)* ('Veroeffentl. d. deutschen wissensch. Inst. in Belgrad', Sonderausg. No. 2), 1940.
3522. Ryckmans, A., *Etude sur les signaux de 'mondo' (tambour-téléphone) chez les Bayaka et Bankanu du territoire de Popokabaka* ('Zaire' X, p. 493 ff.), May, 1956. **D[1]GKL[1]L[2]M**
3523. Rycroft, David R., *Tribal style and free expression* ('African Music' I, No. 1, p. 16 ff.), 1954. **ACJLM**
3523a. —— *Zulu male traditional singing* ('African Music' I No. 4, p. 33 ff.), 1957. **ACJLM**
3524. Rydén, Stig, *Notes on some archaeological whistling arrowheads from Peru* ('Comp. ethnogr. studies' IX), Göteborg, 1930.
3525. Sachau, Eduard, *Arabische Volkslieder aus Mesopotamien* ('Abhandl. d. kais. Akad. d. Wiss. zu Berlin', Phil.-hist. Kl., 1899), Berlin, 1899.
3526. Sachs, Curt [1]), *Ueber eine bosnische Doppelflöte* ('Sammelb. der Intern. Musikges.' IX, p. 313 ff.), 1907–'08. **CDFH[1]L**
3527. —— *Lituus und Karnyx* ('Festschrift-R. von Liliencron'), 1910. **C**
*3528. —— *Reallexikon der Musikinstrumente* (Berlin, 1913). **ACFGIKLL[2]**
3528a. —— *Die Hornbostel-Sachs'sche Klassifikation der Musikinstrumente* ('Die Naturwissenschaften' II, p. 1056 ff.), 1914.
3529. —— *Die Musikinstrumente* (Breslau, Jedermann's Bücherei, 1923). **AC**
3530. —— *Die litauischen Instrumente* ('Intern. Archiv f. Ethnogr.' XXIII, p. 1 ff.), 1915. **ABCD[1]GKL[2]M**
3531. —— *Die Musikinstrumente Indiens und Indonesiens* (Berlin, 1915; 2/1923). **ABCFGIKL[Q]**
3532. —— *Die Maultrommel* ('Z. f. Ethnologie' XLIX, p. 185 ff.), 1917. **ABCD[1]GHKL[1]L[2]M**
3533. —— *Die Musikinstrumente Birmas und Assams* (München, 1917). **ADIK**
3534. —— *Die Namen der altägyptischen Musikinstrumente* ('Z. f. Musikw.' I', p. 205 ff.), 1917–'18. **CDH[1]KL**

---

[1]) For reviews by this author of ethnomusicological publications see 1575a.

3535. ——— *Die Streichbogenfrage* ('Archiv f. Musikw.' I, p. 3 ff.), 1918. **CDFKLL¹**

3536. ——— *Die altägyptische Namen der Harfe* ('Festschrift-Hermann Kretschmar), Leipzig 1918. **C**

3537. ——— Review of W. Schubart, 'Ein griechischer Papyrus mit Noten' ('Z. f. Musikw.' I, p. 75), 1918. **CDH¹KL**

3538. ——— *Kunstgeschichtliche Wege zur Musikwissenschaft* ('Archiv f. Musikw.' I, p. 451 ff.), 1919. **CDFKLL¹**

3539. ——— *Handbuch der Musikinstrumentenkunde* (Leipzig, 1920). **ACEFIKL²**

3540. ——— *Altägyptische Musikinstrumente* ('Der alte Orient' XXI), 1920. **ACD¹IHK**

3541. ——— *Die Tonkunst der alten Aegypter* ('Archiv f. Musikw.' II), 1920. **CDFKLL¹**

3542. ——— *Die Musikinstrumente des alten Aegyptens* (Berlin, 1921). **CIK**

3543. ——— *Der Ursprung der Saiteninstrumente* ('Pater Wilhelm Schmidt-Festschrift', p. 629 ff.), 1928. **JL³**

3544. ——— *Musik des Altertums* (Leipzig, 1924). **AC**

3545. ——— *Die griechische Instrumentalnotenschrift* ('Z. f. Musikw.' VI, p. 289 ff.), 1924. **CDH¹KL**

3546. ——— *Die Entzifferung einer babylonischen Notenschrift* ('Sitzungsber. der Preuss. Akad. d. Wiss.' XVIII, p. 120 ff.), 1924.

3546a. ——— *Altägyptische Musik* ('Faust' III, fasc. 2/3, p. 36 ff.), 1924/'25.

3547. ——— *Die griechische Gesangsnotenschrift* ('Z. f. Musikw.' VII, p. 1 ff.), 1925. **CDH¹KL**

3548. ——— *Ein babylonischer Hymnus* ('Archiv f. Musikw.' VII, p. 1 ff.), 1925. **CDFH¹KLL¹**

3549. ——— *Anfänge der Musik* ('Bull. de l'Union Musicologique' VI, p. 136 ff.), 1926. **ACD¹FGHL**

3549a. ——— *Heidenlärm und Kinderspiel* ('Velhagen u. Klasings Monatshefte' XLI, vol. I, p. 93 ff.), 1926/'27.

3550. ——— *Die Musik der Antike* (in Ernst Bücken, 'Handbuch der Musikwissenschaft'), Berlin, 1929. **CDEFH¹KLL³**

3551. ——— *Zweiklänge im Altertum* ('Festschrift-Johannes Wolf'), Berlin, 1929.

3552. ——— *Der Gamelan* ('50th Jahresbericht der Stl. Akad. Hochschule f. Musik in Berlin', p. 230 ff.), 1929. **A**

*3553. ——— *Geist und Werden der Musikinstrumente* (Berlin, 1929). **ACEFIJKL**

3554. ——— *Vergleichende Musikwissenschaft in ihren Grundzügen* (Leipzig, 1930). **AFL** (Japanese transl. by F. Yosio Nomura, Tokyo, 1953).

3555. ——— *Antike* (in Guido Adler, *Handbuch der Musikgeschichte* I), 1924, 2/1930. **ACEFK**

3556. ——— *A travers un musée d'instruments* ('La Revue musicale' XIII, p. 212 ff.), 1932. **ACDFGHKL**

3557. ——— *Kongress der arabischen Musik zu Kairo 1932* ('Z. f. Musikw.' XIV, p. 448 ff.), Leipzig, 1932. **CDEFH¹KL**

3557a. ——— A series of articles in the 'Reallexikon der Vorgeschichte' (Berlin, 1924/'32): vol. I. *Becken* (p. 376); vol. III. *Flöte* (p. 390); vol. V. *Harfe B. Vorderasien* (p. 125), *Horn* (p. 392); vol. VII. *Leier* (p. 281); vol. IX. *Notenschrift* (p. 123); vol. XI. *Kassel* (p. 23), *Sackpfeife* (p. 178); vol. XIII. *Trommel. B. Naher Orient* (p. 448), *Trompete B. Naher Orient* (p. 450). **D¹GHK**

3558. ——— *Eine aegyptische Winkelharfe* ('Z. f. ägypt. Sprache und Altertumskunde' LXIX, p. 68 ff.), 1933. **D¹GHK**

3559. ——— *Prolegomena zu einer Geschichte der Instrumentalmusik* ('Z. f. vergl. Musikw.' I), 1933. **ACK**

*3560. ——— *Eine Weltgeschichte des Tanzes* (Berlin, 1933). **BCIL**

3560a. ——— *Die Marokkaner* ('Z. f. vergl. Musikw.' I, p. 17 ff.), 1933. **ACK**

3561. ——— *Les instruments de musique de Madagascar* (Paris, 1938). **ACGIJKL³**

3562. ——— *Towards a prehistory of occidental music* ('Papers of the Amer. Musicol. Soc.' 1937, p. 91 ff., and 'The Musical Quarterly' XXIV, p. 147 ff.), 1938. **CDF**

3563. ——— *World History of the Dance* (transl. by Bessie Schönberg), London, 1938. **CIK**

3563a. ——— *Music in the Bible* ('The universal Jewish Encyclopedia' vol. VIII, p. 46 ff.), New York, 1939 ff. **D¹** (ed. 1901/'06) **G** (id.) **H** (id.) **K**

*3564. ——— *The History of Musical Instruments* (New York, 1940). **ACEFIJKL**

3565. ——— *Music History – the two sides of the coin* ('Papers of the Amer. Musicol. Soc.' 1940), p. 137 ff.

3566. ——— *The Road to Major* ('The Musical Quarterly' XXIX), 1943. **CH¹**

3567. ——— *The Rise of Music in the Ancient World East and West* (New York, 1943). **ACGIJK**

3568. ——— *The Mystery of the Babylonian Notation* ('The Musical Quarterly' XXVII, p. 62 ff.), (1941) and 'Papers of the Intern. Congress of Musicology, New York 1939', p. 161 ff.), New York, 1944. **AC**

3569. ——— *The Orient and Western Music* (in A. E. Christy, 'The Asian Legacy and American Life'), p. 56 ff. (New York, 1945).

3570. ——— *The commonwealth of art. Style in the fine arts, music and dance* (New York, 1946). **A**

3570a. ——— *Das Geheimnis der babylonischen*

185

Notenschrift ('Stimmen' I, p. 236 ff.), 1947/'48. **L[1]**

3571. —— *Some remarks about old notation* ('Musical Quarterly' XXIV, p. 65 ff.), 1948. **CDFKL[1]**

3572. —— *A short history of world music* (London, 1949). **I**

3573. —— *The commonwealth of art* (Annual Louis C. Elson Memorial Lecture, delivered April 25th, 1949), Washington D.C., 1950. **ACI**

3574. —— *Notes on Chinese music and dance* ('Journal of the Amer. Musicol. Soc.' III, p. 292 ff.), 1950. **CFK**

3575. —— *Note on Egyptian Music* ('Journal of the Amer. Musicol. Soc.' II, p. 204), 1949. **CFKL**

3576. —— *Rhythm and Tempo: an introduction* ('The Musical Quarterly' XXXVIII p. 384 ff.), 1952. **CDFH[1]IKL[1]**

*3577. —— *Rhythm and Tempo. A Study in Music History* (New York, 1953). **ACF**

3578. —— *Our musical heritage, a short history of music* (Prentice Hall Inc., New York, 1955). **AIK**

3579. —— *Heterophonie* ('Die Musik in Geschichte und Gegenwart' VI, col. 327 ff.), 1957. **ACDEFGH[1]KL**

3579a. —— *Muses and scales* (in: 'Essays on music in honor of A. T. Davison', Cambridge (Mass.), 1957, p. 3 ff.).

3579b. —— *Erich M. von Hornbostel* ('Die Musik in Geschichte und Gegenwart' VI, col. 719 ff.), 1957. **ACDEFGH[1]KL**

3579c. —— *The lore of non-Western music* (in: 'Some aspects of musicology, three essays written for the American Council of Learned Societies', p. 19 ff.), New York, 1957.

3579d. —— *The wellsprings of music. An introduction to Ethnomusicology* (in preparation).

3579e. —— *Babylonische Musik* ('Riemann Musiklexikon' 12th ed.), Mainz, 1958.

3579f. —— *Chinesische Musik* (ibid.), Mainz, 1958.

3579g. —— *Musik der Naturvölker* (ibid.), Mainz, 1958.

3579h. —— *Musen und Töne* ('Jahrbuch der Musikwissenschaft' I, p. 7 ff.), Leipzig, 1957.

3579i. **Sachse, F. J. P.,** *Het eiland Seran en zijne bewoners* (Leyden, 1907), pp. 150 ff. **B**

3579j. —— *Seran* ('Meded. v. h. Encycl. Bureau' XXIX, p. 99 ff.), Weltevreden, 1922. **B**

3580. **Sachsse,** *Palästinische Musikinstrumente* ('Z. d. deutschen Palästinavereins' L, p. 117 ff.), 1927. **D[1]GHL[1]**

3580a. **Saefthingen, W. van,** *Trommeltual* ('Nieuw Afrika' LXXI, No. 3, p. 135 ff.), 1955. **M**

3581. **Safford, W. E.,** *Panpipes* ('J. of the Washington Acad. of Science' IV, No. 8), 1914. **AH**

3582. **Sahukar, Mani,** *The appeal in Indian music* (Rampert Library, Bombay, 1943). **I**

3583. **Saindon, J. Emile,** *Two Cree songs from James Bay* ('Primitive Man' VII, No. 1, p. 6 ff.), Washington, Jan. 1934.

3584. **Sainte-Fare Garnot, Jean,** *L'offrande musicale dans l'Ancienne Egypte* ('Mélanges d'histoire et d'esthétique musicales', vol. I, p. 89 ff.), Paris, 1955.

3585. **Saint-Saëns, Camille,** *Lyres et cithares* (1912) (in Lavignac, 'Hist. de la Mus.' 1re partie, vol. I, p. 538 ff.), 1922. **ACDEFHJ**

3586. **Saionji, Yoshikazu,** *Nihon Minyô Taikan: Kantô-hen* (*A Survey of Japanese Folksong*), vol. I (Japanese Broadcasting Corporation, Tokyo, 1953).

3587. **Salaberry, J. D. J.,** *Chants populaires du pays basque* (Bayonne, 1870).

3588. **Salas, Samuel,** and others, *Historia de la música* (America Latina), Buenos Aires, 1938.

3589. **Salasc, Leon,** *Sur les musiques du Haut Cameroun* ('Togo-Cameroun' Jan. 1934, p. 34 ff.).

3590. **Salazar, Adolfo,** *Música negras* ('Nuestra Música' No. 26), Mexico, 1952.

3591. **Saldivar, Gabriel,** *Historia de la musica en Mexico* (Mexico, 1934).

3592. **Salmen, Walter,** *Alte Volksinstrumente in Westfalen* ('Westfal. Heimatkalender 1952', p. 59 ff.).

3593. —— *Zur Erforschung landschaftlicher Eigentümlichkeiten in den Weisen des westfalischen Volksliedes* ('Rhein. Jahrb. f. Volkskunde' III, p. 135 ff.), 1952. **KL[1]**

3594. —— *Vorschläge zur Aufzeichnung, Anordnung und Katalogisierung deutscher Volkslieder* ('Ber. über d. Algem. volkskundl. Kongress in Jugendheim, 1951', p. 93).

3595. —— *Die Schichtung der mittelalterlichen Musikkultur in der ostdeutschen Grenzlage* (Kassel, 1954).

3596. —— *Zur Verbreitung von Einhandflöte und Trommel im europäischen Mittelalter* ('Jahrbuch des Oesterreichischen Volksliedwerkes' VI, p. 154 ff.), 1957. **AL**

3597. —— *Towards the exploration of national idiosyncrasies in wandering song-tunes* ('Journal of the Intern. Folk Music Council' VI, p. 52 ff.), 1954. **ACJKL**

*3598. —— *Das Erbe des ostdeutschen Volksgesanges. Verzeichnis seiner Quellen und Sammlungen* (Würzburg, 1956).

3599. —— *Mittelalterliche Totentanzweisen* ('Die Musikforschung' IX, p. 189), 1956. **ACEFKLL[1]**

3600. —— 'Ihr Spielleut spielet auf'. Der Spielmann im deutschen Volksliede ('Das Musikleben' VIII, p. 168 ff.), Mainz, May 1955. **ACL**

3601. —— Wie und zu welchen Zwecken sammelt man Volkslieder ('Das Musikleben' VII, Heft 2, p. 50 ff.), 1954. **ACL**

3602. —— Die internationale Wirksamkeit slawischer und magyarischer Musiker (in 'Syntagma Friburgense', Hist. Studien, Hermann Aubin zum 70. Geburtstag dargebracht), Lindau/Konstanz, 1956. **A**

3603. **Salvador-Daniel, Francesco**, La musique arabe, ses rapports avec la musique et le chant grégorien (Alger, 1863). **C**

*3604. —— The Music and Musical Instruments of the Arab, with Introduction on How to appreciate Arab Music (edited with notes, memoir, bibliography and musical examples by Henry George Farmer), London/New York, 1915. **CIK**

3604a. —— Note on a gong of bronze from Katsina, Nigeria ('Man' XXIX, p. 157 ff.), 1929. **B**

3605. **Sambamurthy, P.**, Elements of Karnatic Music (Madras, 1929).

3606. —— The seventy-two melakarta janya raga scheme (Madras, 19..).

3607. —— Catalogue of the musical instruments exhibited in the government museum Madras ('Bull of the Madras Government Museum'), Madras, 1931. **J**

3608. —— South Indian Folk Music ('Indian Art and Letters' VI, p. 32 ff.), 1932. **GK**

3609. —— The teaching of music ('The Journal of the Music Academy, Madras' XI, p. 48 ff.), 1940.

3610. —— Music in training schools (ibid. XIII, p. 33 ff.), 1942.

3611. —— Comparative Music, a reply (ibid. XIII, p. 87 ff.), 1942.

3612. —— The Wallajapet Manuscripts (ibid. XIV, p. 86 ff., XVIII, p. 114 ff.), 1943 and 1947.

3613. —— The Flute; a Study containing a short account of its History, Antiquity and Laws together with full Instructions for Practice (Madras, 2/1943).

3614. —— The origin of some ragas ('The Journal of the Music Academy, Madras' XVI, p. 73 ff.), 1945. **C**

3615. —— Survival of the useful and the beautiful in the realm of music (ibid. XVII, p. 80 ff.), 1946. **C**

3616. —— South Indian Music, vols. I–IV (The Indian Music Publishing House, Madras), 4th ed. 1948–'49; 5th ed. (5 vols.), 1955 seq. **I**

3617. —— Madras as a Seat of Music Learning (Madras, 1949).

3618. —— Syama Sastri and other famous composers (Madras, 1949). **I**

3619. —— A dictionary of South Indian music and musicians I (A–P), Madras, 1953.

3620. —— Tyagaraja's opera's–Nowka Charitan ('Music Festival Souvenir, Jan. 1953, Bombay').

3621. —— Tyagaraja and Bhajana ('Annual Music Festival Souvenir, 1953'), Madras 1953.

3622. —— Tyagaraja ('Great Composers' II), Madras, 1954.

3623. —— Pallavi Seshayyar (1846–1908) ('J. of the Music Academy, Madras' XXV, p. 58 ff.), Madras, 1954. **AC**

3623a. —— The musical content of Bharata Natyam ('Marg' X, No. 4, p. 10 ff.), Sept. 1957.

3623b. —— Karnatic Music ('The March of India' X, No. 1, p. 26 ff.), Jan. 1958. **B**

3624. **Sami, Abdel Rahman**, Folk music and musical trends in Egypt to-day ('J. of the Intern. Folk Music Council' IX, p. 11 ff.), 1957. **ACJKL**

3625. **Saminsky, Lazare**, The music of the peoples of the Russian Orient ('The Mus. Quarterly' VIII, p. 346 ff.), 1922. **C**

3626. —— Music of the Ghetto and the Bible (New York, 1934). **K**

3627. **Sanchez de Fuentes, Eduardo**, El folklore en la musica cubana (Havana, 1923).

3628. —— Influencia de los ritmos africanos en nuestro cancionero (Havana, 1927).

3629. —— Los origines de la musica cubana ('Pro Arte Musical', Habana, 18th Nov. 1929).

3630. —— La canción cubana (Havana, 1930).

3631. —— La musica cubana y sus origines ('Bol. Latino-Americano de Música' IV, p. 177 ff.), Bogotá, 1938.

3632. —— La musica aborigen de America (Havana, 1938). **I**

3633. —— Consideraciones sobre la musica cubana (La Habana, 1936). **K**

3634. —— The musical folklore of Cuba ('Papers Intern. Congress of Musicology, Sept. 1939', p. 284 ff.), 1944. **AC**

3635. **Sanden, Heinrich**, Antike Polyphonie (Heidelberg, 1957).

3636. **Sandvik, O. M.**, Norsk Folkemusik, saerlig Østlandsmusikken (Oslo, 1921).

3637. —— Die norwegische Volksmusik ('Bull. de la Soc. 'Union Musicologique'' IV, p. 121 ff.), The Hague, 1924. **ACD¹FGHL**

3638. —— Norsk folkmusikk ('Nordisk Kultur. Musikk og Musikkinstrumenter', p. 128 ff.), 1934. **A**

3639. —— Keltiske melodier og norsk folkemusikk ('Norsk musikkgranskning' 1939, p. 68 ff.), Oslo, 1940. **K**

3640. —— Østerdalsmusikken (Oslo, 1943). **A**

3641. —— Folkemusikk i Gudbrandsdalen (Oslo, 1948). **AL**

187

3642. —— *Setesdalsmelodier* (Oslo, 1952).

*3643. —— *Norwegian Folk Music* ('Grove's Dictionary' 5th ed. vol. III, p. 322 ff.), 1954. **ACFH¹K**

3644. San Juan, Pedro, *Cuba's popular music* ('Modern Music' XIX, p. 22 ff.), May/June 1942.

3644a. Sannemann, Friedrich, *Ueber eine ungedruckte Sammlung deutscher Volkslieder mit ihren Singweisen in der Altmark und im Magdenburgischen, aus Volksmunde gesammelt von Ludolf Parisius* ('Report of the 4th Congress of the Intern. Musical Soc.', p. 205), London, 1911. **CF**

3645. Santesteban, J. A., *Colección de aires vascongadas* (San Sebastián, 1860).

3646. —— *Chansons basques* (Bayonne, 1870).

3647. Santiago, Francisco, *The development of music in the Philippine Islands* (Manila, 1931, 2/1957). **G**

3648. Sapir, Edward, *Song recitative in Paiute mythology* ('Journal of Amer. Folklore' XXIII, p. 455 ff.), 1910. **GKL²**

3649. —— *Texts of the Kaibab Paiutes and Uintah Utes* ('Proc. Amer. Acad. of Sciences' vol. 65, p. 297 ff.), 1930. **D¹**

3650. —— *Songs for a Comox dancing mask* ('Ethnos' IV, p. 52 ff.), 1939. **L²M**

3651. Sarathchandra, *Folklore and music in Ceylon* (Lake House Book Depot, Colombo, Ceylon).

3652. Sargeant, Winthrop, and J. Lahiri, *A Study in East Indian Rhythm* ('The Musical Quarterly' XVII), 1931. **C**

3653. —— *Types of Quechua melody* ('The Musical Quarterly' XX, p. 230 ff.), 1934. **CD**

3654. —— *Folk and primitive music in Canada* ('J. of the Intern. Folk Music Council' IV, p. 65 ff.), 1952. **AC**

3655. Sarkis, S. J., *A treatise on the similarity between European and Indian music* (Calcutta, 1930). **I**

3655a. Sartiaux, P., *Aspects traditionnels de la musique au Ruanda-Urundi* ('Jeune Afrique' VII, p. 19 ff.), 1954. **M**

3656. Sas, André, *Aperçu sur la musique inca* ('Acta Musicologica' VI, p. 1 ff.), 1934. **CDEH¹KLL¹**

3657. —— *Ensayo sobre la musica nazca* ('Bol. Lat.-Amer. de Música' IV, p. 221 ff.), Bogotá, 1938.

3657a. Sastri, K. Vasudeva, *Music at the time of king Sahaji of Tanjore, A.D. 1710* ('The J. of the Music Academy, Madras' XVII, p. 90 ff.), 1946. **C**

Sastri, Pandit S. Subrahmanya, see: Subrahmanya Sastri, Pandit S.,

3658. Satyadeva, Geeta, *North Indian Music Today* ('United Asia' III No. 1, India Number, p. 57 ff.), 1950. **A**

3659. Saunders, William, *Sailor songs and songs of the sea* ('The Musical Quarterly' XIV, p. 339 ff.), 1928.

3660. Saussine, R. de, *Rythmes et figures du Brésil* ('La Revue musicale' 1931). **CD¹GKL**

3661. Saville, M. H., *A primitive Maya musical instrument* ('American Anthropologist' X (O.S.) No. 8), 1897. **GL²**

3662. —— *The musical bow in ancient Mexico* (ibid. XI (O.S.) No. 9), 1898. **GL²**

3663. Sax, C. von, *Bosnische Musik* ('Wissensch. Mitteil. aus Bosnien und der Hercegowina', Vienna, 1893).

3664. Sayer, Thos., *A sketch of the life of C. Eulenstein, the celebrated performer on the Jew's harp* (London, 1833).

3665. Saygun, Ahmed Adnan, *Le recueil et la notation de la musique folklorique* ('Journal of the Intern. Folk Music Council' I, p. 27 ff.), 1949. **ACKL**

3666. —— *Des danses d'Anatolie et de leur charactère rituel* (ibid. II, p. 10 ff.), 1950. **ACJKL**

3667. —— *Authenticity in Folk Music* (ibid. III, p. 7 ff.), 1951. **ACJKL**

*3668. —— *Turkish Folk Music* ('Grove's Dictionary' 5th ed. vol. III, p. 384 ff.), 1954. **ACFH¹K**

3669. Sbîrcea, George, *Obiceiuri, cîntece si jocuri magice din comuna Toplita* ('Revista de folclor' II, Nos. 1–2, p. 157 ff.), Bucarest, 1957. **AC**

3670. Scarborough, Dorothey, *On the trail of Negro folk songs* (Cambridge, Mass., 1925).

3671. Schad, Gustav, *Musik und Musikausdrücke in der mittelenglischen Literatur* (Diss., Giessen, 1911).

3672. Schaden, Francisco S. G., *Musica e Dança entre os Indios do Brasil* ('Paulistania' XXVI, p. 13 ff.), Sao Paulo, 1948.

3673. Schadenberg, Alex., *Musik-Instrumente der Philippinen-Stämme* ('Z. f. Ethnologie' XVIII, p. (549) ff.), 1886. **ABD¹GHKL¹L²M**

3674. Schäfer, H., *Die Lieder eines ägyptischen Bauern* (Leipzig, 1903).

3675. Schaeffner, André, *Notes sur la musique des Afro-américains* ('Le Ménestrel' 25/6–6/8, 1926). **D**

3676. —— *Projet d'une nouvelle classification méthodique des instruments de musique* ('Revue musicale' XIII, vol. II, p. 215 ff.), 1932. **ACDGJKL**

3677. —— *Note sur la filiation des instruments à cordes* ('Mélanges de Musicologie offerts à M. Lionel de la Laurencie'), Paris, 1933. **A**

3678. —— *Notes sur la musique des populations du Cameroun septentrional* ('Minotaure' II, p. 65 ff.), 1933. **J**

3680. —— *Parmi les origines corporelles des instruments de musique* ('Le Ménestrel' XCVI, p. 65 ff., 77 ff. and 89 ff.), 1934. **K**

*3681. —— *Origines des instruments de musique* (Paris, 1936). **AGIJLM**

3682. —— *Contribution à l'étude des instruments de musique d'Afrique et d'Océanie* (Compte rendu de la 2ième session du Congrès intern. des sciences anthropologiques et ethnologiques, p. 268 ff.), Copenhagen, 1939. **M**

3682a. —— *Musique, danse et danse des masques dans une société nègre* (ibid.), Copenhagen, 1939. **M**

3862b. —— *Le folklore musical* ('Cahiers de Radio-Paris' May 15, 1938, p. 459 ff.).

3863. —— *Musique primitive ou exotique et musique moderne d'Occident* ('Mélanges offerts à Zoltan Kodály', p. 213 ff.), 1943. **ACK**

3684. —— *Sur deux instruments de musique des Batas (Nord-Cameroun)* ('Journal de la Soc. des Africanistes' XIII, p. 123 ff.), 1943. **AGL²M**

3685. —— *Les instruments de musique* (in Dufourq, 'La Musique des origines à nos jours', ed. Larousse, p. 13 ff.), 1946. **ACDEFHJK**

3686. —— *La musique noire d'Afrique* (ibid., p. 460 ff.), 1946. **ACDEFGJK**

3687. —— *Découverte de la musique noire* ('Présence africaine', 1950, p. 205 ff.). **M**

3688. —— *Les Kissi, une société noire et ses instruments de musique* (Paris, 1951). **ACJL²M**

3689. —— *Une importante découverte archéologique: le lithophone de Ndut Lieng Krak (Vietnam)* ('La Revue de Musicologie' XXXIII, p. 1 ff.), 1951. **ACD¹EFKLL¹**

3690. —— *Musique populaire et art musical* ('Journal de Psychologie normale et pathologique', Jan./June 1951, p. 237 ff.). **AD¹HKL¹**

3691. —— *Timbales et longues trompettes* ('Bull. de l'Inst. Français d'Afrique Noire' XIV, p. 1466 ff.), Oct. 1952. **AGL²M**

3691a. —— *Musique et instruments primitifs* (in: 'Guide de la Musique'), Paris, 1951.

3692. —— *Ethnologie musicale ou musicologie comparée?* ('Les Colloques de Wégimont' I, p. 18 ff.), Brussels, 1956. **ACL**

3692a. —— *Musique outre-mer* ('France-Outre-mer' XXV, No. 212, p. 7 ff.), 1947.

3692b. —— *Organologie primitive* (in: Jacques Chailley, 'Précis de Musicologie'), Paris, 1958 (Chapter V).

3693. Schebesta, Paul, *Die Bambuti-Pygmäen vom Ituri* (3 vols.) (Brussels, 1941, '48,

'50). II. Band, I. Teil: Die Wirtschaft der Ituri-Bambuti, p. 243 ff.: *Tänze, musikalische und gesangliche Unterhaltungen;* II. Teil: Das soziale Leben, p. 481 ff.: *Die Lärminstrumente im Nkumbi.* **B**

3694. —— *Pygmy music and ceremonial* ('Man' LVII, p. 62 ff. (No. 78)), April, 1957. **B**

*3695. Scheepers, Will D., *De mondharp* ('Mens & Melodie' XII, p. 275 ff.), 1957. **ACF**

3696. Scheierling, K., *Ich bin das ganze Jahr vergnügt. Lieder für uns alle* (Kassel, 1955).

3696a. Schellong, O., *Musik und Tanz der Papuas* ('Globus' LVI), 1889. **D¹M**

3697. Scherber, F., *Arabische Lieder* ('Die Musik' IV, fasc. 6), 1904/'05. **CDFKL**

3697a. Scherman, L., *Musizierende Genien in der religiösen Kunst des Birmanischen Buddhismus* ('Ostasiatische Zeitschrift' VIII, p. 345 ff.), 1920. **GKL⁶**

3697b. Scherrer, M., *Les dumy ukrainniennes* (1947).

*3698. Scheurleer, D. F., *Nederlandsche liedboeken* (Den Haag, 1912); 1st Suppl. ibid. 1923. **CD**

3699. Schiffer, Brigitte, *Die Oase Siwa und ihre Musik* (Berlin, 1936). **I**

*3700. Schimmerling, H. A., *Folk Dance Music of the Slavic Nations* (New York, 1951). **A**

3701. Schindler, Kurt, *Folk music and poetry of Spain and Portugal. Música y poesia popular de España y Portugal* (New York, 1941).

3702. Schinhan, Jan P., *The music of the Papago and Yurok* ('Bull. of the American Musicol. Soc.' I, p. 13 ff.), 1934.

3703. Schiørring, Nils, *Det 16. og 17. Århundredes verdslige Danske Visesang* (2 vols.), Copenhagen, 1950. **AK**

*3704. —— *Danish Folk Music* ('Grove's Dictionary of Music and Musicians' 5th ed., vol. III, p. 223 ff.), 1954. **ACFH¹K**

3705. —— *Selma Nielsens viser* ('Danmarks Folkeminder' 1956, p. 66 ff.). **AK**

3706. Schipper, Ary, *Enkele opmerkingen over Surinaamse muziek* ('West-Indische Gids' XXVII, p. 209 ff.), 1944/'45. **ABCD¹G**

3707. Schirmunski, V., *Alte und neue Volkslieder aus der bayrischen Kolonie Jamburg am Dnjepr* ('Das Deutsche Volkslied' XXXIII, p. 1 ff. and 35 ff.), 1931.

*3708. Schlager, Ernst, *Bali* ('Die Musik in Geschichte und Gegenwart' I, col. 1109 ff.), 1950. **ACDEFGH¹KL**

3709. —— *Balische Musik* (publ. of the Museum f. Völkerkunde, Basel), Basel, undated. **A**

3710. Schlesinger, Kathleen, *Researches into*

the Origin of the Organs of the Ancients ('Sammelb. der Intern. Musikges.' II, p. 167 ff.), 1900/'01. **CDFH¹L**

3711. —— *The Instruments of the Modern Orchestra and Early Records of the Precursors of the Violin Family* (London, 1910). **CI**

*3712. —— *A Bibliography of Musical Instruments and Archaeology* (London, 1912). **I**

3713. —— *The precursors of the violin family* (London, 1914).

3714. —— *The Basis of Indian Music* ('Musical Times' LVI, p. 335 ff.), 1915. **C**

3715. —— Commentary on the musical instruments in Aurel Stein, 'Serindia' (London, 1921).

3716. —— *Is European Musical Theory indebted to the Arabs.*³ (London, 1925). **C**

3717. —— *The Question of an Arabian Influence on Musical Theory* ('Musical Standard' N.S. XXV, p. 148 ff. and 160 ff.), 1925. **D¹**

3718. —— *The Greek Foundations of the Theory of Music* ('Musical Standard' XXVII N.S., p. 23, 44, 62, 96, 109, 134, 162, 177, 197, 208; XXVIII N.S., p. 31 and 44 (1926). **D¹**

3718a. —— *The significance of musical instruments in the evolution of music* ('O H M '), London, 1929.

3719. —— *The Greek Aulos* (London, 1939). **BC**

3720. Schmeltz, J. D. E., *Das Schwirrholz* ('Verhandl. des Vereins f. naturwiss. Unterhaltung zu Hamburg' IX), 1896.

3721. —— *Bronzepauken im indischen Archipel* ('Intern. Archiv f. Ethnographie' IX, Suppl., p. 41 ff.), 1896. **BH**

3722. —— *A primitive musical instrument* (ibid. XI, p. 89 ff.), 1898. **BD¹GKL³**

3723. —— *Ueber Bronzepauken aus südost-Asien* (ibid. XIV, p. 192 ff.), 1901. **BD¹GKL²**

3724. —— *Messingtrommen von Alor* (ibid. XV, p. 32 ff., 53 and 208), 1902. **BD¹GKL²**

3725. —— *Einige vergleichende Bemerkungen über die Kesseltrommel von Saleyer* (ibid. XVI, p. 158 ff.), 1904. **BD¹GKL²**

3726. Schmidt, Leopold, *Kulturgeschichtliche Gedanken zur Musik im Märchen* ('Musikerziehung' III, 3), Vienna, 1950. **L**

3726a. —— *Die kulturgeschichtlichen Grundlagen des Volksgesanges in Oesterreich* ('Schweizerisches Archiv für Volkskunde' XLV, p. 105 ff.), Basel, 1948.

3727. Schmidt, Father Wilhelm, *Ueber Musik und Gesänge der Karesau Papuas* ('Kongressbericht Intern. Musikges', Vienna, 1910). **AC**

3728. —— *Ueber die Musik west-afrikanischer und ozeanischer Neger* ('Kongressber. der Intern. Musikges.' 1907, p. 60 ff.). **C**

3729. Schmidt-Ernsthausen, V., *Ueber die Musik der Eingebornen von Deutsch Neu-Guinea* ('Vierteljahrschr. f. Musikwiss.' VI, p. 268 ff.), 1890. **ACDFH¹KL**

3730. Schmidt-Lamberg, Herbert, *Chorgesang im schwarzen Afrika* ('Der Chor' III, p. 151 ff.), 1951.

3731. —— *Chorgesang bei exotischen Völkern* (ibid. II, p. 119 ff.), 1950.

3732. Schmitz, Hans Peter, *Flöteninstrumente* ('Die Musik in Geschichte und Gegenwart' IV, col. 311 ff.), 1955. **ACDEFGH¹KL**

3733. Schneerson, G., *Die Musikkultur Chinas* (transl. from the Russian), Leipzig, 1955. **A**

3734. Schneider, Marius, *Geschichte der Mehrstimmigkeit.* 1. *Die Naturvölker* (Berlin, 1934), II. *Die Anfänge in Europa* (Berlin, 1935). **AIL**

3735. —— *Ueber die Anwendung der Tonalitätskreistheorie auf die Musik der orientalischen Hochkulturen und der Antike* (in collab. with J. W. Schottländer) ('Z. f. vergl. Musikw.' III, p. 50 ff.), 1935. **ACK**

3736. —— *Gesänge der Gogadara* (in P. Wirz, 'Die Gemeinde der Gogadara' ('Nova Guinea' XVI)), 1934. **BD¹GH**

3737. —— *Siriono-Gesang* (in H. Snethlage, 'Nachrichten') ('Z. f. Ethnologie' vol. 67), 1935. **BD¹GHKL¹L²M**

3738. —— *Gesänge aus Uganda* ('Archiv f. Musikforschung' 1937). **ACDH¹KL**

3739. —— *Ueber die Verbreitung afrikanischer Chorformen* ('Z. f. Ethnologie' vol. 69, p. 79 ff.), 1937. **ABD¹GHKL¹L²M**

3740. —— *Deutsche Volkslieder aus Argentinien* ('Archiv f. Musikforschung' II, 1937. **CDH¹KL**

3741. —— *Bemerkungen über südamerikanische Panpfeifen* ('Archiv f. Musikforschung', 1937). **CDH¹KL**

3742. —— *Javanese music* (a review of J. Kunst 'De toonkunst van Java') ('Bull. of the Colonial Inst. of Amsterdam' I, p. 274 ff.), Aug. 1938. **ABD¹GHL²**

3743. —— *Ethnologische Musikforschung* (in K. Th. Preuss, 'Lehrbuch der Völkerkunde', p. 125 ff.), 1937, 2/1956. **ABL**

3744. —— *Ueber die wörtliche und gestaltmässige Ueberlieferung wandernder Melodien* ('Archiv f. Musikf.' III, p. 363 ff.), 1938. **CDH¹KL**

3745. —— *Die musikalischen Beziehungen zwischen Urkulturen, Altpflanzern und Hirtenvölkern* ('Z. f. Ethnologie' vol. 70, p. 287 ff.), 1938. **ABD¹GHKL¹L²M**

3746. —— *Kaukasische Parallelen zur mittelalterlichen Mehrstimmigkeit* ('Acta Musicologica' XII), 1940. **DEKLL¹**

3747. —— *Lieder aegyptischer Bauern (Fellachen)* ('Festschrift-Kodaly', p. 154 ff.), Budapest, 1943. **ACK**

3748. —— *Phonetische und metrische Korrelationen bei gesprochenen und gesungenen Ewe-texten* ('Archiv f. vergl. Phonetik' VII), 1943/'44. **D¹GHKL**

3749. —— *El influjo Arabe en España* ('Anuario Musical' I), 1946. **ACIL**

3750. —— *El origin musical de los animales simbolos en la mitología y la escultura antiguas* (Barcelona, 1946). **ACIL**

3751. —— *La canción de cuna en España* ('Anuario Musical' III), 1948. **ACL**

3752. —— *La danza de espadas y la tarantela* (Barcelona, 1948). **ACIL**

3753. —— *Los cantos de lluvia en España. Estudio etnológico comparativo sobre la ideología de los ritos de pluviomagía* ('Anuario Musical' IV, p. 3 ff.), 1949. **ACL**

3754. —— *Australien und Austronesien* ('Die Musik in Geschichte und Gegenwart' I, col. 869 ff.), Kassel, 1950. **ACDEFGH¹KL**

3755. —— *La relation entre la mélodie et le langage dans la musique chinoise* ('Anuario Musical' V, p. 62 ff.), 1950. **ACL**

3756. —— *Die historischen Grundlagen der musikalischen Symbolik* ('Die Musikforschung' IV, p. 113 ff.), 1951. **ACL**

3757. —— *Ist die vokale Mehrstimmigkeit eine Schöpfung der Altrassen?* ('Acta Musicologica' XXIII, p. 40 ff.), 1951. **ACDEFH¹KLL¹**

3758. —— *Música en las Philipinas* ('Anuario Musical' VI, p. 91 ff.), 1951. **ACL**

3759. —— *Catálogo de los instrumentos musicales 'igorrotes' conservados en el Museo Etnológico de Madrid* (in collab. with **M. Garcia Matos**) ('Revista de Anthropología' IV), 1951. **AGL³**

3760. —— *Cancionero de la provincia de Madrid*, vols. I and II (Barcelona, 1951 and 1952). **AIL**

3761. —— *Zur Trommelsprache der Duala* ('Anthropos' XLVII, p. 235 ff.), 1952. **ABD¹GHJKLL¹L²M**

3762. —— *Contribución a la música del Matto Grosso* ('Anuario Musical' VII), 1952. **ACL**

3763. —— *Die Bedeutung der Stimme in der alten Kulturen* ('Tribus, Jahrbuch des Lindenmuseums' II/III, p. 9 ff.), Stuttgart, 1952/'53. **ABGLL¹L²M**

3764. —— *Singende Steine. Die musikalische Grundlagen der Kapitalordnung in drei katalonischen Kreuzgängen des 12. Jahrhunderts* (Kassel, 1955). **ACL**

3764a. —— *Un villancico de Alonso Mudarra procedente de la música popular granadina* ('Anuario Musical' X, 79 ff.), Barcelona, 1955. **ACL**

3765. —— *Arabischer Einfluss in Spanien?* ('Kongressbericht Bamberg 1953' p. 175 ff.), 1954. **ACDEFL**

3765a. —— *Bemerkungen über die spanische Sackpfeife* ('Musikerkenntnis und Musikerziehung', Festgabe für Hans Mersmann, p. 129 ff.), Kassel/Basel, 1957. **A**

3766. —— *Flamenco* ('Die Musik in Geschichte und Gegenwart' IV, col. 283 ff.), 1954. **ACDEFGH¹KL**

3767. —— *Fandango* ('Die Musik in Geschichte und Gegenwart' III, col. 1758 ff.), 1954. **ACDEFGH¹KL**

3767a. —— *Entstehung der Tonsysteme* ('Bericht über den Intern. Musikwiss. Kongress Hamburg 1956', p. 203 ff.), Kassel/ Basel, 1956. **ACEL**

•3768. —— *Primitive Music* ('The New Oxford History of Music' 3rd ed., vol. I, p. 1 ff.), 1957. **ABCD¹FGH¹JKL**

3769. —— *La philosophie de la musique chez les peuples non-européens* ('Editions de la Pléiade, Histoire de la musique'), Paris, 1956.

3770. —— *Pandero und zambomba* ('Spanische Forschungen der Görresgesellschaft' IX, p. 1 ff.), München, 1954. **HK**

3771. —— *Les fondements intellectuels et psychologiques du chant magique* ('Les Colloques de Wégimont' I, p. 56 ff.), Brussels, 1956. **ACL**

3772. —— *Le verset 94 de la sourate VI du Coran étudié en une version populaire et en trois maqamât de tradition hispano-musulmane* ('Anuario Musical' IX, p. 80 ff.), Barcelona, 1954. **ACL**

3773. —— *Die Musik der Naturvölker* (in: Adam u. Trimborn, 'Lehrbuch der Völkerkunde', Stuttgart, 1958. **B**

3774. —— Review of Walter Wiora, 'Zur Frühgeschichte der Musik in den Alpenländern', 'Alpenländische Liedweisen der Frühzeit und des Mittelalters im Lichte vergleichender Forschung' and 'Das echte Volkslied' ('Anuario musical' V, p. 224 ff.), 1950. **C**

3774a. —— *Rhythmische Studien zum Cancionero de Palacio* ('Festschrift-Anglés' 1958).

3774b. —— *Jota* ('Die Musik in Geschichte und Gegenwart' VII, col. 214 ff.), 1958. **ACDEFGH¹KL**

3774c. —— *Vom ursprünglichen Sinn der Musik* ('Kongressbericht Basel 1949', p. 183 ff.), Basel, 1949. **ACDEFL**

3775. **Schneider, Thekla**, *Organum Hydraulicum* ('Die Musikforschung' VII, p. 24 ff.), 1954. **ACEIKLL¹**

3776. **Schoen, Max**, *The effects of music* (London, 1927). **A**

3777. **Schole, H.**, *Tonpsychologie und Musikästhetik* (1930).

3778. Schott, S., *Altägyptische Liebeslieder* (Zurich, 1950).

3779. Schottländer, J. W., *Ueber die Tonalitätskreistheorie auf die Musik der orientalischen Hochkulturen und der Antike* ('Z. f. vergl. Musikwiss.' III, p. 60 ff.), 1935. **ACK**

3780. Schullian, D. M., and M. Schoen, *Music and Medicine* (New York, 1948).

3781. Schünemann, Georg, *Kasantatarische Lieder* ('Archiv f. Musikw.' I, p. 499 ff.), 1918/'19. **CDFKLL[1]**

3782. —— *Ueber die Beziehungen der vergleichenden Musikwissenschaft zur Musikgeschichte* ('Archiv. f. Musikw.' II, p. 175 ff.), 1919/'20. **CDFKLL[1]**

3783. —— *Das Lied der deutschen Kolonisten in Russland* ('Sammelb. d. vergl. Musikwiss.' III), München, 1923. **KL**

3784. —— *Musikinstrumente der Indianer* ('Archiv f. Musikforschung' I, fasc. 3 and 4), 1936. **CDH[1]KL**

3784a. —— *Die Musikinstrumente* ('Atlantisbuch der Musik'), Berlin, 1934.

3784b. Schuster, Carl, *Head-hunting symbolism on the bronze drums of the ancient Dongson culture and in the modern Balkans* ('Proc. 4th Intern. Congress of Anthrop. and Ethnol. Sciences, Vienna' II, p. 278 ff.), 1955. **AB**

3785. Scott, A. C., *The Kabuki theatre of Japan* (Chapter V: *The music of the theatre*), London, 1955.

3786. —— *The classical theatre of China.* (London, 1957). Chapter III. *The music of the Ching hsi theatre.*

*3787. Scott, J. E., *Roman Music* ('The New Oxford History of Music', 3rd ed., vol. I, p. 404 ff.), 1957. **ABCD[1]FGH[1]JK**

3788. Scott, J. G., *Burma* (London, 1921), p. 300 ff.: *Burmese music and musical instruments.* **J**

3789. Scott, Nora E., *The lute of the singer Har-Môse* ('Bull. of the Metropolitan Museum of Art, New York', Jan. 1944). **A**

3790. Scott, R. R., *Kenya Exhibition of musical instruments from Uganda and demonstration of Uganda music* ('African Music Society Newsletter' I, No. 2, p. 22 ff.), 1949. **ACM**

3791. Scully, Nora, *Native tunes, heard and collected in Basutoland* ('Bantu Studies' V, p. 247 ff.), 1931. **KL[2]M**

3792. Scully, William Charles, *Kaffir music* (in his 'By veldt and kopje', p. 285 ff.), Fisher Unwin, 1907.

3793. Seashore, Carl E., *Psychology of Music* (New York/London, 1938). **HI**

3794. —— *Three new approaches to the study of negro music* ('Annals of the Amer. Acad. of Political and Social Science' CXL, p. 191 ff.), 1928.

3795. Seder, Theodor A., *Old World Overtones in the New World* (Philadelphia, University Museum, Bulletin XVI, No. 4), June 1952. **FL[2]**

3796. Seeger, Charles, *U.S.A. Folk Music* ('Grove's Dictionary' 5th ed. vol. III, p. 387 ff.), 1954. **ACFH[1]K**

3797. —— *An instantaneous music notator* ('Journal of the Intern. Folk Music Council' III, p. 103 ff.), 1951. **ACJKL**

3798. —— *Systematic musicology: viewpoints, orientations, and methods* ('J. of the Amer. Musicol. Soc.' IV, p. 240 ff.), 1951. **CKL**

3799. —— *Preface to the description of a music* (in 'Proc. 5th congress of the Intern. Ges. f. Musikwiss.' p. 360 ff.), The Hague, 1953. **ACDEF**

3800. —— *Toward a universal music soundwriting for musicology* ('J. of the Intern. Folk Music Council' IX, p. 63 ff.), 1957. **ACJKL**

*3800a. —— *The Appalachian dulcimer* ('J. of American Folklore' 1958, p. 40 ff.). **AGK**

3801. Seeger, Peter, *How to play the 5-stringed Banjo* (2nd ed., Beacon, N.Y., 1954). **A**

3802. Seemann, E., *Mythen vom Ursprung der Musik* ('Kongressber. Ges. f. Musikf., Lüneburg 1950', p. 151 ff.), 1951. **ACDEFKL**

3803. Seewald, Otto, *Beiträge zur Kenntnis der steinzeitlichen Musikinstrumente Europas* (Vienna, 1934). **ABCJL**

3804. Seidel, J., *Národ v Písni. Tisíc národnich písni* (Prague, 1941).

3805. —— *Zpevy domova. Druhy tisíc národnich písni* (Prague, 1943).

3806. —— and J. Špičak, *Tance českého lidu* (Prague, 1945).

3807. Seidenfaden, Erik, *Rock gongs and rock slides* ('Man' LVII, p. 32, No. 33), 1957. **BD[1]GKL[1]L[2]M**

3807a. Selden, Margery Stomme, *The music of old Iceland* ('American-Scandinavian Review' XLV, p. 369 ff.), winter 1957.

3808. Seler, Eduard, *Mittelamerikanische Musikinstrumente* ('Globus' LXXVI, p. 109 ff.), 1899. **D[1]**

3809. —— *Altmexikanische Knochenrasseln* ('Z. f. Ethnologie' XLVIII), 1916. **BD[1]GHKL[1]L[2]M**

3809a. —— *Drei Gegenstände aus Mexico* (ibid. XXXVII), 1905. **BD[1]GHKL[1]L[2]M**

3809b. —— *Die Lichtbringer bei den Indianenstämmen der Nordwestküste* ('Globus' LXI. p. 195 ff., 212 ff., 230 ff. and 243 ff.), 1892. **D[1]M**

3810. Seligmann, C. G., *Note on a wooden Horn or Trumpet from British New-Guinea* ('Geographical Journal' XXVII, p. 225 ff.), 1906. **D[1]GJK**

3811. **Selvas, Eduardo J.**, *Música y danzas indigenas de Chiapas* ('Ateneo' V, p. 14 ff.), 1954.

3812. **Semenov, A. A.**, *Sredne aziatskii traktat po muzyke Dervisha Ali* (i.e. Central Asiatic treatise on the music of Dervish Ali (from the 17th cent.)), Tashkent, 1946.

3813. **Sempebwa, E. K. K.**, *Baganda folksongs: a rough classification* ('Uganda Journal' XII, p. 16 ff.), March 1948. **L²M**

3814. **Sen, Vuong Hong**, *Note additionnelle à l'étude de M. Nguyen-Dinh Lai sur la musique sino-viêtnamienne et les chants populaires du Viêtnam* ('Bull. de la Soc. des Etudes Indochinoises' N.S. XXXI, No. 1, p. 87 ff.), Saigon, 1956. **BL³**

3815. **Sena, Devar Surya**, *Folk Songs of Ceylon* ('Journal of the Intern. Folk Music Council' VI, p. 11 ff.), 1954. **ACJKL**

*3816. **Sendrey, Alfred**, *Bibliography of Jewish Music* (New York, 1951).

3817. **Serov, Aleksandr Nikolaevič**, *Muzyka južno-russkich pesen* (i.e. The music of the South-Russian folksongs), Moscow, 1953.

3818. **Servier, Jean H.**, *Musique et poésie kabyles* ('Actes du IVe Congres Intern. des Sciences Anthrop. et Ethnol., Vienne 1–8 Sept. 1952', III. Ethnologica, 2nde. partie, p. 19 ff.), Vienna, 1956. **AB**

3819. **Shaffer, Mrs. J. M.**, *Bamboo pipes of the Batetela children* ('African Music' I, No. 1, p. 74 ff.), 1954. **ACJLM**

3820. —— *Experiments in indigenous church music among the Batetela* ('African Music' I, No. 3, p. 39 ff.), 1956. **ACJLM**

*3821. **Sharp, Cecil J.**, *English Folk Songs from the Southern Appalachian Mountains* (edited by Maud Karpeles), London, 1932, 2/1952. **CFL**

3822. ——*Journal of the Folk-Song Society* (London), No. 6 (1905), 18 (1914), 20 (1916) and 31 (1927).

3823. —— *Folksongs of England I–V* (London, Novello, no date). **K**

3824. —— *English Folk Song, Some conclusions* (London, 1907), revised by Maud Karpeles, (London, 3/1954).

3825. **Shastri, M. R.**, *Music of Travancore* ('Sangeet Natak Akadami', Bull. No. 3, p. 57 ff.), New Delhi, July 1955. **BF**

3826. **Shaw, Margaret Fay**, *Folksongs and Folklore of South Uist* (London, 1955). **A**

3827. —— *Gaelic folksongs from South Uist* ('Studia Memoriae Belae Bartók Sacra', p. 427 ff.), Budapest, 1956. **AC**

3828. **Shay, Felix**, *Fife and drum corps of a Uganda chief* ('Nat. Geogr. Magazine' XLVII, pp. 174, 181, 189, 191), 1925. **D¹G**

3829. **Shelford, R.**, *An Illustrated Catalogue of the Ethnographical Collection of the Serawak Museum. Part I. Musical Instruments* ('Journal of the Straits Branch of the R. Asiatic Soc.' No. 40, p. 3 ff.), 1904. **BGKL²L⁵**

3829a. **Shen Tsung-Wen**, *Recent finds in a 2300-year-old tomb* ('China Pictorial' 1958, No. 2, p. 27) (series of bronze bells).

3829b. **Shiba, Sukehiro**, *Score of Gagaku, Japanese classical court music* vol. I. *Kangen-orchestra in Hayagaku and Haya-tada-byōshi* (Tokyo, Ryugin-sha, 1955). **C**

3830. **Shirali, Vishnudass**, *Hindu music and rhythm* (Paris, 1937). **J**

3830a. **Shochikubai**, *Japanese koto music, selected by S. Yamase and G. Yamada* (Tokyo, n.d.).

3831. **Shuldham Shaw, Patrick**, *Scandinavian folk music on British soil* ('J. of the Intern. Folk Music Council' VIII, p. 11 ff.), 1956. **ACJKL**

3832. *Siamese music*, Score and parts (for resp. *Pi nai, Ranad Ek + Ranad Lek, Gong wong yai, Gong wong lek, Ranad Thume, Thume Lek, Ching + Tapone + Klong thad + Charb yai + Mong*) of the piece 'Evening Prelude' (for *Piphat* orchestra), Bangkok, undated. **AB**

3833. **Sicard, Harald von**, *The ancient East African Bantu drum* ('Ethnos' VII, p. 49 ff.), 1942. **L²M**

3833a. —— *Ngoma Lungundu, eine afrikanische Bundeslade* ('Studia ethnographica Uppsaliensia' V), Uppsala, 1952. **M**

3834. **Sichardt, Wolfgang**, *Der alpenländische Jodler und der Ursprung des Jodelns* (Berlin, 1938). **AL**

3835. **Sichel, A.**, *Histoire de la musique des Malgaches* (1907) (in Lavignac, 'Hist. de la Mus.' V, p. 3227 ff.), 1922. **ACDEFHJ**

3835a. **Siebold, Ph. F. von**, *Musik und Tanz in Japan* ('Nippon, Arch. z. Beschreibung v. Japan'), Leyden 1832/'35.

3836. **Siegmeister, Elie**, *Music and Society* (New York, 1938).

3837. **Siedersbeck, Beatrice Dohme, and Hans-Heinz Dräger**, *Fidel. II. Die Fidel im Abendland* ('Die Musik in Geschichte und Gegenwart' IV, col. 158 ff.), 1954. **ACDEFGH¹KL**

3837a. **Sihleanu, Stefan**, *De la musique populaire dans les pays Roumains* (summary) ('Report of the 4th Congress of the Intern. Musical Soc.', p. 205), London, 1911. **CF**

3838. **Sihorkar, K. S.**, *Music under state patronage* ('Silver Jubilee Souvenir of the Marris College of Hindustani music, Lucknow, Nov. 1952'), Lucknow 1953.

3839. Simbriger, Heinrich, *Klangsteine, Steinspiele und ihre Nachbildungen in Metall* ('Anthropos' XXXII, p. 552 ff.), 1937. **ABD¹GHKL¹L²M**

*3840. —— *Gong und Gongspiele* ('Intern. Arch. f. Ethnogr. XXXVI), Leyden, 1939. **ABCD¹EFGJKLL²M**

3841. Simmons, Donald C., *Efik gongs and gong signals* ('Man' LV, p. 107 ff. (No. 117)), July, 1955. **BD¹GKL¹L²M**

3842. Simon, François, *Chansons populaires de l'Anjou* (Angers, 1926).

3843. Simon, Richard, *Quellen zur indischen musik* ('Z. d. Deutschen Musikges.' 1902).

3844. —— *Die Notationen des Somanatha* ('Sitzungber. Phil.-Klasse d. Kgl. Bayrische Akad. d. Wiss.' 1903, p. 452 ff.).

3845. —— *The musical compositions of Somanatha* (Leipzig, 1904).

3846. —— *Notationen der vedischen Liederbücher* ('Wiener Zeitschr. f. d. Kunde d. Morgenlandes' XXVII, p. 305 ff.), 1913. **D¹GHKL¹**

3847. Simpson, George E., *Peasant song and dance of Northern Haiti* ('J. of Negro History' XXV, p. 2 ff.), 1940.

3848. Sinclair, A. T., *Gypsy and Oriental musical instruments* ('J. of Amer. Folklore' XXI, p. 205 ff.), 1908. **GKL²**

3848a. Singh, Jaideva, *Hindostani Music* ('The March of India' X, No. 2, p. 26 ff.), March 1958. **B**

3849. Singh, Rai Bajrang Bahadur, *Punya pratap vina* ('Silver Jubilee Souvenir of the Marris College of Hindustani music, Lucknow, Nov. 1952'), Lucknow, 1953.

3850. Singh, Samar Bahadur, *Pt. Vishnu Narayan Bhatkhande* (ibid.), Lucknow, 1953.

3851. Širola, Božidar, *Sopile i Zurle* (Zagreb, 1932). **A**

3852. —— *Fučkalice sviraljke od kore svježeg drveta* (Zagreb, 1932). **A**

3853. —— *Sviraljke s udarnim jezičkom* (Zagreb, 1937). **A**

3854. —— Summary in German of the foregoing important publication in 'Bull. Intern. de l'Acad. Yougoslave des Sciences et des Beaux Arts' IX, p. 155–184, (1937). **AK**

3855. —— *Hrvatske Narodna Glazba* (Zagreb, 1942). **A**

3856. —— *Kroatische Volksmusikinstrumente* ('Mélanges offerts à Zoltan Kodaly' p. 114 ff.), 1943. **ACK**

3857. —— *Die Volksmusik der Kroaten* ('Studia Memoriae Belae Bartók Sacra', p. 89 ff.), Budapest, 1956. **AC**

3858. —— *Žumberačke narodne popijevke* (Zagreb, 1942).

3859. Skeat, W. A., and C. O. Bladgen, *Pagan races of the Malay peninsula* (London, 1906), vol. II, Chapter V, p. 117 ff.: *Music, songs and feasts.* **BJ**

3859a. Skinner, Alanson, *Songs of the Menomini medicine ceremony* ('American Anthropologist' XXXVIII, p. 290 ff.), 1925. **L²**

3859b. Skinner, H. D., *Three Polynesian drums* ('J. of the Polynesian Soc.' XLII), 1933. **GL²**

3860. Slavenski, Josip, *Naše narodne melodije* ('Musički Glasnik' XI, No. 1–2, p. 3 ff.), Beograd, 1941.

3861. Slonimsky, Nicolas, *Music of Latin America* (New York, 1945). **C**

3862. —— *Cuban Folk Music* ('Grove's Dictionary' 5th ed. vol. III, p. 214 ff.), 1954. **ACFH¹K**

3863. —— *Mexican Folk Music* ('Grove's Dictionary' 5th ed. vol. III, p. 314 ff.), 1954. **ACFH¹K**

3864. Smeding, H., *Bezoekreis naar de Gemeenten in Kediri, Madioen en Modjokerto* ('Mededeelingen vanwege het Nederl. Zendelinggenootschap' V, p. 120 ff. and 245 ff.), 1861. **B**

3865. Smend, *Negermusik und Musikinstrumente in Togo* ('Globus' XCIII), 1908. **D¹L²M**

3866. Smirnov, P., *Kazakhskiye sovetskiye narodnye pesni* (i.e. Kazakh Soviet folk songs) ('Sovetskaya muzyka' 1950, No. 9, p. 54 ff.).

3867. —— *Zametki o khorovom penii v srednei Azii* (i.e. Notes on choral singing in Central Asia) ('Sovetskaya muzyka' 1951, No. 7, p. 54 ff.).

3868. Smith, B. J., *Musical saga of Samoa* ('Etude' LX, p. 369), 1942.

3869. Smith, C. Alphonso, *Ballads surviving in the United States* ('The Musical Quarterly' II, p. 109 ff.), 1916.

3869a. Smith, Carleton Sprague, *The song makers* ('Survey Graphic' XXX, No. 3, p. 179 ff.), March 1941.

3870. Smith, H., *The World's Earliest Music* (London, 1904).

3871. Smith, M. E., *The social functions and meaning of Hausa praise-singing* ('Africa' XXVII No. 1, p. 26 ff.), London, 1957. **BGJKL¹L²M**

3872. Smits van Waesberghe, Jos., *Melodieleer* (Amsterdam, undated). **AEF**

3873. —— *A textbook of Melody* (Amer. Inst. of Musicology, 1955). **A**

3874. —— *Handzeichen. II. Mittelalter* ('Die Musik in Geschichte und Gegenwart' V, col. 1451 ff.), 1956. **ACDEFGH¹KL**

3875. Smyth, H. Warington, *Five years in Siam* (London, 1898), 2 vols. App. 8: *The ken and (other) Lao reed instruments;* App. 15: *Some airs of Siam.* **J**

194

*3876. Snelleman, Joh. F., *Muziek en Mu-ziekinstrumenten* ('Encycl. v. Neder-landsch-Indië', 2nd. ed. vol. II, p. 812 ff.), 1918. ABC

3877. Suethlage, Emil Heinrich, *Musikinstru-mente der Indianer des Guaporégebietes* ('Baessler Archiv', Beiheft, Berlin, 1939). BCD¹GKLL²

3878. Snowden, A. D., *Some Common Musical Instruments found among the Native Tribes of Southern Rhodesia* ('Nada, the Southern Rhodesia Native Affairs Dept. Annual' No. 16, p. 72 ff.), Salis-bury, Rhod., 1939.

3879. Sobieska, Jadwiga, *Wielkopolskie spiew-ki ludowe* (Krakow, 1957). A

3880. Sobieski, Marian, *Wylor Polskich piesni ludowych* (2 vols.), Krakow, 1955. L

3881. —— and Maria Sobolewska, *Piesni ludowe Warmii i Mazur* (Krakow, 1955). AL

3882. Sobieski, Jadwiga and Marian, *Pieśń i muzyka ludowa Wielkopolski i ziemi Lubuskiej w swietle dotychczasowych badań* (i.e. Folk songs and music of Great Poland and the region of Lubusz in the light of present research), Warsaw, und. (1951?). I

3882a. Sobtchenko, A. I., *Pérédatcha sooshe-nii na barabanakh u narodob zapadnoi Afriki* ('Sovietskaia Etnografia' I, p. 120 ff.), 1952. M

3883. Söderberg, Bertil, *Musical Instruments used by the Babembe* ('Ethnos' XVII, p. 51 ff.), 1952. (ABCJM) (= African Music Soc. Newsletter, vol. I no. 6, p. 46 ff.), 1953. ACJM

3883a. —— *Afrikans musik* ('Östergötlands Dagblad' 7th Dec. 1946).

3883b. —— *Sången och musiken i nedre Kon-go* (in: J. E. Lundahl, 'Guds fotspår i dagens missionsvärld', p. 114 ff.), 1946.

*3884. —— *Les instruments de musique du Bas-Congo et dans les régions avoisi-nantes* (Stockholm, 1956). AJL

3884a. —— *Can African music be useful in missionary work?* ('Congo Mission News' No. 129, p. 10 ff.), 1945. M

3884b. —— *The influence of African music on European tunes* ('Congo Mission News' No. 135, p. 16), 1946. M

3885. Soepardi-Handjakiswara, *De heilige gong van Lodojo (Blitar)* ('Jong-Java' V, Nos. 3 and 4, p. 124 ff.).

3886. Soeriadiningrat, Soewardi, *Kinanthie Sandoong.* C

3886a. Soerjowinoto, R., *Beschrijving van ga-melaninstrumenten* ('Ned.-Indië Oud & Nieuw' V, p. 267 ff.), 1920/'21. ABD¹GHL²

3887. Sohne, L. S., *Aeldre og nyere norske Fjeldmelodier* XIV (1907) (cf. No. 2621).

3887a. Sokoli, Ramadan, *Veglat muzikore të popullit tane* ('Buletin për shkencat shoqërore' 1954, No. 4, p. 115 ff.).

3888. Sokolov, F. V., *Roussкié narodnie pesni o Krestrianskija Voinacha i Vossta-niiacha* (i.e. Russian folk songs on peasant revolts) ('Academy of Sciences U.S.S.R.'), Moscow, 1956.

3889. Sokolskaja, T., *Alte deutsche Volkslieder in der oberhessischen Sprachinsel Be-lowjisch (Nord-Ukraine)* ('Hess. Blätter f. Volkskunde' XXIX, p. 140 ff.), 1930. K

3890. Solomons, E. V., *The krontjong, Java's ukelele* ('Lloyd Mail' No. 6, Oct. 1933. p. 236 ff.). B

3890a. Solorzano, Armando, and Raul G. Guerrero, *Ensayo para un estudio sobre la 'Danza de los Concheros de la Gran Tenochtitlán'* ('Bol. Latino-Americano' V, p. 449 ff.), Montevideo, 1941. AGL

3891. Solvijns, F. Baltazard, *Les Hindous* (Paris, 1808/'12) (4 vols.). B

3892. Somervel, T. Howard, *The Music of Tibet* ('The Musical Times' LXIV), 1923. AC

3893. Sonner, Rudolf, *Musik und Tanz* ('Wis-senschaft und Bildung' No. 266), Leip-zig, 1930. C

3894. Sonnerat, Pierre, *Voyage aux Indes Orientales et à la Chine fait par ordre du Roi, depuis 1774 jusqu'en 1782* (Paris, 1782), *passim.* C

3894a. Sonobe, Saburo, *O iaposkikh musykun-takh* ('Sovetskaia muzyka' 1956 No. 5, p. 169 ff.).

3895. Soulié, Georges, *La Musique en Chine* (1911). ACIJKL

3896. —— *Théâtre et musique modernes en Chine, avec une étude technique de la musique chinoise et transcriptions pour piano* (Paris, 1926). GI

3897. Souriau, E., *Autorité humaine de la musique* ('Polyphonie' 1950, No. 7–8, p. 24 ff.). K

3898. Sousberghe, L. de, *Les danses rituelles mungonge et kéla des Bapende (Congo Belge)* ('Acad. Royal des Sciences colo-niales, classe des Sciences morales et politiques' N.S. Memoires in 8vo., vol. IX, No. 1 (Ethnographie), p. 62 ff.), Brussels, 1956.

3899. Southgate, T. L., *On a pair of Egyptian double flutes* ('Proc. of the Musical Association' XVII), 1890/'91. C

3900. —— *Communication on the ancient Egyptian scale* (ibid. 1890/'91). C

3901. —— *Some ancient musical instruments* ('Musical News' XXV), 1903.

3902. —— *Musical instruments in Indian sculpture* ('Z. d. Intern. Musikges.' X), 1908/'09. CDFH¹KL

3903. —— *Ancient flutes from Egypt* ('J. of

195

Hellenic Studies' XXXV), London, 1915. **CD¹GHKL¹**

3904. Sowande, Fela, *African music* ('Africa' XIV, p. 340 ff.), London, 1944. **BGKL¹L²M**

3904a. —— *Three Yoruba songs* ('Odù' No. 3, p. 36 ff.), 1955 (?). **M**

3905. Spanke, H., *La teoría árabe sobre el origen de la lírica romanica a la luz de las ultimas investigaciones* ('Anuario musical' I, p. 5 ff.), 1946. **CL**

3906. Spannaus, Guenther, *Musik und Musikinstrumente* ('Die Kulturen der ausser-europäischen Erdteile in Uebersicht') (Führer durch die Schausammlungen des Inst. f. Völkerkunde, Univ. Göttingen), p. 91 ff. (Göttingen, 1954). **BJ**

3907. Spasow, Vasil, *Volksmusik, Musikinstrumente und Tänze der Bulgaren* (Diss. Vienna, 1931).

3908. —— *Bulgarskite besmensurni pesni i technata ornamentika* ('Izvestia na narodniya etnografski musey' XIV), Sofia, 1943.

3909. Speck, Frank G., *Ceremonial songs of the Creek and Yuchi Indians* ('Anthrop. Publ. Mus. Univers. Pennsylvania' II, p. 155 ff.), 1911. **GIKL²**

3910. —— *Ethnology of the Yuchi Indians* (Philadelphia, 1909).

3911. —— *Penobscot man* (Philadelphia, 1940) (with transcr. by Edw. Sapir).

3912. —— *The Tutelo spirit adoption ceremony* (with transcr. by George Herzog), Harrisburg, 1942.

3913. Spector, Johanna, *On the trail of Oriental music: among the yemenites* ('The Reconstructionist' XVIII, No. 5, p. 7 ff.), April 18th, 1952.

3914. —— *Anthropological approach to Jewish music* ('Jewish Music Notes' IX, p. 3 ff.), Oct. 1954.

3915. —— *Further excursions on the trail of Oriental Jewish music* ('The Reconstructionist' XVIII, No. 11, p. 37 ff.), 1955.

3915a. —— *Musical styles in Near Eastern Jewish lithurgy* ('J. of the Music Acad., Madras' XXVI, p. 122 ff.), 1955. **C**

3916. Speight, W. L., *Notes on South African native music* ('Musical Quarterly' XX, p. 344 ff.), 1934. **CD**

3917. —— *The evolution of native music* ('The Sackbut' XIV, p. 18 ff.), 1933.

3918. Speiser, Felix, *Ethnographische Materialien aus den Neuen Hebriden und den Banks-Inseln* (Berlin, 1923), p. 420 ff.: *Music and dance.* **J**

3919. Speiser, W., *Eine Komposition des Dschou Wen-Gü* (London, 1917).

3920. Spencer Pryse, G., *Talking drums and stools of sovereignty* ('Ill. London News' CLXXII, p. 390 ff.), 1928.

3921. Spies, Walter, *Bericht über den Zustand von Tanz und Musik in der Negara Gianjar* ('Djawa' XVI, p. 51 ff.), 1936. **ABD¹G**

3922. —— *De Gamelanwedstrijd te Gianjar* (ibid. XIX, p. 197 ff.), 1939. **ABD¹**

3923. —— and Beryl de Zoete, *Dance and Drama in Bali* (London, 1938, 2/1953). **BJ**

3924. Spreen, Hildegard N., *Folkdances of South India* (London, 2/1948). **ABC**

3925. Springer, George P., *Language and music: parallels and divergencies* (in: 'For Roman Jakobson', p. 504 ff.), Rijswijk (Neth.), 1956. Sri B. Subba Rao, see: Rao, Sri B.

Subba,

3926. Srinivasan, M. A., *The lure of music* ('Annual Music Festival Souvenir, Madras, 1953').

3927. Srinivasan, R., *The swaras from basis of ragas* ('Silver Jubilee Souvenir of the Marris College of Hindusthani music, Lucknow, Nov. 1952'), Lucknow, 1953.

3928. —— *Democracy and creative music* (ibid.), Lucknow, 1953.

3928a. —— *Teaching of Music-theory* ('J. of the Music Acad., Madras' XXVI, p. 73 ff.), 1955.

3929. Stafford, William C., *Oriental music. The music of Hindustan or India* (in Surindro Mohun Tagore, 'Hindu music from various authors', p. 217 ff.), Calcutta, 1882. **CFIK**

3930. Stainer, John, *Music of the Bible* (new ed. by Fr. Galpin), London, 1914. **IJ**

3931. Stankovic, Zivojin, *Narodne pesme Krajina* (i.e. Folk melodies of the Krajina) (Monographies of the Serbian Academy of Sciences, vol. CLXXV), Beograd, 1951.

3932. Stannus, Hugh, *A rare type of musical instrument from Central Africa* ('Man' XX 3, No. 20), 1920. **BD¹GJKL²M**

3933. —— *The Wayao of Nyasaland* (Harvard African Studies III), Cambridge, Mass., 1922 (p. 365 ff.). **K**

3934. Starkie, Walter, *Gypsy Music* ('Grove's Dictionary' 5th ed. vol. III, p. 859 ff.), 1954. **ACFH¹K**

*3935. —— *Raggle Taggle* (London, 1949).

3936. —— *Spanish Raggle Taggle* (London, 1934).

3937. —— *Don Gypsy: adventures with a fiddle in Barbary, Andalusia and La Muncha* (New York, 1937).

3938. —— *Auf Zigeunerspuren, Von Magie und Musik. Spiel und Kult der Zigeuner in Geschichte und Gegenwart. Mit einem Beitrag von W. Dostal* (transl. from the English by E. Zehnden-Böhm), München, 1957.

3939. **Statius Muller, Wim**, *Enkele aantekeningen over de Antilliaanse dansmuziek* ('Christoffel' I, p. 500 ff.), June 1956. **BD¹GH**

*3939a. **Stauder, W.**, *Die Harfen und Leiern der Sumerer* (Frankfurt a/M., 1957). **AL**

3940. **Stayt, Hugh A.**, *The Bavenda* (Oxford Univ. Press, 1931), Chapter XXIII, p. 316. **J**

3940a. **Stearns, Marshall**, *The story of the jazz* (New York, Oxford Univ. Press, 1956).

3940b. **Stechenko-Kouftina, V. K.**, *Drevnejshie instrumentalnye osnovy gruzinskoj narodnoj musyki. I. Flejta pana* (= The most ancient instruments of the Georgian folk music. I. The Pan-pipe), Tiflis, 1936.

3941. **Stefaniszyn, B.**, *The Hunting Songs of the Ambo* ('African Studies' X, p. 1 ff.), March 1951. **BGKM**

3941a. **Stein, O.**, *Musik in Indien* ('Der Auftakt' 1921).
Stein Callenfels, P. V. van, see Callenfels, P. V. van Stein,

3942. **Steinen, Karl von den**, *Die Marquesaner und ihre Kunst* (Berlin, 1928), vol. II, p. 58 ff. **J**

3943. **Steinitz, Wolfgang**, *Deutsche Volkslieder demokratischen Charakters aus sechs Jahrhunderten* ('Veröffentl. d. Inst. f. Deutsche Volkskunde d. Deutschen Akademie d. Wiss. zu Berlin' IV), Berlin, 1954.

3944. —— *Lied und Märchen als 'Stimme des Volkes'* ('Deutsches Jahrbuch für Volkskunde' II, p. 11 ff.), Berlin, 1956. **AL¹**

3945. **Steinmann, Alfred**, *Ueber anthropomorphe Schlitztrommeln in Indonesien* ('Anthropos' XXIII, p. 240 ff.), 1938. **AD¹GHKL¹L²M**

3946. —— *Een fragment van een keteltrom van het eiland Koer* ('Cultureel Indië' III, p. 157 ff.), 1941. **ABD¹GHL²**

3946a. —— *Die Verwendung von Baumwurzeln als natürliche Gongs* ('Anthropos' XXXIII), 1938. **D¹GHKL¹L²M**

3947. **Stephan, S. H.**, *The smell of the Lebanon: 24 Syrian folk-songs* ('J. of the Palestine Oriental Soc.' 1921, p. 199 ff.). **G**

3948. **Sterling, Adeline**, *Drama and Music in Siam* ('Inter-Ocean' XIII, p. 139 ff.), 1932. **D¹G**

3949. **Stern, Philippe**, *The music of India and the theory of the raga* ('Indian Arts & Letters', N.S. VII, p. 1 ff.), 1933. **GK**

3950. —— *La musique hindoue. Les ragas* ('Revue musicale' III), 1923. **CD¹FGHKL**

3951. —— *Une nouvelle collection musicale consacrée principalement aux musiques de l'orient et des contrées lointaines* (Paris, no date). **A**

3952. —— *Sur les danses de Java, de l'Indo-*chine et de l'Inde* ('Revue musicale' V, No. 4), 1st Febr. 1924. **CD¹FGHKL**

3953. **Stevenson, Robert**, *Music in Mexico* (New York, 1952). **B**

3954. **Stewart, J. L.**, *Northern Gold Coast Songs* ('African Music Society Newsletter' I, No. 5, p. 39 ff.), 1952. **ACJM**

3954a. **Stockmann, Erich**, *Kaukasische und albanische Mehrstimmigkeit* ('Kongressbericht Ges. f. Musikforschung, Hamburg 1956', p. 229 ff.). **CEL**

3955. **Stoïn, Elena**, *Suvremennata Bulgarska pessen* ('Izvestia na Instituta za musika' I, publ. by the Bulgarska Akademia na Naukite), Sofia, 1952.

3956. —— *Lazaruvane v selo naguschevo* (ibid. II–III), Sofia, 1956.

3957. —— *Narodni partizanski pesni* (publ. by the Bulgarska Akademia na Naukite), Sofia, 1955.

3958. **Stoïn, Vasil**, *Kum Bulgarskite narodni napevi* ('Izvestia na narodniya etnografski musey', fasc. III and IV, 4th year), Sofia, 1924.

3959. —— *Hypothèse sur l'origine bulgare de la diaphonie* (Sofia, 1925).

3960. —— *Bulgarska narodna muzika: metrika i ritmika* (Sofia, 1927).

3961. —— *Narodni pesni ot Timok do Vita* (Sofia, 1928). **A**

3962. —— *Bulgarski narodni pesni ot istochna i zapadna Trakia* (i.e. Bulgarian folk music from eastern and western Thracia), Sofia, 1929.

3963. —— *Narodni pesni ot sredna severna Bulgaria* (i.e. Folk music from north Central Bulgaria), Sofia, 1931. **A**

3964. —— *Svirka Dvoyanka* ('Bull. du Musée Nat. d'Ethnogr.' XII, p. 86 ff.), Sofia, 1936.

3965. —— *Narodni pesni ot zapadnite pokraynini* (in preparation).

3966. **Stoll, Dennis Gray**, *The 'Graces' of Indian Music* ('Asiatic Review' N.S. XXXVIII, p. 167 ff.), 1942. **D¹H**

3967. —— *The elements of Indian music* ('The Asiatic Review' XLI, No. 146), April, 1945. **AD¹H**

3968. **Stone, William H.**, *Panpipes (Pandean pipes)* ('Grove's Dictionary of Music and Musicians' 5th ed., vol. VI, p. 538 ff.), 1954 (with additions by Anthony Baines). **ACFH¹K**

3969. **Stooke, Herbert J.**, and **K. Khandalavala**, *The Laud ragamala miniatures. A study in Indian painting and music* (Oxford, 1953).

3970. **Stowel, H. M.**, *An ancient 'flute-song'* ('Journal of the Polynesian Soc.' XXVII, p. 222 ff.), 1918. **BG**

3971. **Strang, Gerald**, *The sliding tones in oriental music* ('Bull. of the Amer. Musicol. Soc.' VIII, p. 29 ff.), 1945.

3971a. Štrekelj, K., and J. Glonar, *Sloven-
ske narodne pesmi iz tiskanih in pisanih
virov* (Ljubljana, 1895–1923).

3972. Strelnikov, J. D., *La musica y la
danza de las tribus indias Kaa-Ihwua
(Guarani) y Botocudo* ('Proc. of the
23rd Congr. of Americanists' 1928, p.
796 ff.), New York, 1930.

3973. Strehlow, T. G. H., *Australian aboriginal songs* ('Journal of the Intern.
Folk Music Council' VII, p. 37 ff.),
1955.   **ACJKL**

3974. Strickland-Anderson, Lily, *Rabindranath Tagore, poet-composer* ('The Musical Quarterly' X, p. 463 ff.), 1924. **C**

3975. —— *Music in Malaya* (ibid. XI, p. 506
ff.), 1925.   **CF**

3977. —— *The Cambodian ballet* (ibid. XII,
p. 206 ff.), 1926.

3978. —— *Aboriginal and animistic influences in Indian music* (ibid. XV, p. 371
ff.), 1929.   **C**

3979. —— *The mythological background of
Hindu music* (ibid. XVII, p. 330 ff.),
1931.   **C**

3980. —— *Devil dances amid eternal snows*
('Asia' Dec. 1925, p. 1039 ff.).   **AD¹**

3981. —— *A sketch of the origin and development of Egyptian music* ('Calcutta
Review' II), 1924.

3982. Struck, Bernhard, *Afrikanische Kugel-
flöten* ('Kol. Rundschau' Heft 2–6, pp.
56 ff., 190 ff., 236 ff.), 1922.   **D¹L²**

3983. Stumme, H., *Tripolitanisch-tunesische
Beduinenlieder* (Leipzig, 1894).

3984. Stumpf, Carl, *Musikpsychologie in
England. Betrachtungen über die Her-
leitung der Musik aus der Sprache
und aus dem tierischen Entwicklungs-
prozess, über Empirismus und Nativis-
mus in der Musiktheorie* ('Vierteljahrschr. f. Musikw.' I, 1885). **CDFKL**

3985. —— *Lieder der Bellakula-Indianer*
(ibid. II, 1886 (CDFKL); repr. in:
'Sammelb. f. vergl. Musikw.' I, 1922).
ACDFGH¹IKLL¹

3986. Review of Alexander J. Ellis, 'On
the musical scales of various nations'
('Vierteljahrschr. f. Musikw.' II, p. 511
ff.), 1886.   **CDFKL**

3987. —— *Mongolische Gesänge* (ibid. III,
1887 (CDFKL); repr. in 'Sammelbände
f. vergl. Musikw.' I, 1922). **ACGH¹IKLL¹**

3988. —— *Tonpsychologie*, vol. I (1883); vol.
II (1890).

3989. —— *Ueber Vergleichungen von Tondis-
tanzen* ('Z. f. Psychol. und Physiol. der
Sinnesorgane' I), 1890.   **D¹GH**

3990. —— *Phonographierte Indianermelodien*
('Vierteljahrschr. f. Musikw.' VIII,
1892 (CDFKL); repr. in 'Sammelb. f.
vergl. Musikw.' I, 1922).
ACDFGH¹IKLL¹

3991. —— *Maassbestimmungen über die Reinheit konsonanter Intervalle* (in collab.
with M. Mayer) ('Z. f. Psychol. und
Physiol. der Sinnesorgane' XVIII),
1898.   **D¹GH**

3992. —— *Tontabellen* (in collab. with K. L.
Schaefer) ('Beiträge zur Akustik und
Musikw.', fasc. 3), 1901.   **L**

3993. —— *Tonsystem und Musik der Siamesen* (ibid., fasc. 3, 1901 (L); 'Sammelb. f. vergl. Musikw.' I, 1922).
ACGH¹IKLL¹

3994. —— *Das Berliner Phonogrammarchiv*
('Intern. Wochenschr.', 1909).   **CHK**

3995. —— *Die Anfänge der Musik* ('Intern.
Wochenschr.' 1909).   **HK**

3996. —— *Ueber die Bedeutung ethnologischer
Untersuchungen für die Psychologie und
Aesthetik der Tonkunst* (in collab. with
E. M. von Hornbostel) ('Kongressbe-
richt 4th Congress of the Gesellsch. f.
experimentelle Psychologie 1911'). **ABI**

3997. —— *Die Anfänge der Musik* (Leipzig,
1911).   **BCEFJLL²**

3998. —— *Singen und Sprechen* ('Z. f.
Psychol. u. Physiol. der Sinnesorgane'
XCVI), 1923.   **D¹GH**

3999. —— *Die Sprachlaute. Experimentell-
phonetische Untersuchungen nebst einem
Anhang über Instrumentalklänge* (Berlin, 1926).

4000. Style, E., *Musical notations of the
Chinese* ('J. of the R. Asiatic Soc.,
North-China branch', O.S. No. 2, p.
176), 1859.   **KL⁵**
Subba Rao, Sri B., see: Rao, Sri B.
Subba,
Subba Rao, T. V., see: Rao, T. V.
Subba,

4001. Subrahmanya Sastri, Pandit S., *The
mela raga malika of Maha Vaidyanatha
Sivan* (Madras, 1937).

4002. Suchy, František, *Lidové písně a tance z
polabí na kralovéněštecku* (Prague, 1955).

4003. Sunaga, Katsumi, *Japanese Music*
(London, 1936).   **AGIJ**

4004. Sušil, F., *Moravské národní písne s
nápevy do textu vraděnymi* (Prague,
1832–'60, 3/1941, 4/1951).

4004a. Švabe, A., K. Strauberg, E. Hauzen-
berga-Šturma, *Latviešu tautas dziesmas*
(Copenhagen, 1952).

4005. Svensson, Sven E., *Studier i eskimo-
musikens intervallförräd och tonalitet*
('Svensk tidskrift för musikforskning'
XXXVIII, p. 135 ff.), Stockholm, 1957.
K

4006. Swan, A., *The nature of Russian folk-
song* ('The Musical Quarterly' XXIX,
p. 498 ff.), 1943.   **CH¹**

4007. Swanton, John R., *Religious beliefs and
medical practices of the Creek Indians*
('Annual Report of the Bur. of Amer.

Ethnology' No. 42 (1924–'25), p. 477 ff.), Washington D.C., 1928. **BGKL²**

4008. **Swartz, J. F. A.**, *A hobbyist looks at Zulu and Xhosa songs* ('African Music' I, No. 3, p. 29 ff.), 1956. **ACJLM**

4009. **Swarup, Rai Bahadur Bishan**, *Theory of Indian Music* (Swarup Brothers, Maithan, Agra, 1933). **I**

4009a. **Swets, W.**, *Het ensemble van de Bulgaarse republiek* ('Grammofoon voor kenner en liefhebber' Dec. 1957, p. 18 ff.). **A**

4010. **Sykes, M.**, *Notes on Musical Instruments in Khorasan with special reference to the Gypsies* ('Man' IX, p. 161 ff., No. 94), 1909. **ABD¹GJKL²M**

4012. **Szabolcsi, Bence**, *Népvándorláskori elemek a magyar népzenében* ('Ethnographia' 1934, p. 138 ff.). – Engl. transl.: *Eastern relations of early Hungarian folk music*) ('J. of the R. Asiatic Soc.' 1935, p. 483 ff.

4013. —— *Egyetemes müvelődéstörténet és ötfoku hangsorok* (i.e. The spread of pentatonic scales and their importance for musical history) ('Ethnographia' 1936, p. 233 ff.).

4014. —— *Ueber Kulturkreise der musikalischen Ornamentik in Europa* ('Z. f. Musikw.' XVII, p. 65 ff.), 1935. **CDH¹KL**

4015. —— *Morgenland und Abendland in der ungarischen Volksmusik* ('Ung. Jahrb.' XVIII, p. 202 ff.), Berlin, 1928.

4016. —— *Adatok a középázsiai dallamtipus elterjedéséhez* (i.e. About the spread of the Central-asian melodytype), Budapest, 1950, 2/1957.

4017. —— *A primitiv dallamosság: a hanglejtéstől az otfokúsdsig* (i.e. Primitive Melodik: vom Tonfall zur Pentatonie) (in: 'Mélanges offerts à Zoltan Kodály à l'occasion de son 60ième anniversaire', p. 19 ff.), Budapest, 1943. **ACK**

4018. —— *Five-tone scales and civilization* ('Acta Musicologica' XV, p. 24 ff.), 1943. **CEKLL¹**

4019. —— *A melódia története* (i.e. Studies on the development of melody), Budapest, 1950, 2/1957.

4020. —— *Népzene és Történelem* (i.e. Folk music and History), Budapest, 1954.

4021. —— *A XVII. szárad Magyar világi dallamai* (i.e. Hungarian wordly melodies from the XVII. century), Budapest, no date. **K**

4021a. —— *Osztyák és vogul dallamok* (i.e. Ostyak and Wogulian melodies) ('Ethnographia' XLVIII No. 4), Budapest, 1937.

4021b. **Szendrey, Zsigmond**, and Zoltán Kodály, *Nagyszalontai guyjtés* (Budapest, 1924).

*4021c. **Szöllősy, András**, *Bartók Béla válogatott zenei irásai* (= Selected articles on music by Bela Bartok), Budapest, 1948. Among them the following may be mentioned:

4. *Magyar népzene és új magyar zene* (1928) (= The Hungarian folk music and the new Hungarian music);

5. *A régi magyar népzenéről* (1933) (= About the ancient hungarian folk music);

6. *Mi a népzene?* (1931) (= What is folk music?);

7. *A parasztzene hatása az újabb müzenére* (1931) (= The influence of peasant music on the modern art music);

8. *A népzene jelentőségéről* (1931) (= On the importance of folk music);

9. *Az összehasonlító zenefolklore* (1912) (= The comparative musical folklore);

10. *Magyarországi népzenei kutatások* (1929) (= Hungarian investigations in the field of folk music);

11. *Magyar népzene* (1935) (= Hungarian folk music);

12. *Román népzene* (1935) (= Rumanian folk music);

13. *Szlovák népzene* (1935) (= Slovakian folk music);

14. *Népdalgyüjtés Törökországban* (1937) (= Collecting folk songs in Turkey) (cf. No. 275);

15. *Az úgynevezett bolgár ritmus* (1938) (= On the so called Bulgarian rhythm);

16. *Miért és hogyan gyüjtsünk népzenét* (1936) (= Why and how should we collect folk music) (cf. No. 281);

17. *Népdalkutatás és nacionalizmus* (1937) (= The study of folk music and nationalism);

18. *Zene és faji tisztaság* (1944) (= Music and racial purity) (cf. No. 278);

24. *Cigányzene? Magyar zene?* (1931) (= Gypsy music? Hungarian music?);

28. *Vita a román népdalgyüjtésről Sereghy Elemérrel és Hubay Jenővel* (1920) I–VI (= Discussion with E. Sereghy and J. Hubay on the collecting of Rumanian folk music) I–VI.

4022. **Tagore, Surindro Mohun**, *Short Notices of Hindu Musical Instruments* (Calcutta, 1877). **ACFG**

4023. —— *Hindu music*, vol. I (Calcutta, 1875). **CH**

4024. —— *Theory of Sanskrit music*, compiled from the ancient authorities (Calcutta, 1875). **CHK**

4026. —— *Yantra Kosha, or a treasury of the musical instruments of ancient and of modern India, and of various other countries* (Calcutta, 1875). **CG**

4026a. —— *Theory of Sanskrit music* (Calcutta, 1875). **CF**

4026b. —— Six principal ragas (Calcutta, 1875). **F**

4026c. —— A Vedic hymn (Calcutta, 1878). **F**

4027. —— A few specimens of Indian songs (Calcutta, 1879). **CF**

4028. —— The ten principal avatara of the Hindus (Calcutta, 1880). **CF**

4029. —— The eight principal rasas of the Hindus (Calcutta, 1880). **CF**

4030. —— The five principal musicians of the Hindus (Calcutta, 1880). **CFGK**

4031. —— Hindu Music from various authors (Calcutta, 1882). **CFIKL²**

4032. —— The musical scales of the Hindus (Calcutta, 1884). **CFK**

4033. Taig, Th., Rhythm and Metre (1930).

4034. Takacs, Jenő von, Arabische Musik in Aegypten ('Auftakt' IX, p. 241 ff.), 1929.

4035. Takano, Kiyosi, Theorie der japanischen Musik ('Tohoku Psychologica Folia' III, fasc. 2–3), Sendai, 1935. **G**

4036. —— Beiträge zur Geschichte der japanischen Musik ('Archiv f. Musikforschung' II, fasc. 3), 1937. **CDH¹KL**

4037. Takeda, Chuichiro, Songs of the Mongols, notations and explanations (' Journal of the Soc. for Research in Asiatic music' 10/11, p. 67 ff.), Dec. 1952.

4038. Taki, R., On the P'i-p'a or Chinese lutes ('Journal of the Soc. f. Research in Asiatic Music' 9, p. 6 ff.), March 1951. **A**

4041. Tanabe, Hideo, Les études récentes concernant les instruments de musique du Japon ('Art populaire' II, p. 130), 1931. **A**

4042. —— The Character of Japanese Music (' Japanese Music'), Tokyo, 1953.

4043. Tanabe, Hisawo, Equal tempered scales of less than 12 tones in the Far East and a new proposal for a 14 tone equal temperament ('Journ. of the Soc. for Research in Asiatic music' IX), March, 1951. **A**

4044. —— Die Weltbedeutung der alten chinesischen Musik ('Die Musikwelt', Shanghai 1923, fasc. 4).

4045. —— Japanese music (Tokyo, 1936, 2/ 1937). **ACI**

4046. Tanaka, S., An Investigation of the Tuning of the Siamese Seven Tone Equal Tempered Scale ('Journal of the Soc. for Research in Asiatic Music' IX, p. 1 ff.), 1951. **A**

4047. Tanghe, Basiel, De ziel van het Ngbandivolk (Congo Bibliotheek), Brugge, De Gruuthuuse Persen, 1929 (p. 95 ff.).

4048. —— De Ngbandi naar het leven geschetst (Congo Bibliotheek), Brugge, De Gruuthuuse Persen, 1929 (p. 9 ff. and 210 ff.).

4049. Tanghe, Joseph, La musique nègre ('La Revue Sincère' XI, p. 274 ff.), Brussels, 1933.

4050. Tannery, P., L'invention de l'hydraulis ('Revue des Études grecques' XXI), 1908. **D¹GL¹**

4051. Tantawi Gawhari, Al-musiqa al-Arabiyya (Alexandria, 1914). **G**

4052. Tappert, Wilhelm, Wandernde Melodien (Leipzig 1868, 2/1890).

4053. Tarenne, G., Recherches sur les Ranz des vaches, ou sur les chansons pastorales des bergers de la Suisse (Paris, 1813). **C**

4054. Tate, H., Australian aboriginal music ('Canon' V, p. 249 ff.), 1951.

4055. Tauern, O. D., Patasiwa und Patalima (Leipzig, 1918), s.v. Lieder (p. 73 ff. and 193 ff.). **B**

4056. Tavares de Lima, Rossini, Melodia et ritmo no folclore de Sao Paulo (Sao Paulo, 1954).

*4057. Taylor, C. R. H., A Pacific Bibliography (Wellington, 1951), pp. 46, 79, 129, 188, 227, 242, 256, 298, 319, 333, 345, 381, 434, and 446. **AB**

4058. Taylor, M., Did Pharaoh Necho's minstrels visit South Africa? ('Ill. London News' CLXXI, p. 1058 ff.), 1927.

4059. Taylor, W. H., Bantu music in Kenya ('Oversea Education' V, p. 168 ff.), 1934.

4060. Tcherepnin, A., Music in modern China ('The Musical Quarterly' XXI, p. 391 ff.), 1935. **CD**

4061. Tegethoff, W., Tendances nouvelles dans la musicologie comparative ('Aequatoria' XVIII), Coquilhatville, 1955. **GL²M**

4062. Telang, Mangesa Ramakrishna, The 22 srutis of Indian music (Poona, 1933). **I**

4062a. Terada, T., A coustical investigation of the Japanese bamboopipe syakuhati (' J. of the College of Science, Imp. Univ. of Tokyo' XXI/10), 1907.

4063. Terry, Richard R., Vooduism music (London, 1934).

4064. Thalbitzer, William, and Hjalmar Thuren, La musique chez les Esquimaux ('Mercure musical', 1911).

4065. —— Eskimomusik und Dichtkunst in Grönland ('Anthropos' VI, p. 485 ff.), 1911. **D¹GKL¹L²M**

4066. —— and Hjalmar Thuren, Melodies from East Greenland with a supplement containing melodies from Nordwest Greenland ('Meddelelse om Grønland' XL, II/1,) Copenhagen, 1911. **GKL¹L²**

4067. —— and —— Musik aus Ostgrönland; eskimoische Phonogramme ('Z. d. Intern. Musikges.' XII), 1910/'11. **CDFH¹KL**

4069. Thalbitzer, William, Cultic games and festivals in Greenland ('Compte rendu de la 21e session du Congrès Intern. des Américanistes' II), Göteburg, 1925. **K**

4070. —— *Légendes et chants esquimaux du Greenland* (1920). **K**

4071. —— *Eskimo-liederen van Oost-Groenland* (Santpoort, 1933). (Dutch transl. by Annie Posthumus). **AK**

4072. —— *Inuit sange og danse fra Grønland* (Copenhagen, 1939). **CK**

4072a. Thilenius/Meinhof/Heinitz, *Die Trommelsprache in Afrika und in der Südsee*) ('Vox' XXVI), 1916. **G**

4073. Thornton, P., *The voice of Atlas: in search of music in Morocco* (London, 1936). **CGIJ**

4074. Thorsteinsson, Bjarni, *Icelandic folktunes* (1906–'09). **K**

4075. —— *Folkelig Sang og Musik paa Island* ('Nordisk Kultur. Musikk och Musikkinstrumenter', p. 139 ff.), 1934. **AK**

4076. Thuren, Hjalmar L., *Tanz, Dichtung und Gesang auf den Färöern* ('Sammelb. d. Intern. Musikges.' III, p. 222 ff.), 1902. **ACDFH¹IKL**

4077. —— *Folkesangen paa Faerøerne* (Copenhagen, 1908) (with German summary). **K**

4078. —— *On the Eskimo music in Greenland* ('Meddelelse om Grønland' XL, II/1), Copenhagen, 1911. **GKL¹L²**

4080. —— *The Eskimo Music* (1912). **CK**

4081. —— *La musique chez les Eskimo* (Paris, 1912). **CK**

4082. —— *Das dänische Volkslied* ('Z. d. Intern. Musikges.' IX, p. 13 ff.), 1907. **CDFH¹KL**

4082a. —— *Tanz und Tanzgesang im nordischen Mittelalter nach der dänischen Balladendichtung* ('Z. d. Intern. Musikges.' IX, p. 209 ff., 239 ff.), 1907. **CDFH¹KL**

4083. —— and William Thalbitzer, *Musik aus Ostgrönland: Eskimoische Phonogramme* ('Z. der Intern Musikges.' XII, p. 33 ff.), 1910. **CDFH¹KL**

4084. —— and H. Gruener-Nielsen, *Faerøske melodier til danske kaempeviser* (Copenhagen, 1923). **K**

4085. Thurston Dart, R., *Notation* ('Grove's Dictionary of Music and Musicians' 5th ed. VI, p. 108 ff.), 1954. **ACFH¹K**

4085a. Tiby, Ottavio, *Corpus di musiche popolari Siciliane* (2 vols.) (Palermo, 1957).

4086. Tiersot, Julien, *Histoire de la chanson populaire en France* (Paris, 1889). **CD¹GHL**

4086a. —— *Les types mélodiques dans la chanson populaire française* (Paris, 1893).

4087. —— *Chansons populaires des Alpes françaises (Savoie et Dauphiné)* (Grenoble, 1903).

*4088. —— *Notes d'Ethnographie musicale. La musique chez les peuples indigènes de l'Amérique du Nord (Etats-Unis et Canada)* ('Sammelb. d. Intern. Musikges.' XI, p. 141 ff.), Leipzig, 1909/'10. **CDFH¹JL**

4089. —— *Chansons nègres* (Paris, 1933). **C**

4090. —— *La musique chez les nègres d'Afrique* (in Lavignac, 'Hist. de la Musique' 1st. Part, vol. V, p. 3197 ff.), Paris, 1922. **AC**

4091. —— *Mediterranean folk-song* ('The Musical Quarterly' XV, p. 522 ff.), 1929. **C**

4092. Tiessen, Heinz, *Musik der Natur. Ueber den Gesang der Vögel, insbesondere über Tonsprache und Form des Amselgesanges* (Atlantis-Verlag, 1953). **A**

4093. Til, Salomon van, *Digt-, sang- en speelkonst, soo der Ouden, als bysonder der Hebreen* (Dordregt, Dirk Goris, 1692). With drawings of musical instruments by A. Houbraken. **C**

4094. Tillema, H., *Uit Apokajan. Muziekinstrumenten (de kediree)* ('Tropisch Nederland' VI, p. 234 ff. and 249 ff.), 1933/'34. **BD¹**

4095. Tillyard, H. Julius W., *Byzantine Music* ('Grove's Dictionary of Music and Musicians' 5th ed. vol. I, p. 1008 ff.), 1954. **ACFH¹K**

4096. Tinoco, Maria F. de, and Guillermo Aguilar Machado, *Una ocarina huetar de 18 notas del Museo Nacional de Costa Rica* (San José, 1937).

4097. Tirén, K., *Die lappische Volksmusik* ('Acta lapponica' III, p. 155 ff.), 1942. **AGKL**

4098. Titiev, Mischa, *Social singing among the Mapuche* (Ann Arbor, 1949). **H**

4099. Tobler, Alfred, *Das Volkslied im Appenzellerlande* (Zürich, 1903).

4100. —— *Kühreihen oder Kühreigen, Jodel und Jodellied in Appenzell* (Zürich, 1890).

4101. Tod, James, *Music* (in Surendro Mohun Tagore, 'Hindu music from various authors' p. 275 ff.), Calcutta, 1882. **CFIKL²**

4102. Törnberg, Gerda, *Musical instruments of the Afro-Cubans* ('Ethnos' XIX, p. 105 ff.), 1954. **ABJL²M**

4103. Tokyo, Academy of Music of, *Collection of Japanese Koto music* (Tokyo, 1888). **J**

4103a. Tonkovič, Pavol, *Spevy z Oravy* (Bratislava, 1953).

4104. —— *Slowakische Volksmusik und ihre Instrumente* ('Musica' 1957, p. 541 ff.). **CKLL¹**

4105. Toor, Frances, *A Treasury of Mexican Folkways*, p. 299 ff. Part. III. Music-Verse-Dance (New York, 5/1956). **J**

4106. Torday, Emil, *Songs of the Balubaof Lake Moero* ('Man' IV, p. 117 ff. (No. 80)), 1904. **BD¹GKL²M**

4107. —— and Thomas Athol Joyce, *Notes on the ethnography of the Ba-Mbala* ('J. of the R. Anthrop. Inst. of Great Britain and Ireland' XXXV, p. 413 ff.), 1905. GIKL¹L²M

4108. —— and —— On the ethnology of the South-West Congo Free State (ibid. XXXVII, p. 150), 1907. GIKL¹L²M

4109. —— and —— Notes ethnographiques sur les populations habitant les bassins du Kasai et du Kwango oriental ('Ann. du Mus. du Congo, Ser. III, Ethnol.' II, part 2, pp. 18 ff., 25, 55 ff., 203, 274 ff.), Brussels, 1922. GKM

4110. Torhout, Nirgidma de, and M. Humbert-Sauvageot, 18 Chants et Poèmes mongols (Paris, 1937). K

4111. Torner, Eduardo Martinez, Cancionero musical de la lirica popular asturiana (Madrid, 1920).

*4112. —— Bibliographie du folklore musical Espagnol ('Art populaire' II, p. 159 ff.), 1931. A

4113. —— La Cancion tradicional Española (in F. Carreras y Candi, 'Folklore y costumbres de España') Barcelona undated.

4113a. Tóth, Kálmán Cs., Halottas énekeskönyveink dullamai (= Melodies from our songs of death books) ('Emlékkönyv Kodály Zoltán 70. születésnapjára' p. 287 ff.), Budapest, 1953. A

4114. Touzé, M., Sur les modes musulmans ('Revue musicale' VII No. 1), 1st Nov. 1925. CD¹GH¹KL

4115. Tracey, Hugh T., Native music and the church ('Native Teacher's Journal' XI, p. 110 ff.), 1931/32.

4116. —— African folk music ('Man' XXXII, p. 118 ff.), 1932. BD¹GKL¹L²M

4117. —— Some observations on native music of Southern Rhodesia ('Nada' VII, p. 96 ff.), Buluwayo, 1929. M

4118. —— The tuning of musical instruments ('Nada' XIII, p. 35 ff. and 107 ff.), Buluwayo, 1935. M

4119. —— Marimbas: os xylophones dos Changanes ('Moçambique' 31st Oct. 1942), p. 49 ff.

4120. —— Música, poesia e ballados Chopes (ibid. 30th June 1942), p. 69 ff.

4121. —— Chief above and Chief below, a musical play for Africans (1944).

4122. —— Ngoma, an introduction to Music for Southern Africans (London, 1948). ACJKM

4123. —— Chopi Musicans. Their Music, Poetry and Instruments (Oxford, 1948). ACIJKLM

4124. —— Organized research in African music ('Rhodes-Livingstone Journal' VI, p. 48 ff.), 1948. L

4125. —— Lalela Zulu (100 Zulu Lyrics), Johannesburg, 1948. J

4126. —— African Dances of the Witwaters-

rand Gold Mines (with photographs by Merlyn Severn), Johannesburg, 1952. AFM

4127. —— Musical Wood ('African Music Society Newsletter' I, No. 2, p. 17 ff.), 1949. ACM

4128. —— The state of Folk Music in Bantu Africa ('Journal of the Intern. Folk Music Council' VI, p. 32 ff.), 1954. ACJKL

4129. —— Bantu Music ('Grove's Dictionary' 5th ed. vol. I, p. 416 ff.), 1954. ACFH¹K

4129a. —— Recording in East Africa and Northern Congo ('African Music Soc. Newsletter' I, No. 6, p. 6 ff.), 1953. ACJM

4129b. —— Short survey of Southern African folk music for the International catalogue of folk music records ('African Music Soc. Newsletter' I, No. 6, p. 41 ff.), 1953. ACJM

4129c. —— Evolution et continuité de la musique africaine ('Education de base et Education des adultes' IV, No. 3, p. 27 ff.), 1952. M

4129d. —— Bantu music ('Theoria' 1953, No. 5, p. 55 ff.). M

4129e. —— African music and dancing ('United Empire' XLIV, p. 252 ff.), 1953. M

4130. —— The social role of African music ('African Affairs' LIII, p. 234 ff.), 1954. BKL¹L²M

4131. —— The problem of the future of Bantu music in the Congo ('Problèmes d'Afrique Centrale' No. 26, p. 272 ff.), 1954. AGJKM

4132. —— African winds ('Woodwind Magazine' V, p. 4 ff.), 1953.

4133. —— The state of folk music in Bantu Africa ('African Music' I, No. 1, p. 8 ff.), 1954. ACJLM

4134. —— Recording African music in the field ('African Music' I, No. 2, p. 6 ff.), 1955. ACJLM

4135. —— Handbook for Librarians (Johannesburg, 1957).

4136. —— Notes on Canon Lury's article ('African Music' I, No. 3, p. 36), 1956. ACJLM

4136a. —— Música africana ('Bol. Soc. Estudos Colon. de Moçambique' XXI, p. 61 ff.), 1951. M

4136b. —— Gentes afortunadas. VI. As tibilas, xilofones dos Chopes. VII. Fabrico de timbilas ('Moçambique' 1948, No. 54, p. 97 ff., No. 55, p. 15 ff.), 1948. M

4136c. —— Human problems in British Central Africa: organised research in african music ('Rhodes-Livingstone Journal' 1948, No. 6, p. 48 ff.). M

4136d. —— Blindness – a sanction ('Nada' 1947, No. 24, p. 94). M

4136e. —— Gentes afortunadas ('Moçambi-

que' No. 46, p. 93 ff., No. 47, p. 103 ff.,
No. 48, p. 77 ff.), 1946. **M**

4136f. —— *Native dancing. A wasted asset*
('Nada' No. 17, p. 28 ff.), 1940. **M**

4136g. —— *African music. A modern view*
('Nada' No. 19, p. 57 ff.), 1942. **M**

4136h. —— *A study of native music in Rhodesia* ('Nada' 1949, No. 26, p. 27 ff.). M

4136i. —— *Songs from the kraals of Southern
Rhodesia* (Salisbury, The Rhod. Prin-
ting and Publ. Co., 1933).

4136j. —— *Recording in the Lost Valley*
('African Music' I No. 4, p. 45 ff.), 1957.
ACJLM

4137. **Traeger, P.**, *Die Deutschen in der Dob-
rudscha* (Stuttgart, 1922), p. 182 ff.

4138. **Traynor, Leo**, and **Shigeo Kishibe**, *The
four unknown pipes of the Sho (mouth
organ) used in ancient Japanese court
music* ('Journal of the Soc. f. Research
in Asiatic Music' IX, p. 26 ff.), March
1951. **A**

4139. **Trebitsch, R.**, *Phonographische Aufnahmen in Irischer Sprache und einiger
Musikinstrumente in Irland und Wales*
(1908).

4140. —— *Phonographische Aufnahmen in
der bretonische Sprache und zweier Musikinstrumente in der Bretagne* (1908).

4141. —— *Baskische Sprach- und Musikauf-
nahmen* (1914). .

4142. **Trefzger, Heinz**, *Die Musik in China*
('Sinica' XI), Frankfurt, 1936. **GK**

4143. —— *Das Musikleben der T'ang-Zeit*
('Sinica' XIII), Stuttgart, 1938. **GK**

4144. —— *Ueber das K'in, seine Geschichte,
seine Technik, seine Notation und seine
Philosophie* ('Schweiz. Musikzeitung'
LXXXVIII, p. 81 ff.), 1948.

4145. —— *Ueber das Sheng* ('Hug's Musik-
kurier' IV, No. 1, p. 2 ff.), Zürich,
March 1948. **A**

4146. —— *Ueber die chinesischen Notenschriften* ('Universitas' VI, p. 753 ff.), 1951.
D¹KL¹

*4147. **Trend, J. B.**, *Spanish Folk Music*
('Grove's Dictionary' 5th ed. vol. III,
p. 368 ff.), 1954. **ACFH¹K**

4148. **Tricon, A.**, and **Ch. Bellan**, *Chansons
cambodgiennes* (Saigon, 1921).

4149. **Trilles, Henri**, *La marimba et l'anzang*
('Revue Musicale' V, p. 473 ff.), 1905.
K

4150. **Troj, F.**, *O muzičkoj osetlivosti Južno-
srbijanaca Sumadinaca i Crnogoraca*
(Skoplje, 1931).

4151. **Troyer, Carlos**, *Indian music lecture:
the Zuñi Indians and their music*
(Philadelphia, 1913). **I**

4152. **Trubetzkoy, Prince N. S.**, *Zur Struktur
der Mordwinischen Melodien* (Akad. d.
Wiss. in Wien, Phil.-hist. Kl., Sitzungsber., vol. 205, p. 106 ff.), 1933.

4152a. **Tsala, Th.**, *'Nkui' ou le tam-tam*
('Presses missionnaires' 1955, No. 22,
p. 3). **M**

4153. **Tucker, A. N.**, *Tribal Music and Dancing in the Southern Sudan* (London,
1933.) **CJ**

4154. —— *Music in South Sudan* ('Man'
XXXII, p. 18 ff.,(No.12)), 1932.
BD¹GKL¹L²M

4155. —— *Childrens games and songs in the
Southern Sudan* ('Journal of the Royal
Anthrop. Inst.' LXIII, p. 165 ff.), Lon-
don, 1933. **ABGIJKL¹L²M**

4156. **Turnbull, Colin M.**, *Pygmy music and
ceremonial* ('Man' LV, p. 23 ff. (No. 31)),
Febr. 1955. **BD¹GKL¹L²M**

4157. —— *Pygmy music and ceremonial* (ibid.
LVII, p. 128 (No. 157)), August, 1957.
BD¹GKL¹L²M

4158. **Tvermose Thyregod, S.**, *Danmarks
Sanglege* (Copenhagen, 1931). **K**

*4159. **Udry, Albert**, *Les vieilles chansons
patoises de tous les pays de France*
(Paris, 1930).

4159a. **Upadyaya, Krishna Deva**, *An introduction to Bhojpuri folksongs and ballads* ('Midwest Folklore' VII, No. 2, p.
85 ff.), summer 1957. **A**

4160. **Ursprung, Otto**, *Um die Frage nach
dem arabischen bzw. maurischen Einfluss
auf die abendländische Musik des Mittelalters* ('Z. f. Musikwiss.' XVI, p. 129 ff.
and 355 ff.), 1934. **CDH¹KL**

4161. **Uspenskij, V. A.**, and **V. Belayev**,
Torkmenskaya muzyka (Moscow, 1928).

4162. —— *Shas-Maqom* (i.e. 6 maqamat),
Bukhara, 1924.

4163. —— *Uzbekskaya vokalnaya muzyka* (i.e.
Uzbek vocal music), UZGIZ 1950.

4164. **Väänänen, Jorma**, *Beobachtungen über
Verbreitung und Art der finnischen
Volkswalzermelodien* (Helsinki, 1946).
IK

4165. **Václavek, Bedrich** and **Robert Smetana**,
České Světské pisne Zlidovělé vol. 1:
Pisně epické (Prag, 1955).

4166. —— and —— *České národní zpevnik.
Pisne české společnosti 19 stoleti* (Prague,
1949).

4167. **Väisänen, A. O.**, *Väinämöisen kantele
kuvissa* ('Kalevalaseuran vuosikirja' V,
p. 191 ff.), Helsinki, 1925. **K**

4168. —— *Das Zupfinstrument gusli bei den
Wolgavölkern* ('Suomalais Ugrilaisen
Seuran Toimituksia' LVIII, p. 303 ff.),
Helsinki, 1928. **K**

4169. —— *Kantele und Streichleier* ('Suomen
Kansan Sävelmiä' V), 1928.

4170. —— *Die Leier der ob-ugrischen Völker*
('Eurasia septentrion. antiqua' VI, p.
15 ff.), Helsinki, 1931. **D¹HK**

4171. —— *Wogulische und ostjakische Melodien* ('Suomalais Ugrilaisen Seuran

Toimituksia' LXXIII), Helsinki, 1937. **KL**

4172. ——— *Wirklichkeitsgrund der finnisch-estnischen Kantelerunen* ('Acta Ethnologica' I, p. 31 ff.), Copenhagen, 1938. **L²**

4173. ——— *Die Ob-ugrische Harfe* ('Finnisch-ugrische Forschungen' XXIV, p. 127 ff.), 1937. **D¹GK**

*4174. ——— *Untersuchungen über die ob-ugrischen Melodien* (Helsinki, 1939). **AK**

4175. ——— *Die Kantele der Wepsen* ('Mélanges offerts à Zoltan Kodaly', p. 337 ff.), 1943. **ACK**

4176. ——— *Finnische Volksmusik* ('Der Norden' XX, p. 196 ff.), 1943. **AK**

4177. ——— *Mordwinische Melodien* (Helsinki, 1948). **AKL**

4178. ——— *Suggestions for the methodical classification and investigation of folk tunes* ('Journal of the Intern. Folk Music Council' I, p. 34), 1949. **ACJKL**

4179. ——— *Finnisch-ugrische Musik* ('Die Musik in Geschichte und Gegenwart' IV, col. 229 ff.), 1954. **ACDEFGH¹KL**

4179a. ——— *Yajö Kilpinens kanteletar-Lieder* ('Kongressbericht Ges. f. Musikforschung, Hamburg 1956', p. 231 ff.). **CEL**

4179b. Vajro, M., *La musica negra e gli studii di afroamericanistica* ('Rivista di Etnografia' III, No. 4, p. 88 ff.), 1949. **M**

4180. Vakarelski, Christo, *La musique de mon village natal: Momina Clissoura, arrondissement Pasardjik* ('Izvestia na Instituta za Muzika (Sofia)' 1952, p. 167 ff. (with a French summary)).

4181. ——— and A. Primovski, *Musikalnofolklorni proyavi v plovdivskoto izlozenie pres 1892* ('Izvestia na instituta za musica', fasc. II–III), 1956.

4181a. Valaštan, Bohuslav, *Slovensky l'udovy spevnik* (Bratislava, 1956).

4182. Valcárcel y Vizcarra, L. E., *Músicos* (On representations of musical instruments in ancient Peruvian art) ('Cuadernos de Arte antiguo del Perú', Lima, 1938. **I**

4182a. Valen, Leigh van, *Talking drums and similar African tonal communication* ('Southern Folklore Quarterly' XIX, p. 252 ff.), Dec. 1955.

4183. Valentijn, François, *Oud en Nieuw Oost-Indiën* (Dordrecht/Amsterdam, 1724). II. *Beschrijvinge van Amboina*: p. 162 ff.: *Van de speeltuigen der Amboineesen*. **AB**

4184. Valentim, Afonso, Antonio Mourinho, and Santo Júnior, *Coreografia popular trasmontana* III. *O Galandum* ('Douro Litoral' VII–VIII, 5th series, p. 3 ff.), Porto, 1953.

4185. Valentin, Karl, *Studien über die schwedischen Volksmelodien* (Leipzig, 1885). **L**

4186. Valle, Flausino Rodrigues, *Elementos de folklore musical brasileiro* (Sao Paulo, 1936).

4187. Valle, Nicola, *Origine e tradizione dei canti caratteristici della Sardegna* ('Ricreazione' July/Aug. 1949, p. 83 ff.).

4187a. Vandewalle, I., *De dans bij de Pamitu* ('Nieuw Afrika' LXVII, p. 261 ff.), 1951. **M**

4188. Vandyopadhyana, Sri Pada, *The music of India. A popular handbook of Hindostani music* (D. B. Taraporevala Sons & Co., Bombay, 1945). **I**

4189. Vansina, J., *Laam, gezongen kwaadsprekerij bij de Bushong* ('Aequatoria' XXVIII, p. 125 ff.), 1955. **GL²M**

4190. Varagnac, A., *De la musique dans l'activité de l'homme* ('Polyphonie' 1950, No. 7–8, p. 31 ff.). **K**

4191. Vargias, Lájos, *Aj falu zenei élete* (i.e. The musical life of the village of Aj), Budapest, 1941.

4192. ——— *Példatar* (coll. of folksongs to the third ed. of Kodály's 'A magyar népzene'), Budapest, 1952.

4193. ——— *Ugor rétek a Magyar népzeneben* (i.e. The Ugrian elements in the Hungarian folk music) (in: 'Emlékkonyv Kodaly. I. 70 Zsulétesnapjára', p. 611 ff.), Budapest, 1953. **AC**

4194. ——— *Kollektives Schaffen in der Volksmusik* ('Acta Ethnographica' IV, p. 395 ff.), Budapest, 1955. **A**

4195. ——— *Die Wirkung des Dudelsacks auf die ungarische Volkstanzmusik* ('Studia Memoriae Belae Bartók Sacra', p. 503 ff.), Budapest, 1956. **AC**

4195a. ——— *Francia párhuzam regösénekeinkhez* (= The New Year begging songs and some French parallels) ('Néprajzi Közlemények' II No. 1–2, p. 1 ff.), Budapest, 1957.

4195b. ——— *Some parallels of rare modal structures in Western and Eastern Europe* ('J. of the Intern. Folk Music Council' X, p. 22 ff.), 1958. **ACIJKL**

*4196. Varley, Douglas H., *African Negro Music, an annotated Bibliography* (1936). **CGIJL²M**

4197. Varnoux, Jean, *Vietnamese Music* (from 'France-Asie' No. 52, July 1950) ('The Journal of the Music Academy, Madras' XXI, p. 136 ff.), 1950. **AC**

4198. Vasiljevic, Miodrag A., *Les bases tonales de la musique populaire serbe* ('Journal of the Intern. Folk Music Council' IV, p. 19 ff.), 1952. **AC**

4199. ——— *Yugoslavenska Musićki Folklora* I. *Serbia* (Beograd, 1952). **A**

4200. ——— *Yugoslavenska Musićki Folklora* II. *Makedonia* (Beograd, 1953). **AL**

4201. —— *Narodne Melodieje. Sandshak* (Beograd, 1953).   **A**

4201a. —— *Jedniglasni solfegio zasnovan na narodnom pevanju* (Beograd, 1958).   **A**

4202. Vatter, Ernst, *Ata Kiwan* (Leipzig, 1932), Chapter X. *Die Insel Solor* (p. 187 ff.); Chapter XIII, *Drei Reisen auf Alor* (p. 230, 238 ff.); Chapter XIV. *Zehn Tage auf Pantar* (p. 267 ff.); Chapter XV. *Die Rassen, Sprachen und Kulturen des Solor-Alor-Archipels* (p. 286).   **AB**

4203. Vattier, M., *Musique et musiciens maures* ('France-Maroc' 15th Febr. 1919).

4204. Vavrinecz, Béla, *Aszimmetrikus ritmusok* (i.e. The asymmetrical rhythms) (in 'Emlékkonyv Kodály. I. 70 Zsulétesnapjára' p. 567 ff.), Budapest, 1953.   **A**

4205. Vazquez Santana, Higinio, *Historia de la canción Mexicana. Canciones, cantares y corridos* (Mexico, Talleres Gráficos de la Nación), 1931.

4205a. *Vechi cintece de Viteji* (culegere alcatuita sub ingrijirea Institutului de Folclor), Bukarest, 1956.

4206. Vechten, C. van, *The Music of Spain* (London, 1920).   **C**

4206a. Veeder, P. V., *Japanese musical intervals* ('Transactions of the Asiatic Soc. of Japan' VII), 1879.

4207. Vega, Carlos, *La flauto de Pan andina* ('Proc. 25th Congress of Americanists, Buenos Aires 1932', p. 333 ff.), Buenos Aires, 1934.   **A**

4208. —— *Cantos y bailes africanos en El Plata* ('La Prensa', Buenos Aires, 1932).

4209. —— *Los instrumentos musicales aborigenes y criollos de la Argentina* (Buenos Aires, 1949).   **J**

4210. —— *Danzas y canciones Argentinas* (Buenos Aires, 1936).

4211. —— *Tonleitern mit Halbtönen in der Musik der alten Peruaner* ('Acta Musicologica' IX, p. 41 ff.), 1939.   **CDEH¹KLL¹**

4212. —— *Panorama de la musica popular argentina* (Buenos Aires, 1944).

4213. —— *Las danzas populares argentinas* (Buenos Aires, Ministerio de Educación, Dirección General de Cultura, Instituto de Musicología, 1952).

4214. Vela, David, *Noticia sobre la marimba* (Guatemala, 1953).
Venkatarama Iyer, Mudikondan C., see: Iyer, Mudikondan C. Venkatarama
Venkatarama Iyer, T. L., see: Iyer, T. L. Venkatarama

4216. Verbeken, A., *Le tambour-téléphone chez les indigènes de l'Afrique centrale* ('Congo' 1920, p. 253 ff.), Brussels, 1920.   **K**

4217. —— *La communication à distance chez les Noirs* (Elisabethville, 1920).

4218. —— *Le langage tambouriné des Congolais* ('African Music Society Newsletter' I, No. 6, p. 28 ff.), 1953. **ACJM**

4219. Verdeil, R. Palikarova, *La musique byzantine chez les Bulgares et les Russes du IXe au XIVe siècle* ('Monumenta Musicae Byzantinae' III), 1953.   **A**

4220. Veress, S., *Folkmusic in musical and general education* ('J. of the Intern. Folk Music Council' I, p. 40 ff.), 1949.   **AC**

4221. Verney, Frederick William, *Notes on Siamese Musical Instruments* (London, 1885).   **I**

4221a. Verwilghen, A., *Wat elk Europeaan weten moet over kongolese muziek* ('Zaïre' IV, No. 5, p. 489 ff.), 1950. **D¹GKL¹L²M**

4222. Vetter, Walther, *Ethos* ('Die Musik in Geschichte und Gegenwart' III, col. 1582 vv.), 1954.   **ACDEFGH¹KL**

4223. —— *Griechenland. A. Antike* ('Die Musik in Geschichte und Gegenwart' V, col. 840 ff.), 1956.   **ACDEFGH¹KL**

4224. —— *Ost und West in der Musikgeschichte* ('Die Musikforschung' I), 1948.
                                                           CEIKLL¹

4225. Vetterl, Karel, *Folk songs of East Czechoslovakia* ('Journal of the Intern. Folk Music Council' I, p. 35 ff.), 1949.
                                                                 ACKL

*4226. —— *Czech Folk Music* ('Grove's Dictionary' 5th ed. vol. III, p. 216 ff.), 1954.   **ACFH¹K**

4227. —— *Lidové písně a tance z valašskokloboucka* (Prague, 1955).   **A**

4228. Veurman, B., and D. Bax, *Liederen en dansen uit West-Friesland* (The Hague 1944).   **A**

4229. Vichitr-Vadakarn, H. E. Nai V., *The Evolution of Thai Music* ('Publ. of the Dept. of Fine Arts, Thailand'), 1942.
                                                                     A

4230. Viellard, Gilbert, *Le chant de l'Eau et du Palmier Doum, poème bucolique du marais nigérien* ('Bull. de l'Inst. Français d'Afrique Noire' II, Nos. 3–4, p. 299 ff.), 1940.   **GL²M**

4231. Viggiano Esain, Julio, *Instrumentologia musical popular argentina* (Buenos Aires, 1948).

4232. —— *La musicalidad de los Tupi Guaraní* (Cordoba, Argentina, 1954).

4233. Viglieti, Cedar, *Folklore en el Uruguay: la guitarra del Gaucho, sus danzas y canciones* (Montevideo, 1947).

4233a. Villemarqué, *Chants populaires de la Bretagne, Barzaz Bretz* (1867).

4234. Villoteau, G. A., *Abhandlung über die Musik des alten Ägyptens* (transl. from the French), Leipzig, 1821.   **CK**

4235. —— *Sur la musique en Egypte* (Paris, 1822/'23).   **C**

4236. Vinogradov, V., *Muzuka sovetskoj Kirgizii* (Moscow, 1939).

4237. —— *Uzeir Gadzhibekov i azerbajdzhanskaya muzyka* (Moscow, 1938).

4238. —— *O traditsiyakh narodnoi muzyki i razvitii khorovoi kultury* (i.e. On traditions of folk music and the developments of choral culture), ('Sovetskaya muzyka' 1951, No. 7, p. 49 ff.).

4239. —— *Piat duganskikh pesen* (i.e. Five Dugan songs) ('Sovetskaya muzyka' 1950, No. 5, p. 51 ff.).

4240. Virollaud, Ch., and Fernand Pélagaud, *La musique Assyro-Babylonienne* (1910) (in Lavignac, 'Hist. de la Mus.' I, p. 35 ff.), 1922. **ACDEFHJ**

Vissa Appa Rao, see: Rao, Vissa Appa.

4241. Vloten, van, and M. A. Brandts Buys, *Nederlandsche baker- en kinderrijmen* (Leyden, 3/1874). **H**

4242. Voegelin, Erminie Wheeler, *Shawnee musical instruments* ('Amer. Anthropol.' XLIV, p. 463 ff.), 1942. **GL²**

4243. Voigt, Alban, *Chinesische Musikinstrumente* ('Deutsche Instrumentenbauzeitschr.' XXXII), 1931.

4244. Vois, P., *La musique des vieux* ('Etudes Mélanésiennes', No. 2, p. 10 ff.), Nouméa 1939.

4245. Vojáček, I., *Folklore musicale du chant populaire de Bohème* ('Rivista Musicale Italiana' 1909). **CKL**

4246. Volland, *Beiträge zur Ethnographie der Bewohner von Armenien und Kurdistan* ('Archiv f. Anthropologie' XXXVI), 1909. **D¹**

4247. Voskuil, J., *De spreekmachine in de loop der eeuwen* ('Luister' No. 44, p. 217 ff.), Amersfoort, 15th May 1956. **AK**

4248. Vries, H. de, *Sprekende trommen van Afrika* (Publ. No. IX of the Exotic Music Soc.), Amsterdam, 1957. **A**

4248a. —— *The Exotic Music Society: its aims and activities* ('Ethnomusicology' II No. 2, p. 68 ff.), May 1958. **AGL**

4249. Vulpesco, M., *La chanson populaire en Roumanie* ('Revue musicale' XI, No. 24), Nov. 1927. **CD¹GKL**

Vuong Hong Sen, see: Sen, Vuong Hong.

4250. Vyasa, Lakshmidasa Adityarama, *Evolution of Indo-Aryan music and its present needs* (Ahmedabad, 1916). **I**

4251. Vysloužil, Jiri, *Folcloristica muzicala in Cechoslovacia* ('Revista de folclor' II, Nos. 1–2, p. 182 ff.), Bucarest, 1957. **AC**

4252. Vyzgo, T., *O rekonstruktsii uzbekskikh narodnykh instrumentov* (i.e. About the rebuilding of Uzbek national instruments ('Sovetskaya muzyka' 1954, No. 12, p. 56).

4253. —— *Muzykal'naja kul'tura sojuznych*

respublik (i.e. Musical culture in the Usbek republic), Moscow, 1954.

4254. Wachsmann, Klaus, *Untersuchungen zum vorgregorianischen Gesang* (Regensburg, 1935). **K**

4255. —— *An approach to African Music* ('Uganda Journal' VI, No. 3, p. 148 ff.), 1939. **L²M**

4256. —— *The Transplantation of Folk Music from one social environment to another* ('Journal of the Intern. Folk Music Council' VI, p. 41 ff.), 1954. **ACJKL**

4257. —— *An Equal-stepped Tuning in a Gandu Harp* ('Nature' Jan. 7th., 1950, p. 40 ff.). **AD¹GL¹M**

4258. —— *Tribal Crafts of Uganda* (in collab. with Margaret Trowell), Part II. *The Sound Instruments* (p. 309 ff.), 1953. **ABJLM**

4259. —— *Musicology in Uganda* ('Journal of the R. Anthrop. Inst. of Great Britain and Ireland' LXXXIII, p. 50 ff.), 1953. **BGIKL¹L²M**

4260. —— *Harp songs from Uganda* ('J. of the Intern. Folk Music Council' VIII, p. 23 ff.), 1956. **ACJKL**

4261. —— *Folk musicians in Uganda* (Uganda Museum occasional papers No. 2), Kampala, 1956. **ABJ**

4262. —— *A study of norms in the tribal music of Uganda* ('Ethnomusicology' Newsletter No. 11, p. 9 ff.), Sept. 1957. **AGL**

4262a. —— *A century of change in the folk music of an African tribe* ('J. of the Intern. Folk Music Council' X, p. 52 ff.), 1958. **ACIJKL**

4263. Waddell, L. A., *The 'Lepchas' or 'Rongs' and their Songs* ('Intern. Archiv f. Ethnogr.' XII, p. 41 ff.), 1899. **BD¹GKL²**

4264. Waengler, Hans-Heinrich, *Ueber südwest-afrikanische Bogenlieder* ('Afrika und Uebersee' XXXIX, p. 49 ff., XL, p. 103 ff.), March 1955 and Sept. 1956. **GKM**

4265. Wagener, G., *Bemerkungen über die Theorie der chinesischen Musik und ihren Zusammenhang mit der Philosophie* ('Mitth. der Deutschen Ges. f. Natur- und Völkerkunde Ostasiens' II, p. 42 ff.), 1877. **G**

4266. Wagner, Eduard, *Verzeichnis chinesischer Musikinstrumenten* ('Jahrb. d. Museums f. Völkerkunde zu Leipzig' XI), 1952. **M**

4267. Wagner, O., *Das rumänische Volkslied* ('Sammelb. der Intern. Musikges.' 1902). **CDFH¹L**

4268. Waldmann, G., *Sammlungen deutscher Volkslieder aus Rumänien und Ungarn*

('Musik und Volk' III, p. 190 ff.), 1935/ '36.

4268a. —— *Zur Tonalität des deutschen Volksliedes* (Wolfenbüttel, 1938). **L**

4269. —— *Musik und Rasse* (Berlin, 1939). **I**

4269a. Wales, H. G. Quaritsch, *The religious significance of the early Dongson bronze drums* ('Proc. 23rd. Intern. Congress of Orientalists', p. 270 ff.), Cambridge, 1954.

4270. Walin, Stig, *Die schwedische Hummel* (Stockholm, 1952). **ACJ**

*4271. Wallaschek, Richard, *Primitive Music* (London, 1893). **AIJ**

4272. —— *On the origin of music* (London, 1891).

4273. —— *Natural selection and music* (London, 1892).

4274. —— *On the difference of time and rhythm in music* (London, 1893).

4275. —— *Musikalische Ergebnisse des Studiums der Ethnologie* ('Globus' 1895). **D¹M**

4276. —— *Anfänge unseres Musiksystems* ('Mitt. der Anthrop. Ges., Wien', 1897). **D¹GHL²**

4277. —— *Urgeschichte der Saiteninstrumente* (ibid.), 1898. **D¹GHL²**

4278. —— *Entstehung der Skala* ('Sitzungsber. der Wiener Kais. Akad. d. Wissensch., mathem.-naturw. Klasse', July 1899).

4279. —— *Anfänge der Tonkunst* (1903) (enlarged ed. of No. 4272). **IK**

4280. Walle, Joh. van de, *Walsen, danza's en tumba's der Antillen* ('Oost & West' XLVII No. 5, p. 11 ff.), 29th May, 1954. **ABD¹G**

4281. —— *De Nederlandse Antillen* (Baarn, 1954), p. 79 ff. and 89 ff. **A**

4282. Walleser, Sixtus, *Die Tanzgesänge der Eingebornen auf Jap* ('Anthropos', X/XI, p. 655 ff.), 1915/'16. **D¹GKL¹L²M**

4283. Walls y Merino, M., *La música popular de Filipinas* (Madrid, 1892). **I**

4284. Walton, James, *Iron gongs from the Congo and Southern Rhodesia* ('Man' LV, p. 20, No. 29, and XVI, p. 16 No. 20), resp. Febr. 1955 and Jan. 1956. **ABD¹GKL¹L²M**

4285. Waly, A., *The No plays of Japan* (London, 1921).

4286. Wang, Betty, *Folk Songs as a Means of Social Control* ('Sociology and Social Research' XIX No. 1, p. 64 ff.), Sept./Oct. 1934. **L¹**

4287. —— *Folk Songs as Regulators of Politics* (ibid. XX, p. 161 ff.), 1935. **L¹**

4288. Wang, En Shao, *Chinessische Kammermusik einst und jetzt* ('Musica' IV, p. 131 ff.), 1950. **CKLL¹**

4289. Wang, Kuang Chi, *Ueber die chinesische Musik* (in: Richard Wilhelm, 'Chinesische Musik'), p. 48 ff. (Frankfurt a/M., 1927). **G**

4290. —— *Ueber die chinesische Notenschriften* ('Sinica' III, p. 110 ff.), 1928. **GK**

4291. —— *Ueber die chinesische klassische Oper (1550–1860)*, Geneva, 1934. **IK**

4292. —— *Musikalische Beziehungen zwischen China und dem Westen im Laufe der Jahrtausende* ('Studien zur Geschichte und Kultur des nahen und fernen Ostens' (Festschrift-Paul Kahle), ed. by W. Heffening and W. Kirfel), Leyden, 1935. **A**

4293. Wang, Kuo Wei, *Das chinesische Theater vor der T'ang-Zeit* ('Asia Major' X), 1935. **D¹GL¹**

4295. Wang, Shih-Hsiang, and Wang Ti, *A 2000-year-old melody* ('China reconstructs' March 1957, p. 18 ff.). **A**

4296. Wantzloeben, S., *Das Monochord als Instrument und als System* (Halle, 1911). **C**

4297. Ward, Herbert, *A voice from the Congo* (New York, Scribner, 1910), p. 298 ff.

4298. Ward, William Ernest Frank, *Music in the Gold Coast* ('Gold Coast Review' III, p. 199 ff.), 1927.

4299. —— *Music of the Gold Coast* ('Musical Times' LXXIII, pp. 707 ff., 797 ff. and 901 ff.), 1932. **C**

4300. —— *Gold Coast music in education* ('Oversea Education' V, p. 64 ff.), 1934.

4301. Warlington Eastlake, D., *The shêng or Chinese reed organ* ('China Review' 1882/'83).

4302. Warman, J. W., *The Hydraulic Organ of the Ancients* ('Proc. of the Musical Association' 1903–'04).

4303. Warmelo, Willem van, *Afrikaanse liederwijsies* (Unie-Volkspers, Capetown, 1948).

4304. —— *Ou Afrikaanse volkswijsies* ('Lantern' III, No. 3, blz. 250 vv.), Jan./Maart 1954. **AC**

4305. —— *Op zoek naar volksliederen in Zuid-Afrika* ('Mens en Melodie' IX, p. 321 ff.), 1954. **ACF**

4306. —— *Het Nederlandse lied bij de Kaapse Maleiers* ('Mens en Melodie' X, p. 351 ff.), Utrecht, 1955. **ACF**

4306a. Warner, W. Lloyd, *A black civilization (a study of an Australian tribe)*, New York, 1937, revised ed. 1958), p. 26, 292, 502 ff. **B**

*4307. Waterman, Richard A., William Lichtenwanger, Virginia Hitchcock Herrmann, Horace I. Poleman, and Cecil Hobbs, *Bibliography of Asiatic Musics* ('Notes', magazine devoted to music and literature with bibliographies, reviews of books, records and music', Second series, V, p. 21 ff. (I. General); p. 178 ff. (II. Southwest Asia). **A.**

General, B. Ancient Civilizations); p. 354 ff. (C. Jews: Ancient and Modern); p. 549 ff. (D. Christians, 2. Caucasians and Transcaucasians), VI, p. 122 ff. (D. Christians cont., 3. Armenians, 4. Georgians; 5. Syrians a.o.); p. 281. (E. Moslems: 1. General, 2. Arabic-speaking peoples); p. 419 (3. Turkic-speaking peoples, 4. Iranians a.o.); p. 570 ff. (III. India: A. General and Art Music, B. Primitive and Folk Music, C. Ceylonese Music); VII. p. 84 ff. (IV. South-East Asia: A. General, B. Burma, C. Siam, D. Indo-China, E. Malaya and Malay Archipelago, F. Philippine Islands); p. 265 (V. Central East Asia: A. General, B. Japan, C. Korea); p. 415 ff. (D. China); p. 613 (D. China cont.); VIII, p. 100 ff. (VI. Central Asia and Siberia: A. General, B. Tibetans, C. Mongols, D. Turkic Peoples, E. Paleo-Siberians, Samoyeds, Tungus, and Manchus), p. 322 ff. (Addenda), Washington D.C., 1947-'51. **DFKL**

4308. —— and —— *Survey of Recordings of Asiatic Music in the United States, 1950-'51* ('Notes' VIII, p. 683 ff.), Sept. 1951. **DFKL**

4309. Waterman, Richard A., *African influence on the music of the Americas* (in: Sol Tax, 'Acculturation in the Americas', p. 207 ff.), Chicago, 1952. **AB**

4310. —— *Hot rhythm in negro music* ('J. of the Amer. Musicol. Soc.' I, No. 2) 1948. **CK**

4311. —— *African patterns in Trinidad Negro music* (unpublished MS., Northwestern Univ., 1943).

4312. —— *Folk music of Puerto Rico* (Library of Congress, Washington, Album No. 18). **I**

4312a. —— *Music in Australian aboriginal culture. Some sociological and psychological implications* ('Music Therapy' 1955, p. 40 ff.), Kansas, 1956.

4313. Watson, R. W. S., *Slovak peasant art and melodies* (London, 1911). **I**

4314. W..., C. P., *The art of Ravi Shankar* (repr. from 'The Times of India') (publ. by the Indian Embassy, The Hague, 1957). **A**

4315. Wead, Charles K., *The Study of Primitive Music* ('Archiv f. Anthrop.' II), 1900. **D¹GHKL²**

4316. —— *Contribution to the history of musical scales* ('Report of the Smithsonian Inst. for 1900', p. 417 ff.), Washington, 1902. **CJL²**

4317. —— *Early Musical Scales in the Light of the Twentieth Century* ('Papers of the Michigan Acad. of Science, Arts and Letters' IV, p. 43 ff.), 1924.

4318. Weber-Kellermann, Ingeborg, *Ludolf Parisius und seine altmärkischen Volkslieder* (for the melodies in collab. with Erich Stockmann) ('Veröffentl. d. Inst. f. Deutsche Volkskunde d. Deutschen Akademie d. Wiss. zu Berlin' VI), Berlin, 1956.

4319. Weber, Max, *Die rationalen und soziologischen Grundlagen der Musik* (München, 1921). **A**

4320. Wegelin, C. A., *Chineesche muziek* ('China' IV, p. 129 ff. and 217 ff.), 1929. **D¹GH**

4321. Wegner, Max, *Das Musikleben der Griechen* (Berlin, 1949). **CKL**

4322. —— *Die Musikinstrumente des alten Orients* (Münster, 1950). **ABCGL²**

4323. —— *Etrurien* ('Die Musik in Geschichte und Gegenwart' III, col. 1595 vv.), 1954. **ACDEFGH¹KL**

4324. —— *Griechenland. B. Griechische Instrumente und Musikbräuche* ('Die Musik in Geschichte und Gegenwart' V, col. 865 ff.), 1956. **ACDEFGH¹KL**

*4325. —— *Hethitische Musik* ('Die Musik in Geschichte und Gegenwart' VI, col. 330 ff.), 1957. **ACDEFGH¹KL**

4326. Weinstock, Herbert, *Mexican music* (New York, Museum of modern art, May 1940). **J**

4326a. Weis, K., *Český jih a Šumava v lidové písni* (Prague, 1928-1941).

4327. Weiss, Josef, *Die musikalischen Instrumente des alten Testaments* (Graz, 1895).

4328. Weiss, Rodica, and Pascal Bentoiu, *100 melodii de jocuri din Ardeal* (Bukarest, 1955).

*4329. Weissmann, John S., *Hungarian Folk Music* ('Grove's Dictionary' 5th ed. vol. III, p. 277 ff.), 1954. **ACFH¹K**

4330. Wellek, Albert, *Das Farbenhören im Lichte der vergleichenden Musikwissenschaft. Urgeschichte des Doppelempfindens im Geistesleben der Orientalen* ('Z. f. Musikw.' XI, p. 470 ff.), 1929. **ACDEH¹KL**

4331. —— *Begriff, Aufbau und Bedeutung einer systematischen Musikwissenschaft* ('Die Musikforschung' I, p. 157 ff.), 1948. **CEIKLL¹**

4332. Wellesz, Egon, *Der syrische Kirchengesang* ('Musica Divina' V, p. 215 ff.), 1917.

4333. —— *Die Kirchenmusik der Kopten und Abessinier* (ibid. p. 244 ff.).

4334. —— *Die armenische Kirche und ihre Musik* (ibid. VI, p. 16 ff.), 1918.

4335. —— *Die armenische Kirchenmusik* (ibid. p. 54 ff.).

4336. —— *Das armenische Hymnar* (ibid., p. 99 ff.).

4337. —— *Probleme der musikalischen Orient-*

forschung ('Jahrbuch der Musikbibl. Peters' XXIV, p. 1 ff.), 1917. **CGKL¹**

4338. —— *Die Orgel im byzantinischen Reiche* ('Musica sacra' LI, p. 51 ff.), April 1918. **F**

4339. —— *Zur Entzifferung der byzantinischen Notenschrift. Untersuchungen über die Bedeutung der byzantinischen Tonzeichen der mittleren und späten Epoche* ('Oriens Christianus' N.S. VII, p. 79 ff.), 1918. **D¹GKL¹**

4340. —— *Vom Geist der chinesischen Musik* ('Musikblätter des Anbruchs' I, p. 42). 1919. **L**

4341. —— *Vom Wesen der orientalischen Musik* (ibid. II, p. 52), 1920. **L**

4342. —— *Studien zur äthiopischen Kirchenmusik* ('Oriens Christianus' N.S. IX, p. 74 ff.), 1920. **D¹GKL¹**

4343. —— *Byzantinische Musik* (Breslau, Jedermann's Bücherei, 1927). **A**

4344. —— *Die Byzantinische und Orientalische Kirchenmusik* (in Guido Adler, 'Handbuch der Musikgeschichte', vol. I, 2nd ed. p. 126 ff.), 1929. **ACEF**

4345. —— *Eastern Elements in Western Chant* (1947). **AC**

4346. —— *A History of Byzantine Music and Hymnography* (Oxford, 1949). **I**

4347. Wells, Evelyn Kendrick, *The Ballad Tree* (New York, 1950; London, 1954). **H**

4348. *Welsh Folk Song Society, Journal of the,* (Wrexham and Llangollen, 1909 – in progress).

4349. Weman, H., *Afrikansk musik för kyrkan och missionsarbetet* ('Svensk Missionstidskrift' XLIII), Uppsala, 1955.

4349a. Wen, Yu, *Selected ancient bronze drums found in China and Southeast Asia* (Shanghai, 1955).

4350. Werckmeister, Heinrich, *Impressions of Japanese music* ('The Musical Quarterly' XIII, p. 100 ff.), 1927.

4351. Werner, Alice, *On a stringed instrument obtained at Ntumbi, Nyasaland* ('Bantu Studies' V, p. 257 ff.), 1931. **KL²M**

4352. Werner, Eric, *Geschichte der jüdischen Volksmusik* (Breslau, 1938).

4353. —— *The oldest sources of octave and octoechos* ('Acta musicologica' XX, p. 1 ff.), 1948. **ACE**

*4354. —— *The Music of Post-Biblical Judaism* ('The New Oxford History of Music', 3rd ed., vol. I, p. 313 ff.), 1957. **ABCD¹FGK**

4355. —— *The philosophy and theory of music in Judaeo-Arabic literature* (Cincinnati, 1941).

4356. —— *The conflict between Hellenism and Judaism in the music of the early Christian church* ('Hebrew Union College Annual' XX, p. 407 ff.), Cincinnati, 1947. **G**

4357. —— *The origin of the eight modes of music* (ibid. XXI), 1948. **G**

4358. —— and Isaiah Sonne, *The Philosophy and Theory of Music in Judaeo-Arabic Literature* ('Hebrew Union College Annual' XVI), 1941. **G**

4358a. —— *Jewish music* ('Grove's Dictionary of Music and Musicians' 5th ed., vol. IV, p. 615 ff.), 1954. **ACFH¹K**

4359. Werner, Heinz, *Die melodische Erfindung im frühen Kindesalter* (Akad. d. Wiss. zu Wien, Phil.-hist. Kl., Sitzungsber. No. 182, Abh. no. 4), 1917. **D¹GIKL¹**

4360. Wertheimer, Max, *Musik der Wedda* ('Sammelb. der Intern. Musikges'. XI, p. 300 ff.), 1909. **ACDFH¹L**

4361. Westarp, Alfred, *A la découverte de la musique Franco-Japonaise* ('Bull. de la Soc. Franco-Japonaise' XXIII/XXIV), Paris, 1912. **C**

4362. Westerman, D., *La langue du tambour à Togo* ('Anthropos' I), 1906. **D¹GKL¹L²M**

4362a. Westphal, E., *Linguistics and the African music research* ('African Music Soc. Newsletter' I, No. 1, p. 15 ff.), 1948. **C**

4363. Wetering, F. H. van de, *De Savoeneezen* ('Bijdr. t.d. Taal-, Land- en Volkenk. v. Ned.-Indië' LXXXII), 1926 (p. 542 ff.). **ABD¹GL²**

4364. Weule, K., *Schädeltrommeln aus dem Otschigebiet* ('Ethnol. Notizblatt', I, fasc. 3, p. 35 ff.), 1896. **K**

4365. Whall, W. B., *Ships, sea songs and shanties* (Glasgow, 1910). **A**

4366. Wheeler, A. J., *Gongs and bells* (in: Hastings, 'Encycl. of Religion and Ethics' VI), London, 1909. **D¹GH**

4366a. White, C. M. N., *The material culture of the Lunda-Lovale peoples* ('Occasional Papers of the Rhodes-Livingstone Museum' 1948, No. 3, p. 3 ff.). **M**

*4367. White, Newman Ivey, *American Negro folksongs* (Cambridge, Mass., 1928).

4368. Whyte, E. T., *Egyptian musical instruments* ('Proc. of the Soc. of Biblical Archaeology' XXI), 1899.

4369. Whyte, Harcourt, *Types of Ibo Music* ('Nigerian Field' XVIII, p. 182 ff.), 1953. **O**

4370. Wieger, L., *Histoire des croyances religieuses et des opinions philosophiques en Chine* (Hien-hien, Ho-Kien-fou, 1917), pp. 13, 52 ff., 94, 118.

4371. Wiegrabe, Paul, *Ewelieder* ('Afrika und Uebersee' XXXVII (Aug. 1953), p. 99 ff.; XXXVIII (Dec. 1953), p. 17 ff.; (June 1954), p. 113 ff.; (Sept. 1954), p. 155 ff.). **GKM**

4372. Wiehmayer, Th., *Musikalische Rhythmik und Metrik* (Magdeburg, 1917).

4373. Wieschhoff, Heinz, *Die afrikanischen Trommeln und ihre ausserafrikanischen Beziehungen* (Stuttgart, 1933). **CJL²M**

4374. Wilbert, Johannes, *Los instrumentos musicales de los Warrau (Guarao, Guarauno)* ('Antropológica' I, p. 2 ff.), Caracas, Sept. 1956. **A**

4375. Wilhelm, Richard, *Das Wesen der chinesischen Musik* ('Sinica' II, p. 203 ff.), 1927. **GK**

4376. —— *Chinesische Musik* (Frankfurt a/ M., China-Institut, 1927). **G**

4377. Wilke, *Archaeologische Parallelen aus dem Kaukasus und den unteren Donauländern* ('Z. f. Ethnologie' XXXVI, p. 39 ff.), 1904. **ABD¹GHKL¹L²M**

4378. Wilkes, J. T., *La ritmica especifica del cantar nativo* ('Revista de Estudios musicales' II, No. 4, p. 11 ff.), Mendoza (Arg.), Aug. 1950. **AKL**

4379. Willard, N. A., *A Treatise on the Music of Hindoostan* (in Surindro Mohun Tagore, 'Hindu Music from various authors', p. 1 ff.), Calcutta, 1882. **CFIKL²**

4380. Willekes Macdonald, P. J., *Het Indonesische toonstelsel, hoe en waarom het afwijkt van andere* ('Orientatie' No. 26, p. 30 ff.), Nov. 1949. **ABD¹GH**

4381. Willems, Edgar, *Le rythme musical: rythme, rythmique, métrique* (Presses universitaires de France, 1956). **AD**

4382. Willems, J. F., *Oude Vlaamsche liederen, ten deele met de melodieën* (Gent, 1848). **L**

4383. Williams, F. E., *Papuans of the Trans-Fly* (Oxford, 1936), App. 4, p. 435 ff.: Musical instruments. **J**

4384. —— *Bull-roarers in the Papuan Gulf* ('Report No. 17 of the Territory of Papua, Anthropology'), Port Moresby, 1936. **J**

4384a. Williamson, Robert W., *The Mafulu, mountain people of British New Guinea* (London, 1912), Chapter XIV. Music and singing dancing and toys and games (p. 212 ff.). **BJ**

4385. Wilson, Lady A. C., *A short account of the Hindu system of music* (Lahore, 1904).

4386. Wilson, E. W., *Prehistoric musical instruments* ('Report of the U.S. National Museum, Washington', 1898, p. 524 ff.).

4387. —— *Gourd in folk music* ('Southern Folklore Quarterly' XV, p. 188 ff.), 1951.

4388. Wilson, Thomas, *Prehistoric Art* ('Report of the U.S. National Museum, Washington' 1896, p. 325 ff., *passim*). **AC**

4389. Wimsatt, G., *Chinese shadow shows* (Cambridge Mass., 1936). **C**

4390. Windakiewiczowa, H., *Pentatonika w muzyce polskiej ludowej* ('Kwartalnik muzyczny', Warsaw, 1933).

4391. Winnington-Ingram, R. P., *Mode in Greek music* (Cambridge, 1936).

4392. —— *Greek Music (ancient)* ('Grove's Dictionary' 5th ed. vol. III, p. 770 ff.), 1954. **ACFH¹K**

4393. Winternitz, Emanuel, *Bagpipes and Hurdy-gurdies in their social setting* ('Bull. of the Metropolitan Mus. of Art', N.S. vol. II, No. 1, p. 56 ff.), 1943. **AJ**

4394. Wiora, Walter, *Die Aufzeichnung und Herausgabe von Volksliedweisen* ('Jahrb. f. Volksliedforschung' VI, p. 53 ff.), 1938. **D¹GKL**

4395. —— *Das Alter der deutschen Volksliedweisen* ('Deutsche Musikkultur' IV/1, p. 15 ff.), 1939. **D¹L**

4396. —— *Systematik der musikalischen Erscheinungen des Umsingens* ('Jahrb. f. Volksliedforschung' VII, p. 128 ff.), 1940. **D¹L**

4397. —— *Die Volksliedweise und der Osten* (1941). **L**

4398. —— *Zur Frühgeschichte der Musik in den Alpenländern* (Basel, 1949). **ACL**

4399. —— *Alpenmusik* (in 'Die Musik in Geschichte und Gegenwart', vol. I, col. 359 ff.), 1949. **ACDEFGH¹KL**

4400. —— *Alpenländische Liedweisen der Frühzeit und des Mittelalters im Lichte vergleichender Forschung* ('Angebinde für John Meier'), 1949. **A**

4401. —— *Das echte Volkslied* (Heidelberg, 1950). **AL**

4402. —— *Die vergleichende Frühgeschichte der europäischen Musik als methodische Forschung* ('Kongressber. d. Intern. Musikges., Basel, 1949', p. 212 ff.), 1950. **ACDEFL**

4403. —— *Concerning the conception of authentic folk music* ('J. of the Intern. Folk Music Council' I, p. 14 ff.), 1949. **AC**

4404. —— *Die Stellung der Volkskunde im Kreise der Geisteswissenschaften* ('Bericht über den 7. deutschen Volkskundetag'), 1952.

4405. —— *Europäischer Volksgesang. Gemeinsame Formen in charakteristischen Abwandlungen* (Heemstede/Cologne, 1952). **ACL**

4406. —— *Die Melodien der 'Souterliedekens' und ihre deutsche Parallelen* ('Transactions Intern. Mus. Congress Utrecht 1952' p. 438 ff.), 1953. **ACD**

4407. —— *Die rheinisch-bergischen Melodien bei Zuccalmaglio und Brahms. Alte Liedweisen in romantischer Färbung* (Godesberg, 1953). **AL**

4408. —— *Der Brautreigen zu Kölbigk in der Heiligen Nacht des Jahres 1020* ('Z. f. Volkskunde' L, Heft 3/4, p. 188 ff.), 1953. **D¹KL¹**

4409. —— and Walter Salmen, *Die Tanzmu-*

sik im deutschen Mittelalter (ibid. p. 164 ff.), 1953. **D¹K**

4410. —— *Grundschichten der deutschen Musik (Frühgeschichte und Volksmusik)* ('*Deutschland in der Musikgeschichte*') ('Die Musik in Geschichte und Gegenwart' III, col. 261 ff.), Kassel, 1953. **ACDEFGH¹KL**

4411. —— *Schrift und Tradition als Quellen der Musikgeschichte* ('Kongressber. Ges. f. Musikforschung, Bamberg, 1953', p. 159 ff.), Kassel, 1954. **CDEFL**

*4412. —— *German Folk Music* ('Grove's Dictionary' 5th ed. vol. III, p. 259 ff.), 1954. **ACFH¹K**

4413. —— *Zur Lage der deutschen Volksliedforschung* ('Z. f. deutsche Philologie' LXXIII, Heft 2, p. 197 ff.), Berlin/Bielefeld/München, 1954. **D¹GHKL¹**

4414. —— *Zwischen Einstimmigkeit und Mehrstimmigkeit* ('Festschrift zum 80. Geburtstag von Prof. Dr. Max Schneider', p. 319 ff.), Leipzig, 1955. **AC**

*4415. —— *Älter als die Pentatonik* ('Studia Memoriae Belae Bartók Sacra', p. 185 ff.), Budapest, 1956. **AC**

4416. —— *Gesungene Erzählung als Strophenlied* ('Les Colloques de Wégimont' I, p. 120 ff.), Brussels, 1956. **ACL**

4417. —— *Volksmusik und hohe Kunst* (in: 'Musikerziehung in der Schule' Vorträge der ersten Bundes-Schulmusikwoche, Mainz 1955, p. 39 ff.), Mainz, 1956.

4418. —— *Das Produktive Umsingen deutscher Kirchenliedweisen in der Vielfalt europäischer Stile* ('Jahrb. f. Liturgik und Hymnologie' II), Kassel, 1956. **KL**

*4419. —— *Europäische Volksmusik und Abendländische Tonkunst* (Kassel, 1957). **ACL**

4420. —— *On the method of comparative melodic research* ('J. of the Intern. Folk Music Council' IX, p. 55 ff.), 1957. **ACJKL**

*4420a. —— *Jodeln* ('Die Musik in Geschichte und Gegenwart' VII, col. 73 ff.), 1958. **ACDEFGH¹KL**

4421. **Wirth, Herman Felix,** *Der Untergang des Niederländischen Volksliedes* (The Hague, 1911). **FL**

4422. **Wirz, Paul,** *A description of Musical Instruments from Central North Eastern New Guinea* (Publ. No. 100 of the Royal Tropical Institute), Amsterdam, 1952. **ABCFG**

4423. —— *Ueber sakrale Flöten und Pfeifen des Sepik-Gebietes* (*Neu-Guinea*) ('Verh. Naturf. Ges. Basel' LXV, p. 97 ff.), 1954. **D¹L²**

4424. **Wisse, Jan,** *China* ('Encyclopedie van de Muziek' I, p. 49 ff.), Amsterdam, 1956. **ACDEFGH¹**

4425. —— *Indianen* (ibid. II, p. 172 ff.), Amsterdam, 1957. **ACDEFGH¹**

4426. **Witte, Father A.,** *Zur Trommelsprache bei den Ewe Leuten* ('Anthropos' V, p. 50 ff.), 1910. **D¹GKL¹L²M**

4427. **Witte, Father Fr.,** *Lieder und Gesänge der Ewe-Neger* ('Anthropos', I, p. 65 ff. and p. 194 ff.), 1906. **D¹GKL¹L²M**

*4428. **Wodehouse, Mrs. Edmund,** *Icelandic Folk Music* ('Grove's Dictionary' 5th ed. vol. III, p. 288 ff.), 1954. **ACFH¹K**

4429. **Wöber, O.,** *Die ungarische Musik und die Zigeuner* ('Die Musik' IV, fasc. 22), 1904/'05. **CDFKL**

4430. **Wolf, Johannes,** *Handbuch der Notationskunde* (vol. I 1913, vol. II 1919). **CEF**

4431. —— *Die Tagung für arabische Musikreform in Kairo* ('Deutsche Tonkunstlerzeitung', Berlin, 1932). **I**

4432. —— *Die Tonschriften* (Breslau, Jedermanns Bücherei, 1924). **ACL**

*4433. **Wolf, Siegfried,** *Zum Problem der Nasenflöte* (Leipzig, 1941). **ABL**

4434. **Wolferen, M. D. van,** *Sociale factoren in de ontwikkeling der Jazzmuziek* ('Mens en Maatschappij' XXXI, p. 125 ff.), May/June 1956. **BD¹HL¹**

4435. **Wolfram, Richard,** *European songdance forms* ('J. of the Intern. Folk Music Council' VIII, p. 32 ff.), 1956. **ACJKL**

4436. **Wood, Alexander,** *The Physics of Music* (London, 1947).

4437. **Worms, E. A., S. A. C.,** *Australian Ghost Drums, Trumpets and Poles* ('Anthropos' XLVIII, p. 278 ff.), 1953. **ABD¹GHJKL¹L²M**

4438. **Wöss, Margareta,** *No, das japanische Gesamtkunstwerk* ('Oesterreichische Musikzeitschrift' X, p. 57 ff.), 1955. **C**

4439. **Woykowitz, R. Nebesky de,** *Hochzeitslieder der Lepchas* ('Z. der Schweiz. Ges. f. Asienkunde' VI, p. 30 ff.).

4439a. **Wright, R.,** *Dictionnaire des instruments de musique. Etude de lexicologie* (London, 1941).

4440. **Wünsch, Walter,** *Die Geigentechnik der südslawischen Guslaren* (Brünn/Leipzig, 1934). **CL**

4441. —— *Heldensänger in Südosteuropa* ('Arb. aus dem Inst. f. Lautforschung. Univ. of Berlin' IV), Berlin 1937. **L**

4442. —— *Gusle* ('Die Musik in Geschichte und Gegenwart' V, col. 1133 ff.), 1956. **ACDEFGH¹KL**

4443. —— *The changing shape and the disappearance of Styrian folk song* ('J. of the Intern. Folk Music Council' IX, p. 45 ff.), 1957. **ACIJKL**

4443a. —— *Die südeuropäische Volksepik, die Ballade und das Tanzlied im Vergleich zu den Frühformen in der abend-*

ländischen Musikkultur ('Kongressber. d. Ges. f. Musikforschung, Bamberg 1953', p. 200 ff.). **CDEFL**

4443b. —— *Die musikalisch-sprachliche Gestalt des Zehnsilblers im Serbokroatischen Volks-epos* ('Kongressber. d. Ges. f. Musikforschung, Hamburg 1956', p. 241 ff.). **CEL**

4443c. Wustmann, Erich, *Klingende Wildnis* (Kassel, 1956). **L**

4444. Yafil, E., and J. Rouanet, *Répertoire de musique arabe et maure; collection de mélodies* (Algers, 1904 et seq.).

4445. Yamanouchi, Seihin, *The Music of the Ryūkyūs (Okinawa)*, Tokyo, 1950. **A**

4446. —— *The History of Music of the Ryukyu* ('Journal of the Soc. f. Research in Asiatic Music' X–XI, p. 3 ff.), Dec. 1952. **A**

4447. Yang, Yin-Lu, *An account of the efforts of Chinese scholars towards the solution of the problem of the equal tempered scale in Chinese music* ('Yenching Hsüeh Pao'o' XXI), 1937.

4448. Yasser, Joseph, *Rhythmical Structure of Chinese Tunes* ('Musical Courier' LXXXVIII, No. 14, p. 44 ff.), April 1924. = German transl. from the Russian in 'Die Musik' XVII fasc. 1), 1924/'25. **CDKL**

4449. —— *Musical Moments in the Shamanistic Rites of the Siberian Pagan Tribes* ('Pro Musica Quarterly' IV, No. 3/4, p. 4 ff.), March/June 1926.

4450. —— *A Theory of Evolving Tonality* (New York, Amer. Libr. of Musicol., 1932).

*4451. —— *A Bibliography of Articles and Books on Jewish Music* (New York, Nat. Jewish Council, 1947).

4452. Yekta, Raouf, *La musique turque* (in Lavignac, 'Hist. de la Mus.' vol. V, p. 2845 ff.), 1922. **ACDEFHJ**

4453. —— *Mutula 'at wa-ara hawla mu'tamar al-musiqi al-'arabiyya* (Cairo, 1934). **G**

4454. Yeomans, W., *The musical instruments of Pre-Columbian Central America* ('Proc. 30th Intern. Congress of Americanists, Cambridge 1952', p. 54 ff.), London, und.

4455. Yin, Fa-Lu, and Yang, Yin-Liu, *Chinese music: its past and promise* ('People's China', Febr. 1957, p. 14 ff.). **A**

4456. Young, R. W., *A table relating Frequency to Cents* (publ. by C. G. Conn, Elkhart, Indiana U.S.A., 1939). **A**

4457. Yoshida, Tsuenzō, *An Introduction to the Shōmyō of the Tendai School.* ('Journal of the Soc. for Research in Asiatic Music', No. 12–13, English Section, p. 3 ff.), Tokyo, Sept. 1954. **A**

4458. Yuan-Ching Li, *Chinese musical instruments* ('China reconstructs' III No. 2,

p. 35 ff.), March/April 1954 (reprinted as 'Traditional Chinese instruments' in 'China in transition''), Peking, 1957.

4459. Yurchenco, Henrietta, *Indian music of Mexiko and Guatemala* ('Bull. of the American Musicol. Soc.' XI–XIII, p. 58 ff.), 1948.

4460. —— *Sobre música indígena* ('Boletin Indigenista' IV), Mexico, 1944.

4461. —— *Investigaciones sobre música indígena* (ibid. VI), Mexico, 1944.

4462. Yusuf, Zakariyya, *Al-misiqi al-'Arabiyya* (Bagdad, 1951). **G**

4463. IJzerdraat, Bernard, and Suhendro Sosrosuwarno, *Bentara senisuara Indonesia* (Djakarta/Groningen, 1954). **ACGJ**

4464. IJzerdraat, Bernard, *Muziekopnamen in Indonesië* ('Mens & Melodie' XI, p. 80 ff.), 1956. **ACF**

4465. Žába, Zbyněk, *Die 'Sackpfeifen-Syrinx' der Berliner Terrakotta No. 8798 und ihre Stellung in der Geschichte der Musikinstrumente* ('Aegyptologische Studien' 1955, p. 411 ff.).

4466. Zagiba, Franz, *Funde zur vorgeschichtlichen Musik in Oesterreich. Knochenflötenfunde aus der Hallstattzeit, Panflötenabbildung aus der Laténezeit* ('Anzeiger der phil.-hist. Klasse der Oesterr. Akad. d. Wiss.' XCI, No. 16, p. 208 ff.), 1954. **AK**

4467. —— *Der strukturelle Charakter des slowakischen Volksliedes* ('Jahrb. des Oesterreichischen Volksliedwerkes' I, p. 46 ff.), Vienna, 1952. **L**

4468. —— *Die Funktion des Volksliedgutes in der Entwicklung der südeuropäischen Musikgeschichte* (in: 'Kongressber. Bamberg 1953' p. 197 ff.), Kassel/Basel, 1953. **CDEFL**

4469. —— *Ungarische Balladenmelodien aus Neutraer Gebiet* ('Jahrbuch des Oesterreichischen Volksliedwerkes' III, p. 63 ff.), Vienna, 1954. **L**

4470. —— *Begriff, Aufbau und Methode einer strukturalistischen musikwissenschaftlichen Arbeit* ('Die Musikforschung' VIII, p. 298 ff.), 1955. **ACEFKL¹**

4470a. Zahan, D., *Notes sur un luth dogon* ('J. d. l. Soc. des Africanistes' XX, p. 193 ff.), 1950. **GL²M**

4471. Zaleŝak, Cyril, *Pohronské tance* (Bratislava, 1953).

4472. Zamfir, Constantin, and Ion Zlotea, *Metodă de cobză* (Bucarest, 1955). **J**

4473. Zatayevitsh, A. B., *Muzykant etnograf* ('Sovetskaya muzyka' 1951, No. 12, p. 104).

4474. —— *1000 pesen kirgizskovo naroda* (i.e. 1000 songs of the Kirghiz people), Örenburg, 1925.

4475. —— *250 Kirgizskikh instrumentalnykh*

pyes i napevov (i.e. 250 Kirghiz songs and melodies), Moscow, 1934.

4476. **Žatko, Rudolf,** *Prispevky k stúdiu Slovenských Bethlehemských hier* ('Slovenský Národopis' IV, p. 117 ff.), 1956. **GK**

4477. **Zaw, U Khin,** *Burmese Music; a Preliminary Inquiry* ('Journal of the Burma Research Soc.' 1940, p. 387 ff.). **AG**

4478. —— *Burmese nursery songs* (Rangoon, 1951). **A**

4478a. —— *Burmese music* ('The Atlantic' Febr. 1958, Suppl. 'Perspective of Burma', p. 163 ff.).

4479. **Zerries, Otto,** *Das Schwirrholz* (Stuttgart, 1942). **BL²**

4480. —— *The bull-roarer among South American Indians* ('Revista do Museu Paulista' N.S. VII, p. 275 ff.), Sao Paulo. **GL²**

4481. —— *Kürbisrassel und Kopfgeister in Südamerika* ('Paideuma' V, Heft 6, p. 323 ff.), June 1953. **BD¹K**

4482. **Žganec, Vinko,** *Kroatische Volksweisen und Volkstänze* (Zagreb, 1944). **A**

4483. —— *Hrvatske Narodne Pjesme Kajkavske* (Zagreb, 1950). **A**

4484. —— and **Nada Sremec,** *Hrvatske Narodne Pjesme i Plesovi* (Zagreb, 1951). **A**

4485. —— *Narodne Popijevke Hrvatskog Zagorja* I. Music (1950), II. Texts (1952). **AKL**

4486. —— *Die Elemente der jugoslawischen Folklore-Tonleitern im serbischen lithurgischen Gesange* ('Studia Memoriae Belae Bartók Sacra', p. 349 ff.), Budapest, 1956. **AC**

4487. —— *Orijantalizmi u Jugoslavenskom muzičkom folkloru* ('Tkalčićevog Zbornika' p. 81 ff.), Zagreb, 1955. **A**

4488. —— *Folklore elements in the Yugoslav orthodox and Roman Catholic liturgical chant* ('J. of the Intern. Folk Music Council' VIII, p. 19 ff.), 1956. **ACJKL**

4489. —— *Pjesme Jugoslavenskih Rusina* (Zagreb, 1946).

4490. —— *Hrvatske pučke popijevke iz Medimurja* (Zagreb, 1925).

4491. —— *Medimurje u svojim pjesmana* (Zagreb, 1957). **A**

4491a. —— *The tonal and modal structure of Yugoslav folk music* ('J. of the Intern. Folk Music' X, p. 18 ff.), 1958. **ACIJKL**

*4491b. —— *Yugoslawien.* II. *Die Volksmusik.* 2. *Kroatien* ('Die Musik in Geschichte u. Gegenwart' VII, col. 348 ff.), 1958. **ACDEFGH¹KL**

4492. **Ziehm, Elsa** (in collab. with **F. Bose),** *Rumänische Volksmusik, dargestellt an den Schallaufnahmen des Institutes für Lautforschung an der Universität Ierlin* (Berlin, 1939). **I**

4493. —— *Volksmusik in Rumänien* ('Volkische Musikerziehung' 1942, p. 135 ff.).

4494. **Zilevicius, Juozas,** *Native Iithuanian musical instruments* ('The Musical Quarterly' XXI, p. 99 ff.), 1935.

4494a. **Zin, U Than,** *Music in Burma* ('Guardian' III No. 14, p. 35 ff.), 1956.

4495. **Zivković, Milenko,** *Le problème tonal des mélodies populaires* ('Zvuk' IV/V, p. 145 ff.), Beograd, 1956. (Serbian text; French translation).

*4496. **Zoder, Raimund,** *Austrian folk music* ('Grove's Dictionary of Music and Musicians' 5th ed., vol. III, p. 187 ff.), 1954. **ACFH¹K**

4497. —— *Eine Methode zur lexikalischen Anordnung von Ländlern,* ('Z. des Vereins f. Volkskunde' 1908, p. 307 ff.). **D¹GHK**

4498. **Zoete, Beryl de,** *Dance and magic drama in Ceylon* (London, Faber & Faber, 1957). **B**

4499. **Züricher, Gertrud,** *Kinderlied und Kinderspiel im Kanton Bern* (Zürich, 1903).

4500. —— *Kinderlieder der deutschen Schweiz* (Basel, 1926).

4501. **Zwingc, Hermann,** *Lieder der Qunantuna-Jugend auf Neubritannien* ('Anthropos' XLVI, p. 399 ff.), 1951. **ABD¹GHJKL¹L²M**

APPENDIX

4502. **Alexandru, Tiberiu,** *Instrumentele muzicale ale poporului Romin* (= The musical instruments of the Rumanian people), Bucarest, 1956.

4503. —— *Béla Bartók despre folclorul rominese* (Bucarest, 1958).

4504. **Alvarenga, Oneyda,** *Melodias registradas por Meios Nao-Mecanicos* (Sao Paulo, 1946).

*4504a. **Arends, H.,** *Koreaanse muziek* (Publ. No. 17 of the Exotic Music Society), 1958. **A**

4504b. **Ball, James Dyer,** *Music (Chinese)* ('Hasting's Encycl. of Religion and Ethics' IX, p. 16 ff.), Edinburgh, 1917. **D¹GH**

4505. **Berner, Alfred,** *Die Berliner Musikinstrumenten-Sammlung* (Berlin, 1952).

4506. **Buçsan, Andrei,** *Jocuri din Ardsalul de Sud* (Bucarest, 1957).

4506a. **Blyau and Tasseel,** *Iepersch Oud-Liedboek* (Ghent, 1900/'02). **G**

*4506b. **Bose, Fritz,** *Die Musik der Chibcha und ihrer heutigen Nachkommen* ('Intern. Archiv f. Ethnographie' XLVIII, p. 1 ff.), 1958. **ABD¹GHK**

4506c. Bücken, Ernst, *Handbuch der Musikwissenschaft* (Berlin, 1929), vol. I. **CDEFGH¹JKLL²**

*4506d. Chailley, Jacques, *Précis de Musicologie* (Paris, 1958). **A**

4506e. Chavannes, Edouard, *Les mémoires historiques de Se-Ma Tsien* (5 vols.), Paris, 1895–1905 (vol. III, p. 230 ff.).

4506f. Cherbuliez, Antoine E., *Systematisches und Geschichtliches zur Alphornmelodik* ('Schweiz. Musikzeitung' 1949, No. 5). **L**

4507. Cock, A. de, and Is. Teirlinck, *Kinderspel en kinderlust in Zuid-Nederland* (8 vols.), Ghent, 1902/'08. **D¹GH**

4508. Claudius, Carl, *Die schwedische ,,Nyckelharpa'* ('Proc. 2nd. Congress I.M.G., Basel 1906'), Leipzig, 1907.

4509. Denver Art Museum, *Indian musical and noise making instruments* ('Leaflet Series' XXIX), 1931.

4510. Dragoi, Sabin V., *Coruri mixte* (Bucarest, 1956).

*4511. Eckardt, Hans, *Kishibe, Shigeo*, ('Die Musik in Geschichte u. Gegenwart' VII, col. 956 ff.), 1958. **ACDEFGH¹KL**

4511a. Florenz, Karl, *Formosanische Volkslieder nach chinesischen Quellen* ('Mitt. d. Deutschen Ges. f. Natur- und Völkerkunde Ostasiens' VII, p. 110 ff.), 1898. **G**

*4511b. Fortassier, Pierre, *La musique byzantine* (in: Jacques Chailley, 'Précis de Musicologie'), Paris, 1958 (Chapter VIII, p. 83 ff.). **A**

4512. Fürer-Haimendorf, Christoph von, *The Reddis of the Biston Hilla* (London, 1945), p. 347 ff.

4513. Gironcourt, Georges de, *La géographie musicale du 14. juillet à Papeete, en Nouvelle-Calédonie et Nouvelle-Zélande* (Extract from the 'Bull. de la Soc. des Etudes Océaniennes', Sept. 1953), Papeete, 1957.

4514. Goikovic, Andrijana, *Folk dance instruments. Double flute* ('The Folclorist' IV, No. 6, p. 165 ff.), summer 1958. **A**

4515. Hammerich, Angul, *Zur Frage nach dem Ursprung der Streichinstrumente* ('Proc. 2nd. Congress I.M.G., Basel, 1906'), Leipzig, 1907.

4516. Hannaas, Torleif, *Hardingfela* ('Bergen's Museums Aarbog' Hist. antikv. raekke No. 1), 1916/'17.

4516a. Harich-Schneider, Eta, *Rôei, the medieval court songs of Japan* ('Monumenta Nipponica' XIII), 1957. **GL¹L⁵**

4516b. Jargy, Simon, *Chant populaire et musique savante en proche orient arabe* ('Orient' II No. 6, p. 107 ff.), 1958. **B**

*4517. Hickmann, Hans, *Die aussereuropäischen und antiken Klarinetteninstrumente. Vor- und Frühgeschichte* ('Die Musik in Geschichte u. Gegenwart' VII, col. 993 ff.), 1958. **ACDEFGH¹KL**

*4518. —— *Klappern* (ibid. VII, col. 980 ff.), 1958. **ACDEFGH¹KL**

4519. —— and Karl Gregorius, Duke of Mecklenburg, *La musique populaire égyptienne et ses rapports avec l'art musical pharaonique* (Strassburg/Kehl, 1958).

4520. Hoboken, P. C. J. van, *Het sitâr-spel van Ustâd Vilâyat Khân* ('Gramofoon voor Kenners en Liefhebbers' Sept./Oct. 1958, p. 18 ff.). **A**

4521. Ilitch, S. L., *Antologia Srpskii narodnii pesama* (Bucarest, 1958).

*4522. Jenkins, Jean, *Musical Instruments* (Publ. of the Horniman Museum), London, 1958. **A**

4523. Jonsson, F., *Das Harfenspiel des Nordens in der alten Zeit* ('Sammelbände der Intern. Musikges.' IX), 1907/'08. **CDFH¹L**

4524. Jurk-Bauer, I., *Volkstümliche Lärminstrumente* (diss.), Heidelberg, 1937.

4525. Kiesewetter, R. G., *Ueber die musikalischen Instrumente und die Instrumentalmusik im Mittelalter* ('Caecilia' XXII), Mainz/Brussels/Antwerp, 1843.

4526. Kirby, Percival R., *The musical practices of the native races of South Africa* (in: 'The Bantu-speaking tribes of South Africa'), London, 1936 (p. 271 ff.).

4527. —— *South African native drums* ('South African Museum's Association Bulletin' III, p. 42 ff.), Durban, 1943.

4528. —— *My museum of musical instruments* (ibid. IV, p. 7 ff.), Durban, 1947.

4529. Kishibe, Shigeo, *The origin of the K'unghou* ('Tôyô-ongaku-kenkyû', 1957).

4530. Kreiger, Herbert W., *Material culture of the people of South Eastern Panama* ('Bull. No. 134 of the United States National Museum, Washington D.C.' p. 115 ff.), 1926.

4531. Larrea Palacin, Arcadio de, *La música hispano-árabe* ('Crece o Muere' No. 111), Madrid, 1957.

*4531a. Liang, Tsai-Ping, *Bibliography on Chinese music* (Taipei, Taiwan, 1956). **A**

4531b. Liétard, Alfred, *Au Yun-nan: les holo P'o, une tribu des aborigines de la Chine Méridionale* ('Anthropos-Bibliothek' vol. I Heft 5), Münster, 1913 (pp. 109 ff. and 111 ff.).

4532. Lobsiger-Dellenbach, M., *Népal* (Geneva, 1954), p. 39 ff.

4532a. Lootens and Feys, *Chants populaires flamands, avec les airs notés et poésies populaires div. receuillis à Bruges* (Bruges, 1879). **GH**

214

4532b. **Maceda, José,** *Music of Southeast Asia:
a report of a brief trip* ('J. of East
Asiatic Studies' V No. 3, p. 297 ff.),
Manila, 1958. **A**

4533. **Machabey, A.,** *Un instrument de musique de l'antiquité: le scabellum* ('Le Ménestrel' XCVI), Paris, 1934. **K**

*4533a. — *L'Antiquité orientale* (in: Jacques
Chailley, 'Précis de Musicologie', Paris,
1958 (Chapter VI, p. 59 ff.). **A**

*4533b. **Marcel-Dubois, Claudie,** *L'Ethnomusicologie* (in: Jacques Chailley, 'Précis
de Musicologie'), Paris, 1958 (Chapter
IV, p. 31 ff.). **A**

*4533c. **Marrou, Henri-Irénée,** *L'Antiquité
classique* (in: Jacques Chailley, 'Précis
de Musicologie'), Paris, 1958 (Chapter
VII, p. 73 ff.). **A**

4534. **Marshall, Harry Ignatius,** *The Karen
people of Burma* ('Ohio State University
Bulletin' vol. 26, p. 161 ff.), 1918.

4535. **Mauny, Raymond,** *Nouvelles pierres
sonores d'Afrique Occidentale* ('Notes
Africaines' No. 79, p. 65), July, 1958.

4535a. **Menon, Narayana,** *Eastern and Western
music* ('The March of India' X, Nos.
4/5, p. 12 ff.), April/May 1958. **B**

4536. **Merriam, Alan P.,** and **Warran L.
D'Azevedo,** *Washo Peyote Songs* ('American Anthropologist' LIX, p. 615 ff.),
1957. **BGL²M**

4536a. **Merriam, Alan P.,** *Statistical classification in anthropology* ('American Anthropologist' LVIII, p. 464 ff.), 1956.
BGL²M

4537. **Moser, Hans Joachim,** *Die Musik der
deutschen Stämme* (Vienna, 1957).

*4537a. **Nettl, Bruno,** *Historical aspects of
ethnomusicology* ('American Anthropologist' LX, p. 518 ff.), June 1958.
ABGL²M

4537b. — *Unifying factors in folk and primitive music* ('J. of the American Musicol.
Soc.'), in preparation. **CFKL**

4538. **Norlind, Tobias,** *Stråkharpan* ('Svensk
Tidskrift för Musikforskning' IV, fasc.
3), 1922. **CK**

4539. **Olrik, Axel,** *Middelalderens vandr. spillemaend i Norden og deres visesang*
('Opuscula philologica'), Copenhagen,
1887.

4540. **Panoff, Peter,** *Die Volksmusik der Bulgaren* ('Melos' IV, No. 1), 1925. **KL**

4541. **Philippines Unesco National Commission,** *Music in Southeast Asia* ('Proc. of
the First Regional Music Conference of
Southeast Asia, Manila, 1955'), Manila,
1956. **A**

4542. **Regner, Hermann,** *Ein altes instrument
wird neu entdeckt. Gedanken und Bericht
über die Wiedereinführung des Alphorns
im Allgäu* ('Pro Musica' 1958, No. 4, p.
101 ff.). **A**

4543. **Ribera y Tarago, J.,** *La música de la
Jota Aragonese. Ensayo histórico* (Madrid, 1928).

4543a. **Robinson, K. R.,** *Venerated rock gongs
and the presence of rock slides in Southern
Rhodesia* ('The South African Archaeological Bulletin' No. 50, vol. XIII, p. 75
ff.), June 1958. **B**

*4543b. **Schaeffner, André,** *Organologie primitive* (in: Jacques Chailley, 'Précis de
Musicologie'), Paris, 1958 (Chapter V,
p. 53 ff.). **A**

4544. **Schletterer, H. M.,** *Geschichte der Spielmannszunft in Frankreich und der Pa-
riser Geigenkönige* (Berlin, 1884).

*4545. **Schneider, Marius,** *Kirby, Percival
Robson,* ('Die Musik in Geschichte u.
Gegenwart' VII, col. 932 ff.), 1958.
ACDEFGH¹KL

4546. **Sharp, Cecil J.,** *Some characteristics of
English folk-music* ('Folklore' XIX, p
132 ff.), London, 1908.

4547. **Stern, Theodore,** *Drum and whistle languages* ('American Anthropologist'
LIX, p. 487 ff.), 1957. **ABGL²M**

4548. **Szegö, Julia,** and **Klára Sebestyen
Dobó,** *Kötöttem Bokrétát. 150 nepdal*
(Bucarest, 1958).

4549. **Truka, Jaroslav,** *La musique et le chant
tchéchoslovaques dans le monde libre*
('Rencontres' Nos. 14/15), Paris, 1958.

4549a. **Vos, F.,** *De Koreaanse cultuur* (Publ.
No. 17 of the Exotic Music Society),
1958. **A**

4549b. **Wang, Kung Ki,** *Ueber die chinesischen Notenschriften* ('Sinica' III, p. 110
ff.), 1928. **GK**

4549c. **Ware, James R.,** *Query No. 114: Were
the ancient Chinese weights and measures
related to musical instruments?* ('Isis'
XXXVII, p. 73 ff.), May 1947. **AGL¹**

4550. **Williams, C. F. Abdy,** *The story of
notation* (London, 1903).

4551. **Winstedt, Richard,** Review of Quaritsch Wales, 'Prehistory in Southeast
Asia' ('J. of the R. Asiatic Soc., Malayan Branche' XXX), 1957 (p. 86: a
new hypothesis on bronze drum figures). **BD¹GKL²L⁵**

4552. **Zamfir, Constantin, Victoria Dosios,**
and **Elisabeta Moldoveanu-Nestor,** *132
cintece şi jocuri din Naăsăud* (Bucarest,
1958).

Fig
1 Since
ELLIS'S y

This is Alexander
Ellis as I remember
him.

G. Bernard Shaw

Ayot Saint Lawrence
28 November
1949

Fig. 1. A. J. ELLIS (1814–1890)[1]

Fig. 2. CARL STUMPF (1848–1936)

Fig. 3. CURT SACHS (b. 1881)

[1] Since the identity of the above portrait was uncertain, an appeal has been made to one of ELLIS's younger contemporaries, namely BERNARD SHAW. I believe I may rightly reproduce his testimony *in facsimile*.

217

Fig. 4. Nils Schiørring (b. 1910)

Fig. 5. Tobias Norlind (1879–1948)

Fig. 6. Johann Sebastian Brandts Buys
(1879–1939)

Fig. 7. A. H. Fox Strangways (1859–1948)
(Courtesy Mr. Jerome Dessain)

218

4532b. **Maceda, José,** *Music of Southeast Asia: a report of a brief trip* ('J. of East Asiatic Studies' V No. 3, p. 297 ff.), Manila, 1958. **A**

4533. **Machabey, A.,** *Un instrument de musique de l'antiquité: le scabellum* ('Le Ménestrel' XCVI), Paris, 1934. **K**

*4533a. — *L'Antiquité orientale* (in: Jacques Chailley, 'Précis de Musicologie'), Paris, 1958 (Chapter VI, p. 59 ff.). **A**

*4533b. **Marcel-Dubois, Claudie,** *L'Ethnomusicologie* (in: Jacques Chailley, 'Précis de Musicologie'), Paris, 1958 (Chapter IV, p. 31 ff.). **A**

*4533c. **Marrou, Henri-Irénée,** *L'Antiquité classique* (in: Jacques Chailley, 'Précis de Musicologie'), Paris, 1958 (Chapter VII, p. 73 ff.). **A**

4534. **Marshall, Harry Ignatius,** *The Karen people of Burma* ('Ohio State University Bulletin' vol. 26, p. 161 ff.), 1918.

4535. **Mauny, Raymond,** *Nouvelles pierres sonores d'Afrique Occidentale* ('Notes Africaines' No. 79, p. 65), July, 1958.

4535a. **Menon, Narayana,** *Eastern and Western music* ('The March of India' X, Nos. 4/5, p. 12 ff.), April/May 1958. **B**

4536. **Merriam, Alan P., and Warran L. D'Azevedo,** *Washo Peyote Songs* ('American Anthropologist' LIX, p. 615 ff.), 1957. **BGL²M**

4536a. **Merriam, Alan P.,** *Statistical classification in anthropology* ('American Anthropologist' LVIII, p. 464 ff.), 1956. **BGL²M**

4537. **Moser, Hans Joachim,** *Die Musik der deutschen Stämme* (Vienna, 1957).

*4537a. **Nettl, Bruno,** *Historical aspects of ethnomusicology* ('American Anthropologist' LX, p. 518 ff.), June 1958. **ABGL²M**

4537b. — *Unifying factors in folk and primitive music* ('J. of the American Musicol. Soc.'), in preparation. **CFKL**

4538. **Norlind, Tobias,** *Stråkharpan* ('Svensk Tidskrift för Musikforskning' IV, fasc. 3), 1922. **CK**

4539. **Olrik, Axel,** *Middelalderens vandr. spillemaend i Norden og deres visesang* ('Opuscula philologica'), Copenhagen, 1887.

4540. **Panoff, Peter,** *Die Volksmusik der Bulgaren* ('Melos' IV, No. 1), 1925. **KL**

4541. **Philippines Unesco National Commission,** *Music in Southeast Asia* ('Proc. of the First Regional Music Conference of Southeast Asia, Manila, 1955'), Manila, 1956. **A**

4542. **Regner, Hermann,** *Ein altes instrument wird neu entdeckt. Gedanken und Bericht über die Wiedereinführung des Alphorns im Allgäu* ('Pro Musica' 1958, No. 4, p. 101 ff.). **A**

4543. **Ribera y Tarago, J.,** *La música de la Jota Aragonese. Ensayo histórico* (Madrid, 1928).

4543a. **Robinson, K. R.,** *Venerated rock gongs and the presence of rock slides in Southern Rhodesia* ('The South African Archaeological Bulletin' No. 50, vol. XIII, p. 75 ff.), June 1958. **B**

*4543b. **Schaeffner, André,** *Organologie primitive* (in: Jacques Chailley, 'Précis de Musicologie'), Paris, 1958 (Chapter V, p. 53 ff.). **A**

4544. **Schletterer, H. M.,** *Geschichte der Spielmannszunft in Frankreich und der Pariser Geigenkönige* (Berlin, 1884).

*4545. **Schneider, Marius, Kirby, Percival Robson,** ('Die Musik in Geschichte u. Gegenwart' VII, col. 932 ff.), 1958. **ACDEFGH¹KL**

4546. **Sharp, Cecil J.,** *Some characteristics of English folk-music* ('Folklore' XIX, p 132 ff.), London, 1908.

4547. **Stern, Theodore,** *Drum and whistle languages* ('American Anthropologist' LIX, p. 487 ff.), 1957. **ABGL²M**

4548. **Szegő, Julia, and Klára Sebestyen Dobó,** *Kötöttem Bokrétát. 150 nepdal* (Bucarest, 1958).

4549. **Truka, Jaroslav,** *La musique et le chant tchéchoslovaques dans le monde libre* ('Rencontres' Nos. 14/15), Paris, 1958.

4549a. **Vos, F.,** *De Koreaanse cultuur* (Publ. No. 17 of the Exotic Music Society), 1958. **A**

4549b. **Wang, Kung Ki,** *Ueber die chinesischen Notenschriften* ('Sinica' III, p. 110 ff.), 1928. **GK**

4549c. **Ware, James R.,** *Query No. 114: Were the ancient Chinese weights and measures related to musical instruments?* ('Isis' XXXVII, p. 73 ff.), May 1947. **AGL¹**

4550. **Williams, C. F. Abdy,** *The story of notation* (London, 1903).

4551. **Winstedt, Richard,** Review of Quaritsch Wales, 'Prehistory in Southeast Asia' ('J. of the R. Asiatic Soc.', Malayan Branche' XXX), 1957 (p. 86: a new hypothesis on bronze drum figures). **BD¹GKL²L⁵**

4552. **Zamfir, Constantin, Victoria Dosios, and Elisabeta Moldoveanu-Nestor,** *132 cintece şi jocuri din Nașăud* (Bucarest, 1958).

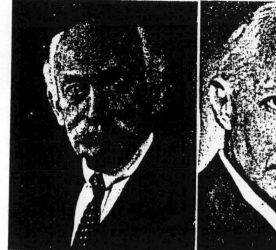

Fig. 8. HENRY BALFOUR (1863–1939)
(Courtesy Messrs. LAFAYETTE Ltd., London)

Fig. 9. BÉLA BARTÓK (1881–1945)

Fig. 10. ZOLTÁN KODÁLY (b. 1882)

Fig. 11. FRANCES DENSMORE
(1867–1957)

Fig. 12. Erich M. von Hornbostel (1877–1935) (l.) with Jacques Handschin (1886–1950)

Fig. 13. Constantin Brailoiu (b. 1893) (l). with Léon Algazi. At the background, from left to right: Zygmunt Estreicher, Claudie Marcel-Dubois and Samuel Baud-Bovy

Fig. 14. Jaap Kunst (b. 1891)

Fig. 15. André Schaeffner (b. 1895)

Fig. 16. A. O. Väisänen (b. 1890)

Fig. 17. Robert Lach (b. 1874)

Fig. 18. Erich M. von Hornbostel (1877–1935)

Fig. 19. Marius Barbeau (b. 1883)

Fig. 20. ROBERT LACHMANN (1892–1939)

Fig. 21. PERCIVAL R. KIRBY (b. 1888)

Fig. 22. MIECZYSLAW KOLINSKI (b. 1901)

Fig. 23. ARNOLD A. BAKE (b. 1899)

Fig. 24. HUGH T. TRACEY (b. 1903)

Fig. 25. MARIUS SCHNEIDER (b. 1903)

Fig. 26. ERNST EMSHEIMER (b. 1904)

Fig. 27. EDITH GERSON-KIWI

Fig. 28. Helen H. Roberts

Fig. 29. Walter Wiora (b. 1906)

Fig. 30. Hans Hickmann (b. 1908)

Fig. 31. Claudie Marcel-Dubois

Fig. 32. Manfred F. Bukofzer
(1910–1955)

224

Fig. 33. ERIK DAL (b. 1922)

Fig. 34. GILBERT ROUGET (b. 1902)

Fig. 35. VINKO ŽGANEČ (l) (b. 1890).
and VALENS VODUŠEK (b. 1912)

Fig. 36. CVJETKO RIHTMAN (b. 1902)

Fig. 37. KLAUS WACHSMANN (b. 1907)

Fig. 38. (from l. to r.): CONSTANTIN BRAILOIU
(b. 1893), AHMED ADNAN SAYGUN (b. 1907)
and RAINA KATZAROVA

Fig. 39. MARIAN (b. 1908) and JADWIGA
SOBIESKI

Fig. 40. LÁSZLÓ LAJTHA (b. 1892)
and ALBERT MARINUS (b. 1886)

Fig. 40a.
GEORGE HERZOG
(b. 1901)

Fig. 40b.
O. M. SANDVIK
(b. 1875)

Fig. 41. MIODRAG VASILJEVIĆ
(b. 1903)

Fig. 42. BRUNO NETTL (b.
1930)

Fig. 43. ALAN P. MERRIAM (b. 1923)

Fig. 44. MANTLE HOOD (b. 1911)

Fig. 45. Buttock-'music' on a ancient Greek vase

Fig. 46. Ancient Egyptian orchestra

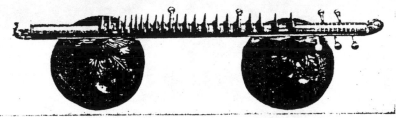

Fig. 47. North Indian *bin* (after HIPKINS)

Fig. 48. Bamboo zithers from Flores
(A = full-tube, B and C = half-tube
instruments)

Fig. 50. Prehistoric *lu(n)komba*. Dra-
kensberg (Basutoland) rock-painting
(after STOW). (Courtesy Mr.P.R.KIRBY
and the Trustees of the South African
Museum)

Fig. 49. Raft-zither from Hindostan
(after SOLVIJNS)

Fig. 51. Modern *lu(n)komba*

Fig. 52. Musical bow from South Africa
(after PERCIVAL R. KIRBY)

229

Fig. 53. Javanese *kemanak*

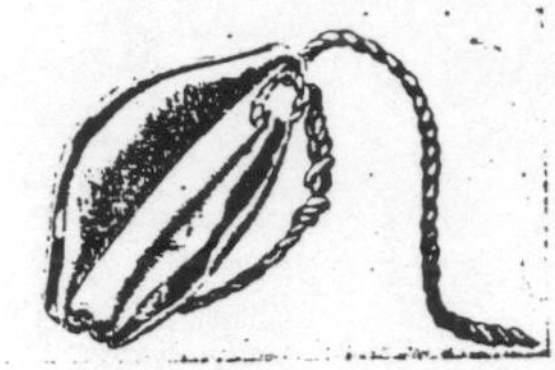

Fig. 54. ,,Kemanak" of the Pangwé, West Central Africa (after von Hornbostel)

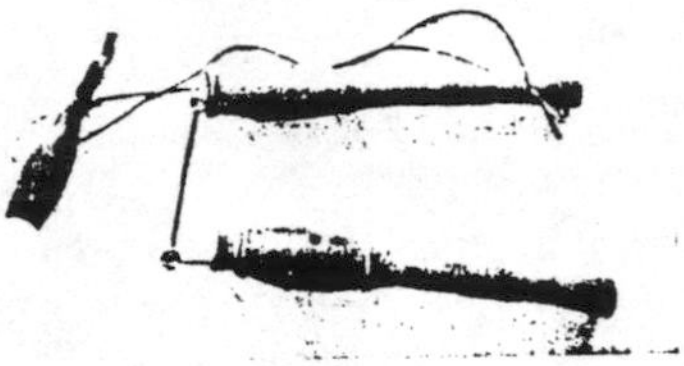

Fig. 55. *Féku* of the Atoni, Central Timor

Fig. 56. *Dunda* from Sokoto, North Nigeria

Fig. 57. Pan-pipe (Central Timor)

Fig. 58. Unconnected pan-pipes (*hoi*) (West-Flores)

Fig. 59. Monochord with scale division

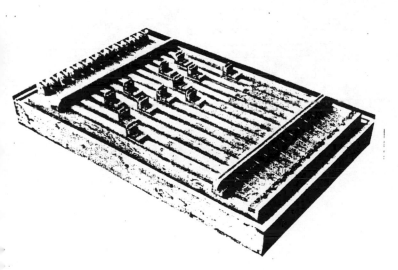

Fig. 60. Dodecachord provided with 12 graduated scales, moveable bridges and tuningpegs, which can duplicate any kind of scale of known vibration numbers

n	0	1	2	3	4	5	6	7	8	9	n
34	0	5	10	15	20	25	30	35	40	45	34
35	50	55	60	64	69	74	79	84	89	94	35
36	98	103	108	113	118	122	127	132	136	141	36
37	146	151	155	160	164	169	174	178	183	187	37
38	192	196	201	206	210	215	219	224	228	232	38
39	237	243	246	250	255	259	263	268	272	276	39
40	281	286	290	294	298	302	306	311	315	319	40
41	324	328	332	336	340	344	349	353	357	361	41
42	365	369	373	377	382	386	390	394	398	402	42
43	406	410	414	418	422	426	430	434	438	442	43
44	446	450	454	458	462	466	469	473	477	481	44
45	485	489	493	496	500	504	508	512	516	519	45
46	523	527	530	534	538	542	546	549	553	557	46
47	560	564	567	571	575	578	582	586	589	593	47
48	596	600	604	607	611	614	618	622	625	629	48
49	632	636	640	643	646	650	654	657	660	664	49
50	667	670	674	678	681	684	688	691	695	698	50
51	702	705	708	712	715	718	722	725	728	732	51
52	735	738	742	745	748	752	755	758	761	765	52
53	768	771	774	778	781	784	788	791	794	797	53
54	800	804	807	810	813	816	820	823	826	829	54
55	832	836	838	842	845	848	851	854	857	860	55
56	863	866	869	872	876	878	882	885	888	891	56
57	894	897	900	903	906	909	912	915	918	921	57
58	924	927	930	933	936	939	942	945	948	951	58
59	954	957	960	962	965	968	971	974	977	980	59
60	983	986	988	991	994	997	1000	1003	1006	1008	60
61	1011	1014	1017	1020	1023	1026	1028	1031	1034	1037	61
62	1040	1042	1045	1048	1051	1054	1056	1059	1062	1064	62
63	1067	1070	1072	1075	1078	1081	1084	1086	1089	1092	63
64	1094	1097	1100	1102	1105	1108	1110	1113	1116	1118	64
65	1121	1124	1126	1129	1132	1134	1137	1140	1142	1145	65
66	1148	1150	1153	1156	1158	1160	1163	1166	1168	1171	66
67	1174	1176	1179	1181	1184	1186	1189	1192	1194	1197	67
68	1200	1202	1204	1207	1210	1212	1214	1217	1220	1222	68
69	1224	1227	1230	1232	1235	1237	1240	1242	1245	1247	69
70	1250	1252	1254	1257	1260	1262	1264	1266	1269	1271	70
71	1274	1276	1279	1281	1284	1286	1288	1291	1293	1296	71
72	1298	1300	1303	1305	1308	1310	1312	1315	1317	1320	72
73	1322	1324	1327	1329	1332	1334	1336	1339	1341	1343	73
74	1346	1348	1350	1353	1355	1358	1360	1362	1364	1366	74
75	1369	1371	1373	1376	1378	1380	1382	1385	1387	1389	75
76	1392	1394	1396	1398	1401	1404	1406	1408	1410	1412	76
77	1415	1417	1419	1422	1424	1426	1428	1430	1433	1435	77
78	1437	1440	1442	1444	1446	1448	1450	1453	1455	1457	78
79	1459	1461	1463	1466	1468	1470	1472	1474	1476	1478	79
80	1481	1483	1485	1487	1490	1492	1494	1496	1498	1500	80
n	0	1	2	3	4	5	6	7	8	9	n

Fig. 61. The cents-table of VON HORNBOSTEL

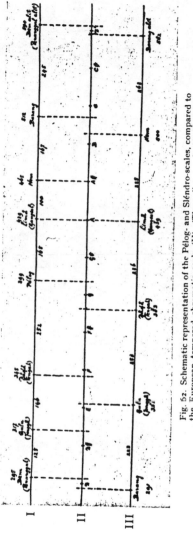

Fig. 52. Schematic representation of the Pélog- and Sléndro-scales, compared to the European tempered chromatic scale (II). (The pélog- and sléndro-scales (resp. I and III) are those of the Gamelan Kyahi Kanyut Mésem, Mangku Nagaran, Solo)

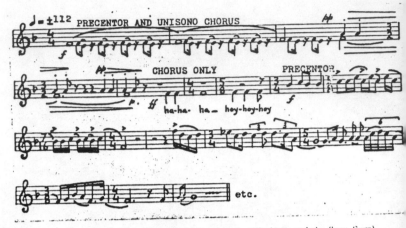

Fig. 63. Transcription after a phonogram of a Florinese melody (lagu Soga)

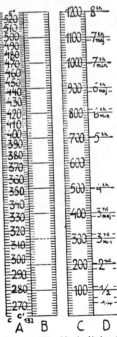

Fig. 64. The Music Rule of
Prof. M. REINER

I

INDEX OF SUBJECTS *)

* Figures between brackets refer to the Bibliography (p. 79 ff.). As a rule a literature reference is only given when the keyword behind which it appears is mentioned in the title of the work concerned or is treated extensively in it. – Figures in *italics* refer to the pages of this book.

239

kim si daw *30*
k'in (1555, 1556, 1557, 1558, 2299a, 4144), *54*
kipi (642)
kirtan (184)
kitab al-iqd al-farid (1191)
kitab al-malahi (1184)
kithara (1552, 1984, 3034, 3094, 3585)
kledi (3829, 4094), *26*
klong thad (3832)
klu'i *57*
kobuz, see: qopuz
Kokusai Bunka Shinkokai *36*
koledo (3466)
kolinde (274)
kom boät *26*
k'ong-heou (k'ung-hou) (3134, 4529)
kora (1502, 3501), *27, 34, 36*
koto (2034, 2686, 3049a, 3830a, 4103), *25, 27, 29, 31, 36, 54*
ko-uta (778)
kowangan *60*
kponingbo *28*
kpwen (1412)
kronchong (758, 978, 1142, 1430 (p. 63 ff.), 1857, 2370 (p. 300), 2399 (p. 375), 2532a, 2724, 2952, 3890)
Kru harp *34*
kudlung (738), *30*
kuhreigen (ranz des vaches) (2894, 4053, 4100)
Kulturkreise *62*
kudyapi (738), *30*
kundi *28*
k'ung-hou, see: k'ong-heou
kunyu (564a)
lang(e)leik, see: Hummel
language and music (428, 564d, 1429, 1710, 2442, 2466, 2984, 3003, 3005b, 3187, 3748, 3755, 3925, 3984, 3998, 3999), *65*. See also: signalling, silbo, talking drums, whistle languages.
Lankavatara Sutra (3342b)
lapka, see: livika
lantuy (738), *30*
launeddas (1152), *35, 66*
lauto *26*
leading notes *42*
Leningrad, phonogram collection in, *21*
Library of Congress, Washington D.C. (1090), *16, 36*
ligombo *27*
Lindström concern, Karl, *23, 24*
linga (3137)
Lingapurana (3284)
linguaphones *60*
lira *32*
lirica (1376, 3905)
lisanzo *28*
lithophones (115, 676, 736, 1145, 1146, 1147, 1473, 2005, 2399 (p. 294), 2444, 2917a, 2962, 3689, 3807, 3839, 4455, 4535, 4543a)
lituus (3527)

livika (lapka, lunuat, nunut) (2308, 2612)
lokole (1456)
lokombe, see: lukumbi
London, phonogram collections in, *21*
lu(n)komba (figs. 50 and 51) (2702), *34, 55*
lukumbi (1423, 1532a)
lunuat, see: livika
lure (509, 1584, 3016, 3059)
lute (112, 312, 852 (p. 92 ff.), 1172H, 1185C, 1185D, 1185F, 1185G, 1389, 1641, 1759 II, 1760 VI, 1761, 1789 XI, 2520b, 2532a, 3039, 3108 (p. 407 ff.), 3179, 3789, 4470a), *25, 28, 30, 32, 34, 36*
lyre (957, 1309, 1759 II, 3034, 3108 (pp. 9, 90 ff.), 3557a, 3585, 3939a, 4125, 4169), *25, 28, 30, 32*
magic and music (119, 128, 154a, 203, 219, 285 (p. 53 ff.), 445, 529, 533, 564d, 730, 731, 873, 891, 1062, 1096, 1097, 1099, 1225, 1459, 2119, 2419, 2421, 2422, 2425, 2545, 2571, 2585 (p. 91 ff.), 2741, 2870, 2871, 2933, 3152a, 3201, 3334a, 3446 (p. 37), 3487, 3491 (p. 2800), 3495a, 3518, 3529, 3549a, 3670, 3753, 3763, 3771, 3892, 3938, 4007, 4437, 4449, 4498), *65*. See also: bull-roarer.
ma-grama, see: grama
Maheswara Sutra (812)
Malaya Broadcasting Corporation *33*
male principle in music *44, 52*
mandola *25*
mandolin *33*
maqam(at) (2017, 2025, 3419, 4162), *64*
maraca(s) (1444), *25, 33, 36*
marimba (balafon) (145, 392, 634, 635, 1433, 1443, 2000, 2122, 2134a, 2221, 2372, 2696, 2699, 2767, 2956, 2959, 3325, 3501, 3932, 4108, 4119, 4149, 4214), *26, 27, 29, 30, 31, 32, 34, 36, 52, 57*
masonquo *28*
Mau-mau [61, 2572]
maung saing *30*
ma ya li *26*
m'bila, see: marimba
m'bilta *28*
m'bira, see: sanza
medicine and music (119, 873, 890, 936, 937, 940, 943, 2421, 2422, 2683, 3005, 3081, 3335b, 3752, 3780, 3859a, 4007), *65*. See also: magic and music.
medieval European musical instruments (93, 132, 208, 209, 342, 455, 517, 532, 841, 852, 1108, 1269, 1310, 1312, 1338, 1363, 1389, 1390, 1753, 2605, 2642, 3031, 3039, 3040, 3041, 3107, 3108, 3109, 3458a, 3528, 3539, 3553, 3564, 3596, 3672, 3713, 4393, 4525, 4539). See also: Alp-horn, bag-pipe, hurdy-gurdy.
mela(-karta) (2043, 2323b, 2704b, 3266, 3509, 3511, 3606, 4001)
Melograph, Seeger's, (3797, 3800), *41*
membranes, vibrating, (219)
membranophones *58*

menda *34*
meringue *32*
metre *64*. See also: rhythm.
mey *26*
meydan saži (12-str. saž) *28*
mganda dance (2096)
midwinter horn (2586, 2588b)
mi gyaung *54*
milli-octave (M.O) *4*
mina *25*
Minnesang (1051, 1115)
mission and music (1151a, 1991a, 2066, 2392, 2663, 2666, 3517, 3884a, 3884b, 4349), *65*
mitote *29*
mizmar (1172F)
mokko (2014, 3019, 3020, 3021, 3724)
mong (3832)
monkeys and music *49*
monochord (fig. 59) (3108 (p. 188 ff.), 4296), *10, 11, 12*
mouth harp, see: jew's harp
mouth organ (3829, 4094), *26, 31*
mrdangga (3298), *27, 28, 33*
multi-faced drum (3306)
multi part music (113, 165, 223a, 324, 405, 550, 1524, 1747, 1794, 1899, 1965, 2209, 2213, 2302, 2401, 2499, 2624, 2740b, 2987, 2999 (p. 77 ff.), 3174 (p. 239), 3176, 3327a, 3326, 3327a, 3422, 3423, 3551, 3635, 3730, 3731, 3734, 3739, 3746, 3757, 3867, 3954a, 4123, 4238, 4414), *19, 44, 64*
Musée de l'Homme, Paris *35* ff.
Musée des Arts et Traditions populaires en France *21*
musette (503), *24.*
musical bow (fig. 52) (210, 388, 570, 599,738, 839, 977, 1016a, 1253a (p. 36 ff.), 2148, 2149, 2214, 2223 (p. 171 ff.), 2225, 2439, 2579, 2777, 3039, 3523a, 3662), *25, 26, 27, 29, 30, 31, 32, 34, 35, 54, 55*
musical instruments in general (3041, 3109, 3528, 3529, 3539, 3553, 3564, 3681, 3685, 3692b, 3712, 3718a, 3784a, 4439a, 4543b)
musical script (general) (610, 827, 1408, 2684, 3557a, 3571, 4085, 4430, 4432, 4550);
  Arabia (2440a, 2534, 2537, 3491 (p. 2733))
  Aztecs (3046)
  Babylonia (3546, 3548, 3568, 3570a)
  Bali (2360 (p. 47 ff.))
  Byzantium (1373 (pp. 547 and 553 ff.), 4339, 4511b (p. 90 ff.))
  China (750 (p. 156 ff.), 1555 (pp. 4/5 and 114 ff.), 1919, 2255, 2603, 3174 (p. 239 ff.), 4000, 4011, 4144, 4146, 4290, 4549b)
  Egypt (ancient) (1812, 1822 (p. 48 ff.))
  Greece (ancient) (1397a (p. 129 ff.), 4533c (p. 78 ff.), 3545, 3547)
  Hebrews (3480a, 4358a (p. 625))
  India (41a, 641, 811 II, 1535 (pp. 300 ff. and 324), 3520, 3844, 3846, 4144)
  Japan (1050a (figs. 2, 5, 6 and 15), 1617, 2498, 3184 (p. 124 ff.))
  Java (474, 489, 2399 (p. 346 ff.))

Khwarizm (318a)
Okinawa (3516)
Persia (2534)
Sumeria (1341 (Chapter IV))
Tibet (3892)
Vietnam (2519 (p. 46 ff.))
Musica Viva firm *33*
music rule (fig. 64) (3369), *8, 9*
Musique Monde *33*
mutivi (3013a)
myth and music (801, 1217, 1218, 3979)
nada (186)
nagara *25, 33*
nagaswara(m) (3287), *27*
nai, see: nay
nanga *27*
Naqqarahkhanah (376)
Nataratnakosa (3255)
Natya-çastra (190, 198c, 499, 2510, 2511), *56*
nay (1172F), *31, 33*
ndingiti *34*
ndongo *34*
negroid elements *44*
neikembe *28*
Netherlands, phonogram collections in the, *21*
Netherlands section of the International Folk Music Council *21*
neums *51*
Nigerian Institute of Music (3065b)
nigûn *64*
Noordse balk (Noardske balke), see: Hummel
noh music (2498, 2686, 3223, 4285, 4438), *19, 36, 64*
noise making instruments (4509, 4524). See also: clappers, rattles, a.o.
nomos *64*
Nonnengeige, see: trumpet marine
nose flute (96, 1253a (p. 52 ff.), 1291, 2044 (p. 327 ff.), 2083b, 2178 (p. 232 ff,), 2402 (p. 34 ff.), 2872, 4433). *25, 32*
notation, mechanical methods of, (512, 822a, 1453a, 1560, 2093, 2445, 2866, 2867, 3150, 3797), *10, 41*
notation, musical, see: musical script
notation of dances, see: choreographic script
notation of ethnic and folk music (3044, 3665, 3800, 4394), *37 ff.* See also: transcription of phonograms.
notched rattle (1630)
nugara *29*
nunut, see: livika
nyamulera *28*
nyckelharpa (85 (p. 199 ff.), 3040 (col. 27 ff.), 3108 (p. 312 ff.), 4508)
oboe (698, 1780), *24, 31, 53*
ocarina (1603, 1604, 1807 II, 2767, 3095, 3982, 4096)
octoechos (842, 2078, 4353, 4357)
Odeon firm *24*
omakola (844a)
omichicahuaztli (582, 2627)
ondes sonores *61*

II

INDEX OF PEOPLES AND REGIONS THE MUSIC
OF WHICH HAS BEEN STUDIED AND/OR RECORDED

3834, 4087, 4398, 4399, 4400, 4443, 4506f).
See also: Switzerland.
Altai-peoples (600, 2029)
Altmark (3644a, 4318)
Alur (4187a, 4260)
Amakwavi *31*
Amami Islands (Northern Ryū-kyū's) *30*
Amazonas (incl. Caishana = Cayuishana, Mundurucu) (205, 1040, 2869, 3126, 3487), *26, 28, 30, 35*
Ambilube *24*. See also: Madagascar.
Ambo (3941)
Ambon (Amboina) (2085, 4183), *25*
Ambrym (1551a)
Amhara *35*
Ami *25*
Amish (2998)
Anatolia (74, 139, 3110, 3176, 3385, 3666, 3668), *35*. See also: Turkey.
Andalusia (1150, 2714, 3937), *25, 30*
Andamans (3219), *51*
Angami Naga *45*
Anglo-Americans (303, 304, 304a, 522, 3002). See also: English Canadian.
Anglo-Egyptian Sudan, see: Sudan
Angola (incl. Bachioko, Chokwe, Lovale, Lunda, Ovimbundu) (844a, 1715, 2046a, 3366a)
Angoulème *29*
Anjou (3842), *29*
Annam (505, 506, 966, 1023a, 1460, 1462, 1463, 2005, 2249, 2251 (p. 3125 ff.), 2252, 3013, 3177 (p. 156 ff.), 3335)
Antigua *33*
Antilles, see: West Indian Archipelago
Aotearoa (1481)
Apache (2802), *29, 32, 36*
Apiaká (2869)
Appalachians (519, 2629a, 3800a, 3821)
Appenzell (4099, 4100)
Arab music (general) (5, 55, 148, 154, 162, 315, 330, 410, 591, 607, 639, 645, 661, 662, 669, 728 (vol. I p. 255), 729, 786, 787, 1051, 1112, 1116, 1117, 1156, 1157, 1158, 1160 – 1166, 1168 – 1179, 1181, 1184, 1185, 1189, 1190, 1191, 1195 – 1198, 1208, 1223, 1317, 1374, 1504, 1624, 1640, 1655, 1750, 1756, 1783, 1840d, 1950, 1979, 2017, 2134, 2201, 2440a, 2465, 2501, 2507, 2508, 2513, 2515, 2532b, 2533, 2534, 2535, 2537, 2569, 2953, 3093, 3153, 3233, 3365, 3426, 3456, 3457, 3491 – 3495, 3557, 3564, 3603, 3604, 3697, 3716, 3717, 3735, 3772, 3905, 4034, 4051, 4114, 4160, 4355, 4358, 4431, 4444, 4453, 4462, 4516b), *19, 28, 29, 31, 35, 43, 64, 65*. See also: Algeria, Arabia, Arabian Spain, Beduin, Biskra, Egypt (modern), Iraq, Libya, Maghreb, Mesopotamia, Morocco, Near East, Palestine, Persia, Syria, Tripolitania, Tunisia, Turkey.
Arabia (incl. Mecca, Yemen) (441, 1172G, 1184, 1185E, 1575, 1686, 2020, 2127, 2762,

2954, 3408, 3409, 3604, 3913, 4150), *28, 29, 31, 32, 35*
Arabian Spain (1115, 1185D, 1203, 1750, 3408, 3409, 3410, 3495, 3748, 3765, 3772, 4444)
Aragon (2552a, 4543), *34*
Arapaho (916, 917, 1994, 2797, 2984, 2989), *25*
Arapai (956)
Arara *28*
Araucanians (149, 2032, 2033, 2568, 2767 (p. 59, 147))
Arecuna (3487)
Argentina (incl. Araucanians, Fuegians, Patagonians) (124, 124a, 149, 401, 580, 586, 1250, 1316, 1961, 1962, 2032, 2033, 2552, 2568, 2579, 3095, 3740, 4208, 4209, 4210, 4212, 4213, 4231, 4378), *31*
Armenia (728 (vol. I p. 262), 842, 1371, 1787, 2297, 2298, 2693, 2966, 3094a, 3207, 3209, 4010, 4246, 4334, 4335, 4336), *26, 32, 33*
Arnhemland (1063, 1063b, 2106), *25, 30, 33*
Aruaks (= Arowaks) (3487)
Aruba (2609, 4280, 4281)
Aru Islands (1864, 2281, 2864), *25*
Arumanians (2740b)
Ashanti (2287, 3167, 3168, 3358), *34*
Ashluslay (205)
Asia Minor (incl. Anatolia, Hittites, Phrygia) (74, 139, 321, 406, 407, 408, 409, 411, 1018, 1182, 1188, 1884, 2678, 3110, 3132, 3176, 3210, 3385, 3666, 3668, 4010, 4322, 4325, 4452), *26, 28, 30, 32, 34, 35*. See also: Armenia, Pontic Greek, Turkey.
Assam (404, 821, 1291, 2973, 2974, 2974a, 3533)
Assiniboin *30*
Assyria (776, 1197F, 1341, 1802, 2971, 3190, 3211, 4204, 4322, 4533a (p. 60 ff.))
Astrolabe Bay (360)
Asturias (565, 3092, 4111), *25, 29*
Atlas mountains (4073). See also: Morocco.
Atjèh (Achin) (2315)
Atoni (fig. 55) (1238 (p. 53 ff.))
Atorai (3487)
Aueto (2869)
/?Auni Bushmen (2227)
Australia, aboriginals of, (211, 288, 401, 457, 606a, 728 (vol. I p. 272), 830, 1063, 1063a, 1063b, 1063c, 1505, 1571, 1973, 2106, 2598, 3166, 3486, 3754, 3973, 4054, 4306a, 4312a, 4437), *25, 30, 31, 33, 45*
Austria (1496, 1551, 2244, 2302, 3726a, 4443, 4466, 4496, 4497), *35*
Austronesia, see: Indonesia, Oceania
Avars (254a)
Ayinara *29*
Azande, see: Zande
Azera (1874, 1875)
Azerbaijan (563, 4237), *26, 29, 31, 32*
Aztecs (76, 250, 575, 582, 601, 602, 603, 761b, 1333, 1393, 1394, 1395, 1603, 1604, 2295, 2477, 2761, 2766, 2767 *(passim)*, 2769,

248

805, 1026, 1027, 1028, 1035, 1056a, 1092, 1093, 1097, 1101, 1120, 1121, 1192, 1205a, 1294, 1295, 1337, 1399, 1437, 1459, 1669, 1854, 1904, 2012, 2012a, 2029, 2067, 2240, 2305, 2335, 2462, 2480, 2481, 2490, 2495, 2500, 2635, 2888, 3066, 3067, 3069, 3085, 3093a, 3105, 3131, 3221, 3387, 3625, 3715, 3781, 3812, 3866, 3867, 3892, 3980, 3987, 4012, 4016, 4037, 4110, 4161, 4162, 4163, 4170, 4171, 4173, 4174, 4192, 4236, 4238, 4239, 4252, 4253, 4263, 4439, 4449, 4473, 4474, 4475), *26, 29, 32, 55, 63*

Central Eskimo (164)

Ceram, see: Seran

Ceylon (141, 225, 728 (vol. I p. 404), 831, 3651, 3815, 4498)

Chaco (incl. Ashluslay, Bororó (S. Amer.), Cashica, Chamakoko, Chané, Choroti, Horió, Makushi, Mbayá, Mosho, Taulipang, Tumereha, Yekuana) (205, 1131, 1925, 3029)

Chahar Mongols (471)

Chaldea (702, 2077, 2679, 4533a (p. 60 ff.)), *43*

Chamakoko (205)

Chané (205)

Chari region (incl. Baya, Bugungo, Moundan, Sará, Tchad) (1348, 1411, 3367), *26, 27, 28, 31*

Chattisgarh (1084)

Chavantes (3407), *30*

Chechino-Ingoutch (1056a)

Cheremiss (2270, 2272, 2480, 2483, 3123)

Cherkessian, see: Circassian Tatars

Cherokee (2437), *25, 36*

Chewa (1712), *25*

Cheyenne (916, 917, 2797, 2846), *25, 36*

Chhattisgarh, see: Chattisgarh

Chiandjur *35*

Chiapas (1550, 3811)

Chibcha (4506b)

Chickasaw *25*

Chile (incl. Araucanians, Fuegians) (56, 57, 58, 149, 1961, 1962, 2032, 2033, 2568, 2796, 3123, 3157), *31*

China (1, 2, 24, 47, 49, 70, 112, 112b, 252, 395, 617, 618, 619, 620, 620a, 621, 630, 631, 632, 664, 676, 703, 715, 717, 728 (vol. I p. 411), 750, 764, 792, 832, 843, 854, 960, 963, 1033, 1036, 1038, 1046, 1047, 1053a, 1141, 1185A, 1192, 1231, 1232, 1233, 1351, 1306, 1322, 1410, 1439, 1474, 1498, 1501, 1509, 1532, 1554 – 1558, 1577, 1618, 1619, 1846, 1846a, 1854, 1869, 1881, 1919, 1969, 1975, 1976, 1977, 1989, 2052, 2081, 2084, 2086, 2138, 2192, 2205, 2207, 2238, 2239, 2240, 2255, 2256, 2259, 2274, 2275, 2299a, 2304, 2313, 2331, 2339a, 2355, 2356, 2374, 2441, 2442, 2443, 2467, 2469, 2528, 2529, 2531, 2601, 2602, 2603, 2604, 2631, 2632, 2633, 2634, 2645, 2664, 2705, 2706, 2713, 2751, 2764, 2791, 2837, 2923, 2925, 2926, 2961a, 2969, 2970, 3035, 3068, 3134, 3170, 3174, 3177 (p. 83 ff.), 3179, 3180, 3181, 3195, 3196,

3381, 3382, 3384, 3386, 3388, 3415, 3455, 3564, 3567, 3574, 3579f, 3733, 3735, 3755, 3786, 3388, 3415, 3455, 3564, 3567, 3574, 3579f, 3733, 3735, 3755, 3786, 3829a, 3839, 3894, 3895, 3896, 3919, 4000, 4038, 4044, 4060, 4142–4146, 4243, 4265, 4266, 4286– 4295, 4301, 4320, 4349a, 4370, 4375, 4376, 4389, 4424, 4447, 4448, 4455, 4458, 4504b, 4506e, 4511a, 4529, 4531b, 4549b, 4549c), *12, 23, 26, 31, 32, 35, 43, 44, 48, 55, 63, 65*

Chindau, see: Mozambique

Chinook (378, 1014)

Chios (3160)

Chipaya (2869)

Chipchin Mongols (1093)

Chippewa (Ojibwa) (554, 857, 867, 869, 902, 948, 2433), *25, 32, 36*

Chiriguano (2869)

Chiriqui (1873)

Chitimacha Indians (932)

Chleuh (653, 655)

Choctaw (926, 2437), *25, 36*

Chokwe (2729, 3060a, 3366a)

Chopi (2122, 4120, 4123, 4136b), *25, 28*

Choroti (205)

Chu'an Miao (24, 1498)

Chuwassians (1056a 2481,)

Circassian Tatars (2495)

Coast Salish (1014, 1713, 1746, 3430). See also: Salish.

Cochiti (947a)

Cocoma (2869), *30*

Cocopa *36*

Coll *25*

Colombia (incl. Chibcha, Chiriqui, Guambia, Kogaba, Saliva, Umauca) (44, 45, 697, 1472, 1873, 1973a, 2614–2617, 2767 (p. 143), 3123, 3154, 3155, 3156, 3487, 4207, 4506b), *31*

Comanche (2797), *25, 36*

Comox (1725, 3650)

Congo, see: Belgian Congo, French Equatorial Africa

Conibo *30*

Cook Islands (525)

Copper Eskimo (3345, 3436)

Copts (1755, 1760, 1765, 1770, 1774, 4333), *27*

Cora Indians (1910, 2767 (pp. 20, 40, 144, 147, 151, 159)), *28*

Corea, see: Korea

Cordilleras de los Andes (309, 4207). See also: Bolivia, Chile, Colombia, Ecuador, Peru.

Corsica *24, 29, 35*

Costa Rica (145, 4095)

Cree Indians (3583), *30*

Creek Indians (2437, 3909, 4007), *25, 36*

Crete (300, 1467, 3241), *30*

Crimea (2480)

Croatia (incl. Dalmatia, Istria, Medimurje) (282, 1376, 1457, 1748, 2138b, 2350, 2354, 2654, 3851, 3855-3858, 4443b, 4482–4485, 4490, 4491), *25, 29, 32, 66*

Fès (644)

Fezzan *24, 35*

Fiji Islands (2190, 2191, 2556, 3362a, 4433 (p. 44 ff.))

Finland (83, 85, 86, 90, 94, 431, 728 (vol. I p. 542), 782, 2328, 2329, 2330, 2333, 2334, 2337, 2338, 2518, 2560, 2562, 2562a, 3123, 3389, 4164, 4167, 4172, 4176, 4179, 4179a), *31.* See also: Scandinavia (general).

Fin-Ugrians (802, 2336, 2462, 2480, 2481, 2931, 4179). See also: Ob-Ugrians, Permiaks, Ugrians, Wotyaks.

Flanders (705a, 726, 746, 757, 852a, 1029, 1030, 3130a, 4382, 4506a, 4507, 4532a), *35.* See also: Netherlands.

Flathead Indians (2848, 2857), *30*

Flores (figs. 48 and 58) (1639, 2369, 2383, 2413), *15, 40, 44, 52, 54*

Florida (910, 947)

Fly River (4383)

Fon (769, 3284), *27, 35*

Formosa (incl. Bunun, Tayal, Tsou) (2015, 2149, 2439, 4433 (p. 34 ff.)), *25, 35*

Foulbe *26*

Fouta Dialon (2690)

Fox Indians (= Meskwaki) (2437, 2797), *32*

France (135, 244, 502, 503, 517, 579, 581, 643, 716, 717, 717a, 728 (vol. I p. 566), 757, 825, 825a, 999, 1000, 1001, 1002, 1022, 2028, 2595, 2605, 2735–2738, 3123, 3191, 3222, 3396, 3842, 4086, 4086a, 4087, 4140, 4141, 4159, 4195a, 4233a, 4544), *24, 29, 31, 34, 35.* See also: Basques.

French Antilles (3115). See also: West Indian Archipelago.

French Canadian (233, 234, 236, 238, 1321, 1607, 3505), *17, 25, 31*

French Congo, see: French Equatorial Africa.

French Equatorial Africa (incl. Baduma, Babali, Batéké, Bawanji, Baya, Bembe, Bong(i)li, Bongongo, Boungomo, Eshira, Fang, Iveïa, Kalai, Kukuya, Kuyu, Lari, Loango, Mbeti, Mbochi, Mboko, Ngoma, Ngundi, Okandi, Pomo, Sará, Vali region, Vili, Wasamba, Yaswa) (153, 219, 807, 1348, 1507, 1508, 1914, 2646a, 2668, 3065a, 3123, 3135, 3136, 3138 – 3141, 3143, 3144, 3148, 3149, 3151, 3151a, 3152, 3307, 3498,3502a, 3883, 3884, 4149, 4433), *24, 27, 28, 31, 35.* See also: Cameroons, Gabon, Tchad, Ubangi-Chari.

French Guinea (2116, 2690, 3123, 3501), *24, 26, 27, 28, 30, 31, 32, 34, 35, 36, 66.* See also: Fulah, Guerzé, Kissi, Kurussa, Malinké, Toma, Wolof.

French Guyana (incl. Kalina, Oayana, Roucouyenne) (3487, 4433 (p. 51 ff.)), *26, 33*

French Sudan (112c, 564a, 2584a, 3109a, 3500), *24, 27, 34, 35.* See also: French Guinea, French West Africa.

French Switzerland (3481, 3483, 3484)

French West Africa (112c, 306, 629a, 1516, 2584a, 2594, 3123, 3359, 3500, 3501, 3682a,

4470a), *26, 31, 32, 35, 36, 66.* See also: Ashanti, Ba'ule, Buguni, Dahomey, Dogon, French Guinea, Ivory Coast, Senegal, Togo.

Frosinone *31*

Fuegians (1961, 1962)

Fulah (= Peul) (1131), *27, 35, 36*

Fulbe (Foulbe) (1017a, 3679), *26*

Fulup (336)

Further India (728 (vol. I p. 232). See also: Annam, Burma, Cambodia, Dong-s'on, Karén, Laos, Moï, Pemsians, Siam, Tonkin, Viet-nam.

Futuna (552, 4433 (p. 44 ff.))

Ga *34*

Gabon (incl. Baduma, Bawanji, Boungomo, Fang, Okandi) (fig. 41) (153, 955, 1507, 1508, 1914, 4149), *24, 26, 27*

Gabrielino Indians (3446)

Gaels (573, 1597, 3826, 3827), *25.* See also: Hebrides.

Galicia (Poland) (2280)

Galicia (Spain) (2340, 3470), *25, 29*

Galway (748)

Gambia (incl. Mandingo, Wolof) (332, 336, 1479, 1502, 2455, 3161), *30*

Ganda (2450, 3474, 3813, 4257, 4258, 4260, 4261), *25, 28*

Ganda/Soga *28*

Gaspésia peninsula (3505)

Gaule (Gallia) (582)

Gazelle peninsula (1039)

Genya *28*

Georgia (202a, 325, 724, 728a, 974, 1100, 2480, 2482, 2928, 2960, 3940b), *26, 33, 34, 35*

Gerais (3393)

Gerebi *25*

German Czechs (2118), *35*

German Switzerland (637, 1052, 1368, 1515, 1526, 1527, 1990, 4099, 4499), *34*

Germany (Germans) (311, 383, 383a, 705a, 728 (vol. I p. 497), 798, 958, 959, 1113, 1114, 1227a, 1307a, 1485, 1548, 1627, 1643, 1860, 1861, 1871, 2118, 2188, 2248, 2248a, 2248b, 2821a, 2862, 3016, 3057, 3383, 3592, 3593, 3594, 3595, 3598, 3600, 3644a, 3696, 3707, 3740, 3783, 3889, 3943, 4137, 4268, 4268a, 4318, 4395, 4407 – 4413, 4417, 4418, 4537), *35*

Geronimo Apache *25*

Ghana, see: Gold Coast

Ghasis (3480)

Ghonds (1523, 2182), *25*

Gilbert Islands (2571)

Gio *30*

Girimaya *25, 28*

Gogadara (3736)

Gogo *28*

Gold Coast (= Ghana) (73, 771a, 1383, 1385, 3025a, 3082a, 3428a, 3463, 3954, 4298, 4299, 4300), *34.* See also: Akan, Ashanti, Ewe, Fanti, Ga, Kabre, Sena, Togo, Upper

Hebrew-Persian, Hebrew-Syrian, Hittites, Iraq, Kurdistan, Libanon, Mesopotamia, Persia, Phoenicia, Sumerians, Syria, Turkey.
Negritos, see: Pygmees, Asiatic,
Nepal (571, 3123, 4532), *30*
Netherlands (518, 518a, 518b, 705a, 746, 852, 1029, 1030, 1302, 1361, 2109, 2110, 2128, 2248b, 2358, 2359, 2405, 2586, 2588a, 2588b, 2886, 3212, 3229, 3698, 4228, 4241, 4406, 4421), *32*. See also: Flanders.
Netherlands Guyana, see: Surinam
Netsilik Eskimo (3344)
Neu Mecklenburg, see: New Ireland
Neu Pommern, see: New Britain
New Britain (= Neu Pommern) (incl. Gazelle peninsula) (1039, 1986, 1987, 1988, 4433 (p. 39 ff.), 4501)
New Caledonia (3072, 4244, 4433 (p. 39 ff.), 4513), *35, 36*
New England (1256)
Newfoundland (1509a, 2140a)
New Guinea (incl. Ali, Astrolabe Bay, Azera, Fly River, Gogadara, Karesau, Karkar, Kate, Kiwai, Lake Murray, Mafulu, Mamberamo Papuans, Mekeo, Orokaiva, Papua, Papuan Gulf, Ramu district, Sepik, Sialum, Tami, Torres Straits, Trans-Fly, Yabim, Yule Island) (307, 360, 373, 382, 642, 667a, 668, 1139, 1253, 1253a, 1314a, 1324a, 1483, 1486, 1488, 1489, 1566, 1567, 1568, 1694, 1695, 1874, 1875, 1983, 2281, 2366, 2367, 2402, 2538, 2949, 2950, 3177 (pp. 176, 178 ff.), 3201, 3696a, 3727, 3729, 3736, 3810, 4383, 4384, 4384a, 4422, 4423, 4433 (p. 39 ff.)), *25, 44, 49, 50, 51, 53*
New Hebrides (incl. Futuna, Malekula) (552, 839, 1253, 3918, 4433 (p. 39 ff.))
New Ireland (= Neu Mecklenburg) (incl. Tombara) (6, 1658, 1662, 1892, 1986, 1987, 1988, 2308, 2612)
New Mexico (919, 3127, 3429), *29*
New Zealand (4513). See also: Maori
Ngada (1639, 2383), *44*
Ngala *28, 34*
Ngbandi (4047, 4048)
Ngoma (3148)
Ngundi *24, 27, 28, 35*
Nias (2376, 3177 (p. 170), 4433 (p. 34 ff.)), *14, 15, 16, 45*
Nicaragua (846, 1604)
Nicobars (4433 (p. 34 ff.)), *54*
Nieder-Lausitz (1627)
Nigeria (fig. 56) (134, 219, 444, 806, 836, 1145, 1146, 1147, 1148, 1580, 1619a, 1621, 1952, 2080, 2203a, 2544, 2687, 2688, 2688a, 2688b, 2935a, 3065b, 3604a, 4230), *30, 31, 32, 45*. See also: Efik, Ewe, Haussa, Ibo, Sokoto, Tiv, Yoruba.
Niger Territory (incl. Bambara, Ba'ule, Bororo (Afr.), Fulah, Haussa, Jarma, Sarakolé, Senoufo, Songhai/Zerma, Sonray, Yefe) (287, 1131, 1479, 1677, 2247, 3123, 3161, 3230, 3231, 3871), *24, 27, 35*

Nikki (339)
Niue (4433 (p. 44 ff.))
Nkanu (= Bankanu) (3522)
Nkumbi (3693)
Nkund(j)o (385, 1456, 1993)
Nogai Tatars (2495)
Nogundi, see: Ngundi
Nootka (923, 1014, 3451), *36, 65*
Norfolk *35*
Normandy *29*
North America, see: Canada, Eskimo, United States
North American Indians (general) (200, 237, 504, 543, 545, 555, 557, 561, 625, 858, 859, 860, 862, 863, 864, 868, 873 – 879, 882 – 892, 894, 895, 899, 900, 901, 904, 908, 911, 913, 914, 920, 924, 927, 928, 929, 930, 935, 936, 937, 939–945, 1103, 1239, 1240, 1241, 1262, 1267, 1334, 1703, 1716–1719, 1728, 1729, 1731, 1735, 1740, 2262, 2421, 2422, 2431, 2608, 2788a, 2801, 2882, 2979, 2981, 2986, 3005a, 3084, 3399, 3400, 3406, 3449, 3784, 3990, 4088, 4425, 4509), *12, 25, 28, 29, 30, 31, 32, 36*. See also: Canada, United States.
North American Negroes (686, 1102, 1235, 1255, 2438d, 2860a, 3056, 3124, 3472, 3671, 4310), *29, 31*. See also: Afro-Americans.
North California (98)
Northern Rhodesia (219, 995, 2093, 2096, 2097, 2102, 3523a, 4136d, 4136h, 4136j, 4366a). See also: Ambo, Bachioko, Barotse, Ila, Lala, Lamba, Luchazi, Luena, Mbunda, Ovimbundu, Thonga, Zambesi.
Northumberland (144, 623), *35*
Northwest Greenland (4066)
Northwest Indians (incl. Bellakula, Chinook, Coast Salish, Haida, Kwakiutl, Nootka, Salish, Tlingit, Tsimshian) (378, 379, 923, 925, 926, 1014, 1242, 1334, 1360, 1713, 1714, 1746, 3404, 3430, 3451, 3809b, 3985), *25, 31*
Norway (30, 89, 93, 333 II, 363–368, 400, 728 (vol. II p. 400), 782, 1056, 1065–1069, 1375, 1497, 1513, 1537, 1560a, 1674, 2538, 2621, 3082, 3636–3643, 3887, 4516), *32, 35*. See also: Scandinavia (general).
Nova Scotia (761a, 2689a), *30*
Novi Pazar (2654)
Nubi *28*
Nubia (1652)
Nuer (4153)
Nuristan, see: Kafiristan
Nyamwezi (1897), *25, 27, 28*
Nyasaland (incl. Chewa, Wayao) (1559, 1712, 2918, 3344a, 2933, 4351), *25*
Nyaturu (3366 (p. 65 ff.))
Nyika/Chonye *28*
Nyika (incl. Wayao) *28*
Nyika/Girimaya *28*
Nyika/Kambe *28*
Nyoro *25, 28*
Nyoro/Haya *28*
Nyoro/Toro *28*

3602, 3700, 3879, 3880, 3881, 3882, 4103a,
4181a, 4390, 4471)
Polynesia (general) (527, 547 – 552, 690, 728
(vol. II p. 471), 1276, 1571, 3051, 3754,
3859b, 4057), *16, 29, 31, 66.* See also:
Aotearoa, Cook Islands, Fatu hiva, Fiji
Islands, Futuna, Gilbert Islands, Hawaii,
Maori, Marquesas, New Zealand, Niue,
Paumotu, Samoa, Society Islands, Tahiti,
Tonga, Tuamotu.
Pomo *35*
Ponape (4433 (p. 44 ff.))
Ponca *25*
Pontic Greeks *30*
Port au Prince (3503)
Portugal (341, 374, 1327, 1329, 1480, 2120,
2121, 2824a, 2898, 3008, 3425, 3470, 3701,
4184), *35*
Portugese East Africa, see: Mozambique
Portugese Guinea (1469a)
Portugese West Africa, see: Angola
Provence (1051, 2737a), *29*
Pskoff *35*
Pueblo Indians (incl. Acoma, Bonito, Cochi-
ti, Hopi, Isleta, Moki, Santo Domingo
Pueblo, Taos, Zuñi) (902, 909, 919, 947a,
1057, 1236, 1438, 1440, 1705, 1721, 2117,
3431, 3451c), *29, 32, 36*
Puerto Rico (560, 847, 1090, 1611, 2652a,
4312), *31*
Puget Sound Indians (3404, 3430), *36*
Puget Sound Salish (3430)
Puinave *25, 35*
Punjab (739), *28*
Pygmies, African (469, 3502a, 3502b, 3693,
3694, 4156, 4157), *12, 26, 28, 36, 51.* See
also: Babinga, Batwa (Twa), Mbuti
Pygmies, Asiatic, (1137)
Pyrenees (3222)
Pyuma *25*
Quebec (236)
Quechua (128a, 128b, 493, 3653), *29*
Queensland (457)
Quicuru *27*
Quileute (923), *36*
Quinault Indians (3404), *36*
Qunantuna (4501)
Rabat (3413)
Rada (2859)
Rajahstan (614), *28*
Ramu district (1483)
Reddi tribe (4512)
Rhaetoromania (2709)
Rhenania (311)
Rhodesia, see: Northern Rhodesia, Southern
Rhodesia
Rhodope mountains (539, 2154). See also:
Rumelia.
Rio Grande do Sul (3008a)
Rio Plata (586)
Rio Xingu, see: Xingu
Roanoke (622)
Roma (3022)

Rong, see: Lepcha
Ronga (2123)
Roté (2584)
Roucouyenne (3487)
Ruanda/Urundi (393, 469, 470, 1020, 1916,
2743a, 2849, 2850, 2860b, 2860d, 3125,
3655a). See also: Batwa (Twa), Hutu,
Tutsi.
Rumania (incl. Banat, Bu' ovina, Dobrucha,
Moldavia, Muntenia, Oltenia, Siebenbürgen, Walachia) (51, 52, 53, 54, 54a, 201,
202, 256, 257, 261, 262, 263, 265, 266, 274,
331, 421, 458, 460, 466, 495, 496, 497, 588,
677–681, 709, 710, 733, 973, 1010, 1010a,
1155, 1451a, 2054, 2055, 2155, 2168, 2520n,
2525a, 2610, 2637, 2908, 3011, 3104, 3123,
3227, 3228, 3228a, 3238, 3239, 3216a, 3418,
3419, 3420, 3459, 3670, 3837a, 3935, 4021c
(Nos. 12 and 28), 4137, 4205a, 4227, 4249,
4267, 4268, 4328, 4377, 4472, 4492, 4493,
4502, 4503, 4506, 4510, 4551), *21, 29, 32,
35.* See also: Arumanians.
Rumelia (300a, 2844). See also: Rhodope
mountains.
Rundi (3047), *34.* See also: Burundi.
Russia (incl. Caucasus) (113, 113a, 202a,
289a, 290, 324, 325, 465, 670, 724, 728a,
974, 1056a, 1094, 1100, 1594, 2137, 2146,
2187, 2278, 2279, 2280, 2280a, 2336, 2347,
2449, 2462, 2480 – 2485, 2493, 2495, 2624,
2625, 2625a, 2708, 2875, 2928, 2960, 2901,
2987, 2992, 3012, 3105, 3106, 3123, 3250,
3512, 3697b, 3700, 3707, 3746, 3781, 3783,
3817, 3888, 3889, 3940b, 3954a, 4006, 4152,
4175, 4177, 4219, 4238, 4377), *31, 32, 35.*
See also: Baltic States.
Ryūkyū's (incl. Amami Islands, Luchuans,
Okinawa) (2135, 2136, 3515, 3516, 4445,
4446), *25, 30, 65*
Sagada (province) (2677a)
Sahara (3123). See also: Tuareg.
Saisett *25*
Sakai (4433 (p. 32)), *35*
Sakalava *24*
Sakhalin (2069)
Salayar (1865, 3725)
Salish (1014, 1713, 1746, 3430)
Saliva (3487)
Saloum (1016a)
Sambesi, see: Zambesi
Samoa (526, 905, 1450, 2282, 3868, 4433 (p.
44 ff.))
San Andres *33*
Sandchak (4201)
San Domingo (143, 744, 1358, 3027)
Sanga *35*
San Ildefonso Indians *29, 32, 36*
San Paolo Matese *31*
San Salvador (232)
Santa Ana Indians *32*
Santa Catharina *35*
Santander (565), *25*
Santo Domingo Pueblo (919)

Tarahumare Indians (2767 (p. 178), 2797)
Tarascans (601, 1550a)
Tariana (3487)
Taruma (3487)
Tasmania (3486)
Tatars (15, 1056a, 2067, 2462, 2480, 2481, 2495, 3093a, 3105, 3781), 33
Tatar Tadjik 33
Taulipang (205, 1925, 1963)
Tayal (44ss (p. 37))
Tchad (1411, 3367)
Tchuwassians (1056a, 2481)
Tembé (2869)
Tembeling (2618)
Temiar (Plé-Temiar) (1569), 28, 30, 33
Terschelling (2358)
Tesot (4260)
Tetela (1423, 1532a, 2049, 2050, 3819, 3820)
Teton Sioux (861, 865)
Thailand, see: Siam
Thonga (N. Rhod., Mozamb.) (2124, 2231, 2755, 3013a, 3523, 3523a), 25, 28
Thracia (2170, 3962)
Tibet (385c, 765, 728 (vol. II p. 631), 1294, 1295, 1854, 1869, 2636, 3177 (p. 137 ff.), 3221, 3892, 3980), 27, 31, 33. 65. See also: Sikkim.
Tigrai (752)
Tiki, see: Marquesas
Timor (figs. 55 and 57) (incl. Atoni, Belu) (22, 1238, 2346, 2927a), 45, 54
Tinguian (1324)
Tirol 35
Tiv (1964, 2542, 2543)
Tlemcen 33
Tlingit (1014)
Togo (747a, 2247, 3865, 4362, 4364), 24, 27. See also: Gold Coast, Otchi region.
Toka (600)
Toltecs (2767 (pp. 58, 90, 120))
Toma 27, 35
Tombara (2308)
Tonga Islands (3362, 4433 (p. 44 ff.))
Tonga (Afr.), see: Thonga
Tonkawa (2797)
Tonkin (1448, 1460, 1462, 3335)
Toraja (2178, 2343, 4433 (p. 34 ff.))
Torres Straits (1566, 1567, 2949, 2950)
Trans-Fly (4383)
Transylvania (201, 266, 2520n)
Travancore (3825)
Tres Zapotes (2767(pp. 95, 112))
Trinidad (105, 456, 590, 1122, 2789, 2859, 2942, 3055, 3071, 3127a, 3239a, 4311), 27, 31, 33, 34
Trio Indians (3487)
Tripolitania (163, 257, 3226, 3699, 3983)
Truk (1706, 4432 (p. 44 ff.))
Tsarisen 35
Tsimshian (1014, 1360)
Tschokwe, see: Chokwe
Tshopi, see: Chopi
Tsou (4433 (p. 37))

Tuamotu (548)
Tuareg (1872, 2606), 24, 32, 35
Tukanó (3487)
Tule Indians (877, 880)
Tumba (687)
Tumereha (205)
Tumet Mongols (1093)
Tun Huang (3715)
Tunisia (5, 1119, 1149, 1446, 1624, 1891, 2496, 2505, 3983), 23, 31
Tupi-Guarani (incl. Apiaká, Aueto, Caingua, Camayura, Chipaya, Chiriguano, Cocoma, Curuaya, Guarani, Guarayú, Karajá, Mauhé, Mundurucú, Omagua, Oyampi, Parintintin, Pauserna, Tembé, Tupinamba, Yuruma, Ywuina) (159, 2869, 3487, 3972, 4232), 27, 30
Tupinamba (159, 2869)
Turfan (3715)
Turkestan (146, 1205a, 2012, 2012a, 2500, 3131, 3177 (p. 136), 3715, 4162). See also: Kirghiz, Turkmenes, Uzbekistan.
Turkey (74, 139, 275, 321, 373b, 406, 407, 408, 409, 411, 412, 1140, 1182, 1188, 1197C, 1379, 1884, 2139, 2354, 3070, 3110, 3176, 3210, 3385, 3387, 3388b, 3426, 3666, 3668, 4021c, (No. 14), 4452), 26, 28, 31, 32, 35
Turkmenes (162, 319, 600, 2495, 3131, 3387, 3388b, 4161), 26, 34, 43
Turko-Afghans (352)
Turk Tatars (2462, 2480, 2481, 2495)
Tutelo Indians (1727, 2424, 2425, 3912), 32
Tutsi (469, 3655a), 28, 29, 31, 34
Twa (469, 3655a), 28, 31, 34
Twi (73)
Tzotzil 29
Uapu (4433 (p. 44 ff.))
Uaupes (3487)
Ubangi (3155, 3137), 26
Ubangi-Chari region (incl. Baya, Bugongo) (3367), 27
Udmurske (1056a)
Uganda (incl. Alur, Bamba, Bunyoro, Ganda, Ganda/Soga, Gwere, Iteso, Konjo, Nyoro/ Toro, Tesot, Usuku) (370, 757a, 2450, 2667, 3460, 3474, 3738, 3790, 3813, 3828, 4257– 4262a), 28
Ugrians (2524, 4193). See also: Fin-Ugrians, Ob-Ugrians.
Uigurs 26
Uintah Utes (3649)
Uist (3826, 3827), 25
Uitoto (415, 3487)
Ukraine (113, 113a, 2278, 2279, 2280, 2280a, 2449, 2987, 2992, 3512, 3697b, 3700, 3889), 30, 31, 35
Ulawa (2036)
Uliasse (2085)
Umauca (3487)
United Kingdom, see: England, Great Britain, Ireland, Man, Scotland, Wales
United States (general) (237, 252a, 252b, 303, 304, 304a, 326, 385d, 437, 504, 519, 520,

267

III

INDEX OF AUTHORS, COLLECTORS AND MUSICIANS

271

Braunwieser, Martin, (493b)
Brazys, Th., (494)
Breazul, G., (495)
Brediceanu, Tiberius, (496, 497)
Brehmer, Fritz, (498, 1938), 48
Breloer, Bernhard, (499)
Brenecke, Ernest, (500)
Briceño, Olga, (501)
Bricqueville, E. de, (502, 503)
Brinton, G., (504)
Bris, E. le, (505, 506)
Briton, H. H., (507)
Britten, Benjamin, (2809)
Broadwood, Lucy, (508)
Brömse, Peter, (510, 511)
Broholm, H. C., (509)
Bronson, Bertrand Harris, (512–515, 638)
Bruce-Mitford, R. L. S., (516)
Brücken, Fritz, (517)
Brugial, Jean, 26
Bruning, Father Elis., (518, 518a, 518b), 21
Bryan, Charles Faulkner, (519–521)
Buchanan, Annabel Morris, (522)
Buchner, Alexander, (523, 524)
Buck, Peter H., (525–528a)
Buçsan, Andrei, (201, 4506)
Budde, Karl, (529)
Bücken, Ernst, (3968, 4506c)
Bücher, Carl, (530), 47, 65
Bürchner, L., (531)
Buhle, Edward, (532)
Bukofzer, Manfred F., (fig. 32) (533–538), 17, 18, 19
Bukoreschliev, A., (539)
Bulut, Tarik, 28
Bundu Khan 33
Bunting, Edward, (540–542)
Burlin, Nathalie, (543–545)
Burnier, Th., (546, 546a)
Burrows, Edwin G., (547–552a), 63
Burssens, A., (553)
Burton, Frederick R., (554), 16
Buttree, Julia M., (555)
Buvarp, Hans, (556, 557)

Cabral, Jorge, (558)
Cabussi-Kabusch, N., (559)
Cadilla de Martinez, Maria, (560)
Cadman, Charles W., (561)
Cadwell, Helen, (562)
Caferoglu, Ahmed, (563)
Cahen, Abraham, (564)
Calame, Blaise, (564b–564d), 26
Calame-Griaule, Geneviève, (564a–564d)
Calleja, R., (565)
Callenfels, P. V. van Stein, (566)
Calmet, Augustin, (567)
Caluza, Reuben Tolakele, (568, 569)
Calvert, W. E., (358)
Camp, Ch. M., (570), 55
Campbell, (571)
Campbell, A., (572)
Campbell, J. L., (573)

Campen, C. F. H., (574)
Campos, Ruben M., (575–577)
Candied, Fr., (577a)
Cano, D. M., (578)
Canteloube, J., (579)
Canziani, Estella, (581)
Canzoneri, V., (581a)
Capitan (582)
Capmañy, A., (583)
Cappelle, H. van, (584)
Capus, M. G., (585)
Carámbula, Rubén, (586)
Carlheim-Gyllenskiöld (587)
Caron, Hubert, (789)
Carp, Paula, (588)
Carpentier, Alejo, (589)
Carpitella, Diego, 66
Carr, Andrew T., (590)
Carra de Vaux (591)
Carreras y Candi, F., (4113)
Carrington, J. F., (592–597a)
Carrol, Father K., (598)
Carybé (599)
Castagné, J., (600)
Castañeda, Daniel, (601–603)
Casteele, J. M. van de, (603a–603e)
Castellanos, Israel, (604)
Castera, J., (252)
Castillo, Jesus, (605)
Castro, José, (606)
Caughie, Catherine, (606a)
Caussin de Perceval, A., (607, 3153)
Cavazzi, P., (608, 2451)
Český, Lid, (609)
Chailley, Jacques, (467a, 610, 610a, 3692b, 4506d), 69
Chaitanya Deva, B., (611, 611a, 611b)
Chaitanya Mahaprabu, Cri, (183, 198d)
Chakravarthi, Suresh Chandra, (612–614)
Chalmers Werner, E., (1033)
Chambers, G. B., (615)
Chandra Vedi, Pandit R. Dilip, (616)
Chantre, E., (340)
Chao, Mei-Pa, (617)
Chao, Wei Pang, (618, 619)
Chao, Y. R., (620, 620a, 621)
Chapin, James P., (621a)
Chapman, Francis S., 31
Chappel, Louis W., (622)
Chardon, Yves, 42
Charlton, George V. B., (623
Charpentier, G., 33
Chartres, Samuel B., 33
Chase, Gilbert, (624–627), 30
Chatur Lál, Pandit, see: Lál, Pandit Chatur,
Chaubey, S. K., (628)
Chauvet, Stéphen, (629, 629a), 57
Chavannes, Edouard, (630–632, 4506e)
Chavez, Carlos, (633), 64
Chavez Franco, M., (634, 635)
Chelebi, Ewliya, (1182)
Chengalavarayan, N., (636)
Cherbuliez, Antoine E., (637, 4506f), 60

273

274

Edge-Partington, J., (1052a)
Edwards, Arthur C., (1053)
Edwards, E. D., (1053a, 1501)
Edwards, L. F., (1054)
Edwards, S. Hylton, (1055)
Eggen, Erik, (1056)
Egorova, V., (1056a)
Ehrenreich, Paul, (1057)
Eichenauer (1058), *12*
Elbert, Johannes, (1059)
Elbert, Samuel H., (1060)
Elia, Piero, (1061)
Eliade, Mircea, (1062)
Elkin, A. P., (1063–1063c), *25, 30, 33, 36, 64*
Elkin, Clarence, (1064)
Elling, Catharinus, (1065–1069)
Ellis, Alexander · John, (fig. 1) (1070–1082, 2411, 3986), *2 ff., 10*
Elwin, Verrier, (1083–1086)
Emerson, Joseph S., (1087)
Emerson, Nathaniel H., (1088)
Emmanuel, Maurice, (1089)
Emrich, Duncan, (1090), *26, 37*
Emsheimer, Ernst, (fig. 26) (1091–1101), *17, 21, 75*
Ende, A. von, (1102, 1103)
Endo, Hirosi, (1104)
Ene, Augustine, (2688b)
Engel, Carl, (1105–1109)
Engel, Hans, (1110)
Ennis, Seamus, *24*
Enright, D. J., (1112)
Erdélyi, János, (1112a)
Erdmann, Hans, (1113)
Erk, Ludwig, (1114)
Erkmann, (1115)
Erlanger, Rodolphe d', (1116–1119), *63*
Erzakovitsch, B., (1120, 1121)
Escobar, M. L., (2551, 2552)
Eskin, Sam, *31, 32*
Espinet, Charles S., (1122)
Essafi (951)
Esser, J., (1122a)
Estella, Pe. H. Olazaran de, (1123)
Estreicher, Zygmunt, (fig. 13) (1124–1133), *41*
Eugène, Prince, *31*
Eulenstein, C., (3664)
Evans, Bessie, (1705)
Evans, Ivor H. N., (1135–1137)
Evans, May G., (1705)
Evrard, W., (1138)
Ewald, Z., *22*
Exner, F., (1139), *17*
Ezgi, Suphi, (1140)

Faber, E., (1141)
Faber, G. H. von, (1142)
Fabó, Bertalan, (1143)
Faddegon, Barend, (1144)
Fagg, Bernard, (1145–1147)
Fagg, William, (1148, 1148a)
Faiyaz Khan, Ustad, (628)

Falck, R. (1212a)
Falconi, Gerardo, (1149)
Falla, Manuel de, (1150)
Falls, J. C. E., (1151)
Faly, I., (1151a)
Fara, Guilio, (1152–1154)
Faragó, József, (1155)
Farmer, Henry George, (1156–1210, 3456, 3604), *46, 63, 75*
Farnsworth, P. R., (1211)
Faroughy, A., (1212)
Faublee, J., (1212a, 3502)
Faulkner, Maurice, (1212b)
Favari, Alberto, (1213)
Feather, Leonard, (1214)
Fedeli, Vito, (1215)
Feilberg, C. G., (1216)
Felber, Erwin, (1217–1222), *17*
Féline, Pierre, (1223)
Fellerer, Karl Gustav, (1224)
Fenton, William N., (1225–1227, 2420), *36*
Fenwick Jones, G., (1227a)
Ferand, Ernst Th., (1228, 1229)
Ferguson, John, (1230)
Fernald, Helen E., (1231–1233)
Ferrars, Bertha, (2743)
Ferrars, Max, (2743)
Ferreira, Ascenso, (1234)
Ferrero, E., (1235)
Ferryman, A. F. M., (836)
Fewkes, J. W., (1236), *16*
Feys (4532a)
Fichter, Jean, *35*
Ficker, Rudolf von, (1237)
Fiedler, Hermann, (1238)
Figueras, José Romeu, see: Romeu Figueras, José.
Filipović, M. S., *29*
Fillmore, John Comfort, (1239–1242)
Finesinger, Sol Baruch, (1243)
Fink, Gottfried Wilhelm, (1244)
Firfov, Givko, (1245–1248a), *22, 64*
Fischer, Adolf, (1249)
Fischer, E., (1250, 1251)
Fischer, Hans, (1252, 1253, 1253a)
Fischer, H. W., (1254)
Fisher, Miles Mark, (1255)
Flanders, Helen Hartness, (1256)
Fleischer, Oskar, (1257, 1258)
Flesche, Francis la, (1259, 1266)
Fletcher, Alice Cunningham, (1261–1267)
Flood, William H. Grattan, (1268, 1269, 1506)
Florenz, Karl, (4511a)
Flornoy, Bertrand, *35*
Focke, II. C., (1270)
Fökövi (1271)
Foldes, A., (1272)
Foley, Rolla, (1273)
Forde, F. von der, (1276)
Fortassier, Pierre, (4511b)
Foucart, F., (1277)
Fourneau, J., (1278)

275

276

281

283

284

Panoff, Peter, (3105, 3106, 4540)
Panum, Hortense, (3107-3109)
Pâques, Mrs., (3109a), *35*
Parisius, Ludolf, (3646a, 4318)
Parisot, J., (3110)
Park, Kyung Ho, *29*
Parker, D. C., (3111)
Parmentier, H., (3112, 3113)
Parrinder, E. G., (3114)
Parry, Milman, (282, 2654)
Parsons, Elsie Clews, (3115)
Parthasarathi, S., (3116)
Parvatikar, Swami D. R., *27, 29*
Pasini, Fr., (3117)
Passin, Herbert, (2677)
Pastor, Willy, (3118)
Pataik, Raphael, *28*
Patel, Dinesh, *34*
Paterson, A., (3119)
Paterson, J. D., (3120)
Pattamal, Mrs. D. K., *27, 29, 35*
Patterson, Annie, (3121)
Paucitis, K., (3122)
Pauli, F. W., (3123, 3124)
Pauwels, P. M., (3125)
Payer (3126)
Peabody, Charles, (3127)
Peacock, Ken, *30*
Pearse, Andrew, (3127a, 3128), *32*
Peate, Iorwerth, (3128a)
Péczely, A., (3128b)
Pedrell, Felipe, (3129)
Pedrosa, Mario, (3130)
Peeters, R. P., (1547)
Peeters, Theophiel, (3130a)
Pekker, Ian, (3131)
Pélagaud, Fernand, (3132, 4240)
Pelay Briz (3133)
Pelliot, Paul, (3134)
Pepper, Herbert, (3135-3152), *63*
Pépratx-Saisset, Henry, (3152a)
Percival, Coussin de, see: Caussin de Percival, A.,
Perdomo Escobar, José Ignacio, (3154-3156)
Pereira Salas, Eugenio, (3157, 3157a)
Péri, Noel, (3158), *63*
Peristerès, Spyros D., (3159), *30*
Pernot, Hubert, (3160)
Perron, Michel, (3161)
Petit, Raymond, (3162)
Petneki, Jenö, (3163)
Petri, George, (3164, 3165)
Pettazzoni, Raffaele, (3166)
Pfister, G. A., (3167, 3168)
Pfrogner, H., (3169)
Phelps, D. L., (3170)
Philips, Ekundayo, (3172)
Phillips, W. J., (3173)
Pichiappa, K., *27*
Picken, Laurence, (3174-3181), *63, 75*
Pigeaud, Th., (3182)
Piggott, Francis, (3183-3185), *63*
Piguet, E., (3483)

Pike, Kenneth L., (3186, 3187)
Pilet, Raymond, (3188)
Pillai, T. N. Rajaratnam, *27, 29*
Pillai, Vidvan Manpoondiya, (3189)
Pillai, Vidvan Palani Subramania, (3189)
Pinches, T. G., (3190)
Pinck, Louis, (3191)
Pingle, Bhavanrao A., (3192)
Pinon, Roger, (2606a, 3193)
Piquet, E., (3483, 3484)
Pischner, Hans, (3195)
Pitts, Harry, (1122)
Plath, Joh, Heinrich, (3196)
Plato (3170), *44*
Platt, W., (3197), *48*
Plessis, I. D. du, (3198, 3199)
Plessis, L. J. du, (440)
Plicka, Karel, (3200)
Plischke, Hans, (3201)
Poduval, R. V., (3202-3204)
Pöch, Rudolf, (1139, 1488), *17*
Poensen, C., (3205)
Pol, Balth, van der, *42*
Poláček, Jan, (3206)
Poladian, Sirwart, (3207-3209)
Polak, A. J., (3210)
Polin, Claire C. J., (3211)
Poleman, Horace L., (4307, 4308)
Pollmann, Jop, (3212), *21*
Poloczek, František, (3213, 3214)
Ponce, M. M., (3215)
Pop, M., (3216a)
Pope (13)
Popley, Herbert A., (3217), *63*
Porée-Maspéro, Eveline, (3218)
Portmann, M. V., (3219)
Potentier, P., *36*
Pott, A. F., (3220)
Pott, P. H., (3221)
Poueigh, J., (3222)
Pound, Ezra, (3223)
Pradines, Emerante de, (3224)
Prado, Germán, (3465)
Prajnanananda, Swami, (3225)
Prasâd, Nandan, *27*
Prasanna, Raghunath, *27*
Pratella, F. B., (708, 3226)
Preuss, Karl Theodor, (1910, 3743)
Price, E. W., (3226a)
Price, Thomas J., *33*
Prichici, Constantin Gh., (3227, 3228, 3228a)
Prick van Wely, Max, (3229)
Prietze, Rudolf, (3230, 3231)
Primovski, A., (4181)
Prin, J. B., (1340, 3232)
Prince, J. D., (3233)
Pringsheim, Klaus, (3234-3236)
Pritchard, W., (3237)
Proca, Vera, (3238, 3239)
Procope, Bruce, (3239a)
Psachos, C. A., (3240, 3241)
Pujol, F., (3242, 3243),
Pulestone, F., (3244)

285

287

289

Venkatarama Iyer, T. L., see: Iyer, T. L.
  Venkatarama,
Verbeken, A., (4216–4218)
Verdeil, R. Palikarova, (4219)
Veress, Sándor, (2520j, 4220)
Verger, Pierre, 26
Verney, Frederick William, (4221)
Vernillat, France, (244)
Verwilghen, Leo, (4221a), 29
Vetter, Walther, (4222–4224)
Vetterl, Karel, (4225–4227), 68
Veurman, B., (4228)
Vichitr-Vadakarn, H. E. Nai V., (4229), 64
Viderø, Finn, (136)
Vidya, Mrs. S., 27
Viellard, Gilbert, (4230)
Viggiano Esain, Julio, (4231, 4232)
Viglieti, Cedar, (4233)
Vilâyat Khân (4520)
Villemarqué (4233a)
Villoteau, G. A., (4234, 4235)
Vinogradov, V., (4236–4239)
Virollaud, Charles, (4240)
Vissa Appa Rao, see: Rao, Vissa Appa,
Visvanathan, T., 27
Vloten, van, (4241)
Vodušek, Valens, (fig. 35), 22
Voegelin, Erminie Wheeler, (4242)
Voigt, Alban, (4243)
Vois, P., (4244)
Vojaček, I., (4245)
Volland (4246)
Volz, W., (1685)
Vos, F., (4549a)
Voskuil, J., (4247)
Vries, H. de, (4248, 4248a)
Vulpesco, M., (4249)
Vuong Hong Sen, see: Sen, Vuong Hong,
Vyasa, Lakshmidasa Adityarama, (4250)
Vysloužil, Jiri, (4251)
Vyzgo, T., (4252, 4253)

Wachsmann, Klaus P., (fig. 37) (4254–4262a),
  63, 75
Waddell, L. A., (4263)
Waengler, Hans-Heinrich, (4264)
Wagener, G., (4265)
Wagnall (1744)
Wagner, Eduard, (4266)
Wagner, O., (4267)
Waldmann, Guido, (4268, 4268a, 4269), 13
Wales, H. G. Quaritsch, (4269a, 4551)
Walin, Stig, (4270)
Wallaschek, Richard, (4271–4279)
Wallle, I. van de, see: Vandewalle, I.,
Walleser, Sixtus, (4282)
Walls y Merino, M., (4283)
Walton, James, (4284)
Waly, A., (4285)
Wang, Betty, (4286, 4287)
Wang, En Shao, (4288), 64
Wang, Kuan Chi, (4289–4292), 64
Wang, Kung-Ki, (4549b)

Wang, Kuo Wei, (4293)
Wang, Shih-Hsiang, (4295)
Wang, Ti, (4295)
Wantzloeben, S., (4296)
Ward, Herbert, (4297)
Ward, William Ernest Frank, (4298–4300)
Ware, James R., (4549c)
Warlington Eastlake, D., (4301)
Warman, J. W., (4302)
Warmelo, Willem van, (4303–4306)
Warner, W. Lloyd, (4306a)
Warnsinck, J. C. M., 15
Wasson, R. G., 33
Wasson, V. P., 33
Waterman, Richard Alan, (1701, 4307–4312a)
  VI, 17, 21, 26, 32, 34, 76
Watson, R. W. S., (4313)
W . . . . . , C. P., (4314)
Wead, Charles K., (4315–4317), 17
Weber-Kellermann, Ingeborg, (4318)
Weber, Max, (4319)
Wegelin, C. A., (4320)
Wegner, Max, (1802, 4321–4325)
Wehrli, Werner, (2709)
Weinstock, Herbert, (4326)
Weis, K., (4326a)
Weiss, Josef, (4327)
Weiss, Rodica, (4328)
Weissman, John S., (4329)
Wellek, Albert, (4330, 4331)
Wellesz, Egon, (4332–4346)
Wells, Evelyn Kendrick, (4347)
Weman, H., (4349)
Werckmeister, Heinrich, (4350)
Werner, Alice, (4351)
Werner, E. Chalmers, (1033)
Werner, Eric, (4352–4358a)
Werner, Heinz, (4359), 48
Wertheimer, Max, (4300)
Westarp, Alfred, (4301)
Westerman, D., (4362)
Westphal, E., (4362a)
Wetering, F. H. van de, (4363)
Weule, K., (4364)
Weyer, Edward, 30
Whall, W. B., (4305)
Wheeler, A. J., (4366)
Whinery, Sara, (2859)
White, C. M. N., (4366a)
White, Newman Ivey, (4367)
Whyte, E. T., (4368)
Whyte, Harcourt, (4369)
Wieger, L., (4370)
Wiegraebe, Paul, (4371)
Wiehmayer, Th., (4372)
Wieschhoff, Heinz, (1959, 4373), 46
Wilbert, Johannes, (4374)
Wilhelm, Richard, (1969, 2645, 4289, 4375,
  4376)
Wilke, (4377)
Wilkes, J. T., (4378)
Willard, N. A., (4379)
Willekes Macdonald, P. J., (4380)

IV

INDEX OF PERIODICALS AND OF SOME
PUBLICATIONS CONTAINING ARTICLES BY VARIOUS AUTHORS

Bulletin de la Société des Etudes Camerounaises (2740a)
Bulletin de la Société des Etudes Indochinoises (968, 1447, 1448, 1449, 2418b, 2519, 3814)
Bulletin de la Société des Etudes Océaniennes (848, 1450, 1451, 4513)
Bulletin de la Société des Recherches Congolaises (1041a)
Bulletin de la Société Neuchâteloise de Géographie (1126, 1131)
Bulletin de la Société Royale Belge de Géographie (701)
Bulletin de la Société Suisse des Américanistes (1607a)
Bulletin de la Société 'Union Musicologique' (3549, 3637)
Bulletin de l'Ecôle Française d'Extrême Orient (736, 1459, 1463, 3112, 3113)
Bulletin de l'Egypte (129)
Bulletin de l'Institut d'Egypte (1793, 1794, 1800, 1812, 1813, 1829a, 1830)
Bulletin de l'Institut des Hautes Etudes Marocaines (2590)
Bulletin de l'Institut d'Etudes Centrafricaines (3150)
Bulletin de l'Institut Français d'Afrique Noire (2594, 3691, 4230)
Bulletin de l'Union des Femmes Coloniales (1565a, 2728)
Bulletin des Amies du Vieux Hué (505, 506)
Bulletin des Recherches Soudanaises (2584a)
Bulletin d'Etudes Orientales (441)
Bulletin du Comité d'Etudes Historiques et Scientifiques de l'Afrique Occidentale Française (2452)
Bulletin du Musée National d'Ethnographie (3964)
Bulletin et Travaux de l'Institut Indochinois pour l'Etude de l'Homme (1978)
Bulletin International de l'Académie Yougoslave des Sciences et des Beaux Arts(3854)
Bulletin of the American Musicological Society (1467, 1724, 1733, 1736, 1738, 1743, 2811, 3702, 3971, 4459)
Bulletin of the British Institute of Recorded Sound (169, 2882a)
Bulletin of the Bureau of American Ethnology (857, 865, 871, 872, 896, 897, 906, 907, 923, 925, 926, 932, 2420, 2433, 2438a)
Bulletin of the Colonial Institute of Amsterdam (3742)
Bulletin of the Deccan College Research Institute (113b, 113c)
Bulletin of the Folk Song Society (1711)
Bulletin of the Institute of Ethnology of the Academia Sinica (2015, 4325a)
Bulletin of the International Folk Music Council (745)
Bulletin of the Metropolitan Museum of Art (3789, 4393)
Bulletin of the New York Public Library (2781a)

Bulletin of the Pan-American Union (57)
Bulletin of the Raffles Museum (566)
Bulletin of the School of Oriental and African Studies of the University of London (198b, 1053a, 2756a, 3453, 3453a)
Bulletin of the Ohio State University (4534)
Bulletin of the United States National Museum, Washington D. C. (4530)

Caecilia (Mainz/Brussels/Antwerp) (4525)
Caecilia en het Muziekcollege (3, 1362)
Cahiers Charles de Foucauld (2606)
Cahiers de Radio-Paris (3682b)
Cahiers d'Histoire Egyptiennes (1788, 1799, 1804, 1814)
Cahiers Musicaux (2731b)
Calcutta Review (3981)
Canon, The, (457, 4054)
Caribbean Quarterly (590, 767, 3127a, 3239a)
Central Africa (2918)
Century (3051)
Chesterian (2564)
China (4320)
China Magazine (1474)
China Pictorial (3829a)
China Reconstructs (1846a, 4295, 4458)
China Review (632, 1036, 4301)
Chinesische Musik (Richard Wilhelm) (1969, 2645, 4289, 4375, 4376)
Christoffel (3939)
Chronique d'Egypte (1780, 1825)
Chor, Der, (3730, 3731)
Colloques de Wégimont, Les, (300, 467, 538, 725, 726, 1513, 2525, 2729, 2736, 3499, 3692, 3771, 4416)
Common Weal, The, (2789)
Communities (1389)
Comptes rendues des Séances de l'Institut Français d'Anthropologie (969a, 3502b)
Congo Mission News (3226a, 3884a, 3884b)
Congo, Revue Générale de la Colonie Belge (384, 1456, 1992, 2701, 4216)
Contact (978)
Contemporary Japan (2788, 3234)
Courier de l'Unesco (688b, 2517)
Crisis (1610)
Cuadernos Americanos (2768, 2769, 2770, 2771)
Cultureel Indië (2377, 2378, 2379, 2381, 2384, 2387, 2389, 2391, 3946)
Cultureel Nieuws (1142)
Curtain Call (2840)
Cyclopaedia of Music and Musicians (Thompson) (2911)
Cypriot Studies (140)

Dance Index (2813)
Dance Observer (2422)
Dansk Musiktidsskrift (783, 2090, 2266)
Debreceni Szemle (2520c)
Deutsche Instrumentenbauzeitung (4243)
Deutsche Literaturzeitung (1926, 1938)
Deutsche Militär-Musiker-Zeitung (2313)

Deutsche Musikkultur (4395)
Deutsches Jahrbuch für Volkskunde (1860, 3313, 3944)
Deutsches Kolonial-Lexikon (1917)
Deutsche Tonkünstlerzeitung (4431)
Deutsche Vierteljahrschrift für Literatur (1115)
Deutsche Volkslied, Das, (2242)
Dictionnaire de la Bible (1402d)
Diliman Review (2696, 2697)
Discovery (1752)
Djawa (472, 473, 474, 475, 476, 477, 480, 483, 484, 485, 486, 487, 488, 489, 2359a, 2359b, 2359c, 2359d, 2378a, 2805, 2806, 2807, 3182, 3921, 3922)
Douro Litoral (341, 4184)
Dufourcq, Norbert, La musique des origines à nos jours (411, 610, 661, 713, 1021, 1372, 1605, 2679, 2680, 2681, 2682, 2706, 2733, 2734, 2914, 3685, 3686)

East Africa and Rhodesia (2105a)
Eastern World (1608)
Edoth (1398, 1402c)
Education de Base et Education des Adultes (4129c)
Egyptienne, L', (2953)
Elsevier's Encyclopaedie van de Muziek (197, 230, 231, 289a, 518, 518a, 728, 1878, 2532a, 2670, 2671, 2672, 4424, 4425)
Emlékkönyv Kodály Zoltán 70. születésnap-jára (283a, 283b, 325a, 1359, 2072, 2194, 2195, 2524, 2904, 3081a, 3335, 4113a, 4193, 4204)
Encyclopaedia Arctica (1124)
Encyclopaedia Brittanica (2207)
Encyclopaedie van Nederlandsch-Indië (3496, 3876)
Encyclopédie Africaine Française (747a)
Encyclopédie Coloniale et Maritime (629a, 663, 3144)
Encyclopédie Mensuelle Outre-Mer (3249a)
Encyclopedia of Social Sciences (759a, 3451a)
Encyclopedia of the Philippines (3471)
Erdball, Der, (1276, 2958)
Erzieher, Der, (422)
Essec (564c)
Estudios Afro-Cubanos (26, 3073, 3076, 3077)
Estudios Latino-Americanos (576, 1471, 2032, 2551, 2616)
Estudios Musicales (846, 1422)
Estudios y Fuentes del Arte in Mexico (2836b)
Estudos Coloniais (2046a)
Ethnographia (151, 257, 2268, 2520a, 2520g, 2520i, 2520q, 2716, 4012, 4013, 4021a)
Ethnographia-Népelet (4016)
Ethnographie, L' (600, 1695, 2632)
Ethnologica (1291)
Ethnologischer Anzeiger (1937, 1943, 3370)
Ethnologisches Notizblatt (99, 4364)
Ethnomusicology (continuation of Ethno-musicology Newsletter) (552a, 728c, 2438c, 2677a, 3005d, 4248a)

Ethnomusicology Newsletter (768, 1879, 2241, 2290, 2438, 2802, 2993, 3388, 3401, 4262)
Ethnos (1091, 1092, 1095, 1096, 1097, 1098, 1536, 1613, 1725, 1844a, 1962, 1994, 2395, 2619, 2766, 3042, 3173, 3650, 3833, 3883, 4102)
Etude (141, 1999, 3868)
Etudes Asiatiques (850)
Etudes Camerounaises (1552a, 1553, 3137)
Etudes Dahomiennes (769, 1354a)
Etudes Mélanésiennes (4244)
Eurasia Septentrionalis Antiqua (4170)
Exotic Music Society, Publ. of., (4504a, 4549a)
Experientia (3369)
Exploration (133)
Exploration and Fieldwork Smithsonian Institute (859, 862, 870, 874, 876, 877, 881, 886, 893, 898, 904, 910, 915)

Faust (2469, 3546a)
Federation Museums Journal (371)
Feuilles Musicales (355a)
Finnisch-Ugrische Forschungen (4173)
Flacara (709)
Flambeau, Le, (703)
Föreningen för Svensk Kulturhistoria (85)
Folkdancer, The, (3519)
Folklore (London) (4546)
Folklore Americano (128)
Folklore Americas (2994, 3003)
Folklore Brabançon, Le, (2747)
Folklore Studies of the Museum of Oriental Ethnology, Catholic University of Peking (618, 619)
Folklorist, The, (783a, 1457a, 1457b, 2305a, 2305b, 4514)
Forschungen und Fortschritte (2492, 2493, 2505, 2959)
France-Maroc (9, 330, 718, 3497, 4203)
France-Outre-Mer (646, 3413, 3692a)

Galpin Society Journal, The, (1776, 3179, 3181)
Garbe (2842)
Geographic Journal (3810)
Géographie, La, (1446)
Getouw, 'T, (1475)
Gids, De, (172)
Giornale de la Societas Asiatica Italiana (1619)
Glasnik Zemaljskog Muzeja u Bosni i Her-cegovine (2349)
Globus (17, 96, 166, 1483, 2012b, 2083b, 2311, 2823, 2872, 3696a, 3809b, 3865, 4275)
Gold Coast Review (4298)
Gramofoon voor Kenners en Liefhebbers (1848, 1849, 1850, 1851, 1852, 1853, 1854, 2312, 2588, 3164, 3221, 3472, 4009a, 4520)
Grands Lacs, Les, (145a, 3047)
Grove's Dictionary of Music and Musicians (158, 195, 637, 711, 746, 765, 766, 828, 998,

Journal of the American Oriental Society (742, 1628, 2013)
Journal of the Burma Research Society (2202a, 2758, 2759, 4477)
Journal of the College of Science, Imperial University of Tokyo (4062a)
Journal of the East African Swahili Committee (2531a)
Journal of the English Folk Dance and Song Society (1111)
Journal of the Folk Song Society (1275, 3822)
Journal of the Galpin Society (1776, 3179, 3181)
Journal of the Indian Society of Oriental Art (3263)
Journal of the International Folk Music Council (185, 191, 241, 295, 363, 438, 438a, 515, 606a, 705, 719, 771, 780, 783b, 1001, 1101, 1246, 1399, 1400, 1497, 1745, 1781, 1836, 1974, 2030, 2073, 2074, 2103, 2127, 2266a, 2302, 2419, 2441, 2637, 2723, 2748, 2749, 2752, 2779, 2878, 2880, 3005b, 3128, 3142, 3178, 3200, 3387, 3388a, 3405a, 3423, 3513, 3597, 3624, 3665, 3666, 3667, 3797,' 3800, 3815, 3831, 3973, 4128, 4178, 4195b, 4225, 4256, 4260, 4262a, 4420, 4435, 4443, 4488, 4491a)
Journal of the Irish Folk Song Society (2031)
Journal of the Manchester Geographic Society (2905)
Journal of the Music Academy Madras (25, 34-40, 115, 438c, 611, 611a, 616, 790, 809, 810, 812, 813, 814, 816, 818a, 822, 822a, 1353a, 2038, 2039, 2040b, 2041, 2042, 2043, 2043a, 2043c, 2185a, 2204, 2280b, 2323a, 2323b, 2756, 2838, 2938, 2973, 3116, 3189, 3252, 3253, 3254, 3257, 3260, 3261, 3262, 3265, 3266, 3267, 3268, 3270-3279, 3282, 3284-3288, 3291, 3293, 3294, 3295, 3296, 3298, 3299, 3300, 3305, 3306, 3307, 3308a, 3308b, 3310, 3314, 3318, 3320, 3320a, 3330, 3335b, 3335c, 3336, 3337, 3339, 3340, 3340a-3340e, 3341, 3342-3342d, 3348, 3350-3353, 3509, 3510, 3511, 3609-3612, 3614, 3615, 3623, 3657a, 3915a, 3928a, 4197)
Journal of the Oriental Institute Baroda (952, 2057)
Journal of the Palestine Oriental Society (3947)
Journal of the Polynesian Society (527, 547, 551, 992, 1060, 1966, 2571, 3302a, 3443, 3444, 3970)
Journal of the Royal Anthropological Institute of Great Britain and Ireland (208, 212, 217, 219, 1621, 2114a, 2219, 2232, 4107, 4108, 4155, 4259)
Journal of the Royal Asiatic Society of Great Britain and Ireland (43, 1158, 1159, 1164, 1165, 1166, 1167, 1175, 1176, 1177, 1178, 1186, 1187, 1188, 1193, 1287, 1768, 1796, 2546, 2675, 2925, 3170, 3219, 3324)

Journal of the Royal Asiatic Society, Korean Branch (393a)
Journal of the Royal Asiatic Society, Malayan Branch (381, 2626, 4551)
Journal of the Royal Asiatic Society, North China Branch (854, 1410, 2081, 2205, 2923, 2926, 4000, 4011)
Journal of the Royal Asiatic Society, Straits Branch (3829)
Journal of the Royal Historical Society of Ceylon (225)
Journal of the Royal Society of Arts (689, 1055, 1082)
Journal of the Science Society of China (2631)
Journal of the Siam Society (2365)
Journal of the Society for Research in Asiatic Music (1557, 1876, 2147, 2202, 2239, 2439, 2685, 3083, 3091, 4037, 4038, 4043, 4046, 4138, 4446, 4457)
Journal of the University of Gauhati (2974a)
Journal of the University of Pennsylvania Museum (1231)
Journal of the Washington Academy of Sciences (892, 894, 895, 3581)
Journal of the Welsh Folk Song Society (4348)
Journal of the West China Border Research Society (24)

Kalevalaseuran Vuosikirja (4167)
Kashmir (32)
Katholieke Illustratie, De, (1870)
Keleti Szemle (2356)
Kemi (1810, 1811)
Kengele (448c)
Koloniale Rundschau (423, 3982)
Koloniale Studiën (471)
Kongo-Overzee (749b, 2049, 2050, 2704, 2796a)
Korean Survey (1212a)
Kosmos (1502)
Kroniek van Kunst en Kultuur (207a, 2380)
Kultur und Schallplatte (1945, 2508)
Kwartalnik Muzycky (1127, 4390)

Lakshya Sangeet (229, 666, 2267, 2899, 2939, 2940, 3354, 3355, 3356, 3357)
Lantern (109, 4304)
Larawan (2711a)
Lavignac, Histoire de la Musique (309, 564, 750, 751, 1089, 1294, 1373, 1535, 1599, 1980, 2250, 2251, 2253, 2262, 2263, 2548, 2550, 2659, 2906, 3132, 3491, 3492, 3585, 3835, 4240, 4452)
Leaflet Series (4509)
Leven en Werken (2608)
Lüneburg 1950, Kongressbericht, (190, 1044, 1099, 1598a, 1614, 2403, 3802)
Luister (1436, 1437, 4247)

Macmillan (2124)
Magasin Pittoresque (960, 963)
Magyar Müvészet (2520d)

299

Transactions of the Glasgow University Oriental Society (1180)
Transactions of the Gold Coast and Togoland Historical Society (3428a)
Transactions of the New Zealand Institute (77, 79, 3010)
Travel (2712)
Tribune de St. Gervais (405)
Tribus, Jahrbuch des Lindenmuseums (250, 1973a, 3763)
Tropiques (3138, 3143)
Tropisch Nederland (4094)
Turismo (3467)

Uganda Journal (757a, 2667, 3813, 4255)
Ukrainian Trend, The, (2987)
Ultra (27)
Unesco Courier (688b, 2517)
Ungarisches Jahrbüchlein (273, 4015)
United Asia (3658)
United Empire (1383, 4129e)
Universal Jewish Encyclopaedia (3563a)
Universitas (4146)

Värmland Förr och Nu (3059)
Vedanta Kesari (3283)
Velhagen und Klasings Monatshefte (3549a)
Verhandelingen der Koninklijk Nederlandse Akademie van Wetenschappen, Afd. Letterkunde (1144, 2532b)
Verhandlungen der Naturforscher Gesellschaft, Basel (4423)
Vie et les Arts Lithurgiques, La, (702)
Vierteljahrschrift für Musikwissenschaft (675, 2537, 3729, 3984, 3985, 3986, 3990)
Visva-Bharati Quarterly, The, (170, 2448)
Voix du Congolais (100a, 3425a)
Vox (1581a, 1649, 1654, 1664, 1666, 1669, 1670, 1675, 1677, 2824, 4072a)

Weekblad voor Nederlandsch-Indië(111,112b)
Welt des Orients, Die, (1767)
Wereld der Muziek, De,(1429,1431,1432,1433)
West-Africa (223)
West African Review (771a, 1320, 1380, 1381, 1382, 1384, 2087, 3360)
Westermann's Monatshefte (104)
Western Folklore (2428)
West-Indische Gids (734, 735, 1454, 1455, 3102, 3103, 3706)
Wiener Beiträge für Kunst und Kulturgeschichte Asiens (175)
Wiener Medizinische Wochenschrift (2463, 2466, 2471, 2491)
Wiener Völkerkundige Mitteilungen (1492, 2136a)
Wiener Zeitschrift für die Kunde des Morgenlandes (2355, 2458, 3846)
Wörter und Sachen (2320a)
Woodwind Magazine (4132)
Word (1741, 1744b)
Y Cerddor (1632a)
Yeda-Am (2599)
Yenching Hsüeh Pa'o (4447)

Ymer (388)

Zaïre (749, 749a, 2849, 2852, 2856, 3522, 4221a)
Zeitschrift der Deutschen Morgenländischen Gesellschaft (1623)
Zeitschrift der Deutschen Musikgesellschaft (1295, 3843)
Zeitschrift der Internationalen Musikgesellschaft (1886, 1887, 1905, 1906, 1909, 2575, 3902, 4067, 4082, 4082a, 4083)
Zeitschrift der Schweizerischen Gesellschaft für Asienkunde (4439)
Zeitschrift des Deutschen Palästinavereins (3580)
Zeitschrift des Vereins für Volkskunde (2276, 4497)
Zeitschrift für Aegyptische Sprache und Altertumskunde (1809, 3558)
Zeitschrift für Aesthetik und Allgemeine Kunstwissenschaft (1922)
Zeitschrift für Angewandte Psychologie (498, 1938)
Zeitschrift für Deutsche Philologie (4413)
Zeitschrift für die Alttestamentischen Wissenschaften (529)
Zeitschrift für die Oesterreichische Gymnasien (2459)
Zeitschrift für Eingeborenen-Sprachen (1637)
Zeitschrift für Ethnologie (97, 167, 402, 800, 976, 1057, 1249, 1253, 1874, 1875, 1883, 1884, 1903, 1913, 2000, 2311, 2574, 2702, 3085, 3126, 3378, 3532, 3674, 3737, 3739, 3745, 3809, 3809a, 4377)
Zeitschrift für Instrumentenbau (420, 1839a)
Zeitschrift für Laryngologie (1946)
Zeitschrift für Missionswissenschaft (3517)
Zeitschrift für Musik (387, 1659, 1660, 2128a, 3379)
Zeitschrift für Musikwissenschaft (257, 258, 312, 1389, 1651, 1652, 1655, 1657, 1658, 1661, 1662, 1668, 1949, 2021, 2335, 2490, 2582a, 3105, 3534, 3537, 3545, 3547, 3557, 4014, 4160, 4330)
Zeitschrift für Phonetik und Allgemeine Sprachwissenschaft (433)
Zeitschrift für Physik (534, 1923)
Zeitschrift für Psychologie und Physiologie der Sinnesorgane (1931, 2876a, 3989, 3991, 3998)
Zeitschrift für Rassenkunde (424, 1683)
Zeitschrift für Semistik (334)
Zeitschrift für vergleichende Musikwissenschaft (415, 550, 653, 654, 657, 743, 1286, 1576, 1693, 1708, 1716, 1950, 1951, 1952, 1954, 1956, 1957, 1958, 1959, 1995, 1996, 2509, 2510, 2511, 2512, 3426, 3448, 3559, 3560a, 3735, 3779)
Zeitschrift für Volkskunde (798, 4408, 4409)
Zenei Szemle (2267, 2520b)
Zvuk, Jugoslovenska Muzička Revija (2063, 4495)
Zuschauer, Der, (2488)